D0509390

Standard Catalog of®

MILITARY FIREARMS

1870 TO THE PRESENT

2nd Edition

NED SCHWING

© 2003 by
Krause Publications, Inc.

Published by

An F&W Publications Company

700 East State Street • Iola, WI 54990-0001
715-445-2214 • 888-457-2873
www.krause.com

Please call or write for our free catalog of publications.
Our toll-free number to place an order or obtain a free catalog is 800-258-0929
or please use our regular business telephone 715-445-2214.

Library of Congress Catalog Number: 2001088596
ISBN: 0-87349-525-X

Printed in the United States of America

Edited by Don Gulbrandsen
Designed by Patsy Howell

Cover photos by Paul Goodwin

CONTENTS

───── DIRECTORY ─────

ACKNOWLEDGMENTS

Orvel Reichert is a collector of World War II-era semi-automatic pistols, especially the P38, and has been an invaluable help in sorting out a sometimes confusing array of pistol variations. He can be reached at P.O. Box 67, Vader, WA 98593, 360-245-3492, e-mail address: mr.p38@localaccess.com

Joe Gaddini, of SWR, has provided invaluable technical assistance on Class III firearms and suppressors. He can be reached at 119 Davis Road, Suite G-1, Martinez, GA 30907, 706-481-9403.

Thanks to Eric M. Larson for his knowledgeable information on Federal gun laws.

A special thanks to Simeon Stoddard, former curator of the Cody Firearms Museum, for his research and contribution on the M1 Garand rifle.

Nick Tilotta is an expert on Thompson submachine guns. He helped to explain all of the subtle differences between models and variations. He can be reached at P.O. Box 451, Grapevine, TX 76099, 817-481-6616.

Don Westmoreland is a serious student of Japanese and German World War II automatic weapons. His knowledge was extremely valuable.

Stan Andrewski, a crackerjack gunsmith, can be reached at 603-746-4387 for those who desire nothing but the best in the way of repair and refinishing work on their Class III firearms.

Dan Shea, editor and publisher of the *Small Arms Review*, lent his mastery of Class III firearms.

Ted Dawidowicz of Dalvar, USA made photos available of currently imported Polish military firearms. He may be reached at 740 E. Warm Springs Rd. Ste. #122, Henderson, NV 89015, 702-558-6707.

I want to thank Jim Alley of I.D.S.A. Books for his expert advice concerning the scope of this book based on his encyclopedic knowledge of military books. He was also generous with the use of his extensive personal library. Jim can be reached at P.O. Box 1457-G, Piqua, OH 45356, 937-773-4203.

Blake Stevens, Collector Grade Publications, shared his vast knowledge of military firearms as well as photos from his first-class publications. Blake can be reached at P.O. Box 1046, Cobourg, Ontario, Canada K9 4W5, 905-342-3434.

A special thanks to all the manufacturers and importers who supplied us with information and photographs on their products.

Ted Willems and Bruce Wolberg of *Gun List* have been most helpful with information and locating hard-to-find firearms.

Many thanks to J.B. Wood for taking the time to point out, "a few discrepancies" in the 1st edition.

Ricky Kumor Sr. spent much of his valuable time making constructive suggestions and sharing his bottomless expertise of military firearms.

James Rankin gave freely of his vast experience as an author and small arms expert to steer this book in the right direction. His assistance is gratefully acknowledged.

Mark Keefe, editor of the *American Rifleman*, is a keen student of military firearms. He was particularly helpful on Lee-Enfield rifles with small but important details that are so useful to the collector.

A special note of appreciation to Chuck Karwan, one of the contributing editors of this book, who gave unselfishly of his enormous store of knowledge of military firearms.

Richard R. Wray, one of the deans of the Class III community with 50 years of experience, and Ken Keilholtz with over 30 years of experience, both extremely knowledgeable Class III collectors, gave generously of their time and expertise to make this a more useful and more accurate publication. Photos of their comprehensive collections are seen throughout this book.

J.R. Moody, a contributing editor, willingly gave of his time and expertise based on his years of practical hands-on experience with Class III weapons and sniper rifles.

Many thanks to Pedro Bello for sharing his extensive experience and knowledge of machine pistols.

Charlie Cutshaw provided valuable assistance on hard-to-find information about rarely encountered weapons.

Paul Miller shared with us his deep knowledge of military firearms.

John M. Miller's, CWO, U.S. Army (Ret), assistance was invaluable by sharing his information from his vast knowledge of firearms built on his extensive collection and practical experience.

Bob Naess is a wealth of information on a wide variety of machine guns and their values as well as their availability. Bob can be reached at 802-226-7204.

Mike LaPlante went out of his way to straighten out the maze of variations that are to be found in the Colt M16 and AR-15 series of weapons.

I want to thank the contributing editors to this publication who have gone out of their way to give of their time and knowledge to make this a better book. Any errors or omissions in this book are entirely the editor's responsibility.

PHOTO CREDITS

Many of the large format photos in this book were taken by Paul Goodwin, a photographer of exceptional ability.

A special acknowledgment to Kris Leinicke, curator of the Rock Island Arsenal Museum, for allowing us full access to the museum's outstanding firearms collection.

Karl Karash supplied photos from his personal Colt 1911 collection.

Jim Rankin has an extensive library of photos he was kind enough to share with the readers.

Robert Fisch, curator of the museum at the United States Military Academy at West Point, was most helpful and cooperative in sharing that institution's wonderful treasure trove of historically important firearms.

Blake Stevens, Collector Grade Publications, furnished many outstanding photos from his comprehensive books.

Robert Segel lent photos of his superb collection of vintage machine guns, beautifully photographed and displayed.

Many thanks to Charles Kenyon for the use of photos for his forthcoming book on Luger pistols.

Chuck Karwan shared many photos from his extensive photo archives of military firearms.

Ricky Kumor Sr. photographed many of the rare and high quality military weapons that flow through his shop.

Tom Nelson of Ironside International Publishers kindly permitted us to reprint some of his photos of rare weapons from his outstanding series of books on automatic firearms.

John M. Miller helped with photos of early military firearms.

INTRODUCTION

One of the most noticeable aspects of this 2nd edition is the complete updating of information concerning prices. We have also revised and expanded this edition to better reflect additional information that is needed to identify various modifications and configurations of weapons. This is especially true in the Colt M16 section as well as the Colt Model 1911 section.

One of the most enlightening aspects of collecting military firearms is that the collector is almost forced to become an amateur historian. Military firearms are inexorably tied to history. A good working knowledge of general history is essential to capture the full enjoyment of military weapons collecting. A detailed knowledge of military history opens a panorama of information concerning a particular weapon's use and its role in victory or defeat. The first combat use of the Maxim gun was by the British in South Africa in 1893. The Mauser Model 1871 was the first German metallic cartridge rifle. Norway was the last of three countries to adopt its own Krag-Jorgensen rifle behind Denmark (1889) and the United States (1892). The German MP-18 submachine gun was the first successful design of its type and

was in limited use during the end of World War I. The Remington Model 1917 rifle was more widely used by U.S. troops in World War I than the Springfield Model 1906. During World War II, the United States was the only nation to fight the war armed primarily with a semiautomatic rifle, the M1 Garand. There are numerous examples of military weapons that shaped not only the outcome of battles but of entire wars. As Major-General J.F.C. Fuller once wrote, "... weapons if only the right ones can be discovered, form 99 percent of victory."

Military history and its accompanying weapons are inexpiably linked. The result is a fascinating collecting field full of affordable guns that have seen the horrors of war and survived. If only they could talk. Oh, the stories they could tell. We hope that this publication will provide the reader with helpful information that will make his or her collecting more enjoyable.

Good luck with your collecting and be safe in your shooting.

Ned Schwing
Editor

GRADING SYSTEM

In the opinion of the editor all grading systems are subjective. It is our task to offer the collector and dealer a measurement that most closely reflects a general consensus on condition. The system we present seems to come closest to describing a firearm in universal terms. We strongly recommend that the reader acquaint himself with this grading system before attempting to determine the correct price for a particular firearm's condition. Remember, in most cases, condition determines price.

NIB—New in Box
This category can sometimes be misleading. It means that the firearm is in its original factory carton with all of the appropriate papers. It also means the firearm is new; that it has not been fired and has no wear. This classification brings a substantial premium for both the collector and shooter.

Excellent
Collector quality firearms in this condition are highly desirable. The firearm must be in at least 98 percent condition with respect to blue wear, stock or grip finish, and bore. The firearm must also be in 100 percent original factory condition without refinishing, repair, alterations, or additions of any kind. Sights must be factory original as well. This grading classification includes both modern and antique (manufactured prior to 1898) firearms.

Very Good
Firearms in this category are also sought after both by the collector and shooter. Firearms must be in working order and retain approximately 92 percent metal and wood finish. It must be 100 percent factory original, but may have some small repairs, alterations, or non-factory additions. No refinishing is permitted in this category. Both modern and antique firearms are included in this classification.

Good
Modern firearms in this category may not be considered to be as collectable as the previous grades, but antique firearms are considered desirable. Modern firearms must retain at least 80 per-

cent metal and wood finish, but may display evidence of old refinishing. Small repairs, alterations, or non-factory additions are sometimes encountered in this class. Factory replacement parts are permitted. The overall working condition of the firearm must be good as well as safe. The bore may exhibit wear or some corrosion, especially in antique arms. Antique firearms may be included in this category if their metal and wood finish is at least 50 percent original factory finish.

Fair
Firearms in this category should be in satisfactory working order and safe to shoot. The overall metal and wood finish on the modern firearm must be at least 30 percent and antique firearms must have at least some original finish or old re-finish remaining. Repairs, alterations, nonfactory additions, and recent refinishing would all place a firearm in this classification. However, the modern firearm must be in working condition, while the antique firearm may not function. In either case, the firearm must be considered safe to fire if in a working state.

Poor
Neither collectors nor shooters are likely to exhibit much interest in firearms in this condition. Modern firearms are likely to retain little metal or wood finish. Pitting and rust will be seen in firearms in this category. Modern firearms may not be in working order and may not be safe to shoot. Repairs and refinishing would be necessary to restore the firearm to safe working order. Antique firearms will have no finish and will not function. In the case of modern firearms, their principal value lies in spare parts. On the other hand, antique firearms in this condition may be used as "wall hangers" or as an example of an extremely rare variation or have some kind of historical significance.

Pricing Sample Format

NIB	Exc.	V.G.	Good	Fair	Poor
550	450	400	350	300	200

PRICING

The prices given in this book are __RETAIL__ prices.

Unfortunately for shooters and collectors, there is no central clearinghouse for firearms prices. The prices given in this book are designed as a guide, not as a quote. This is an important distinction because prices for firearms vary with the time of the year and geographical location. For example, interest in firearms is at its lowest point in the summer. People are not as interested in shooting and collecting at this time of the year as they are in playing golf or taking a vacation.

It is not practical to list prices in this book with regard to time of year or location. What is given is a reasonable price based on sales at gun shows, auction houses, *Gun List* prices, and information obtained from knowledgeable collectors and dealers. The firearms prices listed in this book are **RETAIL PRICES** and may bring more or less depending on the variables discussed above. If you choose to sell your gun to a dealer, you will not receive the retail price but a wholesale price based on the markup that particular dealer needs to operate.

Also, in certain cases there will be no price indicated under a particular condition but rather the notation "**N/A**" or the symbol "—". This indicates that there is no known price available for that gun in that condition or the sales for that particular model are so few that a reliable price cannot be given. This will usually be encountered only with very rare guns, with newly introduced firearms, or more likely with antique firearms in those conditions. Most antique firearms will be seen in the good, fair, and poor categories.

One final note. The prices listed here come from a variety of sources: retail stores, gun shows, individual collectors, and auction houses. Due to the nature of business, one will usually pay higher prices at a retail store than at a gun show. In some cases, auctions will produce excellent buys or extravagant prices, depending on any given situation. Collectors will sometimes pay higher prices for a firearm that they need to fill out their collection, when in other circumstances they will not be willing to pay market price if they don't have to have the gun. The point here is that prices paid for firearms is an ever-changing affair based on a large number of variables. The prices in this book are a **GENERAL GUIDE** as to what a willing buyer and willing seller might agree on. You may find the item for less, and then again you may have to pay more depending on the variables of your particular situation.

Sometimes we lose sight of our collecting or shooting goals and focus only on price. Two thoughts come to mind. First, one long time collector told me once that, "you can never pay too much for a good gun." Second, Benjamin Franklin once said, "the bitterness of poor quality lingers long after the sweetness of a low price."

In the final analysis, the prices listed here are given to assist the shooter and collector in pursuing their hobby with a better understanding of what is going on in the marketplace. If this book can expand one's knowledge, then it will have fulfilled its purpose.

There is one pricing comment that should be made about military firearms in particular. The prices given in this book for foreign firearms are for guns that do not have an importer's stamp affixed to them. This stamping became a federal requirement in 1968. The importer's stamp was required to be placed on the receiver or frame of the firearm in a conspicuous location. To many collectors this makes little difference in their collecting. To others it makes a significant difference and this group will pay more for firearms without an importer's stamp.

Note also that the prices listed below for Class III weapons reflect the gun only with one magazine and no accessories. The prices for medium and heavy machine guns do not include bipods or tripods. These necessary items are extra. Buyer and seller should note that machine gun mounts come in various configurations. Mounts may range in price from several hundred dollars to several thousand dollars depending on type.

A further caution regarding the buying and selling of Class III firearms. These weapons are highly restricted by federal law. Some states do not allow its citizens to own these firearms. Because the value of these Class III firearms lies not only in the historical and technical significance of the weapon, it also lies in the grandfathered paper that accompanied each gun. The values sited in this publication can change overnight if federal or state law changes. Be aware. Be cautious.

EDITOR'S REQUEST: Guns that are rare, scarce, obscure, or seldom traded are difficult if not impossible to price. We have provided prices as an estimate only. The editor welcomes any information that would improve pricing for these uncommon items.

ADDITIONAL CONSIDERATIONS

Perhaps the best advice is for the collector to take his time. Do not be in a hurry and do not allow yourself to be rushed into making a decision. Learn as much as possible about the firearms you are interested in collecting or shooting. Try to keep current with prices through *Gun List* and this publication. Go to gun shows, not just to buy or sell but to observe and learn. It is also helpful to join a firearms club or association. These groups have older, experienced collectors who are glad to help the beginner or veteran. One of the best starting points in firearms collecting is to read as much as possible. There are many first-rate publications available to the beginner and veteran collector alike that will not only broaden his knowledge of a particular collecting field, but also entertain and enlighten as well.

In the preparation of this book, I have encountered a vast number of models, variations, and subvariations. It is not possible to cover these in the kind of detail necessary to account for every possible deviation in every model produced. The collector needs to read in-depth studies of models and manufacturers to accomplish this task. Knowledge and experience together fashion the foundation for successful collecting.

Firearms collecting is a rewarding hobby. Firearms are part of our nation's history and represent an opportunity to learn more about their role in that American experience. If done skillfully, firearms collecting can be a profitable hobby as well.

AUCTION HOUSE CREDITS

The following auction houses were kind enough to allow the Catalog to report unusual firearms from their sales. The directors of these auction concerns are acknowledged for their assistance and support.

Amoskeag Auction Company, Inc.
250 Commercial Street, Unit #3011
Manchester, NH 03101
Attention: Jason or Melissa Devine
603-627-7383
603-627-7384 FAX

Bonhams & Butterfield
220 San Bruno Avenue
San Francisco, CA 94103
Attention: James Ferrell
415-861-7500 ext. 3332
415-861-8951 FAX

Old Town Station Ltd.
P.O. Box 15351
Lenexa, KS 66285
Attention: Jim Supica
913-492-3000
913-492-3022 FAX

Rock Island Auction Company
1050 36th Avenue
Moline, IL 61265
Attention: Patrick Hogan
800-238-8022
309-797-1655 FAX

Cherry's Fine Guns
3402-A W. Wendover Ave.
Greensboro, NC 27407
Attention: Kevin Cherry or Gurney Brown
336-854-4182
336-854-4184 FAX

Little John's Auction Service, Inc.
1740 W. La Veta
Orange, CA 92868
Attention: Carol Watson
714-939-1170
714-939-7955 FAX

THE EDITOR

Ned Schwing is the author of:

The Winchester Model 42, Winchester's Finest: The Model 21, Winchester Slide Action Rifles, Volume I: The Model 1890 and Model 1906, Winchester Slide Action Rifles, Volume II: The Model 61 and Model 62, The Browning Superposed: John M. Browning's Last Legacy. For the past 12 years he has been the editor of the *Standard Catalog of Firearms.* He is also the firearms contributor to the *Standard Catalog of Winchester.* His articles have appeared in the *American Rifleman, Guns Illustrated, Shooting Sportsman, Waffen Digest, Double Gun Journal,* and other firearm publications.

CONTRIBUTING EDITORS

Bob Ball
Springfield Armory & Mauser rifles
P.O. Box 562
Unionville, CT 06085

Bailey Brower
Savage military pistols
P.O. Box 111
Madison, NJ 07940

John Callahan
Savage Historian
53 Old Quarry Road
Westfield, MA 01085

Bruce Canfield
U.S. Military firearms
P.O. Box 6171
Shreveport, LA 71136

Jim Cate
J.P. Sauer pistols
406 Pine Bluff Dr.
Chattanooga, TN 37412
423-892-6320

Gene Guilaroff
Modern military firearms
P.O. Box 173
Alvaton, KY 42122
270-622-7309
e-mail: arclight@nctc.com

Karl Karash
Colt Model 1911 & 1911A1
288 Randall Road
Berlin, MA 01503
978-838-9401
987-589-2060 FAX

Chuck Karwan
Colt New Service, Browning High-Power,
Lee-Enfield, Webley revolvers
958 Cougar Creek Road
Oakland, OR 97462
541-459-4134

Richard M. Kumor Sr.
c/o Ricky's Gun Room
WWII era military firearms
P.O. Box 286
Chicopee, MA 01021
413-592-5000
413-594-5700 FAX
e-mail: Rickysinc@aol.com
Web site: rickysinc.com

CWO John M. Miller (U.S. Army, Ret.)
19th and 20th century military small arms
c/o Ned Schwing
Krause Publications
700 E. State St.
Iola, WI 54990

Gale Morgan
Luger and Mauser pistols
Pre-World War I pistols
P.O. Box 72
Lincoln, CA 95648
916-645-1720

J.R. Moody
Contemporary military small arms
c/o Ned Schwing
Krause Publications
700 E. State St.
Iola, WI 54990

Robert E. Naess
Class III guns of all types
P.O. Box 471
Cavendish, VT 05142
802-226-7204
e-mail: margoc@mail.tds.net

Charles Pate
U.S. military handguns
c/o Ned Schwing
Krause Publications
700 E. State St.
Iola, WI 54990

Jim Rankin
Walther pistols & pre-war auto pistols
3615 Anderson Road
Coral Gables, FL 33134
305-446-1792

Orvel Reichert
World War II-era semiautomatic
pistols
P.O. Box 67
Vader, WA 98593
360-245-3492
e-mail: mr.p38@localaccess.com

Howard Resnick
19th century military handguns
141 S. Smoke Road
Valparaiso, IN 46385
219-477-1045

Joe Schroeder
Steye/Mannlicher pistols
P.O. Box 406
Glenview, IL 60025
847-724-8816
827-657-6500
847-724-8831 FAX

John Stimson Jr.
High Standard pistols
540 W. 92nd St.
Indianapolis, IN 46260
317-831-2990

Simeon Stoddard
Swiss, Swedish, and Finnish rifles
P.O. Box 2283
Cody, WY 82414

Jim Supica
Smith & Wesson
P.O. Box 15351
Lenexa, KS 66285
913-492-3000

Nick Tilotta
Great Western Firearms Co.
Thompson submachine guns
P.O. Box 451
Grapevine, TX 76099
817-481-6616
817-251-5136 FAX

Don Westmoreland
Class III Curio & Relic guns
c/o Ned Schwing
Krause Publications
700 E. State St.
Iola, WI 54990

BIBLIOGRAPHICAL NOTES

There are a number of excellent comprehensive books on military history for the period that this volume covers. Perhaps the best, at least in my opinion, are two outstanding studies by Edward Ezell. They are: *Small Arms of the World,* 12th edition, Stackpole Books, 1983, and *Handguns of the World,* Stackpole Books, 1981.

For early military revolvers, the two-volume work by Rolf H. Muller, *Geschichte und Technik der Europaischen Militarrevolver,* Journal-Verlag Schwend, 1982, is excellent.

For modern military weapons, *Jane's Infantry Weapons* gives a broad overview, with technical data, of just about any modern military weapon in use in recent times.

Donald Webster's book, *Military Bolt Action Rifles, 1841-1918,* Museum Restoration Service, 1993, filled some important gaps in information on early bolt action rifles.

There are additional titles that are of interest and offer beneficial information: *Pistols of the World,* 3rd ed., Hogg and Weeks, DBI Books, 1992. *Rifles of the World,* John Walter, DBI Books, 1993. *Military Small Arms of the 20th Century,* 7th ed., Hogg and Weeks, Krause Publications, 1999. *Small Arms Today,* 2nd ed., Edward Ezell, Stackpole Books, 1988. *The Greenhill Military Small Arms Data Book,* Ian Hogg, Greenhill Books, 1999. *Modern Machine Guns,* John Walter, Greenhill Books, 2000. *The Encyclopedia of Modern Military Weapons,* Chris Bishop, ed., Barnes & Noble, 1999. *The World's Submachine Guns,* Vol. I, Thomas B. Nelson, 1964. *The World's Assault Rifles,* Vol. II, Musgrave and Nelson, 1967. *The World's Fighting Shotguns,* Vol. IV, Thomas F. Swearengen, Ironside, 1978. *Flayderman's Guide to Antique American Firearms...and Their Values,* 7th edition, Krause Publications, 1998. Paul S. Scarlata's *Collecting Classic Bolt Action Military Rifles,* Andrew Mobray Publishers, 2001, gives a good overview of this field for the collector. I have endeavored to give the reader a listing of helpful books of specific weapons at the beginning of each section, where applicable, so that he may easily pursue additional information that is outside the scope of this book.

SNAP SHOTS

This is a new feature for the Military Catalog that intends to give the reader a firsthand look at selected firearms, both old and new, from the writer's individual perspective. Due to space limitations, these reviews are kept to a 300-word maximum. Despite this restriction, we think these commentaries are valuable to the reader. We hope that this will personalize and bring to life what otherwise might be a dispassionate rendition of technical facts and descriptions. We all have our likes and dislikes when it comes to firearms. I hope our readers enjoy our contributors' personal opinions and insights.

CONTRIBUTORS

Charles Cutshaw:

Charles Cutshaw is a decorated veteran of the U.S. Army with service in Vietnam. Mr. Cutshaw also served as a civilian technical intelligence officer for 17 years. He is a recognized authority on small arms and ammunition. He is also the editor of *Jane's Ammunition Handbook,* co-editor of *Jane's Infantry Weapons,* small arms editor of *Jane's International Defense Review Magazine,* and contributing editor to numerous firearms publications. He is also the author of *The New World of Russian Small Arms and Ammo* as well as co-author (with Valery Shilin) of *Legends and Reality of the AK* and (with Dianne Cutshaw) a comprehensive major study of firearms, law enforcement, and crime in the United States. He has published numerous articles in monthly domestic and international periodicals.

David Fortier:

David Fortier's byline first appeared in the September 1999 issue of *Gun World* magazine. Encouraged by *Gun World's* editor, Jan Labourel, he has gone on to write over 140 articles. Currently he is the Precision Shooting editor for *Guns* magazine and a contributing editor to *Gun World, Shotgun News,* and the *Accurate Rifle.* His main interest is post-1886 military small arms, specifically sniper rifles, and has traveled as far as Russia in pursuit of them. He is one of the few westerners to have fired the AN-94 Nikonov. An avid shooter, he also trains regularly. His articles are the result of much help from both friends and colleagues. He resides in rural Maine with his wife/photographer Emily and their two cats.

Dan Shea:

Dan Shea is a U.S. Army veteran, and has been an active machine gun manufacturer, dealer, and importer for well over 20 years. He is the author of *Machine Gun Dealer's Bible,* now in its fourth printing, and for ten years was the Technical Editor of the now defunct *Machine Gun News* magazine. Dan owns Long Mountain Outfitters, one of the nation's largest and oldest Class 3 dealers, and has handled more than 15,000 machine gun transfers. He is also the General Manager and Technical Editor of *Small Arms Review* magazine. (www.smallarmsreview.com)

Peter Kokalis:

Peter G. Kokalis served in the United States Army in the field of technical intelligence. He holds a B.A. degree from

Northwestern University and an M.S. degree in the physical sciences from Arizona State University. He was the technical editor of *Soldier of Fortune* for twenty years and is currently Senior Editor of the *Small Arms Review*. He has participated in four wars, to include Afghanistan in 1983, Angola and South West Africa, Bosnia-Herzegovina and 21 combat missions in El Salvador. He is a member of the board of directors of the International Wound Ballistics Association and has served as an expert witness in a number of important cases in the firearms industry. He is the author of more than one thousand articles on topics ranging from pen guns to 155mm self-propelled artillery and is considered to be a leading authority in the field of modern military small arms.

Chuck Karwan:

Chuck attended and graduated from the U.S. Military Academy where he spent a tremendous amount of time in the West Point Museum firearms study collection learning everything he could about firearms. He eventually graduated from Airborne, Jump Master, Jungle School, Ranger School (Honor Graduate), and the Special Forces Officers Course, among others, and was five time heavyweight wrestling champion of all the military services. He served a combat tour in Vietnam with the 1st Cavalry Division where he acquired a substantial collection of captured weapons that were donated to the West Point Museum.
His gun collecting interests and knowledge are broad, covering everything from muzzle loaders to machine guns. He left the military in 1978 to start a career in writing and has written hundreds of articles in a wide variety of firearms-related magazines including a recent article in the *American Rifleman*. He has authored two books on combat handgunnery and has contributed chapters and articles to several dozen other books. He is an avid hunter and also frequently serves as a legal expert on firearms.

Frank James:

Frank W. James has been writing firearms-related articles and commentaries for over seventeen years. Currently he is a Projects Editor for *Guns & Ammo Handguns* and a contributing editor to *Combat Handguns*.

He has published over 900 articles in seven countries during his career. He is the IDPA Area Coordinator for the states of Indiana and Michigan. He is also a Special Deputy with the White County Sheriff's Department, Monticello, Indiana, as well as that agency's firearms instructor. He is certified by the Indiana Law Enforcement Academy to teach police handgun, shotgun, and patrol carbine. He is an active shooting competitor, primarily in IDPA handgun competition, but he has participated over many years in IPSC (USPSA), NRA Small Bore rifle, NRA Bullseye pistol, and the Masters International Tournament. He has completed training in several of the Heckler & Koch International Training Division courses, as well as Thunder Ranch, the Sigarms Academy, and the Yavapi Firearms Academy. In 1995, he was named the OUTSTANDING WRITER OF THE YEAR by Anchutz-Precision Sales, Inc. He is the author of the *MP5 Submachine Gun Story*, available from Krause Publications.

Paul Scarlata:

Paul is a resident of North Carolina and has been involved in gun collecting and the shooting sports longer than he would care to admit on these pages. For the last twelve years he has been a full time writer and contributes to the *Shotgun News, Shooting Times, American Rifleman, Man at Arms, Military History, SWAT, Combat Handguns, Women & Guns*, a number of Krause annuals and—in his spare time—also writes for gun magazines in eight foreign countries. Paul bought his first military surplus rifle when he was seventeen and has amassed—and disposed of—several rather extensive collections since then and is presently specializing in Krag—Jorgensens. While his writing covers all aspects of the shooting sports, his primary interest lies in military small arms from the 1875—1945 period. His first book, *Collecting Classic Bolt Action Military Rifles,* was published in 2000 and his second, on Mannlicher straight-pull rifles, is due for publication in 2003.

Whenever possible, Paul makes it a practice to test fire the guns he writes about. In this he is greatly aided by 2nd Amendment Research & Development (Tel. 520-642-9314 http://www.ammunitions.com), a company which produces an extensive selection of custom reloaded modern and obsolete ammunition.

CLASS III FIREARMS

Condensed from the article by Joe Moody

One important fact to remember is the basic law of supply and demand. The NFA weapons market has a small supply and a large demand. This always drives prices upward. It is estimated that there are only about 155,000 registered NFA firearms in the hands of individuals in the U.S.

The market price for NFA weapons has been steadily increasing, although in the past year or so the increase has been quite dramatic. Twenty years ago a new M16 rifle cost approximately $350; today it's about $4,500. During the same period, a German light machine gun, the MG42, cost about $900. Today, if one can be found, its cost is approximately $10,000 or more. The most important aspects of the pricing formula are rarity, desirability, and historical significance. Keep in mind that these guns are not bought on the world market at prices much lower than private sales to individuals. These guns bring a premium because the buyer is in essence purchasing the grandfathered registration paperwork of the weapon plus the weapon itself.

In order to better understand the pricing structure of NFA weapons, it is necessary to understand the different chronological sequences that NFA weapons went through. There were periods of time which gradually decreased the incoming supply of NFA weapons entering the NFA registry. The Gun Control Act of 1968 was one of the most crucial. Pursuant to NFA weapons, the 1968 Act stipulated that no more imported machine guns could be brought into the system. As a result, pre-1968 imported guns command a premium because of their original manufacture. During 1968, the NFA branch of the ATF allowed a one-year amnesty period so that returning servicemen from Vietnam could register their war trophies. It was during this period that many AK47s, PPSH41s, and MP40 machine guns were put into the system. Many more U.S. and foreign manufactured guns were also registered at this time as well. All of these guns command a premium because of their originality and registration.

Domestic production of NFA weapons continued until 1986, when the 1986 Gun Control Act prohibited the registration of domestic machine guns. Thus the door was closed to any further production of machine guns available to individuals. NFA weapons already registered could remain in the system and be transferred to qualified individuals. This situation drove prices higher and continues to do so. This group of weapons consists of many desirable semi-automatics that were legally converted into fully automatic weapons. These include the HK94s converted to the MP5, the HK91s converted to the G3, and the HK93 converted to the HK33. There were many Browning .30 and .50 caliber machine guns manufactured during this time frame as well. But remember, pedigree determines price. An original pre-1968 Israeli-manufactured

UZI will fetch over $9,000 whereas a U.S. manufactured UZI built during the same time period will only bring $3,000.

[The reader needs to be aware that there are different classifications of Class 3 guns that are not original guns but are instead referred to as "side-plate guns." These are principally Browning Model 1917s, 1919s, Vickers, and a few others. These are guns with non-original side-plates. There are also re-welds or rewats. These are guns that were deactivated and then reactivated. Pricing for these categories can be confusing, and it is suggested that the collector or shooter seek expert advice before a sale. Editor]

Those individuals who wish to be Class 3 dealers in machine guns have many more NFA weapons to choose from, especially the newer, more contemporary designs. Pre-1986 dealer samples, imported before 1986, can be transferred between dealers only and retained personally by them after they surrender their Class 3 licenses. Only people who wish to engage in active business of buying and selling machine guns should do this as it entails much more paperwork and responsibility. These dealer samples can only be transferred to other dealers. Some of these contemporary guns are very rare and desirable. For example, a pre-1986 dealer sample FN MAG machine gun in excellent condition will bring upwards of $60,000 because only about six of these guns were imported into the country before 1986. Supply and demand rule here.

Post-1986 dealer samples are even more restrictive. Only dealers who can produce a law enforcement letter wishing to demonstrate these weapons can obtain them. Unlike the pre-1986 samples, these post-1986 samples cannot be retained after their license is surrendered. It is for this reason that post-1986 dealer sample prices are not given.

People from all walks of life own and shoot these rare firearms. Sub-machine matches are held around the country for those interested in the competitive aspects of shooting these NFA weapons. Collecting and shooting NFA firearms is as interesting, perhaps more so, as the more traditional firearms. It is always important to keep in mind that these NFA firearms are heavily regulated and strict federal rules must be adhered to. Always follow NFA rules. When in doubt, call or write the ATF for clarification.

J.R. Moody, a degreed historian, has been collecting and shooting Class III firearms for twenty years because he enjoys the historical and technological aspects of these firearms. He competes successfully at sub-machine matches across the country. On several occasions he has defeated the National Champion. In addition he works as a consultant to Knight's Armament Company, one of the country's leading small arms contractors to U.S. military forces and law enforcement agencies.

ADVISORY: For those readers who are interested in advancing their knowledge and understanding of Class III firearms, it is recommended that they subscribe to *Small Arms Review*, a first rate publication that has many informative and useful features. There are sections on the law, new products, and illuminating articles on all aspects of NFA weapons and their history. *Small Arms Review* may be contacted at Moose Lake Publishing, 223 Sugar Hill Rd., Harmony, ME 04942. Telephone 207-683-2959 or FAX 203-683-2172. E-mail SARreview@aol.com. Web site: http://www.small-armsreview.com.

NOTE: *The prices listed for Class III firearms reflect the most current information as of publication date. Class III firearms are very volatile with rapid and sudden price changes. It is highly recommended that the latest market prices be verified in a particular market prior to a sale.*

DEWAT (Deactived War Trophy) MACHINE GUNS

Mention should be made that these guns, which have been rendered inactive according to BATF regulations, have a general value that is a rough percentage of its active counterpart: that percentage is approximately 80%. This percentage is only an approximation because of a wide range of factors ranging from who performed the deactivation, the extent of the work, how difficult it would be to reactivate the gun, and whether or not the work could be done without altering the basic look and function of the orginal. The collector should note that very rare machine guns, DEWAT or not, will bring the same price.

It should be noted also that reactivated machine guns are priced as conversions, because they are no longer in original condition.

Browning Model 1917 (Westinghouse)

ARGENTINA

Argentine Military Conflicts, 1870-Present

During the latter part of the 19th century Argentina suffered from political instability and military coups. This instability continued into the 20th century. Argentina adopted a pre-Axis neutrality during World War II and finally entered the war on the Allied side in 1945. With a military coup in 1944 Colonel Juan Peron rose to power and implemented a popular dictatorship. The subsequent 30 years saw Peron and his wives come and go in power with the eventual coup in 1976 that led to a repressive military junta led by General Galteri. In 1982, Argentina occupied the Falkland Islands and was defeated by the British in the war that followed. The balance of its 20th century history is marked by economic difficulties and austerity measures.

NOTE: Argentina manufactures most of its small arms in government factories located in different locations around the country. This factory is known as the *Fabrica Militar de Armas Portatiles "Domingo Matheu"* (FMAP "DM"). It is located in Rosario.

HANDGUNS

Argentina also used a small number of Star Select fire pistols for its special forces. See *Spain, Handguns, Star Model M.*

FN Model 1935 GP

Designated by the Argentine military as the "Browning Pistol PD." Licensed from FN and manufactured by FMAP "DM." Since 1969, Argentina has built about 185,000 of these pistols some of which have been sold commercially. This 9x19 caliber pistol is marked on the left side of the slide, "FABRICA MILITAR DE ARMAS PORTATILES "D.M." ROSARIO, D.G.F.M., LICENCIA F N BROWNING, INDUSTRAI ARGENTINA."

Exc.	V.G.	Good	Fair	Poor
500	400	300	225	150

BALLESTER—MOLINA

Argentine D.G.F.M.

(Direccion General de Fabricaciones Militares) made at the F.M.A.P. (Fabrica Militar de Arms Portatiles (Military Factory of Small Arms)) Licensed copies SN 24,000 to 112,494 (Parts are generally interchangeable with Colt. Most pistols were marked "D.G.F.M. - (F.M.A.P.)." Late pistols were marked FM

within a cartouche on the right side of the slide. These pistols are found both with and without import markings, often in excellent condition, currently more often in refinished condition, and with a seemingly endless variety of slide markings. None of these variations have yet achieved any particular collector status or distinction, unless "New In Box." A "New In The Box" DGFM recently sold at auction for $1200. In fact, many of these fine pistols have and continue to be used as the platforms for the highly customized competition and target pistols that are currently popular.

Courtesy Karl Karash collection

Exc.	V.G.	Good	Fair	Poor
550	425	350	275	225

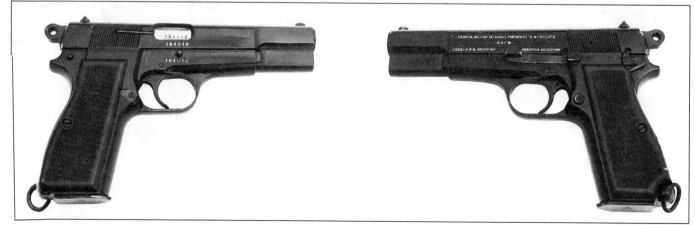

Argentine Hi-Power • Courtesy Blake Stevens, from *The Browning High-Power Automatic Pistol*, Stevens

Argentine Made Ballester Molina

Un-licensed, Argentine re-designed versions (parts are NOT interchangeable with Colt except for the barrel and magazine). These pistols are found both with and without import markings. Pistols without import markings usually have a B prefix number stamped on the left rear part of the mainspring housing and are often in excellent to New original condition. The vast majority of currently available pistols are found in excellent but re-finished condition. Only the pistols with no import markings that are in excellent to New original condition have achieved any particular collector status. Most of these pistols that are being sold today are being carried and shot, rather than being collected. 99%-100% = Exc + 40%; Refinished = Fair/Poor.

Courtesy Karl Karash collection

Exc.	V.G.	Good	Fair	Poor
425	300	250	185	135

SUBMACHINE GUNS

Shortly after World War II, Argentina purchased a number of Beretta Model 38A₂ directly from Beretta. The Argentine military also used the Sterling Mark 4 and the Sterling Mark 5 (silenced version) purchased directly from Sterling against British forces during the Falkland War. The Argentine Coast Guard purchased HK MP5A2 and MP5A3 guns from Germany.

The Argentines have also produced a number of submachine guns of its own design and manufacture. The PAM 1, PAM 2, the FMK series, and the Mems series were, or are, all Argentine submachine guns. It is doubtful if any of these guns were imported into the U.S. prior to 1968 and are therefore not transferable.

RIFLES

In 1879, the Argentine army adopted the Remington Rolling rifle in .43 caliber as its standard issue rifle. This was followed by the Mauser Model 1891 rifle.

The Model 1909 was replaced by the FN FAL series of rifles. This was the standard rifle of the Argentine armed forces. About 150,000 of these rifles have been issued in various configurations and the majority of these were manufactured in Argentina at FMAP "DM" Rosario.

Argentina has also used the U.S. M1 carbine, the Beretta BM59 rifle, and the Steyr SSG sniper rifle.

MAUSER

M1891 Rifle

This rifle was made in Germany with a 19.1" barrel and 5-round magazine. Full stock with straight grip with half-length upper handguard. Rear sight V-notch. Chambered for the 7.65x53mm cartridge. Weight is about 8.8 lbs. Marked with Argentine crest on receiver ring.

Exc.	V.G.	Good	Fair	Poor
400	350	300	150	90

M1891 Carbine

Full stock with straight grip. Front sight protectors and sling loops attached to bottom of stock behind the triggerguard. Turned down bolt. Barrel length is 17.6". Caliber is 7.65x53mm. Weight is about 7.2 lbs.

Exc.	V.G.	Good	Fair	Poor
400	350	300	200	150

M1909 Rifle

Based on the Gew design and fitted with a 29" barrel and tangent rear sight graduated to 2000 meters. Almost full stock with pistol grip. The 5-round magazine fits in a flush box magazine with hinged floor plate. Chambered for the 7.65x53mm cartridge. Some of these rifles were made in Germany and about 85,000 were built in Argentina. Argentine crest on receiver ring. Weight is about 9 lbs.

Courtesy Rock Island Auction Company

Exc.	V.G.	Good	Fair	Poor
500	425	375	250	175

M1909 Sniper Rifle w/o scope

Same as above but for bent bolt and scope. Some telescopes were German-made for the Argentine army.

Exc.	V.G.	Good	Fair	Poor
1500	900	750	600	400

M1909 Cavalry Carbine

Built by the German company DWM and Argentine companies as well. This 7.65x53mm rifle has a full-length stock with straight grip and 21.5" barrel. Upper handguard is 2/3 length. Bayonet fittings. Weight is about 8.5 lbs. About 19,000 of these carbines were produced in Argentina between 1947 and 1959.

Exc.	V.G.	Good	Fair	Poor
400	350	300	225	150

M1909 Mountain Carbine

Sometimes referred to as the Engineers model. This is a cut down Model 1909 rifle with 21.25" barrel with bayonet lug. Rear sight graduated to 1400 meters. Weight is about 8.5 lbs.

Exc.	V.G.	Good	Fair	Poor
400	350	300	225	150

FN FAL (Argentine Manufacture)

A number of these have been imported into the U.S. in semi-automatic configuration. Marked, "FABRICA MILITAR DE ARMAS PORTATILES-ROSARIO, INDUSTRAI ARGENTINA."

Exc.	V.G.	Good	Fair	Poor
3000	2500	1500	900	450

SHOTGUNS

Mossberg Model 500

In 1976, the Argentine navy acquired the Mossberg Model 500 in 12 gauge.

Exc.	V.G.	Good	Fair	Poor
600	500	400	200	100

MACHINE GUNS

The Argentine military has used a wide variety of machine guns from various sources. Obsolete guns include the Browning Model 1917 water-cooled gun. More current machine guns are the Browning .50 caliber M2 HB, the FN MAG, the French AAT-52, and the MG3.

Argentine Maxim Model 1895

This gun was sold to Argentina from both British and German sources. Standard pattern early Maxim gun with smooth brass water jacket and brass feed plates. Most likely chambered for the 7.65x53mm Mauser cartridge. Rate of fire was about 400 rounds per minute. Weight of the gun was approximately 60 lbs. Marked in Spanish on the receiver as well as the country of manufacture.

NOTE: According to Dolf Goldsmith, author of *The Devil's Paintbrush,* some 55 of these guns are in private hands in the U.S.

Pre-1968 (Rare)

Exc.	V.G.	Fair
25000	20000	17500

Pre-1986 conversions

Exc.	V.G.	Fair
12500	10000	9500

Pre-1986 dealer samples

Exc.	V.G.	Fair
N/A	N/A	N/A

British Maxim Nordenfelt M1895 in 7.65mm • Courtesy private NFA collection, Paul Goodwin photo

AUSTRALIA

Australian Military Conflicts, 1870-Present

The period of the last quarter of the 19th century was marked by colonization and westward expansion similar to that in the U.S. In 1901 the various colonies were federated as states into a Commonwealth of Australia. Australia fought on the side of Great Britain in both world wars. Australia sent troops to Vietnam in the 1960s and 1970s.

HANDGUNS

The Australian military currently uses the Browning Model 1935 designated the L9A1. These guns were manufactured by Inglis during World War II and since by FN. Chambered for 9mm cartridge. The first FN built pistols were purchased in 1963.

Australian Model L9A1 Pistol

This model is the standard British issue 9mm Model 1935 pistol built by FN under contract. Marked, "PISTOL, SELF-LOADING" instead of "PISTOL, AUTOMATIC." First ordered in June of 1963.

Exc.	V.G.	Good	Fair	Poor
650	550	400	200	150

SUBMACHINE GUNS

Australian military forces currently use its own designed and produced F1 submachine gun as well as the HK MP5 and MP5SD. The Sterling L34A1 silenced version is also used by special operations units.

Owen

This Australian submachine is chambered for the 9mm cartridge. It features a top mounted 33-round magazine and quick release barrel attachment. The barrel is 9.75" long and the rate of fire is 700 rounds per minute. Weight is about 9.25 lbs. It was produced from 1941 to 1944. Marked "OWEN 9MM MKI LYSAGHT PK AUSTRALIA PATENTED 22/7/41" on the right side of the frame.

Pre-1968

Exc.	V.G.	Fair
7500	7000	6500

Pre-1986 conversions (reweld)

Exc.	V.G.	Fair
5500	5000	4500

Pre-1986 dealer samples

Exc.	V.G.	Fair
4000	3500	3000

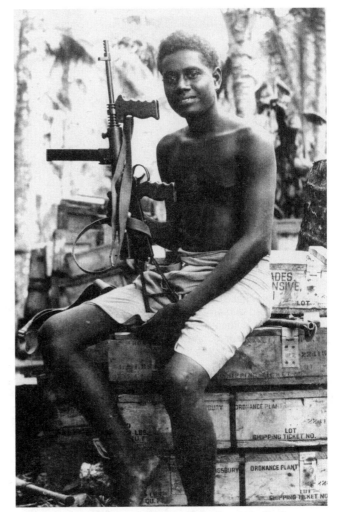

Pacific Theater, WWII. A native boy, armed with a 9mm Australian Owen submachine gun, guards an ammunition supply point • U.S. Army Signal Corps/Lee Holland Collection/Robert Bruce Military Photo Features

Owen • Paul Goodwin photo

Austen Mark I

Introduced in 1943 this gun is a take-off on the British Sten with a folding butt similar to the MP40. Chambered for the 9mm cartridge and fitted with an 8" barrel with forward grip. Uses a 28-round box magazine. Rate of fire is approximately 500 rounds per minute. Weight is about 9 lbs. About 20,000 were produced between 1943 and 1945 by Diecasters and Carmichael in Australia.

Austen Submachine Gun • Courtesy Thomas Nelson, from *The World's Submachine Guns, Vol. 1*

Pre-1968

Exc.	V.G.	Fair
5500	5000	4500

Pre-1986 conversions

Exc.	V.G.	Fair
N/A	N/A	N/A

Pre-1986 dealer samples

Exc.	V.G.	Fair
3000	2500	2000

F-1

First introduced in 1962, this submachine gun was built by the Australian arsenal at Lithgow. Chambered for the 9mm cartridge and fitted with an 8" barrel, this gun has a round receiver with a wooden buttstock with pistol grip and perforated barrel jacket. The 34-round magazine is top mounted. Weight is about 7 lbs. Rate of fire is approximately 600 rounds per minute.

NOTE: It is not known how many, if any, of these guns are in the U.S. and are transferable. Prices listed below are estimates only.

Pre-1968

Exc.	V.G.	Fair
10000	9500	9000

Pre-1986 conversions

Exc.	V.G.	Fair
N/A	N/A	N/A

Pre-1986 dealer samples

Exc.	V.G.	Fair
N/A	N/A	N/A

RIFLES

In 1985 the Australian Defense Ministry adopted the Steyr AUG 5.56mm F8 rifle as its service rifle. Australia also uses the British Parker Hale M82 Sniper Rifle, as well as the U.S. M16A1 rifle.

Vietnam, ca. 1968. Australian soldier on patrol, armed with the powerful 7.62mm NATO caliber L1A1 rifle, probably a license-built version of the Belgian FAL made at the Lithgow Arsenal. Another Aussie behind him carries an American M16 • U.S. Army Military History Institute/Robert Bruce Military Photo Features

Austrialian L1A1 Rifle • Courtesy Blake Stevens, *The FAL Rifle*

L1A1 Rifle

This is the British version of the FN-FAL in the "inch" or Imperial pattern. Most of these rifles were semiautomatic only. This rifle was the standard service rifle for the British army from about 1954 to 1988. The rifle was made in Lithgow, Australia, under license from FN. The configurations for the L1A1 rifle are the same as the standard FN-FAL Belgium rifle. Only a few of these rifles were imported into the U.S. They are very rare. This "inch" pattern British gun will also be found in other Commonwealth countries such as Australia, New Zealand, Canada, and India.

NOTE: Only about 180 Australian L1A1s were imported into the U.S. prior to 1989. These are rare and in great demand.

Exc.	V.G.	Good	Fair	Poor
5000	4500	—	—	—

MACHINE GUNS

Between 1925 and 1930 the Australian firm of Lithgow built the Vickers machine gun. Later, between 1938 and 1940, the same company built the Bren gun in .303 caliber. Approximately 12,000 Vickers and 17,000 Bren guns were built in Australia during this period. After World War II the Australian military adopted the U.S. M60 machine gun, the Browning 1919A4, and the .50 caliber Browning M2HB. More recently, that country's military uses the Belgian FN MAG, and the German MG3.

Australian Bren

This is a slightly modified version of the MK I built by the Small Arms Factory, Lithgow, beginning in 1940. Marked "MA" and "LITHGOW" on the right side of the receiver. A total of 17,429 guns were produced when production stopped August 13, 1945.

Pre-1968 (Extremely Rare)

Exc.	V.G.	Fair
35000	—	—

Pre-1986 conversions

Exc.	V.G.	Fair
N/A	N/A	N/A

Pre-1986 dealer samples

Exc.	V.G.	Fair
N/A	N/A	N/A

Australian Vickers

Manufactured by the Small Arms Factory in Lithgow beginning in 1929. The gun was last built in 1945. Serial numbers began with the number 1 and went to 9,999. From then on the prefix "B" was added. Highest serial number recorded is B2344.

Pre-1968

Exc.	V.G.	Fair
N/A	—	—

Pre-1986 conversions (side-plate using Colt 1915 or 1918 plates)

Exc.	V.G.	Fair
10500	9500	9000

Pre-1986 dealer samples

Exc.	V.G.	Fair
9000	8500	8000

AUSTRIA-HUNGARY AUSTRIA

Austrian/Hungarian Military Conflicts, 1870-Present

In 1867 the Austro-Hungarian monarchy ruled this important and critical part of Europe. Germany and Austria-Hungary entered into an alliance called the Dual Alliance and later, in 1882 when Italy joined, the Triple Alliance. In the same year Serbia and Romania joined this group as well. Eventually this partnership between Germany and Austria-Hungary pitted them against England and France for control of Europe. With the advent of World War I and the defeat of the Dual Alliance, the Austrian-Hungarian rule came to an end. Between 1914 and 1918 Austria-Hungary had a total of 7,800,000 serve in its armed forces. By the end of the war 2,482,870 had been killed or wounded, about 1/3 of total military personnel. In 1918 German Austria became a republic. The small nation was beset by social, economic, and political unrest throughout the 1920s and in 1934 a totalitarian regime was established. Austria became part of the German Third Reich in 1938. After the end of World War II, Austria was restored to a republic and occupied by the allies until 1955 when it became a sovereign nation. Austria joined the European Union in 1995.

HANDGUNS

Model 1870

This revolver is built on a Lefaucheux-Francotte double action solid frame with fixed cylinder with mechanical rod ejection. It is chambered for the 11.3mm cartridge and fitted with a 7.3" round barrel. The non-fluted cylinder holds 6 rounds. The frame and barrel were iron, not steel. Checkered wooden grips with lanyard loop. Built by the Austrian firm of Leopold Gasser, and marked "L.GASSER, WIEN, PATENT, OTTAKRING." Weight is about 53 oz., or 3.3 lbs., making it one of the heaviest military service revolvers of its time. When the Model 1878 was introduced and adopted by the Austro-Hungarian army, the Model 1870 was sold to the Balkan States and was sometimes referred to as the "Montenegrin" revolver.

Courtesy J. B. Wood

Military Unit Marked

Exc.	V.G.	Good	Fair	Poor
1250	750	400	250	150

Non-Unit Marked

Exc.	V.G.	Good	Fair	Poor
900	600	350	225	150

Model 1870/74 Gasser Trooper's Model

Similar to the above model but built with cast steel instead of iron. It was issued from 1874 to 1919. Built by the Austrian firm of Leopold Gasser. Weight is still about 53 oz.

Military Unit Marked

Exc.	V.G.	Good	Fair	Poor
1250	750	400	250	150

Non-Unit Marked

Exc.	V.G.	Good	Fair	Poor
900	600	350	225	150

Model 1878 Officer's Model

Because the Model 1870 revolver was so heavy and large, Johann Gasser, Leopold's younger brother, designed a smaller version chambered for the 9mm (9x26) cartridge. The barrel length was 4.8" and the overall length was reduced as well. The weight of this revolver was about 27 oz.

Exc.	V.G.	Good	Fair	Poor
750	500	350	200	150

Model 1898 • Paul Goodwin photo

Model 1898 Rast & Gasser

This model was built on the Schmidt-Galand double action solid frame with 8-round cylinder with loading gate and mechanical ejection rod. Chambered for the 8mm cartridge and fitted with a 4.5" round barrel. The caliber was too light to be effective as a military sidearm. The firing pin was a spring-loaded frame-mounted plunger instead of the more common hammer mounted type. Checkered wooden grips with lanyard loop. In service from 1898 to 1938. Weight is about 33 oz.

Short Grip

Exc.	V.G.	Good	Fair	Poor
500	300	150	120	90

Short Barrel

Exc.	V.G.	Good	Fair	Poor
3500	2000	1200	400	200

STEYR
Osterreichische Waffenfabrik Gesellschaft GmbH, Steyr (1869-1919)
Steyr-Werke AG (1919-1934)
Steyr-Daimler-Puch, Steyr (1934-1990)
Steyr-Mannlicher GmbH, Steyr (1990-)

Steyr Model 1893 Gas Seal Test Revolver

Chambered for the 8mm cartridge this 7 shot 5.5" barrel revolver was built by Steyr as a prototype for the Austrian army. Fewer than 100 were built. Several different variations. It is recommended that an expert be consulted prior to a sale.

Exc.	V.G.	Good	Fair	Poor
15000	9000	5000	2000	—

Roth Steyr Model 1907

Based on the patents granted to Karel Krnka and Georg Roth, the 8mm Model 1907 had a rotating barrel locking system and was the first self-loading pistol adopted by the Austro-Hungarian army. It was also the first successful double action automatic pistol. Add 20% for early Steyr examples without a large pin visible on right side of frame, or for those made in Budapest instead of Steyr.

Courtesy Joseph Schroeder

Exc.	V.G.	Good	Fair	Poor
750	600	500	350	250

Steyr Hahn Model 1911

The Steyr Hahn was originally introduced as a commercial pistol but was quickly adopted by the Austro-Hungarian, Chilean, and Romanian militaries. Magazine capacity is 8 rounds. Weight is about 30 oz. Commercial examples were marked "Osterreichische Waffenfabrik Steyr M1911 9m/m" on the slide, have a laterally adjustable rear sight, and are rare.

Austrian militaries are marked simply "STEYR" and the date of manufacture, while those made for Chile and Romania bear their respective crests. During WWII the Germans rebarreled a number of Steyr Hahns to 9mm Parabellum for police use, adding "P.08" to the slide along with appropriate Waffenamt markings. The German army designation for this pistol was "Pistole Mod 12(o)."

Courtesy Orvel Reichert

Commercially Marked

Exc.	V.G.	Good	Fair	Poor
1350	1000	750	500	350

P.08 Marked Slides

Exc.	V.G.	Good	Fair	Poor
800	500	350	200	125

Austrian Military

Exc.	V.G.	Good	Fair	Poor
400	300	200	150	100

FEG (Frommer) Stop Model 19

Introduced in 1912 and took a whole new approach compared to any of the pistols this company had produced to that point. It is still unconventional as it uses two recoil springs in a tube above the barrel and resembles an air pistol in this way. It is chambered for 7.65mm or 9mm short and has a 3.75" barrel. The detachable magazine holds 7 rounds, and the sights are fixed. This locked-breech action, semiautomatic pistol was a commercial success. It was used widely by the Austro-Hungarian military during WWI. It was manufactured between 1912 and 1920.

Courtesy James Rankin

Exc.	V.G.	Good	Fair	Poor
350	250	200	150	100

Model 1929

A blowback-operated semiautomatic chambered for the 9mm short cartridge. It has an external hammer and the barrel was retained, as the Browning was, by four lugs. This was a simple and reliable pistol, and it was adopted by the military as a replacement for the Stop. This model was manufactured between 1929 and 1937. It was also produced in .22 Long Rifle.

Courtesy James Rankin

Exc.	V.G.	Good	Fair	Poor
450	325	200	175	125

PA-63

An aluminum frame copy of the Walther PP in a slightly larger size. Chambered for the 9mm Makarov cartridge. This was the standard Hungarian service, until recently.

Exc.	V.G.	Good	Fair	Poor
165	135	120	90	75

R-61

This model is a smaller version of the PA-63. Chambered for the 9mm Makarov. This model is slightly longer than a Walther PPK and was intended for issue to high ranking officers, CID, and police units.

Exc.	V.G.	Good	Fair	Poor
185	150	130	100	80

Glock 17

Adopted by the Austrian military in 1983. This model is chambered for the 9mm Parabellum cartridge. It is a double action only semiautomatic that has a 4.49" barrel and a 17-shot detachable magazine. The empty weight of this pistol is 21.91 oz. This pistol is offered with either fixed or adjustable sights at the same retail price. The finish is black with black plastic grips. It is furnished in a plastic case with an extra magazine. This pistol was introduced in the U.S. in 1985 and is still currently produced.

NIB	Exc.	V.G.	Good	Fair	Poor
600	450	325	300	275	175

Note: Add $70 if equipped with Meprolight night sights. Add $90 if equipped with Trijicon night sights. Add $30 if equipped with adjustable sights.

SUBMACHINE GUNS

Steyr-Solothurn MP 30

Introduced in 1930 and built at the Steyr plant under license from the Swiss firm, Solothurn. It was adopted by the Austrian police. Chambered for the 9x23 Steyr cartridge and fitted with a 7.8" jacketed barrel. It is fed by a 32-round magazine and has a rate of fire of about 500 rounds per minute. Wood buttstock with unusual upswept appearance. It is select fire. Weight is about 9.5 lbs. Produced from 1930 to 1935 with approximately 6,000 manufactured.

Steyr Model 1930 • Courtesy Thomas Nelson, from *World's Submachine Guns, Vol. I*

Pre-1968

Exc.	V.G.	Fair
8000	7500	7000

Pre-1986 conversions (reweld)

Exc.	V.G.	Fair
6000	5500	5000

Pre-1986 dealer samples

Exc.	V.G.	Fair
4000	3500	3000

Steyr-Solothurn S1-100 (MP 34(o))

This gun machine was designed in Germany, perfected in Switzerland, and built in Austria. Steyr-Solothurn was a shell company established to enable the German company Rheinmetall to evade the restrictions of the Versailles Treaty that prevented them from producing military small arms. The gun was used by the Austrian army as well as the German army. It is chambered for the 9x23 Steyr cartridge as well as others. The German army used them in 9mm Parabellum while Austrian troops used the gun chambered for the 9mm Mauser cartridge. The gun was also sold to Portugal where it was designated the Model 42. Barrel length is almost 7.8". Magazine capacity is 32 rounds. Rate of fire is about 500 rounds per minute. Fixed wooden butt and forearm. Weight is approximately 9.5 lbs. Produced from 1934 to 1939. On this gun, a magazine loading device is built into the magazine housing.

Pre-1968

Exc.	V.G.	Fair
8500	8000	7500

Pre-1986 conversions (reweld)

Exc.	V.G.	Fair
6500	6000	5500

Pre-1986 dealer samples

Exc.	V.G.	Fair
4500	4000	3500

Steyr Mpi69

Built in Austria, this submachine gun is chambered for the 9mm cartridge. It was adopted by the Austrian army in 1969. The gun features a 10" barrel and 25- or 32-round magazine. It has a rate of fire of 550 rounds per minute. It is marked "STEYR-DAIMLER-PUCH AG MADE IN AUSTRIA" on top of the receiv-

er. The folding stock is metal. The gun weighs about 7 lbs. Production stopped in 1990.

Photo courtesy private NFA collection

Pre-1968 (Rare)

Exc.	V.G.	Fair
8000	7500	7000

Pre-1986 conversions

Exc.	V.G.	Fair
N/A	N/A	N/A

Pre-1986 dealer samples

Exc.	V.G.	Fair
4500	4000	3500

RIFLES

MANNLICHER
Built by Steyr & Fegyvergyar

Model 1885

This was the first magazine rifle used by Austria-Hungary and the first straight-pull rifle used as a general issue shoulder arm. This model required that a clip be used to load the box magazine, loose cartridges could not be loaded. Like the U.S. M1 Garand, clips were ejected up from the receiver when empty. Chambered for the 11.15mmx58R black powder cartridge. Barrel length is 31" with two barrel bands. Box magazine held 5 clip loaded rounds. Weight was about 10 lbs. Only about 1500 of these rifles were built.

Exc.	V.G.	Good	Fair	Poor
1200	900	700	500	300

Model 1886

This rifle was produced in large numbers and adopted for general service use. This model is similar to the Model 1885 but unlike the M85, the clip of this rifle ejected out of the bottom of the magazine. Still chambered for the 11.15mmx58R black powder cartridge. Barrel length was 30". After 1888 most of these rifles were converted to 8x50R smokeless powder. Two barrel bands with pistol grip stock. This rifle was made at Steyr. Weight was slightly under 10 lbs.

Exc.	V.G.	Good	Fair	Poor
400	300	200	100	75

MP 34 • Paul Goodwin photo

Model 1888/1890 • Courtesy West Point Museum, Paul Goodwin photo

Model 1888

This model is the same as the Model 1886 except chambered for the 8x50R black powder cartridge.

Exc.	V.G.	Good	Fair	Poor
550	400	250	150	100

Model 1888/1890

This variation is the result of the change-over from black powder to smokeless. This model was chambered for the 8x50R smokeless powder cartridge with a stronger bolt locking wedge. Barrel length was 30". New sights were added to accommodate the new cartridge. These sights were graduated. This model was also made at Steyr. A number of these were sold to Bulgaria, Greece, and Chile. A number of these rifles were used during WWI and some were found in irregular units during WWII.

Exc.	V.G.	Good	Fair	Poor
400	275	200	150	75

Model 1890 Carbine

This model represented a departure from previous models, not only in design, but incorporated a stronger action to better handle the 8x50R smokeless cartridge. On this model the bolt head contained the extractor. The result of this new design was that the trigger was behind the end of the bolt handle. Barrel length was 19.5" with a single barrel band and no handguard. There is no bayonet lug on this rifle. The box magazine capacity was 5 rounds of clip loaded ammunition. Weight is about 7 lbs.

Exc.	V.G.	Good	Fair	Poor
650	450	300	200	100

Model 1895 Infantry Rifle

Chambered for the 8x50R cartridge, this straight pull bolt action rifle was fitted with a 30" barrel with an integral clip loaded magazine and wooden handguard. This model has essentially the same action as the Model 1890 Carbine. Fitted with leaf sights. Weight is about 8 lbs. Produced from 1895 to about 1918 both at Steyr and Budapest. The rifle was marked with either of these two locations on top of the receiver ring along with "M95."

This was the primary shoulder arm of the Austro-Hungarian army during WWI and was made in huge quantities. The rifle

was also used by Bulgaria and Greece. Many of these models were used in Italy during WWII, as well as the Balkans during that same period of time.

NOTE: In the 1930s, both Austria and Hungary converted large numbers of these rifles to 8x56Rmm. Many of these rifles were converted to carbines at the same time. Converted rifles will have an "S" or "H" stamped over the chamber.

Between the two world wars, many Model 95s were converted to 8x57mm short rifles and fitted with 24" barrels. These rifles used the standard Mauser stripper clip instead of the Mannlicher system. Receivers were marked "M95M" and "M95/24". Yugoslavia was the main user of these rifles.

Exc.	V.G.	Good	Fair	Poor
250	200	125	75	50

THE M95 STEYR STRAIGHT PULL

The M95 Steyr straight pull rifle was the primary service rifle of the Austro-Hungarian Empire at its peak and consequently was made and used in huge quantities (7 to 8 million). It is by far the most significant of all the straight pull bolt action military rifles. Unlike most others it proved to be reliable under the worst field conditions and served with considerable distinction in WWI. The action of the M95 was actually introduced into Austrian service in 1890 with their M90 carbine. It had controlled round feeding using a non-rotating claw extractor, timed ejection, and a strong breaching system with the bolt head protruding through a collar in the receiver. No Mauser had all these features until their M1898. It was often criticized because the rifle could not function as a repeater without its special clips and the opening in the bottom of the magazine for clip ejection allowed dirt into the magazine. The latter rarely was a real problem since any dirt that got in just fell back out. Since the ammunition was issued already in the clips, the second criticism rarely applied either. Because of its short straight pull action and faster loading Mannlicher clips, the M95 had a higher rate of fire than any Mauser or other bolt action of its day, except the ten shot Lee-Enfield. Originally chambered for the Austrian 8x50Rmm cartridge, in between the world wars many were converted to the hotter 8x56Rmm cartridge for Austria and Hungary and the 8x57mm cartridge for Yugoslavia. Huge numbers in all three chamberings saw service in WWII. The M95 was a far better and more historically significant rifle than most Americans realize. It was stronger, more reliable, faster firing, and more effective than most of its contemporaries.

Chuck Karwan

Model 1886 • Courtesy West Point Museum, Paul Goodwin photo

Model 1895 Short Rifle (Stuzen M95)

This model was designed for non-cavalry use as it was fitted with a bayonet lug and sling swivels on the underside of the rifle. It was also fitted with a stacking hook attached to the barrel band. When the bayonet is attached, a blade sight is integral with the bayonet barrel ring for sighting purposes. Weight is about 7.5 lbs.

Exc.	V.G.	Good	Fair	Poor
400	300	250	125	75

FEGYVERGYAR
Fegyver es Gepgyar Resvenytarsasag, Budapest, (1880-1945)
Femaru es Szersazamgepgyar NV (1945-1985)
FEG Arms & Gas Appliances Factory (1985-)

Model 35 Rifle

This turn-bolt rifle is based on the Romanian Model 1893 Mannlicher turn bolt but chambered for the 8x56Rmm cartridge. It is clip loaded with a full-length stock (two-piece around receiver) and full upper handguard. Barrel length is 23.5". Magazine capacity is 5 rounds. Weight is about 9 lbs.

Exc.	V.G.	Good	Fair	Poor
400	275	200	125	75

Model 1895 Sharpshooter's Rifle

Same configuration as the Infantry rifle except for the addition of double set triggers. Rare.

Exc.	V.G.	Good	Fair	Poor
750	600	500	400	200

Model 1895 Sniper Rifle

Same as the Sharpshooter's rifle but fitted with a telescope sight. Extremely rare.

Exc.	V.G.	Good	Fair	Poor
3000	2500	2000	—	—

Model 1895 Cavalry Carbine

Essentially the same as the Infantry rifle with a shorter barrel. Barrel length is 19.5". The sling swivels are located on the side on the stock and there is no bayonet lug or stacking hook. Weight is about 7 lbs. Produced until 1918.

Exc.	V.G.	Good	Fair	Poor
400	350	275	—	—

Model 35 with close up of receiver ring • Private collection, Paul Goodwin photo

Close up of receiver ring of Model 1895 Steyr Rifle

Model 1895 Steyr Rifle • Courtesy West Point Museum, Paul Goodwin photo

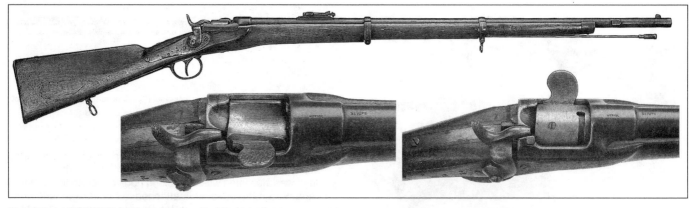

Werndl Model 1867/77 Rifle • Private collection, Paul Goodwin photo

STEYR
Osterreichische Waffenfabrik Gesellschaft GmbH, Steyr (1869-1919)
Steyr-Werke AG (1919-1934)
Steyr-Daimler-Puch, Steyr (1934-1990)
Steyr-Mannlicher GmbH, Steyr (1990-)

Werndl Model 1867 Infantry Rifle

This is a single shot rotary breech block action with external side hammer. It is full stocked with exposed muzzle and bayonet fitting. Chambered for the 11.15x58R Werndl cartridge. Barrel length is 33.6". Weight is about 9.75 lbs. About 600,000 Model 1867 rifles were built.

Exc.	V.G.	Good	Fair	Poor
450	400	300	200	100

Werndl Model 1867 Carbine

Similar to the rifle above but with a 22.4" barrel. Chambered for the 11x36R Werndl cartridge. Weight is approximately 7 lbs. About 11,000 carbines were produced.

Exc.	V.G.	Good	Fair	Poor
550	500	400	250	100

Werndl Model 1873 Infantry Rifle

This model is an improved version of the The Model 1867 with central exposed hammer. Caliber is 11x41RM Werndl. Barrel length is 33.2". Weight is about 9.25 lbs. Total production was about 400,000.

Exc.	V.G.	Good	Fair	Poor
450	400	300	200	100

Werndl Model 1873 Carbine

Similar to the M1873 rifle but with a 22.8" barrel. Chambered for the 11x36R Werndl cartridge. Weight is about 7 lbs. Total production for this model was about 100,000 carbines.

Exc.	V.G.	Good	Fair	Poor
550	500	400	250	100

Werndl Model 1867/77 Rifles and Carbines

This model was the Model 1873 but redesigned for the 11x58R cartridge with a modified rear sight graduated from 200 to 2100 steps.

Exc.	V.G.	Good	Fair	Poor
450	400	300	200	100

Model 95 Rifle (Model 31)

A number of Model 95 rifles and short rifles were modified to accept the 8x56Rmm cartridge after World War I. The letter "H" is stamped on the barrel or the receiver. This is a straight pull rifle with 19.6" barrel and a 5-round fixed magazine. Weight is approximately 7.5 lbs.

Exc.	V.G.	Good	Fair	Poor
125	80	65	40	25

Model 1903

Built for Greece in 6.5x54mm.

Exc.	V.G.	Good	Fair	Poor
400	275	200	125	75

NOTE: For Carbine version add a 50% premium.

Model 1904

Similar to the Dutch Model 1895 but chambered for 8x57mm rimless cartridge. Many of these rifles were sold to China and about 11,000 were sold to the Irish Ulster Volunteer Force.

Exc.	V.G.	Good	Fair	Poor
300	175	125	75	50

NOTE: For Irish Ulster marked versions add a 30% premium.

Model SSG-PI

This model features a black synthetic stock originally designed as a military sniper rifle. Fitted with a cocking indicator, single or double set trigger, 5-round rotary magazine or 10-round magazine. Receiver is milled to NATO specifications for Steyr ring mounts. Barrel length is 26". Rifle weighs about 9 lbs. Offered in .308 Win.

NOTE: This model was originally called the SSG 69.

NIB	Exc.	V.G.	Good	Fair	Poor
1700	1300	1000	—	—	—

Steyr AUG (Armee Universal Gewehr)

Produced by Steyr-Mannlicher beginning in 1978, this rifle is chambered for the 5.56x45mm cartridge. It is a bullpup design with a number of different configurations. Barrel lengths are 13.6" in submachine gun configuration, 16.3" in carbine, 19.8" in rifle, and 24.2" in a heavy barrel sniper configuration. Magazine is 30 or 42 rounds. Carry handle is an optic sight of 1.5 power. Adopted by Austrian army and still in production. Weight is 7.7 lbs. in rifle configuration. Rate of fire is about 650 rounds per minute.

Photo courtesy private NFA collection

Pre-1968

Exc.	V.G.	Fair
N/A	N/A	N/A

Pre-1986 conversions

Exc.	V.G.	Fair
8000	7500	7000

Pre-1986 dealer samples

Exc.	V.G.	Fair
7500	7300	7000

Steyr AUG (Semiautomatic Version)

As above but in semiautomatic only. Two versions. The first with green furniture and fitted with a 20" barrel. The second with black furniture and fitted with a 16" barrel.

First Model

NIB	Exc.	V.G.	Good	Fair	Poor
3900	3250	2250	—	—	—

Second Model

NIB	Exc.	V.G.	Good	Fair	Poor
4200	3700	2750	—	—	—

MAUSER

M1914 Rifle

This rifle is identical to the Model 1912. Austrian rifles are fitted with large sling swivels in order to accommodate the Austrian sling. Some of these rifles are unit marked on the buttplate or buttplate tang.

Exc.	V.G.	Good	Fair	Poor
675	500	425	225	100

MACHINE GUNS

Austrian Hungary also used the Maxim, having purchased some in 1889. These guns were designated the Model 89/1, then with modifications called the M89/04. Austrian Hungary used their own design, the Skoda M1893, but this gun was never considered successful.

Model 07/12 Schwarzlose

The gun was designed by Andreas Wilhelm Schwarzlose and built in Austria by Steyr. First model was the 1907 chambered for the standard military 8x50Rmm cartridge. Successor was the Model 1907/12 which was marked as the M07/12. The gun was built until 1918 in 8x50R. The Czechs built a version called the M7/24 chambered for the 7.92 cartridge. The Romanians converted Steyr M07/12s to 9.92 with lengthened water jackets. The gun was also manufactured by the Dutch, Swedish, and Hungarians. It was adopted by Austria-Hungary in 1905. It was also sold to the Dutch, Greeks, and Germans as well. It saw use in WWI. Barrel length was 24.4" and rate of fire was about 500 rounds per minute. Fed by a 250-round cloth belt. The gun was produced until 1918. Marked "MG SCHWARZLOSE M7/12" on the rear of the receiver. Weight is about 44 lbs. Italy used this gun, as part of World War I reparations, through World War II.

Aircraft versions with modified internals to increase the rate of fire were marked M7/12 (16/A) and M7/12 (16/R), and these have no jackets on the barrel. Note that the gun marked "MG SCHWARZLOSE M7/12," which is correct, but the other side is marked "WAFFENFABRIK STEYR" with the date of manufacture underneath.

No factory Schwarzlose were built with ventilated shrouds. They were either fitted with water-jackets or had bare exposed barrels for aircraft use. No doubt there were field expedients of various sorts, but there is no evidence of any factory ventilated shrouds.

NOTE: The predecessor to this gun was the Model 1907. Its rate of fire was about 350 rounds per minute, and it was fitted with a smaller oil reservoir. An aircraft version of the Model 07/12 was the Model 07/16, which had a rate of fire of about 600 rounds per minute. Early versions were water-cooled, later versions were air-cooled with slotted barrel jacket. Last version had no jacket.

Pre-1968

Exc.	V.G.	Fair
22000	20000	18000

Pre-1986 conversions (reweld)

Exc.	V.G.	Fair
17500	16000	15000

Pre-1986 dealer samples

Exc.	V.G.	Fair
N/A	N/A	N/A

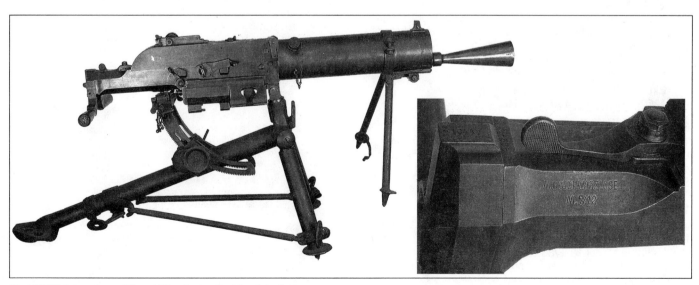

Model 07/12 Schwarzlose • Private NFA collection, Paul Goodwin photo

BELGIUM

Belgian Military Conflicts, 1870 – Present

Throughout the last quarter of the 19th century, Belgium experienced rapid economic growth that led to colonization, mainly in the Belgian Congo. Germany occupied Belgium in both World War I and World War II. During World War I, Belgium had 270,000 men under arms. A total of almost 83,000 were killed or wounded during the war. In World War II, Belgium had 650,000 military personnel of which 23,000 were killed or wounded. Belgium became a member of NATO in 1949 where that organization's headquarters are located in Brussels.

Bibliographical Notes

The best overview of Belgian military firearms are two books by Claude Gaier; *FN 100 Years, The Story of the Great Liege Company, 1889-1989*, 1989, and *Four Centuries of Liege Gunmaking*, 1985.

HANDGUNS

E. & L. NAGANT

Model 1878 Officer's (Fluted Cylinder)
This 6-shot double action centerfire revolver is chambered for the 9mm cartridge. Solid frame with fixed cylinder sliding rod ejection. Octagon barrel is 5.5". Issued to Belgian officers, it is marked with the Nagant address and logo. Wooden checkered grips with lanyard loop. Weight is about 33 oz. Produced from 1878 to 1886.

Exc.	V.G.	Good	Fair	Poor
1750	900	500	300	200

Model 1883 (Non-Fluted Cylinder)
This model was also chambered for the 9mm centerfire cartridge. Fitted with a 5.5" octagon barrel. Wooden checkered grips with lanyard loop. A simplified version of the Model 1878 Officer's revolver. This model was used by NCOs, artillery, and troops in the Belgian army from 1883 to 1940.

Exc.	V.G.	Good	Fair	Poor
1250	750	400	275	150

Model 1878/86 Officer's (Fluted Cylinder)
This 6-shot revolver was issued to officers in the Belgian army. Chambered for the 9mm cartridge and fitted with a 5.5" octagon barrel. Checkered wooden grips with lanyard loop. Produced from 1886 to 1940.

Exc.	V.G.	Good	Fair	Poor
1500	850	450	300	175

Model 1883/86
Similar to the Model 1878/86 Officer's but issued to NCOs as a regular sidearm. Cylinder is non-fluted. The hammer rebounds slightly after the revolver has been fired.

Exc.	V.G.	Good	Fair	Poor
1250	750	400	275	150

GAVAGE, ARMAND

A 7.65mm caliber semiautomatic pistol with a fixed barrel and a concealed hammer. Similar in appearance to the Clement. Markings with "AG" molded into the grips. Some (1,500 est.) have been found bearing German Waffenamts. Manufactured from 1930s to 1940s.

Exc.	V.G.	Good	Fair	Poor
400	300	225	150	100

FABRIQUE NATIONALE

NOTE: For historical and technical information, see Blake Stevens, *The Browning High Power Automatic Pistol*, Collector Grade Publications, 1990.

Model 1903
A considerable improvement over the Model 1900. It is also a blowback-operated semiautomatic; but the recoil spring is located under the barrel, and the firing pin travels through the slide after being struck by a hidden hammer. The barrel is held in place by five locking lugs that fit into five grooves in the frame. This pistol is chambered for the 9mm Browning long cartridge and has a 5" barrel. The finish is blued with molded plastic grips, and the detachable magazine holds 7 rounds. There is a detachable shoulder stock/holster along with a 10-round magazine that was available for this model. These accessories are extremely rare and if present would make the package worth approximately five times that of the pistol alone. There were approximately 58,000 manufactured between 1903 and 1939. This model was one of the Browning patents that the Eibar Spanish gunmakers did so love to copy because of the simplicity of the design.

It should be noted that during World War I the Spanish supplied almost one million Model 1903 copies for the French army.

Production Note: FN had a number of contract sales to foreign countries from 1907 to about 1928. These countries are:

Sweden: 1907-1908	10,000
Russia: 1908-1910	8,200
Ottoman Empire: 1908-1923	8,000
England: 1914	100
Holland: 1922	80
Estonia: 1922-1928	4616
El Salvador: 1927-	?
Paraguay: 1927	324

Courtesy Richard M. Kumor Sr.

Exc.	V.G.	Good	Fair	Poor
500	425	375	275	175

Model 1910 "New Model"
Chambered for 7.65mm and 9mm short. It has a 3.5" barrel, is blued, and has molded plastic grips. The principal difference between this model and its predecessors is that the recoil spring on the Model 1910 is wrapped around the barrel. This gives the slide a more graceful tubular appearance instead of the old slab-sided look. This model has the triple safety features of the 1906 Model 2nd variation and is blued with molded

plastic grips. This model was adopted by police forces around the world. It was manufactured between 1912 and 1954.

Courtesy Orvel Reichert

Exc.	V.G.	Good	Fair	Poor
375	300	250	175	125

Model 1922

Similar to the Model 1910, with a longer 4.5" barrel and correspondingly longer slide. This model was a military success, and approximately 200,000 were produced during the WWII German occupation of Belgium in 1940-1944. These pistols that bear the Waffenamt acceptance marks are known as the "Pistole Modell 626(b)," and are chambered for 7.65mm only. The Germans also had a 9mm version designated the "Pistole Modell 641(b)." These pistols would bring a 10 percent premium. There were approximately 360,000 of these pistols produced during the German occupation. There are a number of subvariations that may effect value. There were also contracts from France, Yugoslavia, and Holland, as well as Belgian military versions. They were manufactured between 1912 and 1959.

Exc.	V.G.	Good	Fair	Poor
300	225	175	125	100

Model 1922 • Paul Goodwin photo

Model 1935

The last design from John Browning and was developed between 1925 and 1935. This pistol is known as the Model 1935, the P-35, High-Power or HP, and also as the GP (which stood for "Grand Puissance") and was referred to by all those names at one time or another. The HP is essentially an improved version of the Colt 1911 design. The swinging link was replaced

with a fixed cam, which was less prone to wear. It is chambered for the 9mm Parabellum and has a 13-round detachable magazine. The only drawback to the design is that the trigger pull is not as fine as that of the 1911, as there is a transfer bar instead of a stirrup arrangement. This is necessary due to the increased magazine capacity resulting in a thicker grip. The barrel is 4.75" in length. It has an external hammer with a manual and a magazine safety, was available with various finishes and sight options, and was furnished with a shoulder stock. The Model 1935 was used by many countries as their service pistol; as such there are many variations. We list these versions and their approximate values. There are books available specializing in this model, and it would be beneficial to gain as much knowledge as possible if one contemplates acquisition of this fine and highly collectible pistol.

Prewar Commercial Model

Found with either a fixed sight or a sliding tangent rear sight and is slotted for a detachable shoulder stock. It was manufactured from 1935 until 1940.

Wood Holster Stock–Add 50%.

Fixed Sight Version

Exc.	V.G.	Good	Fair	Poor
600	525	475	375	275

Tangent Sight Version

Exc.	V.G.	Good	Fair	Poor
1000	850	675	550	400

Prewar & WWII Military Contract

The Model 1935 was adopted by many countries as a service pistol, and some of them are as follows:

Belgium

Exc.	V.G.	Good	Fair	Poor
1200	1050	900	600	375

Canada and China (See John Inglis & Company)
Denmark (See Denmark)
Great Britain

Exc.	V.G.	Good	Fair	Poor
1150	1000	850	550	325

Estonia

Exc.	V.G.	Good	Fair	Poor
1200	1050	900	600	375

Holland

Exc.	V.G.	Good	Fair	Poor
1250	1100	950	650	400

Latvia

Exc.	V.G.	Good	Fair	Poor
1500	1350	1050	775	500

Lithuania

Exc.	V.G.	Good	Fair	Poor
1250	1100	950	650	400

Romania

Exc.	V.G.	Good	Fair	Poor
1500	1350	1050	775	500

German Military Pistole Modell 640(b)

In 1940 Germany occupied Belgium and took over the FN plant. The production of the Model 1935 continued, with Germany taking the output. The FN plant was assigned the production code "ch," and many thousands were produced. The finish on these Nazi guns runs from as fine, as the Prewar Commercial series, to downright crude, and it is possible to see how the war was progressing for Germany by the finish on their weapons. One must be cautious with some of these guns, as there have been fakes noted with their backstraps cut for shoulder stocks, producing what would appear to be a more expensive variation. Individual appraisal should be secured if any doubt exists.

Fixed Sight Model

Paul Goodwin photo

Exc.	V.G.	Good	Fair	Poor
500	450	400	300	250

Tangent Sight Model - 50,000 Manufactured

Courtesy Orvel Reichert

Exc.	V.G.	Good	Fair	Poor
850	750	700	550	400

Captured Prewar Commercial Model

These pistols were taken over when the plant was occupied. They are slotted for stocks and have tangent sights. There were few produced between serial number 48,000 and 52,000. All noted have the "WaA613" Nazi proof mark. Beware of fakes!

Exc.	V.G.	Good	Fair	Poor
1500	1400	1150	750	500

Postwar Military Contract

Manufactured from 1946, and they embody some design changes—such as improved heat treating and barrel locking. Pistols produced after 1950 do not have barrels that can interchange with the earlier model pistols. The earliest models have an "A" prefix on the serial number and do not have the magazine safety. These pistols were produced for many countries, and there were many thousands manufactured.

Fixed Sight

Exc.	V.G.	Good	Fair	Poor
475	425	375	300	250

Tangent Sight

Exc.	V.G.	Good	Fair	Poor
750	675	575	400	300

Slotted and Tangent Sight

Exc.	V.G.	Good	Fair	Poor
1500	1250	750	500	400

Sultan of Oman

This is the only post war Hi-Power that is designated a Curio and Relic pistol. It has a tangent sight. The grip is slotted to accept a shoulder stock which is a legal accessory to this model. Less than 50 of these pistols were brought into the U.S. Canceled contract military sidearm for Oman. Very rare.

NIB	Exc.	V.G.	Good	Fair	Poor
6000	5750	4500	—	—	—

NOTE: For pistols with no shoulder stock deduct $1,000.

SUBMACHINE GUNS

Prior to 1940, Belgium used the MP28 (Model 34) as its standard military submachine gun.

FN also manufactured, under license from Israeli Military Industries (IMI), a copy of the UZI submachine gun.

Vigneron M2

This sub gun was issued to the Belgian army in 1953. It was also used by those same forces in the Belgian Congo. Many of these guns were taken by Congo forces after independence. A number of Vigneron guns may be found over much of Central Africa. The gun is chambered for the 9mm cartridge and has a wire folding stock. Barrel length is 11.75" with the rear portion of the barrel finned. A muzzle compensator is also standard. Magazine capacity is 32 rounds. Rate of fire is about 600 rounds per minute. Capable of select fire. Markings are found on the right side of the magazine housing and read, "ABL52 VIG M1." Also on the right side of the receiver is stamped "LICENCE VIGNERON." Weight is about 7.25 lbs. The gun was in production from 1952 to 1962.

Pre-1968

Exc.	V.G.	Fair
9000	8000	7000

Pre-1986 conversions

Exc.	V.G.	Fair
N/A	N/A	N/A

Pre-1986 dealer samples

Exc.	V.G.	Fair
4000	3500	3000

Mauser/FN Model 1889 Rifle • Paul Goodwin photo

RIFLES

NOTE: For historical information, technical data, and photos on the FN-FAL rifle, see Blake Stevens', *The FAL Rifle, Classic Edition*, Collector Grade Publications, 1993.

MAUSER (FN)

Model 1889 Rifle

The Mauser rifle that Fabrique Nationale was incorporated to manufacture. It is chambered for 7.65mm and has a 30.5" barrel. The magazine holds 5 rounds. The unique feature that sets the Belgian rifle apart from the Mausers made by other countries is the thin steel tube that encases the barrel. This was the first Mauser to use a charger loaded detachable box magazine. The sights are of the military type. The finish is blued, with a walnut stock. This rifle was also made by the American firm of Hopkins and Allen, and is considered rare.

Exc.	V.G.	Good	Fair	Poor
350	300	225	150	100

NOTE: For rare Hopkins and Allen examples, add a premium of 150%.

M1889 Carbine with Bayonet

Barrel length is 21". Fitted for a bayonet. Weight is about 7.5 lbs.

Exc.	V.G.	Good	Fair	Poor
375	350	235	160	100

M1889 Carbine with Yataghan

Barrel length is 21". Fitted for a unique bayonet. Weight is about 7.5 lbs.

Exc.	V.G.	Good	Fair	Poor
375	350	250	200	150

M1889 Carbine Lightened

Fitted with a 15.75" barrel and turned down bolt. A slotted sling bracket mounted on left side of buttstock.

Exc.	V.G.	Good	Fair	Poor
375	320	250	175	100

M1889 Carbine Lightened with Yataghan

Same as above but with longer stock. A unique bayonet, handle has no guard and frequently having a double curved blade, was also issued with this carbine.

Exc.	V.G.	Good	Fair	Poor
375	320	250	175	100

M1890 Turkish Rifle

Captured Turkish Model 1890 rifles with Belgian rear sight similar to the Model 1889 rifle. No handguard. Original Turkish markings remain. Belgian proofs.

Exc.	V.G.	Good	Fair	Poor
350	275	250	200	100

M1916 Carbine

Similar to the Model 1889 with Yataghan bayonet but with different bracket on buttstock.

Exc.	V.G.	Good	Fair	Poor
350	275	225	175	125

M1935 Short Rifle

This model is very similar to the German 7.92 Kar 98k and uses the M98 bolt system. It is fitted with a 5-round flush magazine. Barrel length is 23.5". Weight is about 9 lbs.

Exc.	V.G.	Good	Fair	Poor
400	350	300	225	125

M50 Short Rifle

Post war surplus rifle converted to .30-06 caliber. Barrel length is 23.2". Tangent leaf rear sight graduated to 2000 meters. Marked "B/ABL/DATE." Weight is approximately 9 lbs.

Exc.	V.G.	Good	Fair	Poor
350	300	250	200	100

M1889/36 Short Rifle

This model is a converted Model 1889 with a 23.5" barrel with wooden handguard. The upper barrel band and front sight are of the Model 1935 type. The bolt system appears similar to the Model 98. Chambered for the 7.65mm Mauser cartridge. Weight is about 9 lbs.

Exc.	V.G.	Good	Fair	Poor
250	200	150	90	60

M35/46 Short Rifle

Similar to the M50 short rifle.

Exc.	V.G.	Good	Fair	Poor
350	200	150	100	60

M24/30 .22 Caliber Training Rifle–Army

This is a military training rifle in .22 caliber built for the Belgian army after World War II.

Exc.	V.G.	Good	Fair	Poor
400	300	250	175	125

Model 1889 Carbine • Paul Goodwin photo

Model 1935 Short Rifle • Courtesy West Point Museum, Paul Goodwin photo

M24/30 .22 Caliber Training Rifle–Navy
Same as above but for the Belgian navy.

Exc.	V.G.	Good	Fair	Poor
400	300	250	175	125

FN M30 Postwar Short Rifle (M24/30)
Built after WWII for the Belgian army. It uses the standard M98 action.

Exc.	V.G.	Good	Fair	Poor
350	300	250	200	135

FABRIQUE NATIONALE

Model 1949 or SAFN 49
A gas-operated semiautomatic rifle chambered for 7x57, 7.92mm, and .30-06. It has a 23" barrel and military-type sights. The integral magazine holds 10 rounds. The finish is blued, and the stock is walnut. This is a well-made gun that was actually designed before WWII. When the Germans were in the process of taking over Belgium, a group of FN engineers fled to England and took the plans for this rifle with them, preventing the German military from acquiring a very fine weapon. This model was introduced in 1949, after hostilities had ceased. This model was sold on contract to Egypt, chambered for 7.92mm; to Venezuela, chambered for 7x57; and to Argentina, Columbic, Indonesia, Belgium, and Luxembourg chambered for the .30-06. Argentina models were chambered for the 7.65x53mm as well as the Argentina navy which had its rifles chambered for their 7.62 NATO cartridge.

NOTE: The Egyptian model has recently been imported in large numbers and is worth approximately 25% less. For .30-06 caliber add 20%. For Argentina navy 7.62 NATO examples add 50%.

Courtesy Richard M. Kumor Sr.

Exc.	V.G.	Good	Fair	Poor
500	400	300	225	150

Model 30-11 Sniper Rifle
Chambered for the 7.62 NATO cartridge. It has a 20" heavy barrel and Anschutz sights. There is a flash suppressor mounted on the muzzle. It is built on a highly precision-made Mauser bolt action fed by a 9-round, detachable box magazine. The walnut stock is rather unique in that the butt is made up of two parts, with the rear half being replaceable to suit the needs of different-sized shooters. It is issued with a shooting sling, bipod, and a foam-lined carrying case. This is a rare firearm on the commercial market as it was designed and sold to the military and police markets.

Courtesy Jim Supica, Old Town Station

Exc.	V.G.	Good	Fair	Poor
5000	4500	3500	2750	2000

FN-FAL
A gas-operated, semiautomatic version of the famous FN battle rifle. This weapon has been adopted by more free world countries than any other rifle. It is chambered for the 7.62 NATO or .308 and has a 21" barrel with an integral flash suppressor. The sights are adjustable with an aperture rear, and the detachable box magazine holds 20 rounds. The stock and forearm are made of wood or a black synthetic. This model has been discontinued by the company and is no longer manufactured.

The models listed below are for the metric pattern Type 2 and Type 3 receivers, those marked "FN MATCH." The models below are for semiautomatic rifles only. FN-FAL rifles in the "inch" pattern are found in the British Commonwealth countries of Australia, India, Canada, and of course, Great Britain. These rifles are covered separately under their own country headings.

50.00-21" Rifle Model

NIB	Exc.	V.G.	Good	Fair	Poor
3000	2750	2250	2000	1850	1000

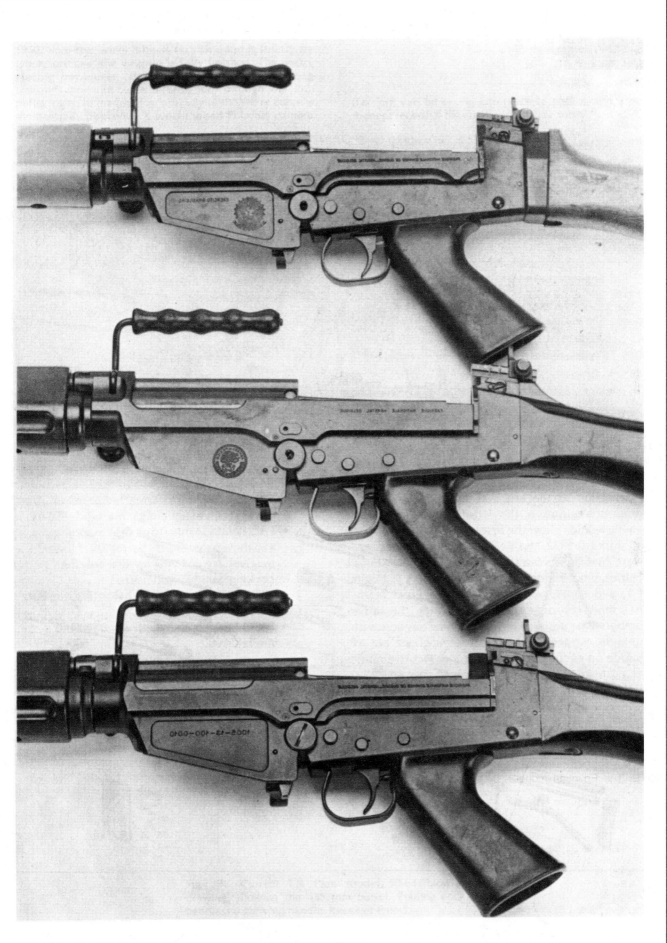

FAL Receivers: Top - Type 2; Middle - Type 3; Bottom - Type 1 • Courtesy Blake Stevens

50.63-18" Paratrooper Model

NIB	Exc.	V.G.	Good	Fair	Poor
3800	3350	2950	2750	2450	1100

50.64-21" Paratrooper Model

NIB	Exc.	V.G.	Good	Fair	Poor
3300	3000	2700	2200	1900	1000

50.41-Synthetic Butt H-Bar

NIB	Exc.	V.G.	Good	Fair	Poor
2800	2400	2000	1800	1200	1000

50.42–Wood Butt H-Bar

NIB	Exc.	V.G.	Good	Fair	Poor
2800	2400	2000	1800	1200	1000

FN FAL "G" Series (Type 1 Receiver)

Converted semiautomatic FAL. These rifles are subject to interpretation by the BATF as to their legal status. A list of BATF legal serial numbers is available. This information should be utilized prior to a sale in order to avoid the possibility of the sale of an illegal rifle. There was a total of 1,160 legal "G" Series FN FAL rifles imported into this country.

Standard

NIB	Exc.	V.G.	Good	Fair	Poor
5000	4500	4000	3000	2000	1000

Lightweight

NIB	Exc.	V.G.	Good	Fair	Poor
5000	4500	4000	3000	2000	1000

NOTE: There are a number of U.S. companies that built FN-FAL receivers and use military surplus parts. These rifles have no collector value as of yet.

FN FAL–Select Fire Assault Rifle

First produced in 1953, this 7.62x51mm select fire rifle has been used world wide. It is fitted with a 20.8" barrel and a magazine that holds 20 rounds. It is available in several different configurations. Weight is about 9.8 lbs. Marked "FABRIQUE NATIONALE HERSTAL." Markings will also indicate many other countries made this rifle under license from FN.

Photo courtesy FN

Pre-1968 (Rare)

Exc.	V.G.	Fair
9000	8500	8000

Pre-1986 conversions

Exc.	V.G.	Fair
5500	5000	4500

Pre-1986 dealer samples

Exc.	V.G.	Fair
4000	3500	3000

FN CAL

Chambered for the 5.56x45mm cartridge and designed with a rotary bolt. It is fitted with an 18.2" barrel and has a magazine capacity of 20 or 30 rounds. Weight is about 6 lbs. With folding stock. Produced from 1966 to 1975 and is marked "FABRIQUE NATIONALE HERSTAL MOD CAL 5.56MM" on the left side of the receiver. This rifle was not widely adopted. A rare rifle. Only about 20 of these rifles were imported into the U.S.

NIB	Exc.	V.G.	Good	Fair	Poor
7000	6500	5000	3000	—	—

FN CAL-Select Fire Assault Rifle

Chambered for the 5.56x45mm cartridge and designed with a rotary bolt. It is fitted with an 18.2" barrel and has a magazine capacity of 20 or 30 rounds. Its rate of fire is 650 rounds per minute. Weight is about 6 lbs. With folding stock. Produced from 1966 to 1975 and is marked "FABRIQUE NATIONALE HERSTAL MOD CAL 5.56MM" on the left side of the receiver. This rifle was not widely adopted.

Photo courtesy private NFA collection

Pre-1968 (Rare)

Exc.	V.G.	Fair
9500	9000	8500

Pre-1986 conversions

Exc.	V.G.	Fair
7500	7000	6800

Pre-1986 dealer samples

Exc.	V.G.	Fair
5500	5000	4500

FNC

A lighter-weight assault-type rifle chambered for the 5.56mm cartridge. It is a gas-operated semiautomatic with an 18" or 21" barrel. It has a 30-round box magazine and is black, with either a fixed or folding stock. This model was also discontinued by FN. The same problem with fluctuating values applies to this weapon as to the L.A.R., and we strongly advise that one research the market in a particular geographic location as prices can fluctuate radically.

Standard–Fixed Stock, 16" or 18" Barrel

NIB	Exc.	V.G.	Good	Fair	Poor
3000	2800	2500	2000	1500	1000

Paratrooper Model–Folding Stock, 16" or 18" Barrel

NIB	Exc.	V.G.	Good	Fair	Poor
3000	2800	2500	2000	1500	1000

NOTE: The above prices are for Belgian-made guns only.

FN FNC–Select Fire Assault Rifle

This model, introduced in 1979, took the place of the CAL. Chambered for the 5.56x45mm cartridge and fitted with a 17.5" barrel, it weighs about 8.4 lbs. It has a 30-round magazine capacity. Rate of fire is 700 rounds per minute. Fitted with a metal folding stock. This model will accept M16 magazines. Marked "FNC 5.56" on left side of receiver. This rifle was adopted by the Belgian, Indonesian, and Swedish militaries.

Pre-1968

Exc.	V.G.	Fair
N/A	N/A	N/A

18" Para Model • Courtesy Blake Stevens from *The FAL Rifle*

21" Para Model • Courtesy Blake Stevens, from *The FAL Rifle*

FN Heavy Barrel Model • Courtesy Blake Stevens, from *The FAL Rifle*

Pre-1986 conversions

Exc.	V.G.	Fair
5500	4500	4000

Pre-1986 dealer samples

Exc.	V.G.	Fair
4000	3800	3500

FN BAR Model D (Demontable)

Photo courtesy Jim Thompson

This was the FN version of the Browning automatic rifle. It is fitted with a quick change barrel, pistol grip, and can be modified to either a belt-fed or box magazine configuration. It was offered in a variety of calibers from 6.5 Swedish Mauser to the 7.92x57mm Mauser. It is fitted with a 19.5" barrel and has a rate of fire of either 450 or 650 rounds per minute. Weight is about 20 lbs. Marked "FABRIQUE NATIONALE D'ARMES DE GUERRE HERSTAL-BELGIQUE" on left side of receiver.

FN sold about 700 Model Ds to Finland in 1940 which the Finns used during their "Winter War" with the Russians. These Finnish BARs were chambered for the 7.63x54R cartridge. Also a small number of FN guns were sold to China (2,000) and Ethiopia in the 1930s. These BARs were chambered for the 7.92x57mm Mauser cartridge. After World War II FN sold its Model 30 BAR to a number of countries around the world.

Pre-1968 (Very Rare)

Exc.	V.G.	Fair
35000	32500	30000

Pre-1986 conversions

Exc.	V.G.	Fair
22000	20000	18000

Pre-1986 dealer samples

Exc.	V.G.	Fair
17500	16000	15000

MACHINE GUNS

Fabrique Nationale has a long history of manufacturing John M. Browning's firearms. These firearms include the Browning Model 1917, M1919, and .50 caliber heavy gun. The light machine guns were chambered in a variety of calibers and sold around the world by FN. During World War II the FN factory was occupied by German troops, but after the war in 1945 when production finally returned to normal levels, the Belgians produced the air-cooled Browning guns in 7.62x63mm

(.30-06) for the Belgian army. When NATO adopted the 7.62x51mm cartridge, FN designed and built the FN MAG machine gun.

FN MAG (Mitrailleuse d'Appui Generale) (M240)

First produced in Belgium in 1955, this machine gun is chambered for the 7.62x51mm cartridge. It is fitted with a 21.3" quick change barrel and has an adjustable rate of fire of 700 to 1000 rounds per minute. It is belt-fed with metal links. The basic configuration uses a wooden buttstock, smooth barrel with bipod attached to gas cylinder, pistol grip, and slotted flash hider. The gun can also be attached to a tripod as well as used with an anti-aircraft mount. Weight is about 22 lbs. Marked "FABRIQUE NATIONALE D'ARMES DE GUERRE HERSTAL BELGIUM" on the right side of the receiver. This gun is still in production and is in use by over 80 countries world-wide.

There is an aircraft version of this gun designated as Model 60-30 (single mount) or 60-40 (twin mount). The gun can also be mounted in a coaxial configuration such as a tank or armored vehicle.

Pre-1968 (Very Rare)

Exc.	V.G.	Fair
125000+	—	—

Pre-1986 conversions (side-plates, 65 registered)

Exc.	V.G.	Fair
55000	50000	47500

Pre-1986 dealer samples

Exc.	V.G.	Fair
85000	—	—

NOTE: This is an extremely rare machine gun with prices based on scarcity and demand. It is possible for prices to exceed $125,000 under certain conditions.

FN Minimi (M249)

Designed as a squad automatic weapon (SAW) and chambered for the 5.56x45mm cartridge, this machine gun has a rate of fire of 700 to 1,000 rounds per minute and is equipped with a 30-round box magazine or 100 to 200-round boxed belts. Rate of fire with box magazine is higher than when using belt. The quick change barrel length is 18" and weight is about 15 lbs. Marked "FN MINIMI 5.56" on the left side of the receiver. First produced in 1982, this gun is called the M249 machine gun in the U.S. Army. It is also in service in a number of other countries such as Canada, Australia, and Italy.

Photo courtesy private NFA collection

Pre-1968 (Extremely Rare, 1 known)

Exc.	V.G.	Fair
100000	—	—

Pre-1986 conversions

Exc.	V.G.	Fair
N/A	N/A	N/A

**Pre-1986 dealer samples
(Extremely Rare, only 6 known)**

Exc.	V.G.	Fair
75000	—	—

WHAT'S IT LIKE:
THE FN MINIMI (M249 SAW)

Chambered for the M855 caliber 5.56x45mm NATO cartridge, the U.S. Army's SAW (Squad Automatic Weapon) was selected from a rigorous competitive evaluation of four candidate systems. But, the M249 has also seen its share of contentious commentary. Gas-operated with a short-stroke piston and two-lug rotary bolt, the M249 fires from the open-bolt position to inhibit "cook-offs," as do most belt-fed machine guns. It was designed to accept either disintegrating link belts or the M16 30-round box magazine with modification.

This has proved to be a major design error for the M249 will not function reliably with any magazine, loaded to any capacity. This weapon should be restricted to belt-fed operation only. Another area of concern is the M249's accuracy potential. During repeated testing it has exhibited pronounced vertical stringing thought to be induced by the design of the barrel-to-receiver interface.

With those exceptions, the M249 is generally the very model of a modern SAW. When belt-fed, reliability exceeds all competing designs. When employed for area-target fire support, as all belt-fed machine guns most often should be, the accuracy potential is adequate. It has numerous desirable features, not the least of which is its weight, which is only 21.3 lbs. with a 200-round assault pack. It has a quick-change, chrome-lined 18.3-inch barrel and exhibits excellent human engineering overall. The overall length is only 41.4 inches. The cyclic rate is about 750 rpm. It provides the firepower required at the squad level in a compact and lightweight envelope. The U.S. Navy has recently adopted a short-barrel version of the M249 and phased out the M60 GPMG. Recent reports out of Afghanistan, however, indiate that the M855 cartridge is performing poorly with regard to wound ballistics, with many requests from special operations personnel for a return to the 7.62x51mm NATO round.

Peter Kokalis

BRAZIL

Brazilian Military Conflicts, 1870–Present

Pedro II was the ruler of Brazil from 1840 until 1889. During this period the country grew and prospered, while at the same time overthrowing several neighboring dictatorships. In 1889 a military revolt overthrew Pedro II and Brazil was proclaimed a republic. In 1891 the country was officially named the United States of Brazil with a constitution similar to that of the U.S. During World War I, Brazil contributed ships and supplies to the Allied forces. After the war, economic difficulties created a series of crises and unrest which led to widespread revolt. Finally, in 1930 a military coup brought relative stability to the country for the next 15 years. Brazil was on the Allied side during World War II and it contributed important military support such as military bases and supplies to the Allied effort. After the end of the war, Brazil suffered through four decades of unstable governments. In 2001, Brazil had a total military force of 287,600, of which 189,000 were in the army. First line reserves number 1,115,000. These include 385,600 para-military forces.

HANDGUNS

NOTE: Brazil used a number of Colt Model 1911A1 pistols (Pst M1911A1). These pistols are still in service in second line units. Mauser shipped a few hundred Model 1912/14 pistols to Brazil. In the 1930s about 500 Mauser Schnellfeuer pistols were purchased and a few are still in service. Brazil has also purchased the Beretta Model 92 from Italy.

In the 1980s Brazil began to produce its own version of the Colt 1911A1 known as the Imbel M973. Other variations of this pistol have been produced in 9x19, 9x17, and .38 Super. No examples of these pistols are known in the U.S.

SUBMACHINE GUNS

Brazil has used or is using in second line units the U.S. M3 gun, the Beretta Model 12, the H&K MP5 and MP5SD. Brazil has additionally issued the Walther MPK. A few Thompson M1s and U.S. Reisings are used as well.

URU Model 2

Chambered for the 9mm parabellum cartridge and fitted with a 7" barrel with slotted barrel jacket. Made of stampings with round receiver. Forward magazine acts as a handgrip. Magazine capacity is 30 rounds. Detachable wooden butt or steel single strut stock. Rate of fire is about 750 rounds per minute. Weight is about 6.5 lbs. Produced in Brazil at Bilbao SA in Sao Paulo.

Pre-1968

Exc.	V.G.	Fair
N/A	N/A	N/A

Pre-1986 conversions

Exc.	V.G.	Fair
N/A	N/A	N/A

Pre-1986 dealer samples

Exc.	V.G.	Fair
3000	2500	2250

RIFLES

Brazil uses the HK 33E, the M16 (Model 614), the M16A2, and the FN FAL and variations, built under license from FN. The Brazilian military also uses the U.S. M1 rifle converted to 7.62 NATO caliber.

MAUSER

M1894 Rifle

Similar to the Spanish Model 1893 but with a cylindrical bolt head. Barrel length is 29". Chambered for the 7x57 cartridge. Magazine is flush mounted and has a 5 round capacity. Adjustable rear sight from 400 to 2,000 meters. Brazilian crest on receiver ring. Produced by DWM and FN.

Exc.	V.G.	Good	Fair	Poor
275	225	125	100	75

M1894 Carbine

As above but with 18" barrel and adjustable rear sight to 1,400 meters. No bayonet lug.

Exc.	V.G.	Good	Fair	Poor
250	200	125	100	75

M1904 Mauser-Verueiro Rifle

Chambered for the 6.5x58Pmm cartridge, this model was fitted with a 29" barrel. Tangent sight graduated to 2,000 meters. Brazilian crest on receiver ring. Produced by DWM.

Exc.	V.G.	Good	Fair	Poor
325	250	200	150	100

M1907 Rifle

Built by DWM from 1904 to 1906. Sold to Brazil in 1907. Chambered for the 7x57mm cartridge. Pistol grip stock. Fitted with a 29" barrel. Tangent rear sight graduated to 2,000 meters. Built by DWM. Brazilian crest on receiver ring.

Exc.	V.G.	Good	Fair	Poor
325	250	200	150	100

M1907 Carbine

As above with shorter barrel. Produced from 1907 to 1912 by DWM.

Exc.	V.G.	Good	Fair	Poor
400	300	250	175	100

M1908 Rifle

Similar in appearance to the Gew 98. Chambered for the 7x57mm cartridge. Built by DWM between 1908 and 1914. Fitted with a 29.25" barrel. Magazine capacity is 5 rounds. Tangent rear sight graduated to 2,000 meters. Brazilian crest on receiver ring.

Courtesy Rock Island Auction Company

Exc.	V.G.	Good	Fair	Poor
275	225	125	100	75

M1908 Short Rifle

Same as the Model 1908 rifle but with a 22" barrel.

Exc.	V.G.	Good	Fair	Poor
250	200	150	100	70

M1922 Carbine

Chambered for the 7x57mm cartridge and fitted with a 19.5" barrel. Magazine capacity is 5 rounds. Tangent rear sight graduated to 1,400 meters. Built by FN. Weight is about 6.5 lbs.

Exc.	V.G.	Good	Fair	Poor
225	175	130	90	60

VZ 24 Short Rifle

This rifle was built in Czechoslovakia and sold to Brazil in 1932. Bent bolt handle with flat bolt knob. Finger grooves in forend. Czech markings (BRNO). About 15,000 sold to Brazil.

Exc.	V.G.	Good	Fair	Poor
250	195	125	90	75

M1935 Mauser Banner Rifle

Chambered for the 7x57mm cartridge. Fitted with a 28.75" barrel. Magazine capacity is 5 rounds. Tangent rear sight graduated to 2,000 meters. Brazilian crest on receiver ring. Finger grooves in forend. Weight is about 10 lbs.

Exc.	V.G.	Good	Fair	Poor
350	300	240	195	120

M1935 Mauser Banner Short Rifle

As above but with 21.5" barrel. Rear sight graduated to 1,400 meters. Bent bolt handle. Stock cut to accommodate the downturn of the bolt handle. Mauser banner logo on the receiver ring. Brazilian crest on receiver ring. Weight is about 9 lbs.

Exc.	V.G.	Good	Fair	Poor
350	300	240	195	120

M1935 Mauser Carbine

Exc.	V.G.	Good	Fair	Poor
350	300	240	195	120

M1908/34 Short Rifle

Built in Brazil at Itajuba. The stock for this model used local wood and not European walnut. Chambered for the .30-06 cartridge. Fitted with a 23.5" barrel. Tangent rear sight graduated to 2,000 meters. Weight is about 9.75 lbs. Brazilian crest on receiver ring. Manufacturer's markings on side rail.

Exc.	V.G.	Good	Fair	Poor
300	250	195	150	90

M1954 Caliber .30-06 Short Rifle

This model was also built in Brazil and chambered for the .30-06 cartridge. Fitted with a 23.25" barrel. Tangent rear sight graduated to 2,000 meters. Pistol grip stock with finger grooves. Nose cap fitted with a bayonet lug. Weight is about 8.75 lbs. Brazilian crest on receiver ring.

Exc.	V.G.	Good	Fair	Poor
300	250	180	125	90

MACHINE GUNS

The Brazilian military uses a wide variety of machine guns. They are: the FN MAG, Browning M1919A4, the Browning .50 M2 HB, the Danish Madsen converted to .30 caliber, and even the Hotchkiss LMG in 7mm. The Brazilian military has also developed, in the 1990s, its own design called the Uirapuru GPMG in 7.62x51mm.

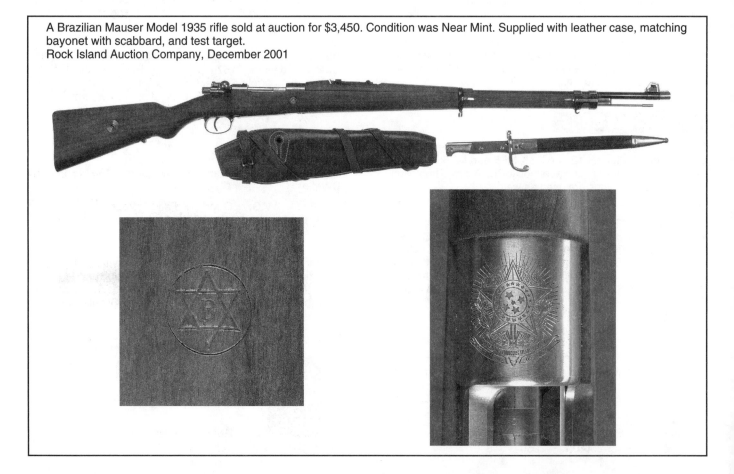

A Brazilian Mauser Model 1935 rifle sold at auction for $3,450. Condition was Near Mint. Supplied with leather case, matching bayonet with scabbard, and test target.
Rock Island Auction Company, December 2001

CANADA

Canadian Military Conflicts, 1870–Present

In 1867, under the British North America Act, the Dominion of Canada was created. In 1982 the British Parliament in London gave Canada's constitution full self control. Because Canada has such close ties to Great Britain, much of Canada's military history closely follows Great Britain, especially during both World Wars and Vietnam.

HANDGUNS

INGLIS, JOHN & COMPANY

Introduction by Clive M. Law

This firm manufactured Browning Pattern .35 semiautomatic pistols for the Canadian, Chinese, and British governments. Pistols are parkerized dark gray and include black plastic grips and a lanyard ring. Premium paid for pistols which still display the Canadian "Lend-Lease" decal on the front grip strap. Fewer than 160,000 pistols were manufactured between 1943 and 1945. Add $350 for original Canadian-produced wood stocks. Prices shown here are for original finish unaltered pistols, prices lower for recent Chinese and British imports.

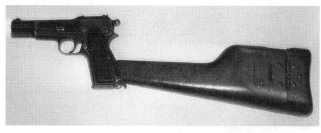

Courtesy Richard M. Kumor Sr.

Mk. 1 No. 1 (Chinese Marked)

The first 4,000 pistols destined for the Chinese government included a six character Chinese marking on the slide, as well as a serial number which incorporated the letters "CH." Includes a tangent rear sight and a stock slot.

Exc.	V.G.	Good	Fair	Poor
2000	1650	1400	950	800

Mk. 1 No. 1

Identical to the Chinese-marked model but without the Chinese characters.

Exc.	V.G.	Good	Fair	Poor
1250	1000	925	825	750

Mk. 1 No. 1*

Externally identical to the No. 1 Mk. 1 but the slide includes the marking Mk. 1*. This mark may be factory applied, or applied in the field after conversion.

Exc.	V.G.	Good	Fair	Poor
750	600	475	425	375

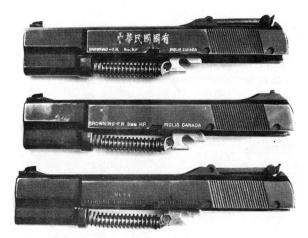

Inglis slides from top to bottom: Chinese pattern No. 1 Mk.1, Canadian forces No. 2 Mk.1, later Chinese type No. 1 Mk. 1* • Courtesy Blake Stevens, *The Browning High-Power,* Stevens

No. 2 Mk. 1

The first 10,000 pistols made for Canada/Britain display the standard slide legend, fixed rear sight in the distinctive Inglis "hump," and no stock slot. All No. 2 type pistols will incorporate the letter "T" within the serial number.

Exc.	V.G.	Good	Fair	Poor
1000	925	850	775	675

No. 2 Mk. 1*

Identical to the No. 2 Mk. 1 externally but the slide includes the marking Mk. 1*. This mark may be factory applied, or applied in the field after conversion. Some examples imported from England or New Zealand may include the "No. 2" stamped or engraved on the slide.

Paul Goodwin photo

Paul Goodwin photo

Exc.	V.G.	Good	Fair	Poor
650	550	475	425	375

No. 2 Mk. 1* Slotted

A small quantity of pistols, mostly in the 3Txxx range, were made up from Chinese frames and includes the stock slot. Beware of fakes.

Exc.	V.G.	Good	Fair	Poor
1300	1150	925	625	500

DP Pistols

Approximately 150 No. 1 type pistols, some with the Chinese inscription, were made up as display and presentation pistols. Serial numbers will range from approximately DP1 to DP150.

Exc.	V.G.	Good	Fair	Poor
2500	2000	1750	1450	1200

Inglis Diamond

In the last week of production, Inglis marked a small quantity of pistols with their trademark, the word Inglis within a diamond. Both the No. 1 and No. 2-style pistols were affected. Some pistols remained in the white while others were parkerized. It is believed that fewer than 50 pistols were marked.

Exc.	V.G.	Good	Fair	Poor
2500	2250	1900	1650	1200

New Zealand Issue

Only 500 pistols were acquired by New Zealand in the 1960s. A serial number list will soon be published which will identify 400 of these pistols. A small quantity was modified, and marked, by the NZ Special Air Service.

Exc.	V.G.	Good	Fair	Poor
1000	800	650	575	525

British Issue

A large quantity of pistols have been imported from the British Ministry of Defense over the past several years. These pistols often display a black "paint" finish and may be marked "FTR" (Factory Thorough Repair) or "AF" (meaning unknown).

Exc.	V.G.	Good	Fair	Poor
600	525	500	475	425

Dutch Issue

The Netherlands used over 10,000 Inglis pistols. Early versions display a small crown over W mark on the rear sight while later models will have Dutch serial numbers, Belgian proofs, and Belgian barrels.

Exc.	V.G.	Good	Fair	Poor
2500	2300	2100	1800	1600

Belgian Issue

Belgium received 1,578 pistols as aid from Canada in the 1950s. These remained in use with the Gendarmerie until recently. Some pistols will display a grey "paint" finish and have numbered magazines. These have been wrongly identified as Danish navy in the past.

Exc.	V.G.	Good	Fair	Poor
3000	2500	2300	2100	1700

SUBMACHINE GUNS

Canadian Sten MK II

These are Canadian built Sten MK II guns built at Long Branch between February 1942 and September 1945. A total of 133,497 guns were produced in this interval. Canadian built Stens are marked "LONG BRANCH" on the magazine housing with the date of manufacture.

NOTE: Canadian Stens do not bring a premium over British-made Stens.

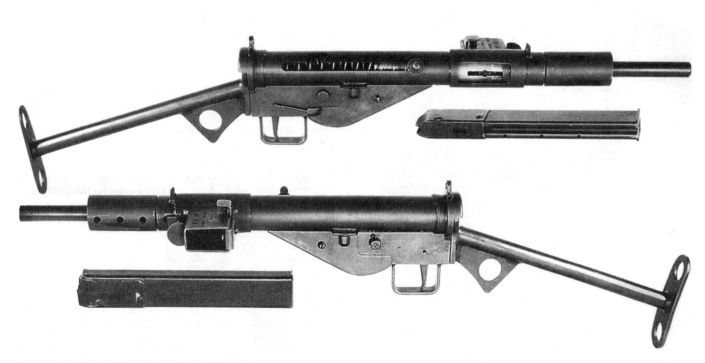

Canadian Sten Mark II • Photo courtesy Robert G. Segel

Pre-1968

Exc.	V.G.	Fair
5000	4500	4000

Pre-1986 conversions (or U.S.-manufactured receivers)

Exc.	V.G.	Fair
3000	2500	2500

Pre-1986 dealer samples

Exc.	V.G.	Fair
2500	2000	1000

Sterling-Canadian C1

Chambered for the 9mm cartridge, this submachine gun features a 7.75" barrel and collapsible metal stock. The rate of fire is 550 rounds per minute. Weight is about 6 lbs. Produced from 1953 to 1988. Still made in India under license. Marked "SMG 9MM C1" on the magazine housing.

The Canadian version of the Sterling is much like the British except for a 30-round magazine without rollers as followers, a different type bayonet (FAL), and internal modifications. A 10-round magazine is also available. Designated the "C1" by the Canadian military. It was first produced in Canada in the late 1950s.

Photo courtesy private NFA collection

Pre-1968 (Very Rare)

Exc.	V.G.	Fair
9000	8000	7000

Pre-1986 conversions

Exc.	V.G.	Fair
5000	4500	4500

Pre-1986 dealer samples

Exc.	V.G.	Fair
5000	4500	3250

RIFLES

PEABODY

Canadian Rifle Musket (1867)

Chambered for the .50-60 Peabody rimfire cartridge and fitted with a 36" barrel. Blued barrel with case hardened furniture. "CM" marked on right side of buttstock and "DWB" on left wrist. Canada purchased 3,000 of these rifles but a total of 5,000 were produced.

Exc.	V.G.	Good	Fair	Poor
—	950	800	500	200

ROSS RIFLE CO.

Designed in 1896 by Sir Charles Ross, this straight pull rifle was manufactured in a variety of styles. Due to problems with the bolt design, it never proved popular and was discontinued in 1915.

Mark I

This rifle was adopted by the Canadian military in 1903. Barrel length is 28". Chambered for .303 caliber with a "Harris Controlled Platform Magazine" that can be depressed by an external lever to facilitate loading. Magazine capacity is 5 rounds. Marked "ROSS RIFLE COM. QUEBEC CANADA" on left side of receiver. About 5,000 of these rifles were built.

Courtesy Buffalo Bill Historical Center, Cody, Wyoming

Exc.	V.G.	Good	Fair	Poor
500	350	250	150	100

Mark I Carbine

As above, with a 26" barrel without bayonet lug.

Exc.	V.G.	Good	Fair	Poor
450	300	250	200	150

Mark II

Introduced in 1905 with a modified rear sight, longer hand-guard, no receiver bridge. Marked "ROSS RIFLE CO. QUEBEC CANADA 1905."

Exc.	V.G.	Good	Fair	Poor
500	350	250	150	100

Mark III

Built between 1910 and 1916 with improved lockwork and stripper clip guides. Extended single column 5-round box magazine. Barrel length is 30". Marked "ROSS RIFLE CO." over "CANADA" over "M10" on receiver ring. About 400,000 of these rifles were produced with about 67,000 sent to England's Home Guard.

Courtesy Buffalo Bill Historical Center, Cody, Wyoming

Exc.	V.G.	Good	Fair	Poor
500	350	275	175	125

Mark III*

As above, with a magazine cutoff.

Exc.	V.G.	Good	Fair	Poor
450	300	250	200	150

Ross Military Match Rifle

A .280 Ross or .303 caliber straight pull military-style rifle with a 30" barrel having peep sights. Blued with a walnut stock. Similar in appearance to the Mark III except for flush magazine with .280 version.

Exc.	V.G.	Good	Fair	Poor
825	600	400	250	125

WINCHESTER

Model 1894 Carbine

This is the Canadian military version of the Winchester saddle ring carbine. Fitted with a 20" barrel and chambered for the .30-30 cartridge. Extra set of sling swivels added to left side of buttstock and forearm. Stamped with the Canadian "Broad Arrow" (an arrow inside the letter C).

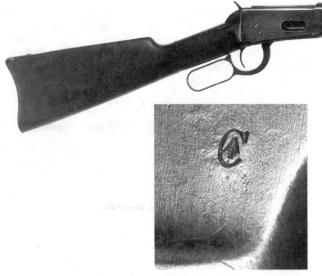

Winchester Model 1894 Carbine • Courtesy Rock Island Auction Company

Exc.	V.G.	Good	Fair	Poor
1750	1500	950	450	250

Fabrique Nationale

C1/C1A1 (FN FAL)

Canada was one of the first countries to adopt the FN-FAL rifle. This is a semiautomatic version with 21" barrel. Twenty-round box magazine. The rear sight on the C1 is a revolving disk with five different sized openings. Ranges calibrated from 200 to 600 yards; numbered 2 to 6 on the sight. The sight may be folded when not in use. Weight is about 9.5 lbs. About 1959 the C1 was modified to use a 2-piece firing pin and a plastic carry handle replaced the wooden type. Both types of rifles utilize the long prong flash hider on the muzzle.

Exc.	V.G.	Good	Fair	Poor
2500	2000	1500	1000	500

NOTE: For C1/C1A1 registered as NFA firearms see prices listed below:

Pre-1968 (Rare)

Exc.	V.G.	Fair
9000	8500	8000

Pre-1986 conversions

Exc.	V.G.	Fair
5500	5000	4500

Pre-1986 dealer samples

Exc.	V.G.	Fair
4000	3500	3000

C2/C2A1

This is Canada's version of the FN heavy barrel Squad Light Automatic Rifle. Select fire with a rate of fire of about 700 rounds per minute. Barrel length is 21". Magazine capacity is 30 rounds. Weight is approximately 15 lbs. Built by Long Branch Arsenal, Ontario.

Pre-1968 (Rare)

Exc.	V.G.	Fair
10000	9000	8000

Pre-1986 conversions

Exc.	V.G.	Fair
6000	5500	5000

Pre-1986 dealer samples

Exc.	V.G.	Fair
5000	4500	4000

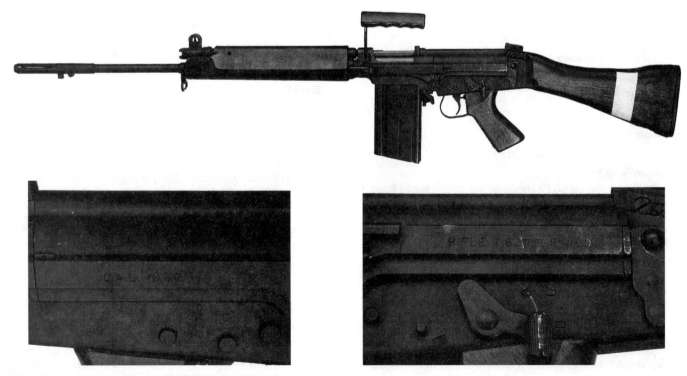

C1A1 • Courtesy West Point Museum, Paul Goodwin photo

C7/C8 (M16A2)

In 1985 the Canadian firm of Diemaco began producing a Canadian version of the Colt M16A2 rifle. There are differences between the Colt-built M16 and the Diemaco version. However, due to import restrictions on Class 3 weapons, no Diemaco M16s were imported into the U.S. for transferable civilian sale. Therefore, no Diemaco lowers are available to the civilian collector. There are Diemaco uppers in the U.S. that will fit on Colt lowers. The 20" rifle version is designated the C7 while the 16" carbine version is called the C8. There are a number of other Diemaco Canadian uppers that may be seen in the U.S., such as the LMG and 24" barreled versions. Prices should be comparable with Colt uppers.

MACHINE GUNS

NOTE: Canada used the Lewis and Vickers machine guns during World War II. The Toronto firm of John Inglis produced Mark I and Mark II Bren guns in .303 caliber in large quantities for British and Canadian troops. Beginning in 1943 Canada produced almost 60 percent of the total Bren gun production for World War II. This amounted to about 186,000 guns produced during the war. Canada also uses the Browning Model 1919A4, called the C1 machine gun in 7.62mm (.308) as its primarily light machine gun.

See *Great Britain Machine Guns, Bren.*

Canadian Bren Mk I and Mk II

The first examples of the Canadian Bren were built in 1940 by the Inglis Company. A total of 186,000 Brens were built in Canada with 56,000 going to the Canadian army. Marked with the date and manufacturer (Inglis) on the right side of the receiver.

Pre-1968

Exc.	V.G.	Fair
35000	30000	27500

Pre-1986 conversions

Exc.	V.G.	Fair
20000	18500	17500

Pre-1986 dealer samples

Exc.	V.G.	Fair
N/A	N/A	N/A

Inglis Bren Mk I • Courtesy Blake Stevens, *The Bren Gun Saga*, Dugelby

Canadian Chinese Bren Mk II

Full production of Mk II Bren guns in 7.62x57mm began in January of 1944 and ended in 1945. These guns were produced under a Chinese contract. About 39,300 of these guns are marked with Chinese characters and Inglis with the date of manufacture. Some 3,700 guns were sent to resistance groups in Europe. These were not marked in Chinese, but marked with "OT" prefix serial numbers.

Pre-1968 (Very Rare)

Exc.	V.G.	Fair
40000	37500	35000

Pre-1986 conversions

Exc.	V.G.	Fair
N/A	N/A	N/A

Pre-1986 dealer samples

Exc.	V.G.	Fair
N/A	N/A	N/A

CHINA & PEOPLE'S REPUBLIC OF CHINA

Chinese Military Conflicts, 1870–2000

By 1870 China was affected by foreign influence from Great Britain, France, Germany, and Russia. The central government in China was further weakened by its defeat in the Sino-Japanese War of 1894-1895. The decade of the 1890s ended with China's fierce attempt to overthrow foreign influence by means of the Boxer Rebellion, 1898 to 1900. The period of the early 20th century was marked by internal strife which eventually led to Chinese warlords gaining control of the government in 1916. These warlords were eventually ousted in 1927 by the Nationalist leader Chiang Kai-shek in alliance with the Communists. The year 1927 marked the beginning of a long Chinese civil war between the Nationalist and the Communists ending with the Communists' Long March of 1934-35 and their exile. In 1931 Japan occupied Manchuria, and in 1937 the Japanese mounted a full scale invasion of China. Both the Nationalists and the Communists fought in an uneasy alliance against the Japanese. By the end of World War II, the civil war again ignited and the Communists became victorious in 1949 when the People's Republic of China was proclaimed. China entered the Korean War on the side of the North Koreans in 1950. In the last 50 years China has been occupied with intellectual turmoil (Cultural Revolution) and other domestic ferment.

HANDGUNS

MAUSER

Between the two world wars, the Chinese military purchased a number of Mauser 1896 pistols directly from Mauser and other commercial sources. These purchases consisted mainly of Bolos and Model 1930s. In addition to these purchases, China made its own copies of the Mauser broomhandle as well as the Astra. *See Germany, Handguns, Mauser for more detailed descriptions and prices.*

CHINESE MAUSERS

The Chinese government purchased a large quantity of Mauser pistols directly from Mauser and continued to do so until they began purchasing Browning Hi-Power pistols from FN in the mid 1930s. The Chinese bought many Bolos and Model 1930 pistols. Some of these pistols are marked with Chinese characters, many are not. The Chinese also made their own copies of Mauser broomhandles as well as Spanish copies. Some of the more commonly encountered varieties are listed here.

CHINESE MARKED, HANDMADE COPIES

Crude copies of the Model 96; unsafe to fire.

Exc.	V.G.	Good	Fair	Poor
500	400	350	250	175

Taku-Naval Dockyard Model

Approximately 6,000 copies of the Model 96 were made at the Taku-Naval Dockyard. Values listed below include a correct shoulder stock/holder.

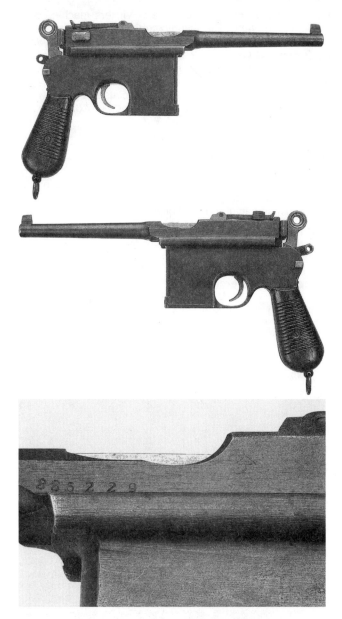

Taku Naval Dockyard Model • Private collection, Paul Goodwin photo

Exc.	V.G.	Good	Fair	Poor
2500	1500	1000	500	400

Shansei Arsenal Model

Approximately 8,000 Model 96 pistols were manufactured in .45 ACP caliber at the Shansei Province Arsenal in 1929. Magazine capacity is 10 rounds.

CHINESE SHANSEI .45 BROOMHANDLE

Among all the Chinese variants of the C-96 Mauser, the most exotic is the big .45 caliber Broomhandle. Referred to as the "Yen" type pistol in China, it was made by the Shansei warlord, Yen Hsi-Shan. In the mountainous province of Shansei, Yen's railway was often under attack by bandits and other warlords. So he armed his men with a local copy of the Model 1921 Thompson and a C-96 Broomhandle, both chambered for a 11.43 cartridge similar to our .45 ACP. Production of the big Broomhandle began in 1929 with its formal designation being Type 18. Examining one shows it to be simply a scaled up C-96. Now a regular Broomhandle is already a large pistol so the Shansei is quite a handful. In the hand it reminded me of the old cap-and-ball horse pistols, huge but still manageable. Operating it is the same as for a regular C-96. Simply pull the bolt to the rear until it locks back and insert a 10-round stripperclip and briskly push the fat rounds into the action. If no clips are available, they're rarer than the guns, you can load single rounds. Let the bolt run forward and you're ready to go. Triggers on C-96s tend to be fairly light, and my test specimen was quite good. The sights though are typical German Mauser, hard to see, slow to pick up, and generally useless. Squinting for the sights touch the trigger and the Shansei barks. As the bore sits very high above the hand, muzzle jump is more pronounced over, say, an M1911. Recoil though, being only a .45, is still quite comfortable, the gun simply jumps in the hand. Empties eject straight up and sometimes hit you on the head on the way back down. While surprisingly accurate, I feel Yen would have been better off making a copy of the M1911 to go with his Thompsons.

David Fortier

NOTE: Within the past several years, a large quantity of Model 96 pistols exported to or made in China have been imported into the United States. It has been reported that some *newly* made copies of the Shansei .45 were recently exported from China. **Proceed with caution.**

NOTE: Copies of the Model 96 were made by Unceta (Astra), Eulogio Arostegui (Azul), and Zulaica y Cia (Royal) and marketed by the firm of Beistegui Hermanos. These copies are covered in their own sections of this text.

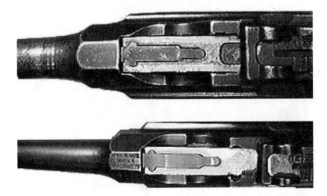

Courtesy Gale Morgan

Shansei Panel Marking

Courtesy Gale Morgan

Exc.	V.G.	Good	Fair	Poor
5000	3500	2250	1500	1300

CHINA STATE ARSENALS

Type 51/54 Pistol (TT33)

A 7.62mm semiautomatic pistol with a 4.5" barrel and 8-shot magazine. This model was produced in a number of communist countries. It is essentially a Soviet Tokarev TT-33.

NOTE: For cut-aways add 200%.

Exc.	V.G.	Good	Fair	Poor
500	450	375	225	100

From top to bottom: M20 export model, K54, K51 • Courtesy Chuck Karwan

TT33 • Courtesy Richard M. Kumor Sr.

Type 59 Makarov

This semiautomatic pistol is similar in appearance to the Walther PP pistol and is chambered for the 9mm Makarov (9x18mm) cartridge. It has a double-action trigger and is fitted with fixed sights. Barrel length is 3.6" and overall length is 6.4". Weight is approximately 25 oz. Magazine capacity is 8 rounds.

Exc.	V.G.	Good	Fair	Poor
150	100	80	60	50

Type 80

A Chinese version of the Mauser 96 pistol chambered for the 7.63x25mm cartridge. Fitted with a 7" barrel and detachable 10- or 20-round magazine, this pistol is capable of select fire. Weight is approximately 40 oz. *See Mauser Schnellfeuer.*

SUBMACHINE GUNS

Type 43/53

This is a Chinese copy of a Soviet PPS 43 built during the Korean War.

Pre-1968

Exc.	V.G.	Fair
5500	5000	4500

Pre-1986 conversions

Exc.	V.G.	Fair
N/A	N/A	N/A

Pre-1986 dealer samples

Exc.	V.G.	Fair
N/A	N/A	N/A

Type 50

This model is a Chinese copy of the Soviet PPSh-41 submachine gun. It is chambered for the 7.62 Soviet pistol cartridge. Barrel is 10.5" and magazine capacity is 25, 32, or 40 rounds. Rate of fire is 600 rounds per minute. Weight is approximately 7.5 lbs. Markings are located on top of the receiver.

Pre-1968

Exc.	V.G.	Fair
7000	6500	6000

Pre-1986 conversions

Exc.	V.G.	Fair
N/A	N/A	N/A

Pre-1986 dealer samples

Exc.	V.G.	Fair
N/A	N/A	N/A

North Vietnamese K-50M

Similar to the Type 50 but unlike the Soviet model, this gun features a telescoping metal stock and no muzzle compensator.

North Vietnamese Type 50 M • Paul Goodwin photo

Pre-1968

Exc.	V.G.	Fair
7000	6500	6000

Pre-1986 conversions

Exc.	V.G.	Fair
N/A	N/A	N/A

Pre-1986 dealer samples

Exc.	V.G.	Fair
N/A	N/A	N/A

RIFLES

MAUSER

Mauser Rifles

The Chinese used a wide variety of Mauser rifles from the Gew 71 to the Chinese Model 1924. Some of these are marked with Chinese characters and others are not.

For in-depth information on Chinese Mausers, see Robert W.D. Ball's, *Mauser Military Rifles of the World*, 3rd Edition, Krause Publications, 2003.

G71 Rifle

This rifle is identical to the German model of the same designation.

Exc.	V.G.	Good	Fair	Poor
400	325	250	190	120

K71 Carbine

This carbine is identical to the German model of the same designation.

Exc.	V.G.	Good	Fair	Poor
400	350	225	200	150

M1895 Rifle

This model is identical to the Chilean Model 1895 rifle.

Exc.	V.G.	Good	Fair	Poor
225	200	175	130	90

Hunyaug Rifle

Exc.	V.G.	Good	Fair	Poor
225	200	175	130	90

M1907 Rifle

This model is based on the German Model 1904. Chambered for the 7.92x57mm cartridge. Fitted with a 29" barrel and 5-round magazine. Tangent rear sight to 2,000 meters. Made with a pistol grip stock and upper handguard. On the receiver ring two superposed diamonds are marked with the Chinese date for rifles made in China. German built rifles will have Mauser or DWM stamped on them. Weight is about 8.25 lbs.

Exc.	V.G.	Good	Fair	Poor
225	195	175	125	90

Type 53 Rifle • Courtesy West Point Museum, Paul Goodwin photo

M1907 Carbine

As above but with 21.75" barrel and tangent sight to 1,400 meters. Turned down bolt handle and full stock. No bayonet. Weight is about 8 lbs.

Exc.	V.G.	Good	Fair	Poor
225	195	150	90	60

M1912 Steyr Rifle

Chambered for the 7x57mm cartridge and fitted with a 28.75" barrel. Weight is about 9 lbs. Built in Austria.

Exc.	V.G.	Good	Fair	Poor
275	225	175	120	90

M98/22 Rifle

Manufactured by CZ in BRNO, this rifle is based on the Mexican Model 1912 with a Model 98 action. It is half cocked with a full-length upper handguard with pistol grip. Chambered for the 7.92x57mm Mauser cartridge. Barrel length is 29" with a 5-round integral magazine. Weight is about 9.5 lbs. China purchased about 70,000 of these rifles.

Exc.	V.G.	Good	Fair	Poor
250	200	160	110	90

FN M24 and 30 Short Rifles

Exc.	V.G.	Good	Fair	Poor
150	120	90	60	40

M21 Short Rifle

A Chinese copy of the FN Model 30 Short Rifle. Pistol grip stock with upper handguard from receiver to upper band. Chambered for the 7.92x57mm cartridge and fitted with a 23.6" barrel. Tangent rear sight to 2,000 meters. Weight is about 8.5 lbs. Chinese characters marked on the receiver ring.

Exc.	V.G.	Good	Fair	Poor
175	150	120	90	50

Chiang Kai-shek Short Rifle

Chambered for the 7.92x57mm cartridge. Fitted with a 23.6" barrel. Tangent rear sight to 2,000 meters. Magazine capacity is 5 rounds in a flush mounted box magazine. Weight is approximately 8.75 lbs. Chinese markings on the receiver ring. Manufactured between 1936 and 1949, this rifle became the standard issue for Chinese troops.

Exc.	V.G.	Good	Fair	Poor
165	130	100	80	50

VZ24 Short Rifle

This is the Czech Model 24 short rifle purchased from Czechoslovakia in the mid-1930s. Approximately 100,000 were purchased and all have a "P" prefix in the serial number. All are dated 1937. Many of these rifles were captured by the Japanese during World War II and issued to Japanese troops. After the war these rifles were reissued to Chinese troops.

Exc.	V.G.	Good	Fair	Poor
90	80	60	50	30

M1933 Standard Model Short Rifle

Chambered for the 7.92x57mm cartridge and fitted with a 23.6" barrel. Magazine capacity is 5 rounds in a flush-mounted box magazine. Tangent rear sight to 2,000 meters. Mauser Banner trademark is marked on the receiver ring. Weight is about 8.75 lbs. Stock has a pistol grip and upper handguard. Straight bolt handle.

Exc.	V.G.	Good	Fair	Poor
190	170	140	110	90

M1933 Standard Model Carbine

As above but with turned down bolt handle and sling swivels mounted on left side of stock. Chambered for the 7.92x57mm cartridge but also offered in 7.65x53mm and 7x57mm. Mauser trademark on receiver ring. Weight is about 8.5 lbs.

Exc.	V.G.	Good	Fair	Poor
190	170	140	110	90

VZ24 with Japanese Folding Bayonet (Chinese copy)

A copy of the VZ24 and fitted with a Japanese Model 44 folding bayonet. Pistol grip stock and straight bolt handle. Barrel length is 23". Chambered for the 7.92x57mm cartridge. Rear tangent sight to 2,000 meters. Chinese markings on the receiver. Weight is about 9 lbs.

Exc.	V.G.	Good	Fair	Poor
200	175	150	120	100

Manchurian Mauser Rifle (Mukden Arsenal)

See Japan, Rifles.

Type 53

This is a Chinese copy of the Soviet Model 1944 Mosin-Nagant carbine. Production began in 1953. Early models up to 1959 have Chinese characters for the model designation stamped on the receiver. Rifles made after 1959 do not have these characters. Chinese rifles have the bolt, magazine, floorplate, and buttplate serial-numbered to the rifle. Production ended sometime in the early 1960s.

Exc.	V.G.	Good	Fair	Poor
200	150	125	75	50

Type 56 Carbine (SKS)

A 7.62x39mm semiautomatic rifle with a 20.5" barrel and 10-shot fixed magazine. Blued with oil finished stock. This rifle was a standard service arm for most Eastern Bloc countries prior to the adoption of the AK-47.

Pre-Ban Rifles

Exc.	V.G.	Good	Fair	Poor
400	300	—	—	—

SKS Carbine • Paul Goodwin photo

NOTE: The importation of post-ban SKS rifles has resulted in an oversupply of these rifles with the result that prices are less than $100 for guns in excellent condition. However, this situation may change and if that occurs the price will adjust accordingly. Study local conditions before purchase or sale of this firearm.

North Korean Type 56 Carbine (SKS)

Same overall design as the Chinese version but with high quality fit and finish. Reddish-brown laminated stock. Rare.

Pre-Ban Rifles

Exc.	V.G.	Good	Fair	Poor
1400	1000	800	600	300

Chinese Type 56 Rifle

A close copy of the AK-47 and first produced in 1958, this select fire rifle is chambered for the 7.62x39mm cartridge. It is fitted with a 16" barrel and has a magazine capacity of 30 rounds. This model has a folding bayonet hinged below the muzzle. Weight is about 8.4 lbs. Rate of fire is 600 rounds per minute. Markings on left side of receiver. Still in production. This rifle was adopted by Chinese forces and was seen in Cambodia as well.

There are a number of subvariations of the Type 56. Early guns had machined receivers with Chinese characters for selector markings, some of which are marked "м22" to designate export sales. Another style is fitted with a folding spike bayonet as well as a machined receiver. Still another style has a stamped receiver, Chinese characters for selector markings, and a folding spike bayonet. All are direct copies of the Soviet model AK-47.

Another variation of the Type 56 was the Type 56-1, which featured prominent rivets on a folding metal butt. No bayonet. Other variants of the Type 56-1 are fitted with a folding spike bayonet and folding metal buttstock. The Type 56-2 has a skeleton tubular stock which folds to the right side of the receiver with no bayonet. There is also the Type 56-C with plastic furniture, side folding butt with cheekpiece, and improved sights with no bayonet.

NOTE: Type 56 rifles manufactured by China North Industries (NORINCO) will have stamped on the left side of the receiver the number "66" in a triangle.

Pre-1968

Exc.	V.G.	Fair
17500	16000	15000

Pre-1986 conversions

Exc.	V.G.	Fair
6000	5500	5000

Pre-1986 dealer samples

Exc.	V.G.	Fair
8000	7000	6000

Type 56 (AK Clone semiautomatic versions)

Imported from China in semiautomatic versions and built by Poly Tech and Norinco in different styles and configurations, some of which are listed below.

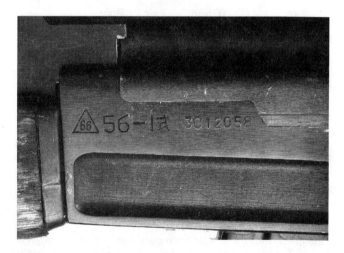

Chinese Type 56 • Paul Goodwin photo

Milled Receiver–Poly Tech

Exc.	V.G.	Good	Fair	Poor
1500	1200	800	500	250

Stamped Receiver–Poly Tech

Exc.	V.G.	Good	Fair	Poor
1100	800	500	300	150

Stamped Receiver–Norinco

Exc.	V.G.	Good	Fair	Poor
950	700	450	250	150

NOTE: For folding stock version add 20%.

Type 79

A Chinese copy of the Soviet Dragunov SVD sniper rifle.

Exc.	V.G.	Good	Fair	Poor
3000	2500	1500	1000	750

MACHINE GUNS

NOTE: See also *Great Britain, Machine Guns, Bren MK2.*

Type 24

The Chinese copy of the German Model 1909 commercial Maxim built under the supervision of German engineers.

Pre-1968

Exc.	V.G.	Fair
20000	18000	17000

Pre-1986 conversions

Exc.	V.G.	Fair
8500	8000	7000

Pre-1986 dealer samples

Exc.	V.G.	Fair
N/A	N/A	N/A

Type 26

This is the Czech VZ26 purchased in the 1930s.

Pre-1968

Exc.	V.G.	Fair
15000	14000	13000

Pre-1986 conversions

Exc.	V.G.	Fair
13000	12500	12000

Pre-1986 dealer samples (Rare)

Exc.	V.G.	Fair
N/A	N/A	N/A

Type 53

This is a Chinese copy of the Soviet DPM machine gun.

Pre-1968

Exc.	V.G.	Fair
13000	11000	11000

Pre-1986 conversions

Exc.	V.G.	Fair
8000	7000	6000

Pre-1986 dealer samples

Exc.	V.G.	Fair
N/A	N/A	N/A

Type 54

The Chinese made a variation of the Soviet DShK 38/46 gun.

Pre-1968

Exc.	V.G.	Fair
—	35000	30000

Pre-1986 conversions

Exc.	V.G.	Fair
—	27000	—

Pre-1986 dealer samples (Rare)

Exc.	V.G.	Fair
—	20000	20000

Type 56

This is a Chinese copy of the Soviet Model RPD light machine gun.

Pre-1968 (Very Rare)

Exc.	V.G.	Fair
35000	32500	30000

Pre-1986 conversions (rewelds)

Exc.	V.G.	Fair
30000	27500	25000

Type 56 • Courtesy West Point Museum, Paul Goodwin photo

Type 57 with mount • Courtesy West Point Museum, Paul Goodwin photo

Pre-1986 conversions

Exc.	V.G.	Fair
10000	9000	8000

Pre-1986 dealer samples (Rare)

Exc.	V.G.	Fair
N/A	N/A	N/A

Pre-1986 dealer samples (Rare)

Exc.	V.G.	Fair
20000	20000	20000

Type 57

This is a Chinese copy of the Soviet SG-43.

Pre-1968

Exc.	V.G.	Fair
25000	20000	18000

Pre-1986 conversions

Exc.	V.G.	Fair
20000	18000	15000

Pre-1986 dealer samples (Rare)

Exc.	V.G.	Fair
N/A	N/A	N/A

Type 58

This is a licensed Chinese-made copy of the Soviet RP-46.

Pre-1968

Exc.	V.G.	Fair
19000	18000	16000

Type 58 • Courtesy West Point Museum, Paul Goodwin photo

CZECHOSLOVAKIA

Czechoslovakian Military Conflicts, 1918–1993

Czechoslovakia, as an independent nation, was established at the end of World War I from the ruins of the Austro-Hungarian Empire. In 1939 the country was invaded and occupied by Germany. After the war ended in 1945, Czechoslovakia was re-established under Communist rule. Czechoslovakia was split in 1993 into the Czech Republic and Slovakia, both independent states.

Bibliographical Notes:

Perhaps the best general work on Czech firearms is *Czech Firearms and Ammunition*, by Dolinek, Karlicky, and Vacha, Prague, 1995. Jan Still, *Axis Pistols*, 1986.

NOTE: The term "VZ" stands for model (*Vzor*) in Czech. This abbreviation is used in place of the English word Model. The author has sometimes used both terms but never together.

HANDGUNS

Most Czech handguns are of domestic design and manufacture. See below.

Army Pistole 1922

Semiautomatic pistol chambered for the .380 ACP (9x17mm short) cartridge. Barrel length is 3.5". Magazine capacity is 8 rounds. Weight is approximately 22 oz. Adopted by the Czech army in 1922 and called the M22. This was the first Czech designed and manufactured service semiautomatic pistol. It was based on a German locked breech design and made under license from Mauser. Blued with checkered plastic grips. Manufactured between 1921 and 1923. Because of production difficulties, only about 22,000 were built.

Exc.	V.G.	Good	Fair	Poor
650	500	350	200	150

CZ 1924

The first large production military pistol produced by CZ. It is a locked-breech pistol with a 3.5" rotating barrel chambered for the 9mm short cartridge, external hammer, and a magazine safety. It features a rounded slide and is blued with a wraparound walnut grip. Magazine capacity is 8 rounds. The slide is marked "Ceska Zbrojovka A.S. v Praze." Weight is approximately 24 oz. About 170,000 of these pistols were produced between 1922 and 1938.

NOTE: For Nazi-Proofed add 50%.

Exc.	V.G.	Good	Fair	Poor
475	375	300	200	100

NOTE: A limited number of pistols have been noted marked "CZ 1925" and "CZ 1926." There are various minor design changes on each model, and it is conjectured that they were prototypes that were manufactured on the road to the production of the less complicated, blowback-operated CZ 1927 pistol.

CZ 1927

A semiautomatic pistol chambered for the 7.65mm cartridge (.32 ACP), marked the same as the CZ 1924, but the cocking grooves on the slide are cut vertically instead of sloped as on the earlier model. This model was blued with checkered, wraparound, plastic grips. These early guns were beautifully made and marked "Ceska Zbrojovka AS v Praze."

This version remained in production during the German occupation of Czechoslovakia between 1939 and 1945. Occupation pistols are marked, "BOHMISCHE WAFFENFABRIK IM PRAG." The Germans used the code "fnh" on these wartime pistols and designated the model the "PISTOLE MOD 27(t)." The finish declined as the war progressed, with the very late guns rough but functional. There are several subvariations of this pistol that may affect value (see Still). A total of about 450,000 were produced during the German occupation. After the war, these pistols continued in production until 1951. There were almost 700,000 manufactured.

NOTE: For Nazi-Proofed add 50%.

Early CZ 27 with Nazi production markings • Courtesy Orvel Reichert

Exc.	V.G.	Good	Fair	Poor
450	375	300	200	165

NOTE: Some of these pistols were made with an extended barrel for the use of a silencer. This variation brings a large premium. Less than 10 CZ 27s were made in .22 caliber. An expert opinion is suggested if a sale is contemplated.

CZ 1938

It is chambered for the 9mm short cartridge (.380 Auto) and has a 4.65" barrel. Except for a few examples with a conventional sear and slide safety, it is double action-only with exposed hammer, and difficult to fire accurately. It utilizes a 9-round, detachable box magazine; and the slide is hinged at the muzzle to pivot upward for ease of cleaning and disassembly. It is well made and well finished, but is as large in size as most 9mm Parabellum pistols. Production began in 1938, and the Germans adopted it as the "Pistole Mod 39" on paper; but it is doubtful that any were actually used by the German army. It now appears that the P39(t), which is the Nazi designation, were all sent to Finland and a large number with "SA" (Finnish) markings have recently been surplused along with their holsters. A few SA marked guns have been modified by the Finnish army to function single or double action. About 40,000 of these pistols were manufactured.

Exc.	V.G.	Good	Fair	Poor
450	400	350	250	175

CZ 1938–Nazi Proofed (P39(t))

Fewer than 1,000 of these pistols were Nazi proofed late in the war. E/WaA76 acceptance stamp on left frame and barrel.

Exc.	V.G.	Good	Fair	Poor
—	1500	1250	600	300

CZ 1950

This is a blowback-operated, semiautomatic, double action pistol chambered for the 7.65mm cartridge with a 3.75" barrel. Magazine capacity is 8 rounds. Weight is about 23 oz. It is patterned after the Walther Model PP with a few differences. The safety catch is located on the frame instead of the slide; and the triggerguard is not hinged, as on the Walther. It is dismantled by means of a catch on the side of the frame. Although intended to be a military pistol designed by the Kratochvil brothers, it proved to be under-powered and was adopted by the police. There were few released on the commercial market.

CZ 1950 • Courtesy Chuck Karwan

Exc.	V.G.	Good	Fair	Poor
275	200	150	100	75

Model 1970

This model was an attempt to correct dependability problems with the Model 50. There is little difference to see externally between the two except for markings and the grip pattern. Markings are "VZOR 70 CAL 7.65." Production began during the 1960s and ended in 1983.

Courtesy Rock Island Auction Company

Exc.	V.G.	Good	Fair	Poor
250	200	150	100	75

CZ 1952

Since the Czechoslovakian army was not happy with the under-powered CZ 1950 pistol, they began using Soviet weapons until 1952, when this model was designed. It was designed for a new cartridge known as the 7.62mm M48. It was similar to the Soviet cartridge but loaded to a higher velocity. This is a single action, semiautomatic pistol with a 4.5" barrel. It has a locked breech that utilizes two roller cams. Magazine capacity is 8 rounds. This was an excellent pistol that has been replaced by the CZ 75, a pistol that is decidedly inferior to it.

Exc.	V.G.	Good	Fair	Poor
150	125	100	75	65

CZ 75 B

Introduced in 1994, this CZ model is an updated version of the original CZ 75. It features a pinned front sight, a commander hammer, non-glare ribbed barrel, and a squared triggerguard. Also offered in .40 S&W chamber. Offered in both commercial and military versions the CZ 75 B is used by more than 60 countries around the world in 9mm. Approximately 1,250,000 military pistols are in service. The Czechs use the pistol in their Special Forces units.

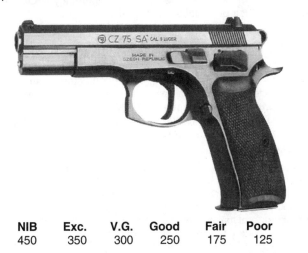

NIB	Exc.	V.G.	Good	Fair	Poor
450	350	300	250	175	125

NOTE: For .40 S&W add $30. For glossy blue add $20, for dual tone finish add $25, and for nickel add $25. For tritium night sights add $80.

CZ 82/83

This is a fixed barrel .380 caliber pistol. It features an ambidextrous safety and magazine catch behind the triggerguard. The pistol is stripped by means of a hinged triggerguard. Barrel length is 3.8", overall length is 6.8", and weight is about 23 oz.

The Model 82 designation is the military model, while the Model 83 is the commercial version. The Model 83 is offered in 3 calibers: the 9x18, .380, and 9mm. The military Model 82 is offered in only 1 caliber, the 9mm Makarov. The Model 82 is the side arm of the Czech army. The Model 82 is no longer in production, but the Model 83 is currently manufactured.

NIB	Exc.	V.G.	Good	Fair	Poor
315	250	200	175	150	125

SUBMACHINE GUNS

The Czechs built the CZ 247 and the CZ 47 after World War II, but did not adopt these guns for their own military use. Instead they were exported to South America and other countries. These submachine guns are chambered for the 9mm Parabellum cartridge and are similar in appearance to the CZ 1938 gun but with a 40-round magazine.

CZ 23/25

The Model 23 has a wooden stock while the Model 25 has a folding metal stock; otherwise all other dimensions are the same. Introduced in 1948, this submachine gun is chambered for the 9mm cartridge. Magazine capacity is 25- or 40-round box type. Rate of fire is about 600 rounds per minute. Weight is approximately 8 to 8.5 lbs., depending on model. This gun introduced the hollow bolt that allows for the short length of the gun (17.5" with butt folded, 27" with butt extended) and was copied in the UZI. The magazine well is located in the pistol grip, another feature copied by the UZI. The trigger mechanism is designed so that light pressure gives semiautomatic fire while full trigger pressure gives full automatic fire. Weight of the gun is about 7 lbs. A variation of this model is called the Model 24/26 and is the same except for the caliber: 7.62mm.

NOTE: Prices listed are estimates only.

Courtesy Thomas Nelson, *The World's Submachine Guns, Vol. 1*

Pre-1968

Exc.	V.G.	Fair
9000	8000	7000

Pre-1986 conversions

Exc.	V.G.	Fair
N/A	N/A	N/A

Pre-1986 dealer samples

Exc.	V.G.	Fair
5000	4500	4000

ZK 383

This submachine gun was first introduced in 1933. It is chambered for the 9mm Parabellum cartridge and fitted with a 12.8" quick change barrel with jacket. Adjustable rate of fire from 500 to 700 rounds per minute by means of a removable insert in the bolt. This model fitted with a bipod. Rear sight is a V-notch tangent graduated to 800 meters. Weight is about 9.5 lbs. This gun was sold to Bulgaria, some South American countries, and was used by the German army from 1938 to 1945.

A variation of this model called the ZK 383P was used by police units and does not have a bipod or quick change barrel. The ZK 383H was a limited production version with a folding magazine housing fitted to the bottom of the gun rather than the side.

Pre-1968

Exc.	V.G.	Fair
14000	13000	12000

Pre-1986 conversions

Exc.	V.G.	Fair
N/A	N/A	N/A

Pre-1986 dealer samples

Exc.	V.G.	Fair
N/A	N/A	N/A

ZK 383 • Courtesy Thomas Nelson, *The World's Submachine Guns, Vol. 1*

Skorpion Samopal VZ61

Introduced in 1960 this weapon is sometimes referred to as a machine pistol because of its size. Chambered for the 7.65x17SR Browning (.32 ACP) cartridge. Export models of this gun are chambered for the 9x17mm (.380 ACP(VZ63)), 9x18mm Makarov (VZ64), and the 9x19mm Parabellum (VZ68). The gun has a 4.5" barrel and is fitted with a wooden pistol grip. Overall length with butt folded in 10.5", with butt extended the length is 20.5". Weight is approximately 3 lbs. Rate of fire is about 700 rounds per minute. A licensed copy is made in Yugoslavia called the Model 84.

Pre-1968		
Exc.	V.G.	Fair
N/A	N/A	N/A

Pre-1986 conversions		
Exc.	V.G.	Fair
N/A	N/A	N/A

Pre-1986 dealer samples (Rare)		
Exc.	V.G.	Fair
9500	9000	8500

RIFLES

Immediately after World War I the Czechs continued to use the Mannlicher Model 1895 rifle until 1924 when they began production of their own Mauser action rifles.

MAUSER

Ceskoslovensha Zbrojovaka (ZB), Brno

NOTE: In 1924 the Czechs began to manufacture a number of Mauser-designed rifles for export, and for its own military use. Czech Mausers were based on the Model 98 action. Many of these rifles were sold to other countries and will be found under *Germany, Mauser, Rifles.*

M1898/22 Rifle

Manufactured by CZ in Brno this rifle is based on the Mexican Model 1912 with a Model 98 action. It is half cocked with a full-length upper handguard with pistol grip. Chambered for the 7.92x57mm Mauser cartridge. Barrel length is 29" with a 5-round integral magazine. Weight is about 9.5 lbs. This rifle was used by Turkey as well as other countries.

Skorpion • Courtesy West Point Museum, Paul Goodwin photo

Exc.	V.G.	Good	Fair	Poor
100	90	70	40	25

VZ23 Short Rifle

Used by the Czech army this 7.92x57mm rifle was fitted with a 21.5" barrel and 5-round magazine. Tangent leaf rear sight graduated to 2000 meters. Most were marked, "CZECHOSLOVAKIAN FACTORY FOR ARMS MANUFACTURE, BRNO" on the receiver ring. Weight is about 9 lbs.

Exc.	V.G.	Good	Fair	Poor
120	100	80	60	40

VZ24 Short Rifle

Chambered for the 7.92x54mm cartridge and fitted with a 23.25" barrel. Weight is about 9 lbs. This was the standard Czech rifle prior to World War II and was used by a number of countries such as Romania, Yugoslavia, and China. This rifle was also used by the German army at the beginning of WWII.

Exc.	V.G.	Good	Fair	Poor
100	80	60	40	25

VZ12/33 Carbine

This rifle was produced primarily for export. It has a pistol grip stock with 3/4 length upper handguard and two barrel bands fairly close together. Bolt handle is bent down. Barrel length is 21.5" with 5-round magazine. Rear leaf sight is graduated to 1400 meters. Weight is about 8 lbs. Country crest stamped on receiver.

Exc.	V.G.	Good	Fair	Poor
125	110	90	75	50

VZ16/33 Carbine

Designed for paramilitary units this rifle has a 19.25" barrel. Chambered for the 7.92x57mm cartridge as well as other calibers depending on country. Magazine capacity is 5 rounds. Tangent rear leaf sight graduated to 1000 meters. Czech crest stamped on receiver ring. This rifle formed the basis on the German Model 33/40 paratroop carbine used during WWII.

Exc.	V.G.	Good	Fair	Poor
300	260	220	160	120

CZECH STATE

Ceskoslovenska Zbrojovka Brno (BRNO) was established in 1919 as the state arms factory. It was originally state owned but later, in 1924, was reorganized as a limited liability company.

Model 24 (VZ24)

This rifle marks the first Czech produced military rifle for the Czech army. It was based on the Mauser 98 action. The rifle was in wide use by other countries such as Germany prior to WWII. Chambered for the 7.92mm cartridge and fitted with a 23" barrel, this model had a 5-round non-detachable box magazine. The rear sight was graduated from 300 to 2000 meters in 100 meter increments. Weight is about 9 lbs.

Exc.	V.G.	Good	Fair	Poor
300	200	100	75	50

NOTE: Prices are for rifles with matching numbers and original markings.

Model ZH29

Introduced in 1929, this semiautomatic rifle was designed by Emmanuel Holek of CZ at Brno. It is chambered for the 7.92x57mm cartridge and is fitted with a 21.5" barrel with aluminum cooling jacket over the barrel. Fitted with a bayonet lug. The detachable box magazine has a 10- or 25-round capacity. Weight is about 10 lbs. Exported to Thailand and Ethiopia. Very rare.

Exc.	V.G.	Good	Fair	Poor
9500	8500	7500	—	—

Model ZK420S

Chambered for the 7.92x57mm cartridge this rifle was first introduced in 1942 but did not appear in its final form until 1946. It was also offered in 7mm, .30-06, and 7.5mm Swiss. This was a gas operated semiautomatic rifle with 21" barrel and upper handguard. The detachable magazine has a 10-round capacity. Front sight is hooded. Rear sight is notched tangent with ramp. Weight is about 10 lbs. Not adopted by Czech military but tested by many countries. Built by CZ Brno in limited numbers. Very rare.

Exc.	V.G.	Good	Fair	Poor
10500	9000	8000	—	—

Model 52

Chambered for 7.62x45 caliber, this gas operated semiautomatic rifle is fitted with a 20.5" barrel. This model has a full

Czech VZ24 with receiver markings and crest • Paul Goodwin photo

stock with pistol grip. Folding non-detachable bayonet. Hooded front sight and notched tangent rear sight with ramp. Detachable box magazine with 10-round capacity. Weight is about 9.7 lbs. First produced in 1952.

Exc.	V.G.	Good	Fair	Poor
400	300	250	—	—

Model 52/57

Similar to the Model 52 except chambered for the 7.62x39 cartridge.

Courtesy Richard M. Kumor Sr.

Exc.	V.G.	Good	Fair	Poor
650	500	400	300	150

Model 1954 Sniper Rifle

This rifle, introduced in 1954, is built on a Mosin Nagant 1891/30 action and fitted with a 28.7" barrel chambered for the 7.62x54mmR cartridge. Magazine capacity is 5 rounds. Half stock with pistol grip and handguard. Rifle is supplied with a 2.5x telescope. Weight is approximately 9.5 lbs. Built by CZ in Brno. Production ended in 1957.

Exc.	V.G.	Good	Fair	Poor
750	600	500	400	200

VZ58

First produced in 1959, this select fire assault rifle is chambered for the 7.62x39mm Soviet cartridge. Its appearance is similar to an AK-47 but it is an entirely different design. It is gas operated but the bolt is locked to the receiver by a vertically moving block similar to the Walther P-38 pistol. Early rifles were fitted with a plastic fixed stock while later rifles used a folding metal stock. Barrel length is 16". Rate of fire is about 800 rounds per minute. Weight is approximately 7 lbs. Production ceased in 1980. Made at CZ Brno and Povaske Strojarne. The two versions of this gun are designated the vz58P with fixed stock and the vz58V for metal folding stock.

Pre-1968

Exc.	V.G.	Fair
9500	8500	8000

Pre-1986 conversions

Exc.	V.G.	Fair
N/A	N/A	N/A

Pre-1986 dealer samples

Exc.	V.G.	Fair
7000	6500	6000

MACHINE GUNS

The Czechs used the Steyr-built Schwarzlose Model 7/24 adopted to 7.92mm immediately after World War I. Czechoslovakia has also used the Soviet SG43 and the Soviet DT. Today the Czech army uses the ZB 59 as its primary machine gun. The ZB 59 is called a universal machine gun when mounted on a bipod. It is also used by the Czech military with a light barrel.

ZB VZ26

Manufactured by CZ Brno, this weapon is a light air-cooled gas-operated select-fire machine gun chambered for the 7.92x57mm Mauser cartridge. Fitted with a 23.7" finned barrel, it has a rate of fire of 500 rounds per minute. It is fed by a 20- or 30-round box magazine. Bipod and carry handle standard. Wooden butt with pistol grip. Quick change barrel. It was adopted by over two dozen countries around the world. It was the fore-runner of the famous British Bren gun (model designation ZGB33). Produced from 1925 to 1945. On left side of receiver marked "BRNO," and on right side marked "LEHKY KULOMET ZB VZ26." Weight is about 21 lbs. This gun was, and still is, used in large numbers throughout the world.

ZB made small improvements to the vz26 along with the date of the improvements. These guns are essentially the same as the ZB 26, but are known as the ZB vz27 and vz28.

Pre-1968

Exc.	V.G.	Fair
15000	14000	13000

Pre-1986 conversions

Exc.	V.G.	Fair
13000	12500	12000

Pre-1986 dealer samples

Exc.	V.G.	Fair
N/A	N/A	N/A

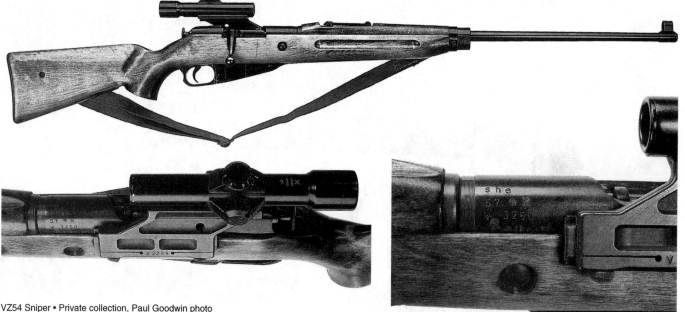

VZ54 Sniper • Private collection, Paul Goodwin photo

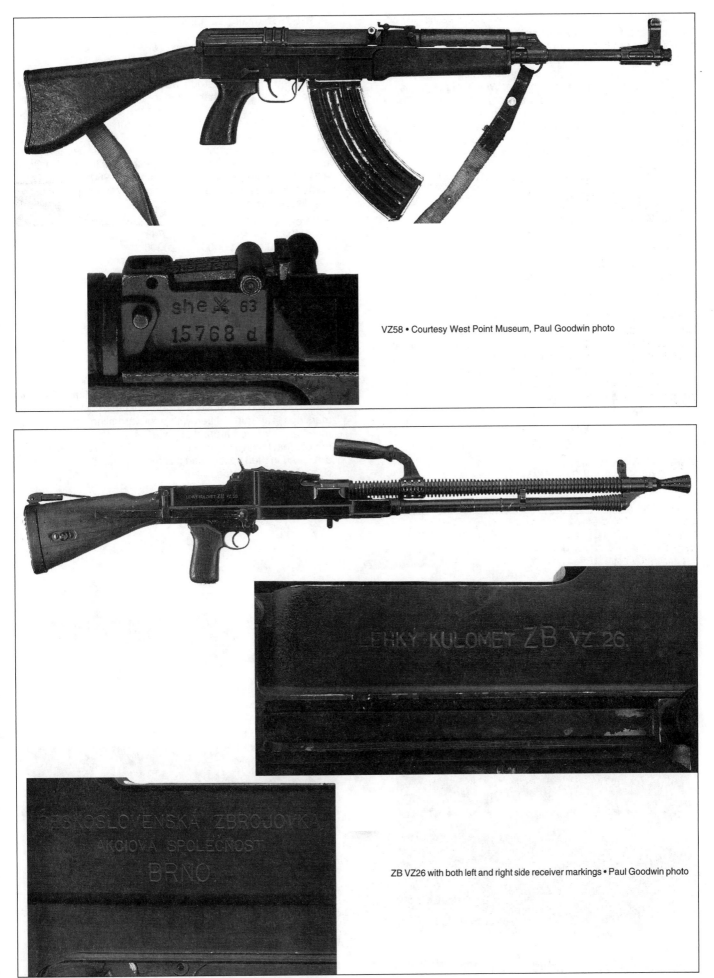

VZ58 • Courtesy West Point Museum, Paul Goodwin photo

ZB VZ26 with both left and right side receiver markings • Paul Goodwin photo

ZB VZ30

This weapon has an outward appearance almost identical to that of the VZ26 but with the exception of a new bolt movement design different from the VZ26. It has a 26.5" finned barrel and uses a 30-round top mounted straight box magazine. The rate of fire is about 600 rounds per minute. Weight of the gun is approximately 21 lbs. This model was adopted by China, Spain, and Iran. Between 1939 and 1945 it was also used by the German army. A variation of the ZB VZ30 is the ZB VZ30J (Yugoslavian or Venezuelan) similar to the VZ30 but with a heavy knurled portion of the barrel at the breech end.

Pre-1968

Exc.	V.G.	Fair
20000	18500	17000

Pre-1986 conversions

Exc.	V.G.	Fair
14000	13500	13000

Pre-1986 dealer samples

Exc.	V.G.	Fair
N/A	N/A	N/A

ZGB VZ30 (VZ32/33/34)

Same as the VZ30 but modified to fire the British .303 cartridge. Uses a curved 20-round magazine to accommodate the .303 cartridge. Improved versions of this gun are known as the VZ32, the VZ33, and the VZ34. These later versions use a 30-round magazine and a slightly shorter barrel. Reduced rate of fire to 500 rounds per minute.

Pre-1968

Exc.	V.G.	Fair
18500	17000	16000

Pre-1986 conversions

Exc.	V.G.	Fair
14000	13500	13000

Pre-1986 dealer samples

Exc.	V.G.	Fair
N/A	N/A	N/A

ZB VZ37 (Model 53 for export)

Introduced in 1937 this gun was designed as a medium air-cooled machine gun chambered for the 7.92x57mm cartridge. The finned barrel was 26.5" in length. Uses a 100- or 200-round metal belt. Grips mounted under the receiver with trigger. Rate of fire was either 500 or 700 rounds per minute. Weight is approximately 40 lbs. This gun is usually tripod mounted. A number of these guns were supplied to Viet Cong and North Vietnamese forces during the 1960s. Some 4,000 were sold to Israel in 1949. Many more were exported to the Middle East and Africa.

Pre-1968 (Very Rare)

Exc.	V.G.	Fair
30000	25000	20000

Pre-1986 conversions

Exc.	V.G.	Fair
N/A	N/A	N/A

Pre-1986 dealer samples

Exc.	V.G.	Fair
N/A	N/A	N/A

ZB 39

In 1939 the Czechs exported a small number (est. less than 100) of this gun to Bulgaria in 8x56R Austrian Mannlicher caliber. This gun is stamped with the Bulgarian crest and other markings. The gun is fitted with a forward sling swivel, a ring-mounted extension around the wrist of the stock, and a different compact sight mounting system is used. Some examples are found in .303 caliber and it is thought that these examples come from South Africa.

ZB53 (VZ37) with both left and right side receiver markings • Paul Goodwin photo

VZ39 Export Gun • Courtesy Robert E. Naess

Pre-1968
(Extremely Rare, only 1 transferable example known)

Exc.	V.G.	Fair
Too Rare To Price		

Pre-1986 conversions

Exc.	V.G.	Fair
N/A	N/A	N/A

Pre-1986 dealer samples

Exc.	V.G.	Fair
N/A	N/A	N/A

VZ52/57

This gun is based on the ZB VZ30. It is chambered for the 7.62x39 rimless cartridge (Warsaw Pact). The gun was originally chambered for the 7.62x45 rimless cartridge (VZ52). Barrel length is 27" and is quick change. It is fed by a 100-round belt or 25-round detachable box magazine. Rate of fire is 900 rounds per minute with box magazine and about 1,100 rounds per minute with belt. Weight is about 17.5 lbs. with bipod. This is a select fire weapon with the finger pressure on the trigger determining full auto or single-round fire. The gun was introduced in 1952. This gun is often seen in Central America.

VZ52/57 • Courtesy Blake Stevens, *The Bren Gun Saga*

Pre-1968 (Very Rare)

Exc.	V.G.	Fair
25000	22500	20000

Pre-1986 conversions

Exc.	V.G.	Fair
N/A	N/A	N/A

Pre-1986 dealer samples

Exc.	V.G.	Fair
N/A	N/A	N/A

Model 07/24 Schwarzlose

This is a Czech built Schwarzlose chambered for the 7.92 cartridge.

Pre-1968
(Extremely Rare, 1 transferable example known)

Exc.	V.G.	Fair
25000	—	—

Pre-1986 conversions

Exc.	V.G.	Fair
N/A	N/A	N/A

Pre-1986 dealer samples

Exc.	V.G.	Fair
N/A	N/A	N/A

DENMARK

Danish Military Conflicts, 1870–Present

After losing part of its territory to Prussia and Austria in 1862, Denmark concentrated its energies on improving its domestic, economic, and social conditions. Denmark maintained a peaceful coexistence with its European neighbors until it was occupied in 1940 by the German army. Following the end of the war, Denmark joined NATO in 1949, and in 1973 joined the European Union.

HANDGUNS

In addition to the handguns listed below, the Danes used the Browning Hi-Power 9mm pistol designated the Model 46. They also used the Swedish Model 40 Lahti, called the Model 40S by the Danes. In the late 1940s the Danes adopted the SIG 9mm Model 47/8 pistol (P-210-2).

Model 1871

This 6-shot revolver was built on a Lefaucheux-Francotte solid frame fixed cylinder with non-mechanical ejection. This is an 11mm pin-fire revolver. Octagon barrel length is 5". Weight is about 34 oz. Smooth wooden grips with lanyard loop. Built by the Belgian firm of Auguste Francotte. Issued to the Danish navy from 1871 to 1882.

Exc.	V.G.	Good	Fair	Poor
750	500	375	200	125

Model 1871/81

This model is a converted centerfire 11mm Model 1871. The conversion was done at the Danish navy yard in Copenhagen in 1881. All other specifications are the same as the Model 1871.

Exc.	V.G.	Good	Fair	Poor
600	375	200	125	75

Model 1865/97

This revolver is built on the Chamelot-Delvigne solid-frame, fixed-cylinder action with non-mechanical ejection. It was originally issued to the Danish navy in 1865 as an 11mm pinfire sidearm and was later converted in Kronberg to 11.45mm centerfire revolver. The revolver is fitted with a lever-type safety that blocks the hammer from the cylinder when engaged. Barrel length is 5". Checkered wood grips with lanyard loop located behind the hammer. Weight is about 30 oz. Issued to the Danish navy from 1897 to 1919.

Exc.	V.G.	Good	Fair	Poor
1750	1000	600	350	200

Model 1882

This revolver was built on the Lefaucheux-Francotte solid-frame fixed cylinder with non-mechanical ejection. Capacity was 6 rounds and the gun was chambered for the 9mm cartridge. The half-round half-octagon barrel was 5.5". This revolver was issued to Danish NCOs from 1888 to 1919.

Exc.	V.G.	Good	Fair	Poor
1200	650	400	200	125

Model 1886

This revolver was chambered for the 9.5mm cartridge and fitted with a 3" barrel. Built by Auguste Francotte in Liege, Belgium, and issued to military police units in the Danish army beginning in 1886.

Exc.	V.G.	Good	Fair	Poor
500	350	200	125	75

Model 1891

This revolver employed top-break, hinged frame with latch. This model was chambered for the 9mm cartridge and fitted with a 6.3" half-round half-octagon barrel. Checkered wooden grips with lanyard loop. Built by J.B. Ronge in Liege, Belgium. Weight is about 33 oz. Issued to Danish navy units from 1891 to 1941.

NOTE: A training version of this revolver was also used by the Danish navy and was chambered for the 5.1mm cartridge. All other specifications are the same.

Standard Model

Exc.	V.G.	Good	Fair	Poor
1000	500	350	250	150

Model 1891/96 Training Version

Exc.	V.G.	Good	Fair	Poor
3500	1750	800	500	300

Bergmann-Bayard Model 1908

Built by the Belgium firm of Pieper SA from 1908 to about 1914. Caliber is 9x23mm Bergman-Bayard with 4" barrel. Many foreign contracts were built in this model.

Courtesy Rock Island Auction Company

Exc.	V.G.	Good	Fair	Poor
1250	950	700	400	200

Bergmann-Bayard Model 1910-21

After WWI Pieper could no longer supply Bergmann-Bayard pistols to the Danish army, so Denmark made their own at their two national arsenals, Haerens Rustkammer and Haerens Tojus as the Model 1910-21. Most pre-war Pieper-made pistols were modified to 1910-21 configuration during the post-war years.

Courtesy Rock Island Auction Company

Exc.	V.G.	Good	Fair	Poor
1500	1100	850	700	300

Model 46

This is the Danish designation for the post-war Browning Hi-Power. Marked "M 1946 HV" on the left side of the frame. Fixed sights.

Courtesy Orvel Reichert

Exc.	V.G.	Good	Fair	Poor
1250	1100	950	650	400

P210 (Model 49)

See *Switzerland, Handguns, SIG*

SUBMACHINE GUNS

The Danish military has also used the Finnish Suomi MP41, the Swedish Model 37/39, and the HK MP5A2 and MP5A3 submachine guns.

Danish Hovea M49

Introduced in 1949 this submachine gun is chambered for the 9mm Parabellum cartridge and fitted with an 8.5" barrel. Folding metal butt. Magazine capacity is 35 rounds. Rate of fire is about 600 rounds per minute. Weight is approximately 7.5 lbs. This gun was originally developed by Husqvarna for the Swedish army. Denmark purchased the rights and built the gun for its own forces.

Courtesy private NFA collection

Pre-1968

Exc.	V.G.	Fair
9000	8000	7000

Pre-1986 conversions

Exc.	V.G.	Fair
N/A	N/A	N/A

Pre-1986 dealer samples

Exc.	V.G.	Fair
N/A	N/A	N/A

Madsen M50

This submachine gun was produced from 1945 to 1953 by the Danes. It is chambered for the 9mm cartridge and is fitted with a 7.8" barrel. Its rate of fire is about 500 rounds per minute. Marked "MADSEN" on the right side of receiver. Weight is approximately 7 lbs.

This gun has some unusual features, such as a flat receiver with barrel attached with locking nut that when unscrewed allows the left side of the receiver to fold back to expose the right side, which contains all the moving parts. Fitted with a quick change barrel. Very simple design allows for fast and economical construction.

Photo courtesy private NFA collection

Pre-1968

Exc.	V.G.	Fair
6000	5500	5000

Pre-1986 conversions

Exc.	V.G.	Fair
4000	3500	3000

Pre-1986 dealer samples

Exc.	V.G.	Fair
3000	2500	2000

RIFLES

More recently Danish military forces have used the U.S. M16A1 rifle, the HK G3, the M1 Garand converted to 7.62 NATO, and the Enfield Model 1917 rifle.

REMINGTON ROLLING BLOCK

Bibliographical Note: For detailed information, photos and technical data see *The Military Remington Rolling Block Rifle*, George Layman, 4th ed., 1999.

Model 1867 Rifle

This rifle was modified from rimfire to centerfire. Chambered for the 11.7x42R Danish/Remington cartridge. Fitted with a 35.7" barrel. Weight is approximately 9.25 lbs. Full stocked with exposed muzzle and bayonet bar with lug on right side. Three barrel bands. On the left side of the receiver is marked "M.1867" with the Danish Crown. The upper tang is marked with either "REMINGTON" or "KJOBENHAVN" with the year of manufacture.

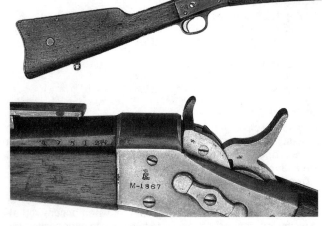

Model 1867 Rifle with loading indicator shown in close up • Private collection, Paul Goodwin photo

Exc.	V.G.	Good	Fair	Poor
—	600	450	300	125

Model 1867 Carbine

Similar to the rifle but with half length walnut stock with one barrel band and 21" barrel. Three variations were produced: Artillery, Engineer, and Cavalry. Weight is approximately 7 lbs.

Exc.	V.G.	Good	Fair	Poor
—	750	600	400	200

Model 1867/93 Marine Rifle

This rifle was built in Denmark at Kjobenhavn Arsenal. It was essentially a Model 1867 rifle re-built to fire the 8x58R Danish Krag cartridge. Barrel length is 21" and weight is about 7 lbs. Nose-cap has bayonet fittings.

Exc.	V.G.	Good	Fair	Poor
—	600	450	300	125

Model 1867/96 Cavalry Carbine

This model was also built in Denmark and was a Model 1867 carbine re-chambered for the 11.7x51R Danish cartridge.

Exc.	V.G.	Good	Fair	Poor
—	750	600	400	200

MAUSER

The rifles listed below represent war surplus captured from the Germans at the end of World War II. These rifles were converted by the Danes to military target rifles.

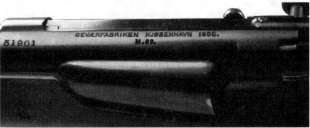

G98 Action Military Target Rifle (Model 52)

Exc.	V.G.	Good	Fair	Poor
400	250	200	150	100

G98 Action Military Target Rifle (Model 52)

Exc.	V.G.	Good	Fair	Poor
400	250	200	150	100

K98k Action Military Target Rifle (Model 58)

Exc.	V.G.	Good	Fair	Poor
400	250	200	150	100

KRAG JORGENSEN

The Krag rifle was developed in Norway and first adopted by Denmark for standard issue through World War II. For a list of U.S. models and prices see *United States, Rifles, Krag Jorgensen*. For those collectors who are interested in the Danish Krags, the only major difference, other than caliber, lies in the operation of the loading gate. Prices listed below are for unaltered Danish Krags. The forerunner of the U.S. Krags was the Model 1889 rifle.

NOTE: All Danish Krags are chambered for the 8x58Rmm cartridge.

Danish Model 1889

This rifle was developed by Ole Krag and Eric Jorgensen. It used a single forward bolt locking lug plus a bolt guide rib. Chambered for the 8x58Rmm cartridge, the rifle was fitted with a 33" barrel with full stock and no pistol grip. The barrel is fitted with a full-length metal handguard. A flush loose-loaded box magazine was used. The bolt handle was straight. There were a number of different carbine versions but all of these were full stocked and fitted with 23.5" barrel with bayonet lugs on all but one variation: the artillery carbine (see below). These guns are marked prior to 1910 "GEVAERFABRIKEN KJOBENHAVN" [date] over "M89" on the left side of the receiver. Approximately 140,000 of these rifles and carbines were manufactured prior to 1930. During the German occupation in WWII, the Germans reintroduced the rifle for its own use.

Exc.	V.G.	Good	Fair	Poor
450	350	250	150	100

Model 1889 Infantry Carbine

Introduced in 1924, this model is a converted Model 1889 rifle with metal barrel jacket and bayonet stud. Barrel length is 24". Tangent rear sight. Magazine capacity is 5 rounds. Weight is about 8.5 lbs. Marked "F" before the serial number.

Exc.	V.G.	Good	Fair	Poor
550	450	300	200	100

Model 1889 Artillery Carbine

Similar to the Infantry carbine and also introduced in 1924, this model features a turn down bolt handle, a triangle shaped upper sling swivel, and a hanger stud on the left side of the stock.

Exc.	V.G.	Good	Fair	Poor
550	450	300	200	100

Danish Model 1889 Rifle • Courtesy West Point Museum, Paul Goodwin photo

Model 1889 Engineer Carbine

This model was introduced in 1917. It is fitted with a wooden handguard and a slightly shorter barrel, about 1/2". Marked with "I" before the serial number.

Exc.	V.G.	Good	Fair	Poor
550	450	300	200	100

Model 1889 Cavalry Rifle

Introduced in 1914, this model is fitted for a bayonet. Straight bolt handle. Marked with "R" before the serial number.

Exc.	V.G.	Good	Fair	Poor
450	350	250	150	100

Model 1928 Sniper Rifle

This model is based on the Model 1889 with half stock but fitted with a 26" heavy barrel, micrometer rear sight, and hooded front sight. Wooden handguard. Turned down bolt. Similar in appearance to the U.S. 30 caliber-style "T" rifle. Weight is approximately 11.5 lbs.

Exc.	V.G.	Good	Fair	Poor
1250	950	700	500	200

MADSEN

Model 47

Sometimes referred to as the Madsen light military rifle, this post-WWII bolt-action rifle was sold to Colombia in limited quantities of 5,000 guns. Fitted with a rubber buttplate. Chambered in a number of calibers including the .30-06. Barrel length was 23" with a magazine capacity of 5 rounds. Weight was about 8 lbs.

Courtesy Richard M. Kumor Sr.

Exc.	V.G.	Good	Fair	Poor
600	500	350	—	—

NOTE: Add $75 for rifles with numbered matching bayonet.

MACHINE GUNS

After World War II Denmark used the British Bren gun chambered for the .303 caliber, the Swedish Model 37 6.5mm gun, the U.S. Model 1919A4 and A5 versions, and the .50 M2 Browning. More recently the Danes use the German MG 42/59.

Madsen

This was the first practical light machine gun. It was produced from 1897 to 1955. It is chambered for several calibers from 6mm to 8mm. It is fitted with a 22.7" barrel and a top feeding 25-, 30-, or 40-round magazine. Rate of fire is 450 rounds per minute. Its weight is approximately 20 lbs. Marked "MADSEN MODEL" on the right side of the receiver. Found all over the world during a fifty year period.

Pre-1968

Exc.	V.G.	Fair
10000	9000	8000

Pre-1986 conversions

Exc.	V.G.	Fair
N/A	N/A	N/A

Pre-1986 dealer samples

Exc.	V.G.	Fair
5000	4500	4000

Madsen-Satter

First produced in 1952, this belt-fed machine gun is chambered for the 7.62x51mm NATO cartridge. Designed to be used on a tripod for sustained fire, it had a rate of fire of 650 to 1000 rounds per minute (adjustable). Fitted with a 22" barrel. Weight is approximately 23.4 lbs. Marked "MADSEN-SETTER" on left front side of receiver. Many South American countries used this gun as do many other countries around the world. Production stopped on this gun in 1960 in Denmark but continued under license to Indonesia until the 1970s.

Photo courtesy private NFA collection

Pre-1968 (Very Rare)

Exc.	V.G.	Fair
25000	23000	22000

Pre-1986 conversions

Exc.	V.G.	Fair
N/A	N/A	N/A

Pre-1986 dealer samples (Rare)

Exc.	V.G.	Fair
20000	18000	17000

Chilean Madsen Model 1950 with receiver markings and crest • Paul Goodwin photo

The excellent Danish Madsen machine rifle was adopted by several European armies prior to WWI and continued in active service well into the 1950s. This is the Model 1950 on an ingenious light tripod • U.S. Army Ordnance Corps National Archives, Robert Bruce Military Photo Features

FINLAND

Finnish Military Conflicts, 1870-Present

Finland was annexed by Russia in 1809 but was allowed considerable independence throughout the 19th century. Finnish nationalism began to grow during the latter part of the 19th century, and, by the early 20th century, Finland established its own parliament in 1906. Finnish independence was declared in 1917. Beginning in 1918, a civil war erupted in which the White Guard aided by German troops defeated the leftist Red Guard supported by the Soviet Union. As a result of this conflict a republic was established in 1919. In 1939 Soviet troops invaded Finland, and by 1940 Finnish forces were defeated, despite a heavy cost to the Soviet troops. Finland joined the German attack on the Soviet Union in 1941. Finland was again defeated by Soviet forces by 1944. Finland was then forced to expel the Germans which resulted in a massive loss of life and property to the Finnish people. A 1947 treaty between Finland and the Soviet Union ceded some Finnish territory to the Soviets, and in 1948 the Finns signed a mutual defense pact with the Soviets. During the post-war period, Finland attempted to stay neutral and preserve its independence. By 1990, with the collapse of the Soviet Union, the 1948 treaty was moot and in 1995 the Finns joined the European Union.

NOTE: The Finns established their own arms factory soon after independence. It was called *Souojeluskuntain Ase-ja Konepaja Oy* (SAKO). In 1926 the Finns constructed a state rifle factory called the *Valtion Kivaaritehdas* (VKT, later Valmet). Also in the 1920s another state arms plant was built called *Tikkakoski* (TIKKA).

HANDGUNS

NOTE: During the 1920s and 1930s the Finnish army relied primarily on the Model 1895 Russian Nagant revolver and the Spanish 7.65mm self-loading pistols, the Ruby (Model 19). During World War I the Finns were supplied with the Mauser M1896 Broomhandle in a late wartime commercial configuration. In the early 1920s the Finns adopted a commercial model of the DWM Luger, called by the Finns the Model 23. By the late 1920s the Finnish military decided to adopt and domesticly produce a 9mm self-loading pistol of their own. It was called the Lahti.

The Finns, more recently, have used the FN M1935 in 9mm and the French MAB PA-15 pistol in 9mm.

M35 Lahti

This 9x19mm semiautomatic pistol was adopted in 1935 and built at VKT. This pistol is a locked-breech semiautomatic that features a bolt accelerator that does much to make this a reliable firearm. This pistol is the same as the Swedish Model 40 Lahti, 4.7" barrel and 8-round magazine, except that it has a loaded chamber indicator on top of the pistol, a different assembled recoil spring, and the Finnish pistol's grips are marked "VKT." Finnish army markings on top of slide. This pistol was designed to function in extreme cold and has a reputation for reliability. About 5,700 wartime Lahti pistols were produced.

Finnish M35 Lahti • Courtesy J.B. Wood

Exc.	V.G.	Good	Fair	Poor
1250	1000	800	550	300

Model 1931 • Paul Goodwin photo

SUBMACHINE GUNS

The first Finnish submachine gun was developed by Aimo Lahti in 1922. This gun later became the Model 1926 with only about 200 built in 7.65mm caliber. A perfected design was later built called the Model 1931 Suomi. Since the end of World War II the Finns have used the Sten Mark II and Mark III guns.

Suomi Model 1931

First produced in Finland in 1931, this submachine gun is chambered for the 9mm cartridge. It was widely used by Scandinavian armies as well as several countries in South America. It features a 12.25" barrel with wooden stock and 71-round drum magazine. Box magazine capacity is 20 or 50 rounds. Rate of fire is 900 rounds per minute. Weight is about 10 lbs. Marked on the end cap and left side of the receiver. Production stopped in 1944. A total of about 80,000 were produced by TIKKA.

This gun was also made in Sweden where it was designated the Model 37-39. In Switzerland it was called the Model 43/44. In Denmark it was made by Madsen.

Pre-1968

Exc.	V.G.	Fair
7500	6500	6000

THE SUOMI M31

This Finnish submachine gun is often overlooked whenever one lists some of history's best submachine guns, but it is one that should be included. Designed and built long before World War II it was definitely a First Generation Subgun as it was constructed of heavy, precisely machined steel. Naturally, the precise machining required for this gun made it both expensive in terms of machine time and heavy. Unloaded it weighed 10.34 pounds which is close to the weight of the Thompson Model 1928, but the difference here is this was a 9mm Parabellum weapon. The really unique aspect to the design of the Suomi Model 31 was the magazine. It was a box type design holding a total of 50 rounds. It consisted of two compartments with a follower and spring for each compartment, both of which fed to a single position. The Suomi M31 was capable of select-fire and featured a safety/selector lever on the front of the triggerguard. When this lever was pushed completely to the rear the gun was placed on SAFE and the bolt was locked against movement. The cocking handle for the bolt was a little unusual at the time because it was found at the rear of the receiver and required a full pull to the rear to cock the open-bolt action. The Suomi M31 was without question the most accurate open-bolt operating submachine gun ever produced anywhere, but then its size and weight more closely resembled a conventional rifle than it did a traditional submachine gun. Used by a number of countries the Suomi saw action in the Spanish Civil War and, of course, the Finnish Winter War of 1939 against Russia. By the time World War II broke out, the design was outdated simply because it required so much to manufacture, but it has remained one of the most accurate 9mm Parabellum submachine guns ever produced, open-bolt or otherwise.

Frank James

Pre-1986 conversions

Exc.	V.G.	Fair
N/A	N/A	N/A

Pre-1986 dealer samples

Exc.	V.G.	Fair
4500	4000	3500

Suomi Model 1944

This Finnish gun is based on the Russian Model PPS-43, but the Model 1944 fires the 9mm cartridge. It is fitted with a 9.66" barrel and accepts a 36-round box magazine or 71-round drum magazine. Rate of fire is 650 rounds per minute. Weight is about 6.35 lbs. Production stopped in 1945. Marked on left side of receiver. TIKKA built about 10,000 of these guns.

Pre-1968

Exc.	V.G.	Fair
7500	6500	6000

Pre-1986 conversions

Exc.	V.G.	Fair
N/A	N/A	N/A

Pre-1986 dealer samples

Exc.	V.G.	Fair
4500	4000	3500

RIFLES

NOTE: Prior to 1917 Finland was part of Russia. All Finnish military rifles are built on Russian Model 1891 Mosin Nagant actions.

For technical data and photos, see Terence Lapin's, *The Mosin-Nagant Rifle,* and Doug Bowser's *Rifles of the White Death.*

Model 1891 (Finnish Army Variation)

Basically a Russian Model 1891 but with a Finnish two-piece stock, sights calibrated to meters, trigger modified to two stage pull, and frequently with the addition of sling swivels. Large numbers of captured Russian Model 1891s were reconfigured this way as late as 1944. Many, but not all, have Finnish-made barrels with a length of 31.6".

Exc.	V.G.	Good	Fair	Poor
175	125	100	75	60

NOTE: There are a number of subvariations of this rifle that are beyond the scope of this book and may be of interest to the collector. It is suggested that the Lapin and Bowser books be consulted.

Model 1891 Dragoon (Finnish Army Variation)

Basically a Russian Model 1891 Dragoon rifle modified as above with a side mounted Mauser Kar 98 type sling. Barrel length is 28.8". About 19,000 of these rifles were produced. Rare.

Exc.	V.G.	Good	Fair	Poor
350	200	150	100	75

Close up of rear sight of Model 91 Dragoon • Private collection, Paul Goodwin photo

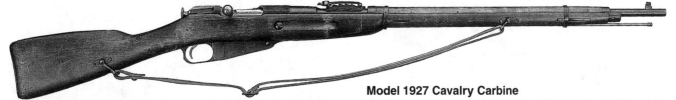

Model 91 Dragoon • Private collection, Paul Goodwin photo

Model 1924 Civil Guard Infantry Rifle

This model built by SAKO and consisted of new heavy Swiss or German barrels fitted to reworked Model 1891 Russian actions. Due to the larger diameter barrel, some barrels were turned down at the muzzle end so it would be the same diameter as the Russian barrel and accept the Russian bayonet. In other cases the larger barrel diameter was left and the bayonets modified instead. Chambered for 7.62x54R cartridge and fitted with 32" barrel. Box magazine capacity was 5 rounds. Weight is about 9.4 lbs.

Exc.	V.G.	Good	Fair	Poor
250	200	125	75	50

Model 1924 Civil Guard Carbine

As above but with 24" barrel. It is estimated that 650 of these carbines were produced. Very Rare.

Exc.	V.G.	Good	Fair	Poor
650	500	400	300	150

Model 1927 Army Short Rifle

This rifle was made by Valmet, is a shorter version of the Model 1924, and fitted with a 27" barrel instead of 31". It has a full stock with bayonet lug with a ramp and leaf rear sight, graduated to 800 meters, and front sight guards for the blade front sight. Early stocks were modified from the Model 1891 stocks, and this made for a very weak forend, which was prone to breakage with the bayonet installed. The fore cap was a hinged, two-piece affair. Weight is about 9 lbs.

Exc.	V.G.	Good	Fair	Poor
275	225	150	75	50

Model 1927 Rifle with modified front barrel band

The front band on these rifles was reinforced with two extensions along the forend to help with the split stock problem on the first type Model 1927 rifles. Many were also fitted with new stocks that were larger in diameter at the front of the fore stock to add strength as well. These rifles have a higher survival rate because many early rifles were modified with this type of front barrel band.

Exc.	V.G.	Good	Fair	Poor
250	200	125	75	50

Model 1927/91-30 Modified Rifle

During the Winter War with Russia, any rifle that could shoot was needed by the Finnish army. Many Model 1927 rifles were restocked with Model 91-30 stocks to make them useable.

Exc.	V.G.	Good	Fair	Poor
275	225	150	75	50

Model 1927 Cavalry Carbine

Similar to the Model 1927 rifle but fitted with a 24" barrel and turned down bolt. Side mounted sling. Weight is approximately 8.75 lbs. About 2,500 were produced with serial numbers between 72,800 and 74,900. Very rare as most were converted to rifles. Some of these were imported into the U.S. in the 1960s and modified into inexpensive hunting rifles.

M27 Rifle on top and M27 Carbine at bottom • Courtesy Chuck Karwan

M27 Carbine action at bottom • Courtesy Chuck Karwan

Exc.	V.G.	Good	Fair	Poor
750	500	350	225	150

Model 1928 Civil Guard Short Rifle

Similar to the Model 1927 except with minor differences such as a non-hinged front barrel band that was stonger and a fore stock enlarged in diameter to help prevent splitting. It weighs about 9.2 lbs. The letters "SY" are stamped on the receiver ring. Built by SAKO.

Exc.	V.G.	Good	Fair	Poor
275	225	175	75	50

Model 1928/30 Civil Guard Short Rifle

This is the same as the Model 1928 Short Rifle but with an improved magazine and different rear sight graduated to 2,000 meters. It weighs about 9.6 lbs. On the receiver is stamped

Model 1927 Short rifle with close up of receiver, notice reinforcing in forearm near muzzle • Private collection, Paul Goodwin photo

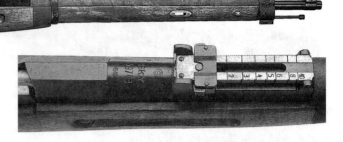

Model 28/30 showing rear sight and receiver markings • Private collection, Paul Goodwin photo

with an "S" topped with three fir sprigs in a gear wheel. Built by SAKO.

Exc.	V.G.	Good	Fair	Poor
250	200	150	75	50

Finnish Model 91-30
Many Russian Model 91-30s were captured during the war. All were marked with the Finnish army property mark "SA", and many restocked with heavier Finnish produced stocks.

Exc.	V.G.	Good	Fair	Poor
135	100	70	40	25

Model 1939 Short Rifle (Army and Civil Guard)
Similar to the Model 1928/30 but with larger diameter bore to accommodate a heavier bullet (201 grains). One piece stock with pistol grip and new rear sight fitted to this model. Barrel length is 27" but lighter in weight than the Model 28/30. Weight is about 10 lbs. Produced by SAKO, TIKKA, and VKT. The rifle was produced until 1944 but a few examples were produced in 1945. Approximately 5,000 to 6,000 of these rifles had barrels made in Belgium. These are marked with a "B" on the barrel.

Exc.	V.G.	Good	Fair	Poor
200	175	125	75	50

NOTE: Add a 25% premium for SAKO-built rifles. Rifles marked "Sk.Y" (Civil Guard) will command a 100% premium.

Swedish Model 1896 Rifle
Used by the Finns without modifications, these rifles have "SA" Finnish army property markings on the receiver. Some of these rifles were lent to the Finnish government, some were sold to them.

Exc.	V.G.	Good	Fair	Poor
175	140	100	75	50

Italian Carcanco
Marked with the "SA" property marking on the rear left side of the barrel.

Exc.	V.G.	Good	Fair	Poor
100	75	40	30	15

FINNISH SNIPER RIFLES
Beginning in 1937 the Finns began to develop a sniper rifle built around the Mosin-Nagant rifle. Approximately 400 M37 sniper rifles were built with a 3X Physica telescope. These scopes were a prismatic box design for use, not only on rifles, but on machine guns and mortars as well. During World War II the Finns used the Model 39 rifle with German Ajacks scope.

About 500 of these rifles were built, and were known as the Model 39/43. Finland also used Soviet scopes on its rifles with Ajacks mounts. These Soviet scopes were designated the PE and PEM. The only difference was that the PEM scope has no focusing ring on the eyepiece.

NOTE: There are no known examples of Finnish sniper rifles in the U.S.

TRG-21
The receiver is similar to the TRG-S, but the polyurethane stock features a unique design. The trigger is adjustable for length and two-stage pull and also for horizontal or vertical pitch. This model also has several options that would affect the price: muzzle brake, one-piece scope mount, bipod, quick detachable sling swivels, and military nylon sling. The rifle is offered in .308 Win. only. It is fitted with a 25.75" barrel and weighs 10.5 lbs.

NIB	Exc.	V.G.	Good	Fair	Poor
3500	2750	1850	—	—	—

TRG-22
This model is similar to the TRG-21 but meets the exact specifications to comply with the Finnish military requirements. Introduced in 2000.

NIB	Exc.	V.G.	Good	Fair	Poor
2700	2000	—	—	—	—

TRG-41
Exactly the same as the TRG-21 except chambered for the .338 Lapua Magnum cartridge.

NIB	Exc.	V.G.	Good	Fair	Poor
4350	3500	2500	1500	—	—

Model 1939 with close up of rear sight • Private collection, Paul Goodwin photo

TRG-42

This model is similar to the TRG-41 but meets the exact specifications to comply with the Finnish military requirements. Introduced in 2000.

NIB	Exc.	V.G.	Good	Fair	Poor
3100	2300	—	—	—	—

Valmet M62

Based on the third model AK-47 but with internal differences built by Valmet. SAKO also built many of these rifles. Machined receiver. Perforated plastic forend and handguard. Tube butt. Barrel length is 16.5". Magazine is 30 rounds. Rate of fire is about 650 rounds per minute. Weight is about 9 lbs. Production in Finland began in 1965. Rifles produced from 1965 to 1969 were designated "M 62 PT." PT stands for day sight. In 1969 Model 62s were produced with folding night sights. Beginning in 1972 these night sights were fitted with tritium inserts.

NOTE: There are a number of different versions of this rifle: the M62-76-a Finnish AKM; the M62-76M plastic stock; M62-76P wood stock; M62-76T tubular steel folding stock.

Pre-1968

Exc.	V.G.	Fair
N/A	N/A	N/A

> ## FINNISH SAKO TRG-22
>
> The current trend in European bolt action sniper rifles is to develop them from successful competition rifles. Sometimes this works, sometimes it doesn't. In the case of the SAKO TRG-21 this formula proved highly successful and led to the development of an outstanding sniper rifle. As good as the TRG-21 was though, there was room for improvement and this has led to the new TRG-22. A thoroughly modern sniper rifle chambered in .308 Winchester, the TRG-22 features an enclosed receiver mated to a 26" hammer-forged Match barrel. The bolt features three locking lugs and a short 60 degree lift. The rifle's synthetic stock is fully adjustable and extremely comfortable. In my opinion the SAKO is not simply a rifle but an accuracy machine. You learn this the first time you flop with it. Sitting on its low-slung wide-footed bipod it's very stable. With the stock properly adjusted it's a very comfortable rifle to lay behind, even for hours at a time. Lock a 10-round magazine into place and work the bolt, which feels like it rides on greased ball bearings. When it's time to make your shot, simply push the Garand-style safety forward and touch the trigger. A .30 caliber hole will appear wherever you placed the crosshairs. The rifle's muzzle brake almost eliminates muzzle jump allowing an operator to spot his shots. With a flick of the wrist an empty is sent spinning and another round loaded into the chamber. Fast multiple shots are easy with the TRG-22. Accuracy? Putting 5 rounds into an inch or less at 300 yards, under field conditions, is no big deal for this rifle. Offhand, sitting, kneeling, or prone the rifle is equally comfortable. While many rifles can be made to shoot, the TRG-22 is more than this. It's a well thought out sniper system that's not only extremely accurate but robust and user friendly as well.
>
> **David Fortier**

Pre-1986 conversions

Exc.	V.G.	Fair
5000	4750	4500

Pre-1986 dealer samples

Exc.	V.G.	Fair
4000	4000	3850

Valmet M62S

A semiautomatic version of the M62 imported for sale in the U.S. by Interarms. Offered in both 7.62x39mm and 5.56x45mm calibers.

NIB	Exc.	V.G.	Good	Fair	Poor
3000	2800	2300	900	750	300

Valmet M71

A different version of the M62 with solid plastic butt and rear sight in front of chamber. Sheet metal receiver. Chambered for the 7.62x39mm and the 5.56x45mm cartridges. Weight reduced to 8 lbs.

Pre-1968

Exc.	V.G.	Fair
N/A	N/A	N/A

Pre-1986 conversions

Exc.	V.G.	Fair
5000	4750	4500

Pre-1986 dealer samples

Exc.	V.G.	Fair
4000	4000	3850

Valmet M71S

A semiautomatic version of the M71 imported for sale in the U.S. by Interarms.

Model 71S • Courtesy Blake Stevens, *Kalashnikov: Arms and the Man*, Ezell

NIB	Exc.	V.G.	Good	Fair	Poor
1350	1000	850	650	450	300

Valmet M76

This model has a number of fixed or folding stock options. It is fitted with a 16.3" barrel and has a magazine capacity of 15, 20, or 30 rounds. Its rate of fire is 700 rounds per minute. It is chambered for the 7.62x39mm Soviet cartridge or the 5.56x45mm cartridge. Weight is approximately 8 lbs. Marked "VALMET JYVAKYLA m78" on the right side of the receiver. Produced from 1978 to 1986.

There are a total of 10 variants of this model.

Model 76 (stamped receiver) • Courtesy Blake Stevens, *Kalashnikov: Arms and the Man*, Ezell

Pre-1968

Exc.	V.G.	Fair
N/A	N/A	N/A

Pre-1986 conversions

Exc.	V.G.	Fair
8000	7000	6500

Pre-1986 dealer samples

Exc.	V.G.	Fair
4000	4000	3850

NOTE: For rifles in 7.62x39mm caliber add a 20% premium. For rifles chambered for .308 caliber deduct $2,500.

Model 78 (Semiautomatic)

As above, in 7.62x51mm, 7.62x39mm, or .223 with a 24.5" heavy barrel, wood stock, and integral bipod. Semiautomatic-only version.

NIB	Exc.	V.G.	Good	Fair	Poor
1750	1350	1000	850	600	300

MACHINE GUNS

During the early years the Finns used the Maxim Model 09, Maxim Model 21, and the Maxim Model 09-32, all chambered for the 7.62mm cartridge.

Lahti Saloranta Model 26

Designed and built as a light machine gun this model was chambered for the 7.62mm rimmed cartridge. Fitted with a 20-round box magazine or a 75-round drum magazine. The rate of fire was about 500 rounds per minute. Weight is approximately 23 lbs. This gun was also chambered for the 7.92mm cartridge for sale to the Chinese prior to World War II.

Pre-1968

Exc.	V.G.	Fair
10000	9000	8500

Pre-1986 conversions

Exc.	V.G.	Fair
N/A	N/A	N/A

Pre-1986 dealer samples

Exc.	V.G.	Fair
N/A	N/A	N/A

Valmet M62

First introduced in 1966, this machine gun is chambered for the 7.62x39mm cartridge. Designed as a light air-cooled machine gun it is based on the Czech ZB26. Fitted with a wood butt with pistol grip and 18.5" heavy barrel with bipod. Fed by a 100-round metal link belt with a rate of fire of about 1000 rounds per minute. Gun weighs approximately 18 lbs. Produced between 1966 and 1976.

Model 62 • Courtesy Blake Stevens, *Kalashnikov: Arms and the Man*, Ezell

Pre-1968

Exc.	V.G.	Fair
N/A	N/A	N/A

Pre-1986 conversions

Exc.	V.G.	Fair
6500	6000	5500

Pre-1986 dealer samples

Exc.	V.G.	Fair
4500	4000	3500

Valmet M78

This model is a heavy-barrel version of the Valmet M76. Barrel length is 18.75". It is offered in 7.62x39mm and 5.56x45mm calibers. Marked "VALMET Jyvaskyla M78" on the right side of the receiver. Rate of fire is about 650 rounds per minute and magazine capacity is 15 or 30 rounds. Weight is about 10.3 lbs. Produced from 1978 to 1986.

Photo courtesy private NFA collection

Pre-1968

Exc.	V.G.	Fair
N/A	N/A	N/A

Pre-1986 conversions

Exc.	V.G.	Fair
7500	7000	6000

Pre-1986 dealer samples

Exc.	V.G.	Fair
5000	4500	4000

NOTE: For guns chambered for 7.62x39 add 20%.

Valmet Model 78 • Courtesy Chuck Karwan

FRANCE

French Military Conflicts, 1870–Present

With the French defeat in the Franco-Prussian War, 1870-1871, Napoleon III was ousted and the Third Republic established. France was involved in overseas colonial expansion in North Africa and Indochina. The French army bore the brunt of heavy fighting during World War I. During the war, France had 8,600,000 men under arms, of which 5,714,000 were killed or wounded, a casualty rate of 66%. France surrendered to Germany in 1940 and was occupied by German troops. In unoccupied France the Vichy government was headed by Marshall Petain. General Charles de Gaulle led the Free French government in exile. In the summer of 1944 the allied armies drove the German troops out of France, and when the end of the war came in 1945 a Fourth Republic was formed in 1946. The French army received a stunning defeat in Indochina at Dien Bien Phu (1954) and other elements of the French military were busy in Algeria in that country's war for independence against France. In 1958 Charles de Gaulle returned to power to lead the Fifth Republic and attempted to restore French world prestige. France was involved with the U.S. in Desert Storm in Kuwait as well as a NATO member in various "peacekeeping" ventures.

HANDGUNS

NOTE: At the outbreak of the Franco-Prussian War the French military purchased a large number of revolvers from Colt, Remington, and Starr. These revolvers were percussion arms.

Bibliographical Note: For additional historical information, technical data, and photos, see Eugene Medlin and Jean Huon, *Military Handguns of France, 1858-1958*, Excalibur Publications, 1993.

Model 1870 Navy (Navy Contract)

This 6-shot solid-frame fixed-cylinder revolver uses a mechanical ejection system. Chambered for the 11mm cartridge and fitted with a 4.7" round barrel. Smooth wooden grips with lanyard loop. Adopted by the French navy in 1870 and remained in service until 1900. Built by the French firm "LEFAUCHEUX" in Paris. Marked "E LEFAUCHEUX" on the top of the frame, and on the right side "BVT. S.G.D.G. PARIS" with a naval anchor on the butt cap of the grip. This revolver was the first centerfire handgun to be adopted by any nation's military. About 6,000 revolvers were built under contract.

A modified version of this pistol was built by the French arsenal at St. Etienne (MAS) designated the Model 1870N. About 4,000 of these revolvers were produced and are marked, "MODEL 1870" on the top strap and "MODIFIE N" on the right side of the sighting groove. The military arsenal proof of MAS is on the cylinder and the underside of the barrel.

Revolvers fitted with military extractors have the extractor located along the barrel while civilian revolvers have the extractor located offset from the barrel.

Military Extractor

Exc.	V.G.	Good	Fair	Poor
5000	3500	2000	1000	500

Civilian Extractor

Exc.	V.G.	Good	Fair	Poor
3000	2000	1500	600	300

Model 1873 Navy

Built on a Chamelot-Delvigne type locking system with a solid frame, fixed cylinder, and mechanical rod ejection. Chambered for the 11mm cartridge and fitted with a 4.7" half-round half-octagon barrel. Non-fluted cylinder. It is both a single- and double-action revolver. Finish was left in the white. Marked "MRE D'ARMES ST. ETIENNE" on the right side of the frame. On top of the barrel marked "MLE 1873 M" or "NAVY." There are many other small markings on the revolver as well. Weight is approximately 36 oz. Used by the French navy for its NCOs from 1874 to 1945. Built by French military armory at St. Etienne. Between 1873 and 1886 approximately 350,000 of these revolvers were produced.

NAVY

Exc.	V.G.	Good	Fair	Poor
950	600	500	300	175

"MLE 1873"

Exc.	V.G.	Good	Fair	Poor
400	300	200	100	75

ARMY

Exc.	V.G.	Good	Fair	Poor
400	350	200	150	100

Model 1873 with barrel and frame markings • Paul Goodwin photo

Model 1874

The Model 1874 was essentially the same as the Model 1873 but with a fluted cylinder. Used by French naval officers from 1878 to 1945. Between 1874 and 1886 approximately 36,000 of these revolvers were produced.

ARMY

Exc.	V.G.	Good	Fair	Poor
750	550	400	300	175

NAVY

Exc.	V.G.	Good	Fair	Poor
2500	1500	750	350	200

Model 1892

Model 1892 with frame markings • Paul Goodwin photo

Chambered for an 8mm centerfire cartridge and has a 4.6" barrel with a 6-shot cylinder. Weight is about 30 oz. It is erroneously referred to as a "Lebel," but there is no certainty that Nicolas Lebel had anything to do with its design or production, but was the chairman of the selection board that chose the design. This revolver is a simple double action, with a swing-out cylinder that swings to the right side for loading. The design of this weapon is similar to the Italian Model 1889. There is one redeeming feature on this revolver, and that is a hinged side plate on the left side of the frame that could be swung away after unlocking so that repairs or cleaning of the lockwork could be performed with relative simplicity. The cartridge for which this weapon was chambered was woefully inadequate. This revolver remained in use from its introduction in 1893 until the end of WWII in 1945, mainly because the French never got around to designing a replacement.

NOTE: There are a number of commercial variations of this revolver, some of which are Spanish-made copies and others are St. Etienne commercial examples.

NAVY (anchor on butt)

Exc.	V.G.	Good	Fair	Poor
600	400	200	150	100

ARMY

Exc.	V.G.	Good	Fair	Poor
400	250	175	125	75

Model 1892 "A Pompe"

As above, except that the cylinder latch is a sleeve around the ejector rod that can be moved forward to release the cylinder.

Exc.	V.G.	Good	Fair	Poor
750	500	250	125	75

FRENCH MODEL 1892 REVOLVER

While the French are often mocked for poor weapons design, they did produce several very serviceable pieces. One notable example is the Model 1892 service revolver in 8x27R. Designed during the Golden Age of firearms, the Model 1892 was easily one of the better European military revolvers of its day. Its only drawback being the ballistically unimpressive 8x27R cartridge. The Model 1892 itself is a simple double-action design with a swing out cylinder. However, of interest is the fact that the cylinder swings out to the right instead of the left. This was done to allow an officer to wield a saber in his right hand and use his revolver with his left. The design features a rebounding hammer with a swiveling striker nose to prevent pierced primers and broken firing pin tips. In addition, a movable but captive side plate allowed easy access to the lock mechanism. However, one of the virtues of this revolver is how reliable it is. Examining it, one notes that it is a very well made piece. To load, simply pull back on the loading gate and swing the cylinder out to the right. Six rounds can then be easily dropped in two at a time. Swing the cylinder back and snap the gate shut. Bringing the revolver up one notes the excellent sights which are fast to index on man size targets. The hammer is easily thumb cocked for single-action fire and the trigger pull in this mode is light. The revolver barks but felt recoil is fairly mild. Accuracy is excellent. Switching to double action the trigger pull is still quite good allowing one to place their shots with speed. Empties eject smoothly. While the cartridge it fires is under powered, the Model 1892's ruggedness, reliability, accuracy, and fine handling characteristics made it highly popular among French troops in the trenches. Today it is an interesting collector's piece and a fun shooter.

David Fortier

Le Francais Model 28 Type Armee

A unique pistol chambered for the 9mm Browning cartridge. It is a large pistol with a 5" barrel that was hinged with a tip-up breech. This is a blowback-operated semiautomatic pistol that has no extractor. The empty cases are blown out of the breech by gas pressure. The one feature about this pistol that is desirable is that it is possible to tip the barrel breech forward like a shotgun and load cartridges singly, while holding the contents of the magazine in reserve. This weapon has fixed sights and a blued finish, with checkered walnut grips. It was manufactured in 1928 and built by Manufrance.

Courtesy James Rankin

Exc.	V.G.	Good	Fair	Poor
1250	950	750	500	200

Le Francais Police Model (Type Policeman)

A blowback-operated, double action semiautomatic that is chambered for the .25 ACP cartridge. It has a 3.5" barrel and a 7-round magazine. It has the same hinged-barrel feature of the Model 28 and is blued, with fixed sights and Ebonite grips. This model was manufactured 1913 to the 1920s.

Courtesy James Rankin

Exc.	V.G.	Good	Fair	Poor
700	600	400	300	150

Le Francais Officer's Model (Pocket Model)

May also be referred to as a "Staff Model." Also a blowback-operated semiautomatic chambered for the .25 ACP cartridge. It has a 2.5" barrel and a concealed hammer. It has fixed sights and the finish is blued. The grips are Ebonite. This model was manufactured between 1914 and 1958 in two variations: early and second type.

Early Variation Pocket • Courtesy James Rankin

Second Variation Pocket • Courtesy James Rankin

Exc.	V.G.	Good	Fair	Poor
350	250	200	150	100

Model 1935A

A 7.65mm French Long caliber semiautomatic pistol with a 4.3" barrel. Magazine capacity is 8 rounds. Fixed sights. Weight is about 26 oz. Eventually became known as the Model 1935A. This pistol was designed and built for the French military and about 10,000 were produced up to June 20, 1940, when the factory, SACM (Societe Alsacienne des Constructions Mecaniques, Cholet, France), was occupied by German troops. About 24,000 were built and used by the German army during World War II.

Model 1935A • Courtesy private collection

Model 1935A • Courtesy private collection

German Waffenamt Model (7.65mm Pistole 625f)

Exc.	V.G.	Good	Fair	Poor
500	425	250	125	100

Standard Model

Exc.	V.G.	Good	Fair	Poor
375	250	125	100	75

Model 1935S

As above, with an enlarged chamber area that locked into the ejection port and a 4.3" barrel. Built by MAC Chatellerault, MAS, SAGEM, and MF (Manufrance). About 85,000 pistols were produced between 1939 and 1953.

Model 1935S • Courtesy Richard M. Kumor Sr.

Exc.	V.G.	Good	Fair	Poor
250	150	125	100	75

MAB Model D

This semiautomatic pistol is built along the lines of the FN Model 1910. Built in Bayonne, France (MAB). Chambered for the 7.65mm cartridge. Early examples had a steel frame and later ones had an alloy frame. German army test and acceptance marks stamped on pistol. About 50,000 were produced during World War II.

Exc.	V.G.	Good	Fair	Poor
500	400	300	350	150

MAC/MAS Model 1950

A 9mm Parabellum caliber semiautomatic pistol with a 9-shot magazine. Barrel length is 4.4". Weight is about 34 oz. Blued, with ribbed plastic grips. The pistol's design was strongly influenced by the Model 1935S. The Model 1950 was used by all of the French military forces as the standard issue sidearm, including nations that were former French colonies. Approximately less than 350,000 Model 1950s were produced.

MAS Model 1950 • Private collection, Paul Goodwin photo

Exc.	V.G.	Good	Fair	Poor
525	425	350	275	200

MAS G1

This is a Beretta 92G, which is a double action 9mm pistol with decocking lever. Barrel length is 4.9". Magazine capacity is 15 rounds. Weight is about 34 oz. Military marked.

Exc.	V.G.	Good	Fair	Poor
N/A	—	—	—	—

MAB PA-15

This pistol is a French military version of the commercial Unique Model R Para. Chambered for the 9mm Parabellum cartridge and fitted with a 4.5" barrel. Magazine capacity is 15 rounds. Weight is about 38 oz. Sources indicate that this pistol was never officially adopted by the French military. However, a target version of this pistol, the F1 Target, was adopted by the French air force and army.

Exc.	V.G.	Good	Fair	Poor
550	450	300	200	100

UNIQUE

When the French Vichy government signed an armistice with Germany in 1940, the Germans occupied Handaye in France, the site of Manufacture D'Armes Des Pyrenees. This factory then produced for the German army the Model 16 and Model 17.

Model 16

Chambered for the 7.65mm cartridge this pistol was fitted with a 7-round magazine. German army proof test and acceptance stamp. Hard rubber grips. About 2,000 were built under German supervision.

Exc.	V.G.	Good	Fair	Poor
250	175	150	100	75

Model 17

Similar to the above but with a 9-shot magazine. About 30,000 of these pistols were built under German control.

Exc.	V.G.	Good	Fair	Poor
300	250	200	150	100

Unique Kriegsmodell

This is an improved Model 17 with exposed hammer. Approximately 18,000 were manufactured under German occupation.

Exc.	V.G.	Good	Fair	Poor
500	400	300	200	100

SAVAGE

Model 1907 (French Model)

A .32 or .380 semiautomatic pistol with a 3.75" or 4.25" barrel, depending upon caliber, and a 9- or 10-shot magazine. Blued with hard rubber grips. The .380 caliber model is worth approximately 30% more than the values listed below. This pistol was sold to the French government during World War I and used by the French military. These guns were not stamped with French acceptance marks. The first shipment was made in 1914. Most of these pistols were fitted with a lanyard ring. French contract Model 1907 pistols were chambered for the 7.65mm cartridge and are fitted with a chamber indicator. Most French pistols will have the caliber designation in both ".32 CAL" and "7.65MM" stamped on the slide. Approximately 30,000 of these pistols were sold to France.

Courtesy Orvel Reichert

Exc.	V.G.	Good	Fair	Poor
700	600	450	300	150

NOTE: It is very rare to find a military Savage in very good or better condition. Be aware of refinished pistols.

SUBMACHINE GUNS

The French used the German 9mm Erma submachine gun prior to World War II. The first French designed and built submachine gun was the MAS 35, designated the SE-MAS Type L, chambered for the 7.65 long pistol cartridge and built at Manufacture d'Armes de St. Etienne, St. Etienne, France. This gun was quickly superseded by the more common MAS 38.

MAS 35 SE

This model is the forerunner of the MAS 38. Chambered for the 7.65mm long cartridge. Barrel length is 8.8". Rate of fire is approximately 600 rounds per minute. Full auto fire only. Fed by a 32-round box magazine. Rear sight has 100 and 200 meter settings. Weight is about 6.25 lbs.

Pre-1968

Exc.	V.G.	Fair
5500	5000	4500

Pre-1986 conversions

Exc.	V.G.	Fair
N/A	N/A	N/A

Pre-1986 dealer samples

Exc.	V.G.	Fair
N/A	N/A	N/A

MAS 38

Built in France and chambered for the 7.65mm French Long cartridge. Fitted with an 8.75" barrel and a magazine capacity of 32 rounds. Fitted with a fixed wooden butt. Rate of fire is about 650 rounds per minute. Uses a folding trigger for safety. Weight is approximately 6.5 lbs. On the left side of the receiver marked "CAL 7.65 L MAS 1938." Produced from 1938 to 1946.

Private NFA collection • Gary Gelson photo

MAS 35 SE • Private NFA collection, Paul Goodwin photo

MAS 38 • Courtesy West Point Museum, Paul Goodwin photo

Pre-1968

Exc.	V.G.	Fair
6500	6000	5500

Pre-1986 conversions

Exc.	V.G.	Fair
N/A	N/A	N/A

Pre-1986 dealer samples

Exc.	V.G.	Fair
N/A	N/A	N/A

MAT 49

This French submachine gun was first produced in 1949 and is no longer in production. Built at the French arsenal at Tulle using a stamped steel frame and receiver. It is chambered for the 9mm cartridge and fitted with a 9" barrel. The magazine housing acts as a forward grip and folds forward under the barrel. Fitted with an ejection port cover. It was used by French forces and is still found in former French colonies. The magazine capacity is 32 rounds and the weight is about 8 lbs. Rate of fire is 600 rounds per minute. Markings are "M.A.T. MLE 49 9M/M" on the left side of the receiver.

MAT 49 with receiver markings • Paul Goodwin photo

Pre-1968

Exc.	V.G.	Fair
7500	7000	6500

Pre-1986 conversions (reweld)

Exc.	V.G.	Fair
5000	4500	4000

Pre-1986 dealer samples

Exc.	V.G.	Fair
N/A	N/A	N/A

Hotchkiss Type Universal

Introduced in 1949 and intended as a police weapon. Select fire. It is a basic blowback design and chambered for the 9mm Parabellum cartridge. Fitted with a 10.8" barrel. Magazine capacity is 32 rounds. Rate of fire is about 650 rounds per minute.

The gun is made so that it can be folded to a very compact size. The stock, magazine, and barrel collapse to make the overall length of the gun only 17.2". Weight is approximately 7.5 lbs. This submachine gun saw limited use in Indo-China and a small number of guns were sold to Venezuela in the early 1950s.

Courtesy Robert E. Naess

Pre-1968
(Extremely Rare, 1 transferable sample known)

Exc.	V.G.	Fair
20000	—	—

Pre-1986 conversions

Exc.	V.G.	Fair
N/A	N/A	N/A

Pre-1986 dealer samples

Exc.	V.G.	Fair
N/A	N/A	N/A

RIFLES

CHASSEPOT

Model 1866 Rifle

This needle gun, bolt-action, single-shot model was an improvement over the German Dreyse. Chambered for the 11mm nitrated paper or cloth cartridge with an internal priming pellet. Barrel length is 32.5" with full stock with two barrel bands. These rifles were adopted by the French military in 1866. The rifle was made by a number of different French arsenals as well as contractors in England, Belgium, Spain, and Austria. About 600,000 of these rifles were captured by the Germans during the Franco-Prussian War in 1870-71. Some of these were converted to 11x50.2R Bavarian Werder cartridge, and stamped with German acceptance marks. Some rifles were then later converted to the 11.15x60R Mauser cartridge. A total of 1,000,000 rifles were built by 1870.

Exc.	V.G.	Good	Fair	Poor
550	450	300	200	100

Model 1866 Carbines

Several different variations of carbines were built on the Chassepot action. Some were half stocked and others had full stocks. Some were fitted with brass buttplates, triggerguards, and barrel bands.

Exc.	V.G.	Good	Fair	Poor
1250	1000	850	700	300

PEABODY

Spanish Rifle (1869)

Identical to the Spanish Rifle. Chambered for the .43 Spanish centerfire cartridge and fitted with a 33" barrel. Full stock with two barrel bands. Blued barrel and case hardened furniture. About 33,000 rifles were produced for the French government.

Exc.	V.G.	Good	Fair	Poor
—	750	600	350	150

GRAS

Model 1874 & M1874/M14 & M80

An 11x59Rmm caliber bolt action single shot rifle with a 32" barrel with a walnut stock, two iron barrel bands, and a metal tip. The bayonet is a spike blade with a wood handle and a brass butt cap. Many of these rifles were converted early in WWI to 8x50.5Rmm Lebel caliber by sleeving the barrel and re-chambering. This converted rifle was designated the 1874/M14. Many of the conversions were fitted with wooden handguards. The rifle was built at Chatellerault, Mutzig, Tulle and so marked.

There was a Musketoon version, model designation M1874, with 27" barrel and 3 brass barrel bands. The Musketoon did not have a bayonet lug. It was made at St. Chatellerault and so marked.

A Carbine version was also built at St. Etienne and so marked. It was designated the M80 and was fitted with a 20" barrel with two brass barrel bands.

Rifle

Exc.	V.G.	Good	Fair	Poor
1250	850	650	450	150

Musketoon

Exc.	V.G.	Good	Fair	Poor
1500	1150	800	550	200

Carbine

Exc.	V.G.	Good	Fair	Poor
1500	1150	800	550	200

Model 1874 Rifle (ramrod is missing) • Courtesy Rock Island Auction Company

THE FRENCH MODEL 1874 GRAS

As much as many English-speaking gun collectors may be loathe to admit it, the French get credit for many of the most important developments in firearms technology. Our Gallic brethren developed the Minie ball, pinfire, rimfire, and center cartridges, the first cartridge-firing revolvers and shotguns and—perhaps most important of all—smokeless gunpowder. As a result of their loss in the Franco-Prussian War (1871-72), the French set about developing a rifle to counter Germany's new Gewehr M.71 Mauser. The resulting Fusil Infanterie Modele 1874, developed by Captain Basile Gras, was a single shot, bolt action rifle chambered for the Balle Mle. 1874 (11x59R) cartridge loaded with a 387 gr. lead bullet which 81 gr. of black powder pushed to 1490 fps. An epee bayonet with a 20.5" blade was used. In 1880 most Gras had a channel cut into the left side of the bolt way to safely vent gas from a ruptured case. Modified rifles have "M.80" on the left receiver wall. The Gras I tested was made at the Chatellerault arsenal and, considering it had spent its service lives firing black powder, had a bright bore with plenty of sharp rifling. Its ruggedness was apparent and, unlike many military rifles of the time, possessed a well-balanced feel, although this was counter-balanced by a rather heavy trigger. With its lowest sight setting of 200 meters it tended to shoot high, but once I had the measure of it I put five rounds into an impressive 2.5" group. The bolt worked smoothly, chambering and ejecting cartridges easily. In my opinion, the Gras is a better-handling rifle than either the Gewehr 71 Mauser or British Martini-Henry and—despite not having the most user friendly sights—was as accurate as my M1873 Trapdoor Springfield. With the Gras, the French Poilu was equipped with a rifle equal—if not superior—to those used by other armies of that era.

Paul Scarlata

Model 1878 & 1878/M84 Navy

This rifle was produced at Steyr on contract with the French navy and marines. It was fitted with a 29" barrel and chambered for the 11x59R Gras cartridge. It has a 6-round magazine tube in the forend. The rifle was loaded through the action with the bolt open. These rifles will probably be marked "STEYR MLE. 1878 MARINE" on the left side of the receiver.

The 1878/M84 variation had the magazine extending slightly beyond the forend cap. The 1878/84 was produced at Chatellerault and St. Etienne. It was not made by Steyr.

Exc.	V.G.	Good	Fair	Poor
650	500	300	100	50

LEBEL

The Lebel system was invented by Nicolas Lebel in 1886. The French replaced the single shot Gras Model 1874 rifle with this weapon. This was the first successful smallbore rifle and sent the rest of the European continent into a dash to emulate it. The Lebel was chambered for the 8mm Lebel cartridge with smokeless powder. The Lebel system was used until it was made obsolete by the Berthier rifle in the 1890s.

Model 1886 "Lebel"

Chambered for the 8mm Lebel cartridge. While the cartridge was the first to use smokeless powder, the rifle was based on the old Gras Model 1874. It has a 31" barrel and holds 8 shots in a tubular magazine that runs beneath the barrel. This design is long and heavy and was not in use for long before being replaced by the more efficient box magazine weapons, such as those from Mauser. This rifle has a two-piece stock with no upper handguard. It is held on by two barrel bands, and a cruciform bayonet could be fixed under the muzzle. Weight of the rifle was about 9.5 lbs. Although this rifle was made obsolete rather quickly, it did have the distinction of being the first successful smokeless powder smallbore rifle; there were shortened examples in use until the end of WWII. This rifle was made at Chatellerault, St. Etienne, and Tulle arsenals and so marked.

Courtesy Richard M. Kumor Sr.

Exc.	V.G.	Good	Fair	Poor
650	450	200	100	50

FRENCH MODEL 1886 M93 LEBEL

With the adoption of the Fusil d'Infanterie Model 1886 Lebel, the French Army fielded the most advanced combat rifle in the world. However, it was the 8x51R cartridge loaded with smokeless powder that was revolutionary, not the rifle. Today people look at the Model 1886 as woefully obsolete by the beginning of World War I. While this may be true, it says much that with it the French Poilus fought the invading Germans, equipped with the vastly overrated Mauser G98, to a standstill. Picking a Lebel up one notes that despite the long overall length (51.3") it balances well and hangs nicely offhand. A conventional turnbolt with dual opposed front-locking lugs, it feeds from a tubular magazine. To load, open the bolt, depress the shell carrier, thumb 8 rounds into the magazine, place a round on the carrier and one in the chamber, and close the bolt. For ranges less than 400m, flip the rear sight all the way forward to expose the 250m battlesight underneath it. The rifle shoulders nicely and is comfortable with a 13.5" length of pull. Align the hard-to-see sights and squeeze. When the hammer drops the Lebel slaps hard on both ends. The bolt handle is a bit of a reach due to its forward placement, but the action is fairly smooth and easy to run from the shoulder. You just have to give it a bit of a tug at the end to snap the shell carrier up. While the Lebel sports a magazine cutoff, no safety is provided. French thinking being if action is imminent why do you have the safety on, and if not why do you have a round in the chamber? With quality ammunition and a good bore these rifles are capable of fine accuracy. A rugged and reliable design, the Lebel soldiered on far longer than it should have.

David Fortier

Model 1886/M93/R35

A shorter version of the above. Fitted with a 17.7" barrel and a 3-round tubular magazine. Weight was about 7.8 lbs. Issued in 1935.

NOTE: Add 50% for Nazi marked models.

Courtesy Richard M. Kumor Sr.

Exc.	V.G.	Good	Fair	Poor
550	400	250	150	75

BERTHIER-MANNLICHER

Adolph Berthier was a French army officer. He developed his new design to accommodate the new, more modern 8mm cartridge. His bolt action rifles employed Mannlicher-style clips which were used to form part of the box magazine design. These clips fell out of the bottom of the action when the last round was chambered. Most of the Berthier rifles used 3-round clips.

Model 1890 Cavalry Carbine

This bolt action model as sling swivels mounted on the left side of the stock. The carbines did not have a bayonet lug. One-piece stock had a straight grip without a handguard. The stock just forward of the triggerguard was swelled giving a potbelly appearance. This swell contained the magazine. Stock had two cross bolts. Bolt handle was extra long. Barrel length was 17.7". Weight was approximately 6.8 lbs. These carbines were built at Chatellerault and St. Etienne arsenals and so marked in script on the left side of the receiver.

Exc.	V.G.	Good	Fair	Poor
450	325	250	150	75

Model 1892 Artillery

This model was similar in appearance to the Model 1890 carbine with the exception that it was fitted with a bayonet lug and bottom sling swivels. No handguard.

Exc.	V.G.	Good	Fair	Poor
450	325	250	150	75

Model 1892 Carbine

Chambered for the 8x50.5Rmm Lebel cartridge and fitted with a 17.5" barrel. One-piece stock bellied forward to fully enclose a box magazine with a 5 round capacity. Original Model 1892 carbine were not fitted with upper handguards, but conversions were so fitted. Turned down bolt handle. Marked "MLE. 1892" on the left side of the receiver.

Exc.	V.G.	Good	Fair	Poor
650	500	400	200	150

Model 1892/M16

This is a conversion of the Model 1892 with the addition of a 5-round extended magazine and upper handguard. Conversion was done during WWI, hence the 1916 designation.

Exc.	V.G.	Good	Fair	Poor
250	175	125	90	70

NOTE: For rifles originally chambered for .22 rimfire add 100%.

Model 1902

This model was based on the Model 1890 and 1892 carbines. It was designed for use by colonial troops in Indo-China. It was fitted with a 25" barrel with no upper handguard. One piece stock with straight grip with swell for magazine in front of triggerguard. Long bolt handle. Two cross bolts. These rifles were built at Chatellerault, St. Etienne, and Tulle arsenals, and so marked on the left side of the receiver. Weight was about 8 lbs.

Model 1902 • Courtesy West Point Museum, Paul Goodwin photo

Exc.	V.G.	Good	Fair	Poor
250	150	100	75	50

Model 1907

Similar to the Model 1902 but with a 31.5" barrel. No upper handguard. Other specifications the same as the Model 1902 except weight was about 8.5 lbs.

Exc.	V.G.	Good	Fair	Poor
275	200	150	100	75

Model 1907/15

Similar to the Model 1907 except for a straight bolt design. Barrel length was 31.5" with upper handguard. Besides being built at the three French arsenals, this rifle was also made by Remington-UMC on contract in 1914 and 1915. These examples are so marked on the left side of the receiver. Weight is about 8.25 lbs.

Exc.	V.G.	Good	Fair	Poor
275	200	150	100	75

NOTE: Add 300% for Remington built rifles.

Model 1916 Rifle

Similar to the Model 1907/15 except fitted with a 5-round extended magazine.

Exc.	V.G.	Good	Fair	Poor
275	200	150	100	75

Model 1907/15 • Courtesy West Point Museum, Paul Goodwin photo

MAS Model 1917 • Courtesy West Point Museum, Paul Goodwin photo

Model 1916 Carbine

This is a Model 1916 rifle with a 17.7" barrel and 5-round magazine. Weight is about 7 lbs.

Exc.	V.G.	Good	Fair	Poor
350	250	200	150	100

Model 1907/15-M34

This model was fitted with a 23" barrel and a new Mauser-type 5-round staggered column magazine. Clips were no longer needed in this design. It was chambered for the 7.5x54 rimless cartridge. Weight is about 8 lbs. Some of these rifles were used during WWII.

Exc.	V.G.	Good	Fair	Poor
650	500	350	250	100

Model 1886/74/1917 Signal Rifle

A scarce variation of the military issue rifle.

Courtesy Richard M. Kumor Sr.

Exc.	V.G.	Good	Fair	Poor
950	700	400	200	100

MAUSER

Post-WWII Modified K98k Carbine

Exc.	V.G.	Good	Fair	Poor
550	450	350	175	100

DAUDETEAU

St. Chamond

Model 1896

Chambered for the 6.5x53.5SRmm Daudeteau No. 12 cartridge. Fitted with a 32.5" barrel. Fixed box charger-loaded magazine with 5 round capacity as part of triggerguard. Full stock with half length upper handguard. Weight is approximately 8.5 lbs. Several thousand rifles were made for military trials. All of these rifles were produced between 1896 and 1897.

Courtesy Rock Island Auction Company

Exc.	V.G.	Good	Fair	Poor
600	475	350	250	150

FRENCH STATE ARSENALS

MAS, MAT

Model 1917

An 8x50mm Lebel caliber semiautomatic gas operated rifle with a 31.4" barrel, 5-shot half-oval charger loaded magazine, and full-length walnut stock with cleaning rod. Weight is about 11.5 lbs. Produced by MAT.

Exc.	V.G.	Good	Fair	Poor
1500	1200	800	—	—

Model 1918

As above in an improved version, with a 23.1" barrel. Uses a standard cartridge charger. Weight is about 10.5 lbs.

Exc.	V.G.	Good	Fair	Poor
1700	1400	800	—	—

NOTE: This note applies to both the Models 1917 and 1918. Many of these rifles had their gas systems deactivated and were issued to colonial troops as straight pull rifles. Deduct 50% for these examples.

MAS 36

A 7.5x54mm caliber bolt action rifle with a 22.6" barrel and 5-shot magazine. Bolt handle slants forward. Blued with a two

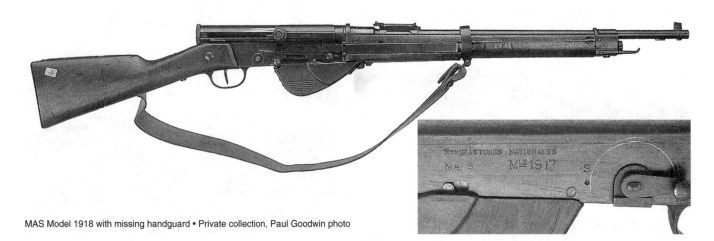

MAS Model 1918 with missing handguard • Private collection, Paul Goodwin photo

MAS 36 LG48 with grenade launcher built into barrel • Courtesy private collection, Paul Goodwin photo

piece walnut stock. Weight is about 8.25 lbs. The standard French service rifle from 1936 to 1949. The post-war version of this rifle has a grenade launcher built into the end of the barrel (see below). This was the last bolt action general service rifle to be adopted by a major military power.

Courtesy Rock Island Auction Company

Exc.	V.G.	Good	Fair	Poor
250	175	150	100	75

MAS 36 LG48

This is an MAS 36 rifle with a grenade launcher built into the barrel of the rifle. A folding sight arm was located on the left side of the barrel. Grenade range was varied by rotating the collar around the muzzle. Produced from about 1948 to 1951 and used extensively by the French army in Indo-China.

Exc.	V.G.	Good	Fair	Poor
550	400	300	200	100

MAS 36 CR39

As above, with an aluminum folding stock and 17.7" barrel. Weight is about 8 lbs. Designed for parachute and mountain troops. This is a rare variation.

Courtesy Richard M. Kumor Sr.

MAS 36 Para rifle in arsenal refinish with wooden stock • Courtesy Richard M. Kumor Sr.

Exc.	V.G.	Good	Fair	Poor
1500	1150	750	350	150

MAS 36 Sub-Caliber

This variation is an MAS 36 but with a special cartridge case designed for .22 caliber long rifle ammunition. Marked "5.5 RE-DUCED CALIBER" on the receiver.

Close-up of the MAS 36 .22 caliber training rifle • Private collection, Paul Goodwin photo

Exc.	V.G.	Good	Fair	Poor
700	600	500	400	300

MAS 44

This model was the first semiautomatic adopted by the French military. It was built in 1944. It later developed into the Model 49.

Courtesy Richard M. Kumor Sr.

Exc.	V.G.	Good	Fair	Poor
650	500	400	250	100

MAS 49

Introduced in 1949, this model is a 7.5x54mm gas-operated semiautomatic rifle with a 22.6" barrel and full-length walnut stock. It has a grenade launcher built into the front sight. Fitted with a 10-round magazine. No bayonet fittings. Weight is about 9 lbs.

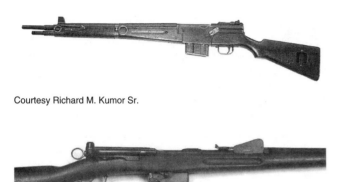

Courtesy Richard M. Kumor Sr.

MAS 49 Sniper Rifle • Courtesy Richard M. Kumor Sr.

Exc.	V.G.	Good	Fair	Poor
500	400	300	275	100

MAS 49/56

This model is a modification of the Model 49. It is fitted with a 20.7" barrel. Principal modification is with NATO standard grenade launcher. A special grenade sight is also fitted. This model has provisions to fit a bayonet. Weight is about 8.5 lbs.

Courtesy Richard M. Kumor Sr.

Exc.	V.G.	Good	Fair	Poor
400	300	250	175	100

Model FR-F 1 Sniper Rifle

Introduced in 1964, this 7.5x54mm rifle is based on the MAS 36 and uses the same style two-piece stock with pistol grip. Barrel length is 22" with bipod attached to forend. Barrel is fitted with a muzzle brake. Fitted with open sights but 3.8 power telescope often used. Magazine capacity is 10 rounds. Many of these rifles were converted to 7.62mm caliber.

Exc.	V.G.	Good	Fair	Poor
5500	4500	4000	—	—

Model FR-F 2 Sniper Rifle

A 1984 improved version of the F 1 rifle. The forearm has a plastic covering. The bipod is now attached to a yoke around the barrel, and the barrel is covered with a thermal sleeve to reduce heat. The features and dimensions the same as the F 1.

Exc.	V.G.	Good	Fair	Poor
6500	5500	5000	—	—

FAMAS F 1 Assault Rifle

Introduced in 1980, this bullpup design rifle is chambered for the 5.56x45mm cartridge and fitted with a 19.2" barrel with fluted chamber. Select fire with 3-shot burst. Muzzle is designed for grenade launcher and fitted with flash hider. This model is also fitted for a bayonet and a bipod. Magazine

capacity is 25 rounds. Rate of fire is about 950 rounds per minute. Weight is approximately 8 lbs.

Pre-1968

Exc.	V.G.	Fair
N/A	N/A	N/A

Pre-1986 conversions

Exc.	V.G.	Fair
N/A	N/A	N/A

Pre-1986 dealer samples

Exc.	V.G.	Fair
8000	7500	7000

FAMAS F 1 Rifle

Same as above but in semiautomatic version only. Scarce.

FAMAS Rifle • Courtesy Chuck Karwan

Exc.	V.G.	Good	Fair	Poor
8000	6000	—	—	—

MACHINE GUNS

Model 1907 St. Etienne

Built by the French arsenal MAS, this is a reversed gas-action gun chambered for the 8x50R Lebel cartridge. It was an unsuccessful attempt to improve on the Hotchkiss gun. The rate of fire is between 400 and 500 rounds per minute and is regulated by changing the gas cylinder volume. Barrel jacket is half-length over a 28" barrel. Fitted with spade grips with trigger. Fed by 24 or 30 metal strips. Weight is approximately 57 lbs. with tripod. This gun was not able to withstand the rigors of trench warfare and was withdrawn from combat in Europe.

Model 1907 St. Etienne • Robert G. Segel collection

round belt. Its rate of fire is about 500 rounds per minute. Barrel length is 31" and weight is about 55 lbs. The tripod for the Hotchkiss weighed another 55 lbs. by itself. In production from 1914 to 1930. Marked "MILTRAILLEUSE AUTOMATIQUE HOTCHKISS M1914 SDGD CALIBERE ——" on left side of receiver. The gun was used by the French army in both WWI and WWII. During WWI it was used by a number of Allied forces as well. As a matter of fact, American forces used the Hotchkiss more widely than any other machine gun. After World War II the gun appeared with French forces in Indo-China where the Viet Minh and later the Viet Cong used the gun.

NOTE: An earlier version of this gun, the Model 1909, was fitted with brass cooling fins instead of steel. The original design of the Hotchkiss was the Model 1897. This gun was fed by 30 round metal strips and had a rate of fire of about 600 rounds

Model 1907 St. Etienne blow forward mechanism • Robert G. Segel collection

1914 HOTCHKISS

Opportunities to fire the original World War I style Hotchkiss machine gun are few and far between. This French design utilizes flat metal trays to hold the cartridges for feeding. Trays can be hooked to each other to achieve a continuous feed. In the original caliber of 8mm Lebel, with its tapered case, the 1914 Hotchkiss is a smooth shooter. This is due to the mass of the weapon system as well as the recoiling parts.

The tripods are very heavy, and if a 1917 "Omnibus" tripod, with its 360 degree traverse ring is used, it takes four men and a boy to carry it around then set it up. These guns were made when men were Men and there were no "light lifting" profiles in the military. Shipping one of these tripods is perhaps one of the most difficult tasks in all of the gun world—there don't seem to be any boxes made that will handle the job.

Once at the range, with the trays loaded and prepared, the assistant gunner slides a tray into the feedblock and the machine gunner charges the weapon. The bolt is a smooth yet strong draw to the rear, and on release of the trigger, in front of an oddly shaped brass pistol grip, the large bolt carrier mass goes home and seats and fires a round. The gunner can hold and direct the machine gun with the odd grip at the back of the receiver while holding the pistol grip. Rate of fire is very slow, and the 1914 Hotchkiss is very accurate when the tripod is properly set up and weighted.

An item of note: the 8mm Lebel ammunition available is very often ancient stock and prone to hang fires. On any old machine gun such as this, it is wise to wait and count slowly to four before extracting a cartridge that has been fired but not gone off. We have seen the cases "explode" in mid air after they were extracted immediately on a misfire. The hangfire should be given a chance to go off in the chamber. When the gun is heated up, this seated cartridge may go off from a "cook-off" which is a different animal, and just as dangerous. Use care and proper safe handling procedures when firing one of these with ancient ammunition.

Dan Shea

Pre-1968
Exc.	V.G.	Fair
10000	9000	8000

Pre-1986 conversions
Exc.	V.G.	Fair
N/A	N/A	N/A

Pre-1986 dealer samples
Exc.	V.G.	Fair
N/A	N/A	N/A

Model 52 (AAT Mle. 52)
Introduced in 1952 as a general purpose machine gun with light 19" quick-change barrel with flash hider and bipod. This gun employs a blowback operation with two-piece bolt and fluted chamber. Chambered for the 7.62mm cartridge. The buttstock is a single-piece metal folding type. Rate of fire is about 700 rounds per minute and is belt-fed from the left side. Weight is about 21 lbs.

A heavy barrel version of this gun is built around a 23.5" barrel. Weight is about 24 lbs. Gun is usually placed on a U.S. M2 tripod. All other specifications same as light barrel version.

Pre-1968
Exc.	V.G.	Fair
18000	16000	14000

Pre-1986 conversions
Exc.	V.G.	Fair
N/A	N/A	N/A

Pre-1986 dealer samples
Exc.	V.G.	Fair
N/A	N/A	N/A

Hotchkiss Model 1914

Model 1914 Hotchkiss • Robert G. Segel collection

This model is an improvement over the original Model 1897 gun but with steel cooling fins instead of brass. Otherwise it remains an air-cooled gun chambered for the 8x50R Lebel cartridge. It is fed by a 24- or 30-round metal strip or by a 250-

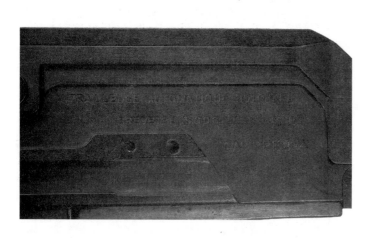

Model 1914 Hotchkiss with receiver markings • Paul Goodwin photo

per minute. Similar in appearance to the Model 1909. This gun was very popular with the Japanese who used it during the Russo-Japanese War of 1904-1905. This led the Japanese to develop the Type 92 for Japan's use during World War II.

Pre-1968

Exc.	V.G.	Fair
8500	8000	7500

Pre-1986 conversions

Exc.	V.G.	Fair
N/A	N/A	N/A

Pre-1986 dealer samples

Exc.	V.G.	Fair
N/A	N/A	N/A

A Von Karner modified Model 1914 rechambered for the 7.62x54Rmm Russian cartridge. Modified for the Dutch government prior to World War II for use in the East Indies against Japanese forces. Most were sunk by Japanese subs before reaching their destination. Courtesy John M. Miller

Chauchat Model 1915 (C.S.R.G.)

This model is a light air-cooled machine gun using a long recoil operation with a rotating bolt. It is chambered for the 8x50R Lebel and features an 18.5" barrel with barrel jacket. The 20-round magazine is a semi-circular type located under the receiver. Wooden buttstock and bipod. Rate of fire is about 250 rounds per minute. Used during WWI. The gun was inexpensively built and was not considered combat reliable.

CHAUCHAT MODEL 1915

The much mocked "Chauchat" machine gun has some rather distinctive features and is historically deserving of a much better reputation. It was born of the trench fighting styles of early World War I, and it must be taken in context to be understood.

This is because it is a truly awful machine gun to fire.

In its original caliber of 8mm Lebel (The later US version was in .30-06), the strangely, radically curved magazine is necessary because 30 cartridges of the tapered Lebel make almost a half moon when laid next to each other. Magazines are hard to insert and locate properly because of each end needing to line up with the gun to mount.

The real problem with firing the Chauchat is in the direction of the line of recoil. The stock is situated such that the full force of the recoil is directed into the shoulder of the operator. This has a jarring effect and, on its flimsy and unstable bipod, the gun chatters and batters the operator quite severely. The relatively slow rate of fire keeps the weapon from stabilizing and it tends to wander off target very quickly.

In defense of the Chauchat, it was made in a time where the troops were being mowed down by heavy, water-cooled, emplaced machine guns. The idea was to make a highly mobile machine gun that an assaulting company could use to bring suppressive fire down on the enemy trenches while the company maneuvered. As such, it succeeded in comparison to the alternatives that were fielded. The Germans had the MG08/15 Maxim, which was a bipod-supported, water-cooled Maxim gun, and in forward assault it was slung at the hip of the gunner. I picked one of these full of water up once, with a full spool of ammo, and fired it. While the MG08/15 as such was listed at around 100 lbs., I assure you that it was more like 975 lbs., or at least felt like it. The very idea of slogging over muddy terrain under fire, carrying that MG08/15 made the idea of the Chauchat much more palatable.

Dan Shea

A U.S. version firing the .30-06 cartridge was designed and built by the French and called the Model 1918. Used by U.S. forces during WWI, the M1918 has a 16-round magazine and a rate of fire of about 300 rounds per minute. U.S. military purchased about 19,000 of these guns chambered for the .30-06 cartridge.

Chauchat Model 1915 with "C.S.R.G." stamped on the receiver with serial number • Paul Goodwin photo

After World War I Belgium used the M1918 chambered for the 7.65mm cartridge and by Greece (Gladiator) chambered for the 8mm Lebel.

Pre-1968

Exc.	V.G.	Fair
4000	3500	3000

Pre-1986 conversions

Exc.	V.G.	Fair
N/A	N/A	N/A

Pre-1986 dealer samples

Exc.	V.G.	Fair
N/A	N/A	N/A

Chatellerault M1924/M29

This is an air-cooled light gas piston machine gun that the French referred to as an automatic rifle. It is chambered for the 7.5x54mm French cartridge. Fitted with a 19.7" barrel with flash hider and bipod. Wooden butt and forearm. Select fire with two triggers. Fed by a 25-round detachable top-mounted box magazine. Rate of fire is about 500 rounds per minute. Weight is approximately 24 lbs. with bipod. Introduced in 1929, the gun was used extensively in combat by French troops.

Another version of this model is known as the M1931A introduced in 1931. It is essentially an M1924/29 for use on a tank as a fixed place machine gun with tripod. Fitted with a 23" heavy barrel. The gun can use a 36-round box magazine or 150-round drum, both of which attach to the right side of the gun. Its rate of fire is 750 rounds per minute.

Pre-1968

Exc.	V.G.	Fair
8500	8000	7500

Pre-1986 conversions

Exc.	V.G.	Fair
N/A	N/A	N/A

Pre-1986 dealer samples

Exc.	V.G.	Fair
N/A	N/A	N/A

Montreux Vieux, France, August 1918. U.S. soldiers of the 114th Infantry Regiment on the range with the French 8mm Mle. 1915 C.S.R.G. machine rifle. This crude but interesting weapon, a forerunner of today's stamped metal assault rifles, was not well liked by Doughboys who had to carry it into combat • U.S. Army Signal Corps/National Archives/Robert Bruce Military Photo Features

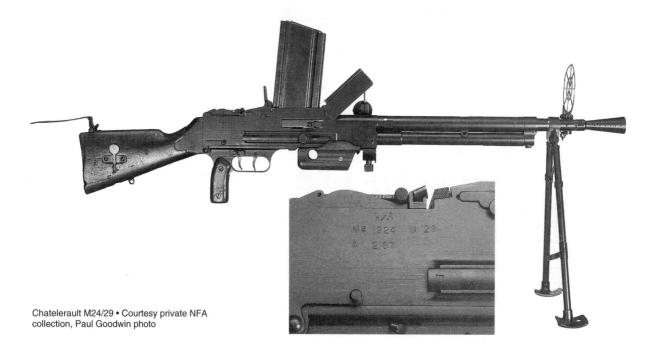

Chatelerault M24/29 • Courtesy private NFA
collection, Paul Goodwin photo

WHAT'S IT LIKE: THE CHATELLERAULT MODEL 1924/29 LMG

The French Chatellerault Model 1924/29 LMG is gas-operated, air-cooled and fires from the open-bolt position. It uses a locked-breech, short-recoil method of operation and is chambered for the odd, but effective, caliber 7.5x54mm round which served the French army admirably for many decades. The Chatellerault weighs 20.25 pounds, empty—about average for weapons of this type and era. The overall length is 42.6 inches. At 19.7 inches, the four-groove barrel with left-hand twist has the gas plug permanently attached. There is no gas regulator. This is a deficiency, although access to the gas port for cleaning is made available by means of a threaded plug at the bottom of the gas block. Most interesting is the gun's double trigger system. The front trigger provides semiautomatic fire and pulling the rear trigger will yield full auto fire at a rate of 635 rpm (substantially higher than stated by most open sources). While it saw little action in World War II, the Chatellerault was to write itself into the pages of glory in the fifteen years subsequent, when the French Foreign Legion and paras fought a series of wars in Indochina, Tunisia, Morocco and Algeria. It was in the conflict in Indochina that the Chatellerault was to prove once and for all that it ranked among the better machine guns of its era.

Although no military small arms are without their individual idiosyncrasies, and the Chatellerault Model 1924/29 is no exception, in general it was an excellent squad automatic when compared to its contemporaries. Its peculiar-looking, conical-shaped flash hider was not terribly effective; the wooden forearm is a bit too short; and the bipod is fairly clumsy as it swings wildly about in its 360-degree arc, but that said it was exceptionally reliable and its magazines hold five more rounds than the highly over-rated BAR, which falls considerably short when compared to its French contemporary.

Peter Kokalis

GERMANY

German Military Conflicts, 1870–Present

Prussia, under Otto von Bismark, achieved unification of the German states with victories in the Austro-Prussian War of 1866 and the Franco-Prussian War of 1870-1871. In 1871 William I of Prussia was named emperor of Germany and the nation's economic and military power began to grow and spread throughout the world. The outbreak of World War I was in part due to German expansion, threatening British and French interests. German military strength totaled 13,400,000. By war's end the total of killed and wounded was 6,400,000. With the end of World War I, and Germany's defeat, came a period of political and economic instability that led to the rise of the Nazi party. In 1933 Adolf Hitler was named Chancellor of Germany. With the invasion of Poland on September 1, 1939, World War II began. A total of 17,900,000 served in the German armed forces during World War II, and of those 7,856,600 were killed and wounded. After the war ended, parts of eastern Germany were absorbed by Poland and Russia. In 1949 West and East Germany were formed. The military weapons in this section cover Germany up to the formation of both East and West Germany with the post-war period only concerned with firearms produced in West Germany. East German military firearms are covered under the Russian, U.S.S.R. section. Both East and West Germany were reunited in 1990.

HANDGUNS

Bibliographical Note: For information on a wide variety of German military handguns see Jan Still, *Axis Pistols*, 1986.

REICHS REVOLVER
Germany

There are two basic versions of the German Standard Service Revolver designed by the Small Arms Commission of the Prussian army in the 1870s. Revolvers of this type were produced by the Erfurt Royal Arsenal, F. Dreyse of Sommerda, Sauer & Sohn, Spangenberg & Sauer, and C.H. Haenel of Suhl. Normally, the maker's initials are to be found on an oval above the triggerguard.

Model 1879

A 10.55mm caliber revolver with a 7.2" stepped octagon barrel, 6-shot cylinder and fixed sights. Standard finish is browned with smooth walnut grips having a lanyard ring at the base. These revolvers are fitted with a safety catch. In use from 1882 until 1919.

Exc.	V.G.	Good	Fair	Poor
1000	700	500	300	200

NOTE: Add 20% for Mauser-built revolvers.

Model 1883

As above with a 5" stepped octagon barrel and round bottom grips with lanyard loop. The finish on early production guns was browned, and on the balance of production the finish was blued. In use from 1885 until 1919. Mauser-built M1883s are rare.

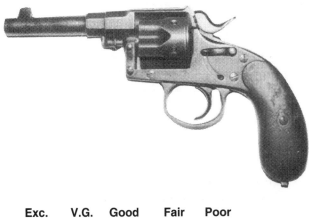

Exc.	V.G.	Good	Fair	Poor
750	500	375	250	175

NOTE: For Mauser-built revolvers add 250%.

STEYR

Steyr Hahn Model 1911

The Steyr Hahn was originally introduced as a commercial pistol but was quickly adopted by the Austro-Hungarian, Chilean, and Romanian militaries. Commercial examples were marked "Osterreichische Waffenfabrik Steyr M1911 9m/m" on the slide, have a laterally adjustable rear sight, and are rare. Austrian militaries are marked simply "STEYR" and the date of manufacture, while those made for Chile and Romania bear their respective crests. During WWII the Germans rebarreled a number of Steyr Hahns to 9mm Parabellum for police use, adding "P.08" to the slide along with appropriate Waffenamt markings.

Courtesy Orvel Reichert

Commercially marked

Exc.	V.G.	Good	Fair	Poor
1350	1000	750	500	350

German WWII Issue (P.08 marked)

Exc.	V.G.	Good	Fair	Poor
800	500	350	200	125

DREYSE

Dreyse 7.65mm

As above, but chambered for the 7.65mm cartridge, with a 3.6" barrel and a 7-shot magazine. The slide marked "Dreyse Rheinmetall Abt. Sommerda." Blued with plastic grips.

Courtesy Orvel Reichert

Exc.	V.G.	Good	Fair	Poor
350	250	175	100	75

Dreyse 9mm

As above, but chambered for the 9mm cartridge with a 5" barrel and an 8-shot magazine. The slide marked "Rheinische Mettellwaaren Und Maschinenfabrik, Sommerda." Blued with plastic grips.

Courtesy James Rankin

Exc.	V.G.	Good	Fair	Poor
3000	2000	800	450	300

MAUSER

MODEL 1896 "BROOMHANDLE MAUSER PISTOL"

Manufactured from 1896 to 1939, the Model 1896 Pistol was produced in a wide variety of styles as listed below. It is recommended that those considering the purchase of any of the following models should consult Breathed & Schroeder's *System Mauser,* Chicago, 1967, as it provides detailed descriptions and photographs of the various models. See also Wayne Erickson and Charles Pate, *The Broomhandle Pistol, 1896-1936,* 1985.

NOTE: A correct, matching stock/holster will add approximately 40 percent to value of each category.

"BUYER BEWARE" ALERT by Gale Morgan: Over the past several years large quantities of "Broomhandle" Mausers and Astra "copies" have been imported into the United States. Generally these are in poor or fair condition and have been offered for sale in the $125 to $300 price range, primarily as shooters or parts guns. Over the past year or so, a cottage industry has sprung up where these very common pistols have been "converted" to "rare, exotic, near mint, original" specimens selling well into the four figure price range. I have personally seen English Crest, the U.S. Great Seal, unheard-of European dealers, aristocratic Coats-of-Arms, and Middle East Medallions beautifully photo-etched into the magazine wells and rear panels of some really common wartime commercials with price tags that have been elevated to $2,500 plus. They are quite eye-catching and if they are sold as customized/modified Mausers, the seller can price the piece at whatever the market will bear. However, if sold as a factory original–BUYER BEWARE.

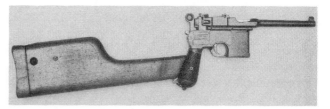

Courtesy Wallis & Wallis, Lewes, Sussex, England

Turkish Contract Cone Hammer

Chambered for 7.63mm Mauser cartridge and fitted with a 5.5" barrel. Rear sight is marked in Farsi characters. Grips are grooved walnut with 21 grooves. Proof mark is a 6-pointed star on both sides of the chamber. Marked in Turkish script and bearing the crest of Sultan Abdul-Hamid II on the frame. Approximately 1,000 were sold to Turkey.

Courtesy Joe Schroeder

Courtesy Gale Morgan

Exc.	V.G.	Good	Fair	Poor
12000	8000	6500	3000	2000

THE MAUSER M1896

Although it was not officially adopted by the German military until 1915, the Mauser M1896 pistol served in the armies of many nations and was the choice of such notable individuals as Sir Winston Churchill, who carried one during the Boer War. The Mauser was also a favorite of Russians and the "Bolo" Model, with its shortened barrel, took its name from the pistols supplied to the Bolshevik Soviet Union. The pistol was also supplied in large numbers to China, where it remained in service from the 1930s until the 1950s. Most had a groove in the grip to allow attachment of a buttstock. The M1896 was originally chambered for the 7.63x25mm Mauser cartridge and later for the 9x19mm Luger round. The high velocity 7.63 remains one of the "hottest" pistol rounds in terms of velocity and overall penetration. The M1896 is awkward in appearance, but actually handles very well. Recoil is mild and the pistol is well-balanced, with most of the weight directly over the shooting hand. The sights of the 1930 Commercial version that we evaluated for this brief article consist of a "barleycorn" at the pistol's business end and a tangent notch rear sight. The latter is hugely optimistic, with graduations to 1,000 meters. One of the most notable features of the M1896 Mauser is the absence of a single pin in its construction and only one screw that retains the grips. The pistol fits together like an oriental puzzle, with all parts manufactured to very close tolerances. Despite this, the M1896 is generally reliable. Disassembly is not overly difficult, but at the same time isn't exactly intuitive and requires a small screwdriver and a non-marring punch or similar tool. The Mauser M1896 is one of those landmark pistols whose use around the world has earned it a justifiable place in firearms history.

Charlie Cutshaw

Contract Transitional Large Ring Hammer

This variation has the same characteristics of the "Standard Cone Hammer" except the hammer has a larger, open ring. It is fitted with a 5.5" barrel and an adjustable sight marked from 50 to 500 meters. Grips are walnut with 23 grooves. Some of these pistols were issued to the German army for field testing.

Courtesy Gale Morgan

Exc.	V.G.	Good	Fair	Poor
3500	2800	2500	1150	800

Model 1899 Flat Side–Italian Contract

Similar to the above, with a 5.5" barrel, adjustable rear sight, and the frame sides milled flat. Left flat of chamber marked with "DV" proof. A "crown over AV" is stamped on the bottom of the barrel. All parts are serial numbered. Approximately 5,000 were manufactured in 1899.

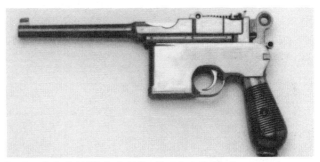

Courtesy Butterfield & Butterfield, San Francisco, California

Exc.	V.G.	Good	Fair	Poor
4000	3000	1500	1200	900

Contract Flat Side

Fitted with a 5.5" barrel with adjustable rear sight marked 50 to 500 meters. Grips are walnut with 23 grooves. The proof mark is the German military acceptance proofs. This model was used for field testing by the German army in 1899 or 1900. Number of pistols is unknown but most likely very small.

Exc.	V.G.	Good	Fair	Poor
2700	2200	1500	1000	750

Persian Contract

Persian rising sun on left rear barrel extension. Persian Lion crest in center of rear frame panel. Barrel length is 5.5" and grips are walnut with 34 grooves. Adjustable rear sight marked from 50 to 1000 meters. Prospective purchasers should secure a qualified appraisal prior to acquisition. Serial numbers in the 154000 range.

Exc.	V.G.	Good	Fair	Poor
4200	3500	2250	1400	1000

Standard Wartime Commercial

Identical to the prewar Commercial Model 96, except that it has 30 groove walnut grips and the rear of the hammer is stamped "NS" for new safety. A number of these have the Austrian military acceptance marks in addition to the German commercial proofs. These pistols were also used by the German army as well.

Courtesy Gale Morgan

Exc.	V.G.	Good	Fair	Poor
1800	1300	1000	500	350

9mm Parabellum Military Contract

As above, in 9mm Parabellum caliber with 24-groove grips, stamped with a large "9" filled with red paint. Rear sights are adjustable with 50 to 500 meter markings. This model has German military acceptance marks on the right side of the chamber. Fit and finish on these pistols are poor. Some examples have the Imperial German Eagle on the front of the magazine well. About 150,000 of these pistols were built for the German government.

Exc.	V.G.	Good	Fair	Poor
2500	2000	1200	700	450

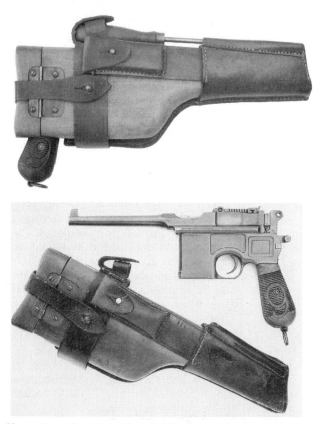

Mauser 9mm military contract "red nine" rig • Courtesy Gale Morgan

1920 Rework

A Model 96 modified to a barrel length of 3.9" and in 7.63mm Mauser or 9mm Parabellum caliber. Rear sight on this model is fixed. German military acceptance marks are located on the right side of the chamber. Often encountered with police markings.

Courtesy Gale Morgan

Courtesy Butterfield & Butterfield, San Francisco, California

Exc.	V.G.	Good	Fair	Poor
1500	1000	500	400	350

Late Postwar Bolo Model

Chambered for the 7.63mm Mauser cartridge and fitted with a 3.9" barrel. Rear sight marked for 50 to 500 meters or 50 to 1000 meters. Grips are walnut with 22 grooves. Some of these pistols will bear Chinese characters. The Mauser banner trademark is stamped on the left rear panel.

Courtesy Gale Morgan

Courtesy Gale Morgan

Exc.	V.G.	Good	Fair	Poor
1800	1200	700	400	200

Early Model 1930

A 7.63mm caliber Model 96 with a 5.2" stepped barrel, 12-groove walnut grips and late style safety. The rear adjustable sight is marked in 50 to 1000 meters. Some of these pistols have Chinese characters on the left side of the magazine well.

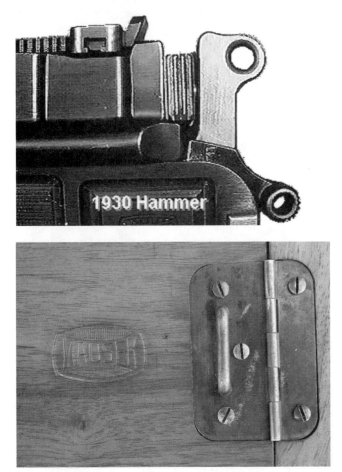

Courtesy Gale Morgan

Exc.	V.G.	Good	Fair	Poor
2700	2200	1200	800	500

Late Model 1930

Identical to the above, except for solid receiver rails.

Exc.	V.G.	Good	Fair	Poor
2500	2000	1000	700	400

Model 1930 Removable Magazine

Similar to the above, but with a detachable magazine. Prospective purchasers should secure a qualified appraisal prior to acquisition. Too rare to price.

Mauser Schnellfeuer (Model 712 or Model 32)

This is not a submachine gun but rather a machine pistol. Chambered for 7.63mm Mauser cartridge. Barrel length is 5.5" and rear sight is adjustable from 50 meters to 1000 meters. Walnut grips with 12 grooves. Magazine capacity is 10 or 20 rounds with a detachable magazine. This pistol is often encountered with Chinese markings as it was very popular in the Orient. Approximately 100,000 were produced. Rate of fire is between 900 and 1,100 rounds per minute. It should be noted that the Model 712 was used to some limited extent by the Waffen SS during World War II as well as the German Luftwaffe. Stamped with army test proof.

NOTE: The prices listed below are for guns with commercial markings and correct Mauser Schnellfeuer stock. Schnellfeuer stocks are cut larger inside to accommodate selector switch. For German army acceptance stamped pistols add 5% to 10% depending on condition. For pistols without stock or incorrect stock deduct $750 to $1,000.

MAUSER 712 SCHNELLFEUER-PISTOLE

The 7.63mm Mauser Schnellfeuer-pistole is one of those fantastic ideas that simply doesn't deliver when put to the test. The final evolution of the Mauser C-96 Military Pistol to be German issue, it was designed to fulfill three functions. It could be used as a normal full size service pistol, plus by attaching a wooden shoulder stock/holster it became a useful carbine, then by adding full automatic capability it could function as a submachine gun. It was a very attractive package. Compact and lightweight it fed from detachable 10 or 20 round magazines and had a cyclic rate of 900 rpm. That's 15 rounds per second. With undeniable sex appeal, the problem was trying to use the lightweight weapon effectively in the fully auto mode. To use a Mauser 712 you simply hit the button on the wooden shoulder stock/holster and the top will flip open. Draw the pistol and insert a 20-round magazine. Pull back and release the bolt. The safety is easily thumbed forward for Safe or back to Fire. In the hands you either love or hate the feel of this pistol, there is no in-between. The sights are small and difficult to see but the trigger is quite good. Used as a conventional pistol the Mauser works OK. Snap the stock on the weapon and in the semi-auto mode the Mauser becomes deadly. Firing as fast as you can pull the trigger riddles targets at 25 and 50 yards. Magazines change easily and taking your time you can hit man-sized targets out to 150-200 yards. Slide the selector to Auto though and the weapon turns into a scalded cat. Brass erupts from the weapon as it viciously climbs off target. I like the Mauser, but at other than conversation distances the full auto feature is useless. Used as a semi-auto carbine though it can be surprisingly effective.

David Fortier

Photo courtesy Joseph Schroeder

Pre-1968

Exc.	V.G.	Fair
7500	7000	6500

Pre-1986 conversions

Exc.	V.G.	Fair
N/A	N/A	N/A

Pre-1986 dealer samples

Exc.	V.G.	Fair
3000	3000	2500

LUGER

Bibliographical Note: See Charles Kenyon's, *Lugers at Random*, Handgun Press, 1969, for historical information, technical data, and photos. See also Jan Still, *Axis Pistols*, 1986.

Just before the turn of the 20th century, Georg Luger (1849-1923) redesigned the Borchardt semiautomatic pistol so that its mainspring was housed in the rear of the grip. The resulting pistol, the German army's Pistole '08, was to prove extremely successful and his name has become synonymous with the pistol, despite the fact his name never appeared on it.

The following companies manufactured Luger pattern pistols at various times:

1. DWM – Deutsch Waffen und Munitions – Karlsruhe, Germany
2. The Royal Arsenal of Erfurt, Germany
3. Simson & Company – Suhl, Germany
4. Mauser – Oberndorf, Germany
5. Vickers Ltd. – England
6. Waffenfabrik Bern – Bern, Switzerland, *see Switzerland, Handguns, Luger.*
7. Heinrich Krieghoff – Suhl, Germany

NOTE: The model listings below contain the commonly accepted Lugers that are considered military issue. It should be pointed out that in wartime commercial pistols were often diverted to military use if necessary.

DEUTSCHE WAFFEN UND MUNITIONS

1900 Swiss Contract

4.75" barrel, 7.65mm caliber. The Swiss Cross in Sunburst is stamped over the chamber. The military serial number range is 2001-5000; the commercial range, 01-21250. There were approximately 2,000 commercial and 3,000 military models manufactured.

Wide Trigger–Add 20%.

Velikie-Luki, western Russia, ca. 1942. With a Pistole 08 (Luger) in hand, a German soldier warily searches a log building. Judging from the cylindrical spare barrel carrier on his back, he is a member of a machinegun crew • Captured German Records/National Archives/Robert Bruce Military Photo Features

Paul Goodwin photo

Swiss Cross & Sunburst • Courtesy Gale Morgan

Exc.	V.G.	Good	Fair	Poor
5500	4000	2000	1500	1000

1900 American Eagle

4.75" barrel, 7.65mm caliber. The American Eagle crest is stamped over the chamber. The serial range is between 2000-200000, and there were approximately 11,000-12,000 commercial models marked "Germany" and 1,000 military test models without the commercial import stamp. The serial numbers of this military lot have been estimated at between 6100-7100.

Paul Goodwin photo

Exc.	V.G.	Good	Fair	Poor
4500	3200	1500	850	600

1900 Bulgarian Contract

An old model, 1900 Type, with no stock lug. It has a 4.75" barrel and is chambered for the 7.65mm cartridge. The Bulgarian crest is stamped over the chamber, and the safety is marked in Bulgarian letters. The serial range is 20000-21000, with 1,000 manufactured. This is a military test model and is quite rare as most were rebarreled to 9mm during the time they were used. Even with the 9mm versions, approximately 10 are known to exist. It was the only variation to feature a marked safety before 1904.

Paul Goodwin photo

Exc.	V.G.	Good	Fair	Poor
12000	8000	4000	2500	1800

1902 American Eagle Cartridge Counter

As above, with a "Powell Indicating Device" added to the left grip. A slotted magazine with a numbered window that allows visual access to the number of cartridges remaining. There were 50 Lugers altered in this way at the request of the U.S. Board of Ordnance, for U.S. army evaluation. The serial numbers are 22401-22450. Be especially wary of fakes!

Paul Goodwin photo

Exc.	V.G.	Good	Fair	Poor
30000	25000	16000	6000	3500

1904 Navy

6" thick barrel, 9mm caliber. The chamber area is blank, and the extractor is marked "Geladen." The safety is marked "Gesichert." There were approximately 1,500 manufactured in the one- to four-digit serial range, for military sales to the German navy. The toggle has a "lock" comparable to 1900 types.

Paul Goodwin photo

Exc.	V.G.	Good	Fair	Poor
40000	30000	16000	6000	4500

1906 U.S. Army Test Luger .45 Caliber

5" barrel, .45 ACP caliber. Sent to the United States for testing in 1907. The chamber is blank; the extractor is marked "Loaded," and the frame is polished under the safety lever. The trigger on this model has an odd hook at the bottom. Only five of these pistols were manufactured.

Exc.	V.G.	Good	Fair	Poor
Too Rare To Price				

1906 Swiss Military

Same as the Swiss Commercial, with the Geneva Cross in shield appearing on the chamber.

Courtesy Rock Island Auction Company

Exc.	V.G.	Good	Fair	Poor
4500	3100	2000	900	700

1906 Swiss Police Cross in Shield

As above, with a shield replacing the sunburst on the chamber marking. There were 10,215 of both models combined. They are in the 5000-15215 serial number range.

Paul Goodwin photo

1906 Swiss Police Cross in Shield • Courtesy Gale Morgan

Exc.	V.G.	Good	Fair	Poor
4500	3300	2200	900	700

1906 Dutch Contract

4" barrel, 9mm caliber. It has no stock lug, and the chamber is blank. The extractor is marked "Geleden" on both sides, and the safety is marked "RUST" with a curved upward pointing arrow. This pistol was manufactured for military sales to the Netherlands, and a date will be found on the barrel of most examples encountered. The Dutch refinished their pistols on a regular basis and marked the date on the barrels. There were approximately 4,000 manufactured, serial numbered between 1 and 4000.

Courtesy Gale Morgan

Paul Goodwin photo

Exc.	V.G.	Good	Fair	Poor
4200	3000	1500	800	600

1906 Royal Portuguese Navy

4" barrel, 9mm caliber, and has no stock lug. The Royal Portuguese naval crest, an anchor under a crown, is stamped above the chamber. The extractor is marked "CARREGADA" on the left side. The frame under the safety is polished. There were approximately 1,000 manufactured with one- to four-digit serial numbers.

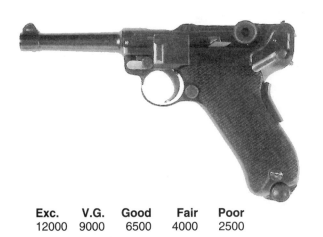

Exc.	V.G.	Good	Fair	Poor
12000	9000	6500	4000	2500

1906 Royal Portuguese Army (M2)

4.75" barrel, 7.65mm caliber. It has no stock lug. The chamber area has the Royal Portuguese crest of Manuel II stamped upon it. The extractor is marked "CARREGADA." There were approximately 5,000 manufactured, with one- to four-digit serial numbers.

Portuguese Army "M2" • Courtesy Gale Morgan

Exc.	V.G.	Good	Fair	Poor
3200	2700	1200	600	500

1906 Republic of Portugal Navy

4" barrel, 9mm caliber. It has no stock lug, and the extractor was marked "CARREGADA." This model was made after 1910, when Portugal had become a republic. The anchor on the chamber is under the letters "R.P." There were approximately 1,000 manufactured, with one- to four-digit serial numbers.

Exc.	V.G.	Good	Fair	Poor
11000	9000	5500	3500	2500

1906 Brazilian Contract

4.75" barrel, 7.65mm caliber. It has no stock lug, and chamber area is blank. The extractor is marked "CARREGADA," and the frame under the safety is polished. There were approximately 5,000 manufactured for military sales to Brazil.

Paul Goodwin photo

Exc.	V.G.	Good	Fair	Poor
3000	2400	1100	750	450

1906 Bulgarian Contract

4.75" barrel, 7.65mm caliber. It has no stock lug, and the extractor and safety are marked in cyrillic letters. The Bulgarian crest is stamped above the chamber. Nearly all of the examples located have the barrels replaced with 4" 9mm units. This was done after the later 1908 model was adopted. Some were refurbished during the Nazi era, and these pistols bear Waffenamts and usually mismatched parts. There were approximately 1,500 manufactured, with serial numbers of one to four digits.

Courtesy Rock Island Auction Company

Exc.	V.G.	Good	Fair	Poor
9500	7000	5000	3500	1500

1906 Russian Contract

4" barrel, 9mm caliber. It has no stock lug, and the extractor and safety are marked with cyrillic letters. Crossed Nagant rifles are stamped over the chamber. There were approximately 1,000 manufactured, with one- to four-digit serial numbers; but few survive. This is an extremely rare variation, and caution should be exercised if purchase is contemplated.

Paul Goodwin photo

Close-up of 1906 Russian Contract • Courtesy Gale Morgan

Exc.	V.G.	Good	Fair	Poor
14000	12000	6500	4000	2500

1906 Navy 1st Issue

6" barrel, 9mm caliber. The safety and extractor are both marked in German, and the chamber area is blank. There is a stock lug, and the unique two-position sliding navy sight is mounted on the rear toggle link. There were approximately 12,000 manufactured for the German navy, with serial numbers of one to five digits. The wooden magazine bottom features concentric rings.

NOTE: Many of these pistols had their safety changed so that they were "safe" in the lower position. Known as "1st issue altered." Value at approximately 20% less.

Close-up of 1906 Navy 1st Issue • Courtesy Gale Morgan

Paul Goodwin photo

Paul Goodwin photo

Exc.	V.G.	Good	Fair	Poor
6000	5000	2000	1300	950

1906 Navy 2nd Issue

As above, but manufactured to be safe in the lower position. Approximately 11,000 2nd Issue Navies manufactured, with one- to five-digit serial numbers—some with an "a" or "b" suffix. They were produced for sale to the German navy.

Paul Goodwin photo

Exc.	V.G.	Good	Fair	Poor
4900	3500	1500	950	700

1908 Navy

As above, with the "Crown M" military proof. They may or may not have the concentric rings on the magazine bottom. There were approximately 40,000 manufactured, with one- to five-digit serial numbers with an "a" or "b" suffix. These Lugers are quite scarce as many were destroyed during and after WWI, although a total of 40,000 were produced.

Exc.	V.G.	Good	Fair	Poor
4200	3200	2000	1100	800

1914 Navy

Similar to the above, but stamped with the dates from 1914-1918 above the chamber. Most noted are dated 1916-1918. There were approximately 30,000 manufactured, with one- to five-digit serial numbers with an "a" or "b" suffix. They are scarce as many were destroyed or altered as a result of WWI, even though about 40,000 were built.

Paul Goodwin photo

Exc.	V.G.	Good	Fair	Poor
4500	3000	1500	950	700

1908 Military 1st Issue

4" barrel, 9mm caliber. This was the first Luger adopted by the German army. It has no stock lug, and the extractor and safety are both marked in German. The chamber is blank. There were approximately 20,000 manufactured, with one- to five-digit serial numbers—some with an "a" suffix.

Exc.	V.G.	Good	Fair	Poor
1500	850	600	500	350

1908 Military Dated Chamber (1910-1913)

As above, with the date of manufacture stamped on the chamber.

Exc.	V.G.	Good	Fair	Poor
1200	900	600	500	350

1914 Military

As above, with a stock lug.

Exc.	V.G.	Good	Fair	Poor
1000	800	650	500	350

1914 Artillery

Fitted with an 8" barrel and chambered for the 9mm Parabellum cartridge, it features a nine-position adjustable sight that has a base that is an integral part of the barrel. This model has a stock lug and was furnished with a military-style flat board stock and holster rig (see Accessories). The chamber is dated from 1914-1918, and the safety and extractor are both marked. This model was developed for artillery and machine gun crews; and many thousands were manufactured, with one- to five-digit serial numbers—some have letter suffixes. This model is quite desirable from a collector's standpoint and is rarer than its production figures would indicate. After the war many were destroyed as the allies deemed them more insidious than other models for some reason.

Courtesy Rock Island Auction Company

Close-up of rear sight on 1914 Artillery • Courtesy Gale Morgan

Exc.	V.G.	Good	Fair	Poor
2400	1800	1300	900	600

NOTE: For models stamped with 1914 date add 50%.

DWM Double Dated

Has a 4" barrel, 9mm cartridge. The date 1920 or 1921 is stamped over the original chamber date of 1910-1918, creating the double-date nomenclature. These are arsenal-reworked WWI military pistols and were then issued to the German military and/or police units within the provisions of the Treaty of Versailles. Many thousands of these Lugers were produced.

Courtesy Rock Island Auction Company

Courtesy Rock Island Auction Company

Exc.	V.G.	Good	Fair	Poor
900	700	550	400	300

1920 Police/Military Rework

As above, except that the original manufacture date was removed before the rework date was stamped. There were many thousands of these produced.

Exc.	V.G.	Good	Fair	Poor
800	650	500	350	300

1920 Navy Carbine

Assembled from surplus Navy parts with the distinctive two position, sliding navy sight on the rear toggle link. Most are marked with the export stamp (GERMANY) and have the naval military proofmarks still in evidence. The safety and extractor are marked, and rarely one is found chambered for the 9mm cartridge. Few were manufactured.

1920 Navy Carbine • Paul Goodwin photo

Exc.	V.G.	Good	Fair	Poor
6250	5000	3000	1800	900

1923 Dutch Commercial & Military

Fitted with a 4" barrel, 9mm caliber. It has a stock lug, and the chamber area is blank. The extractor is marked in German, and the safety is marked "RUST" with a downward pointing arrow. This model was sold commercially and to the military in the Netherlands. There were approximately 1,000 manufactured in the one- to three-digit serial range, with no letter suffix.

Exc.	V.G.	Good	Fair	Poor
3200	2400	1000	850	550

Royal Dutch Air Force

Fitted with a 4" barrel, 9mm caliber. Marked with the Mauser Oberndorf proofmark and serial numbered in the 10000 to 14000 range. The safety marked "RUST."

Exc.	V.G.	Good	Fair	Poor
3500	2500	1000	800	550

VICKERS LTD.

1906 Vickers Dutch

Has a 4" barrel, 9mm caliber. There is no stock lug, and it uses a grip safety. The chamber is blank, and the extractor is marked "Geleden." "Vickers Ltd." is stamped on the front toggle link. The safety is marked "RUST" with an upward pointing arrow. Examples have been found with an additional date as late as 1933 stamped on the barrel. These dates indicate arsenal refinishing and in no way detract from the value of this variation. Arsenal reworks are matte finished, and the originals are a higher polished rust blue. There were approximately 10,000 manufactured in the 1-10100 serial number range.

Paul Goodwin photo

Exc.	V.G.	Good	Fair	Poor
3500	2800	1800	1200	750

ERFURT ROYAL ARSENAL

1908 Erfurt

Has a 4" barrel, 9mm caliber. It has no stock lug, and the year of manufacture, from 1910-1913, is stamped above the chamber. The extractor and safety are both marked in German, and "ERFURT" under a crown is stamped on the front toggle link. There were many thousands produced as Germany was involved in WWI. They are found in the one- to five-digit serial number range, sometimes with a letter suffix.

Exc.	V.G.	Good	Fair	Poor
1000	850	600	400	350

1914 Erfurt Military

Has a 4" barrel, 9mm caliber. It has a stock lug and the date of manufacture over the chamber, 1914-1918. The extractor and safety are both marked in German, and the front link is marked "ERFURT" under a crown. The finish on this model is rough; and as the war progressed in 1917 and 1918, the finish got worse. There were many thousands produced with one- to five-digit serial numbers, some with letter suffixes.

Courtesy Rock Island Auction Company

Exc.	V.G.	Good	Fair	Poor
1000	800	600	400	350

1914 Erfurt Artillery

Fitted with an 8" barrel, 9mm caliber. It has a stock lug and was issued with a flat board-type stock and other accessories, which will be covered in the section of this book dealing with same. The sight is a nine-position adjustable model. The chamber is dated 1914-1918, and the extractor and safety are both marked in German. "ERFURT" under a crown is stamped on the front toggle link. There were a great many manufactured with one- to five-digit serial numbers, some with a letter suffix. This model is similar to the DWM Artillery except that the finish is not as fine.

Paul Goodwin photo

Exc.	V.G.	Good	Fair	Poor
2500	1600	1100	800	600

Double Date Erfurt

Has a 4" barrel, 9mm caliber. The area above the chamber has two dates: the original 1910-1918, and the date of rework, 1920 or 1921. The extractor and safety are both marked in German, and this model can be found with or without a stock lug. "ERFURT" under a crown is stamped on the front toggle link. Police or military unit markings are found on the front of the grip straps more often than not. There were thousands of these produced by DWM as well as Erfurt.

Exc.	V.G.	Good	Fair	Poor
750	600	500	400	350

WAFFENFABRIK BERN

See *Swiss, Handguns, Bern*

SIMSON & CO.
SUHL, GERMANY

Simson & Co. Rework

Fitted with a 4" barrel, and chambered for either the 7.65 or 9mm caliber. The chamber is blank, but some examples are dated 1917 or 1918. The forward toggle link is stamped "SIMSON & CO. Suhl." The extractor and safety are marked in German. Most examples have stock lugs; some have been noted without them. The only difference between military models and commercial models is the proofmarks.

Exc.	V.G.	Good	Fair	Poor
2000	1300	900	600	500

Simson Dated Military

Has 4" barrel, 9mm caliber. There is a stock lug, and the year of manufacture from 1925-1928 is stamped above the chamber. The extractor and the safety are both marked in German. The checkered walnut grips of Simson-made Lugers are noticeably thicker than others. This is an extremely rare variation. Approximately 2,000 were manufactured with one- to three-digit serial numbers, and few seem to have survived.

Paul Goodwin photo

Exc.	V.G.	Good	Fair	Poor
3200	2200	1800	900	650

Simson S Code

Has a 4" barrel, 9mm caliber. The forward toggle link is stamped with a Gothic "S". It has a stock lug, and the area above the chamber is blank. The extractor and the safety are both marked. The grips are also thicker. There were approximately 12,000 manufactured with one- to five-digit serial numbers—some with the letter "a" suffix. This pistol is quite rare on today's market.

Paul Goodwin photo

Exc.	V.G.	Good	Fair	Poor
4000	3000	1500	1000	750

EARLY NAZI ERA REWORKS MAUSER

Produced between 1930 and 1933, and normally marked with Waffenamt markings.

Death's Head Rework

Has a 4" barrel, 9mm caliber. It has a stock lug, and a skull and crossbones are stamped, in addition to the date of manufacture, on the chamber area. This date was from 1914-1918. The extractor and safety are both marked. The Waffenamt proof is present. It is thought that this variation was produced for the 1930-1933 era "SS" division of the Nazi Party. Mixed serial numbers are encountered on this model and do not lower the value. This is a rare Luger on today's market, and caution should be exercised if purchase is contemplated.

Exc.	V.G.	Good	Fair	Poor
2500	1500	950	600	450

Kadetten Institute Rework

4" barrel, 9mm caliber. It has a stock lug, and the chamber area is stamped "K.I." above the 1933 date. This stood for Cadets Institute, an early "SA" and "SS" officers' training school. The extractor and safety are both marked, and the Waffenamt is present. There were only a few hundred reworked, and the variation is quite scarce. Be wary of fakes.

Exc.	V.G.	Good	Fair	Poor
3200	2500	1100	800	600

Mauser Unmarked Rework

4" barrel, 9mm caliber. The entire weapon is void of identifying markings. There is extensive refurbishing, removal of all markings, rebarreling, etc. The stock lug is present, and the extractor and safety are marked. The Waffenamt proofmark is on the right side of the receiver. The number manufactured is not known.

Exc.	V.G.	Good	Fair	Poor
1450	1000	850	600	450

MAUSER MANUFACTURED LUGERS 1930-1942 DWM

Mauser Oberndorf

4" barrel, 9mm caliber. It has a stock lug, blank chamber area, and a marked extractor and safety. This is an early example of Mauser Luger, and the front toggle link is still marked "DWM" as leftover parts were intermixed with new Mauser parts in the production of this pistol. This is one of the first Lugers to be finished with the "Salt" blue process. There were approximately 500 manufactured with one- to four-digit serial numbers with the letter "v" suffix. This is a rare variation.

Exc.	V.G.	Good	Fair	Poor
4000	3200	2000	1500	900

1935/06 Portuguese "GNR"

4.75" barrel, 7.65mm caliber. It has no stock lug but has a grip safety. The chamber is marked "GNR," representing the Republic National Guard. The extractor is marked "Carregada"; and the safety, "Seguranca." The Mauser banner is stamped on the front toggle link. There were exactly 564 manufactured according to the original contract records that the Portuguese government made public. They all have four-digit serial numbers with a "v" suffix.

Paul Goodwin photo

Exc.	V.G.	Good	Fair	Poor
3400	2900	1600	900	750

S/42 K Date

4" barrel, 9mm caliber. It has a stock lug, and the extractor and safety are marked. This was the first Luger that utilized codes to represent maker and date of manufacture. The front toggle link is marked "S/42" in either Gothic or script; this was the code for Mauser. The chamber area is stamped with the letter "K," the code for 1934, the year of manufacture. Approximately 10,500 were manufactured with one- to five-digit serial numbers—some with letter suffixes.

Courtesy Richard M. Kumor Sr.

Exc.	V.G.	Good	Fair	Poor
5000	3800	2200	1200	1000

S/42 G Date

As above, with the chamber stamped "G," the code for the year 1935. The Gothic lettering was eliminated, and there were many thousands of this model produced.

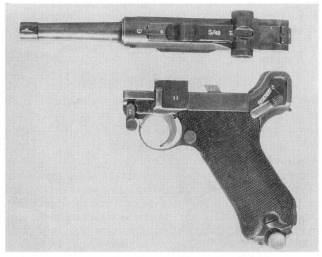

Courtesy Orvel Reichert

Exc.	V.G.	Good	Fair	Poor
2300	1500	1000	650	450

Dated Chamber S/42

4" barrel, 9mm caliber. The chamber area is dated 1936-1940, and there is a stock lug. The extractor and safety are marked. In 1937 the rust blue process was eliminated entirely, and all subsequent pistols were salt blued. There were many thousands manufactured with one- to five-digit serial numbers—some with a letter suffix.

Paul Goodwin photo

Exc.	V.G.	Good	Fair	Poor
1600	1100	750	500	400

NOTE: Rarest variation is early 1937 with rust blued and strawed parts, add 20%.

Code 42 Dated Chamber

4" barrel, 9mm caliber. The new German code for Mauser, the number 42, is stamped on the front toggle link. There is a stock lug. The chamber area is dated 1939 or 1940. There were at least 50,000 manufactured with one- to five-digit serial numbers—some have letter suffixes.

Exc.	V.G.	Good	Fair	Poor
1100	850	650	400	350

41/42 Code

As above, except that the date of manufacture is represented by the final two digits (e.g. 41 for 1941). There were approximately 20,000 manufactured with the one- to five-digit serial number range.

Exc.	V.G.	Good	Fair	Poor
1600	1350	900	700	500

byf Code

As above, with the "byf" code stamp on the toggle link. The year of manufacture, either 41 or 42, is stamped on the chamber. This model was also made with black plastic, as well as walnut grips. There were many thousands produced with the one- to five-digit serial numbers—some with a letter suffix.

Paul Goodwin photo

Exc.	V.G.	Good	Fair	Poor
1300	950	750	450	350

Persian Contract 4"

4" barrel, 9mm caliber. It has a stock lug, and the Persian crest is stamped over the chamber. All identifying markings on this variation—including extractor, safety, and toggle—are marked in Farsi, the Persian alphabet. There were 1,000 manufactured. The serial numbers are also in Farsi.

Persian Contract 4" • Paul Goodwin photo

Exc.	V.G.	Good	Fair	Poor
6500	5000	3500	2500	2000

Persian Contract Artillery

As above, with an 8" barrel and nine-position adjustable sight on the barrel. This model is supplied with a flat board stock. There were 1,000 manufactured and sold to Persia.

Courtesy Rock Island Auction Company

Exc.	V.G.	Good	Fair	Poor
3500	2850	1800	1300	1000

1934 Mauser Dutch Contract

4" barrel, 9mm caliber. The year of manufacture, 1936-1939, is stamped above the chamber. The extractor is marked "Geladen," and the safety is marked "RUST" with a downward pointing arrow. The Mauser banner is stamped on the front toggle link. Checkered walnut grips. This was a military contract sale, and approximately 1,000 were manufactured with four-digit serial numbers with a letter "v" suffix.

Paul Goodwin photo

Exc.	V.G.	Good	Fair	Poor
3500	3000	2000	1100	850

1934 Mauser Swedish Contract

4.75" barrel, 9mm or 7.65mm caliber. The chamber is dated 1938 or 1939. The extractor and safety are both marked in German, and there is a stock lug. The front toggle link is stamped with the Mauser banner. There were only 275 dated 1938 and 25 dated 1939 in 9mm. There were only 30 chambered for 7.65mm dated 1939. The serial number range is four digits with the letter "v" suffix.

Exc.	V.G.	Good	Fair	Poor
4000	3000	2000	1500	700

1934 Mauser German Contract

4" barrel, 9mm caliber. The chamber is dated 1939-1942, and the front toggle link is stamped with the Mauser banner. There is a stock lug, and the extractor and safety are both marked. The grips are either walnut or black plastic. There were several thousand manufactured with one- to five-digit serial numbers—some with letter suffixes. They were purchased for issue to police or paramilitary units.

Exc.	V.G.	Good	Fair	Poor
2800	2300	1500	800	550

Austrian Bundes Heer (Federal Army)

4" barrel, 9mm caliber. The chamber is blank, and there is a stock lug. The extractor and safety are marked in German, and the Austrian federal army proof is stamped on the left side of the frame above the triggerguard. There were approximately 200 manufactured with four digit serial numbers and no letter suffix.

Exc.	V.G.	Good	Fair	Poor
2500	1850	1200	700	500

Mauser 2 Digit Date

4" barrel, 9mm caliber. The last two digits of the year of manufacture—41 or 42—are stamped over the chamber. There is a stock lug, and the Mauser banner is on the front toggle link. The extractor and safety are both marked, and the proofmarks were commercial. Grips are either walnut or black plastic. There were approximately 2,000 manufactured for sale to Nazi political groups. They have one- to five-digit serial numbers—some have the letter suffix.

Mauser 2 Digit Date • Courtesy Gale Morgan

Exc.	V.G.	Good	Fair	Poor
2800	2200	1500	900	650

KRIEGHOFF MANUFACTURED LUGERS

S Code Krieghoff

4" barrel, 9mm caliber. The Krieghoff trademark is stamped on the front toggle link, and the letter "S" is stamped over the chamber. There is a stock lug, and the extractor and safety are both marked. The grips are brown checkered plastic. There were approximately 4,500 manufactured for the Luftwaffe with one- to four-digit serial numbers.

Courtesy Rock Island Auction Company

Exc.	V.G.	Good	Fair	Poor
5000	3200	1800	950	750

Grip Safety Krieghoff

4" barrel, 9mm caliber. The chamber area is blank, and the front toggle link is stamped with the Krieghoff trademark. There is a stock lug and a grip safety. The extractor is marked "Geleden," and the safety is marked "FEUER" (fire) in the lower position. The grips are checkered brown plastic. This is a rare Luger, and the number produced is not known.

Exc.	V.G.	Good	Fair	Poor
6000	4000	2800	1400	900

36 Date Krieghoff

4" barrel, 9mm caliber. It has a stock lug and the Krieghoff trademark on the front toggle link. The safety and extractor are marked, and the grips are brown plastic. The two-digit year of manufacture, 36, is stamped over the chamber. There were approximately 700 produced in the 3800-4500 serial number range.

Paul Goodwin photo

Exc.	V.G.	Good	Fair	Poor
4500	3850	2200	1200	950

4 Digit Dated Krieghoff

As above, with the date of production, 1936-1945, stamped above the chamber. There were approximately 9,000 manufactured within the 4500-14000 serial number range.

Courtesy Gale Morgan

Exc.	V.G.	Good	Fair	Poor
3750	3000	1850	950	750

LUGER ACCESSORIES

Detachable Carbine Stocks

Approximately 13" in length, with a sling swivel and horn buttplate.

Exc.	V.G.	Good	Fair	Poor
4000	3500	1500	700	500

Artillery Stock with Holster

The artillery stock is of a flat board style approximately 13.75" in length. There is a holster and magazine pouches with straps attached. This is a desirable addition to the Artillery Luger.

Exc.	V.G.	Good	Fair	Poor
1500	1000	500	400	300

Navy Stock without Holster

As above, but 12.75" in length with a metal disc inlaid on the left side.

Exc.	V.G.	Good	Fair	Poor
2000	1500	1000	500	400

NOTE: With holster add 100%.

Ideal Stock/Holster with Grips

A telescoping metal tube stock with an attached leather holster. It is used in conjunction with a metal-backed set of plain grips that correspond to the metal hooks on the stock and allow attachment. This Ideal Stock is U.S. patented and is so marked.

Exc.	V.G.	Good	Fair	Poor
2000	1400	1000	700	450

Drum Magazine 1st Issue

A 32-round, snail-like affair that is used with the Artillery Luger. It is also used with an adapter in the German 9mm submachine gun. The 1st Issue has a telescoping tube that is used to wind the spring. There is a dust cover that protects the interior from dirt.

Exc.	V.G.	Good	Fair	Poor
1200	800	600	350	300

Drum Magazine 2nd Issue

As above, with a folding spring winding lever.

Exc.	V.G.	Good	Fair	Poor
1000	700	500	350	300

Drum Magazine Loading Tool

This tool is slipped over the magazine and allows the spring to be compressed so that cartridges could be inserted.

Exc.	V.G.	Good	Fair	Poor
600	550	500	300	200

Drum Magazine Unloading Tool

The origin of this tool is unknown and caution should be exercised prior to purchase.

Drum Carrying Case

The same caveat as above applies.

Exc.	V.G.	Good	Fair	Poor
250	200	125	100	50

Holsters

Produced in a wide variety of styles.

Exc.	V.G.	Good	Fair	Poor
350	275	150	60	50

LANGENHAN, FRIEDRICH

Langenhan Army Model

A blowback-operated semiautomatic pistol chambered for the 7.65mm Auto Pistol cartridge. It has a 4" barrel and a detachable magazine that holds 8 rounds. The pistol was made with a separate breechblock that is held into the slide by a screw. This feature doomed this pistol to eventual failure as when this screw became worn, it could loosen when firing and allow the breechblock to pivot upwards—and the slide would then be propelled rearward and into the face of the shooter. This is not a comforting thought. This pistol was produced and used in WWI only and was never offered commercially. It is marked "F.L. Selbstlade DRGM." The finish is blued, and the grips are molded rubber, with "F.L." at the top.

CAUTION: This is an unsafe weapon to fire.

Exc.	V.G.	Good	Fair	Poor
300	225	200	150	100

P.38

THE GERMAN WWII SERVICE PISTOL

Walther developed its German military service pistol, the P.38 or Model HP (Heerespistole), in 1937. It was adopted by the German military as its primary handgun in 1938. The background behind this adoption by the German military is an interesting one. In the 1930s, the German Army High Command wanted German arms manufacturers to develop a large caliber semiautomatic pistol to replace the Luger, which was difficult and costly to manufacture. The army wanted a pistol that was easy to manufacture as well as simple to assemble and disassemble. It also required a pistol that could be produced by several manufacturers if necessary and one whose parts would be interchangeable among manufacturers. Walther had just completed its Model HP for worldwide distribution and had the advantage over the other German companies. The German High Command approved Walther's design with only a few mechanical changes. This designation, the P.38, was not used by Walther on its commercial guns. Production began in late 1939 for both civilian and military use. Both military and commercial versions were produced throughout the war years. The civilian pistol was referred to as the MOD HP until late in the war, when a few were marked "MOD P.38" to take advantage of the identity of the military pistol. In late 1942, Mauser and Spreewerke began production of the P.38. Mauser was assigned the code "BYF" and in 1945 the code was changed to "SVW." Spreewerke's code was "CYQ." Late in the war the die stamp broke and the code appears as "CVQ."

The P.38 is a double action semiautomatic pistol that is short-recoil operated and fires from a locked breech by means of an external hammer. It is chambered for the 9mm Parabellum and has a 5" barrel. The detachable magazine holds 8 cartridges and the front sight is adjustable for windage. Initially the finish was a high quality blue, but when the war effort increased, less time was spent on the finish. The P.38 was equipped with two styles of plastic grips. Early pistols have a checkered grip and later grips are the military ribbed variety; the later style is much more common. The P.38 was produced by three companies and each had its own distinct markings and variations as outlined below. Despite the large number of variations that the P.38 collector will encounter, it is important for him to be aware that there are no known documented examples of P.38s that are factory engraved, nickel-plated, have barrels that are longer or shorter than standard, or built as military presentation pistols.

Collectors should be made aware of a final note. The P.38 pistol was first adopted more than 50 years ago. During that period of time the pistol has seen use all over the world. After the end of WWII several governments came into possession of fairly large quantities of P.38s and used them in their own military and police agencies. Many countries have reworked these older P.38s with both original and new component parts. The former U.S.S.R. is the primary source of reworked P.38s. Many of these pistols have been completely refinished and re-proofed by a number of countries. The collector should be aware of the existence of reworked P.38s and examine any P.38 carefully to determine if the pistol is original German military issue. These reworked pistols bring substantially lower prices than original P.38s.

NOTE: As of 1997 the Ukraine is now the primary source of pistols. Almost all are importer marked and have been cold dipped blued. Some are reworked and others are original except for the finish.

WALTHER COMMERCIAL

The Commercial version of the P.38 is identified by commercial proofmarks of a crown over N or an eagle over N. Production started at around serial number 1000 and went through serial number 26659. This was the first of the commercial pistols and was a high-quality, well-made gun with a complete inscription on the left slide. A few of these early pistols were equipped with checkered wooden grips. The quality decreased as the war progressed. There are many variations of these commercial models and values can vary from $1,000 to $16,000. It is suggested that these pistols be appraised and evaluated by an expert. For postwar Walther P.38 pistols see the Walther section.

A few of the Walther Commercial Model variations follow:

MOD HP–Early w/High Gloss Blue

Courtesy Orvel Reichert

Exc.	V.G.	Good	Fair	Poor
2800	1750	950	750	450

MOD HP–Early w/High Gloss Blue & Alloy Frame

Courtesy Orvel Reichert

Exc.	V.G.	Good	Fair	Poor
8000	5500	3500	2000	1000

MOD HP–Late w/Military Blue Finish

Courtesy Orvel Reichert

Exc.	V.G.	Good	Fair	Poor
1850	1200	750	550	350

NOTE: Add $200 for "Eagle/359" on right side.

Selected P.38 Stampings

Late Mauser 44-45 right slide

Late war cog hammer

fnh barrel code

Reject mark * (asterisk)

Early 42-43 right slide

Post-War East German military

cyq right slide

Walther right slide

All photos courtesy Orvel Reichert

MOD P38–Late with Military Blue (1800 produced)

Courtesy Orvel Reichert

Exc.	V.G.	Good	Fair	Poor
1800	1200	750	600	40

WALTHER MILITARY

Courtesy Orvel Reichert

Courtesy Orvel Reichert

ZERO SERIES

This was the first of the military P.38s and they are well made with a high polish finish. These pistols have the Walther banner and the designation P.38. The serial number began with 01 and went through about 013714. The First Zero Series has a concealed extractor and rectangular firing pin. About 1,000 First Zero Series were built. The Second Zero Series has a rectangular firing pin and standard extractor, with a production of about 2,300. The Third Zero Series has a standard firing pin and standard extractor and has the highest production with 10,000 built.

First Issue Zero Series

Courtesy Orvel Reichert

Exc.	V.G.	Good	Fair	Poor
7500	5000	3500	2500	1500

Second Issue Zero Series

Courtesy Orvel Reichert

Exc.	V.G.	Good	Fair	Poor
6500	4000	3250	2000	1000

Third Issue Zero Series

Courtesy Orvel Reichert

Exc.	V.G.	Good	Fair	Poor
2500	1750	1250	800	500

480 CODE

This code was utilized by Walther in late 1940 and represents the first true military contract pistols. There were approximately 7,250 guns produced under this code. There are two sub-variations: one with a round lanyard loop and the other with a rectangular lanyard loop.

Courtesy Orvel Reichert

Exc.	V.G.	Good	Fair	Poor
5000	3500	2500	1750	1000

"AC" CODES

This variation follows the 480 code.

"ac" (no date)

This variation has on the slide "P.38ac" then the serial number only. This is the first use of the "ac" code by Walther. There were approximately 2,700 pistols produced with this code and this is the rarest of all military P.38s.

Courtesy Orvel Reichert

Exc.	V.G.	Good	Fair	Poor
7500	4800	3750	2800	2000

"ac40"

There are two types of "ac40s." The first variation is the ac with the 40 added, that is the "40" was hand stamped below the "ac". There are about 6,000 of these produced. The second variation is the "ac40" rolled on together. There are also about 14,000 of these produced as well. The "ac" 40 added is more valuable than the standard "ac40."

"ac40" (added)

Courtesy Orvel Reichert

Exc.	V.G.	Good	Fair	Poor
3500	2500	1750	1000	600

"ac40" (standard)

Courtesy Orvel Reichert

Exc.	V.G.	Good	Fair	Poor
2000	1200	950	700	500

"ac41"

There are three variations of the "ac41." The first variation has "ac" on left triggerguard and features a high gloss blue. About 25,000 of this variation were made. The second variation, about 70,000 were produced, also has a high gloss blue but does not have "ac" on the triggerguard. The third variation features a military blue rather than a high gloss blue and had a production run of about 15,000 pistols.

"ac41" (1st variation)

Courtesy Orvel Reichert

Exc.	V.G.	Good	Fair	Poor
1700	900	700	500	350

"ac41" (2nd variation)

Courtesy Orvel Reichert

Exc.	V.G.	Good	Fair	Poor
1300	750	600	450	300

"ac41" (3rd variation)

Courtesy Orvel Reichert

Exc.	V.G.	Good	Fair	Poor
1100	550	475	400	300

"ac42"

There are two variations of the "ac42" code. The first has an eagle over 359 stamped on all small parts as do all preceding variations and a production of 21,000 pistols. The second variation does not have the eagle over 359 stamped on small parts. This second variation has a large production run of 100,000 pistols.

"ac42" (1st variation)

Courtesy Orvel Reichert

Exc.	V.G.	Good	Fair	Poor
900	450	400	350	275

"ac42" (2nd variation)

Exc.	V.G.	Good	Fair	Poor
800	500	400	300	250

"ac43"

This code has three variations. The first is a standard date with "ac" over "43". It has an early frame and extractor cut. The second variation has the late frame and extractor cut. Both variations are frequently encountered because approximately 130,000 were built.

"ac43" (1st variation)

Courtesy Orvel Reichert

Exc.	V.G.	Good	Fair	Poor
700	400	300	250	200

"ac43" (2nd variation)

Exc.	V.G.	Good	Fair	Poor
550	350	300	250	200

"ac43" single line slide

This variation represents the beginning of the placement of the date on the same line with the production code. There were approximately 20,000 built in this variation.

Courtesy Orvel Reichert

Exc.	V.G.	Good	Fair	Poor
900	550	450	350	250

"ac44"

This variation also has the date stamped beside "ac" and is fairly common. About 120,000 were produced.

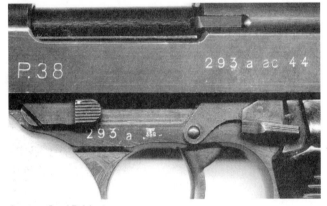

Courtesy Orvel Reichert

Exc.	V.G.	Good	Fair	Poor
650	400	300	250	200

Note: Add $50 for FN frame (Eagle/140).

ac44 FN Slide left and right sides • Courtesy Orvel Reichert

"ac45"

This code has three variations. The first has all matching numbers on a plum colored frame. About 32,000 of this first variation were produced. The second variation has a capital "A" in place of the lowercase "a." The third variation has all major parts with factory mismatched numbers, with a single eagle over 359 on the slide. The first variation is the most common of this code.

"ac45" (1st variation)

Courtesy Orvel Reichert

Exc.	V.G.	Good	Fair	Poor
650	400	325	300	250

"ac45" (2nd variation)

Courtesy Orvel Reichert

Exc.	V.G.	Good	Fair	Poor
750	400	325	300	250

"ac45" (3rd variation)

Courtesy Orvel Reichert

Exc.	V.G.	Good	Fair	Poor
500	350	325	300	250

Note: Add $50 for pistols with Czech barrels; barrel code "fnh."

"ac45" Zero Series

This is a continuation of the commercial pistols with a military marked slide. This series has "ac45" plus the 0 prefix serial number on the left side as well as the usual P.38 roll stamp. It may or may not have commercial proofmarks. A total of 1,800 of these "ac45" Zero Series guns were produced in 1945. They are often seen with a plum colored slide.

Exc.	V.G.	Good	Fair	Poor
1500	900	700	450	325

MAUSER MILITARY

The following P.38s were produced by Mauser and are identified by various Mauser codes.

Courtesy Orvel Reichert

Courtesy Orvel Reichert

"byf42"

Approximately 19,000 P.38s were manufactured in this variation. Some of these pistols will have a flat blue finish.

Courtesy Orvel Reichert

Exc.	V.G.	Good	Fair	Poor
1500	950	700	500	300

"byf43"

A common variation of the P.38 with approximately 140,000 produced.

Courtesy Orvel Reichert

Exc.	V.G.	Good	Fair	Poor
700	400	300	250	200

"byf44"

Another common variation with a total production of about 150,000 guns.

Courtesy Orvel Reichert

Exc.	V.G.	Good	Fair	Poor
700	400	300	250	200

Note: Add $100 for dual tone finish that is a combination of blue and gray components.

AC43/44-FN slide

Courtesy Orvel Reichert

Exc.	V.G.	Good	Fair	Poor
1500	950	725	600	450

"svw45"

The Mauser code is changed from "byf" to "svw." This variation was produced until the end of the war when France took over production and continued through 1946. French-produced guns will have a 5-point star on the right side of the slide. A large number of these French pistols have been imported thereby depressing values.

"svw45"-German Proofed

Courtesy Orvel Reichert

Exc.	V.G.	Good	Fair	Poor
1500	900	650	450	300

"svw45"-French Proofed

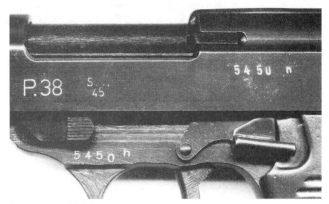

Courtesy Orvel Reichert

Exc.	V.G.	Good	Fair	Poor
500	300	275	250	200

"svw46"-French Proofed

Courtesy Orvel Reichert

Exc.	V.G.	Good	Fair	Poor
600	450	400	350	300

MAUSER "POLICE" P.38

Mauser produced the only Nazi era Police P.38 during the 1943 to 1945 period. It is generally believed that only 8,000 guns were serially produced, although a few "oddballs" show up beyond that range.

Police guns are easily recognized by the appearance of a commercial proof (eagle over N) instead of the Military proof (eagle over swastika). They also have a civilian (Police) acceptance stamp (either an Eagle L or Eagle F).

The guns will have a stacked code with date below the code. Earliest guns were coded "byf" over "43" and later, "byf" over "44". In the late 1944 production, a group of slides manufactured for Walther at the FN plant in Belgium were received and used. These slides all have the "ac" over "43" or "ac" over "44" code. Finally, in 1945, a few "svw" over "45" coded guns were made. These Walther coded slides are hard to find .... the 1945 guns are *quite* rare.

Because of the increased value of these guns, it is wise to have them examined by an expert before purchasing.

"byf/43"

Exc.	V.G.	Good	Fair	Poor
2200	1500	1200	800	500

"byf/44"

Exc.	V.G.	Good	Fair	Poor
2200	1500	1200	800	500

"ac/43"

Exc.	V.G.	Good	Fair	Poor
4200	3000	2000	1250	800

"ac/44"

Exc.	V.G.	Good	Fair	Poor
4200	3000	2000	1250	800

"svw/45"

Exc.	V.G.	Good	Fair	Poor
5200	4000	2250	1600	1000

SPREEWERKE MILITARY

Production of the P.38 began at Spreewerke (Berlin) in late 1942 and Spreewerke used the code "cyq" that had been assigned to it at the beginning of the war.

"cyq" (eagle/211 on frame, 2 known)

Exc.	V.G.	Good	Fair	Poor
3500	—	—	—	—

"cyq" (1st variation)

The first 500 of these guns have the eagle over 359 on some small parts and command a premium. Value depends on markings and an expert should be consulted for values.

Courtesy Orvel Reichert

Exc.	V.G.	Good	Fair	Poor
1250	950	750	600	500

"cyq" (standard variation)

There were approximately 300,000 of these pistols produced in this variation which makes them the most common of all P.38 variations.

Courtesy Orvel Reichert

Exc.	V.G.	Good	Fair	Poor
500	300	275	250	200

Note: If "A" or "B" prefix add $250.

A "cyq" series with an "A" prefix serial number • Courtesy Orvel Reicher

"cyq" Zero Series

This variation features a Zero ahead of the serial number and only about 5,000 of these guns were produced.

Courtesy Orvel Reichert

Exc.	V.G.	Good	Fair	Poor
1100	500	400	350	275

NOTE: Add $250 for AC43 or AC44 marked "FN" slide.

Walther Model P-1

This is a post-war P.38. This model was adopted by the German army as the standard sidearm in 1957, and remained in service until 1980.

Exc.	V.G.	Good	Fair	Poor
500	300	275	250	200

MAUSER POCKET PISTOLS

Bibliographical Note: For historical information, technical data, and photos see Roy Pender III, *Mauser Pocket Pistols, 1910-1946*, Houston, 1971.

Model 1914

Courtesy Butterfield & Butterfield, San Francisco, California

A 7.65mm caliber semiautomatic pistol with a 3.5" barrel, fixed sights, and wrap-around walnut grips. The slide marked "Waffenfabrik Mauser A.G. Oberndorf A.N. Mauser's Patent." The frame has the Mauser banner stamped on its left side. Manufactured between 1914 and 1934. Almost all model 1914 pistols built between serial numbers 40,000 and 180,000 will be seen with German military acceptance stamps. A few will have the Prussian Eagle stamped on the front of the triggerguard.

Courtesy Wallis & Wallis, Lewes, Sussex, England

Exc.	V.G.	Good	Fair	Poor
450	300	225	150	100

Model 1934

Similar to the Model 1910 and Model 1914, with the slide marked "Mauser-Werke A.G. Oberndorf A. N." It has the Mauser banner stamped on the frame. The reverse side is marked with the caliber and "D.R.P. u A.P." Manufactured between 1934 and 1939. Those with Nazi Waffenamt markings are worth approximately 20 percent more than the values listed below. Those marked with an eagle over the letter "M" (navy marked) are worth approximately 100% more than the values listed below.

Courtesy Gale Morgan

Exc.	V.G.	Good	Fair	Poor
525	400	300	150	100

Model HSC

A 7.65mm or 9mm short caliber double action semiautomatic pistol with a 3.4" barrel, 7- or 8-shot magazine and fixed sights. Introduced in 1938 and produced in the variations listed below.

Courtesy Orvel Reichert

Low Grip Screw Model

As above, with screws that attach the grip located near the bottom of the grip. Highly polished blue, checkered walnut grips, and the early address without the lines and has the Eagle N proof. Some have been observed with Nazi Kreigsmarine markings. Approximately 2,000 were manufactured.

Exc.	V.G.	Good	Fair	Poor
3500	2500	1400	750	650

Early Commercial Model

A highly-polished blued finish, checkered walnut grips, the standard Mauser address on the slide, and the Eagle N proofmark. The floorplate of the magazine stamped with the Mauser banner.

Exc.	V.G.	Good	Fair	Poor
650	500	350	175	125

Transition Model

As above, but not as highly finished.

Exc.	V.G.	Good	Fair	Poor
525	400	300	150	100

Early Nazi Army Model

Highly polished with Waffenamt No. 135 or 655 markings. Checkered walnut grips. Acceptance marks are located on the left side of the triggerguard.

Courtesy Orvel Reichert

Exc.	V.G.	Good	Fair	Poor
650	550	400	200	125

Late Nazi Army Model

Blued or parkerized, with walnut or plastic grips, and the 135 acceptance mark only. It also has the Eagle N proof.

Exc.	V.G.	Good	Fair	Poor
450	375	250	150	100

Early Nazi Navy Model

Highly polished with checkered walnut grips and the eagle over "M" marking on the front grip strap.

Exc.	V.G.	Good	Fair	Poor
1000	800	550	400	300

Wartime Nazi Navy Model

Similar to the above, with the navy acceptance mark on the side of the triggerguard. Blued, with either checkered walnut or plastic grips. It has the standard Mauser address and banner and also the Eagle N proof.

Exc.	V.G.	Good	Fair	Poor
700	600	500	400	200

Early Nazi Police Model

Identical to the Early Commercial Model with an eagle over "L" mark on the left side of the triggerguard.

Courtesy Orvel Reichert

Exc.	V.G.	Good	Fair	Poor
600	500	425	250	175

Wartime Nazi Police Model
As above, with a three-line Mauser address.

Exc.	V.G.	Good	Fair	Poor
500	400	350	250	175

Wartime Commercial Model
As above, without acceptance markings on the triggerguard.

Exc.	V.G.	Good	Fair	Poor
425	350	300	200	125

French Manufactured Model
Blued or parkerized with walnut or plastic grips and the trigger-guard marked on the left side with the monogram "MR."

Exc.	V.G.	Good	Fair	Poor
325	275	225	150	100

SAUER, J. P. & SON
Bibliographical Note: For historical information, technical data, and photos see Jim Cate's text.

Text and prices by Jim Cate

SAUER MODEL 1913
FIRST SERIES, which incorporates an extra safety button on the left side of the frame near the trigger and the rear sight, is simply a milled recess in the cocking knob itself. The serial number range runs from 1 to approximately 4750 and this first series is found only in 7.65mm caliber. All were for commercial sales as far as can be determined. Some were tested by various militaries, no doubt.

A. European variation—all slide legends are in the German language.

B. English Export variation—slide legends are marked J.P. Sauer & Son, Suhl - Prussia, "Sauer's Patent" Pat'd May 20 1912.

Both were sold in thick paper cartons or boxes with the color being a reddish purple with gold colored letters, etc. Examples of the very early European variation are found with the English language brochure or manual as well as an extra magazine, cleaning brush, and grease container. These were shipped to England or the U.S. prior to Sauer producing the English Export variation.

A. European variation:

Exc.	V.G.	Good	Fair	Poor
1100	900	650	400	250

B. English Export variation:

Exc.	V.G.	Good	Fair	Poor
1450	1150	800	500	300

Original box with accessories and manual: Add $500 if complete and in very good to excellent condition.

SECOND SERIES, extra safety button eliminated, rear sight acts as cocking knob retainer.

A. Commercial variation
Normal European/German slide markings are normally found; however, it has been called to my attention that there are English Export pistols in this **SECOND SERIES** which have the English markings on the slide which are similar to those found on the **FIRST SERIES** of the Model 1913. This is applicable to both the 7.65mm and 6.35mm model pistols. These are exceptionally scarce pistols and should command at least a 50% premium, perhaps more due to their rarity. This commercial variation had factory manuals printed in English, Spanish, and German which came with the cardboard boxed pistols. With the original Sauer box accessories and manual: Add $300 if in very good to excellent condition.

Caliber 7.65mm variation

Exc.	V.G.	Good	Fair	Poor
450	375	300	250	100

Caliber 7.65mm variation with all words in English (i.e Son, Prussia, etc.)

Exc.	V.G.	Good	Fair	Poor
700	575	450	300	200

Caliber 6.35mm variation
This particular pistol must be divided into three (3) subvariations.

This variation appears to be in a serial number range of its own. The first subvariation appears to run from 1 to 40,000. It is highly doubtful if this quantity was manufactured. The second subvariation incorporates a Zusatzsicherung or Additional Safety which can be seen between the normal safety lever and the top of the left grip. It locked the trigger bar when in use. This second range appears to run from approximately serial number 40,000 to 51,000, which probably was continuous in the number produced. Lastly, the third subvariation examples were manufactured during or after 1926. The triggerguard has a different shape; the slide has a greater area of vertical milled finger grooves; the added Additional Safety (Zusatzsicherung) now acts as the hold open device as well. These are found up to approximately 57,000. Then a few examples of the first subvariation are found from 57,000 up to about 62,500. This was, no doubt, usage of remaining parts.

Caliber 6.35mm first subvariation

Exc.	V.G.	Good	Fair	Poor
350	300	250	150	75

Caliber 6.35mm second subvariation

Exc.	V.G.	Good	Fair	Poor
350	300	250	150	75

Caliber 6.35mm third subvariation

Exc.	V.G.	Good	Fair	Poor
450	375	300	200	100

Caliber 6.35mm English export variation (all words in English; i.e. Son, Prussia, etc.) **Very Rare, only one example known.**

Exc.	V.G.	Good	Fair	Poor
850	700	500	300	200

Please note that any commercial pistol could be special ordered with a factory nickel finish, special grip material (pearl, wood, etc.), as well as different types of engraving. It would be in your best interest to have these pistols examined by an expert.

B. Police variations

These will be of the standard German Commercial configuration but nearly always having the Zusatzsicherung (Additional Safety) added to the pistol. This safety is found between the regular safety lever and the top of the left grip. Police used both calibers, 7.65mm and 6.35mm, but the 7.65 was predominant. After the early part of the 1930s the 6.35 was not available to police departments. Thus the 6.35mm police marked Sauer is rather scarce in relation to the 7.65mm caliber. A few in 7.65mm are dated 1920 on the left side of the frame and were used by auxiliary policemen in Bavaria. Normal police property markings are on the front or rear grip-straps. Most were originally issued with at least two magazines and a police accepted holster. The magazines were usually numbered and the holsters are found with and without pistol numbers.

Caliber 6.35mm police marked but without Zusatzsicherung

Exc.	V.G.	Good	Fair	Poor
400	350	275	200	75

Caliber 6.35mm police marked with Zusatzsicherung

Exc.	V.G.	Good	Fair	Poor
450	375	275	200	75

Caliber 7.65mm police marked without Zusatzsicherung

Exc.	V.G.	Good	Fair	Poor
375	325	275	175	125

Caliber 7.65mm police marked with Zusatzsicherung

Exc.	V.G.	Good	Fair	Poor
400	350	275	175	125

NOTE: Add 10% for one correctly numbered magazine, or 20% if found with both correctly numbered magazines. Add 30% if found with correct holster and magazines.

C. R.F.V. (Reich Finanz Verwaltung)

This Sauer variation is rarely found in any condition. The R.F.V. markings and property number could be 1 to 4 digits. This variation is found in both calibers and was used by the Reich's Customs and Finance Department personnel.

Caliber 6.35mm R.F.V. marked pistols

Exc.	V.G.	Good	Fair	Poor
800	650	500	350	250

Caliber 7.65mm R.F.V. marked pistols

Exc.	V.G.	Good	Fair	Poor
750	600	400	300	200

D. Imperial Military variations

These were normal German commercial variations of the time period having either the Imperial Eagle acceptance marking applied on the front of the triggerguard and having the small Imperial Army inspector's acceptance marking (crown over a scriptic letter) on the right side of the frame close to the Nitro proof; or having just the Imperial Army inspector's marking alone. Usually these pistols are found in the 40,000 to 85,000 range. However, the quantity actually Imperial Military accepted is quite low even though thousands were privately purchased by the officer corps. There are examples in 6.35mm which are Imperial Military accepted but these are very scarce.

Caliber 7.65mm Imperial Military accepted pistols

Exc.	V.G.	Good	Fair	Poor
550	450	350	275	150

Caliber 6.35mm Imperial Military accepted pistols

Exc.	V.G.	Good	Fair	Poor
700	500	375	300	150

E. Paramilitary marked Sauer pistols, of the 1925-35 period

A very few of the Model 1913 pistols will have been marked by paramilitary groups or organizations of this period. Usually this marking is no more than a series of numbers above another series of numbers, such as 23 over 12. These are found usually on the left side of the frame next to the left grip. Most of these numbers are indicative of property numbers assigned to a particular pistol's belonging to a particular SA Group, Stahlhelm, or a right-wing organization such as the Red Front (early communist). Any pistol of this type should be examined by an expert to determine if it is an original example.

Exc.	V.G.	Good	Fair	Poor
350	300	275	200	100

F. Norwegian police usage, post World War II

After the war was over many surplus German weapons were put back into use by the government of Norway. The Germans had occupied this country and large numbers of weapons remained when the fighting ended. This included a large number of surplus Sauer pistols being utilized by the police (POLITI)

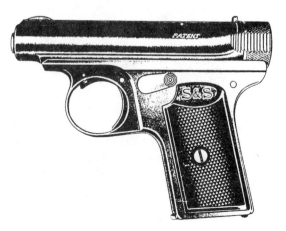

forces. Most of the Sauers that were used by the Politi which have been imported into the U.S. have been the Model 1913; however, there were a number of the Model 1930 pistols which reached our country as well. All examples, regardless of the model, have the word POLITI stamped on the slide as well as a rampant lion on a shield under a crown marking. Following this is the property number and this number is also stamped into the left side of the frame. Most saw much usage during the postwar period. All are in 7.65mm caliber.

Exc.	V.G.	Good	Fair	Poor
350	300	200	150	100

MODEL 38 AND 38-H (H MODEL) VARIATIONS
A. MODEL 38
This pistol started at 260,000. It is Crown N Nitro proofed, has a cocking/decocking lever, and a loaded indicator pin, and is double action. It has a high polish blue; is in 7.65mm (the standard production pistol); is found without the thumbsafety on the slide; with a pinned mag release. VERY RARE.

1. One Line Slide Legend variation (about 250 produced)

Exc.	V.G.	Good	Fair	Poor
2500	1600	1200	600	300

2. Two Line Slide Legend variation C/N proofs, blued, with pinned magazine release (about 850 produced). VERY RARE.

Exc.	V.G.	Good	Fair	Poor
1850	1400	1000	500	275

3. Two Line Slide Legend variation C/N proofs, blued, magazine release button retained by a screw. RARE.

Exc.	V.G.	Good	Fair	Poor
1000	850	600	400	275

NOTE: Add $250 for factory nickel; $350 for factory chrome; $1000 for engraving; $500 for NIROSTA marked barrel.

4. SA der NSDAP Gruppe Thuringen marked variation
blued, C/N proofs, with mag release button held by a screw. VERY RARE.

Exc.	V.G.	Good	Fair	Poor
3000	2000	1000	500	275

B. MODEL 38-H or H MODEL
This model has a thumbsafety on the slide, Crown N Nitro proof, high polish blued finish, a cocking/decocking lever, double action, and is found in 7.65mm caliber as the standard production pistol. This model is found only with the two line slide legend or logo. Type 1, variation 2.

1. Standard Commercial variation as described above:

Exc.	V.G.	Good	Fair	Poor
850	700	475	300	175

NOTE: Add $100 for factory nickel (factory chromed has not been identified); $1000 for factory engraving; $250 for exotic grip material; $500 for NIROSTA marked stainless barrel.

2. SA der NSDAP Gruppe Thuringia variation
Same as 1 above except having SA markings on slide, with blued finish. VERY RARE.

Exc.	V.G.	Good	Fair	Poor
2500	1800	600	350	200

NOTE: Add $700 for SA marked ankle holster in excellent condition.

3. L.M. MODEL
(Leicht Model–lightweight model); frame and slide made of DURAL (Duraluminum), in the 264800 range, with thumb safety, and regular black bakelite grips. EXTREMELY RARE.

Exc.	V.G.	Good	Fair	Poor
3850	3250	2500	1500	850

4. Police accepted variation; found with Police Eagle C acceptance on left triggerguard and having Crown N proofs. RARE.

Exc.	V.G.	Good	Fair	Poor
850	700	500	300	175

TYPE TWO MODEL 38-H (H MODEL)
There are no Model 38 pistols in the Type Two description, only the H Model with thumbsafety. These begin at serial number 269100 and have the Eagle N Nitro proofs, with a blued high polish finish and black bakelite grips. The normal caliber is 7.65mm.

A. H Model
1. Standard Commercial

Exc.	V.G.	Good	Fair	Poor
750	550	475	300	200

NOTE: Add $1500 for boxed examples complete with factory manual, clean ring rod, all accessories, extra magazine, etc. $250 for factory nickel, $350 for factory chrome, $1000 for factory engraving.

2. .22 Caliber variation, found in 269900 range
Slide and magazines are marked CAL. .22 LANG. (Some with steel frame and slides; some with Dural frames and slides.) VERY RARE.

Exc.	V.G.	Good	Fair	Poor
2500	1800	1000	400	250

3. Jager Model

A special order pistol in .22 caliber which is similar in appearance to Walther's 1936 Jagerschafts pistol. VERY RARE, and watch for fakes.

Exc.	V.G.	Good	Fair	Poor
2500	1850	1200	600	250

4. Police Eagle C and Eagle F acceptance variations

These are the first Eagle N (post January 1940) police accepted pistols and are found in the 270000 to 276000 ranges. (Add 25% for E/F.)

Exc.	V.G.	Good	Fair	Poor
650	500	400	325	200

5. German Military variation

This is the first official military accepted range of 2000 pistols. It is in a TEST range found between 271000 and 273000. Two Eagle 37 military acceptance marks are found on the triggerguard.

Exc.	V.G.	Good	Fair	Poor
1200	900	675	475	300

6. Second Military variation

These pistols are found with the high polish finish but have only one Eagle 37 acceptance mark. The letter H is found on all small parts.

Exc.	V.G.	Good	Fair	Poor
600	425	350	275	175

7. Police Eagle C acceptance variation

This variation includes the remainder of the high polish blued police accepted pistols.

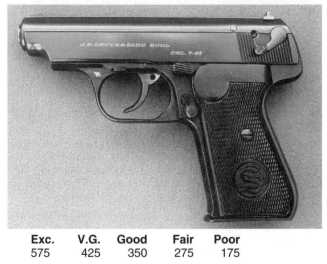

Exc.	V.G.	Good	Fair	Poor
575	425	350	275	175

NOTE: Add $50 for matching magazine, $200 for both matching magazines and correct police holster; $300 for both matching mags and correct matching numbered, police accepted & dated holster.

TYPE THREE 38-H MODEL (H MODEL)

This terminology is used because of the change of the exterior finish of the Sauer pistols. Due to the urgency of the war, the order was received to not polish the exterior surfaces of the pistols as had been done previously. There was also a change in the formulation of the grip's material. Later in this range there will be found stamped parts, zinc triggers and magazine bottoms, etc. used to increase the pistol's production. Type Three has a full slide legend.

A. H Model

1. Military accepted with one Eagle 37 Waffenamt mark

Exc.	V.G.	Good	Fair	Poor
500	450	350	275	150

2. Commercial, with only Eagle N Nitro proofmarks

Exc.	V.G.	Good	Fair	Poor
450	400	350	250	150

NOTE: See Type Two Commercial info above, prices apply here also.

3. Police accepted with the Police Eagle C acceptance

Exc.	V.G.	Good	Fair	Poor
500	425	350	250	150

NOTE: See Type Two Police info above, prices apply here also.

TYPE FOUR 38-H MODEL (H MODEL)

This is a continuation of the pistol as described in Type Three except the J.P. Sauer & Sohn, Suhl legend is dropped from the slide and only CAL. 7.65 is found on the left side. The word PATENT may or may not appear on the right side. Many are found with a zinc trigger.

A. H Model

1. Military accepted with one Eagle 37 Waffenamt mark

Exc.	V.G.	Good	Fair	Poor
500	450	350	275	150

2. Commercial, having only the Eagle N Nitro proofs

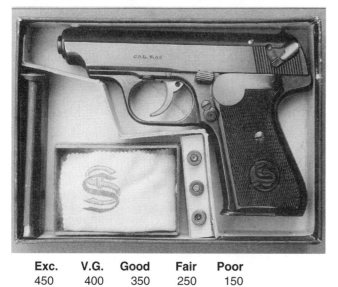

Exc.	V.G.	Good	Fair	Poor
450	400	350	250	150

NOTE: See Type Two Commercial info above, prices apply here also.

3. Police accepted with the Police Eagle C acceptance

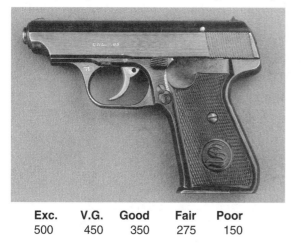

Exc.	V.G.	Good	Fair	Poor
500	450	350	275	150

NOTE: See Type Two price info above, prices apply here also.

4. Eigentum NSDAP SA Gruppe Alpenland slide marked pistols

These unique pistols are found in the 456000 and 457000 serial number ranges. They have thumb safety levers on the slides.

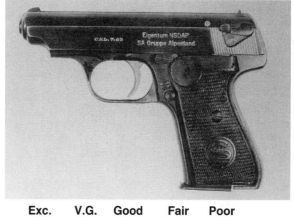

Exc.	V.G.	Good	Fair	Poor
2800	1800	1000	450	250

5. NSDAP SA Gruppe Alpenland slide marked pistols

These unique pistols are found in the 465000 serial number range. They have thumb safety levers on the slide.

Exc.	V.G.	Good	Fair	Poor
2800	1800	1000	450	250

6. H. Himmler Presentation Pistols

These desirable pistols have a high polish finish with DEM SCHARFSCHUTZEN - H. HIMMLER on the left side of the slide (with no other markings), and J.P. SAUER & SOHN over CAL.7.65 on the right side (opposite of normal). These pistols came in imitation leather cover metal cases with cloth interiors having a cleaning brush, extra magazine and cartridges.

Exc.	V.G.	Good	Fair	Poor
15000	12000	8500	3500	1000

B. MODEL 38

To speed up production even more, the thumb safety (Hand-sicherung-Hammer safety) was eliminated. The side continues to be marked only with CAL. 7.65. The frame's serial number changes from the right side to the left side at 472000 with overlaps up to 489000.

1. Military accepted with one Eagle 37 Waffenamt mark

Exc.	V.G.	Good	Fair	Poor
450	400	350	250	175

2. Commercial, having only the Eagle N Nitro proofs

Exc.	V.G.	Good	Fair	Poor
450	400	350	250	175

NOTE: See Type Two Commercial info above, prices apply here also.

3. Police accepted with the Police Eagle C acceptance

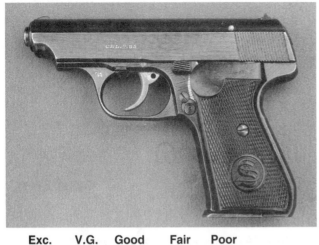

Exc.	V.G.	Good	Fair	Poor
575	450	400	300	200

4. Police accepted with the Police Eagle F acceptance

Exc.	V.G.	Good	Fair	Poor
475	400	350	250	175

NOTE: (3&4) See Type Two Police info above, prices apply here also.

TYPE FIVE MODEL 38 & H MODEL PISTOLS

There are two different basic variations of the Type Five Sauer pistols. Either may or may not have a thumbsafety lever on the slide. The main criteria is whether the frame is factory numbered as per normal and follows the chronological sequence of those pistols in the preceding model. After the frames were used, which were already numbered and finished upon the arrival of the U.S. army, the last variation came about. Neither variation has any Nitro proofmarks.

A. First variation

Factory numbered sequential frames starting on or near serial number 506800. Slides and breech blocks may or may not match.

Exc.	V.G.	Good	Fair	Poor
475	350	275	225	100

B. Second variation

Started with serial number 1; made from mostly rejected parts, generally have notched triggerguards, may or may not be blued, no Nitro proofs, slides may or may not have factory legends, etc. Approximately 300 assembled.

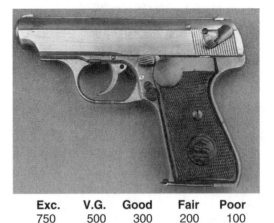

Exc.	V.G.	Good	Fair	Poor
750	500	300	200	100

NOTE: There are some pistols which have postwar Russian Crown N Nitro proofs. The Russians may have assembled a very few pistols after the U.S. army left this section after the war. Several have been found with newly made barrels in 7.65mm with a C/N proof.

WALTHER

Bibliographical Note: For technical details, historical information, and photos see James Rankin, *Walther*, Volumes I, II, and III, 1974-1981.

Model 6

A 9mm semiautomatic pistol. The largest of the Walther numbered pistols. Approximately 1,500 manufactured. Blued with checkered hard rubber grips with the Walther logo on each grip. Sometimes seen with plain checkered wood grips. Introduced 1915.

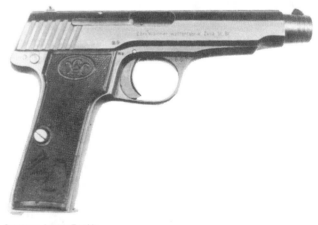

Courtesy James Rankin

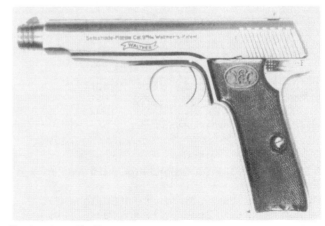

Courtesy James Rankin

Exc.	V.G.	Good	Fair	Poor
7000	5000	3000	1500	700

Model PP

Courtesy James Rankin

Courtesy James Rankin

A semiautomatic pistol in .22, .25, .32, and .380 caliber. Introduced in 1928. It was the first successful commercial double action pistol. It was manufactured in finishes of blue, silver, and gold, and with three different types of engraving. Grips were generally two-piece black or white plastic with the Walther banner on each grip. Grips in wood or ivory are seen, but usually on engraved guns. There are many variations of the Model PP and numerous NSDAP markings seen on the pre-1946 models that were produced during the Nazi regime. All reflect various prices.

Model PP .22 Caliber
Exc.	V.G.	Good	Fair	Poor
800	600	350	250	150

Model PP .25 Caliber
Exc.	V.G.	Good	Fair	Poor
5800	4000	2500	1500	600

Model PP .32 Caliber High Polished Finish
Exc.	V.G.	Good	Fair	Poor
450	325	275	225	175

Model PP .32 Caliber Milled Finish
Exc.	V.G.	Good	Fair	Poor
425	325	250	200	125

Model PP .380 Caliber
Exc.	V.G.	Good	Fair	Poor
950	750	550	475	350

Model PP .32 Caliber with Duraluminum Frame
Exc.	V.G.	Good	Fair	Poor
800	675	550	400	200

Model PP .32 Caliber with Bottom Magazine Release
Exc.	V.G.	Good	Fair	Poor
1100	800	600	400	200

Model PP .32 Caliber with Verchromt Finish
Exc.	V.G.	Good	Fair	Poor
2000	1450	1000	700	400

Courtesy Orvel Reichert

Model PP .32 Caliber in Blue, Silver, or Gold Finish and Full Coverage Engraving

Blue
Exc.	V.G.	Good	Fair	Poor
5000	3500	3000	1200	700

Silver
Exc.	V.G.	Good	Fair	Poor
6000	4000	3000	1200	700

Gold
Exc.	V.G.	Good	Fair	Poor
6500	4500	3500	1500	700

NOTE: Add $250 for ivory grips with any of the three above.
Add $700 for leather presentation cases.
Add $500 for .22 caliber.
Add $1000 for .380 caliber.

Model PP .32 Caliber, Allemagne Marked
Exc.	V.G.	Good	Fair	Poor
850	700	550	325	250

Model PP .32 Caliber, A.F. Stoeger Contract
Exc.	V.G.	Good	Fair	Poor
2500	1750	1050	700	400

Model PP .32 Caliber with Waffenamt Proofs. High Polished Finish

The Waffenamt proofs were the military eagle over 359 on the early models. Military eagle over WaA359 on later models. The Waffenamt proof was on the left side of the frame to the rear of the trigger and on the left side of the slide in front of the slide serrations. The 9mmk models have a bottom magazine release. Rare in both .22 LR and 9mmk calibers.

Model PP Waffenamt • Courtesy James Rankin

Exc.	V.G.	Good	Fair	Poor
1200	800	375	275	150

Model PP .32 Caliber with Waffenamt Proofs. Milled Finish

Exc.	V.G.	Good	Fair	Poor
450	375	325	250	150

Model PP .32 Caliber. Police Eagle/C Proofed. High Polished Finish

The police proofs were the police eagle over the swastika with the letter "C" to the right of the swastika. Later models have the eagle over the swastika with the letter "F" (see below). The police proof was on the left side of the frame to the rear of the trigger.

Model PP Police • Courtesy James Rankin

Exc.	V.G.	Good	Fair	Poor
1200	800	375	250	150

Model PP .32 Caliber. Police Eagle/C and Police Eagle/F Proofed. Milled Finish

Exc.	V.G.	Good	Fair	Poor
900	600	375	275	150

Model PP .32 Caliber. NSKK Marked On The Slide

The NSKK, National Sozialistisches Kraftfahr Korps, Transport Corps. These pistols were issued to officers in the corps. The NSSK emblem is on the left side of the frame in front of the slide serrations.

Model PP NSKK Marked • Courtesy James Rankin

Exc.	V.G.	Good	Fair	Poor
2500	2000	850	550	300

NOTE: Add $700 with proper NSKK DRGM AKAH holster.

Model PP .32 Caliber. NSDAP Gruppe Markings

The SA, Sturm Abteilung, was comprised of various districts throughout Germany and each was separately named. The proof was SA der NSDAP on the top line with the name of the district below. These proofs were found on the front grip strap. Some later models had the SA proof on the rear grip strap. A few SA models had a two digit number following the district name. The .22 LR model is rare.

Listed below are the SA districts:

Alpenland, Berlin-Brandenburg, Bayerische Ostmark, Bayerwald, Donau, Eibe, Franken, Hansa, Hessen, Hochland, Kurpflaz, Mitte, Mittelrhein, Neckar, Nordsee, Neiderrhein, Neidersachsen, Nilfswerk Nordwest, Oder, Ostmark, Osterreich, Oberrhein, Ostland, Pommern, Schlesien, Sachsen, Sudmark, Sudeten, Sudwest, Tannengberg, Thuringen, Standarte Feldherrnhalle, Weichsel, Westfalen, Westmark.

Model PP NSPAD Marked • Courtesy James Rankin

Exc.	V.G.	Good	Fair	Poor
2000	1500	1000	500	300

NOTE: Add $600 with proper SA DRGM AKAH holster.

Model PP .32 Caliber PDM Marked with Bottom Magazine Release

The PDM, Polizei Direktion Munchen, Police Department Munich. The PDM mark was placed on equipment belonging to the Munich police. It can be found on the left side of the frame behind the trigger and is followed by one to four numbers. The PDM pistol has a bottom magazine release.

Model PP PDM marked • Courtesy James Rankin

Exc.	V.G.	Good	Fair	Poor
850	700	550	475	300

Model PP .32 Caliber. RJ Marked

The RJ, Reich Jugend, Hitler Youth Organization. The RJ proof is on front grip strap. Some models are in .22 caliber.

Model PP RJ marked • Courtesy James Rankin

Exc.	V.G.	Good	Fair	Poor
750	600	475	400	150

Model PP .32 Caliber. RFV Marked. High Polished or Milled Finish

Model PP RFV marked • Courtesy James Rankin

Exc.	V.G.	Good	Fair	Poor
700	600	475	400	150

Model PP .32 Caliber. RBD Munster Marked

The RBD Munster, State Railway Directorate Munster in Westfalen. The RPD Munster is on the front grip strap followed by (Westf.).

Model PP RBD • Courtesy James Rankin

Exc.	V.G.	Good	Fair	Poor
2200	1750	1200	650	400

Model PP .32 Caliber. RpLt Marked

The RpLt, Rigspoliti, Danish State Police, is on the left side of the frame directly above the forward part of the triggerguard. The RpLt is followed by "Nr". The number is from one to four digits, and is an inventory number within the police department.

Model PP RpLt marked • Courtesy James Rankin

Exc.	V.G.	Good	Fair	Poor
950	750	475	375	200

Model PP .32 Caliber RZM Marked

The RZM, Reichs Zueg Meisterei, was the equipment office of the NSDAP, and the RZM model of the PP was carried by an NSDAP member who was awarded the use of the pistol. The RZM emblem is on the left side of the slide in front of the slide serrations. Rare.

Exc.	V.G.	Good	Fair	Poor
2500	2000	1250	600	300

Model PP .32 Caliber. Statens Vattenfallsverk Marked

The Statens Vattensfallsverk was contracted by Sweden for use in hydro-electric plant security. The Staten Vattenfallsverk is on the right side of the slide to the front of the slide serrations. There is an "Nr" above each inscription for inventory control. Some of these pistols have Duraluminum frames.

Model PP Statens Vattenfallsverk • Courtesy James Rankin

Exc.	V.G.	Good	Fair	Poor
1000	800	550	375	200

Model PP .32 Caliber. AC Marked

The Model AC was a late wartime pistol with a milled finish. The AC proofmark was usually found on either side of the slide. These pistols sometimes did not have the Walther inscription or trademark. Wood grips replaced the plastic.

Model PP AC marked • Courtesy James Rankin

Exc.	V.G.	Good	Fair	Poor
450	375	300	250	150

Model PP .32 Caliber. Duraluminum Frame

Exc.	V.G.	Good	Fair	Poor
750	600	500	400	150

Model PP .380 Caliber. Bottom Magazine Release and Waffenamt Proofs

Exc.	V.G.	Good	Fair	Poor
2000	1500	700	500	300

Model PP Persian Contract

This model was contracted by Persia for its police units. It is a bottom magazine release model with the Persian Royal Crest and Farsi inscription on the left side of the slide, and the Walther Banner and inscription on the right side of the slide.

Model PP Persian Contract • Courtesy James Rankin

Exc.	V.G.	Good	Fair	Poor
3500	2950	2250	1000	500

Model PPK

A semiautomatic pistol in .22, .25, .32, and .380 caliber. Introduced six months after the Model PP in 1929. A more compact version of the Model PP with one less round in the magazine and one-piece wrap-around checkered plastic grips in brown, black, and white with the Walther banner on each side of the grips. The Model PPK will be found with the same types of finishes as the Model PP as well as the same styles of engraving. Grips in wood or ivory are seen with some of the engraved models. As with the Model PP there are many variations of the Model PPK and numerous NSDAP markings seen on the pre-1946 models that were produced during the Nazi regime. All reflect various prices.

Courtesy Orvel Reichert

Courtesy James Rankin

Model PPK .22 Caliber

Exc.	V.G.	Good	Fair	Poor
1200	700	475	325	175

Model PPK .25 Caliber

Exc.	V.G.	Good	Fair	Poor
6000	4000	1850	1000	500

Model PPK .32 Caliber. High Polished Finish

Exc.	V.G.	Good	Fair	Poor
550	450	325	250	150

Model PPK .32 Caliber. Milled Finish

Exc.	V.G.	Good	Fair	Poor
500	400	325	250	150

Model PPK .380 Caliber

Courtesy Orvel Reichert

Exc.	V.G.	Good	Fair	Poor
2200	1750	1300	750	375

Model PPK .32 Caliber with Duraluminum Frame

Exc.	V.G.	Good	Fair	Poor
950	800	600	400	200

Model PPK .32 Caliber with Verchromt Finish

Exc.	V.G.	Good	Fair	Poor
2500	1800	1200	700	350

Model PPK .32 Caliber in Blue, Silver, or Gold Finish and Full Coverage Engraving

Blue

Exc.	V.G.	Good	Fair	Poor
5000	3500	2500	1200	700

Silver

Exc.	V.G.	Good	Fair	Poor
6000	4000	3000	1200	700

Gold

Exc.	V.G.	Good	Fair	Poor
6500	4500	3500	1500	700

Add $750 for ivory grips with any of the three above.
Add $700 for leather presentation cases.
Add $500 for .22 caliber.
Add $1000 for .380 caliber.

Model PPK .32 Caliber Marked Mod. PP on Slide

Exc.	V.G.	Good	Fair	Poor
5000	4000	2500	1500	1000

Model PPK .32 Caliber with Panagraphed Slide

Exc.	V.G.	Good	Fair	Poor
650	550	450	300	200

Model PPK .32 Caliber. Czechoslovakian Contract

Exc.	V.G.	Good	Fair	Poor
1850	1500	1000	550	300

Model PPK .32 Caliber. Allemagne Marked

Exc.	V.G.	Good	Fair	Poor
800	700	600	400	250

Model PPK .32 Caliber with Waffenamt Proofs and a High Polished Finish

The Waffenamt proofs were the military eagle over 359 on the early models. Military eagle over WaA359 on later models. The Waffenamt proof was on the left side of the frame to the rear of the trigger and on the left side of the slide in front of the slide serrations. The 9mmk models have a bottom magazine release. Rare in both .22 LR and 9mmk calibers.

Exc.	V.G.	Good	Fair	Poor
1200	800	550	400	250

Model PPK .32 Caliber with Waffenamt Proofs and a Milled Finish

Exc.	V.G.	Good	Fair	Poor
800	600	375	300	175

Model PPK .32 Caliber. Police Eagle/C Proofed. High Polished Finish

Exc.	V.G.	Good	Fair	Poor
675	575	450	300	175

Model PPK .32 Caliber. Police Eagle/C Proofed. Milled Finish

The police proofs were the police eagle over the swastika with the letter "C" to the right of the swastika. Later models have the eagle over the swastika with the letter "F" (*see below*). The police proof was on the left side of the frame to the rear of the trigger.

Exc.	V.G.	Good	Fair	Poor
650	500	375	275	175

Model PPK .32 Caliber. Police Eagle/F Proofed. Duraluminum Frame. Milled Finish

Exc.	V.G.	Good	Fair	Poor
900	700	550	350	225

Model PPK .22 Caliber. Late War, Black Grips

Exc.	V.G.	Good	Fair	Poor
1200	750	600	450	300

Model PPK .32 Caliber. Party Leader Grips. Brown

The Party Leader-gripped PPK was the honor weapon of the NSDAP and was given to political leaders from the Fuhrer. The Party Leader grip is usually mottled brown plastic with the NSDAP eagle holding a swastika circled by a wreath on each side of the grip. Near the end of WWII a small number of Party Leader grips were black (*see below*).

Courtesy Rock Island Auction Company

Exc.	V.G.	Good	Fair	Poor
2750	2550	2350	2250	2000

Model PPK .32 Caliber. Party Leader Grips. Black

Exc.	V.G.	Good	Fair	Poor
3250	3000	2750	2550	2500

NOTE: If grips are badly cracked or damaged on the two Party Leaders above, reduce $2000 each valuation.
Add $500 with proper Party Leader DRGM AKAH holster.

Model PPK .32 Caliber. RZM Marked

Courtesy Rock Island Auction Company

Exc.	V.G.	Good	Fair	Poor
900	700	500	400	300

Model PPK .32 Caliber. PDM Marked with Duraluminum Frame and Bottom Magazine Release

The PDM, Polizei Direktion Munchen, Police Department Munich. The PDM mark was placed on equipment belonging to the Munich police. It can be found on the left side of the frame behind the trigger and is followed by one to four numbers. The PDM pistol has a bottom magazine release. This model is much rarer than the PP version.

Exc.	V.G.	Good	Fair	Poor
2500	1800	1150	750	450

Model PPK .32 Caliber. RFV Marked

Exc.	V.G.	Good	Fair	Poor
2000	1750	1150	650	400

Model PPK .32 Caliber. DRP Marked

The DRP, Deutsche Reichs Post, German Postal Service. The DRP is found on the left side of the frame behind the trigger.

Model PPK DRP marked • Courtesy James Rankin

Exc.	V.G.	Good	Fair	Poor
800	650	550	450	275

Model PPK .32 Caliber. Statens Vattenfallsverk

The Statens Vattensfallsverk was contracted by Sweden for use in hydro-electric plant security. The Staten Vattenfallsverk is on the right side of the slide to the front of the slide serrations. There is an "Nr" above each inscription for inventory control. Some of these pistols have Duraluminum frames.

Exc.	V.G.	Good	Fair	Poor
1400	1200	700	450	300

Model P99 Military

Similar to the P99 but with military finish.

NIB	Exc.	V.G.	Good	Fair	Poor
625	475	375	—	—	—

HECKLER & KOCH

VP 70Z

This is a blowback-operated semiautomatic chambered for the 9mm Parabellum cartridge. It is striker-fired and double action only. The barrel is 4.5" long, and the double-column magazine holds 18 rounds. The finish is blued, and the receiver and grips are molded from plastic. This model was discontinued in 1986.

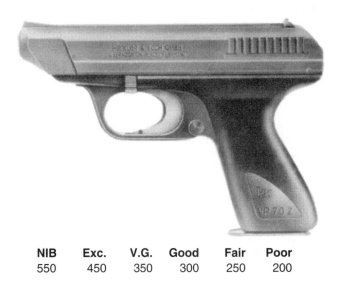

NIB	Exc.	V.G.	Good	Fair	Poor
550	450	350	300	250	200

NIB	Exc.	V.G.	Good	Fair	Poor
1500	1200	850	500	400	300

VP 70M

This is similar to the VP 70Z except for a very important feature: When a shoulder stock is added, the internal mechanism is altered to fire full automatic 3-round burst. When the shoulder stock is removed, the pistol reverts back to semiautomatic. The rate of fire is a very high 2,200 rounds per minute. This version has no safety devices. First produced in 1972 and discontinued in 1986.

H&K VP 70M • Courtesy Thomas Nelson, *World's Machine Pistols, Vol. II*

Pre-1968

Exc.	V.G.	Fair
N/A	N/A	N/A

Pre-1986 conversions

Exc.	V.G.	Fair
15000	—	—

Pre-1986 dealer samples

Exc.	V.G.	Fair
N/A	N/A	N/A

P9

This is a single action, delayed-blowback semiautomatic pistol chambered for 9mm or 7.65mm Parabellum. The action is based on the G-3 rifle mechanism and is single action only. The barrel is 4" in length, and the pistol has an internal hammer and a thumb-operated hammer drop and decocking lever. There is also a manual safety and a loaded-chamber indicator. The finish is parkerized, and the grips are molded plastic and well contoured. It has fixed sights. This model was manufactured between 1977 and 1984. This model is rarer than the P9S model. This was H&K's first military pistol.

SUBMACHINE GUNS

MP18/1 (WWI)

This was the first German submachine gun and it was designed by Hugo Schmeisser in 1916. It was used by German military forces in WWI. The gun was chambered for the 9mm Parabellum cartridge. The barrel length is 7.5" and the snail magazine holds 32 rounds. The rate of fire is about 450 rounds per minute. Markings are "MP 18 L" above the chamber and "C.G HANEL WAFFENFABRIK SUHL" on the left side of the receiver. Not produced after 1945. Weight is about 9 lbs.

Pre-1968

Exc.	V.G.	Fair
6000	5500	5000

Pre-1986 conversions

Exc.	V.G.	Fair
5500	5000	4500

Pre-1986 dealer samples

Exc.	V.G.	Fair
4000	3500	3000

MP18/1 (Post-war)

Introduced into combat by German troops in 1918. Designed by Hugo Schmeisser and built by Bergmann. Chambered for 9mm cartridge. In place of the 32-round snail drum, a box magazine holds 20 or 32 rounds. The magazine is essentially the only difference between the WWI guns and the post-war examples. Barrel length is 8". Rate of fire is about 400 rounds per minute. Was in use from 1918 to 1930s. Weight is about 9 lbs.

Private NFA collection • Gary Gelson photo

Pre-1968

Exc.	V.G.	Fair
7000	6500	6000

MP 18/1 with markings • Paul Goodwin photo

Pre-1986 conversions

Exc.	V.G.	Fair
5500	5000	4500

Pre-1986 dealer samples

Exc.	V.G.	Fair
4000	3500	3000

Bergman MP28

This model is an improved version of the MP18. It is fitted with a tangent sight and straight magazine. It also has a selector switch to allow for semi-auto fire. Rate of fire is approximately 500 rounds per minute. Chambered for a variety of calibers including 9mm Parabellum, 9mm Bergmann, 7.65mm Parabellum, 7.63mm, and .45 ACP. Magazine capacity is 20, 32, or 50 rounds with special 25-round magazine for .45 ACP models. Built in Belgium by Pieper. Many of these guns were sold to South American countries. They were also used by German Police units including SS units. It was never adopted by the German army. Markings over the chamber are "MP 28 II SYSTEM SCHMEISSER PATENT." Weight is 8.8 lbs.

Courtesy Richard M. Kumor Sr.

Pre-1968

Exc.	V.G.	Fair
6500	6000	5500

Pre-1986 conversions

Exc.	V.G.	Fair
5500	5000	4500

Pre-1986 dealer samples

Exc.	V.G.	Fair
3500	3000	3000

Erma EMP

First developed in Germany in 1934, this submachine gun was chambered for the 9mm cartridge. It was fitted with a wooden vertical fore-grip. The gun was fitted with a 9.75" barrel with a 20- or 32-round magazine. The rate of fire was 500 rounds per minute. The weight was about 8.25 lbs. Marked "EMP" on rear receiver cap. Production ceased in 1945. This gun was used extensively in the Spanish Civil War.

Erma EMP • Paul Goodwin photo

Pre-1968

Exc.	V.G.	Fair
6500	6000	5000

Pre-1986 conversions

Exc.	V.G.	Fair
4500	4000	3500

Pre-1986 dealer samples

Exc.	V.G.	Fair
3500	3000	3000

HK MP5

First produced in 1965, this submachine gun is quite popular world-wide, being in service in a number of countries. It is produced in 9mm, .40 S&W, and 10mm. It is offered in a number of variations. The basic model is fitted with an 8.75" barrel with retractable stock. Magazine capacity is 15 or 30 rounds. Rate of fire is 800 rounds per minute. Weight is approximately 5.5 lbs. Marked "MP5 KAL 9MMX19" on top rib of receiver.

Courtesy Richard M. Kumor Sr.

Pre-1968 (Rare)

Exc.	V.G.	Fair
12500	11000	10000

Pre-1986 conversions

Exc.	V.G.	Fair
8500	8000	7000

NOTE: Add 15% for registered receiver using OEM parts.

Pre-1986 dealer samples

Exc.	V.G.	Fair
6000	5500	5000

HK MP5 K

This model is essentially the same as the MP5 with the exception of a 4.5" barrel. Weight is about 4.4 lbs.

Photo courtesy Heckler & Koch

Pre-1968 (Rare)

Exc.	V.G.	Fair
N/A	N/A	N/A

Pre-1986 conversions

Exc.	V.G.	Fair
8500	8000	7500

NOTE: Add 15% for registered receiver using OEM parts.

Pre-1986 dealer samples

Exc.	V.G.	Fair
4500	4000	3500

HK MP5 SD

This variation of the MP5 uses a suppressor, making it one of the quietest submachine guns ever. The barrel is ported so that supersonic 9mm ammunition can be used at subsonic levels. Rate of fire is 800 rounds per minute. Magazine capacity is 15 or 30 round magazines. Barrel length is 7.7" and weight is approximately 7 lbs. This model comes in six different configurations that may affect price.

Courtesy Heckler & Koch

Pre-1968

Exc.	V.G.	Fair
N/A	N/A	N/A

THE HECKLER & KOCH MP5

When it comes to law enforcement tactical teams or even military special operations squads, the choice of the vast majority for a pistol caliber submachine gun is the MP5. The reason is quite simple: This submachine gun is so easy to control and use effectively at typical room distances it allows each operator to exhibit on target skills that could only be matched by a world class pistol shooter. Unlike many other submachine guns, the MP5 did not start out as an original design. It is a variation of a pre-existing design, which was the G-3 service rifle adopted by West Germany in the mid-1950s. The MP5 employs the same style of roller-locked, delayed blowback firing mechanism found with the far more powerful G-3 and that is the big secret to the MP5 in terms of its ease of control. The MP5 fires from a closed bolt which increases the first shot accuracy exponentially. The roller lock mechanism dampens the recoil forces experienced by the shooter and the overall light weight (5.6 pounds, empty) of the gun makes it easy to handle and control. The MP5 features both an upper and lower receiver and is more or less a component gun because the lower receivers can be changed out according to the type of trigger group that is required. The MP5 originally was used with a straight double column, two position feed magazine, but the current 30-round curved box magazine was designed for use with hollowpoint ammunition. The biggest criticism to the MP5 has been its cost. It is an expensive submachine gun to manufacture and some view its design overly complicated. The Heckler & Koch MP5 will go down in history as one of the most successful submachine gun designs ever, if not the most successful.

Frank James

Pre-1986 conversions

Exc.	V.G.	Fair
8500	8000	7000

NOTE: Add 15% for registered receiver using OEM parts.

Pre-1986 dealer samples

Exc.	V.G.	Fair
5000	4800	4500

HK 53

This submachine gun fires the 5.56x45mm cartridge. It is fitted with an 8.25" barrel and retractable stock. Magazine capacity is 25 rounds. Rate of fire is about 700 rounds per minute. Weight is approximately 6.7 lbs. Marked "MP53 KAL 5.56x45" on top rib of receiver. The gun is in service in several military and police units around the world.

Courtesy Heckler & Koch

Pre-1968

Exc.	V.G.	Fair
N/A	N/A	N/A

Pre-1986 conversions

Exc.	V.G.	Fair
8000	7500	6500

Pre-1986 dealer samples

Exc.	V.G.	Fair
5000	4500	4000

Steyr-Solothurn (Solothurn SI-100 or MP34(o))

See Austria, Submachine Guns, Steyr.

MP34/I & MP35/I

Similar in appearance to the MP28, and produced in Germany by Walther in Zella Mehlis. Chambered for the 9mm cartridge and fitted with a 7.8" or 12.6" barrel. Other calibers were offered such as the 9mm Bergmann, 9mm Mauser, .45 ACP, and 7.63 Mauser. Rear sight had a V-notch tangent graduated to 1000 meters. The gun had a cocking handle much like a rifle located at the rear of the receiver. Fitted with two triggers, the outer one fired semiautomatic and the inner one fired full automatic. The 24- or 32-round magazine fed from the right side. Rate of fire was about 650 rounds per minute and weight is approximately 9 lbs. The MP35/I was a modified MP34/I and was used by the German SS. Built by Junker & Ruh. Many more MP35/I guns were built than MP34/I.

Private NFA collection, Gary Gelson photo

Pre-1968

Exc.	V.G.	Fair
6500	6000	5500

Pre-1986 conversions

Exc.	V.G.	Fair
—	—	—

Pre-1986 dealer samples

Exc.	V.G.	Fair
3500	3000	2500

MP38

This German submachine gun was first produced in 1938. It is often called the Schmeisser but that is incorrect. It was designed by Vollmer and built by the Erma company. It is chambered for the 9mm cartridge and is fitted with a 9.75" barrel. It has a folding stock and a magazine capacity of 32 rounds. Its rate of fire is 500 rounds per minute. Full automatic fire only. Weight is approximately 9 lbs. Marked "MP38" on the rear receiver cap. Production ceased in 1940. Produced by Erma. This was the standard submachine gun of the German army during World War II. Over 1,000,000 were produced.

NOTE: In 1940 and 1941 some Model 38s were modified to prevent accidental discharges. By replacing the one-piece retracting handle with a two-piece one that incorporated a cutout which could be locked to prevent firing. This modified Model 38 is designated the Model 38/40.

HK 53 in firing port configuration • Paul Goodwin photo

MP38 • Paul Goodwin photo

Pre-1968 (Rare)

Exc.	V.G.	Fair
20000	18000	17000

Pre-1986 conversions (or U.S. manufactured parts)

Exc.	V.G.	Fair
6500	6000	5500

Pre-1986 dealer samples

Exc.	V.G.	Fair
N/A	N/A	N/A

German Manufacturing Codes for the MP38 & MP40:

Erma	1938 to 1940	"27"
Erma	1940 to 1944	"afy"
Haenal	1938 to 1940	"122"
Haenal	1940 to 1944	"fxo"
Steyr	1939-1940	"660"
Steyr	1940 to 1944	"bnz"

MP40

This model was the successor to the MP38 with faster manufacturing components. The steel receivers pressed with a corrugated magazine housing. The grip frame is pressed steel as well. Weight and barrel length are the same as the MP38 as is magazine capacity and rate of fire. This model was produced from 1940 to 1945 by Erma. Marked "MP40" on the rear receiver cap. Approximately 1,000,000 of these guns were produced.

NOTE: There is a rare modification of this submachine gun designated the MP40/II, which is fitted with a magazine housing that holds two magazines. These magazines fit in an oversized sliding housing that moves laterally, allowing a full magazine to be moved into place when the first magazine becomes empty. Not developed until late 1943. Not considered a successful attempt to increase ammunition capacity.

Pre-1968

Exc.	V.G.	Fair
8000	7500	7000

Pre-1986 conversions (or U.S. manufactured receivers)

Exc.	V.G.	Fair
5500	4500	4000

Pre-1986 dealer samples

Exc.	V.G.	Fair
4000	3500	3000

MP41

This model was built by Schmeisser to compete with the official adopted military MP40. The gun was not adopted by the German army. The result is that very few of these guns exist. The MP40-style receiver and barrel were fitted to a wooden buttstock and a select fire mechanism was added. Weight is about 8 lbs. Marked "MP41 PATENT SCHMEISSER C.G.HAENEL SUHL" on the top of the receiver. About 27,500 of these guns were built between 1941 and 1945.

THE MP40

The MP40 was preceded by the MP38 and they were the first submachine guns designed specifically for use from armored personnel carriers as well by airborne paratroops. They were the first to feature a folding stock, even if it was somewhat wobbly when extended. The MP40 was the easier-to-produce version of the earlier MP38, but it proved it was every bit as reliable. The MP40 was constructed with a thin tubular steel receiver and had a lower receiver constructed from steel sheet metal that was covered with a hard plastic-like bakelite material. The bolt is one piece and powered by a mainspring in a telescoping tube that also contained the firing pin at the end. The stick magazine held 32 rounds in a double column design, but fed from a single position. The bolt handle reciprocated with the bolt when the weapon was fired and the MP38 caused many unintentional deaths because dropping it allowed the weapon to fire when a loaded magazine was in place. As a result, the MP40 exhibits a two-piece bolt handle that enabled the operator to lock the bolt forward on an empty chamber. The MP40 was not a tack driver, but its relatively slow cyclic rate of 500 rpm (far slower than the examples seen in Hollywood films) enabled an experienced operator to accurately engage man-size targets out to distances of 75 yards, and in some cases even farther. Featuring an empty weight of approximately 8.5 pounds, and with the magazine out and the stock folded, the MP40 was an easy gun to transport. Like most submachine guns, the MP40 fired from an open bolt and there is the decided momentum factor as the bolt moves. The Germans made more than 1.2 million MP40s during World War II, so obviously many learned to compensate for this deficiency. The MP40 was a good, not a great, submachine gun, but it will always be a historically important one.

Frank James

MP 40 • Paul Goodwin photo

MP41 • Private NFA collection, Gary Gelson photo

Pre-1968 (Rare)

Exc.	V.G.	Fair
13000	12000	10000

Pre-1986 conversions

Exc.	V.G.	Fair
6500	6000	5500

Pre-1986 dealer samples

Exc.	V.G.	Fair
7000	6000	5000

Walter MPK and MPL

This German submachine gun was first produced in 1963. The MPK is a short barrel (6.7") version and the MPL is the long barrel (10.14") version. Magazine capacity is 32 rounds of 9mm. Rate of fire is 55 rounds per minute. Weight empty is 6.1 lbs. Markings are on the left side of the receiver. Production of this model ceased in 1985.

Photo courtesy private NFA collection

Pre-1968 (Rare)

Exc.	V.G.	Fair
10000	9000	8500

Pre-1986 conversions

Exc.	V.G.	Fair
N/A	N/A	N/A

Pre-1986 dealer samples

Exc.	V.G.	Fair
5000	4000	3500

RIFLES

MAUSER MILITARY BOLT ACTION RIFLES FOR COUNTRIES NOT LISTED UNDER SEPARATE HEADING

Argentina
See Argentina, Rifles, Mauser.

Austria
See Austria, Rifles, Mauser.

Belgium
See Belgium, Rifles, Mauser.

Bolivia

M1895 Rifle

Exc.	V.G.	Good	Fair	Poor
200	165	120	100	70

M1907 Rifle

Exc.	V.G.	Good	Fair	Poor
325	275	225	150	100

M1907 Short Rifle

Exc.	V.G.	Good	Fair	Poor
325	275	225	150	100

VZ24 Short Rifle

Exc.	V.G.	Good	Fair	Poor
400	350	275	225	125

M1933 Standard Model Export Model Short Rifle

Exc.	V.G.	Good	Fair	Poor
325	275	225	150	100

M1950 Series B-50 Rifle

Exc.	V.G.	Good	Fair	Poor
400	350	275	225	125

Brazil
See Brazil, Rifles, Mauser.

Chile

M1893 Rifle

Exc.	V.G.	Good	Fair	Poor
250	200	150	100	60

M1895 Rifle

Courtesy Rock Island Auction Company

Exc.	V.G.	Good	Fair	Poor
250	200	150	100	60

M1895/61 7.62 NATO Conversion

Exc.	V.G.	Good	Fair	Poor
350	300	240	195	120

M1895 Short Rifle

Exc.	V.G.	Good	Fair	Poor
225	190	150	90	60

M1896 Carbine

Exc.	V.G.	Good	Fair	Poor
225	190	150	90	60

M1912 Steyr Rifle

Courtesy Rock Island Auction Company

Exc.	V.G.	Good	Fair	Poor
250	190	140	100	70

M1912 Steyr Short Rifle

Exc.	V.G.	Good	Fair	Poor
250	190	140	100	70

M1912/61 7.62 NATO Conversion

Exc.	V.G.	Good	Fair	Poor
350	300	250	200	125

M1935 Carabineros Carbine

Exc.	V.G.	Good	Fair	Poor
350	320	275	225	180

China
See China, Rifles, Mauser.

Colombia

M1891 Rifle (Argentine Pattern)

Exc.	V.G.	Good	Fair	Poor
120	90	75	55	35

M1904 Rifle

Exc.	V.G.	Good	Fair	Poor
190	160	130	100	75

M1912 Steyr Rifle

Exc.	V.G.	Good	Fair	Poor
170	130	110	90	55

VZ23 Short Rifle

Exc.	V.G.	Good	Fair	Poor
170	130	110	90	55

Steyr-Solothurn A-G M1929 Short Rifle

Exc.	V.G.	Good	Fair	Poor
190	160	130	100	75

FN M24 and 30 Short Rifles

Exc.	V.G.	Good	Fair	Poor
150	120	100	75	45

VZ12/33 Carbine

Exc.	V.G.	Good	Fair	Poor
170	130	110	90	55

FN M1950 Short Rifle

Exc.	V.G.	Good	Fair	Poor
170	130	110	90	55

Costa Rica

M1895 Rifle

Exc.	V.G.	Good	Fair	Poor
120	100	80	60	35

M1910 Rifle

Exc.	V.G.	Good	Fair	Poor
140	110	90	70	40

FN M24 Short Rifle

Exc.	V.G.	Good	Fair	Poor
130	110	90	70	40

Czechoslovakia
See Czechoslovakia, Rifles, Mauser.

Denmark
See Denmark, Rifles, Mauser.

Dominican Republic

M1953 Rifle

Exc.	V.G.	Good	Fair	Poor
325	290	275	175	90

M1953 Short Rifle

Exc.	V.G.	Good	Fair	Poor
325	290	250	160	90

Ecuador

M71/84 Rifle

Exc.	V.G.	Good	Fair	Poor
175	150	100	80	50

M1891 Rifle (Argentine Pattern)

Exc.	V.G.	Good	Fair	Poor
125	90	70	50	30

M1907 Rifle

Exc.	V.G.	Good	Fair	Poor
150	120	90	70	45

M1910 Rifle

Exc.	V.G.	Good	Fair	Poor
150	110	80	60	50

VZ24 Short Rifle

Exc.	V.G.	Good	Fair	Poor
80	60	50	30	20

VZ12/33 Carbine

Exc.	V.G.	Good	Fair	Poor
125	110	90	70	40

FN M30 Short Rifle

Exc.	V.G.	Good	Fair	Poor
110	90	70	60	40

El Salvador

M1895 Rifle

Exc.	V.G.	Good	Fair	Poor
125	90	80	60	40

VZ12/33 Carbine

Exc.	V.G.	Good	Fair	Poor
125	110	90	70	40

Estonia

Czech Model L Short Rifle

Exc.	V.G.	Good	Fair	Poor
400	350	300	250	200

Ethiopia

FN M24 Carbine

Exc.	V.G.	Good	Fair	Poor
400	375	325	275	225

M1933 Standard Model Short Rifle

Exc.	V.G.	Good	Fair	Poor
450	375	350	300	250

M1933 Standard Model Carbine

Exc.	V.G.	Good	Fair	Poor
450	375	350	300	250

France

See France, Rifles, Mauser.

Greece

M1930 Short Rifle

Exc.	V.G.	Good	Fair	Poor
350	300	220	120	60

M1930 Carbine

Exc.	V.G.	Good	Fair	Poor
N/A	—	—	—	—

Guatemala

M1910 Rifle

Exc.	V.G.	Good	Fair	Poor
150	120	80	60	40

VZ25 Short Rifle (Model 24)

Exc.	V.G.	Good	Fair	Poor
175	130	90	70	40

VZ33 Carbine

Exc.	V.G.	Good	Fair	Poor
190	160	120	90	60

Haiti

FN M24/30 Short Rifle

Exc.	V.G.	Good	Fair	Poor
175	140	90	60	30

Honduras

G 71 Rifle

Exc.	V.G.	Good	Fair	Poor
300	250	200	130	90

M1895 Rifle (Chilean Pattern)

Exc.	V.G.	Good	Fair	Poor
150	110	90	60	25

M1933 Standard Model Short Rifle

Exc.	V.G.	Good	Fair	Poor
350	280	230	175	120

Iraq

Post-WWII-style Carbine

Exc.	V.G.	Good	Fair	Poor
200	160	120	80	40

Ireland

G 71 Rifle

Exc.	V.G.	Good	Fair	Poor
400	325	250	200	150

Israel

See Israel, Rifles, Mauser.

Japan

See Japan, Rifles, Mauser.

Latvia

VZ24 Short Rifle

Exc.	V.G.	Good	Fair	Poor
190	150	110	80	60

Liberia

FN M24 Short Rifle

Exc.	V.G.	Good	Fair	Poor
200	160	75	80	40

Lithuania

FN M30 Short Rifle

Exc.	V.G.	Good	Fair	Poor
225	190	160	110	80

FN M246 Short Rifle

Exc.	V.G.	Good	Fair	Poor
275	250	200	130	100

Luxembourg

M1900 Rifle

Exc.	V.G.	Good	Fair	Poor
500	400	300	190	110

FN M24/30 Short Rifle

Exc.	V.G.	Good	Fair	Poor
175	140	90	60	30

Manchuria

See Japan, Rifles.

Mexico

See Mexico, Rifles, Mauser.

Morocco

Post-WWII FN Carbine

Exc.	V.G.	Good	Fair	Poor
225	190	150	110	80

Netherlands

See Netherlands, Rifles, Mauser.

Nicaragua

VZ23 Short Rifle

Exc.	V.G.	Good	Fair	Poor
300	250	200	125	90

VZ12/33 Carbine

Exc.	V.G.	Good	Fair	Poor
350	300	225	140	100

Norway

See Norway, Rifles, Mauser.

Orange Free State

M1895 Rifle

Exc.	V.G.	Good	Fair	Poor
325	275	225	150	100

M1895 Chilean-marked Rifle

Exc.	V.G.	Good	Fair	Poor
325	275	225	150	100

M1896 Loewe & Co. Rifle

Exc.	V.G.	Good	Fair	Poor
350	275	225	175	100

M1897 DWM Rifle

Exc.	V.G.	Good	Fair	Poor
400	350	275	225	125

Paraguay

M1895 Rifle (Chilean Pattern)

Exc.	V.G.	Good	Fair	Poor
150	110	80	40	20

M1907 Rifle

Exc.	V.G.	Good	Fair	Poor
225	200	160	100	80

M1907 Carbine

Exc.	V.G.	Good	Fair	Poor
225	190	160	110	80

M1909 Haenel Export Model Rifle

Exc.	V.G.	Good	Fair	Poor
300	240	190	120	90

M1927 Rifle

Exc.	V.G.	Good	Fair	Poor
180	130	90	60	30

M1927 Short Rifle

Exc.	V.G.	Good	Fair	Poor
180	130	90	50	30

FN M24/30 Short Rifle

Exc.	V.G.	Good	Fair	Poor
225	190	150	100	80

M1933 Standard Model Short Rifle

Exc.	V.G.	Good	Fair	Poor
300	250	200	150	90

M1933 Standard Model Carbine

Exc.	V.G.	Good	Fair	Poor
300	250	200	150	90

Persia/Iran

M1895 Rifle

Exc.	V.G.	Good	Fair	Poor
200	150	120	90	70

FN M24/30 Short Rifle

Exc.	V.G.	Good	Fair	Poor
275	225	175	100	70

M98/29 Long Rifle

Exc.	V.G.	Good	Fair	Poor
425	350	300	250	150

VZ24 Short Rifle

Exc.	V.G.	Good	Fair	Poor
350	300	250	200	100

M30 Carbine

Exc.	V.G.	Good	Fair	Poor
500	400	300	175	100

M49 Carbine

Exc.	V.G.	Good	Fair	Poor
550	450	300	175	100

Peru

M1891 Rifle M1891 Carbine

Exc.	V.G.	Good	Fair	Poor
175	140	100	75	35

M1895 Rifle

Exc.	V.G.	Good	Fair	Poor
190	150	100	75	35

M1909 Rifle

Exc.	V.G.	Good	Fair	Poor
425	350	275	225	100

VZ24 Short Rifle

Exc.	V.G.	Good	Fair	Poor
325	275	225	150	100

VZ32 Carbine

Exc.	V.G.	Good	Fair	Poor
275	225	150	100	65

M1935 Short Rifle (converted to .30-06)

Exc.	V.G.	Good	Fair	Poor
225	225	175	125	90

M1935 Short Rifle

Courtesy Rock Island Auction Company

Exc.	V.G.	Good	Fair	Poor
425	350	275	225	100

Poland

See Poland, Rifles, Mauser.

Portugal

M1904 Mauser-Verueiro Rifle

Courtesy Rock Island Auction Company

Exc.	V.G.	Good	Fair	Poor
250	170	110	80	50

M1904/M39 Rifle

Exc.	V.G.	Good	Fair	Poor
250	200	125	80	50

M1933 Standard Model Short Rifle

Exc.	V.G.	Good	Fair	Poor
300	250	200	150	90

M1933 Standard Model Carbine

Exc.	V.G.	Good	Fair	Poor
300	250	200	150	90

M1937-A Short Rifle

Exc.	V.G.	Good	Fair	Poor
325	280	220	160	90

M1941 Short Rifle

Exc.	V.G.	Good	Fair	Poor
395	300	200	140	80

Romania

See Romania, Rifles.

Saudi Arabia

FN M30 Short Rifle

Exc.	V.G.	Good	Fair	Poor
250	190	120	80	40

Serbia/Yugoslavia

See *Yugoslavia, Rifles, Mauser.*

Slovak Republic

VZ24 Short Rifle

Exc.	V.G.	Good	Fair	Poor
375	300	225	150	90

South Africa

M1896 ZAR Rifle

Exc.	V.G.	Good	Fair	Poor
395	300	250	180	100

ZAE M1896 B Series Rifle

Exc.	V.G.	Good	Fair	Poor
395	300	230	160	100

M1896 ZAR Loewe Long Rifle

Exc.	V.G.	Good	Fair	Poor
375	290	200	150	90

M1895/1896 C Series

Exc.	V.G.	Good	Fair	Poor
375	300	225	160	90

Spain

See Spain, Rifles, Mauser.

Sweden

See Sweden, Rifles, Mauser.

Syria

M1948 Short Rifle

Exc.	V.G.	Good	Fair	Poor
150	125	100	80	40

Courtesy Rock Island Auction Company

Thailand/Siam

G 71 Rifle

Exc.	V.G.	Good	Fair	Poor
350	300	200	150	110

M1903 (Type 45) Rifle

Exc.	V.G.	Good	Fair	Poor
225	175	140	110	90

M1904 Rifle

Exc.	V.G.	Good	Fair	Poor
325	290	260	190	150

M1923 (Type 66) Short Rifle

Exc.	V.G.	Good	Fair	Poor
225	175	150	120	90

Transvaal

G 71 Rifle

Exc.	V.G.	Good	Fair	Poor
450	400	300	200	150

Turkey

See Turkey, Rifle, Mauser.

Uruguay

G 71 Rifle

Exc.	V.G.	Good	Fair	Poor
350	300	200	150	110

M1895 Rifle

Exc.	V.G.	Good	Fair	Poor
175	140	90	60	30

M1908 Rifle

Exc.	V.G.	Good	Fair	Poor
190	160	130	100	70

M1908 Short Rifle

Exc.	V.G.	Good	Fair	Poor
190	160	160	100	70

FN M24 Short Rifle

Exc.	V.G.	Good	Fair	Poor
225	190	170	110	70

VZ37 (937) Short Rifle

Exc.	V.G.	Good	Fair	Poor
400	300	200	120	80

VZ37 (937) Carbine

Exc.	V.G.	Good	Fair	Poor
400	300	200	120	80

Venezuela

G 71/84 Rifle

Exc.	V.G.	Good	Fair	Poor
290	200	150	100	70

M1910 Rifle

Exc.	V.G.	Good	Fair	Poor
200	160	140	100	80

VZ24 Short Rifle

Exc.	V.G.	Good	Fair	Poor
250	200	150	100	70

FN M24/30 Short Rifle

Courtesy Cherry's Fine Guns

Exc.	V.G.	Good	Fair	Poor
400	300	200	120	80

FN M24/30 Carbine

Courtesy Rock Island Auction Company

Exc.	V.G.	Good	Fair	Poor
400	300	200	100	70

FN M24/30 Military Target Rifle

Exc.	V.G.	Good	Fair	Poor
350	300	200	125	90

Yemen

FN M30 Short Rifle

Exc.	V.G.	Good	Fair	Poor
300	220	175	110	80

For historical information, technical data, and photos see Hans Dieter Gotz, *German Military Rifles and Machine Pistols, 1871-1945*, Schiffer Publishing 1990.

MAUSER

Established in 1869 by Peter and Wilhelm Mauser, this company came under the effective control of Ludwig Loewe and Company of Berlin in 1887. In 1896 the latter company was reorganized under the name *Deutsches Waffen und Munition* or, as it is better known, DWM.

For history and technical details, see Robert W.D. Ball's, *Mauser Military Rifles of the World*, 3rd edition, Krause Publications, 2003.

NOTE: There are a number of variations to the Mauser rifle listed below that are found in various countries, approximately 54, throughout the world. These can be identified by the country crest stamped most likely on the receiver ring of the rifle. The rifles listed below form the basis of whatever variations may be encounter elsewhere.

Model 1871

This was the first German metallic cartridge rifle. It was a 11x60Rmm caliber single shot bolt action rifle with a 33.5" barrel with bayonet lug, full-length stock secured by two barrel bands, and a cleaning rod. There is no upper handguard on this model. This model did not have an ejector so empty shells had to be removed manually. The rear sight was a leaf type with graduations out to 1600 meters. Weight was about 10 lbs. The barrel marked "Mod. 71" together with the year of production and the manufacturer's name, of which there were several. First produced in 1875. Blued with a walnut stock.

Courtesy Milwaukee Public Museum, Milwaukee, Wisconsin

Exc.	V.G.	Good	Fair	Poor
750	500	400	300	150

Model 1871 Jaeger Rifle

As above, with a 29.4" barrel and finger grip extension behind the triggerguard. Weight is about 10 lbs.

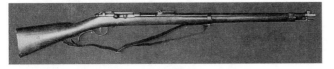

Courtesy Bob Ball

Exc.	V.G.	Good	Fair	Poor
800	650	550	450	300

Model 1871 Carbine

As above, with a 20" barrel and no bayonet lug. It was full stocked to the muzzle. Weight is about 7.5 lbs.

Courtesy Bob Ball

Exc.	V.G.	Good	Fair	Poor
750	500	425	350	225

Model 1871 Short Rifle

As above, but with upper and lower barrel bands and bayonet lug.

Exc.	V.G.	Good	Fair	Poor
700	500	425	350	225

Model 79 G.A.G. Rifle (Grenz-Aufsichts-Gewehr)

Fitted with a 25" barrel and built by Haenel in Suhl and so marked. It is also marked "G.A.G." Used by German border guards. It is full stock almost to the muzzle. It is chambered for the 11x37.5mm cartridge. Weight is about 7 lbs. Single shot.

Exc.	V.G.	Good	Fair	Poor
600	500	400	250	100

Model 71/84 Rifle

The Model 71 modified by the addition of a tubular 8-round magazine. This model was fitted with an ejector. Barrel length 31.5". Weight is approximately 10 lbs. Issued in 1886. About 900,000 were produced. Marked "I.G.MOD.71/84" on the left side of the receiver.

Exc.	V.G.	Good	Fair	Poor
800	600	500	350	275

Model 88 Commission Rifle

A 7.92x57mm caliber bolt action rifle with a 29" barrel, 5-shot magazine, full-length stock, bayonet lug, and cleaning rod. Marked "GEW. 88" together with the year of manufacture and the maker's name. This was the first military rifle to take a rimless cartridge. Weight is about 9 lbs. About 1,000,000 of these rifles were produced. Many of these rifles were later modified to charger loading, therefore original Model 88 rifles are uncommon. These rifles were used in World War I by German, Austro-Hungarian, Bulgarian, and Turkish armies.

Exc.	V.G.	Good	Fair	Poor
300	250	200	150	90

Model 71/84 Rifle • Courtesy Rock Island Auction Company

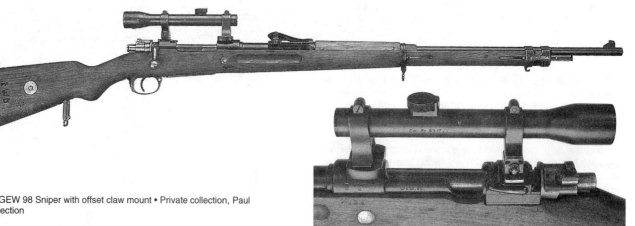

World War I GEW 98 Sniper with offset claw mount • Private collection, Paul Goodwin collection

Model 98 Rifle (Gewehr 98)

The best known of all Mauser rifles. A 7.92mm bolt action rifle with a 29" barrel, 5-shot flush fitting magazine, full-length stock, half-length handguard, cleaning rod, and bayonet lug. Pre-1915 versions had a steel grommet through the buttstock and finger grooves on the forend. These early guns also were fitted with a V-notch rear sight adjustable from 400 to 2,000 meters. Rifles built after World War I were fitted with tangent rear sights graduated from 100 to 2,000 meters. Marked "GEW. 98" together with the date of manufacture and maker's name. Weight is about 9 lbs. About 3,500,000 of these rifles were built from its introduction in 1898 to 1918.

This rifle was built by the following government arsenals and commercial firms: Amberg, Danzig, Erfurt, Spandau, Mauser, DWM, J.P. Sauer & Sohn, V. Chr. Schilling, C.G. Haenel, Simson & Co., and Waffenwerke Oberspree Kornbusch & Co.

Exc.	V.G.	Good	Fair	Poor
500	400	300	150	80

As above, with 17" barrel and full stock to the muzzle without handguard. Not fitted for a bayonet. Produced at the Erfurt arsenal from 1900 to 1902. About 3,000 were produced. In 1902 the Model 98A, with bayonet bar and cleaning rod, was also produced at Erfurt until 1905. Weight was about 7.5 lbs.

Exc.	V.G.	Good	Fair	Poor
800	650	400	250	150

Mauser GEW 98 with trench cover • Courtesy John M. Miller

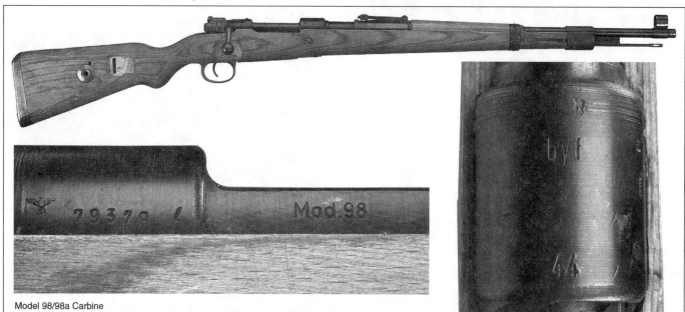

Model 98/98a Carbine

Model 98 AZ • Courtesy West Point Museum, Paul Goodwin photo

Model 98 AZ Carbine/Model 98a

This model has the same stock as the Model GEW 98 but with a slot through the buttstock. Barrel length was 24". Bolt handle was turn down type and the full stock went to the muzzle with full upper handguard. Fitted with a bayonet stud and curved stacking bar on the forearm cap. Magazine capacity is 5 rounds. Weight is about 8 lbs. Introduced in 1908 with about 1,500,000 total production. Stamped "KAR 98" on the left side of the receiver. After WWI these rifles were renamed the Model 98a. Fitted with a small ring receiver.

Exc.	V.G.	Good	Fair	Poor
400	300	225	150	100

Model 98 Transitional Rifle

As a result of the armistice, Model 98 rifles were modified with a simple tangent rear sight, the markings were ground off, and they were arsenal refinished.

Exc.	V.G.	Good	Fair	Poor
400	300	225	150	100

Model 98 KAR 98b Rifle

Also a product of the armistice the Model 98 rifle was altered with the addition of a flat tangent rear sight, removed stacking hook, and a slot was cut for a sling in the buttstock. Otherwise this is a Model 98 rifle.

Exc.	V.G.	Good	Fair	Poor
350	300	275	200	150

Model 98k Carbine (Short Rifle)

This was the standard shoulder arm of the German military during World War II. Introduced in 1935 about 11,000,000 were produced. Barrel length is 23.6". Magazine capacity is 5 rounds of 7.92mm. Rear sight was a tangent leaf graduated to 2000 meters. Weight is about 8.5 lbs. Produced by a numbers of German arsenals using a variety of different identifying codes. Date of production is found on the receiver ring.

Courtesy Buffalo Bill Historical Center, Cody, Wyoming

Exc.	V.G.	Good	Fair	Poor
500	400	300	175	90

Model 98k Carbine (Short Rifle with extended magazine)

This model is a 98k with a non-removable 25-round magazine. It was an attempt to solve the problem of the limited magazine capacity of the standard 98k. This magazine could be filled singly or with 5-round clips.

NOTE: Beware of after-factory add-ons. Prices listed below are for verifiable samples.

Courtesy Amoskeag Auction Company

Exc.	V.G.	Good	Fair	Poor
4000	3000	2500	1500	750

German Sniper Rifles

The German sniper rifle used the K98k rifle as its foundation from 1914 to the end of WWII, although other models such as the G41 and G43 were as employed in that role later in World War II. To simplify a somewhat complex subject, German Sniper rifles are separated into five distinct types. These varieties are based on the type of telescope sight used on the rifle.

The 1st Type is the short rail system.

The 2nd type is the ZF41 and ZF41/1 scopes.

The 3rd type is the turret mount system in both low and high variations.

The 4th type is the long rail system.

The 5th type is the claw mount system.

Different systems were used at different times and often overlap each other. Each system has its own varieties of telescopes made by different manufacturers. Some scopes are numbered to the rifle while others are not. Some rifles and scopes bear the markings of the Waffen-SS, and these will bring a premium.

There were a number of different manufacturers of sniper scopes during the period between 1914 and 1945, and each of these manufacturers was assigned a production code. For example, Schneider & Co. was "dkl". These codes and other pertinent information, including historical information, data,

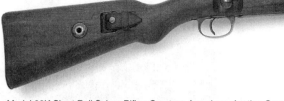

Model 98K Short Rail Sniper Rifle • Courtesy Amoskeag Auction Company

and photos, can be seen in *The German Sniper, 1914-1945*, Peter R. Senich, Paladin Press, 1982.

NOTE: Prices listed below are for the rifle and the correct scope and base, i.e verifiable examples. Sometimes the scope and base are not numbered. It is recommended that an expert opinion be sought prior to a sale. It should be further noted that the prices for German sniper rifles are subject to variations with different scope and mount combinations. Proceed with caution.

Model 98k Sniper Rifle (High Turret Model)

A sniper version of the 98K with different manufactured scopes. This variation has a 6.35mm recess depth greater in the front base cone than the low turret mount. Thus the distinguishing feature in these sniper rifles is the mount, although high-quality German-made scopes will bring a premium.

Mauser 98k with high turret scope • Courtesy private collection, Paul Goodwin photo

Exc.	V.G.	Good	Fair	Poor
10000	7500	5000	2000	1000

Model 98k Sniper Rifle (Low Turret Model)

As above but with a lower front base cone than the high turret mount.

Exc.	V.G.	Good	Fair	Poor
10000	7500	5000	2000	1000

Model K98k Sniper Rifle (Short Rail System)

This mounting system was originally intended for police use during the mid-1930s. Beginning in 1941 this mounting was adopted for general combat use with 98k rifles. Ajack, Zeiss, Hensoldt, and Kahles in 4x are the often-encountered scopes on these mounts. Some of these short rail models were produced specifically for the Waffen-SS and these will command a considerable premium for correctly marked rifles and scopes.

Exc.	V.G.	Good	Fair	Poor
8000	5000	3000	2000	1000

Model K98k Sniper Rifle (Long Rail System)

This mounting system was not utilized in the German military until 1944. This system required that the 98k rifle be modified by having an enlarged receiver flat machined to accommodate the mounting base. This receiver flat has three large tapped screw holes and two smaller holes for tapered pins.

Exc.	V.G.	Good	Fair	Poor
10000	7500	5000	2000	1000

Model K98k Sniper Rifle (Claw Mount System)

According to Senich about 10,000 "bnz" code 98k rifles were produced with claw mounts from late in 1943 to 1944. Various 4x scopes were used on these mounts but the most often encountered is the Hensoldt, Wetzlar (code "bmj"). Original issue rifles will have the rifle, base, and scope with matching numbers.

Exc.	V.G.	Good	Fair	Poor
10000	7500	5000	2000	1000

Russia, 1942-43. A German sniper armed with Mauser Kar 98k rifle equipped with what appears to be a 1.5 power ZF41 scope • Captured German Records/National Archives/Robert Bruce Military Photo Features

Model K98k Sniper Rifle (ZF 41)

This version of the 98K is fitted with a ZF41 scope (1.5x). It is not, in the true sense of the word, a sniper rifle but rather the scope is fitted as an aid to marksmanship. More than 300,000 were produced in this configuration between 1941 and 1945.

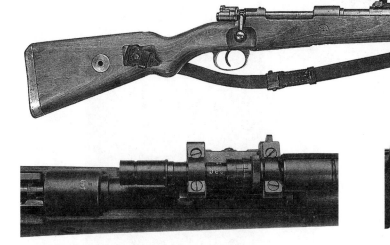

Mauser K98k with ZF41 scope • Private collection, Paul Goodwin photo

Exc.	V.G.	Good	Fair	Poor
3500	2500	1250	750	400

K98k Dual Rail Sniper Rifle • Courtesy Richard M. Kumor Sr.

Model K98k Sniper Rifle (Dual Rail)

This sniper version is fitted with a dual rail scope mount. It is estimated that only about 25 of these rifles were built using this sight system.

Exc.	V.G.	Good	Fair	Poor
Too Rare To Price				

Model 1933 Standard Model Short Rifle

Introduced in 1933 and fitted with a 23.6" barrel full stock with pistol grip and finger grooves in forend. Short upper hand-guard. Weight is about 8.75 lbs. Used extensively by the German Condor Legion in the Spanish Civil War, 1936 to 1939. Stamped with Mauser banner on receiver ring with date of manufacture.

Exc.	V.G.	Good	Fair	Poor
350	275	225	150	100

Model 1933 Standard Model Carbine

Similar to the Model 98k but forearm has finger grooves. Mauser banner stamped on top of receiver ring with date of manufacture. Weight is about 8.5 lbs.

Exc.	V.G.	Good	Fair	Poor
600	500	375	200	125

Model 1933 Standard Model • Courtesy West Point Museum, Paul Goodwin photo

Model 33/40 • Courtesy West Point Museum, Paul Goodwin photo

Model 33/40 Carbine

This carbine was made in Brno in Czechoslovakia during World War II after it was occupied by the German army. This model featured a laminated stock with full upper handguard. Fitted with a 19.2" barrel and marked "G. 33/40" together with the year of production and the maker's code. Marked "dot" over the date or "945" over the date. Weight is about 8 lbs.

Exc.	V.G.	Good	Fair	Poor
800	650	400	300	200

Model 29/40 Rifle (G29o)

This rifle was built by Steyr for the German Luftwaffe. It has a bent bolt and an "L" marked stock. There is some confusion over the origins of this model and its correct designations and configurations. Consult an expert prior to a sale to avoid vexation.

Exc.	V.G.	Good	Fair	Poor
800	675	425	300	200

Model 24 (t) Rifle

This is the German version of the Czech VZ24 rifle built during the German occupation of that country during WWII.

Courtesy Rock Island Auction Company

Exc.	V.G.	Good	Fair	Poor
650	500	300	150	100

Model VG-98

These are crude half-stocked 7.92mm weapons produced near the end of the war to arm the German population. Barrel length is about 21" and some use a 10-round magazine while other examples are single shot. Weight is about 7 lbs. It is made from parts of older, often unserviceable Mausers. Will command premium prices.

Exc.	V.G.	Good	Fair	Poor
3000	2500	2000	1200	600

Model VG-1 (Volksturm Gewehr)

This rifle was made in the last days of WWII and is crudely made. It used the magazine of a semiautomatic Model 43 rifle. Beware of firing this weapon. It is roughly made but because of historical interest and high demand, prices command a premium.

Exc.	V.G.	Good	Fair	Poor
4500	4000	3000	—	—

Model VG-2

Chambered for the 7.9mm cartridge and fitted with a 10-round G43 magazine. This bolt action rifle has a 21" barrel with no bayonet lug. Cheaply built. Receiver is a "U" shaped stamping. Rare.

Exc.	V.G.	Good	Fair	Poor
5500	5000	4000	—	—

Model VG-5

Another last-ditch, locally produced rifle made at the very end of World War II. Chambered for the 7.92x33mm Kertz cartridge. Stamped receiver. Magazine is MP44 type. Simply and roughly made.

Exc.	V.G.	Good	Fair	Poor
5500	5000	4000	—	—

Model 1918 Anti-Tank Rifle

Chambered for the 13x92SR cartridge, this was the first Mauser anti-tank rifle. Barrel length is 39" and weight is about 37 lbs. The Mauser banner is stamped on the upper receiver over the date "1918." Used successfully by the Germans against Allied tanks during WWI.

Courtesy Amoskeag Auction Co., Inc.

VG-1 Rifle • Courtesy West Point Museum, Paul Goodwin photo

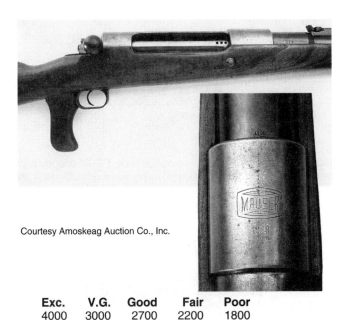

Courtesy Amoskeag Auction Co., Inc.

Exc.	V.G.	Good	Fair	Poor
4000	3000	2700	2200	1800

GERMAN WWII MILITARY RIFLES

Model G 41 Rifle(M)

First produced in 1941. Built by Mauser (code S42). Not a successful design and very few of these rifles were produced. These are extremely rare rifles today. Chambered for the 7.92mm Mauser cartridge. Semiautomatic gas operated with rotating bolt. It was full stocked with a 10-round box magazine. Barrel length is 21.5" and weight is about 11 lbs. The total produced of this model is estimated at 20,000 rifles.

Courtesy Richard M. Kumor Sr.

Exc.	V.G.	Good	Fair	Poor
—	6000	—	—	—

Model G 41(W)

Similar to the above model but designed by Walther and produced by "duv" (Berlin-Lubeck Machine Factory) in 1941. This rifle was contracted for 70,000 units in 1942 and 1943. Correct examples will command a premium price.

Courtesy Richard M. Kumor Sr.

Exc.	V.G.	Good	Fair	Poor
3000	2500	1500	—	—

Model G 43(W) (K43)

An improved version of the G 41(W), introduced in 1943, with a modified gas system that was the more typical gas and piston design. Built by Carl Walther (code "ac"). Full stocked with full-length handguard. Wood or plastic stock. Receiver has a dovetail for telescope sight (#43@4 power). Barrel length is 22" and magazine capacity is 10 rounds. Weight is approximately 9.5 lbs. It is estimated that some 500,000 of these rifles were produced. On the right side of the breech housing, machined into it, there is a telescope rail about .28" in length.

Used by German sharpshooters during World War II and also by the Czech army after WWII.

Exc.	V.G.	Good	Fair	Poor
3000	2500	1500	—	—

NOTE: Add 150% for original scope.

Courtesy Richard M. Kumor Sr.

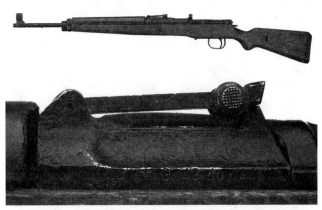

G 43 left side with receiver markings, note rough finish • Paul Goodwin photo

Exc.	V.G.	Good	Fair	Poor
1250	1000	750	250	100

A Walther G 43 rifle sold at auction for $1,650 without the scope. The rifle had all matching numbers and was in very good condition. The scope for the G 43 with mount sold separately for $1,760. It was in excellent condition with steel and rubber sunshade and original leather/cork lens cap.
Amoskeag Auction Company Inc., May 1999

Model FG 42 (Fallschirmjager Gewehr)

This select fire 7.92x57mm rifle was adopted by the Luftwaffe for its airborne troops. It was designed to replace the rifle, light machine gun, and submachine gun. It incorporates a number of features including: straight line stock and muzzle brake, reduced recoil mechanism, closed bolt semiautomatic fire, and open bolt full auto fire. Rate of fire is about 750 rounds per minute. It had a mid-barrel bipod on early (1st Models, Type "E") models and front mounted barrel bipod on later (2nd Models, Type "G") models. Barrel attachment for pike-style bayonet. First Models were fitted with steel buttstocks, sharply raked pistol grips, and 2nd Models with wooden stocks and more vertical pistol grips. The 20-round magazine is left side mounted. Fitted with a 21.5" barrel, the rifle weighs about 9.5 lbs. This breech mechanism was to be used years later by the U.S. in its M60 machine gun.

Pre-1968

Exc.	V.G.	Fair
45000	35000	25000

Pre-1986 conversions

Exc.	V.G.	Fair
N/A	N/A	N/A

Pre-1986 dealer samples

Exc.	V.G.	Fair
N/A	N/A	N/A

NOTE: For rifles fitted with original German FG 42 scopes add between $5,000 and $10,000 depending on model. Consult an expert prior to a sale.

France, July 1944. Army PFC James Durkin shows a captured German FG 42 Type 1 automatic rifle. This light, selective-fire weapon was developed for parachute troops and is chambered for full powered 7.92mm Mauser rifle ammunition • U.S. Army Signal Corps/National Archives/Robert Bruce Military Photo Features

FG 42 with original German FG 42 ZF 4 scope and without scope and wooden buttstock • Courtesy private NFA collection, Paul Goodwin photo

A German ZF 4 Sniper Scope sold at auction for $3,565. Condition is mint with original wooden case. Complete with leather sling and sun shade.
Amoskeag Auction Company Inc., January 2003

STURMGEWEHR GROUP

Because the German military thought the 7.92x57mm cartridge too powerful for its needs, a new cartridge was developed to provide less recoil, lighter weight, and less expensive production. This new cartridge, developed in the mid 1930s by Gustav Genschow, Polte, and others, was called the 7.92x33mm Kurtz (Short) cartridge. The entire cartridge was 1.89" in length and had a bullet weight of 125 grains. This new cartridge was introduced in 1943 and spawned a new series of firearms designed for that cartridge.

FG 42 with original German ZFG 42 scope and without scope and steel buttstock
• Courtesy private NFA collection, Paul Goodwin photo

MKb42(W) • Courtesy West Point Museum, Paul Goodwin photo

MKb42(W)

This select fire open bolt machine carbine built by Walther was used on the Russian front. It was fitted with a 30-round box magazine and 16" barrel. Rate of fire was about 600 rounds per minute. It was fitted with a wooden stock and metal forearm. The rest of the weapon, with the exception of the barrel and bolt, was made from sheet metal to save cost and weight. Weight was about 9.75 lbs. A total of about 8,000 of these weapons were built by Walther.

Pre-1968 (Very Rare)		
Exc.	V.G.	Fair
18000	16500	15000

Pre-1986 conversions		
Exc.	V.G.	Fair
N/A	N/A	N/A

Pre-1986 dealer samples		
Exc.	V.G.	Fair
N/A	N/A	N/A

MKb42(H)

This was a similar design (open bolt) to the Walther version except for a 14.5" barrel and other internal differences. It was built by Haenel, and also saw extensive use on the Eastern Front. This version proved to be better than the Walther design. Its rate of fire was a somewhat slower 500 rounds per minute. Weight was approximately 11 lbs. Some 8,000 of these weapons were also produced.

Walther Arms Plant, Germany, 9 April 1945. 1st Sergeant George Band examines a prototype Maschinenkarbiner Mkb42(W) • U.S. Army Signal Corps/National Archives/Robert Bruce Military Photo Features

MKb42(H) • Courtesy West Point Museum, Paul Goodwin photo

Pre-1968

Exc.	V.G.	Fair
14000	10000	8000

Pre-1986 conversions

Exc.	V.G.	Fair
N/A	N/A	N/A

Pre-1986 dealer samples

Exc.	V.G.	Fair
N/A	N/A	N/A

MP43, MP43/1

With some redesign this model was a newer MKb42(H). This weapon was adopted by the Waffenamt as standard issue in 1944. Originally built by Haenel, it was later produced by Mauser and Erma. This model was the forerunner of the MP44 and StG44.

MP43 • Paul Goodwin photo

Pre-1968

Exc.	V.G.	Fair
8500	7500	7000

Pre-1986 conversions

Exc.	V.G.	Fair
6000	5500	5000

Pre-1986 dealer samples

Exc.	V.G.	Fair
N/A	N/A	N/A

MP44

This German automatic rifle was first produced in 1943 and chambered for the 7.92x33 Kurz cartridge. Fitted with a solid stock and 16.3" barrel, it has a magazine capacity of 30 rounds. The rate of fire is 500 rounds per minute. Weight is about 11.5 lbs. Marked "MP44" on top of the receiver. Production ceased in 1945. This rifle was used extensively on the Eastern Front during World War II.

Pre-1968

Exc.	V.G.	Fair
8500	7500	7000

Pre-1986 conversions

Exc.	V.G.	Fair
6000	5500	5000

Pre-1986 dealer samples

Exc.	V.G.	Fair
N/A	N/A	N/A

StG44

This version of the MP43-MP44 series is nothing more than a name change from the MP44.

Pre-1968

Exc.	V.G.	Fair
12000	11000	10500

Pre-1986 conversions

Exc.	V.G.	Fair
6000	5500	5000

Pre-1986 dealer samples

Exc.	V.G.	Fair
N/A	N/A	N/A

Model 86 SR

Introduced in 1993, this bolt action .308 is sometimes referred to as the Specialty Rifle. Fitted with a laminated wood and special match thumbhole stock or fiberglass stock with adjustable cheekpiece. Stock has rail in forearm and an adjustable recoil pad. Magazine capacity is 9 rounds. Finish is a non-glare blue. The barrel length with muzzle brake is 28.8". Many special features are found on this rifle, from adjustable trigger weight to silent safety. Mauser offers many options on this rifle as well that will affect the price. Weight is approximately 11 lbs.

NIB	Exc.	V.G.	Good	Fair	Poor
3300	2950	2500	1750	1250	750

Model 93 SR

Introduced in 1996, this is a tactical semiautomatic rifle chambered for the .300 Win. Mag. or the .338 Lapua cartridge. Barrel length is 25.5" with an overall length of 48.4". Barrel is fitted with a muzzle brake. Magazine capacity is 6 rounds for .300 and 5 rounds for .338 caliber. Weight is approximately 13 lbs.

NIB	Exc.	V.G.	Good	Fair	Poor
N/A	—	—	—	—	—

HECKLER & KOCH

Model 91

This rifle is recoil-operated, with a delayed-roller lock bolt. It is chambered for the .308 Winchester cartridge and has a 17.7" barrel with military-style aperture sights. It is furnished with a 20-round detachable magazine and is finished in matte black with a black plastic stock. This model is a semiautomatic version of the select fire G3 rifle. Some areas of the country have made its ownership illegal.

NIB	Exc.	V.G.	Good	Fair	Poor
3100	2750	2300	1550	1200	800

Model 91 A3

This model is simply the Model 91 with a retractable metal stock.

NIB	Exc.	V.G.	Good	Fair	Poor
3250	3000	2500	1600	1300	900

Model 93

This model is similar to the Model 91 except that it is chambered for the .223 cartridge and has a 16.4" barrel. The magazine holds 25 rounds, and the specifications are the same as for the Model 91. This is a semiautomatic version of the select fire HK33 rifle.

NIB	Exc.	V.G.	Good	Fair	Poor
3100	2750	2300	1500	1200	800

Model 93 A3

This is the Model 93 with the retractable metal stock.

NIB	Exc.	V.G.	Good	Fair	Poor
3250	3000	2500	1650	1300	900

Model 94

This is a carbine version chambered for the 9mm Parabellum cartridge, with a 16.5" barrel. It is a smaller-scaled weapon that has a 15-shot magazine.

NIB	Exc.	V.G.	Good	Fair	Poor
4200	3850	3300	2750	2200	1500

Model 94 A3

This model is a variation of the Model 94 with the addition of a retractable metal stock.

NIB	Exc.	V.G.	Good	Fair	Poor
4500	3900	3400	2900	2300	1500

HK G3

First adopted by the German army in 1959. Chambered for the 7.62x51mm cartridge and fitted with a 17.5" barrel. Solid wooden stock on early models and plastic stock on later models (A3). Folding stock (A2) also offered. Magazine capacity is 20 rounds with a rate of fire of 550 rounds per minute. Weight is about 9.7 lbs. Marked "G3 HK" on left side of magazine housing. This select fire rifle has seen service with as many as 60 military forces around the world. There are several variations of this model.

Photo courtesy Heckler & Koch

Pre-1968

Exc.	V.G.	Fair
9000	8750	8500

Pre-1986 conversions

Exc.	V.G.	Fair
7000	6500	6000

Pre-1986 dealer samples

Exc.	V.G.	Fair
4000	3800	3500

Saudi Arabia, 1990, Operation Desert Shield. Saudi National Guardsmen on the range with what are likely to be license-built versions of the 7.62mm NATO caliber HK G3, made at the Al-Khardj Arsenal. Note their telescoping stocks • U.S. Department of Defense/Robert Bruce Military Photo Features

HK 33

This model is a reduced caliber version of the standard HK G3. First produced in 1968 this model is chambered for the 5.56x45mm NATO cartridge (.223 caliber). This rifle is available in several variants, namely a sniper version with set trigger, telescope sight and bipod; a retractable stock version (A3); and a carbine version (12.68"). The HK 33 features a 15.35" barrel without flash hider, and a magazine capacity of 25 or 40 rounds. The rate of fire is 750 rounds per minute. The rifle is marked "HK 33 5.56MM" with serial number on the left side of the magazine housing. The rifle is still in production and is in service in Chile, Brazil, various countries in southeast Asia, and Africa. Weight is approximately 8 lbs. for standard model.

HK 33 K • Photo courtesy Heckler & Koch

Pre-1968 (Very Rare)

Exc.	V.G.	Fair
10000	9500	9000

Pre-1986 conversions

Exc.	V.G.	Fair
8500	8000	7500

Pre-1986 dealer samples

Exc.	V.G.	Fair
5000	4500	4000

NOTE: The HK 33 K is the same as the HK 33 with the exception of a 13" barrel. Prices may differ slightly for the HK 33 K version.

HK G41

First produced in 1983, this 5.56x45mm chambered select fire rifle is fitted with a 17.5" barrel and has a magazine capacity of 30 rounds. Rate of fire is about 850 rounds per minute. Marked "HK G41 5.56MM" on the left side of the magazine housing. This model will accept M16 magazines. This model is also available with fixed or retractable stock. Weight is 9.7 lbs.

Pre-1968

HK G41 • Courtesy Heckler & Koch

Exc.	V.G.	Fair
N/A	N/A	N/A

Pre-1986 conversions

Exc.	V.G.	Fair
N/A	N/A	N/A

Pre-1986 dealer samples (Very Rare)

Exc.	V.G.	Fair
9000	8000	7500

PSG-1

This rifle is a high-precision sniping rifle that features the delayed-roller semiautomatic action. It is chambered for the .308 Winchester cartridge and has a 5-shot magazine. Barrel length is 25.6". It is furnished with a complete array of accessories including a 6x42-power illuminated Hensoldt scope. Rifle weighs 17.8 lbs.

NIB	Exc.	V.G.	Good	Fair	Poor
14500	12500	9000	7500	6000	4000

Model SL8-1

This is a new generation .223 rifle modeled after the military Model G36 (not available to civilians) and introduced in 2000. It is built of carbon fiber polymer and is gas operated. Thumbhole stock with cheekpiece. Barrel length is 20.8". Magazine capacity is 10 rounds. Adjustable sights. Weight is approximately 8.6 lbs.

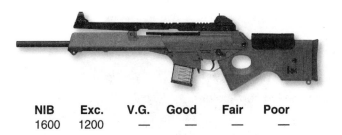

NIB	Exc.	V.G.	Good	Fair	Poor
1600	1200	—	—	—	—

Model USC

Introduced in 2000, this semiautomatic blowback carbine is derived from HK's UMP submachine gun (not available to civilians). Chambered for the .45 ACP cartridge and fitted with a 16" barrel. Skeletonized stock. Accessory rail on top of receiver. Adjustable sights. Magazine capacity is 10 rounds. Weight is approximately 6 lbs.

NIB	Exc.	V.G.	Good	Fair	Poor
1200	900	—	—	—	—

SHOTGUNS

SAUER, J.P. & SON

Luftwaffe Survival Drilling

A double barrel 12 gauge by 9.3x74R combination shotgun/rifle with 28" barrels. Blued with a checkered walnut stock and marked with Nazi inspection. Stampings on the stock and barrel breech. Normally furnished with an aluminum case.

NOTE: Add 50% to prices below for case.

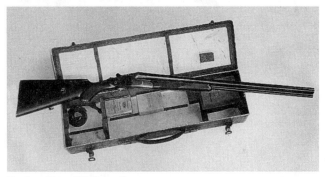

Courtesy Richard M. Kumor Sr.

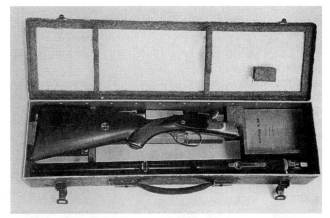

Courtesy Richard M. Kumor Sr.

Exc.	V.G.	Good	Fair	Poor
6000	5500	3800	2500	—

MACHINE GUNS

Germany adopted the Maxim gun and designated it the MG 01, which was built on the Belgian Maxim pattern Model 1900. It was not until 1908 that Germany produced its own version of the Maxim called the MG 08.

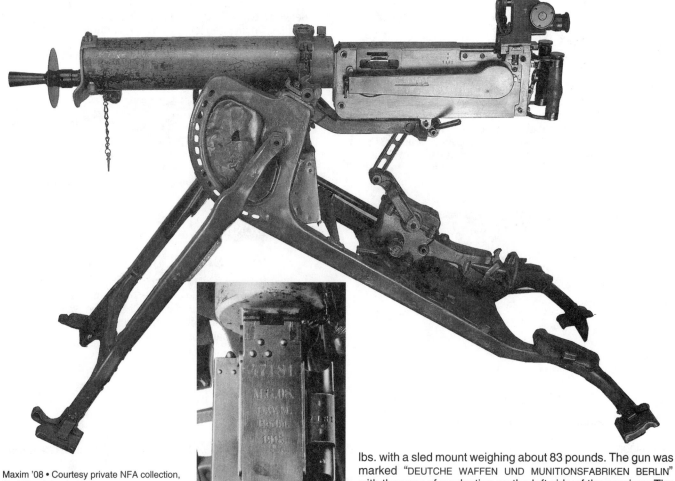

Maxim '08 • Courtesy private NFA collection, Paul Goodwin photo

Bibliographical Note: For information on a wide variety of German machine guns, see Daniel D. Musgrave, *German Machineguns,* 2nd edition, Ironside International Publishers, 1992. Also Folke Myrvang, *MG 34-MG42, German Universal Machineguns*, Collector Grade Publications, 2002. Dolf L. Goldsmith, *The Devil's Paintbrush*, (*the Maxim Gun*) Collector Grade Publications, 2002

Maxim '08 (MG 08)

Germany adopted this gun at the turn of the 20th century. In 1908 they began to produce the gun themselves. This was the standard German heavy machine gun during WWI. Chambered for the 7.92x57mm cartridge this gun had a rate of fire of 400 to 500 rounds per minute from its 28" barrel. It was fed with a 100 or 250-round fabric belt. The gun weighed about 41

lbs. with a sled mount weighing about 83 pounds. The gun was marked "DEUTCHE WAFFEN UND MUNITIONSFABRIKEN BERLIN" with the year of production on the left side of the receiver. The serial number was located on the top of the receiver. The gun was produced from 1908 to about 1918.

Pre-1968		
Exc.	**V.G.**	**Fair**
15000	13000	12000

Pre-1986 conversions		
Exc.	**V.G.**	**Fair**
9000	8000	7000

Pre-1986 dealer samples		
Exc.	**V.G.**	**Fair**
N/A	N/A	N/A

Maxim '08/15

A more movable version of the Maxim Model '08. Chambered for the 7.92x57mm Mauser cartridge and fitted with a 28" water-cooled barrel with bipod, it weighs about 31 lbs. It is fed by

MG 08/15 • Courtesy West Point Museum, Paul Goodwin photo

a 100-round cloth belt housed inside of a special drum with a rate of fire of 500 rounds per minute. Marked "LMG 09/15 SPANDAU" on top of the receiver. Spandau proded 50,000 guns.

Other manufacturers of the gun were:
Erfurt–33,000
Maschinen Fabrik Augsburg, Nurnburg (M.A.N.)–14,000
Siemens & Halske (S&H)–13,000
J.P. Sauer & Sohn, Suhl–11,000
Rheinsche Maschinen & Metallwaren Fabrik (Rh.M. & M.F)–7,000
Deutche Waffen und Munitions Fabriken (D.W. & M.F.)–2,000
Another version of this gun with an air-cooled slotted barrel jacket was used in aircraft. Called the IMG 08/15.

1909 Brass Maxim

The venerable Maxim machine gun is always a pleasure to shoot. In the case of the Brass Maxims, which would be the original guns including the 1905 Russians, assorted Swiss and other models, and the Argentine Model of 1909, the opportunity to fire one comes up very rarely indeed. The Brass Maxims that an American is apt to find at a shoot in the United States will likely be an Argentine Model of 1909 with 1895 markings, on the Ackland high mount or adapted to a Finnish or other low mount. Records show that approximately 200 were made for the Argentine contract, and the last 20 or so had a steel water jacket instead of the brass. All of the ones I have seen in the US were of the brass jacket variety. Tripods were all originally the Ackland type with a seat, serial numbered to the gun.

In 1961, 100 of these rare guns were brought into the United States. There were "Issues" that arose on the import, and many have never been located. Many of the mounts were separated from the guns, thus the improvised mounts. The original caliber of the Argie guns is 7.65 Argentine. This is a fairly short round as far as its contemporary rifle calibers, so conversions are generally limited to .308 (7.62x51 mm NATO).

The cloth belt is meticulously loaded by hand, or if you are fortunate enough, using a belt loading machine. Once the belts have been lined up in their boxes on the right side of the gun, a belt is pulled through the feedblock until it "clicks" into place. On the right of the receiver is a charging handle, which is rotated to the rear—to pull the cartridge from the belt and present it to the chamber. The Maxim is a closed bolt firing system, so the cartridge is in the chamber with a firing pin under tension facing the primer.

Grabbing the spade grips firmly and depressing the firing pin starts the cycle of fire. Since the Maxim is so heavy with its water jacket full, and the tripod, it is extremely stable when firing. You can "keep the hammer down" and traverse your target area with long bursts, until the steam pours out of the jacket, clouding up your shooting area and raising cheers from the crowd. Maxims are generally reliable to shoot, and a rare and beautiful Brass Maxim is certainly a crowd pleaser.

Dan Shea

Pre-1968

Exc.	V.G.	Fair
10000	9500	9000

Pre-1986 conversions

Exc.	V.G.	Fair
N/A	N/A	N/A

Pre-1986 dealer samples

Exc.	V.G.	Fair
N/A	N/A	N/A

Model 1909

A DWM commercial version of the Model 1908 built for export. Fitted with a muzzle booster. Some were sent to Costa Rica as well as Brazil, Mexico, Romania, Switzerland, Belgium, China, and Persia. Some of these countries, like Switzerland and China, built their own military versions of the DWM 1909 commercial. A seldom-seen variation.

Maxim 1909 Commercial • Courtesy Blake Stevens, *The Devil's Paintbrush*, Goldsmith

Pre-1968

Exc.	V.G.	Fair
12000	10000	9000

Pre-1986 conversions (side-plate)

Exc.	V.G.	Fair
8000	7500	7000

Pre-1986 dealer samples

Exc.	V.G.	Fair
N/A	N/A	N/A

Dreyse Model 1910/15

Chambered for the 7.92x57mm Mauser cartridge, this gun was based on the Louis Schmeisser patents of 1907. Built by Rheinmetall in Sommerda, Germany. Named in honor of Johann Niklaus von Dreyse who died in 1875. This is a water-cooled gun designed for sustained fire. Rate of fire is about 550 to 600 rounds a minute. Weight is approximately 37 lbs. Most of these guns were converted by Germany to MG 13s during the 1930s, so few original Dreyse models still survive. Very rare in unaltered condition.

Pre-1968

Exc.	V.G.	Fair
20000	18000	17000

Pre-1986 conversions

Exc.	V.G.	Fair
N/A	N/A	N/A

Pre-1986 dealer samples

Exc.	V.G.	Fair
N/A	N/A	N/A

Parabellum MG 14

Chambered for the 7.9mm cartridge, this was a water-cooled light machine gun. There was also an air-cooled version with

Dreyse Model 1915 • Courtesy private NFA collection, Paul Goodwin photo

a slotted water jacket. Barrel length is 27.75". Rate of fire is about 700 rounds per minute. Weight is about 21.5 lbs. This gun was derived from the Maxim but the main spring is located behind the receiver and is compressed during recoil. The gun was much lighter than the Maxim. Also, the Parabellum has no dead stop on the crank handle. The gun was the standard observer's machine gun in German two-seat aircraft during World War I. The gun was also used in Zeppelins as well as a ground gun. Built by DWM.

Pre-1968

Exc.	V.G.	Fair
Too Rare To Price		

Pre-1986 conversions

Exc.	V.G.	Fair
N/A	N/A	N/A

Pre-1986 dealer samples

Exc.	V.G.	Fair
N/A	N/A	N/A

MG 13

In 1932 the German army adopted the MG 13 as its standard machine gun. Chambered for the 7.92x57mm cartridge and fitted with a 28" air-cooled barrel, this gun is recoil operated. The butt is a single arm metal type with pistol grip. The bipod is attached close to the muzzle. A 25-round box magazine or a 75-round saddle drum magazine can be used. Weight is about 25

Parabellum with original scope • Courtesy private NFA collection, Paul Goodwin photo

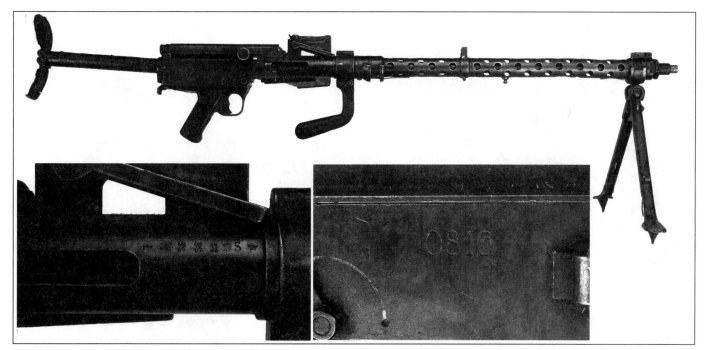

MG 13 • Courtesy West Point Museum, Paul Goodwin photo

lbs. with bipod. Who manufactured the gun is unclear, but Simson of Suhl, Germany, is often reported to be the manufacturer, perhaps because the company was the only legal machine gun manufacturer under the Versailles Treaty. Evidence suggests that the gun was made at Sommerda by Rheinmetall.

NOTE: The 75-round drum for use with the MG 13 is rare because it uses an MG15 drum with a special magazine extension to fit into the side of the MG 13 magazine well.

Pre-1968

Exc.	V.G.	Fair
15000	13000	11000

Pre-1986 conversions

Exc.	V.G.	Fair
N/A	N/A	N/A

Pre-1986 dealer samples

Exc.	V.G.	Fair
N/A	N/A	N/A

MG15 Aircraft Gun

Used by the German air force in its bombers, this air-cooled gun is chambered for the 7.92x57JS cartridge. Rate of fire is about 850 rounds per minute. Barrel length is 28". Saddle drum magazine with 75-round capacity was used. Weight is about 28 lbs. Built by Krieghoff. Made by Rheinmetall beginning in 1932.

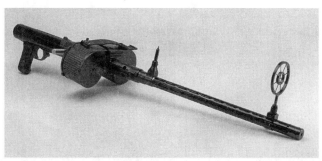

Private NFA collection, Gary Gelson photo

Pre-1968

Exc.	V.G.	Fair
13000	12000	11500

Pre-1986 conversions

Exc.	V.G.	Fair
N/A	N/A	N/A

Pre-1986 dealer samples

Exc.	V.G.	Fair
N/A	N/A	N/A

MG15 Water-Cooled Ground Gun

A converted aircraft machine gun, this water-cooled model was used by ground forces from 1944 to 1945. Barrel length was 30" and weight is about 33 lbs. Chambered for the 7.92x57JS cartridge. Rate of fire is about 750 rounds per minute. Ammunition capacity is a 75-round saddle drum magazine. Built by Krieghoff.

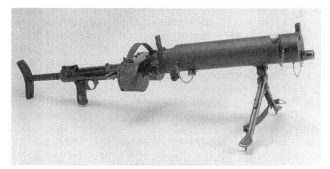

Private NFA collection, Gary Gelson photo

Pre-1968

Exc.	V.G.	Fair
12000	11000	10500

Pre-1986 conversions

Exc.	V.G.	Fair
N/A	N/A	N/A

Pre-1986 dealer samples

Exc.	V.G.	Fair
N/A	N/A	N/A

MG15 Air-Cooled Ground Gun

Same as the aircraft gun but converted to ground use in 1944 and 1945 by attaching a bipod and single strut buttstock.

Pre-1968

Exc.	V.G.	Fair
13000	12000	11500

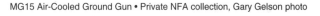

MG15 Air-Cooled Ground Gun • Private NFA collection, Gary Gelson photo

Pre-1986 conversions

Exc.	V.G.	Fair
N/A	N/A	N/A

Pre-1986 dealer samples

Exc.	V.G.	Fair
N/A	N/A	N/A

MG34

Designed and built by Mauser, this was the first general purpose machine gun to be produced in large numbers. It was introduced into the German army in about 1936, and stayed in production until the end of the war in 1945. Chambered for the 7.92x57mm Mauser cartridge, this gun had a 25" barrel with a 50-round belt or 75-round saddle drum. Rate of fire was about 800 to 900 rounds per minute. Marked "MG34" with its serial number on top of the receiver. Weight was approximately 26.5 lbs. There were a number of different bipod and tripod mounts for this gun, as well as different gun configurations such as antiaircraft use, use in armored vehicles, and one configuration where only automatic fire was possible. After WWII the gun was used by the Czechs, French, and Israelis, as well as the Viet Cong. Superseded by the MG42.

MG34 with receiver markings • Paul Goodwin photo

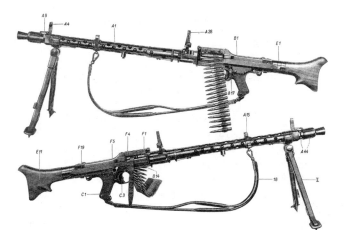

MG34 • Courtesy Blake Stevens, *MG34-MG42 German Universal Machine Guns*, Myrvang

Operation Barbarossa, Russia, June 1941. A German machine gun crew with the versatile MG34 on sturdy tripod and equipped with the Model 34 optical sight • Captured German Records/National Archives/Robert Bruce Military Photo Features

Pre-1968

Exc.	V.G.	Fair
16500	15000	15000

Pre-1986 conversions

Exc.	V.G.	Fair
N/A	N/A	N/A

Pre-1986 dealer samples

Exc.	V.G.	Fair
N/A	N/A	N/A

MG42-MG42/59-MG1-MG3

This gun replaced the MG34 and was chambered for the 7.92x57mm Mauser cartridge. It has a 20.8" quick change barrel and is fed by a 50-round belt. Its rate of fire is about 1,000 to 1,200 rounds per minute. The butt is synthetic with pistol grip. The gun weighs about 25 lbs. Marked "MG42" on the left side of the receiver. This gun was produced from 1938 until the end of the war in 1945. Its design was the result of wartime engineering which used roller locks – at the time a revolutionary design concept.

Post-war models, the MG42/59 followed by the MG1 then the MG3, are still in use by the German army. These post-war guns are chambered for the 7.62x51mm cartridge. These models utilize many important improvements in manufacturing and design, and are in use by many countries throughout the world. There are a number of licensed versions of the MG42/59 made in Austria, Italy, Spain, Portugal, Turkey, Yugoslavia, and Switzerland.

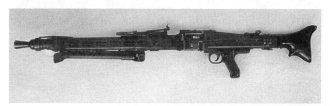

MG3 • Photo courtesy private NFA collection

MG42 • Private NFA collection, Gary Gelson photo

MG42

Pre-1968

Exc.	V.G.	Fair
22500	20000	18500

Pre-1986 conversions

Exc.	V.G.	Fair
15000	13500	12500

Pre-1986 dealer samples

Exc.	V.G.	Fair
12000	10000	9000

NOTE: For MG42/5 and MG42/59 add 75% premium (8 known). For MG3 add 125% (3 known).

Ardennes, Belgium, December 1944. This famous photo from the Battle of the Bulge shows a German SS patrol enjoying a smoke break during the early offensive phase. The MG42 gunner in the center is also holding what appears to be a Browning M35 High Power pistol in his left hand • Captured German Records/National Archives/Robert Bruce Military Photo Features

HK11 (HK11A1-HK11E)

Designed as a light air-cooled machine gun chambered for the 7.62x51mm cartridge, this gun uses a roller-delayed bolt. The quick change barrel is 17.7" long. Fixed synthetic stock with pistol grip and bipod. Uses a 20-round box magazine or 80 dual drum. Rate of fire is about 850 rounds per minute. Weight is approximately 15 lbs.

NOTE: There is no drum magazine on the HK11A1.

Pre-1968

Exc.	V.G.	Fair
N/A	N/A	N/A

Pre-1986 conversions

Exc.	V.G.	Fair
13000	11000	9000

Pre-1986 dealer samples

Exc.	V.G.	Fair
13000	11000	9000

WHAT'S IT LIKE: THE GERMAN MG42

One of the finest weapons to emerge from WWII, the MG42 was often referred to as "Hitler's Zipper" by Allied troops because it spewed bullets at the then amazing rate of up to 1,300 rpm. In tactical concept it was to be identical to its predecessor, the MG34 - the world's first GPMG, which had proved to be overly dust sensitive and too complex. The MG42 is conspicuous for its extensive use of stamped sheet metal and assembly by riveting, spot and fusion welding, brazing and other methods not requiring specialized skills.

The method of operation is best described as short recoil, gas-assisted and roller locked. Because the bolt head's rollers lock into the barrel extension, the MG42's receiver serves as little more than a structural frame for holding the reciprocating parts. The design's greatest deficiency was premature unlocking before the barrel has completed its recoil and while chamber pressures were still too high. This problem was never solved until after the war with the development of the M3, a 7.62x51mm NATO version. A spring-loaded plunger, inserted into the bolt body, forces the firing pin housing forward to press against the locking rollers and increase resistance to unlocking. This device has the added benefit of reducing the cyclic rate by as much as half.

However, German gunners were trained to fire extremely short bursts with the MG42. As long as no more than three or four rounds were fired, the group dispersion downrange was quite low and the hit probability quite high. This was especially so when the gun was fired off its "soft" mount. While disassembly of the MG42 presents no problems, there are a number of ergonomic deficiencies. There is no forearm or carrying handle and the gun must be carried by a two-piece sling wrapped over the top of the gun. These small issues aside, the MG42 is an outstanding design and is still fielded in its .308 versions throughout the world.

Peter Kokalis

HK13 (HK13E)

This gun is similar to the HK11 but is chambered for the 5.56x45mm cartridge. Quick change 17.7" barrel. Fed by a 20-, 30-, or 40-round box magazine, or 100-round dual drum. Rate of fire is about 800 rounds per minute. Weight is approximately 12 lbs.

NOTE: There are a number of variants to this model. The HK13C has a baked-on forest camouflage finish. The HK13E is a modernized version with selective improvements, such as a 3-round burst capability. The rifling has been changed to stabilize 62 grain bullets. The HK13E1 is the same as the HK13E with rifling twist to accommodate 54 grain bullets. The HK13S has a baked-on desert camouflage scheme.

Pre-1968

Exc.	V.G.	Fair
N/A	N/A	N/A

Pre-1986 conversions

Exc.	V.G.	Fair
12000	11000	9000

Pre-1986 dealer samples

Exc.	V.G.	Fair
12000	11000	9000

NOTE: There is a semiautomatic version of this gun. Value would be around $6,000 for one in excellent condition.

HK21 (HK21E-HK23E)

These guns form a series of general purpose machine guns. The 21 series is chambered for the 7.62x51mm cartridge while the 23E is chambered for the 5.56x45mm cartridge. The HK21 is fitted with a 17.5" barrel and has a rate of fire of 900 rounds per minute. Its weight is about 17 lbs. Marked on the top of receiver. The HK21 was first produced in 1970 but is no longer in production, while the HK21E and 23E are still produced.

This series of guns has variations similar to the HK13 series of guns.

HK23 • Courtesy Heckler & Koch

HK23E • Courtesy Heckler & Koch

Pre-1968 Model 21

Exc.	V.G.	Fair
40000	37500	35000

Pre-1986 conversions

Exc.	V.G.	Fair
20000	18000	17000

Pre-1986 dealer samples

Exc.	V.G.	Fair
20000	18000	17000

NOTE: The HK21E and HK23E will bring a premium of 75% over the older HK21/2

GREAT BRITAIN

British Military Conflicts, 1870-Present

The period from 1870 to 1901 marked the height of Britain's economic, political, commercial, and military influence. During this period, the far-flung British empire required the country to police its possessions frequently with force. The British army was involved in Africa, Asia, the Middle East, and even Ireland during this period. The Boer War in the last years of the 19th century, for example, required extensive military presence in South Africa. In 1914, Britain entered World War I. By the end of the war in 1918, the country had exhausted its wealth and manpower. During the war 5,700,000 served in the armed forces and of those 2,365,035 were killed or wounded, about 41% of those who served.

During the period between the two world wars, Britain tried to consolidate its remaining power which led to the appeasement of Nazi Germany and eventually World War II in 1939. At war's end, 5,896,000 had served. Of those, 582,900 were killed or wounded, about 10%. With the end of the war in 1945, Britain gave independence to many of its colonies and concentrated on domestic, economic, and social affairs. In 1982, the country was involved in a successful military engagement with Argentina over the Falkland Islands. As a member of NATO Britain continued to carry out its military responsibilities. As of 2001, the United Kingdom military forces had 211,430 personnel, of which 113,950 were in the army.

HANDGUNS

NOTE: During World War I, the British government contracted with two Spanish firms to build what was called the Old Pattern No.1 Mark I revolver by Garate y Compania and the Old Pattern No. 2 Mark I revolver by Trocaola, Aranzabal y Compania. Both companies were located in Eibar, Spain. These revolvers were chambered for the .455 caliber cartridge and were fitted with 5" barrels. Britain also acquired Colt New Service and Smith & Wesson First Model and Second Model Ejector .455 revolvers from the U.S. Approximately 75,000 of these S&W and Colt revolvers were sent to England between 1914 and 1916.

Adams Model 1872 Mark 2, 3, and 4

A .450 caliber double action revolver with a 6" octagonal barrel and 6-shot cylinder. Blued with walnut grips. Built by Adams Patent Small Arms Company. Weight was about 40 oz. This was the first breechloading revolver issued to the British mounted units. In service from 1872 to 1919.

Exc.	V.G.	Good	Fair	Poor
—	1250	600	400	200

WEBLEY & SCOTT, LTD.

Bibliographical **Note:** For historical information, technical data, and photos see William Dowell's, *The Webley Story*, Skyrac Press, 1987.

Mark I

A .455 caliber double action top break revolver with a 4" barrel and 6-shot cylinder. Blued with hard rubber grips. Manufactured from 1887 to 1894. Models issued to the Royal Navy have the letter "N" stamped on top of the frame behind the hammer.

Courtesy Faintich Auction Services, Inc., Paul Goodwin photo

Exc.	V.G.	Good	Fair	Poor
350	200	175	125	100

NOTE: Military version chambered for .455 cartridge only while commercial versions were chambered for the .442 and .476 cartridges.

Mark II

As above, with a larger hammer spur and improved barrel catch. Manufactured from 1894 to 1897.

Exc.	V.G.	Good	Fair	Poor
350	200	175	125	100

Mark III

As above, with internal improvements. Introduced in 1897.

Courtesy Rock Island Auction Company

Exc.	V.G.	Good	Fair	Poor
350	225	200	150	125

Mark IV

As above, with a .455 caliber and 4" or 6" barrel. Sometimes referred to as the "Boer War" model because it was supplied to British troops in South Africa between 1899 and 1902.

NOTE: This model was also commercially available in .22 caliber with 6" barrel, .32 caliber with 3" barrel, and .38 caliber with 3", 4", or 5" barrel.

Courtesy Faintich Auction Services, Inc., Paul Goodwin photo

Exc.	V.G.	Good	Fair	Poor
375	300	225	175	125

Mark V

As above, with a 4" (standard) or 6" barrel. Manufactured from 1913 to 1915.

Courtesy Faintich Auction Services, Inc., Paul Goodwin photo

Exc.	V.G.	Good	Fair	Poor
375	325	250	200	150

Mark IV .380 (.38S&W)

Webley produced a military version of its .38 revolver for military use during World War II. This model was intended to supplement the .38 Enfield revolvers.

Exc.	V.G.	Good	Fair	Poor
400	325	250	200	150

Mark VI

As above, with 6" barrel and square buttgrip. Introduced in 1915 and replaced in 1928.

Courtesy Faintich Auction Services, Inc., Photo Paul Goodwin

Exc.	V.G.	Good	Fair	Poor
375	300	250	175	125

Model 1913-Semiautomatic Pistol

The Model 1913 was the result of years of development in conjunction with the British government and was finally adopted in 1913 as the Model 1913 MK1N for Royal Navy issue. It has the same breech-locking system as the Model 1910, but has an external hammer and is chambered for the .455 Webley self-loading cartridge. About 1,000 Model 1913s were sold commercially and serial numbered along with the smaller caliber pistols. In 1915, a variation of the Model 1913 with butt slotted for a shoulder stock, an adjustable rear sight, and a hammer safety was adopted for use by the Royal Horse Artillery. Shoulder stocks are very rare, and will double values shown for the RHA model. All militaries were numbered in their own series; about 10,000 made in both variations.

Model 1913

Exc.	V.G.	Good	Fair	Poor
1500	1200	800	500	300

Model 1913 (RHA model)

Courtesy Joseph Schroeder

Exc.	V.G.	Good	Fair	Poor
2500	2000	1500	850	600

Webley-Fosbery Model 1914

This is an automatic revolver that is recoil-operated by the barrel-cylinder group sliding across the frame to cock the hammer and revolve the cylinder using the zig-zag grooves in the cylinder. Chambered for the .455 cartridge. Cylinder has a 6-round capacity. Barrel length is 6". Weight is about 30 oz. This sidearm was not officially adopted by British forces but was widely used by them during World War I.

Webley-Fosbery Model 1914 • Courtesy Rock Island Auction Company

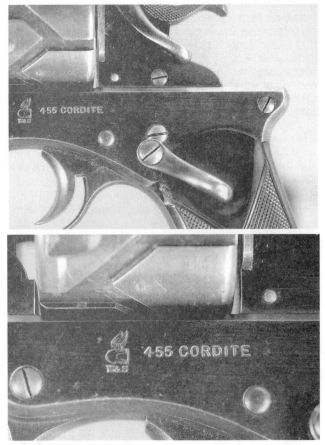

Webley-Fosbery Model 1914 • Courtesy Rock Island Auction Company

Exc.	V.G.	Good	Fair	Poor
4500	3750	2750	1750	1250

ENFIELD ROYAL SMALL ARMS FACTORY

In 1879, the British army needed revolvers, and the Royal Small Arms Factory was commissioned to produce them. The result was that on August 11, 1880, the Enfield Mark 1 was accepted for duty.

Enfield Mark 1 Revolver

A 6-shot, hinged-frame, break-open revolver. It has an odd ejection system—when the barrel is pulled down, the cylinder moves forward; and the extractor plate remains in place, retaining the spent cartridges. This revolver is chambered for the .476 cartridge and has a 6-shot cylinder. The barrel is 6" long, and the finish is blued with checkered walnut grips. Weight is about 40 oz.

Exc.	V.G.	Good	Fair	Poor
400	275	200	150	100

Enfield Mark 2

The Mark 2 is similar externally, with some design improvements—such as a rounded front sight, taper-bored cylinders, an integral top strap, and plain grips. The Mark 2 was introduced in 1881 and was replaced by the Webley Mark I in 1887.

Exc.	V.G.	Good	Fair	Poor
375	250	175	140	100

Enfield-Produced Webley Mark 6

This model is identical to the Webley-produced versions. It is of .455 caliber and is stamped "Enfield" on the frame.

Exc.	V.G.	Good	Fair	Poor
375	250	175	140	100

Enfield No. 2 Mark I/Mark 1*

Originally chambered for the .380 (.38 S&W). It is a 6-shot, break-open double action, with a 5" barrel. The finish is blued, with black plastic checkered grips. This model was actually a modified Webley design and was adopted in 1932. In 1938, the bullet was changed from a 200-grain lead "soft-nosed" to a 178-grain jacketed, in response to pressure from the Geneva Conference.

Exc.	V.G.	Good	Fair	Poor
275	200	150	125	100

Enfield No. 2 Mark 1* • Courtesy West Point Museum, Paul Goodwin photo

Enfield No. 2 Mark 1 • Paul Goodwin photo

Enfield No. 2 Mark I*

The same as the Mark I with the hammer spur and single action lockwork omitted in response to the Royal Tank Regiment's fear that the spur would catch on the tank as the crews were entering and exiting their confines.

Exc.	V.G.	Good	Fair	Poor
275	200	175	150	125

NOTE: During WWII these pistols were also manufactured by Albion Motors Ltd. of Glasgow, Scotland. These pistols were produced between 1941 and 1943, and approximately 24,000 were made. They are marked "Albion" on the right side of the frame. These examples would not be valued differently than Enfield-made pistols. Enfield pistols with the marking "SM" or "SSM" will also be noted, and this refers to various parts produced by Singer Sewing Machine Company of England. These pistols were assembled at Enfield. Used until 1957, when the FN-Browning GP35 semiautomatic pistol replaced them.

SUBMACHINE GUNS

NOTE: For historical information and technical details see Laider and Howroyd, *The Guns of Dagenham; Lanchester, Patchett, Sterling*, Collector Grade Publications, 1999. Laider, *The Sten Machine Carbine*, Collector Grade Publications, 2000.

Lanchester Mk1/Mk1*

The British submachine gun was produced from 1940 to about 1942. It is chambered for the 9mm cartridge and is fitted with a 7.75" barrel. The magazine capacity is 50 rounds. Rate of fire is 600 rounds per minute. Weight is about 9.5 lbs. This British gun is almost an exact copy of the Bergmann MP28. The magazine housing is made of brass. The bayonet lug will accept a Model 1907 pattern bayonet. Most of these weapons were issued to the Royal Navy and stayed in service there until the 1960s. Markings are "LANCHESTER MARK I" on the magazine housing.

The Mk1* has had the fire selector switch in front of the triggerguard removed thus making the weapon capable of full automatic fire only.

Pre-1968

Exc.	V.G.	Fair
5000	4500	4000

Pre-1986 conversions

Exc.	V.G.	Fair
N/A	N/A	N/A

Pre-1986 dealer samples

Exc.	V.G.	Fair
2500	2000	1500

NOTE: Add a premium of 15% for the Mark 1 version.

Sten Mark II

The Mark II is the most common version of the Sten models. It is chambered for the 9mm cartridge and features a removable stock and barrel. The magazine capacity is 32 rounds. Barrel length is 7.66". The rate of fire is 550 rounds per minute. Markings are located on top of the magazine housing and are stamped "STEN MK II." Weight is approximately 6.6 lbs. Produced from 1942 to 1944 with about two million built in Britain, Canada, and New Zealand.

France, 1944. A French partisan armed with a Mark II Sten submachine gun and an American lieutenant with an M1911 auto pistol, keep a sharp eye out for German snipers • U.S. Army Signal Corps/National Archives/Robert Bruce Military Photo Features

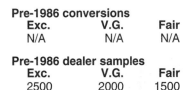

Lanchester Mark I* • Courtesy West Point Museum, Paul Goodwin photo

Courtesy Richard M. Kumor Sr.

Pre-1968

Exc.	V.G.	Fair
5000	4500	4000

Pre-1986 conversions (or U.S.-manufactured receivers)

Exc.	V.G.	Fair
3000	2500	2500

Pre-1986 dealer samples

Exc.	V.G.	Fair
2500	2000	1000

NOTE: The Mark II S is the silenced version of the Mark II. Fitted with a canvas foregrip. Weight is about 7.75 lbs. and rate of fire is about 450 rounds per minute.

Sten Mark III

This model was an improved version of the Marks 1 and 2, and featured a one-piece receiver and barrel jacket of welding tubing with a non-removable barrel. No flash hider. Built at Lines and Long Branch arsenals. All other specifications are the same as the Marks I and II.

Pre-1968

Exc.	V.G.	Fair
5000	4500	4000

Pre-1986 conversions (or U.S.-manufactured receivers)

Exc.	V.G.	Fair
3000	2500	2500

Pre-1986 dealer samples

Exc.	V.G.	Fair
2500	2000	1000

THE STEN MARK II SMG

The British Sten Mark II is probably second only to the Russian PPSh 41 for the most prolific submachine gun of all time. While there were other production Sten models (Mark 1, 3, and 5) , there were many more Mark II Stens made than all other Sten variations combined. Even more important is the fact that none of the other Sten variations, except the silenced Mark IIS and Mark 6, had any performance advantage over the Mark II. The Mark IIS was the most prolific silenced submachine gun ever produced and many were still in use as late as the Vietnam War. While it looked a bit crude and ugly, the Mark II Sten is lighter and handier than most of its competitors. It was also extremely reliable as long as the shooter had good magazines. Unfortunately, many Sten magazines were either poorly made or badly maintained. The Mark II was produced in England, Canada, and New Zealand during WWII and in Taiwan after the war, with an exact copy made in Germany late in the war probably to arm Germans dressed in British uniforms operating behind Allied lines. Many thousands of the Mark II Stens were also supplied to the Allied resistance forces by parachute. These Stens were packaged partially disassembled in small boxes. The barrel would be fitted, the butt stock attached, and the magazine well rotated into firing position in under a minute. Their ease of disassembly made it easier for friendly resistance fighters to hide and to smuggle these guns. Produced in England for as little as $11, the Sten performed as well as any SMG used in the war and better than most. It offered more bang for the buck than any other firearm of its time and is extremely significant historically.

Chuck Karwan

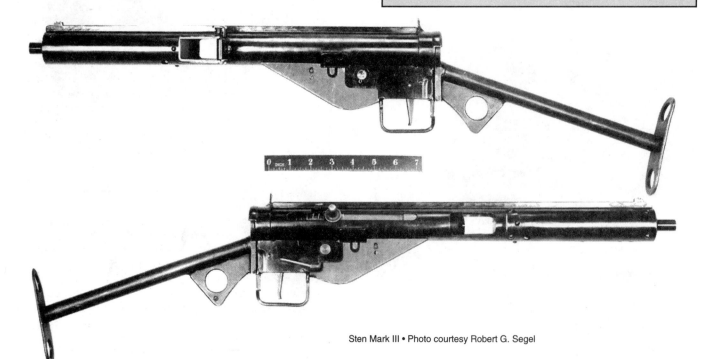

Sten Mark III • Photo courtesy Robert G. Segel

Korea, 1951. A British Commonwealth Forces soldier shows his 9mm Sten Mark V submachine gun to a American GI. The Mark V is readily identified by its rifle-type front sight, wooden stock and pistol grip • U.S. Army Signal Corps/National Archives/Robert Bruce Military Photo Features

Sten Mark V

This version of the Sten was first produced in 1944. It featured a wooden stock and pistol grip. The barrel could accept a bayonet. Finish was better than standard service of the period. Barrel length was 7.75" and magazine capacity was 32 rounds. Rate of fire was 600 rounds per minute. Weight was increased to 8.6 lbs. over the Mark II. Marked "STEN M.C. MK V" on top of the magazine housing. Production ceased on this version in 1946.

Sten Mark V • Photo courtesy Robert G. Segel

Pre-1968

Exc.	V.G.	Fair
5500	4500	4250

Pre-1986 conversions

Exc.	V.G.	Fair
3500	3000	2500

Pre-1986 dealer samples

Exc.	V.G.	Fair
2500	2000	1500

NOTE: The Mark VI is the silenced version of the Mark V. Fitted with a long barrel and silencer assembly. Weight is about 9.8 lbs. and rate of fire is about 450 rounds per minute.

Sterling Mk 4 (L2A3)

Chambered for the 9mm cartridge this submachine gun features a 7.75" barrel, 34-round side mounted magazine, collapsible metal stock. The last version of the Sterling, the Mk 4, is a result of a long line of improvements to the gun beginning with the Pachett. The Pachett was originally developed during WWII and produced by the Sterling Co. in Dagenham, England and the Royal Ordnance Factory in Fazakerley, England. Next came the Mk 2 and the Mk 3 beginning in 1953 and the Mk 4 during the late 1950s.

It has seen wide use throughout the world having been adopted by the British army, New Zealand and approximately 40 other countries. The rate of fire is 550 rounds per minute. Weight is about 6 lbs. Produced from 1953 to 1988. Still made in India under license. Marked "STERLING SMG 9MM" on the magazine housing.

BRITISH STEN MARK V

During the desperate hours of World War II the British fielded the rather crude Sten submachine gun. A simple blowback design cobbled together from simple metal parts it nonetheless proved effective. As the war progressed and things improved, the British took another look at the Sten and decided that maybe it was just a little too crude. This led to the introduction of the Sten Mark V. While basically operating the same as the earlier models, the Mark V was a little bit more refined. It featured a wooden buttstock and pistol grip, front sight assembly from the No. 4 rifle, accepted the No. 4's bayonet, and was generally better finished. Wooden stock or not though, it's still very much a Sten and will never be confused with a Thompson. Still it is a simple and fairly effective weapon. To use, simply insert a 32-round magazine into the mag well located on the left side of the weapon. Retract the bolt and turn the bolt handle up into the safety notch. In front of the trigger there's a button which acts as a selector. Pushing the button to "R" provides semi-auto fire, to "A" provides fully automatic fire. The sight picture mimics that of the No. 4 rifle and is quite good. Drop the bolt handle out of the safety slot, lean into the weapon, and squeeze the mushy trigger. Over 1 pound of bolt jumps forward and then flies to the rear. On full auto, the cyclic rate is low and controllability good. Accuracy on semi-auto depends on the operator's ability to hold the weapon steady as the bolt flies forward. Handling is compromised by the 32-round magazine sticking out of the left side of the receiver and rear of the pistol grip being cut out to allow the stock to be removed. While a serviceable enough design for the time, I'd of rather had a PPSh-41.

David Fortier

Photo courtesy private NFA collection

Pre-1968 (Rare)

Exc.	V.G.	Fair
9500	8500	8000

Pre-1986 conversions

Exc.	V.G.	Fair
5000	4500	4000

Pre-1986 dealer samples

Exc.	V.G.	Fair
5000	4500	3750

Sterling L34A1

This is a silenced version of the L2A3 Mark 4 gun. The silencer is fitted with a short wooden forearm. Barrel length is the same as the unlicensed version. Weight is about 8 lbs.

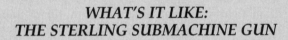

WHAT'S IT LIKE:
THE STERLING SUBMACHINE GUN

The Sterling is a second generation Lanchester without the fine machining. In use throughout the world by Britain and its Commonwealth countries, the Sterling has proven itself in combat on many occasions. It is lighter than the Uzi and uses a two-stage recoil spring that softens recoil thus allowing multiple hits. The rate of fire of about 600 rounds a minute makes it a very controllable gun even with long burst. The bolt has a series of ribs cut into it that allow dirt and other foreign matter to be swept out of the way so that the gun continues to function. Sterling called this feature the "sand-mud-proof" bolt. The Sterling uses a unique 34-round curved magazine with rollers to facilitate loading with fingers only. The loading pressure is almost the same from the first round to the 34th. The gun feeds flawlessly. Sights are adequate with the front adjustable for windage as well as elevation, and fitted with stout protectors. The rear sight is a flip-up device for 100 or 200 yards settings. The one characteristic of this submachine gun that is most noticeable is its smoothness while firing. The muzzle appears not to move making it very easy to stay on target, either with single shots or bursts. Its relatively light-weight makes it easy to carry and handle. The ventilated barrel jacket allows the user to grip the jacket during firing without fear of burning the hand. The folding metal stock, while a bit complex to assemble and takedown, is very strong and stable.

Ned Schwing

Pre-1968 (Rare)

Exc.	V.G.	Fair
9500	8500	8000

Pre-1986 conversions

Exc.	V.G.	Fair
4500	4000	3500

Pre-1986 dealer samples

Exc.	V.G.	Fair
4000	3500	3000

RIFLES

NOTE: For historical information and technical data see: Reynolds, E.G.B., *The Lee-Enfield Rifle*, Herbert Jenkins, Ltd., 1960. *The Lee-Enfield Story*, Ian Skennerton, 1993. Stevens, Blake, *UK and Commonwealth FALs*, Vol. 2, The FAL Series, Collector Grade Publications, 1980. Skennerton has also writen a number of monographs on other British rifles that are well worth study by the collector.

SNIDER

This design was the invention of Jacob Snider, an American from New York. The idea was to convert, in a simple way, muzzle-loading rifles to cartridge-firing-breech loaders. Snider cut away a rear section of the barrel and inserted a breech block with firing pin hinged at the side so that it could be opened and a cartridge inserted. The rifle was fired by an external hammer. Despite extraction problems, this design was used by the British Army, beginning in 1868 in the Ethiopian campaign, for six years and remained in service in second line units into the 1880s. It was the first general issue breech-loader in the British army, and perhaps more important was the parallel development of the Boxer cartridge for use in this rifle. The Boxer cartridge was a .577 caliber with steel rim and rolled heavy paper cartridge case (factory made, see photo below) that held the powder. The bullet was a soft lead.

NOTE: All Snider rifles and carbines are scarce. Examples in excellent condition are rarely encountered.

Bibliographical Note: It is strongly suggested that the reader interested in the myriad of details and variations of the Snider see Ian Skennerton's, *A Treatise On the Snider*, 1977.

Pattern 1 Rifled Musket

Converted Enfield muzzle-loading rifle. Barrel length is 36.5". Brass furniture with flat hammer face. Rear sight marked to 950 yards. Approved 1866.

Exc.	V.G.	Good	Fair	Poor
1500	1200	800	500	300

Pattern 1*

Similar to the Pattern 1 but with a countersunk barrel at the rear of the chamber to accommodate the cartridge rim. The asterisk (*) was marked on top of the receiver to indicate the conversion. Approved in May 1967.

Exc.	V.G.	Good	Fair	Poor
1500	1200	800	500	300

Pattern 2*

Similar to the Pattern I* but it is a direct conversion from the muzzle-loading Enfields and not the Pattern I*. The top of the receiver is marked "Mark II*". Also introduced in May 1867.

Exc.	V.G.	Good	Fair	Poor
1500	1200	800	500	300

Pattern 2**

This conversion is the most-often-encountered conversion. It has the cartridge recess like the earlier conversion, but also has a cupped hammer face, a better shaped extractor, and a larger breech block face. Introduced in May 1867.

Pattern 2* • Courtesy Rock Island Auction Company

Exc.	V.G.	Good	Fair	Poor
1250	1000	650	450	300

Pattern 3

Similar in outward appearance to the earlier conversions but with a flat hammer face and a spring-loaded locking latch on the left side of the breech block. The receiver is marked "III". Introduced in January 1869.

Exc.	V.G.	Good	Fair	Poor
1500	1200	800	500	300

Short Enfield Rifle P60 Mark II**

This conversion used an Enfield Pattern 1860 with the barrel cut to 30.5" from 33". Cupped hammer face. Two barrel bands, a sword bar, and case hardened furniture. Sling swivels on butt and upper barrel band. Sights marked to 400 yards on the rear sight and 1,000 yards on the leaf sight. Top of the receiver marked "II**". Introduced in March of 1867.

Exc.	V.G.	Good	Fair	Poor
1500	1200	800	500	300

Short Enfield Rifle P60 Mark II** Naval Rifle

Similar to the Mark II** army version except that brass furniture is used in place of iron. Some Naval rifles were not fitted with a butt sling swivel. Introduced in August of 1867.

Exc.	V.G.	Good	Fair	Poor
1500	1200	800	500	300

Short Enfield Rifle P60 Mark III

When this conversion was introduced in January of 1869, the steel barrel was also introduced, but a few early examples (about 1,200) were fitted with iron barrels. This rifle was actu-

ally a newly manufactured gun instead of a conversion of a muzzleloader. The top of the receiver is marked "III".

Exc.	V.G.	Good	Fair	Poor
1500	1200	800	500	300

Mark II** Engineers (Lancaster) Carbine

This is a converted Lancaster rifle with a 29" barrel length, brass furniture, and cupped hammer face. Two barrel bands with sling swivel on upper band. Butt-mounted rear swivel. "LANCASTER'S PATENT" stamped on the barrel. Rear leaf sight marked to 1,150 yards. Introduced in 1867 with about 5,000 riles converted.

Exc.	V.G.	Good	Fair	Poor
1850	1450	950	600	350

Artillery Carbine P61 Mark II**

Introduced in May of 1867. It has 2 barrel bands, a sword bar, brass buttplate and trigger guard. The hammer face is cupped. The rear sight has a maximum range of 600 yards. Barrel length is 21.5". Receiver is marked "II**". About 60,000 were converted.

Exc.	V.G.	Good	Fair	Poor
1850	1450	950	600	350

Snider Pattern 2** showing views of breech and cartridge • Private collection, Paul Goodwin photo

Artillery Carbine P61 Mark III

This was a newly manufactured conversion with a spring loaded locking latch on the left side of the breech block. The barrel is steel and is 21.5" long. Brass furniture with flat hammer face. Marked "III" on the top of the action. Introduced in 1869.

Exc.	V.G.	Good	Fair	Poor
1850	1450	950	600	350

Artillery Carbine P61 Mark IV

This rifle uses the Mark III breech and is fitted with a 21.5" barrel. Rear sight graduated to 900 yards. Two barrel bands with the stock coming to within 1.125" of the muzzle. Brass furniture. Introduced in 1891.

Exc.	V.G.	Good	Fair	Poor
1850	1450	950	600	350

Cavalry Carbine P61 Mark II**

This carbine was fitted with a half stock. The butt was fitted with a trap for a 2-piece cleaning rod. Sling bar and ring on left side although some may not have the bar fitted. Brass furniture. Barrel length is 19.25" Rear sight is a ladder type to 600 yards fitted with a leather protector secured by a screw on each side of the stock. A snap cap is secured by a chain screwed into the triggerguard. No sling swivels. Introduced in May of 1867.

Exc.	V.G.	Good	Fair	Poor
1850	1450	950	600	350

Cavalry Carbine Mark III

This is a newly manufactured carbine using the Mark III breech. Only a few early examples used iron barrel, the rest used steel. Brass furniture. Flat hammer face. The stock was newly made. Introduced in January of 1869.

Exc.	V.G.	Good	Fair	Poor
1850	1450	950	600	350

Yeomanry Carbine Mark I

This carbine was converted from Snider long rifles and issued to volunteer cavalry forces. Fitted with a 19.2" barrel. Brass furniture. Flat hammer face. The side nail cups are from the long rifle and made of brass instead of steel. Introduced in July of 1880.

Exc.	V.G.	Good	Fair	Poor
1850	1450	950	600	350

Naval Rifle P58

Approved in August 1867 and fitted with a 30.5" barrel with brass furniture. Many were not fitted with a lower sling swivel.

The receiver is marked, "II**" on the top near the barrel. Leaf sight is graduated to 1,000 yards with a ramp step from 100 to 400 yards. About 53,500 of these rifles were produced.

Exc.	V.G.	Good	Fair	Poor
1500	1200	800	500	300

Irish Constabulary Carbine Mark II** P56

This carbine is a conversion of the Enfield Pattern 1856 short rifle. Barrel length is 22.5". Iron furniture. Cupped hammer face. Sword bar. Two barrel bands. Stock stops 1.4" from muzzle. Sling swivels on upper barrel band and butt stock. Brass triggerguard. Stamped "II**" on receiver. Introduced in July of 1867.

Exc.	V.G.	Good	Fair	Poor
1850	1450	950	500	350

Irish Constabulary Carbine Mark III

Similar to the Mark II** but with flat hammer face and spring loaded locking latch on left side of breech block. Fitted with an iron barrel. Rear sight graduated to 900 yards. Introduced in January of 1869.

Exc.	V.G.	Good	Fair	Poor
1850	1450	950	500	300

Convict Civil Guard Carbine P53

This carbine was issued especially for penal service. Rounded forend, two barrel bands, no rear sight or sling swivels. Converted from Pattern 1853 rifle. Stamped II** on breech. Some of these carbines are rifled, while others are smoothbore with choked muzzle for shot cartridges. Introduced September of 1867.

Exc.	V.G.	Good	Fair	Poor
1850	1450	950	600	350

Martini-Henry

This single shot rolling block rifle was built on the Martini block action (a modification of the American Peabody action) and a rifled barrel by Alexander Henry. Early rifles built prior to 1885 used a fragile rolled cartridge case while later post 1885 versions used a solid case. The rifle was chambered for the .577-450 cartridge that used a paper patch bullet. The British army built these rifles with three different buttstock lengths and marked the 1/2" shorter than standard rifles with an "s" on the stock while longer stocks were marked with an "L." Standard length buttstocks were not marked. Martini-Henry rifles and carbines were used by British military forces all over the world during the latter quarter of the 19th century. Produced by Enfield, BSA, and LSA.

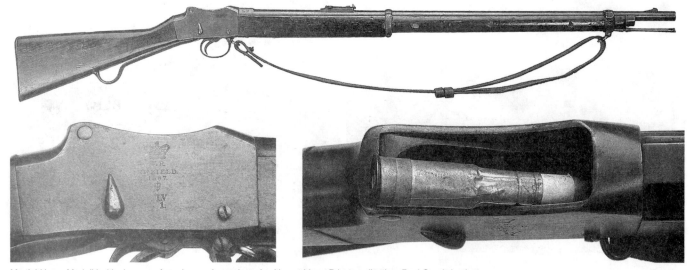

Martini-Henry Mark IV with close up of receiver and open breech with cartridge • Private collection, Paul Goodwin photo

> When 'arf of your bullets fly wide in the ditch,
> Don't call your Martini a cross-eyed old bitch;
> She's human as you are - you treat her as sich,
> An' she'll fight for the young British soldier.
>
> **Rudyard Kipling**

Mark 1 Rifle

Chambered for the .577-450 Martini-Henry cartridge and fitted with a 33.2" barrel, this lever operated single shot rifle was fitted with a steel bayonet and was full stocked with no upper handguard. Weight is about 8.75 lbs. Introduced in 1874.

Exc.	V.G.	Good	Fair	Poor
1250	900	700	400	250

Mark 2 Rifle

Similar to the Mark 1 but with an improved trigger in 1877.

Exc.	V.G.	Good	Fair	Poor
1250	900	700	500	250

Mark 3 Rifle

An improved version introduced in 1879 of the Mark 2 with double lump barrel and wider breech block. Weight is slightly heavier than the Marks 1 and 2 at about 9 lbs.

Exc.	V.G.	Good	Fair	Poor
1250	900	700	500	250

Mark 4 Rifle

Introduced in 1887, this Mark was fitted with a longer lever, a thinner breech block with modified extractor, narrow buttstock with bayonet fitting to accommodate a P1887 sword bayonet. Weight is about 9.25 lbs.

Exc.	V.G.	Good	Fair	Poor
1250	900	700	500	250

Cavalry Carbine Mark 1

This configuration was introduced in 1877 and is a short version of the rifle with full stock, no handguard, front sight with protectors, and a reduced charge carbine cartridge; the .577-450 Martini-Henry Carbine cartridge. Barrel length is about 21.25". Weight is approximately 7.5 lbs.

Exc.	V.G.	Good	Fair	Poor
1500	1250	950	700	350

Artillery Carbine Mark 2

This model is similar to the Cavalry Carbine but with bayonet fittings. Introduced in 1879. Weight is about 7.7 lbs.

Exc.	V.G.	Good	Fair	Poor
1500	1250	950	700	350

LEE-METFORD

NOTE: The Lee-Metford rifles were produced at the Royal Small Arms Factory, Enfield; the Birmingham Small Arms Co.; Sparkbrook, Vickers, Birmingham, and the London Small Arms Co., and so marked on the right side under the bolt handle for rifles and on the left side for carbines.

The British used the MARK and * system to denote improvements. The "MARK" indicated a major design change or improvement. The "*" indicated a minor change.

TRIALS RIFLES

The first trials for magazine rifles for the British army began in 1880. There were a number of initial contenders which will not be covered here. By 1883, the number of serious competitors was reduced to those listed below.

Owen Jones

This model was an adaptation of the Martini action and fitted with a 33" barrel chambered for the .402 caliber Enfield-Martini cartridge. Five-round magazine. Folding rear sight graduated to 2,000 yards. Weight is about 10.5 lbs. An unknown number of these rifles were built with different type magazine feeds and styles.

Exc.	V.G.	Good	Fair	Poor
5500	4750	4000	2500	—

Lee-Burton

This rifle used the Lee action, the first British rifle to do so. Chambered for the .402 caliber Enfield-Martini cartridge and fitted with a 30.2" barrel. Built by Enfield. Magazine capacity is 5 rounds. Marked "ENFIELD 1886" of left side of the receiver. Weight is about 10 lbs. About 300 were produced.

Exc.	V.G.	Good	Fair	Poor
5500	4750	4000	2500	—

Improved Lee

These rifles were purchased directly from Remington in 1887. Chambered for the .43 caliber Spanish cartridge and fitted with a 32" barrel. Folding leaf rear sight was graduated to 1,200 yards. Magazine capacity was 5 rounds. Weighs approximately 10 lbs. Marked with the Remington address on the receiver. About 300 were used in the trials. The only indication that this is a trials rifle is the marking "WD" on the right side of the butt.

Exc.	V.G.	Good	Fair	Poor
3750	3000	2500	1500	—

.303 Magazine Rifle-1888 Trials Model

Developed from the Improved Lee but chambered for the .303 cartridge and fitted with a 30.2" barrel. No upper handguard.

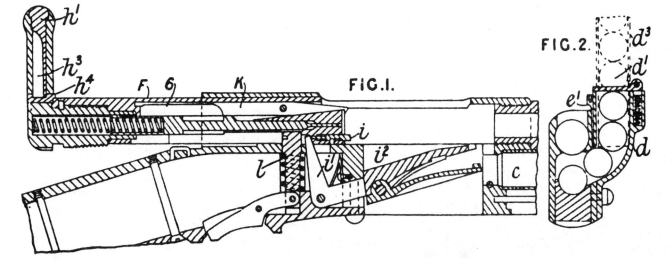

Burton Patent #4046, Oct. 5, 1880, showing receiver and magazine hopper system in Fig. 2 • British Small Arms Patents

Lee-Metford Mark 1* • Paul Goodwin photo

Magazine capacity is 7 rounds. Marked, "ENFIELD 1888." Weight is about 9 lbs. Some 387 of these rifles were produced.

Exc.	V.G.	Good	Fair	Poor
4500	3750	3000	1750	—

Mark I

A bolt action service rifle chambered for the .303 black powder British cartridge. It was designed by James Paris Lee and incorporated rifling developed by William Metford. This rifling was specifically designed to alleviate the problem of black powder fouling. 30.2" barrel and an 8-round, detachable box magazine located in front of the triggerguard. Furnished with magazine cutoff, it features military-type sights and a cleaning rod mounted underneath the barrel and a trap in the steel buttplate to house cleaning tools. Finger grooves in forend. The finish is blued, with a full-length walnut stock held on by two barrel bands. Weight is about 10 lbs. It was introduced in 1888. Approximately 358,000 were produced.

Exc.	V.G.	Good	Fair	Poor
600	450	300	200	100

Mark I*

Similar to the Mark 1 except that the safety catch was removed from the cocking piece and a brass disc was inletted into the buttstock for regimental markings. There were a number of internal improvements, as well as the fitting of a different, blade-type front sight and V-notch rear sight graduated to 1,800 yards. This model was fitted with an 8-round magazine. It was introduced in 1892.

Exc.	V.G.	Good	Fair	Poor
600	450	300	200	100

Mark II

Has a modified magazine that holds 10 rounds in a double column. A half-length cleaning rod was located under the 30.2" barrel. No finger grooves in forend. Fitted with brass buttplate with long heel tang. Rear leaf sight graduated to 1,800 yards. No butt marking disk. It was introduced in 1892. Weight reduced to 9.25 lbs. About 250,000 were produced.

Exc.	V.G.	Good	Fair	Poor
600	450	300	200	100

Mark II*

Has a lengthened bolt, with the addition of a safety catch. Barrel length is 30.2". No finger grooves in forend. All parts are interchangeable with the Mark II rifle. It was introduced in1895. About 13,000 were produced.

Exc.	V.G.	Good	Fair	Poor
550	400	300	200	100

Mark I Carbine

Has a 20.75" barrel. Rear sight is graduated to 2,000 yards. Buttstock is fitted with a marking disk. No bayonet fittings. Weight was about 7.5 lbs. It was introduced in 1894. Approximately 18,000 were produced.

Exc.	V.G.	Good	Fair	Poor
850	700	500	300	150

NOTE: Many Lee-Metford rifles were modified after 1902 to accept a stripper clip guide which required the removal of the dust cover. Such modification results in a deduction of 10% from original Lee-Metford rifles.

ENFIELD ROYAL SMALL ARMS FACTORY

NOTE: This series of rifles is marked by the presence of deeper Enfield rifling rather than the shallow Metford rifling. The same manufacturers that built the Lee-Metford built the Lee-Enfield along with Ishapore, India, and Lithgow, Australia.

Lee-Enfield Mark I Rifle

Chambered for the .303 cartridge and has a 30" barrel. The attached box magazine holds 10 rounds, and the sights are military-styled. Rear leaf sight graduated to 1,800 yards. The stock is full-length walnut, and there is a cleaning rod beneath it. There is a magazine cutoff located on the right side of the receiver. There are two barrel bands and a bayonet lug. The upper handguard extended from the receiver ring to the rear sight. The buttplate is brass with extended upper tang with trap for cleaning equipment. Weight is about 9.25 lbs. This model was manufactured between 1895 and 1899. Approximately 315,000 were manufactured.

Paul Goodwin photo

Exc.	V.G.	Good	Fair	Poor
900	750	600	400	200

Lee-Enfield Mark I* Rifle

No attached cleaning rod, otherwise the same as the Mark I rifle. It was introduced in 1899. Almost 600,000 of these rifles were produced.

Exc.	V.G.	Good	Fair	Poor
900	750	600	400	200

NOTE: Many long Lee-Enfield rifles were modified for charger loading (stripper clip). Prices are 10% less than unmodified rifles.

Lee-Enfield Mark I Carbine

This model is the same as the Lee-Medford except for the Enfield rifling and so marked. Slight different rear sight marked "EC" on bottom right hand corner of leaf. Introduced in 1896.

Mark 1 RIC Carbine with close-up of unique muzzle modification • Private collection, Paul Goodwin photo

Rear sight leather protector is standard on this carbine. Weight is about 7.5 lbs. Approximately 14,000 were produced.

Exc.	V.G.	Good	Fair	Poor
850	700	500	300	150

Lee-Enfield Mark I* Carbine

Same as the Mark I carbine but with no cleaning rod and no left side sling bar. Rear sight leather protector. Introduced in 1899. A little more than 26,000 were produced.

Exc.	V.G.	Good	Fair	Poor
850	700	500	300	150

Lee-Enfield Mark I RIC Carbine

This model was converted from Lee-Enfield carbines and was fitted with a bayonet lug for a Pattern 1888 bayonet. This required a collar to be added at the muzzle to increase the barrel diameter to accept the bayonet ring. It was first converted in 1905 for the Royal Irish Constabulary. About 11,000 were converted.

Exc.	V.G.	Good	Fair	Poor
500	400	250	100	75

No. 1 SMLE SERIES

The SMLEs were not designated No. 1s until the British changed their rifle nomenclature system in 1926. Guns made prior to that date were marked "SMLE," not No. 1.

France, August 1918. American soldiers, armed with British SMLE and US M1903 rifles, undergoing gas warfare training • U.S. Army Signal Corps/Center for Military History/Robert Bruce Military Photo Features

SMLE Trials Rifle

About 1,000 of these rifles were built for trials in 1902. Fitted with a full-length handguard and a charger loading system. Barrel length is 25.2" with a .303 chamber. Sheet metal buttplate. Weight is about 8 lbs. A number of different features appeared on this rifle that were later incorporated into the regular production SMLE. Most of these rifles were converted to Aiming Tube Short Rifles in 1906 and are extremely rare.

Exc.	V.G.	Good	Fair	Poor
1500	1150	800	500	200

No. 1 SMLE Mark I

Introduced in 1902 this was the first of the "**S**hort, **M**agazine **L**ee-**E**nfield" or No. 1 series of rifles. It was fitted with a full stock with pistol grip and a 25.2" barrel. It also had a full upper handguard. Rear sight is leaf-type graduated to 2,000 yards. The bayonet mountings are integral with the nosecap. Magazine capacity was 10 rounds. Magazine cutoff on right side of receiver. Weight was about 8 lbs. A little more than 360,000 of these rifles were produced.

Exc.	V.G.	Good	Fair	Poor
750	600	400	300	150

No. 1 SMLE Mark I*

A minor modification of the SMLE Mark I. Introduced in 1906. Fitted with a buttplate trap and a new style butt sling swivel. About 60,000 of these rifles were produced.

Exc.	V.G.	Good	Fair	Poor
650	550	400	250	100

No. 1 SMLE Mark II

The Mark I and II Long Lee converted by fitting a shorter and lighter barrel (25.2"), modifying the action to accept a stripper clip, and fitting new sights. It was introduced in 1903. Approximately 40,000 Mark IIs were manufactured.

Exc.	V.G.	Good	Fair	Poor
250	200	175	150	100

No. 1 SMLE Mark II*

A modification of the Mark II SMLE to add features from the SMLE Mark III so that it would correspond with that model. Introduced in 1908. About 22,000 were converted.

Exc.	V.G.	Good	Fair	Poor
250	200	175	150	100

No. 1 SMLE Mark III

Chambered for .303 British and has a 25.2" barrel with a 10-round magazine. The magazine has a cutoff, and the sights are military-styled with volley sights on the left side and open sights at top rear. The action is modified to accept a stripper clip and automatically eject it when the bolt is closed. Weight is approximately 8.5 lbs. This model was introduced in 1907. The Mark III was one of the more successful and famous British military rifles. It was used extensively in World War I and World War II. In many areas of the old British Commonwealth it is still used today. Almost 7,000,000 of these were produced.

NOTE: Add 30% for non-imported models.

Courtesy Richard M. Kumor Sr.

Exc.	V.G.	Good	Fair	Poor
200	150	100	60	30

Mark II • Courtesy West Point Museum, Paul Goodwin photo

THE NO. 1 MARK III SHORT MAGAZINE LEE-ENFIELD

Introduced in 1907 and called the Mark III SMLE for short, this rifle and its slightly simplified brother the Mark III* were the primary service rifles of the entire British Commonwealth in WWI, between the wars, and for the first few years of WWII. Indeed, while it was replaced by the No. 4 Lee-Enfield in Canada and supplemented by the latter in British service, the Mark III continued to be made and used in large quantities by the British until the end of WWII. It stayed the standard service rifle of Australia well into the 1950s and in India into the 1960s. It was made in India in .303 as late as 1964. In addition the Indians made a slight modification of the Mark III in 7.62mm NATO called the 2A1 as late as 1968 and possibly later. That's over 60 years of continuous production somewhere in the world. Also used in quantity in India's border conflict with China in the '70s and by the Afghan freedom fighters against the Russians in the '80s, the old Mark III is one of the most historically significant military rifles in history. Probably the main reason for the Mark III's longevity is the simple fact that it was an incredibly good rifle. Extremely rugged and incredibly reliable in even the worst field conditions, the Mark III was capable of very good accuracy and probably the fastest rate of aimed fire of any bolt action military rifle. The latter was the result of a more conveniently located bolt handle, a much shorter bolt lift and bolt throw than other military bolt actions, and its 10-round magazine. Of all the smokeless powder bolt action military rifles, no other combines the degree of historical significance and excellence of performance of the Mark III SMLE.

Chuck Karwan

No. 1 Mark III and Mark III* Drill Rifles

These rifles were modified for drill use and stamped "DP." They feature a firing pin with no tip and on occasion a bolt head with the firing pin hole welded closed.

Exc.	V.G.	Good	Fair	Poor
75	50	40	30	15

No. 1 Mark III Single Shot Rifles

Converted to single shot at Ishapore, India, and have magazine well filled. Intended for use with "unreliable" Indian troops.

Exc.	V.G.	Good	Fair	Poor
150	100	85	60	30

No. 1 Mark III and Mark III* Grenade Launching Rifles

Built on the standard Mk III and Mk III* rifles with the addition of a wire wrapping on the front of the barrel. These rifles are usually marked "E.Y." to indicate only ball ammunition used be used in an emergency. A cup-type grenade launcher was fitted.

No. 1 Mark III* • Courtesy West Point Museum, Paul Goodwin photo

No. 1 rifle (World War II version) with grenade launcher
• Courtesy private collection, Paul Goodwin photo

Exc.	V.G.	Good	Fair	Poor
200	125	100	70	40

NOTE: For rifles without launcher deduct $50.

Lee-Enfield .410 Musket

Built around the No. 1 Mark III rifle and converted in Ishapore, India to a single shot .410 shotgun. Intended for guard duty. The rifle fired a special .303 case that was not necked down. This model, if in original configuration, will not accept a modern .410 shotshell. Those rifles that have been altered to accept modern .410 shells will be worth less.

.410 Musket with close-up of wood-filled magazine • Private collection, Paul Goodwin photo

Exc.	V.G.	Good	Fair	Poor
120	75	50	40	20

No. 1 SMLE Mark IV

This model was Lee-Metford and Lee-Enfield rifles converted to Mark III configuration. The receiver was modified for a charger bridge and safety catch. The dust cover lugs were also removed from the bolt. Adopted in 1907. Almost 100,000 of these rifles were converted.

Exc.	V.G.	Good	Fair	Poor
175	125	100	75	50

Rifle Charger Loading Long Lee-Enfield Mark I/I*

These are converted Lee-Enfield rifles adapted to charger loading. Many of these rifles were used in the early days of World War I by the British Royal Navy. Over 180,000 of these rifles were produced.

Exc.	V.G.	Good	Fair	Poor
800	700	550	300	150

No. 1 SMLE Mark III*

This variation does not have a magazine cutoff, the rear sight windage adjustment, left side auxiliary long rang sights, a center swivel lug, or a brass buttstock marking disc. Over 2 million of this model were made during World War I. It was last built in England in 1944 by B.S.A. This model was also manufactured in India at Ishapore until 1964, and in Australia at Lithgow through the 1950s, and are so marked. Weight is about 9 lbs.

Exc.	V.G.	Good	Fair	Poor
175	125	95	75	50

NOTE: For rifles built in Australia add 20%; for rifles built in India deduct 20%.

No. 1 SMLE Mark III* H

Built only at Lithgow arsenal in Australia and features a heavier barrel marked with an "H" near the receiver.

Exc.	V.G.	Good	Fair	Poor
400	300	200	150	100

No. 1 SMLE Mark V

Similar to the Mark III except for the use of a receiver mounted wide aperture rear sight. The folding sight is graduated from 200 yards to 1,400 yards with even number on the right side and odd on the left. Serial numbers range from 1 to 9999, then an "A" prefix was used. The standard pattern 1907 sword bayonet was issued with the rifle. Between 1922 and 1924 only 20,000 were produced. A scarce model.

No. 1 SMLE Mark IV • Paul Goodwin photo

Courtesy Richard M. Kumor Sr.

Close-up of Mark V rear sight • Courtesy Richard M. Kumor Sr.

Exc.	V.G.	Good	Fair	Poor
650	550	350	—	—

No. 1 SMLE Mark VI

This model had the rear sight located on the receiver bridge. It also used a heavier barrel, lighter nose cap, and smaller bolt head than previous models. It did have the magazine cutoff. Checkered forend. There were three variants of this rifle: Pattern A introduced in 1926, Pattern B, introduced in 1929 to 1931 and Pattern C introduced in 1935. About 1,000 trials rifle were built in Pattern B.

Exc.	V.G.	Good	Fair	Poor
4000	2750	1750	—	—

NO. 4 SERIES

Rifle No. 4 Mark 1 Trials Model

Introduced in 1931 with about 2,500 being produced. This is a No. 1 Mark VI with the exception of the shape of the action, and designation markings. Some had no markings at all. Many were later converted to No. 4 Mark I (T) sniper rifles. Markings are commonly found on the right side of the butt socket.

Exc.	V.G.	Good	Fair	Poor
2500	1750	1100	—	—

Rifle No. 4 Mark I

An improved version of the No. 1 Mark VI that featured a stronger action with an aperture sight. It was issued in 1931. It was redesigned in 1939 for mass production with shortcuts taken for wartime production. Barrel length is 25.2" with 10-round magazine. The barrel diameter is larger than the SMLE series and extended almost 3" out of the forend. Weight is about 8.75 lbs. This model was used extensively during WWII. It is still in use today. About 2 million of these rifles were produced but none were built at Enfield. Other factories were at Longbranch in Canada and Savage-Stevens.

NOTE: Add 30% for non-imports.

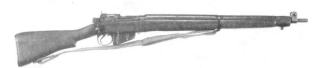

No. 4 Mark 1 with U.S. property stamp, made by Stevens • Courtesy Rock Island Auction Company

Exc.	V.G.	Good	Fair	Poor
300	200	100	75	50

Rifle No. 4 Mark I*

This model was almost identical to the No. 4 Mark I, but was produced in North America during WWII. The principal U.S. producer was Savage-Stevens (marked U.S. PROPERTY); in Canada marked "LONG BRANCH." The Savage-Stevens guns have a "C" in the serial number for Chicoppe Falls and guns with "L" serial numbers were produced at Longbranch. This model differed from the Mark 1 in that the bolt-head catch was eliminated and a cut-out on the bolt head track was used for its removal. Over 2 million were produced during the war.

Exc.	V.G.	Good	Fair	Poor
300	200	100	75	50

Rifle No. 4 Mark 2

This model was fitted with a trigger that was pinned to the receiver rather than the triggerguard. Introduced in 1949. This rifle had a higher quality finish than its wartime predecessors.

Courtesy Rock Island Auction Company

Exc.	V.G.	Good	Fair	Poor
250	175	125	80	50

Rifle No. 4 Mark 1/2 (converted No. 4 Mark I) & No. 4 Mark 1/3 (converted No. 4 Mark I*)

These models have new trigger mechanism installed to more closely emulate the Mark 2 and upgraded components. The conversion required altering the old markings. This was done with an electric pencil instead of a stamp. The result is quite obvious.

Exc.	V.G.	Good	Fair	Poor
200	150	100	75	50

JUNGLE CARBINES

No. 1 Shortened & Lightened Rifle

Fitted with a 20" barrel and a shortened forend. The rear aperture sight is mounted on the charger bridge and graduated for 200 and 500 yards. Fitted for a blade bayonet. Weight is about 8.75 lbs. About 32 of these rifle were built at Lithgow. The serial number has an "XP" prefix.

NOTE: Extremely rare. Beware of fakes. Seek expert advice prior to a sale.

Exc.	V.G.	Good	Fair	Poor
N/A	—	—	—	—

Malaya (no date). A British sergeant of the Malay Regiment teaches jungle fighting tactics to a native recruit, armed with a bolt action, .303 caliber Enfield Number 5 Mark 1 "Jungle Carbine" • U.S. Information Agency/National Archives/Robert Bruce Military Photo Features

Rifle No. 6 Mark I & Mark I/I (AUST)

This model was essentially a trials rifle built in Australia at Lithgow. Similar to the No. 5 but with a No. 1 receiver. Metal components have been milled for lightening. Barrel length is 20.5" with flash hider. The Mark I differs from the Mark I/I in rear sight. Rear sight is open and graduated to 2,000 yards on the Mark I and the Mark I/I uses an aperture sight graduated from 200 to 800 yards. Both models have serial numbers with an "XP" prefix. Each model has two variations of buttplates: one standard brass and the other composition padded with hinges at bottom for trap access.

NOTE: Beware of fakes. Seek expert advice prior to a sale.

Exc.	V.G.	Good	Fair	Poor
2750	2000	1000	—	—

Rifle No. 5 Mark 1

Also known as the "Jungle Carbine." It is chambered for the .303 British cartridge and has a 20.5" barrel with an attached flash suppressor and a shorter forend and handguard. It is furnished with a rubber buttpad and modified rear sight graduated to 800 yards. This was not a popular weapon with the soldiers who carried it, as the recoil was excessive due to the lighter weight. Weight is approximately 7 lbs. About 250,000 were built. This model has its own distinctive knife bayonet.

Courtesy Richard M. Kumor Sr.

Exc.	V.G.	Good	Fair	Poor
500	400	300	175	125

SNIPER RIFLES

SMLE Sniper (Optical Sights)

These rifles are Mark III and Mark III* mounted with optical sights. These sights are comprised of a special front and rear sight that when used together form a telescope with a magnification of 2 to 3 power. About 13,000 of these rifles were fitted with these optical sights. Three different optical makers were used with Lattey being the largest. Conversions were performed by unit armorers beginning in 1915.

NOTE: Beware of fakes. Seek expert advice prior to a sale.

Exc.	V.G.	Good	Fair	Poor
3500	3000	2000	—	—

SMLE Sniper (Telescope Sights)

As above, but fitted with conventional telescope sights made by Periscope, Aldis, Winchester, and others. A total of about 9,700 of these rifles were fitted with telescope sights using Mark III and Mark III* rifles during World War I.

NOTE: Beware of fakes. Seek expert advice prior to a sale.

Exc.	V.G.	Good	Fair	Poor
3500	3000	2000	—	—

No. 1 Mark III* H.T. (Australian) Sniper

Introduced toward the end of World War II, this rifle used mostly rebuilt Mark III actions dating to between 1915 and 1918. Fitted with both high and low mounts. The standard bracket telescope tube is marked, "SIGHT TELESCOPE PATT 1918 (AUS)." These rifles are fitted with a heavy barrel. Only about 1,500 of these rifles were converted.

Exc.	V.G.	Good	Fair	Poor
3000	2500	1500	—	—

SCOPE NOTE: The No. 32 (Marks 1-3) scope was the most commonly used on British-made guns. The No. 32 and the Alaskan are not the same scope. About 100 Lyman Alaskan scopes were fitted to Longbranch No. 4 Mark 1*(T) rifles in 1944-1945. In addition to the British-made scopes, R.E.I. Ltd. in Canada made its own version of the No. 32 and these are usually found on Longbranch guns. The No. 67 scope, used on about 100 Longbranch (T)s was made by R.E.I. and differs from the design of the No. 32.

Rifle No. 4 Mark I (T) & Mark I* (T)

These are sniper versions of the No. 4 Mark I and the Mark1*. Fitted with scope mounts on the left side of the receiver and a wooden cheekpiece screwed to the buttstock. A No. 32 or a No. 67 (Canadian) telescope was issued with these rifles. Many of these rifles were converted by Holland & Holland. About 25,000 rifles using various telescopes were converted.

No. 4 Mark I (T) on top and Standard No. 4 Mark I at bottom • Courtesy Chuck Karwan

No.2 Mark I (T) close-up of action and scope • Courtesy Chuck Karwan

Exc.	V.G.	Good	Fair	Poor
1500	1150	700	500	350

NOTE: Prices above are for rifles in original wood case and scope numbered to the rifle. For rifles without case deduct 10%. A subvariation of this model has no scope fitted to the rifle and is not stamped with a "T" on the butt.

A No. 4 Mark I (T) Sniper rifle sold at auction for $4,600. Original scope, with case and wooden transit. Condition is 98% factory original. Scope is No. 32 Mk3.
Rock Island Auction Company, September 2002

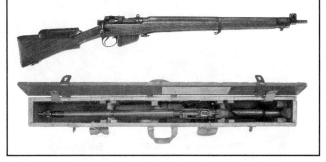

BRITISH LEE-ENFIELD No. 4 MARK I (T)

Without a doubt or argument the finest turn-bolt magazine rifle ever fielded for combat was the British Lee-Enfield. Blessed with one of the smoothest and fastest actions ever designed, the Lee-Enfield was also extraordinarily rugged and extremely accurate. In actual combat, this rifle has proven time and time again its superiority over lesser rifles, like the overrated Mauser K98. In addition to making a superb combat rifle, Holland and Holland showed that the No. 4 Mark I could also be made into an excellent sniper rifle. Rifles, hand picked for their accuracy, were converted by this prestigious firm by the addition of optics and mount, cheekpiece, modified rear sight, and careful rebedding. The result was one of the finest sniper rifles of World War II. What makes the No. 4 Mark I (T) great? A day in the field will show you. The rifle carries and balances well and the action is almost impervious to mud and dirt, unlike front locking designs that had problems in the trenches. Plus the scope and mount are as tough as a brick. Open the bolt, load 10 rounds into the magazine, and close it smartly. Adjust the U.S. M1907 shooting sling and peer through the scope. This is the ONLY sniper rifle of this time period, that I know of, that offers a really good cheek weld. Looking through the No. 32 telescope, simply put the tip of the reticle's post onto your target and squeeze. The rifle jumps. As you recover from recoil, automatically work the bolt and get back on the scope. At long range, 850 yards or so, you have enough time to get back on target and watch your 174 grain FMJ smack home. Not a target rifle and certainly not a sporting rifle, the No.4 (T) was made for hunting men, who shoot back. Rugged, accurate, and topped with a bullet-proof scope it was an impressive rifle in its day.

David Fortier

L42A1

Introduced in 1970, this rifle is a converted No. 4 (T) chambered for the 7.62mm cartridge. Half stocked with upper handguard with 27.6" heavy barrel. A converted No. 32 Mark 3 scope is used marked, "TEL. STRT. STG. L1A1." Weight is about 12.5 lbs. Some 10,000 were converted at Enfield.

NOTE: Prices listed below are for rifles with original wood case.

Exc.	V.G.	Good	Fair	Poor
2500	2000	1500	700	350

LEE-ENFIELD .22 CALIBER RIFLES

Short Rifle Mark I

This single shot .22 caliber model is converted from the Lee-Metford Mark I* rifle but with a 25" barrel. Introduced in 1907.

Exc.	V.G.	Good	Fair	Poor
550	450	300	200	100

Long Rifle Mark II

This single shot .22 caliber rifle was converted from long Lee-Enfield rifles. Adopted in 1912.

Exc.	V.G.	Good	Fair	Poor
550	450	300	200	100

Short Rifle Mark I*

This .22 caliber single shot conversion is modified from the Lee-Metford Mark I* rifle.

Exc.	V.G.	Good	Fair	Poor
1200	950	700	500	200

Short Rifle Mark III

This .22 caliber conversion is from the SMLE Mark II and Mark II*. Adopted in 1912.

Courtesy Rock Island Auction Company

Exc.	V.G.	Good	Fair	Poor
500	400	300	150	100

Rifle No. 2 Mark IV

This model uses converted SMLEs. Some of these conversions are fitted with new .22 caliber barrels and others use .303 barrels with .22 caliber bore liners. These rifles have special bolt heads. Weight is about 9 lbs.

Courtesy Rock Island Auction Company

Exc.	V.G.	Good	Fair	Poor
400	350	250	150	100

L42 A1 rifle • Courtesy private collection, Paul Goodwin photo

No. 7 Mark 1 with close up views of receiver • Private collection, Paul Goodwin photo

Rifle No. 2 Mark IV*

A subvariation of Rifle No. 2 Mark IV.

Exc.	V.G.	Good	Fair	Poor
400	350	250	150	100

Rifle C No. 7

This model was developed at the Long Branch Canadian arsenal. It is a single shot .22 caliber version of the No. 4. Canadian nomenclature is "Rifle "C" No. 7 .22 in Mark I. This model was also made by B.S.A. with a 5-round magazine. About 20,000 were produced.

Exc.	V.G.	Good	Fair	Poor
450	400	300	175	125

Rifle No. 7 Mark 1

This is a conversion of the No. 4, not a new rifle. Introduced in 1948. Different bolt from the Canadian version Rifle C No. 7 Mark 1. This rifle was intended for use at 25 yards. About 2,500 were built at BSA.

Exc.	V.G.	Good	Fair	Poor
450	400	300	175	125

NOTE: Be aware that A.G. Parker built a commercial version of this rifle. For those models deduct $100.

No. 5 Trials Rifle

This rifle was the forerunner of the No. 8. It was designed as a competition small bore rifle with special sights and half stock. It is fitted with a No.4 butt that has a checkered grip. The upper handguard is a No. 5 in length. It uses a No. 1 magazine converted to .22 caliber. It could be used as a single shot or magazine feed. Rear sight is micrometer graduated to 100 yards. Target tunnel front sight. Barrel length is 19". Weight is about 8.5 lbs. About 100 of these rifles were built.

Exc.	V.G.	Good	Fair	Poor
1250	900	650	—	—

Rifle No. 8 Mark 1

This rifle was adopted in 1950. This is a single shot rifle with 24" barrel fitted with a rear peep sight. Half stocked with three sling swivels, the middle one is attached in front of the trigger-guard. Weight is 9 lbs. Approximately 17,000 of these rifles were produced.

No. 8 Mark 1 rifle • Private collection, Paul Goodwin photo

Exc.	V.G.	Good	Fair	Poor
700	550	300	200	100

Rifle No. 9 Mark 1

This .22 caliber single shot conversion was done by Parker Hale using No. 4 rifles. Main differences are the bolt, barrel, magazine, and rear sight. The magazine is an empty case without spring or follower. Weight is about 9.25 lbs. The conversion was done between 1956 and 1960. About 3,000 of these rifles were converted for the Royal Navy.

Exc.	V.G.	Good	Fair	Poor
700	550	300	200	100

7.62x51mm CONVERSIONS & MANUFACTURE

NOTE: The NATO cartridge 7.62x51mm was agreed upon by NATO in December of 1953. Conversions began soon after.

L8 Series

This series consists of converted No. 4 rifles from .303 to 7.62mm. Conversions involved a new barrel, and a new magazine stamped, "CR12A." The old receiver marks were eliminated and new ones using an electric pencil were substituted. Some rear sights graduated to 1,300 *meters*, and other graduated to 1,000 *meters*. Series conversions are as follows:

L8A1 converted from No. 4 Mk2
L8A2 converted from No. 4 MK 1/2
L8A3 converted from No. 4 Mk 1/3
L8A4 converted from No. 4 MK I
L8A5 converted from No. 4 MK I*

Exc.	V.G.	Good	Fair	Poor
900	700	450	300	150

L8A4 conversion by Sterling • Private collection, Paul Goodwin photo

L39A1

This conversion uses a No. 4 Mark 2 action and is similar to a L42A1 sniper rifle without the scope. Fitted with target-type front and rear sights. Half stocked. Weight is about 10 lbs.

Exc.	V.G.	Good	Fair	Poor
1500	1100	750	400	200

NOTE: For 7.62 NATO magazine add $75. For English match sights by Parker Hale add $125.

L42A1

See Sniper Rifles.

Rifle 7.62mm 2A and 2A1 (India)

This rifle is based on a No. 1 Mark III* rifle utilizing newly made receivers of stronger steel to handle the higher .308 pressures. The Indians referred to it as "EN" steel. New rear sight graduated to 800 meters. New detachable box magazine with 10-round capacity. The buttplate is cast alloy. Manufactured in India at Ishapore. Weight is about 9.5 lbs. Most imported rifles are in the 2A1 configuration.

Exc.	V.G.	Good	Fair	Poor
200	125	50	30	15

ENFIELD FENCING MUSKETS

These are not firearms but rather fabricated or converted rifles made to look and feel like the real thing. They were used for bayonet practice and drilling practice. There are a large number of variations, at least 17, and to cover each is beyond the scope of this book. The prices listed below only represent a possible range of prices. Some rifles were late converted to fencing muskets.

Exc.	V.G.	Good	Fair	Poor
125	100	75	50	20

OTHER BRITISH RIFLES

Boys Anti-Tank Rifle

Developed in the 1930s, this rifle was chambered for the .55 caliber armor piercing cartridge. It was fitted with a 36" barrel with muzzle brake. It had a detachable 5-round box magazine. Weight was approximately 36 lbs. Available in two versions: a long barrel (36") and a short barrel airborne model. Not used much after 1940 due to inability to penetrate modern armor. Some of these rifles were used by the U.S. Marine Corp. in the Pacific during World War II.

NOTE: The Boys Rifle is listed as a destructive device by the ATF and is therefore subject to all NFA rules.

Exc.	V.G.	Good	Fair	Poor
3750	3000	2500	2000	1000

L39A1 rifle • Courtesy private collection, Paul Goodwin photo

At top Indian No. 2 with British .303 rear sight. At bottom No. 2A with 7.62mm rear sight • Courtesy private collection, Paul Goodwin photo

No. 3 Mark I (Pattern 14)

Built on a modified Mauser-type action and was chambered for the .303 British cartridge. It is fitted with a 26" barrel and 5-round magazine. It was a secondary-issue arm during WWI and was simpler to mass-produce than the SMLE. These rifles were produced in the U.S.A. by Remington and Winchester. There are a number of marks for this model divided between Remington, Eddystone, and Winchester.

The Mark IE was built at Remington Arms at Eddystone, Pennsylvania. The Mark IR were built at Remington Arms in Ilion, New York.

The Mark IW was built at Winchester Repeating Arms in New Haven, Connecticut.

Exc.	V.G.	Good	Fair	Poor
250	150	100	65	35

No. 3 Mark I* Pattern 14W(F) (T)

This is a No. 3 Mark I that has been converted to a sniper configuration. These rifles were built by Winchester during World War I. The (F) model has a long range aperture and dial sight along with the scope. On the (T) model the long range sights were removed. It is estimated that about 1,500 of these rifles were built. A rare rifle. Caution should be used prior to a sale.

Courtesy Richard M. Kumor Sr.

Boys Anti-Tank Rifle • Courtesy West Point Museum, Paul Goodwin photo

No. 3 Mark I • Courtesy West Point Museum, Paul Goodwin photo

Close-up of sniper scope and mount • Courtesy Richard M. Kumor Sr.

Exc.	V.G.	Good	Fair	Poor
5000	4500	3500	—	—

STERLING

De Lisle Carbine

This rifle is built on a Lee-Enfield action with a .45 ACP caliber barrel fitted inside a large suppressor tube. Barrel length is 8.25". Magazine capacity is 8 rounds using a Colt Model 1911 magazine. Weight is about 7.5 lbs. About 100 to 150 of these rifles were built by Sterling during World War II for use in special operations. Most were destroyed after the war. All NFA rules apply to the purchase of these weapons. Rare.

Exc.	V.G.	Good	Fair	Poor
—	6000	5000	—	—

L1A1 Rifle

This is the British version of the FN-FAL in the "INCH" or Imperial pattern. Most of these rifles were semiautomatic only.

This rifle was the standard service rifle for the British army from about 1954 to 1988. The rifle was made in Great Britain under license from FN. The configurations for the L1A1 rifle is the same as the standard FN-FAL Belgium rifle. Only a few of these rifles were imported into the U.S. They are very rare. This "inch" pattern British gun will also be found in other Commonwealth countries such as Australia, New Zealand, Canada, and India.

Exc.	V.G.	Good	Fair	Poor
—	6000	5000	—	—

NOTE: The only known pre-1986 L1A1 rifles imported into the U.S. are Australian and Canadian. See that country for prices. See also *Canada* for its C1 and C2 versions of the FN FAL.

There are a number of U.S. companies that build or import L1A1 rifles, (imported rifles are in a sporter configuration) but these have no collector value. Rifles built with military surplus parts and U.S.-made receivers also have no collector value as of yet.

Exc.	V.G.	Good	Fair	Poor
N/A	—	—	—	—

ACCURACY INTERNATIONAL

Founded in 1980 by Malcom and Sarah Cooper, they designed snipers rifles which were later adopted by the British Army as the L96A1. This English company, located in Portsmouth, provides its rifles to military forces in over 43 countries, and these models have been used in Northern Ireland, Sri Lanka, Somalia, Bosnia, Rwanda, and in Desert Storm. Most of these rifles are currently NATO codified.

FN-FAL L1A1 Rifle • Paul Goodwin photo

Model AE

Chambered for the 7.62x51 cartridge and fitted with a 24" heavy barrel. Stock is a black synthetic. Magazine capacity is 5 rounds. Weight is approximately 13.25 lbs.

Exc.	V.G.	Good	Fair	Poor
2500	—	—	—	—

Model AW

Chambered for the 5.56 NATO cartridge and the 7.62x51 NATO cartridge, this bolt action rifle is fitted with a 26" heavy match grade barrel with muzzle brake. Magazine capacity is 8 rounds for the 5.56 and 10 rounds for the 7.62x51. Olive green or black stock with adjustable buttstock. Optional bipod, scope, and other accessories can be included in a complete kit. Prices below are for rifle only. Weight is about 14.25 lbs.

Exc.	V.G.	Good	Fair	Poor
4700	—	—	—	—

Model AWP

Similar to the Model AW but with black stock and metal and 24" barrel. Offered in .243 and .308 calibers. Weight is about 14 lbs.

Exc.	V.G.	Good	Fair	Poor
4400	—	—	—	—

Model AWS

A suppressed version of the AW model. Weight is about 13 lbs.

Exc.	V.G.	Good	Fair	Poor
N/A	—	—	—	—

Model AWM

Similar to the Model AW but chambered for the .300 Winchester Magnum or .338 Lapua Magnum cartridge. Fitted with a 26" barrel with muzzle brake. Magazine capacity is 5 rounds. Weight is about 15.5 lbs.

Exc.	V.G.	Good	Fair	Poor
5000	—	—	—	—

Model AW 50

Chambered for the .50 caliber Browning cartridge. Barrel length is 27" with muzzle brake. Magazine capacity is 5 rounds. Weight is about 33 lbs. Supplied with metal case, spare magazine, carry handle, sling, and tool kit.

Exc.	V.G.	Good	Fair	Poor
10925	—	—	—	—

PARKER-HALE

Founded in Birmingham, England in 1890, this firm converted Lee-Enfield rifles into sporting guns. During World War II it manufactured military ammunition and repaired service rifles.

In 1992, the company was sold to Navy Arms who then established a subsidiary called Gibbs Rifle Co. to produce and sell the Parker-Hale line.

M82

This bolt action rifle uses a Mauser 98 action fitted to a heavy 26" barrel chambered for the 7.62x51mm cartridge. Magazine capacity is 4 rounds. Used as a sniper rifle by the Australian, New Zealand, and Canadian military. Marked "PARKER-HALE LTD BIRMINGHAM ENGLAND 7.62 NATO" on top of the barrel. Produced from 1982 to about 1984.

Exc.	V.G.	Good	Fair	Poor
2500	2000	1500	850	—

M85

This is an improved version of the M82 with a Mauser 98 type bolt action designed to compete for a British military contract against the Accuracy International rifle. It did not win the trials. It is fitted with a removable 10-round magazine, 27.5" heavy barrel with iron sights, and telescope mounts on the receiver. Rifle is half stocked with adjustable buttplate. Bipod is attached to forend rail. Weight is about 12.5 lbs. with scope. Chambered for the 7.62x51mm NATO round.

Exc.	V.G.	Good	Fair	Poor
3500	3000	2500	1500	—

MACHINE GUNS

NOTE: For historical information and technical details see: Dugelby, *The Bren Gun Saga*, Collector Grade Publications, 1999. Goldsmith, *The Grand Old Lady of No Man's Land, The Vickers Machinegun*, Collector Grade Publications, 1994.

A British soldier demonstrates the light and controllable Vickers-Berthier, standard machine gun of the Indian Army and in limited use by the UK until full scale production of the BREN began (no date or location, ca. 1930s) • U.S Army Ordnance Corps/National Archives/Robert Bruce Military Photo Features

Bren MK1

Introduced in 1938 and designed in Czechoslovakia as the ZB vz2,6 this British version is chambered for the .303 British cartridge during the early part of its service. After WWII it was adapted to the 7.62x51mm cartridge. It was fitted with a top mounted magazine of 30 rounds. Rate of fire is 500 rounds per minute. The gun was set up to fire selectively as well. The gun has a 24.8" barrel and an empty weight of 22 lbs. The rear sight is an offset drum type. The buttstock has a hand grip and top strap. The bipod has fixed legs, and the cocking handle folds away. Marked "BREN MK" on the rights side of the receiver.

The Bren MK2 (1941) has a leaf type rear sight and a simplified buttstock. The Bren MK3 (1944) is lighter (19 lbs) and fitted with a shorter barrel (22.2"). The Bren MK4 (1944)

has minor differences in the buttstock. The L4A1 (1958) is a converted MK 3 to 7.62mm caliber. The L4A2 (1958) is a converted MK3 with lighter bipod. The L4A3 is a converted MK2 to 7.62mm caliber: used by navy and RAF. The L4A4 (1960) is similar to the L4A2 except for a chrome lined barrel. The L4A6 is a converted L4A1 with chrome lined barrel.

In 1941, the MK2 was produced in Canada for the Chinese Nationalist army in 7.92x57mm caliber. (*see Canada*) A .30-06 version was made in Taiwan.

Be aware that there are a number of different mounts for the Bren gun besides the traditional bipod. There is a tripod mount as well as an antiaircraft mount.

NOTE: The Vickers-Berthier gun is similar in external design, caliber, and general appearance as the Bren except it has a distinctive operating mechanism and other significant differences. This gun is made in India and that country used the gun in World War II. It is still in use in that country. This gun is extremely rare as only a few known transferable examples exist. For pre-1968 Vickers-Berthier guns a price of $35,000 in excellent condition would be a good starting place for value.

Bren MK I • Photo courtesy private NFA collection

Bren MK1

Pre-1968 (Rare)
Exc.	V.G.	Fair
27500	25000	20000

Pre-1986 conversions
Exc.	V.G.	Fair
18000	17000	15000

Pre-1986 dealer samples
Exc.	V.G.	Fair
15000	12500	11000

Bren MK2

Pre-1968 (Rare)
Exc.	V.G.	Fair
30000	27500	25000

Korean War. This British Commonwealth soldier, operating with U.N. forces in Korea, is armed with the superlative BREN Mark 1 light machine gun. Its curved, top-mounted magazine holds 30 rounds of rimmed .303 caliber ammunition • U.S. Army Signal Corps/National Archives/Robert Bruce Military Photo Features

Pre-1986 conversions
Exc.	V.G.	Fair
18000	17000	15000

Pre-1986 dealer samples
Exc.	V.G.	Fair
17500	15000	15000

Lewis 0.303in, Mark 1

This gas-operated machine gun is chambered for the .303 British cartridge. Though perfected by an American army officer, Colonel Isaac Lewis (1858-1931), it was first produced in Belgium in 1912 where it was used extensively by British forces during WWI. In fact, it was the principal British light machine gun used in WWI. It has a 26" barrel and a rate of fire of about 550 rounds per minute. Called by the Germans the "Belgian Rattlesnake." Magazine capacity is 47- or 97-round drum. Its weight is approximately 26 lbs. Marked "LEWIS AUTOMATIC MACHINE GUN/MODEL 1914 PATENTED" behind the magazine drum. The gun was produced by BSA and Savage Arms of the U.S. Production stopped in 1925. A number of other countries used the gun as well, such as France, Norway, Japan, Belgium, Honduras, and Nicaragua.

The Lewis MK2 was introduced in 1915 which was a MK1 without the radiator and barrel jacket. The buttstock was removed and spade grips attached for aircraft use. The Lewis MK2* modified the gun to increase the rate of fire to about 800 rounds per minute. See also *United States, Machine Guns, Savage-Lewis M1917*.

Vickers-Berthier • Courtesy private NFA collection, Paul Goodwin photo

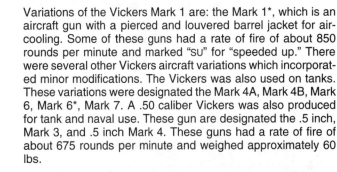

Lewis Mark 2 Aircraft Gun • Paul Goodwin photo

Private NFA collection • Photo by Gary Gelson

Pre-1968

Exc.	V.G.	Fair
15000	14000	12500

Pre-1986 conversions

Exc.	V.G.	Fair
N/A	N/A	N/A

Pre-1986 dealer samples

Exc.	V.G.	Fair
N/A	N/A	N/A

The 1912 "Light Model" Vickers machine gun on versatile Model J tripod • U.S. Army Ordnance Corps/National Archives/Robert Bruce Military Photo Features

Vickers Mark 1

This British water-cooled machine gun was first produced in 1912 and chambered for the .303 British cartridge. In essence, an improved Maxim with the action inverted. It has a 28" barrel with corrugated water jacket and is fed by a 250 cloth belt. Its rate of fire is 450 rounds per minute. Its weight is approximately 40 lbs. It was also used in aircraft and stayed in service in various countries until the 1970s. Besides use in British forces, the gun was sold to South American countries between the two World Wars. Serial number is marked on top rear of water jacket. The Vickers gun was capable of sustained fire of 100,000 rounds without stopping.

Variations of the Vickers Mark 1 are: the Mark 1*, which is an aircraft gun with a pierced and louvered barrel jacket for air-cooling. Some of these guns had a rate of fire of about 850 rounds per minute and marked "SU" for "speeded up." There were several other Vickers aircraft variations which incorporated minor modifications. The Vickers was also used on tanks. These variations were designated the Mark 4A, Mark 4B, Mark 6, Mark 6*, Mark 7. A .50 caliber Vickers was also produced for tank and naval use. These gun are designated the .5 inch, Mark 3, and .5 inch Mark 4. These guns had a rate of fire of about 675 rounds per minute and weighed approximately 60 lbs.

NOTE: For the Colt produced version in .30-06 caliber see *United States, Machine Guns.*

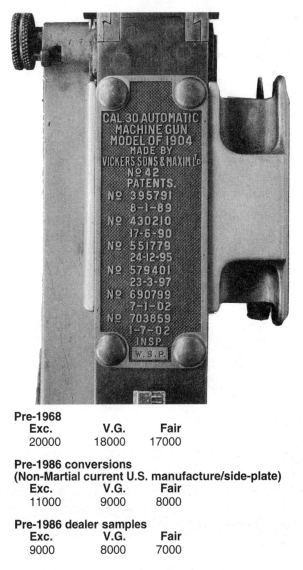

Pre-1968

Exc.	V.G.	Fair
20000	18000	17000

Pre-1986 conversions
(Non-Martial current U.S. manufacture/side-plate)

Exc.	V.G.	Fair
11000	9000	8000

Pre-1986 dealer samples

Exc.	V.G.	Fair
9000	8000	7000

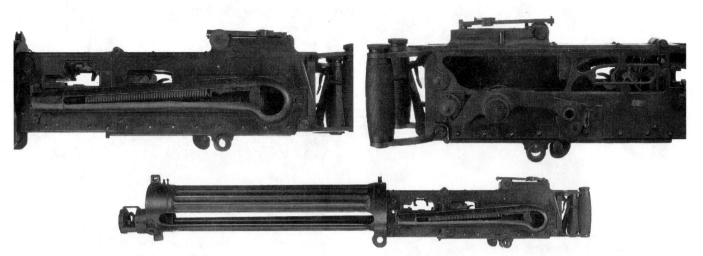

Colt Vickers cut-away • Paul Goodwin photo

British Vickers Mark IV • Courtesy Blake Stevens, *The Grand Old Lady of No Man's Land*

Hotchkiss Mark I

Although a French design, the British army purchased the rights to manufacture the Hotchkiss during World War I. These British guns were known as the Mark 1 and Mark 1* and were built in the Royal Small Arms factory in England. The British Hotchkiss was chambered for the .303 British cartridge. This version was fed by a 30-round metallic strip and had a rate of fire of about 500 rounds per minute. The gun weighed about 27 lbs. Barrel length was 23.5". The British Hotchkiss stayed in service in the British army until 1946. A belt-fed version (Mark I*) for use on tanks used a 250-round belt.

Pre-1968

Exc.	V.G.	Fair
8500	8000	7500

Courtesy Butterfield & Butterfield

Pre-1986 conversions

Exc.	V.G.	Fair
5000	4500	4000

Pre-1986 dealer samples

Exc.	V.G.	Fair
N/A	N/A	N/A

Besa

Introduced in 1939, this gun was a design bought from the Czech's ZB vz53 and produced in Britain by BSA in a slightly modified form. It was used primarily on tanks. It was an air-cooled gun chambered for the 7.92x57mm cartridge. It was gas operated but with a recoiling barrel. It has a rate of fire of approximately 500 or 800 rounds per minute using a selector switch for high or low rate. Weight of the gun is about 48 lbs. Feeds from a 250-round belt.

There are a number of variations of the initial model. The Mark 2 has some minor modifications. The Mark 3 has a single rate of fire of 800 rounds per minute. The Mark 3* has a single rate of fire of 500 rounds per minute.

Pre-1968

Exc.	V.G.	Fair
8500	8000	7500

Pre-1986 conversions

Exc.	V.G.	Fair
N/A	N/A	N/A

Pre-1986 dealer samples

Exc.	V.G.	Fair
N/A	N/A	N/A

HUNGARY

Hungarian Military Conflicts, 1918-Present

Hungary followed a similar history to Austria following the break-up of the Austro-Hungarian Empire in 1918. In 1941, Hungary joined the Axis Alliance and in 1944 was invaded by the USSR. In 1946, a republic was established, but was overthrown by a Communist coup in 1948. In 1956, an anti-Communist revolution was suppressed by Soviet military forces. In 1990, democratic reform swept the country. In 1994, the Socialists won control of the government with the result that economic and social reforms are almost nonexistent.

HANDGUNS

STEYR
Osterreichische Waffenfabrik Gesellschaft GmbH, Steyr (1869-1919)
Steyr-Werke AG (1919-1934)
Steyr-Daimler-Puch, Steyr (1934-1990)
Steyr-Mannlicher GmbH, Steyr (1990-)

Model 1929

A blowback-operated semiautomatic chambered for the 9mm short cartridge. It has an external hammer, and the barrel was retained by four lugs. This was a simple and reliable pistol, and it was adopted by the military as a replacement for the Stop. This model was manufactured between 1929 and 1937. It was also produced in a .22 Long Rifle.

Courtesy James Rankin

Exc.	V.G.	Good	Fair	Poor
400	300	200	175	125

Model 1937

An improved version of the Model 1929, with a grooved slide to make cocking easier. It was adopted as the M1937 by the Hungarian Military, and in 1941 the German government ordered 85,000 pistols chambered for 7.65mm to be used by the Luftwaffe. These pistols were designated the "P Mod 37 Kal 7.65." They were also marked "jhv," which was the German code for the Hungarian company. These German pistols also have a manual safety, which is not found on the Hungarian military version and bears the Waffenamt acceptance marks. This model was manufactured from 1937 until the end of WWII.

Courtesy James Rankin

Nazi Proofed 7.65mm Version (Pistole Modell 37(u))

Exc.	V.G.	Good	Fair	Poor
300	250	200	150	100

9mm Short Hungarian Military Version

Hungarian Military Model 37 • Courtesy Rock Island Auction Company

Exc.	V.G.	Good	Fair	Poor
275	225	175	125	75

Model 48 (7.62mm)

This is a Hungarian copy of the Soviet 7.62mm TT33 pistol. The pistol has a molded plastic grips with the Hungarian coat of arms.

Hungarian M48 • Courtesy Chuck Karwan

Exc.	V.G.	Good	Fair	Poor
250	175	150	100	75

Tokagypt

A licensed copy of the TT33 pistol produced by Fegyvergar (FEG) of Hungary. Chambered for the 9mm cartridge, and intended for, but never issued to, the Egyptian army in the 1950s. Barrel length is 4.5" and magazine capacity is 7 rounds. Manual thumb safety. Weight is approximately 32 oz.

Hungarian Tokagypt • Courtesy Chuck Karwan

Exc.	V.G.	Good	Fair	Poor
750	650	500	350	150

NOTE: For pistols without markings deduct 25%. For pistols with importer stamps deduct 50%.

PA-63

An aluminum frame copy of the Walther PP in a slightly larger size. Chambered for the 9mm Makarov cartridge. This was the standard Hungarian service until recently.

Exc.	V.G.	Good	Fair	Poor
175	135	120	90	75

R-61

This model is a smaller version of the PA-63. Chambered for the 9mm Makarov. This model is slightly longer than a Walther PPK and was intended for issue to high-ranking officers, CID, and police units.

Exc.	V.G.	Good	Fair	Poor
200	150	130	100	80

SUBMACHINE GUNS

Model 39

Produced by Danuvia in Budapest, this submachine gun is chambered for the 9x25mm Mauser Export cartridge. It is fitted with a 19.5" barrel and a full stocked rifle-style wooden stock. Magazine capacity is 40 rounds. The magazine folds into a recess in the forward part of the stock. Fitted with a bayonet lug. Gun features a two-part bolt design. Introduced in the late 1930s but not issued until 1941. Weight is about 8 lbs. Rate of fire is approximately 750 rounds per minute. About 8,000 were produced.

NOTE: It is not known how many, if any, of these guns are in the U.S. and are transferable. Prices listed below are estimates only.

Model 39M • Courtesy Thomas Nelson, *The World's Submachine Guns, Vol. 1*

Pre-1968

Exc.	V.G.	Fair
6500	6000	5500

Pre-1986 conversions

Exc.	V.G.	Fair
4500	4000	3500

Pre-1986 dealer samples

Exc.	V.G.	Fair
N/A	N/A	N/A

Model 43

This model, introduced in 1942, is an improved version of the Model 39. It has a shorter barrel at 16.5", a folding stock, pistol grip, and an improved magazine. Weight is about 8 lbs. Rate of fire and caliber remains the same. Produced until 1945.

NOTE: It is not known how many, if any, of these guns are in the U.S. and are transferable. Prices listed below are estimates only.

Model 43M • Courtesy Thomas Nelson, *The World's Submachine Guns, Vol. 1*

Pre-1968

Exc.	V.G.	Fair
6500	6000	5500

Pre-1986 conversions

Exc.	V.G.	Fair
4500	4000	3500

Pre-1986 dealer samples

Exc.	V.G.	Fair
N/A	N/A	N/A

Operation Barbarossa, Russia, 1942. A Hungarian soldier armed with a Solothurn Model 43 light machine gun • Captured German Records/National Archives/Robert Bruce Military Photo Features

Model 48

This is a Hungarian copy of the Soviet PPSh-41 submachine gun. See also *Russia, Submachine Guns.*

Pre-1968

Exc.	V.G.	Fair
7000	6500	6000

Pre-1986 conversions

Exc.	V.G.	Fair
4500	4000	3500

Pre-1986 dealer samples

Exc.	V.G.	Fair
3250	2750	2250

RIFLES

MANNLICHER
Built by Steyr & Fegyvergyar

Model 1935 Short Rifle

This model is based on the Romanian Model 1893. However, it is chambered for the 8x56R Hungarian Mannlicher cartridge. Barrel length is 23.6". Magazine capacity is 5 rounds in a clip loaded box magazine. Full stock with full-length handguard. Weight is approximately 9 lbs.

Exc.	V.G.	Good	Fair	Poor
300	200	150	100	75

FEGYVERGYAR
Fegyver es Gepgyar Resvenytarsasag, Budapest, (1880-1945)
Femaru es Szersazamgepgyar NV (1945-1985)
FEG Arms & Gas Appliances Factory (1985-)

Model 43 Rifle

This is a Model 35 redesigned on the German Model 98 and chambered for the 7.92mm cartridge. Barrel length is 23.75". Magazine capacity is 5-rounds fixed box. Rear sight is tangent with notch. Weight is approximately 8.5 lbs. Almost full stock with German bayonet fittings. Issued to the Hungarian army in 1943. Rare.

Model 43 rifle • Private collection, Paul Goodwin photo

Exc.	V.G.	Good	Fair	Poor
550	350	250	125	75

44.M (Mosin-Nagant)

This is the Hungarian copy of the Soviet 1944 Mosin-Nagant. Produced in 1952-1955 by FEG. This rifle can be identified by the Communist national crest (a star on top of a globe with a hammer but no sickle) on top of the receiver ring. Stocks are marked with a "B" in a circle and may have "02" on top of the receiver ring that is the code for Hungary.

Exc.	V.G.	Good	Fair	Poor
100	75	60	—	—

48.M (Mosin-Nagant)

This is a Hungarian copy of the M91/30 Mosin Nagant Soviet rifle chambered for the 7.62mm cartridge. Barrel length is 28.5". Five-round magazine. Weight about 8.5 lbs. Exported world-wide.

Exc.	V.G.	Good	Fair	Poor
85	60	40	—	—

NOTE: Model 48 Sniper rifle was also made in Hungary and it is the same as the Soviet M91/30 Sniper rifle. See *Russia, Rifles.*

STEYR
Osterreichische Waffenfabrik Gesellschaft GmbH, Steyr (1869-1919)
Steyr-Werke AG (1919-1934)
Steyr-Daimler-Puch, Steyr (1934-1990)
Steyr-Mannlicher GmbH, Steyr (1990-)

Model 95 Rifle (Model 31)

A number of Model 95 rifles and short rifles were modified to accept the 8x56mm cartridge after World War I. The letter "H" is stamped on the barrel or the receiver. This is a straight pull rifle with 19.6" barrel and a 5-round fixed magazine. Weight is approximately 7.5 lbs.

Exc.	V.G.	Good	Fair	Poor
125	80	65	40	25

Model Gewehr 98/40

Built by FEG but with many Mannlicher and Mauser components in its design. Based on Hungarian M1935 short rifle. Chambered for the 7.92x57mm cartridge and Mauser charger loaded. Two-piece stock. Barrel length is 23.6". Weight is about 9 lbs.

Model 98/40 • Private collection, Paul Goodwin photo

Exc.	V.G.	Good	Fair	Poor
150	125	100	50	—

HUNGARIAN AK CLONES

AKM-63

A close copy of the AKM but with plastic furniture. Fitted with a vertical grip under the forend. Weighs about 1/2 lb. less than the Russian AKM.

Pre-1968

Exc.	V.G.	Fair
18000	15000	13000

Pre-1986 conversions

Exc.	V.G.	Fair
8000	7000	6000

Pre-1986 dealer samples

Exc.	V.G.	Fair
9000	8000	7000

AKM-63 (Semiautomatic version)

This semiautomatic version of the AKM-63 is in a pre-ban (1994) configuration.

Exc.	V.G.	Good	Fair	Poor
1400	1100	800	—	—

NOTE: Add 20% for folding stock (AMD-65-style).

AMD-65

This model is an AKM-63 with a 12.5" barrel, two-port muzzle brake, and a side folding metal butt. Rate of fire is about 600 rounds per minute. Weight is approximately 7 lbs.

Pre-1968

Exc.	V.G.	Fair
18000	15000	13000

Pre-1986 conversions

Exc.	V.G.	Fair
8000	7000	6000

Pre-1986 dealer samples

Exc.	V.G.	Fair
9000	8000	7000

NGM

This assault rifle is the Hungarian version of the AK-74 chambered for the 5.56x45mm cartridge. Fitted with a 16.25" barrel. Magazine capacity is a 30-round box type. Rate of fire is about 600 rounds per minute. Weight is approximately 7 lbs.

Pre-1968

Exc.	V.G.	Fair
N/A	N/A	N/A

Pre-1986 conversions

Exc.	V.G.	Fair
10000	9500	9000

Pre-1986 dealer samples

Exc.	V.G.	Fair
N/A	N/A	N/A

MACHINE GUNS

Hungary was supplied with a wide variety of Soviet machine guns after World War II from the RPD to the DShK38. Many of these machine guns were later copied by the Hungarians while retaining the Soviet model designations.

ISRAEL

Israeli Military Conflicts, 1870-Present

In the late 19th century, Zionist movement called for a Jewish homeland in Palestine. In World War I, Britain captured the area and appeared to support this purpose. In 1922, the League of Nations approved the British mandate of Palestine with the result of a large Jewish immigration into the area. This influx was opposed by the Arabs and with the end of World War II the U.N. divided Palestine into Jewish and Arab states. In 1948, the state of Israel was proclaimed. The Arabs rejected this proclamation and the result was the 1948-1949 war between Israel and Lebanon, Syria, Jordan, Egypt, and Iraq. Israel won the war and increased its territory by 50%. Arab opposition continued with subsequent conflicts: the Sinai campaign of 1956, the Six-Day War of 1967, and the Yom Kippur War of 1973. Israel won all of these conflicts. Israel and Egypt signed a peace treaty in 1979 with Israel withdrawing from the Sinai. The balance of the 1980s and 1990s is marked by fierce fighting in Lebanon and with the PLO. In 1993, Israel signed an accord with the PLO for self rule in Gaza and the West Bank. A peace treaty was signed with Jordan in 1994. The area remains highly volatile.

HANDGUNS

NOTE: Israel has used a number of different handguns during its early fight for independence and in the turbulent years after. These handguns included Enfield and Webley revolvers as well as Browning Hi-power, Lugers and P-38 pistols. They also built a modified copy of the Smith & Wesson Military & Police model chambered for the 9x19 cartridge which required the use of two three-round half-moon clips.

An Israeli-built copy of a Smith & Wesson Military & Police revolver sold at auction for $4,025. Cased with bring back papers dated 1954. One of 50 built in Israel for presentation purposes. Condition is excellent.
Rock Island Auction Company, September 2002

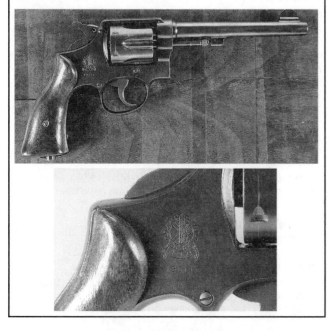

Beretta M1951

This 9mm semiautomatic pistol is the standard Israeli military sidearm. *See Italy, Handguns, Beretta.*

Jericho

A 9mm or .41 Action Express double action semiautomatic pistol with a 4.72" barrel, polygonal rifling, ambidextrous safety and fixed sights. Blued with plastic grips. Weight is approximately 36 oz. Magazine capacity is 16 rounds in 9mm. This pistol is primarily used by the Israeli police and other government agencies, generally in 9mm.

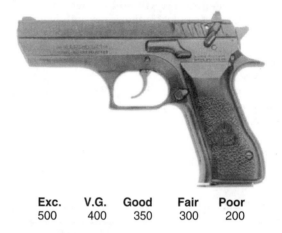

Exc.	V.G.	Good	Fair	Poor
500	400	350	300	200

SUBMACHINE GUNS

NOTE: Prior to the development of the UZI the Israelis used British Sten guns and other World War II submachine guns that were available for purchase on the arms market.

UZI

First produced in Israel in 1953, this submachine gun is chambered for the 9mm cartridge. It was designed by Uzi Gal and was based on the Czech designs that were used by Israeli forces in the 1947-48 conflicts. It is fitted with a 10.14" barrel and metal folding stock. It has a magazine capacity of 25, 32, or 40 rounds. Empty weight is about 7.7 lbs. Rate of fire is 600 rounds per minute. This gun enjoys widespread use and is found in military and police units all over the world. Marked "UZI SMG 9MM" on left side of receiver.

Pre-1968 (Very Rare)

Exc.	V.G.	Fair
10000	9000	8000

WHAT'S IT LIKE:
THE UZI SUBMACHINE GUN

Developed in the early 1950s, the Uzi proved to be a most formidable weapon not only in the hands of the Israelis but by many armies throughout the world. A simple open bolt concept with few moving parts, the Uzi is an extremely dependable and tough weapon. It will function in the desert heat, in wind-driven sand, and a host of other difficult environments. Fitted with either a detachable wood stock or a very stable and strong folding metal stock the gun feels solid. The Uzi will feed any 9mm ammunition without fail. It will break down without tools in a matter of seconds. Its sights are satisfactory and easy to adjust. It is accurate out to 200 meters. With a rate of fire of about 600 rounds per minute and a weight of about 8 lbs, multiple hits on target are accomplished with ease. It is, in short, the ideal second generation submachine gun. What it is not is a finely machined weapon, but that is the secret of its success. Without close tolerances and ease of manufacture the gun is simply not a high maintenance weapon. It is a joy to shoot and never fails to bring a smile to the faces of those who do.

Ned Schwing

Pre-1986 conversions

Exc.	V.G.	Fair
3000	2500	2300

Pre-1986 dealer samples

Exc.	V.G.	Fair
2000	1500	1000

Israel (no date). A soldier of the Israeli Defense Force squints to aim his 9mm UZI submachine gun, balanced on the base of its centrally-mounted magazine • Tal Yodkovik/Israeli Defense Forces/Action Arms Corp./Robert Bruce Military Photo Features

Vector UZI pre-1986 conversion

The receiver was produced, marked, and registered by Group Industries, Louisville, KY, prior to May 1986. Receiver fixed parts manufacturing and receiver assembly is done by Vector Arms, Inc. of North Salt Lake, UT. A total of 3,300 receivers built. All parts (South African) interchangeable with original IMI guns. Receiver parkerized. All other specifications same as original UZI.

Pre-1986 conversions

NIB/Exc.	V.G.	Fair
3000	2500	2300

Mini-UZI

First produced in 1987, this is a smaller version of the original UZI. It functions the same as its larger counterpart. Accepts 20-, 25-, and 32-round magazines. Rate of fire is about 900 to 1,100 rounds per minute. Weight is about 6 lbs. Overall length is about 14" with butt retracted and 23" with butt extended. Still in production in Israel, some South American countries, and U.S. Special Forces.

Photo courtesy private NFA collection

Pre-1968

Exc.	V.G.	Fair
N/A	N/A	N/A

Pre-1986 conversions

Exc.	V.G.	Fair
5500	5000	4500

Pre-1986 dealer samples

Exc.	V.G.	Fair
3500	2750	2500

RIFLES

NOTE: During the 1950s, Israel converted Mauser 98 rifles to 7.62mm caliber. Some of these were sold as surplus. The Israeli military employed a large number, about 150,000 Colt-built M16A1 rifles and M16A1 carbines during the 1970s. This weapon is still popular with the IDF today. They also have used FN-built and IMI-assembled FN-FAL rifles. Israeli military forces were even issued AKM rifles. In 1975 the U.S. government sold about 22,000 M14 rifles to the Israeli military.

Mauser

Czech Post-WWII 98k Short Rifle

This model is identical to the German Model K98k with the exception of an oversize triggerguard. Some have been converted to 7.62x51mm.

Exc.	V.G.	Good	Fair	Poor
275	225	190	125	80

FN 98k-style Short Rifle (7.62 conversion)

This model was purchased directly from FN in the 1950s and is the same configuration as the German Model 98k carbine. It is marked with Israeli markings on the receiver ring.

FN 98k Short Rifle • Private collection, Paul Goodwin photo

Exc.	V.G.	Good	Fair	Poor
300	250	200	125	90

Galil ARM-Select Fire Assault Rifle

This automatic rifle is produced in Israel and is chambered for the 5.56x45mm cartridge. Similar in appearance to the AK-47 this rifle is fitted with an 18" barrel and folding stock. Magazine capacity is 35 or 50 rounds. Rate of fire is 550 rounds per minute. Model markings on the left side of the receiver are in Hebrew. Weight is approximately 8.7 lbs. First produced in 1971. Still in production.

Photo courtesy private NFA collection

Pre-1968

Exc.	V.G.	Fair
N/A	N/A	N/A

Pre-1986 conversions

Exc.	V.G.	Fair
10000	7500	7000

Pre-1986 dealer samples (Rare)

Exc.	V.G.	Fair
9000	9000	8500

Galil SAR-Select Fire Assault Rifle

Similar to the ARM but with a folding metal stock and a barrel length of 13". Weight of SAR is about 8.25 lbs.

Pre-1968

Exc.	V.G.	Fair
N/A	N/A	N/A

Pre-1986 conversions

Exc.	V.G.	Fair
10000	9000	8500

Model ARM Assault Rifle • Courtesy West Point Museum, Paul Goodwin photo

Galil SAR • Photo courtesy private NFA collection

Pre-1986 dealer samples

Exc.	V.G.	Fair
9000	9000	8500

Model AR

This rifle is an Israeli variant of the AK-47 based on the Valmet. It is also used by the South African military where it is called the R-4 rifle. It is a .223 or .308 caliber semiautomatic rifle with 16" or 19" barrels. Parkerized with the flip "Tritium" night sights and folding stock. The .308 version would bring about a 10 percent premium.

NIB	Exc.	V.G.	Good	Fair	Poor
2800	2400	2000	1500	900	700

Model ARM

As above, with a ventilated wood handguard and a folding bipod and carrying handle. The .308 will bring about a 10 percent premium.

NIB	Exc.	V.G.	Good	Fair	Poor
3000	2700	2000	1500	900	700

Galil Sniper Rifle

Introduced in 1983 and similar to the above rifle chambered for the 7.62x51 NATO caliber, with a 20" heavy barrel, adjustable wooden stock, and a 6/40 scope is furnished in addition to the Tritium night sights. Supplied to military in semiautomatic version only. Weight is about 14 lbs. Supplied with two 25-shot magazines and a fitted case.

NIB	Exc.	V.G.	Good	Fair	Poor
8500	7500	6000	4000	3000	2000

IDF Mauser Rifle Model 66SP

This is a bolt action rifle chambered for the .308 Win. cartridge. Adjustable trigger for pull and travel. Barrel length is 27". Specially designed stock has broad forend and a thumb hole pistol grip. Cheekpiece is adjustable as is the recoil pad. The rifle is fitted with an original Swarovsky 6x24 BDC Mil-Spec scope. Supplied with case. This rifle is military issue, built by Mauser for the Israel Defense Force in the early 1980s. Less than 100 imported into the U.S by Springfield Armory.

Exc.	V.G.	Good	Fair	Poor
2500	2000	—	—	—

MACHINE GUNS

Israel uses a variety of foreign-built machine guns from the FN MAG, Browning 1919 and Browning .50 caliber heavy machine gun. There are no known transferable Israel machine guns in the U.S.

ITALY

Italian Military Conflicts, 1870-Present

The period of the last quarter of the 19th century was one of the final nationalistic efforts at unification of the Italian states. By the end of the century this effort was achieved. In 1915 Italy entered World War I on the allied side, and by the end of the war in 1918 Italy was awarded additional territories, but social unrest and economic discord brought about the rise of fascism, and in 1922 Mussolini seized power. He created a totalitarian state and expand Italian influence through armed aggression into Ethiopia in 1936, Albania in 1939, and entered World War II on the side of the Germans. In 1943 Italy surrendered to the Allies. In 1946, Italy became a republic. By 1947 Italy shed its colonies. The last 50 years has seen a rapid succession of governments trying to govern the country without much success.

HANDGUNS

Modello 1874

This was the first handgun adopted by the Kingdom of Italy's military forces. It was very similar to the French Model 1874 and is chambered for the 10.35mm cartridge. It is fitted with a 6.3" octagon barrel. Cylinder is fluted and grips are checkered wood with lanyard loop. Built by Siderugica Glisenti and others. Weight is about 40 oz. In use by the Italian military from 1872 to 1943.

Courtesy Supica's Old Town Station

Exc.	V.G.	Good	Fair	Poor
600	400	300	200	125

System Bodeo Modello 1889 (Enlisted Model)

A 10.4mm caliber revolver with a 4.5" octagonal barrel and 6-shot cylinder. Built on a Chamelot-Delvigne frame with loading gate on the right side. This revolver was adopted as the Italian service revolver in 1889 and was replaced by the Glisenti in 1910. Manufactured by various Italian arms companies. This revolver, in different configurations, remained in service until 1945.

Courtesy Richard M. Kumor Sr.

Exc.	V.G.	Good	Fair	Poor
300	200	150	100	75

Modello 1889 (Officers Model)

Essentially the same as the enlisted man's model with a round barrel, non-folding trigger, and conventional triggerguard.

Exc.	V.G.	Good	Fair	Poor
300	200	150	100	75

Glisenti Model 1910

A 9mm Glisenti caliber semiautomatic pistol with a 3.9" barrel, fixed sights, and 7-shot magazine. Weight is about 30 oz. Manufactured from 1910 to 1915. As many as 100,000 of these pistols were produced and used during World War II.

WARNING: *Standard 9x19 ammo must not be shot in this gun.*

Courtesy Faintich Auction Service • Photo Paul Goodwin

THE BODEO MODELLO 1889 REVOLVER

Why is it that the Europeans can't design a decent looking revolver? And the worst of the lot are those from the 19th century! While we Americans took the smooth, flowing lines and excellent ergonomics of our Colts and S&Ws for granted, our Continental brethren have been stuck with some of the oddest looking and worst handling round guns to ever come down the pike. Even the highly regarded British Webleys are so ugly that they don't bear commenting upon. In 1872 the neophyte Italian army adopted a Chamelot-Delvigne type revolver with a DA/SA trigger, solid frame, and rod ejector. In 1889 it was replaced with Pistola a Rotazione, System Bodeo, Modello 1889 which was chambered for the same 10.35mm cartridge as the 1872 model. There were three versions: Du Officiali (officers), the Alleggerito (light weight), and Du Trup (enlisted personnel). The latter was unique in having a folding trigger and no trigger-guard. All Mo. 1889 revolvers utilized the same frame with a very straight "broom handle" shaped grip, a prominent lanyard ring, six round cylinders, and a Nagant-style rod ejector. Manufacture of the Mo. 1889 continued until 1939. Last year my local gunsmith asked me to indentify an old revolver a customer had brought in. It turned out to be a very nice Mo. 1889 Alleggerito made by Metallurgica Bresciana in 1932. The customer kindly let me borrow it to test fire. Much to my surprise, the grip provided good handling characteristics and it pointed quite naturally, which was counterbalanced by one of the heaviest DA trigger pulls I have ever experienced. It was so bad that at seven yards I found it impossible to keep rounds on a man-sized combat target. Firing it SA at least allowed me to hit the target, although it printed about 6" above point of aim! If I had my druthers, I would have opted for one of the aforementioned Webleys!

Paul Scarlata

BERETTA, PIETRO

Model 1915

A 7.65mm caliber semiautomatic pistol with 3.5" barrel, fixed sights, and 7-shot magazine. Blued with walnut grips. Weight is about 20 oz. The slide is marked "PIETRO BERETTA BRESCIA CASA FONDATA NEL 1680 CAL. 7.65MM BREVETTO 1915." Manufactured between 1915 and 1922. Used by the Italian military during World War I and World War II. About 65,000 were produced, most of which were not martially marked.

Courtesy Rock Island Auction Company

Exc.	V.G.	Good	Fair	Poor
350	300	225	150	100

Model 1915 2nd Variation

As above, in 9mm Glisenti caliber with 3.75" barrel. Checkered wood grips. Weight is about 32 oz.

Exc.	V.G.	Good	Fair	Poor
425	350	275	200	125

Model 1915/1919

This model is an improved version of the above pistol but chambered for the 7.65mm cartridge. It also incorporates a new barrel-mounting method and a longer cutout in the top of the slide. Produced from 1922 to 1931 for the Italian military with about 50,000 manufactured, most without military markings.

Courtesy Orvel Reichert

Model 1910 with black plastic grips with crown • Courtesy Richard M. Kumor Sr.

Exc.	V.G.	Good	Fair	Poor
750	500	375	250	150

Courtesy Orvel Reichert

Exc.	V.G.	Good	Fair	Poor
350	300	225	150	100

Model 1923

A 9mm caliber semiautomatic pistol with 4" barrel and 8-shot magazine. Blued with steel grips. The slide is marked "Brev 1915-1919 Mlo 1923." Exposed hammer. Italian army markings on left grip tang. Some pistols are cut for a shoulder stock. Manufactured from 1923 to 1935. Approximately 10,000 manufactured.

Exc.	V.G.	Good	Fair	Poor
575	450	350	225	150

Model 1931

A 7.65mm caliber semiautomatic pistol with 3.5" barrel and open-top slide. Blued with walnut grips and marked "RM" separated by an anchor. Issue limited to the Italian navy. Produced from 1931 to 1934 for the Italian navy. Approximately 8,000 manufactured.

Exc.	V.G.	Good	Fair	Poor
450	375	275	200	150

Model 1934

As above, with 9mm Corto (Kurz) caliber. The slide is marked, "P. Beretta Cal. 9 Corto-Mo 1934 Brevet Gardone VT." This inscription is followed by the date of manufacture that was given numerically, followed by a Roman numeral that denoted the year of manufacture on the Fascist calendar, which began in 1922. This model was the most common pre-war Beretta pistol and was widely used by all branches of the Italian military. Examples are marked "RM" (navy), "RE" (army), "RA" (air force), and "PS" (police). Manufactured between 1934 and 1959.

Courtesy Orvel Reichert

Exc.	V.G.	Good	Fair	Poor
400	325	225	150	100

Air Force "RA" marked

Exc.	V.G.	Good	Fair	Poor
550	475	325	225	150

Navy "RM" marked

Exc.	V.G.	Good	Fair	Poor
625	550	375	250	175

Model 1934 Rumanian Contract

See Romania, Handguns.

Model 1935

As above, in 7.65mm caliber. A number of these pistols were built and used by the German army during the occupation of Italy in World War II. Some of these pistols are marked with the German army acceptance stamp. Pistols produced in 1944 and 1945 were likely used by the German army without markings. Some of these wartime pistols are marked with

Italian navy or air force markings. Production between 1934 and 1943 was about 200,000 pistols. Postwar versions are known. Manufactured from 1935 to 1959.

Courtesy Orvel Reichert

Exc.	V.G.	Good	Fair	Poor
400	325	225	150	100

Model 1951

Chambered for the 7.65 or 9mm cartridges, this model was fitted with a 4.5" barrel and had an 8-round magazine. Fixed sights. Weight was about 31 oz. This pistol was used by the Italian military as well as by Egypt (Helwan) and Israel. Sold commercially under the name "Brigadier."

Exc.	V.G.	Good	Fair	Poor
300	250	200	100	75

NOTE: For Egyptian copies deduct 50%.

Model 92

A 9mm caliber double action, semiautomatic pistol with a 5" barrel, fixed sights, and a 16-round, double-stack magazine. Blued with plastic grips. Introduced in 1976 and is now discontinued. This model was used by the Italian State Police forces. The U.S. military version, the M9, is based on this series.

NOTE: There are a number of different versions of this pistol. The main differences lie in the safety type and magazine release, barrel length, and magazine capacity.

NIB	Exc.	V.G.	Good	Fair	Poor
450	400	375	300	250	200

BERNARDELLI, VINCENZO

Model PO 18

A 7.65mm or 9mm Parabellum caliber, double action, semiautomatic pistol with a 4.75" barrel and a 16-shot, double-stack, detachable magazine. All steel construction. Blued with plastic grips. Walnut grips are available for an additional $40. Introduced in 1985. The 7.65mm was designed for commercial sales while the 9mm was for military sales and should be so marked.

NIB	Exc.	V.G.	Good	Fair	Poor
650	550	400	275	200	100

Model PO 18 Compact

As above, with a 4" barrel and a shorter grip frame with a 14-shot, double-column magazine. Introduced in 1989.

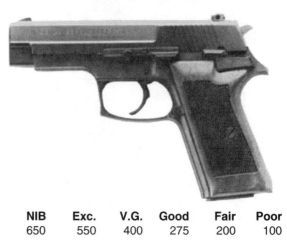

NIB	Exc.	V.G.	Good	Fair	Poor
650	550	400	275	200	100

SUBMACHINE GUNS

Italy also uses the HK MP5A3 and MP5SD in its police and anti-terrorist units.

Villar Perosa Model 1915

This was the first submachine gun adopted by any military force. Chambered for the 9x19mm Glisenti cartridge. Barrel length is 12.5". Its rate of fire was about 1200 rounds per minute. Fed by a 25-round box top-mounted magazine. This gun was designed to be mounted in pairs on aircraft, various types of vehicles, and from fixed mounts with its spade grip. Weight of pair is about 14 lbs.

Pre-1968 (Very Rare)

Exc.	V.G.	Fair
25000	22500	20000

Pre-1986 conversions

Exc.	V.G.	Fair
N/A	N/A	N/A

Pre-1986 dealer samples

Exc.	V.G.	Fair
N/A	N/A	N/A

Villar Perosa Model 1918 (Beretta)

This gun is an adapted Villar Perosa fitted into a wooden stock with new trigger mechanism. Most of the original M1915 Villar Perosa's were converted to the Model 1918. Barrel length is 12.5". Magazine capacity is 25 rounds. Rate of fire is about 900 rounds per minute. Select fire. Weight is about 8 lbs. This gun was used by the Italian army from the end of World War I to World War II.

Beretta Model 1918 • Courtesy Thomas Nelson, *The World's Submachine Guns, Vol. 1*

Twin Villar Perosa guns in simulated aircraft mount • Courtesy private NFA collection, Paul Goodwin photo

Pre-1968 (Extremely Rare)

Exc.	V.G.	Fair
9500	9000	8000

Pre-1986 conversions

Exc.	V.G.	Fair
N/A	N/A	N/A

Pre-1986 dealer samples

Exc.	V.G.	Fair
N/A	N/A	N/A

Beretta Model 1938A

This Italian-made submachine gun is chambered for the 9mm Parabellum cartridge and was produced from 1938 to about 1950. It was in use by German, Italian, and Romanian armies in different eras. Argentina also purchased a number of Model 38As directly from Beretta. It is fitted with a 12.25" barrel, full rifle-style stock, and has a magazine capacity of 10, 20, 30, or 40 rounds. Its rate of fire is 600 rounds per minute. Markings on top of receiver are "MOSCHETTI AUT-BERETTA MOD 1938A BE-REVETTO NO 828 428 GARDONE V.T. ITALIA." This weapon was fitted with two triggers: The front trigger fires in the semiautomatic mode, and the rear trigger fires in the automatic mode. A few early models were fitted with a bayonet lug. Weight is about 9.25 lbs.

Private NFA collection • Photo by Gary Gelson

Pre-1968

Exc.	V.G.	Fair
7000	6500	6000

Pre-1986 conversions

Exc.	V.G.	Fair
4000	3500	3000

Pre-1986 dealer samples

Exc.	V.G.	Fair
3500	3000	2500

Beretta Model 38/42

This is an improved wartime version of the Model 1938 without the barrel shroud. This was a less-well-finished model than the Model 1938A. Barrel length is a little over 8". Rate of fire is about 550 rounds per minute. Magazine capacity is 20 or 40 rounds. Produced from 1943 to about 1975. Weight is approximately 7 lbs. Marked "M.P. BERETTA MOD 38/42 CAL 9" on the top of the receiver. This model was used by Italian and German troops in Italy in the latter stages of World War II. Some of these guns were sold to Romania in 1944.

NOTE: A simplified version of the Model 38/42 is designated the Model 38/44 and features a lighter and more simple bolt design and main operating spring. This main spring is very similar to the one used in the British Sten gun. The Model 38/44 was sold to Syria, Pakistan, Iraq, and Costa Rica, among others, following World War II.

Pre-1968

Exc.	V.G.	Fair
5000	4500	4000

Pre-1986 conversions

Exc.	V.G.	Fair
N/A	N/A	N/A

Beretta Model 38/42 • Private NFA collection, Paul Goodwin photo

Pre-1986 dealer samples

Exc.	V.G.	Fair
3000	2500	2000

Beretta Model 12

Chambered for the 9mm Parabellum cartridge, this sub gun was produced from 1959 to about 1978. It was manufactured basically from steel stampings. Fitted with a bolt that wraps around the barrel. Also fitted with a front vertical hand grip and

---

THE BERETTA 38/42

The Beretta 38/42 was a major weapon of the Italian forces in World War II. Italy surrendered and quit the war in September 1943, but the Beretta 38/42 continued to see heavy use by both the Nazi forces fighting the Allies and by Italian partisan forces opposed to fascist rule. The Beretta Model 38/42 was a submachine gun designed for easier production versus previous 1st generation models. The barrel jacket of previous models was eliminated, the barrel was shorter, the magazine housing was made from sheet metal and spot welded to the receiver, and machine cuts on the end of the barrel were used in place of a compensator. The Beretta 38/42 was seen by many as more of a traditional carbine than a submachine gun because of its appearance with the wooden stock and double trigger firing mechanism. The Beretta 38/42 was a select-fire weapon as the front trigger produced only semi-auto fire, while the rear trigger produced full-auto fire with a cyclic rate of fire of only 550 rpm. The best part of the Beretta 38/42 was its magazine. It was a double column, two position feed box magazine in either 20-round capacity or 40 round capacity. If you examine an UZI magazine you will note a distinct similarity between it and the magazine for the 38/42 and for good reason. It was copied from Beretta. Most of the examples in the United States returned as wartime trophies from the North African campaign. The Beretta 38/42 was a solid performer and well built with the biggest negative being the quality of the wood used for wartime production. Most of the models examined feature a very open grain, somewhat soft wood, for the stocks. It remains, however, a solid design and one that is encountered frequently in far away places like Africa and the Middle East.

Frank James

---

either a folding metal stock or detachable wood stock. First used by Italian military in 1961. Also used in South America and Africa. Barrel is 7.75" long with a magazine capacity of 20, 30, or 40 rounds. Rate of fire is 500 rounds per minute. Marked "MOD12-CAL9/M PARABELLUM" on the top of the receiver. Weight is about 6.5 lbs.

Pre-1968 (Rare)

Exc.	V.G.	Fair
8000	7000	6500

Pre-1986 conversions

Exc.	V.G.	Fair
N/A	N/A	N/A

Pre-1986 dealer samples

Exc.	V.G.	Fair
4000	3500	3000

Beretta Model 12S

Similar to the Model 12 but with an improved safety system, sights, and folding stock fixture. Production began in 1978 when it replaced the Model 12.

Photo courtesy private NFA collection

Pre-1968

Exc.	V.G.	Fair
N/A	N/A	N/A

Pre-1986 conversions

Exc.	V.G.	Fair
N/A	N/A	N/A

Pre-1986 dealer samples

Exc.	V.G.	Fair
5000	4500	4000

Franchi LF-57

First produced in Italy in 1960, this submachine gun is chambered for the 9mm cartridge. It was placed in service with the Italian navy. Produced until 1980. It is fitted with an 8" barrel and has a magazine capacity of 20 or 40 rounds. Equipped with a folding stock. Rate of fire is about 500 rounds per minute. Marked "S P A LUIGI FRANCHI-BRESCIA-CAL9P." Weight is 7 lbs.

Pre-1968

Exc.	V.G.	Fair
5500	5000	4500

Pre-1986 conversions

Exc.	V.G.	Fair
N/A	N/A	N/A

Pre-1986 dealer samples

Exc.	V.G.	Fair
2500	2000	1500

Beretta Model 93R

Built of the Beretta Model 92 frame and slide, this machine pistol is chambered for the 9mm Parabellum cartridge. It is fitted with a 6.1" barrel with muzzle brake and uses a 15- or 20-round magazine. Can be fitted with a shoulder stock. Rate of fire is about 1,100 rounds per minute. Has a 3-round burst mode, and a small swing-down metal foregrip mounted on the front of the triggerguard. Weight is about 2.5 lbs. Used by the Italian anti-terrorist units.

Pre-1968

Exc.	V.G.	Fair
8500	8000	7500

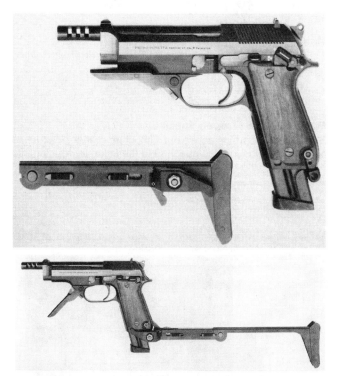

Beretta Model 93R • Courtesy Thomas Nelson, *The World's Machine Pistols, Vol. II*

Pre-1986 conversions

Exc.	V.G.	Fair
N/A	N/A	N/A

Pre-1986 dealer samples

Exc.	V.G.	Fair
4500	4000	3500

RIFLES

Prior to 1965 Italy used the U.S. M1 carbine as well as the M1 Garand. Beretta manufactured as large number of these rifles and many are still in use by some military units. Also used by counter-terrorist units is the HK G3 SG1 sniper rifle and the Mauser Model 66 sniper rifle.

VETTERLI

NOTE: See also *Switzerland, Rifles, Vetterli.*

Model 1870 Rifle

This rifle was produced at Brescia and Torino arsenals under license from the Swiss firm Vetterli. It was chambered for the 10.35x47Rmm centerfire cartridge. Single shot and full stock. This rifle was fitted with a sheet steel bolt opening cover which rotates left to right to close over the receiver opening. The barrel was 34" in length with the rear portion hexagonal. Marked on the upper left barrel flat with the maker's name and on the left barrel flat, the date. There is also a short barrel (24") version of this rifle.

Exc.	V.G.	Good	Fair	Poor
400	300	200	100	50

Model 1870 Carbine

Same as above but fitted with a 17.5" barrel. The stock was half stocked with brass or steel forearm bands. The bayonet folded under the barrel with the blade tip inserted into the forearm.

Exc.	V.G.	Good	Fair	Poor
750	600	500	250	100

Model 1882 Naval Rifle

This rifle used the Model 1870 action. Fitted with a 28.75" barrel and chambered for the 10.4x47R Vetterli-Vitali cartridge. Full stocked. Weight is approximately 9 lbs. This model had no loading port but was charged by loading through the open action. The tube held 8 rounds. Made at Turni.

Exc.	V.G.	Good	Fair	Poor
750	600	500	250	100

Model 1870 Rifle • Private collection, Paul Goodwin photo

Model 1870/87 Vetterli-Vitali • Private collection, Paul Goodwin photo

Model 1870/87 Rifle/Carbine (Vetterli-Vitali)

This rifle was the same as the Model 1870 with the important exception of having been converted to magazine feed. The 4-round magazine was developed by Guiseppe Vitali. The magazine is unusual because the charger had to be fully inserted and then withdrawn with a string as the cartridge stripped away. Over 1,000,000 of these rifles were issued. A large number of these converted rifles and carbines were sold to Russia.

NOTE: Some of these rifles were converted to 6.5mm caliber and designated the Model 1870/87/15.

Exc.	V.G.	Good	Fair	Poor
700	600	500	250	100

CARCANO

NOTE: For drawings, data, and history see, *The Carcano: Italy's Military Rifle* by Richard Hobbs, 1997.

Fucile Modello 1891 Rifle

Designed by Salvator Carcano, the Model 1891 was adopted as Italy's standard service rifle in 1892. A 6.5x52mm caliber bolt action rifle with a 30.6" barrel, 6-shot Mannlicher clip loading magazine, full-length stock, split bridge receiver, and a tangent rear sight with a wooden handguard and barrel bands retaining the stock. Fitted for a knife-type bayonet. On early versions the barrel behind the rear sights is octagonal. Weight is about 8.5 lbs. Produced at the Brescia and Terni arsenals. On post-1922 examples Roman numerals appear on the upper right barrel flat, denoting the year of the Mussolini rule. Many millions of this rifle were produced through World War II.

Exc.	V.G.	Good	Fair	Poor
225	175	125	75	40

Model 1891 Carbine

Same as above but half stocked with an 18" barrel with folding bayonet attached to the muzzle. Weight is about 6.5 lbs.

Exc.	V.G.	Good	Fair	Poor
250	175	125	75	40

Model 1891 TS (Truppe Speciali)

Similar to the Carbine above but without permanently attached bayonet. The bayonet is attached to the fitting by rotating into position over the barrel.

Exc.	V.G.	Good	Fair	Poor
250	175	125	75	40

Model 1891 Rifle • Courtesy West Point Museum, Paul Goodwin photo

Model 91 TS Carbine showing bayonet fitting • Private collection, Paul Goodwin photo

Model 1891/24 Carbine

Similar to the Model 1891 but with different rear sights.

Courtesy Richard M. Kumor Sr.

Exc.	V.G.	Good	Fair	Poor
250	175	125	75	40

Model 1891/28 T.S. Carbine

Chambered for the 6.5x52mm cartridge. Fitted with an 18" barrel. Otherwise similar in appearance to the Model 1891/24 carbine. This rifle was produced between 1928 and 1938 with barrel dates so stamped. Rear sight adjustable from 600 to 1,500 meters. Produced at a number of different Italian arsenals. Weight is about 6.75 lbs.

NOTE: A variation was built with a grenade launcher called the "Tromboni Launchi Bombe."

M91/28 Carbine with grenade launcher • Courtesy Richard M. Kumor Sr.

NOTE: Model 91/28 Carbine is rare and will command a substantial premium. Models in excellent condition can sell as high as $5,000. This model is encountered so seldom that prices are not given. Consult an expert prior to a sale.

Model 1938 Short Rifle (Prototype)

This model is chambered for the 7.35x51mm cartridge and fitted with a 22" barrel. It has a 6-round detachable box magazine. Bent bolt handle. It is full stocked with one barrel band and exposed barrel and bayonet lug. Long handguard. Simple fixed rear sight. Weight is about 7.5 lbs. Produced at the Terni arsenal. Very rare.

Exc.	V.G.	Good	Fair	Poor
N/A	—	—	—	—

Model 1938 Short Rifle (Production version)

As above but with two barrel bands and half-length handguard. The left side of the butt stock is marked in large letters "cal. 7.35." Rear sight is fixed at 200 meters. Weight is about 6.5 lbs.

NOTE: This rifle marked the first new caliber for Italian military rifles, the 7.35mm. When World War II began, about 285,000 rifles had been built in 7.35mm. From then on all Model 1938 Short Rifles and their variants were produced in the older 6.5mm caliber.

Exc.	V.G.	Good	Fair	Poor
175	140	100	60	25

NOTE: For original 7.35mm rifles add a premium of 50%.

Model 1938 Cavalry Carbine

This model has a 17.75" barrel. It is fitted with a round-up bayonet that fits under the barrel when not deployed. Chambered for the 7.35x53mm or 6.5mm cartridge, this carbine was issued to Italian paratroopers in the late 1930s. Built by FNA in Brescia and other Italian firms. The rear sight is a fixed 200 meter sight for rifles chambered for the 7.35mm cartridge and an adjustable rear sight for rifles chambered for the 6.5mm cartridge. About 100,000 were produced, but it is not often seen in North America. Weight is about 6.5 lbs. Carbines built in Gardone were equipped with grenade launchers.

NOTE: A very scarce carbine. No pricing information available.

Model 1938 Carbine • Courtesy West Point Museum, Paul Goodwin photo

Exc.	V.G.	Good	Fair	Poor
N/A	—	—	—	—

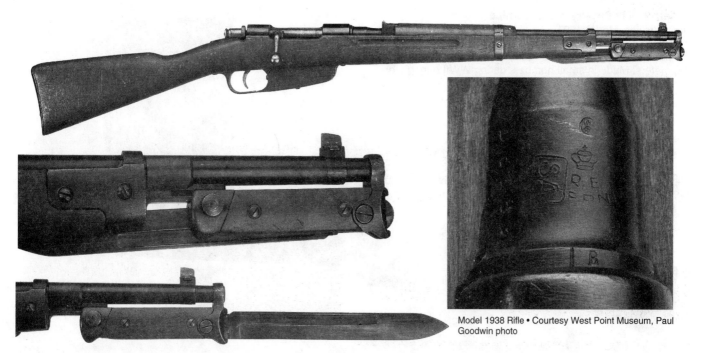

Model 1938 Rifle • Courtesy West Point Museum, Paul Goodwin photo

THE ITALIAN MANNLICHER-CARCANO RIFLE

In the 1890s, the newly formed Kingdom of Italy began the process of reequipping their army with a small bore, smokeless powder rifle—the Fucile Fanteria Modello 1891. A slim, light rifle, the Mo. 1891 used a Mannlicher packet loaded magazine and a bolt that combined features of both the German Mauser and Gew. 88 Commission rifles and was designed by a committee headed by Lt. Col. Salvatore Carcano. It was chambered for the Cartucce a Paliottola cal. 6.5 (a.k.a. 6.5x52) which pushed a round nosed 162 gr. FMJ bullet with a velocity of 2395 fps. I cannot understand why Mo. 1891 rifles have earned a reputation as unsafe junk. It is ludicrous to suppose that any army would purposely equip its troops with unsafe rifles, no matter how badly off they were. While they might appear crudely made and don't operate as smoothly as a Mauser or Lee-Enfield, the Mo. 1891 series of rifles were rugged, dependable weapons and served the Italian army through two world wars and remained in service with police until the 1980s. I recently test fired a Moschetto Mo. 1938 short rifle chambered for the short lived Cartucce a Paliottola cal. 7.35 (7.35x52) cartridge. While loading the six-round Mannlicher magazine was fast and smooth—in my opinion, much easier than a Mauser—bolt operation was very stiff. The fixed rear sight and inverted V blade up front provided a less-than optimal sight picture, but the trigger pull was rather decent and after a few attempts my best group at 75 yards measured exactly three inches. I have fired other, more highly regarded, military rifles that did not perform as well. While they usually generate little interest from American collectors or shooters, the Italian Mannlicher-Carcano rifle has earned a notorious place in this nation's history. This is because on November 22, 1963, Lee Harvey Oswald used a 6.5mm Moschetto Mo. 1938, serial number C2766, to assassinate President John F. Kennedy.

Paul Scarlata

Model 1938 T.S. Carbine

Same as above but with bayonet not permanently attached. Weight is about 6.75 lbs. Approximately 200,000 of these rifles were built.

Courtesy Richard M. Kumor Sr.

Exc.	V.G.	Good	Fair	Poor
150	100	75	40	20

NOTE: For original 7.35mm rifles add a premium of 50%.

Model 1938/43 Cavalry & T.S. Carbine

Similar to the Model 1891 but with 6 round magazine. Also chambered for the 7.9mm German cartridge. "7.9" is marked behind the rear sight. Barrel length is 18". Rear sight is fixed at 200 meters. Made in small numbers during WWII during German occupation of Italy.

Exc.	V.G.	Good	Fair	Poor
400	300	200	100	75

Model 1941 Rifle

This is a 6.5mm rifle fitted with a 27.25" barrel and 6-round detachable box magazine. Very similar to the Model 1891 but for length and rear sight from 300 to 1,000 meters. Weight about 8.2 lbs. Total production is estimated at 820,000 rifles.

Courtesy Richard M. Kumor Sr.

Exc.	V.G.	Good	Fair	Poor
200	150	120	75	50

NOTE: A few of these rifles were sold to Israel at the end of World War II and these are marked with the Star of David.

Italian Youth Rifle

Smaller version of full size military and chambered for 6.5mm cartridge. Barrel length is 14.4".

Breda Model PG • Paul Goodwin photo

Model BM59 • Courtesy West Point Museum, Paul Goodwin photo

NOTE: Add $75 for dedication plaque.

Courtesy Richard M. Kumor Sr.

Exc.	V.G.	Good	Fair	Poor
450	375	250	150	75

Breda Model PG

Chambered for the 7x57mm rimless cartridge, this is a gas operated self-loading rifle with an 18" barrel and 20-round detachable box magazine. The particular rifle was made by Beretta for Costa Rica and is marked "GOBIERNO DE COSTA RICA," with the date 1935 and Roman numerals XIII. Weight was about 11.5 lbs. Fitted for a Costa Rican Mauser bayonet.

Exc.	V.G.	Good	Fair	Poor
450	375	250	150	75

Beretta Model BM59-Select Fire Assault Rifle

This select fire rifle closely resembles the U.S. M1 Garand rifle. Chambered for the 7.62x51mm cartridge, it is fitted with a 19" barrel and 20-round magazine. It has a rate of fire of 750 rounds per minute. Weight is about 10 lbs. Marked "P BERETTA BM59" on the top rear of the receiver. Produced from 1961 to 1966. This rifle did see service in the Italian army. There are number of variations to this rifle, including the BM59 Alpini with folding stock short forearm and bipod for use by Alpine troops, and the BM59 Parachutist Rifle with 18" barrel, folding stock, and detachable muzzle brake (the Italians referred to it as a Tri-Comp).

Pre-1968

Exc.	V.G.	Fair
5500	5000	4500

Pre-1986 conversions

Exc.	V.G.	Fair
3500	3250	3000

Pre-1986 dealer samples

Exc.	V.G.	Fair
3000	2750	2500

Beretta AR70/.223 Select Fire Assault Rifle

Chambered for the 5.56x45mm cartridge, this select fire rifle was fitted with a 17.5" barrel and a 30-round magazine. Most were fitted with a solid buttstock while others were fitted with a folding stock. Weight was about 8.3 lbs. Marked "P BERETTA AR 70/223 MADE IN ITALY" on the left side of the receiver. This rifle was not widely adopted. Produced from 1972 to 1980.

Photo courtesy private NFA collection

Pre-1968 (Rare)

Exc.	V.G.	Fair
12000	8000	8000

Pre-1986 conversions

Exc.	V.G.	Fair
10000	7500	5000

Pre-1986 dealer samples

Exc.	V.G.	Fair
6500	5000	5000

Beretta SC 70 Select Fire Assault Rifle

Similar to the AR 70 and chambered for the 5.56x45mm cartridge. It feeds from a 30-round magazine. The SC 70 has a folding stock and is fitted with a 17.5" barrel. Weight is about 8.8 lbs. The SC 70 short carbine also has a folding stock and is fitted with a 13.7" barrel. Weight is about 8.3 lbs. Both of these rifles are still in production and used by the Italian army since approved for service in 1990.

SC 70 Carbine • Photo courtesy private NFA collection

SC 70 Short Carbine • Photo courtesy private NFA collection

Pre-1968

Exc.	V.G.	Fair
12000	9500	8500

Pre-1986 conversions

Exc.	V.G.	Fair
10000	8000	6500

Pre-1986 dealer samples

Exc.	V.G.	Fair
8000	6500	5500

AR-70

A .223 caliber, semiautomatic rifle with a 17.7" barrel, adjustable diopter sights, and an 8- or 30-shot magazine. Black epoxy finish with a synthetic stock. Weight is approximately 8.3 lbs.

NIB	Exc.	V.G.	Good	Fair	Poor
2500	2200	1900	1500	1000	—

BM-59 Standard Grade

A gas-operated semiautomatic rifle with detachable box magazine. Chambered for .308 cartridge. Walnut stock. Barrel length is 19.3" with muzzle brake. Magazine capacity is 5, 10, or 20 rounds. Weight is about 9.5 lbs.

NIB	Exc.	V.G.	Good	Fair	Poor
2200	1700	1200	700	400	—

SHOTGUNS

Franchi SPAS 12

A 12 gauge slide action or semiautomatic shotgun with a 21.5" barrel and 9-shot magazine. Anodized black finish with a composition folding or fixed stock. Weight is about 9.25 lbs.

NIB	Exc.	V.G.	Good	Fair	Poor
950	800	600	500	400	300

Franchi SPAS 15

Similar to the SPAS 12 but with a detachable 6-round box magazine. Tubular steel folding stock and 18" barrel or fixed stock with 21" barrel. Weight is about 8.5 lbs. Very few imported into the U.S.

NIB	Exc.	V.G.	Good	Fair	Poor
4500	4000	3500	2500	—	—

NOTE: For guns with folding stock and 18" barrel add $1,000.

MACHINE GUNS

Italy used the Maxim Model 1906 and Model 1911. Both of these models were chambered for the 6.5mm cartridge. During World War I, Italy purchased a number of Colt Model 1914 guns (Potato Diggers) chambered for the 6.5mm cartridge. When the war ended, Italy received a large number of Austrian Schwarzlose Model 1907/12 as war reparations. The first Italian light machine gun was the Breda Model 1924, the forerunner of the Breda Model 30.

After World War II, Italy adopted the U.S. Model 1919A4 and .50 NM2 HB guns, as well as the MG42/59, for which several Italian firms make the components under license.

Beretta M70/78

Similar to the Model 70/223 but fitted with a heavy 17.5" barrel. Magazine capacity is 30 or 40 rounds. Rate of fire is 700 rounds per minute. Marked "P BERETTA FM 70/78 MADE IN ITALY"

on left side of the receiver. First produced in 1978 with production ending in 1983.

Pre-1968

Exc.	V.G.	Fair
N/A	N/A	N/A

Pre-1986 conversions

Exc.	V.G.	Fair
N/A	N/A	N/A

Pre-1986 dealer samples (Rare)

Exc.	V.G.	Fair
9000	9000	8500

World War I Italian machine gun team with Model 1914 Revelli • Robert G. Segel collection

Revelli Model 1914

This was the first Italian-designed medium machine gun to be made in quantity. It was chambered for the 6.5mm cartridge and fitted with a 26" barrel. It was fed by a unique 50-round magazine with 10 compartments holding 5 rounds each. Because of its blowback system where the barrel moved a short distance rearward before the bolt moved away from the breech, there was no extraction system other than to oil the cartridges so that they did not rupture. Rate of fire was about 400 rounds per minute. Weight was 38 lbs. without tripod, 50 lbs. with tripod. The gun was manufactured by Fiat. Many of these guns were used by the Italians in World War II as well as in the first world war.

Pre-1968

Exc.	V.G.	Fair
7500	7000	6500

Pre-1986 conversions

Exc.	V.G.	Fair
N/A	N/A	N/A

Pre-1986 dealer samples (Rare)

Exc.	V.G.	Fair
N/A	N/A	N/A

Fiat Model 1928 (SAFAT)

This is a light version of the Revelli Model 1914. Chambered for the 6.5 Carcano cartridge. Magazine is a 20-round magazine. Rate of fire is 500 rounds per minute. Weight is approximately 21 lbs. Only a few thousand were manufactured during its limited production. Very Rare.

Revelli Model 1914 • Courtesy private NFA collection, Paul Goodwin photo

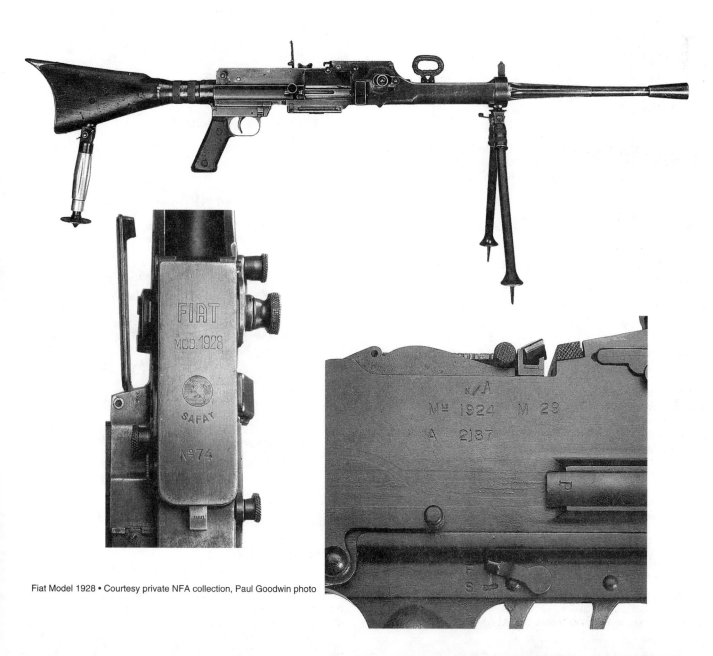

Fiat Model 1928 • Courtesy private NFA collection, Paul Goodwin photo

Fiat Model 35 • Courtesy private NFA collection, Paul Goodwin photo

Pre-1968

Exc.	V.G.	Fair
N/A	N/A	N/A

Pre-1986 conversions

Exc.	V.G.	Fair
N/A	N/A	N/A

Pre-1986 dealer samples (Rare)

Exc.	V.G.	Fair
N/A	N/A	N/A

Revelli/Fiat Model 35

This is a converted Revelli Model 1914 to 8mm. It is an air-cooled gun. It is fed by a 300-round belt. It's fired from a closed bolt. It was not a successful gun. Weight without tripod was 40 lbs.

Pre-1968

Exc.	V.G.	Fair
6000	5000	4500

Pre-1986 conversions

Exc.	V.G.	Fair
N/A	N/A	N/A

Pre-1986 dealer samples

Exc.	V.G.	Fair
N/A	N/A	N/A

Breda Model 30

First produced in Italy in 1930, this machine gun was chambered for the 6.5x52mm cartridge. It is fitted with a 20.3" barrel. Magazine capacity is 20 rounds. Rate of fire is 475 rounds per minute. Marked "MTR LEGG MOD 30….BREDA ROMA" on top of receiver. Weight is about 22 lbs. Production on this model ceased in 1937. This was the primary Italian machine gun of World War II.

NOTE: A number of pre-1968 7mm Costa Rican contract guns are in the U.S. These are valued the same as the 6.5mm guns.

Pre-1968

Exc.	V.G.	Fair
9500	8500	8000

Pre-1986 conversions

Exc.	V.G.	Fair
N/A	N/A	N/A

Pre-1986 dealer samples (Rare)

Exc.	V.G.	Fair
5500	5000	4000

Breda Model 37

Chambered for the 8x59 Breda cartridge, this gas operated machine gun had a rate of fire of 450 rounds per minute. It was fitted with a 26.5" barrel and weighs approximately 43 lbs. It was fed with a 20-round strip. Marked "MITRAGLIATRICE BREDA MOD 37" on the left side of the receiver. Produced from 1936 to

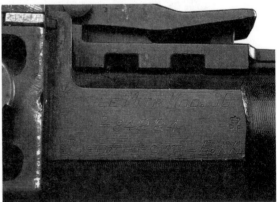

Breda Model 30 with receiver markings • Paul Goodwin photo

1943, this was the standard heavy machine gun of the Italian army during World War II. The Model 37 was considered to be one of the best Italian machine guns used in World War II, mainly because of its reliability and accuracy.

Pre-1968

Exc.	V.G.	Fair
25000	22500	20000

Pre-1986 conversions

Exc.	V.G.	Fair
N/A	N/A	N/A

Pre-1986 dealer samples (12 known)

Exc.	V.G.	Fair
15000	14000	12000

Mignano, Italy, December 1943. Italian Army Bersaglieri of the 51st Battalion (Special Infantry) guard a command post with a Breda 8mm M37 machine gun. This serviceable gun has the unusual distinction of feeding, firing, and replacing empties in its ammo tray system • U.S. Army Signal Corps/National Archives/Robert Bruce Military Photo Features

Breda Model 37 with receiver markings • Paul Goodwin photo

JAPAN

Japanese Military Conflicts, 1870-1945

The year 1868 marks the beginning of Japanese adoption of Western civilization and rapid modernization into an industrial and military power. The Japanese military was successful in the First Sino-Japanese War (1894-1895), as well as the Russo-Japanese War (1904-1905). In 1910, Japan annexed Korea and established a puppet-state in Manchuria in 1932. In 1937, the Japanese invaded northern China to begin the Sino-Japanese War (1937-1945). On December 7, 1941, the Japanese bombed Pearl Harbor, thus entering World War II. The war ended in August 1945. During World War II Japan had 9,100,000 men under arms. At the end of the war 1,834,000 had been killed or wounded. Since the end of World War II the Japanese military has operated on a very small scale, mostly for domestic defense.

Bibliographical Note: Little has been written about Japanese military weapons. For a good overview see A.J. Barker, *Japanese Army Handbook, 1939-1945*, 1979.

HANDGUNS

Bibliographical Note: For technical data, history, and photos see Fred Honeycutt, Jr., *Military Pistols of Japan*, 3rd Ed., Julian Books, 1994.

Type 26 Revolver

A 9mm caliber double action hinged-barrel revolver with a 6-shot cylinder. Because this pistol does not have a hammer spur, it only functions in double action. Fitted with a 4.75" barrel. Checkered beech grips. Grips from later examples have 19 serrations. Weight is about 31 oz. Manufactured from 1893 to 1924 in various government arsenals. Marked on right side of frame. This revolver was used by NCOs during WWII. Less than 60,000 of these revolvers were manufactured.

Courtesy Amoskeag Auction Co., Inc.

Exc.	V.G.	Good	Fair	Poor
400	300	200	150	100

4th Year Type Nambu Pistol

This is a quality-built semiautomatic pistol chambered for the 8mm cartridge. It is fitted with a 4.7" barrel and has a magazine capacity of 8 rounds. It can be identified by the grip safety lo-

cated on the front strap and tangent sights. The early models, known as "Grandpa" to collectors, can be identified by a wooden-bottom magazine and stock slot. Later pistols, known as "Papa" Nambu, have aluminum-bottom magazines and only a very few "Papas" were slotted for stocks. The values shown here are only approximate. Different variations may bring different prices and an appraisal is recommended. Pistols with original wooden stocks are worth considerably more.

It is estimated that approximately 8,500 of these pistols were produced.

Grandpa

Grandpa • Courtesy of James Rankin

Exc.	V.G.	Good	Fair	Poor
5000	3500	2000	1500	800

NOTE: Add $1,500 for original matching shoulder stock-holster.

Papa

Papa • Courtesy of James Rankin

Exc.	V.G.	Good	Fair	Poor
1500	900	650	450	300

Baby Nambu

As above, with a 3.5" barrel. 7mm cartridge is unique to the gun. A much smaller version of the Papa 8mm pistol. It is a well-made piece. Production ceased in 1927 with about 6,500 pistols produced.

Courtesy Rock Island Auction Company

Exc.	V.G.	Good	Fair	Poor
2500	2000	1500	1000	750

14th Year Type Nambu Pistol/T-14

Similar to the 4th Year Type but without a grip safety and with grooved grips and a larger triggerguard. Manufactured until 1945. Early guns have a small triggerguard. Later models have a much larger triggerguard. Early guns will bring a premium of 20 percent. The month and year of production are indicated on the right side of the receiver, just below the serial numbers on both the Type 14 and Type 94 pistols. The guns are dated from the beginning of the reign of Hirohito (Sho-wa period), which stared in 1925. Thus 3.12 means 1928-Dec. and 19.5 means 1944-May.

From 1926 to 1939 (small triggerguard) about 66,700 pistols were manufactured. From 1939 to to 1945 (large triggerguard) approximately 73,000 pistols were produced.

Courtesy Orvel Reichert

Courtesy Orvel Reichert

Later pistol with large triggerguard • Courtesy Orvel Reichert

Exc.	V.G.	Good	Fair	Poor
350	250	200	150	100

Type 94 Pistol/T-94

An 8mm caliber semiautomatic pistol with a 3.8" barrel and 6-shot magazine. Weight is about 27 oz. This was a secondary service pistol issued in WWII. Most late-war examples are poorly constructed and finished. Manufactured from 1935 to 1945. Approximately 70,000 of these pistols were produced.

Courtesy Rock Island Auction Company

Exc.	V.G.	Good	Fair	Poor
350	300	250	175	125

Hamada Skiki (Type) 2

Designed in 1942. There were several variations of this pistol chambered for both 7.65mm and 8mm Nambu. Production started in 1942 and ended in 1945. Probably less than 1,500 pistols were assembled. Rare. An expert opinion should be sought prior to a sale.

Courtesy James Rankin

Exc.	V.G.	Good	Fair	Poor
4500	3500	2500	2000	1500

SUBMACHINE GUNS

The Japanese military used Bergmann submachine guns built by SIG. These guns were similar to the MP 18 but chambered for the 7.63 Mauser cartridge and used a box magazine. These gun were fitted for a bayonet. It was not until the late 1930s that the Japanese began a development program to produce their own submachine gun; the first one was the Type 100/40.

Type 100/40

Adopted for use in 1940, this submachine gun is chambered for the 8x21mm Nambu cartridge and fitted with a 9" barrel with perforated jacket, fitted with a bayonet bar. It is mounted on a wooden half stock with tubular receiver made at the Kokura arsenal. These guns will also be seen with a folding stock made at the Nagoya arsenal. It is estimated that some 10,000 guns were built with fixed stocks and about 6,000 were built with folding stocks. Both types had 30-round box magazines. Rate of fire is approximately 450 rounds per minute. Weight was about 7.5 lbs. This model was issued primarily to paratroopers.

Japanese Type 100/40 • Courtesy Thomas Nelson, *World's Submachine Guns, Vol. I*

Pre-1968

Exc.	V.G.	Fair
5500	5000	4500

Pre-1986 conversions

Exc.	V.G.	Fair
N/A	N/A	N/A

Pre-1986 dealer samples

Exc.	V.G.	Fair
N/A	N/A	N/A

Type 100/44

This model was first produced in Japan in 1944. It is chambered for the 8mm Nambu cartridge. The barrel is 9.2" long with a honeycombed barrel jacket without bayonet bar. The side-mounted magazine capacity is 30 rounds. Markings are in Japanese on the rear of the receiver. Produced until the end of the war. Weight is about 8.5 lbs. Rate of fire is 800 rounds per minute. Approximately 8,000 were produced at the Nagoya arsenal. This improved version was issued to the infantry.

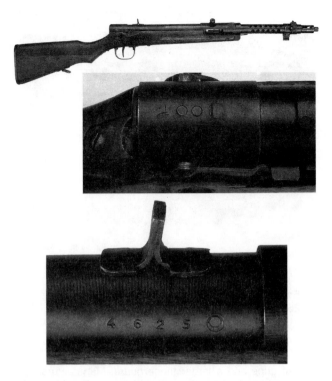

Type 100/44 • Courtesy West Point Museum, Paul Goodwin photo

Pre-1968

Exc.	V.G.	Fair
5500	5000	4500

Pre-1986 conversions

Exc.	V.G.	Fair
N/A	N/A	N/A

Pre-1986 dealer samples

Exc.	V.G.	Fair
N/A	N/A	N/A

RIFLES

Bibliographical Note: For historical information, technical data and photos see *Military Rifles of Japan*, 4th edition. Fred Honeycutt Jr., 1993.

MARTINI

Model 1874 Peabody-Martini Rifle

Chambered for the .45 Turkish centerfire cartridge and fitted with a 32.5" barrel. Blued barrel and furniture with case hardened or blued receiver. Numbered in Arabic script. About 7,000 built for Japanese Navy.

Exc.	V.G.	Good	Fair	Poor
—	750	500	350	150

MURATA

This series of Japanese military rifles was designed by Major Tsuneyoshi, superintendent of Japanese small arms in the late 1870s. These first single-shot bolt action rifles were based on the French Gras design. Later, Murata was influenced by the French Lebel with its tubular magazine.

Murata Type 13 (M.1880)

This was the first Japanese-designed bolt action rifle. This was a single-shot rifle with no extractor or safety. Chambered for the 11x60Rmm cartridge with a barrel length of 31.25". One piece full-length stock with two barrel bands. The machinery to build this rifle was purchased from Winchester. The rear barrel flat is stamped with the Imperial chrysanthemum. The left side of the receiver is stamped with Japanese characters.

Exc.	V.G.	Good	Fair	Poor
2000	1500	1000	600	400

Murata Type 16
Same as above but fitted with a 25" barrel for cavalry use.

Exc.	V.G.	Good	Fair	Poor
2200	1650	1200	700	500

Murata Type 18 (M.1885)
An 11mm caliber bolt-action rifle with a 31.25" barrel, and full-length stock secured by two barrel bands. This was an improved version of the Type 13, which added receiver gas escape ports, a flat-top receiver ring, and a safety. These rifles was used in the Sino-Japanese War of 1894 and the Russo-Japanese War as well.

Courtesy Buffalo Bill Historical Center, Cody, Wyoming

Exc.	V.G.	Good	Fair	Poor
1650	1200	800	200	100

Murata Type 22 (M.1889)
Produced circa 1889-1899 in caliber 8x53Rmm. Fitted with a 29.50" barrel with 8-round tubular magazine located in the forearm. This model was full stocked to the muzzle with straight grip. There were two variations of this rifle. The early version had a barrel band forward of the forend band. In the later version, this extra band was eliminated. This was Japan's first smokeless powder military rifle and was the standard rifle issued to Japanese forces in the Sino-Japanese War of 1894. It remained in service until the Russo-Japanese War of 1904.

Rifle
Exc.	V.G.	Good	Fair	Poor
1600	1400	1000	300	200

Murata Type 22 Carbine
Introduced in 1894 and fitted with a 19.5" barrel and 5-round magazine. No bayonet fitting. A rare carbine.

Courtesy Richard M. Kumor Sr.

Exc.	V.G.	Good	Fair	Poor
2200	1900	1400	350	200

ARISAKA
This series of Japanese military rifles was developed by Colonel Nariake Arisaka, Superintendent of the Tokyo Arsenal. His task was to find a replacement for the Murata rifles that showed some defects during the Sino-Japanese War of 1894.

Arisaka Type 30 Rifle (aka Hook Safety) (M.1897)
A 6.5x51SRmm Arisaka caliber bolt action rifle with a 31.5" barrel, 5-shot magazine and full-length stock secured by two barrel bands and a wooden upper handguard. This was the first box-magazine Mauser-Mannlicher design used by the Japanese military. Straight handle bolt. This was the primary shoulder arm of Japanese troops during the Russo-Japanese War of 1904. Some of these rifles remained in service until WWII. A number of these rifles were sold to Great Britain and Russia during World War I. The Type 30 was also built for Siam (Thailand) and marked by that county's crest on the receiver bridge. It was designed by Nariaki Arisaka. Manufactured from 1897 to 1905. The rifle gets its nickname, "hook-safety," from the prominent hook projecting from the left side of the rear of the bolt.

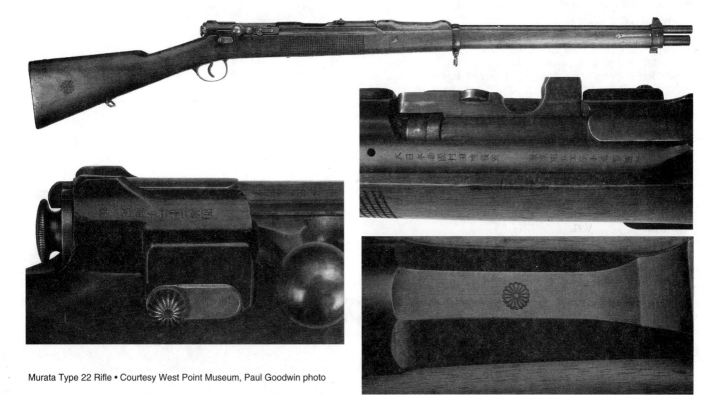

Murata Type 22 Rifle • Courtesy West Point Museum, Paul Goodwin photo

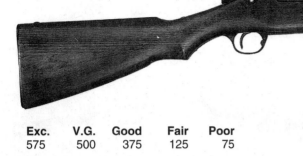

Japanese Type 30 Carbine • Courtesy West Point Museum, Paul Goodwin photo

Exc.	V.G.	Good	Fair	Poor
575	500	375	125	75

Arisaka Type 30 Carbine (aka Hook Safety Carbine)
As above, with a 20" barrel and no upper handguard.

Courtesy Richard M. Kumor Sr.

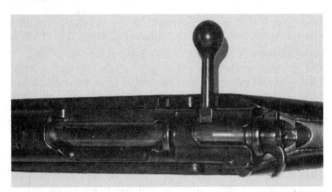

Courtesy Richard M. Kumor Sr.

Exc.	V.G.	Good	Fair	Poor
600	550	400	150	100

NOTE: Deduct 30% if mum stamping is ground off.

Arisaka Type 35 Navy (M.1902)
Adopted by the Japanese navy in 1902, this was an improved version of the Type 30 rifle. Some main differences are that the hook safety was reduced in length and checkered. The receiver included a spring-latched bolt cover. Used during the Russo-Japanese War of 1904. About 40,000 were built. Many of these were sold to Great Britain and Russia during World War I. All dimensions are the same as the Type 30 rifle.

Exc.	V.G.	Good	Fair	Poor
450	350	250	150	100

Arisaka Type 38 Rifle (M.1905)
A 6.5mm Arisaka caliber bolt action rifle with a 31.5" barrel, 5-shot magazine and large bolt handle. Full-length stock secured by two barrel bands with finger grooves. It was based on the Model 1893 Spanish Mauser. This model was built with a separate sheet steel action cover sliding with the bolt action. This rifle saw extensive use as late as World War II. Some of these rifles were sold to England in 1914 and 1915 and about 600,000 were sold to Russia in 1915 and 1916 in 7mm Mauser caliber. These rifles were originally intended for Mexico and have the Mexican crest of the receiver. These Russian-purchased rifles ended up in Germany in 1917 and were used in the Russian Civil War of 1917. Manufactured from 1905 to 1945. Most production switched to the Type 99 in 7.7mm beginning in 1939.

Exc.	V.G.	Good	Fair	Poor
175	150	125	90	65

Arisaka Type 38 Carbine
As above, with a 19" barrel and upper handguard. Equipped for a bayonet. Weight is about 7.25 lbs.

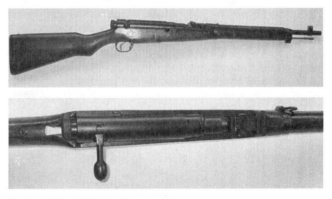

Courtesy Richard M. Kumor Sr.

Exc.	V.G.	Good	Fair	Poor
300	250	175	125	85

NOTE: Deduct 30% if mum stamping is ground off.

Japanese Type 35 rifle with close up of breech and hook safety • Private collection, Paul Goodwin photo

Arisaka Type 38 Rifle • Courtesy West Point Museum, Paul Goodwin photo

Thai Type 38 Conversions

Short Rifle-.30-06

Exc.	V.G.	Good	Fair	Poor
600	475	350	250	150

Half-Stock Carbine-6.5mm

Exc.	V.G.	Good	Fair	Poor
550	425	300	200	100

Manchurian Mauser Rifle (Mukden Arsenal)

This rifle has many features from both the Mauser 98 and the Arisaka. Barrel length is 29" and most rifles are chambered for the 7.92x57mm cartridge while some are chambered for the Japanese 6.5mm cartridge. Magazine capacity is 5 rounds. Bolt handle is pear shaped. Marked on top of receiver ring with Mukden arsenal symbol.

Exc.	V.G.	Good	Fair	Poor
750	600	450	250	100

Arisaka Type 44 Carbine

Similar to the Type 38 carbine but with an 18.5" barrel and folding bayonet that hinged into the forearm. Weight was about 9 lbs.

Courtesy Rock Island Auction Company

Exc.	V.G.	Good	Fair	Poor
450	350	225	150	100

Arisaka Type 97 "Sniper's Rifle"

The Type 38 with a side-mounted 2.5-power telescope and a bipod. Introduced in 1937. The telescope mounted on each rifle was factory fitted and stamped with the serial number of the rifle. The rear sight was a peep with folding from 400 to 2200 meters. Weight is approximately 11 lbs. with scope.

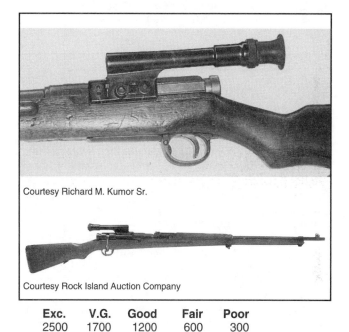

Courtesy Richard M. Kumor Sr.

Courtesy Rock Island Auction Company

Exc.	V.G.	Good	Fair	Poor
2500	1700	1200	600	300

Arisaka Type 99 Short Rifle

A 7.7mm caliber bolt action rifle with a 26" barrel and full-length stock secured by two barrel bands. Non-detachable magazine capacity is 5 rounds. Fitted with a folding wire monopod. Weight is about 8.5 lbs. Adopted for military use in 1939. The rear sight on this rifle was a graduated leaf-type with

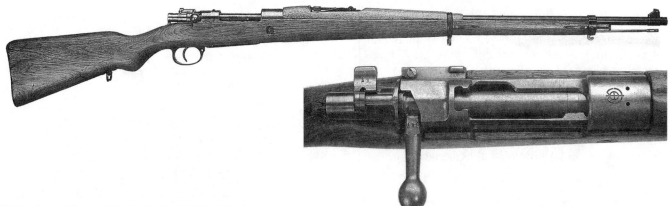

Mukden Arsenal Mauser • Private collection, Paul Goodwin photo

folding arms to help aiming at aircraft. The monopod and anti-aircraft sight were phased out as the war progressed.

NOTE: Add 15% for monopod.

Exc.	V.G.	Good	Fair	Poor
175	140	100	80	60

Arisaka Type 99 Long Rifle
This variation is the same as the above model but fitted with a 31.4" barrel. Weight is about 9 lbs. This is a scarce variation.

NOTE: Add 30% for monopod and dust cover.

Exc.	V.G.	Good	Fair	Poor
500	400	300	100	50

THE TYPE 99 ARISAKA

Introduced in 1939 chambered for the 7.7x58mm cartridge, the adoption of the Type 99 Arisaka was intended to solve several problems for the Japanese Army. The first was to use a cartridge that would be better than the then-standard 6.5x50mm for machine gun use and still be suitable for rifles. The second was that the Type 99 could be manufactured much more inexpensively and easily than the Type 38 Arisaka it was to replace. Finally the Type 99 was a medium length rifle that could serve both infantry or cavalry. The Type 99 had several advantages over the other bolt action military rifles of its day. The most unique and significant was the fact that it had a chrome-lined barrel. This was a huge advantage since most of the ammunition at that time on both sides had corrosive priming that could rust a barrel badly in short order without immediate cleaning.

The chrome-lined barrel is largely impervious to this problem. The Type 99 has an incredibly simple, but tremendously strong, action design. The bolt has only six parts and that includes one of the best safeties ever put on a military rifle. The latter requires a deliberate act to engage, locked both the bolt and the firing pin securely, but could be disengaged with a simple forward and upward push of the shooter's thumb. The bolt can be completely disassembled in ten seconds without any tools and reassembled nearly as quickly. This is a huge advantage for field maintenance, cleaning, and parts replacement. I would rate the Type 99 as no worse than the 2nd or 3rd best bolt action rifle of WWII and would prefer it over any other in damp tropical environments or for amphibious operations. Often thought of as a poor rifle by the uninformed, the Type 99 was actually one of the best of its breed.

Chuck Karwan

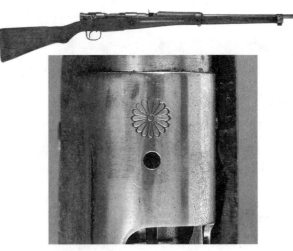

Courtesy Rock Island Auction Company

NOTE: Deduct 30% if mum stamping is ground off.

Arisaka Type 99 "Last Ditch" Rifle
This is a Type 99 simplified for easier production. Typical features include a cylindrical bolt knob, a fixed peep sight, no front sight guards and a wooden buttplate. Not all rifles have each of these features.

Exc.	V.G.	Good	Fair	Poor
250	200	150	125	100

Test Type 1 Paratroop Rifle
Bolt action rifle chambered for 6.5mm Japanese. Barrel length is 19". Cleaning rod is 17 3/16" long. The stock is a two-piece buttstock with full-length handguard and a hinge attached at the wrist. Metal finish is blued. Total number produced is approximately 200-300 rifles.

Exc.	V.G.	Good	Fair	Poor
1800	1500	1000	500	125

Type 100 Paratroop Rifle
Chambered for 7.7mm Japanese cartridge. Barrel length is 25-1/4" long. Blued cleaning rod 21-5/16" long. Rear sight is adjustable from 300 to 1500 meters. Two-piece buttstock with full handguard can be disassembled with an interrupted-thread connector. Bolt handle is detachable. Metal finish is blued. Total number produced is estimated at 500 rifles.

Courtesy Rock Island Auction Company

Exc.	V.G.	Good	Fair	Poor
4500	4000	3000	—	—

Type 2 Paratroop Rifle
Similar to the model above but with a different style of take-down. This model uses a wedge and bail wire connector. This rifle production began in late 1943.

Exc.	V.G.	Good	Fair	Poor
1500	1250	750	400	100

Type 99 "Sniper's Rifle"
The standard Type 99 with a 25.5" barrel and either a 2-1/2 power or 4-power telescope.

Exc.	V.G.	Good	Fair	Poor
2000	1700	1200	500	200

NOTE: The 4x scope is more rare than the 2-1/2 power scope. For 4x scope add $350.

A Japanese Type 2 Paratroop rifle sold at auction for $1,995. Condition is 95% original blue with mint bore. Mum intact. Amoskeag Auction Company, January 2003

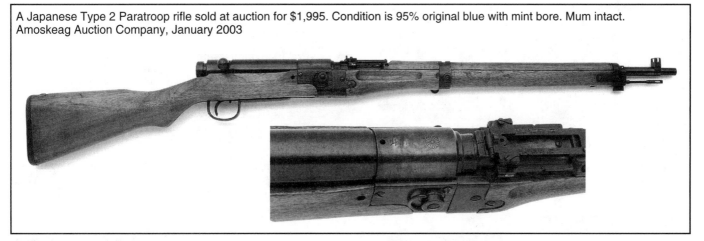

Type 5 Semiautomatic Rifle

A 7.7mm semiautomatic rifle with a 10-round box magazine patterned after the U.S. M1. Made at the Kure Naval Arsenal in 1945. It is believed that approximately 20 were made. Prospective purchasers should secure a qualified appraisal prior to acquisition.

Courtesy Richard M. Kumor Sr.

Exc.	V.G.	Good	Fair	Poor
22000	19000	14000	—	—

MAUSER

G 71 Rifle

Exc.	V.G.	Good	Fair	Poor
400	325	250	200	150

MACHINE GUNS

The Japanese used the Hotchkiss gun during the Russo-Japanese War and later adopted the Model 1914 Hotchkiss. Both of these guns were chambered for the 6.5mm cartridge.

Japanese Type 1

Introduced in 1941 as an improvement over the Type 92. Barrel length is 23" with cooling fins the same diameter through its length. The muzzle is fitted with a flash hider. Fed by a 30-round metal strip and chambered for the 7.7mm cartridge. Rate of fire is approximately 550 rounds per minute. Weight is about 77 lbs. with tripod.

Pre-1968

Exc.	V.G.	Fair
8500	7500	7000

Pre-1986 conversions

Exc.	V.G.	Fair
N/A	N/A	N/A

Pre-1986 dealer samples

Exc.	V.G.	Fair
N/A	N/A	N/A

Type 99 with 4x external scope • Courtesy private collection, Paul Goodwin photo

Type 99 with 2-1/2 power scope • Courtesy private collection, Paul Goodwin photo

Japanese Type 3

Medium air-cooled gun chambered for 6.5x51SR Arisaka cartridge and introduced in 1914. The Hotchkiss Model 1897 influenced the design of this gun. Cooling fins on the barrel. Spade grips and tripod mount with sockets for carrying poles. Weight was about 63 lbs. Barrel length was 29.5". Fed from a metal 30-round strip. Rate of fire was about 400 rounds per minute. Introduced in 1914.

Pre-1968
Exc.	V.G.	Fair
15000	14000	13000

Pre-1986 conversions
Exc.	V.G.	Fair
N/A	N/A	N/A

Pre-1986 dealer samples
Exc.	V.G.	Fair
N/A	N/A	N/A

Japanese Type 11

First produced in 1922, this is a light air-cooled machine gun chambered for the 6.5x51SR Arisaka cartridge. The gun utilizes a 30-round hopper feed system. The 19" barrel is finned. Weight is about 22.5 lbs. Rate of fire is 500 rounds per minute. Fitted with a bipod.

A Japanese machine gun crew in full marching order. The distinctive bend in the weapon's stock indicates it is a 6.5mm Type 11. The ammunition bearer on the right is probably armed with a 6.5mm Type 38 bolt action rifle • Captured Japanese Records/National Archives/Robert Bruce Military Photo Features

Pre-1968
Exc.	V.G.	Fair
6000	5000	4500

Pre-1986 conversions
Exc.	V.G.	Fair
N/A	N/A	N/A

Pre-1986 dealer samples
Exc.	V.G.	Fair
N/A	N/A	N/A

Japanese Type 89

This gun was produced in 1929 and is a copy of the British Vickers aircraft gun but chambered for the 7.7x56R (.303 British) cartridge. Weight is about 27 lbs.

Japanese Type 89 Vickers Aircraft • Courtesy Blake Stevens

Pre-1968
Exc.	V.G.	Fair
11000	10000	9500

Pre-1986 conversions
Exc.	V.G.	Fair
N/A	N/A	N/A

Pre-1986 dealer samples
Exc.	V.G.	Fair
N/A	N/A	N/A

Japanese Type 92

This is an improved version of the Type 3 gun introduced in 1932. Chambered for the 7.7x58SR cartridge. It was fitted with dropped grips behind and below the receiver instead of spade grips. Barrel length is 28". Fed by a metal 30-round strip. Rate of fire was about 450 rounds per minute. Weight is about 100 lbs. with tripod. Gun alone weighs approximately 60 lbs. The mount was designed so that two men could carry it by means of poles or pipes fitted into the legs of the mount. This was the most widely used Japanese machine gun of World War II.

NOTE: The Type 92 designation was also applied to the Japanese copy of the Lewis gun. See *Great Britain, Machine Gun, Lewis 0.303in, Mark 1.*

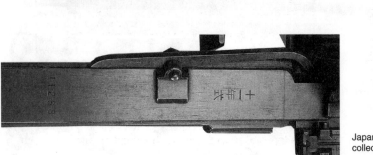

Japanese Type 11 • Courtesy private NFA collection, Paul Goodwin photo

Type 92 on the only known privately held AA mount • Courtesy Robert E. Naess

Pre-1968

Exc.	V.G.	Fair
15000	14000	13000

Pre-1986 conversions

Exc.	V.G.	Fair
11000	10000	9000

Pre-1986 dealer samples

Exc.	V.G.	Fair
N/A	N/A	N/A

Type 92 • Private NFA collection, Gary Gelson photo

JPN 92 MG

The "Woodpecker" of World War Two Island fighting fame, it is so called for the distinctive sound it makes when fired. Heard from a distance, the unique staccato can echo in a jungle as if there was indeed a hard object being hammered onto something. This brass tray-fed Hotchkiss machine gun variant has some very complex and interesting attributes, as well as an Achilles' heel—the rounds must be lubricated from an oiler in the top cover, with brushes inside to deliver the lubrication as cartridges enter the feed slot, driven from their metallic tray.

The tripod is an excellent design, with three attaching points that allow for special carrying handles—making four positions for four soldiers to carry the weapon to its position. The smooth elevation and traversing mechanisms are well designed and a leather "Boot" covers the bottom of the elevation rod to keep it from the dirt.

Ammunition for the Type 92 machine gun is scarce, and it is usually found on brass trays in wooden crates. Setting up the gun is fairly quick once you know the tricks of the tripod, and the oiler is taken care of in the top cover. The Type 3 machine gun, a much rarer gun, has fixed spade grips. The Type 92 has a button on each side that when depressed, allows the grips to swing out and down, making a wide angled grip for the operator. The thumbs are used for firing. Like most air cooled Hotchkiss guns, this is a smooth shooting firearm due to the mass of the weapon and its reciprocating parts.

Don Shea

A Japanese 7.7mm Type 92 heavy machine gun on tripod mount and fitted with a telescopic sight. This efficient and hard-hitting air-cooled gun was well respected by allied troops who faced it in WWII • Captured Japanese Records/National Archives/Robert Bruce Military Photo Features

Japanese Type 92 Lewis

This is a licensed copy of the British Lewis gun. Caliber is .303. Built in both ground and aircraft configurations. There are some minor technical differences between the two. Spade grips. The Japanese tripod for this gun is unique to the gun.

NOTE: Prices listed below are for the gun _and_ original Japanese tripod. Deduct $2,500 for no tripod or incorrect tripod.

Pre-1968

Exc.	V.G.	Fair
10000	9500	9000

Pre-1986 conversions

Exc.	V.G.	Fair
N/A	N/A	N/A

Pre-1986 dealer samples

Exc.	V.G.	Fair
N/A	N/A	N/A

Japanese Type 96

Introduced in 1936, this light, air-cooled machine gun is chambered for the 6.5mm cartridge. It was considered an improvement over the Model 11. This model has a top-mounted box magazine with a 30-round capacity. The cartridges are oiled when loaded into the magazine by an oiler built into the magazine loader. Barrel length is a finned 22" quick-change affair with carrying handle. The wood buttstock has a pistol grip. Rate of fire is about 550 rounds per minute. Weight is approximately 20 lbs. These guns are sometimes seen with a 2.5 power scope fitted on the receiver.

Pre-1968

Exc.	V.G.	Fair
6000	5000	4500

Pre-1986 conversions

Exc.	V.G.	Fair
4000	3000	2500

Pre-1986 dealer samples

Exc.	V.G.	Fair
N/A	N/A	N/A

Japanese Type 97

This model was designed in 1937 to be fired from a tank or aircraft. It was to replace the Type 92 gun and is chambered for the 7.7mm cartridge. Its barrel length is 28" and the barrel is finned for cooling. Design is similar to the Czech VZ26. This was the first Japanese machine gun that did not require oiled ammunition. Weight is about 24 lbs. Rate of fire is approximately 500 rounds per minute. Fed by a 30-round box magazine.

Pre-1968

Exc.	V.G.	Fair
7000	6000	5500

Pre-1986 conversions

Exc.	V.G.	Fair
N/A	N/A	N/A

Pre-1986 dealer samples

Exc.	V.G.	Fair
N/A	N/A	N/A

Japanese Type 98

This is a copy of the German MG 15-ground gun. First used in 1938. Fed by a 75-round saddle drum with a rate of fire of 900 rounds per minute.

Pre-1968

Exc.	V.G.	Fair
8500	7500	7000

Pre-1986 conversions

Exc.	V.G.	Fair
N/A	N/A	N/A

Pre-1986 dealer samples

Exc.	V.G.	Fair
N/A	N/A	N/A

Japanese Type 99

Chambered for the 7.7x58mm Arisaka cartridge, this machine was first produced for the Japanese army in 1939, and is an improved version of the Type 96. It is fitted with a 21.3" quick change barrel and a 30-round top feed magazine. Its rate of fire is 850 rounds per minute. It weighs about 23 lbs. The gun is marked on the right front side of the receiver with date of manufacture and marker's symbols. The gun has a bipod under the barrel and a monopod under the toe of the buttstock. Production ceased with the end of WWII.

Pre-1968

Exc.	V.G.	Fair
8000	7000	6500

Japanese Model 96 with plaque that reads, "Presented to U.S.M.A. by two former superintendents: General Douglas MacArthur and Lt. Gen. Robert L. Eichelberger captured at Buna, New Guinea, Dec. 27, 1942" • Courtesy West Point Museum, Paul Goodwin photo

Japanese Type 97 Tank • Courtesy private NFA collection, Paul Goodwin photo

Pre-1986 conversions

Exc.	V.G.	Fair
5000	4000	3000

Pre-1986 dealer samples

Exc.	V.G.	Fair
N/A	N/A	N/A

Japanese Machine Gun Trainer

These guns were built in small machine shops all over Japan in the 1930s and 1940s so that young school-age males could be taught the basic techniques and operations of machine guns. Blowback operation. This gun does in fact fire a reduced load of either 6.5mm or 7.7mm cartridges, as well as blanks and is registered as a machine gun under the NFA. These guns, as a group, are different enough so that no two will be exactly the same. **CAUTION: DO NOT FIRE THIS GUN, IT IS UNSAFE.**

Pre-1968

Exc.	V.G.	Fair
2000	1500	1000

Pre-1986 conversions

Exc.	V.G.	Fair
N/A	N/A	N/A

Pre-1986 dealer samples

Exc.	V.G.	Fair
N/A	N/A	N/A

Type 99 • Courtesy private NFA collection, Paul Goodwin photo

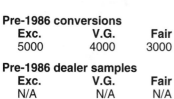

Japanese Machine Gun Trainer • Paul Goodwin photo

MEXICO

Mexican Military Conflicts, 1870-1945

The first three quarters of the 19th century were periods of almost constant strife and civil war for Mexico. Beginning in 1876 Mexico was ruled by Porfirio Diaz. The country was relatively stable and at peace for the 35 years of his rule. Beginning in the early 20th century, a new generation of revolutionaries demanded power for the people. Such men as Emiliano Zapata and Pancho Villa threatened the stability of the government. It was Francisco Madero who overthrew Diaz in 1911. A succession of reformist governments followed with the eventual formation of the PRI party in 1929 and a stable political climate through the Second World War and beyond.

HANDGUNS

NOTE: Other than the Obregon, the Mexican military has relied on foreign purchases of its military handguns. The principal sidearm is the Colt Model 1911 in .45 ACP, purchased from the U.S. government. Mexico has also purchased pistols from Heckler & Koch, the P7M13, and numerous Smith & Wesson revolvers and pistols for its police forces.

OBREGON

Pistola Automatica Sistema Obregon

This is a .45 caliber semiautomatic pistol with a 5" barrel. Similar to the Colt M1911A1 but with a combination side and safety latch on the left side of the frame. The breech is locked by rotating the barrel, instead of the Browning swinging link. This unusual locking system results in a tubular front end appearance to the pistol. Originally designed for the Mexican military, it was not adopted as such and only about 1,000 pistols were produced and sold commercially, mostly to Mexican military officers. The pistol is 8.5" overall and weighs about 40 ozs. The magazine holds seven cartridges. This is a rare pistol, therefore an independent appraisal is suggested prior to sale.

Exc.	V.G.	Good	Fair	Poor
4500	2500	1250	750	400

Colt Model 1911A1

This is the standard service pistol of the Mexican military in .45 ACP.

SUBMACHINE GUNS

NOTE: The Mexican military availed itself of the Thompson submachine gun in various models, from the Model 1921 to the Model M1A1. The Mexican government has also purchased directly from the U.S. government a number of M3A1 .45 ACP submachine guns. From Germany the Mexican government purchased the HK MP5 and the HK 53. The MP5 is currently made in Mexico under license from HK.

Mendoza (HM-3)

Developed by Rafael Mendoza in the 1950s, this submachine gun is produced by Productos Mendoza S.A. in Mexico City. This is a relatively small select-fire gun chambered for the .45 ACP, .38 Super, or 9mm cartridges. Barrel length is 10", although some examples are found with 16" barrels in full automatic fire only. The box magazine capacity is 20 rounds. Rate of fire is about 550 rounds per minute. Weight is about 5 lbs. Stock is tubular steel. An unknown number of these guns are used by the Mexican army.

RIFLES

NOTE: Mexico used a number of different models of the Mauser bolt action rifle. Since the end of World War II, the Mexican military has purchased a number of foreign rifles for military use. These consist of U.S. M1 and M2 carbines, Colt M16A1 rifles in the 1970s, FN-FAL rifles, some of which were assembled in Mexico beginning in 1968 with FN supplied parts. In 1979 Mexico began to produce, under license from HK, the G3 rifle (G3A3 and G3A4).

PEABODY

Spanish Rifle (1869)

Identical to the Spanish rifle. Chambered for the .43 Spanish centerfire cartridge and fitted with a 33" barrel. Full stock with two barrel bands. Blued barrel and case hardened furniture. About 8,500 rifles were produced for the Mexican government.

Exc.	V.G.	Good	Fair	Poor
—	1500	1000	500	200

WHITNEY

Model 1873 Rifle

This is a rolling block design similar to the Remington. It does not use the hammer to lock the block. Fitted with a 35" barrel and full stock with three barrel bands. Chambered for the 11.15x58T Spanish Remington cartridge. Weight is about 9.5 lbs. On the right side of the receiver is the Mexican crest. Upper tang is marked with "Whitney Arms."

Exc.	V.G.	Good	Fair	Poor
—	1500	900	500	200

Model 1873 Carbine

Similar to the rifle but with 20.5" barrel and two-piece stock. Fitted with cavalry bar sling and ring on stock. Weight is about 7.25 lbs.

Exc.	V.G.	Good	Fair	Poor
—	1500	900	500	200

REMINGTON ROLLING BLOCK

Model 1897 Rifle

Chambered for the 7x57mm Spanish Mauser cartridge. Full stocked with two barrel bands. Barrel length is 30". Weight is about 8.5 lbs. Marked Remington on upper tang. Rear sight is ladder-type marked to 2,300 yards.

Exc.	V.G.	Good	Fair	Poor
—	750	500	300	100

MAUSER

M1895 Rifle

This was the standard rifle for the Mexican army under the Diaz regime. It is similar to the Spanish Model 1893. Fitted with an almost full stock with straight grip with no finger grooves. Barrel length is 29" and chambered for the 7x57mm cartridge. Rear leaf sight graduated to 2000 meters. Bayonet lug. Magazine capacity is 5 rounds. Weight is about 8.5 lbs. Produced by both DWM and the Spanish firm Oviedo.

Exc.	V.G.	Good	Fair	Poor
150	110	90	60	25

M1895 Carbine

Similar to the Model 1895 rifle except with 17.25" barrel, bent bolt handle, and side-mounted sling. No bayonet fittings. Weight is about 7.5 lbs. Some but not all are marked with Mexican crest on receiver ring.

Exc.	V.G.	Good	Fair	Poor
150	100	80	50	25

M1902 Rifle

This model has an improved Model 98 action. Nearly full-length stock with half-length upper handguard. This model was built by DWM and Steyr. Barrel length is 29". Caliber is 7x57mm. Straight bolt handle. Rear sight graduated to 2000 meters. Mexican crest on receiver ring. Weight is about 8.75 lbs.

Exc.	V.G.	Good	Fair	Poor
300	225	170	100	60

M1907 Steyr Rifle

This rifle was fitted with an almost full-length stock with pistol grip. Upper barrel band has a stacking hook. Bayonet lug accepts Model 98 bayonet. Barrel length is 29". Caliber is 7x57mm. Straight bolt. Weight is about 8.75 lbs. Marked, "STEYR.MODEL 1907/DATE" on receiver ring.

Exc.	V.G.	Good	Fair	Poor
300	225	190	140	90

M1910 Rifle

This was the first Mauser produced by Mexico at the *Fabrica Nacional de Cartuchos* and the *Fabrica Nacional de Armas* in Mexico City. Similar to the Model 1902 rifle. Straight grip stock. Bayonet stud for Model 1895 bayonet. Barrel length is 29" and caliber is 7x57mm. Marked on top of receiver ring.

Exc.	V.G.	Good	Fair	Poor
125	100	80	60	20

M1910 Carbine

Very similar to the Model 1895 carbine with the addition of the Model 98 action and barley corn front sights. Mexican crest on receiver ring. Weight is about 8 lbs. Barrel length is 17.5" and caliber is 7x57mm.

Exc.	V.G.	Good	Fair	Poor
125	100	80	70	25

M1912 Steyr Rifle

Mexico bought these rifles directly from Steyr. This model is fitted with a 29" barrel and large receiver ring with straight bolt. Nearly full-length stock with pistol grip. Chambered for the 7x57mm cartridge. Receiver ring marked "MODEL 1912" over "STEYR" over the date. Weight is about 8.75 lbs.

Exc.	V.G.	Good	Fair	Poor
300	230	175	100	75

M1912 Steyr Short Rifle

This short rifle is the same as the Model 1912 rifle except for turned down bolt handle and barrel length.

Exc.	V.G.	Good	Fair	Poor
300	230	175	100	75

FN M24 Short Rifle

Approximately 25,000 of these rifles were bought from FN by Mexico in 1926 and 1927. This then is the standard FN Model 1924 version with pistol grip stock without finger grooves. Barrel length is 23.5" and caliber is 7x57mm. Weight is about 8.5 lbs.

Exc.	V.G.	Good	Fair	Poor
150	120	90	70	40

FN M24 Carbine

Same as above but with 16" barrel and no bayonet fittings. Weight is about 7.5 lbs.

Exc.	V.G.	Good	Fair	Poor
150	130	100	80	50

VZ12/33 Carbine

This is the Czech export Model 12/33 carbine. Pistol grip stock. Barrel length is 22" and caliber is 7x57mm. Weight is about 8.5 lbs. Marked with Mexican crest on receiver ring.

Exc.	V.G.	Good	Fair	Poor
225	195	170	125	90

ARISAKA

Model 1905

Identical to the Japanese service rifle of the same model but chambered for the 7x57mm cartridge. The rear sight has been modified for this cartridge. The nose cap has been modified to accept the standard Mexican bayonet. The Mexican eagle and "REPUBLICA MEXICANA" are marked on the barrel near the breech. About 40,000 rifles were ordered but only 5,000 delivered in 1910. Manufactured in Japan in Koishikawa.

Exc.	V.G.	Good	Fair	Poor
750	600	450	300	200

NOTE: A few carbines were also built. These will bring a premium of 60%.

MONDRAGON

Model 1908 & Model 1915

Firearms designed by Manuel Mondragon were produced on an experimental basis first at St. Chamond Arsenal in France and later at SIG in Neuhausen, Switzerland. The latter company was responsible for the manufacture of the two known production models: the Model 1908 and 1915.

The Model 1908 Mondragon semiautomatic rifle holds the distinction of being the first self-loading rifle to be issued to any armed forces. Only about 400 of these rifles were delivered to the Mexican army in 1911 when the revolution broke out. The rifle was chambered for the 7x57mm Mauser cartridge and featured a 24.5" barrel. It has an 8-round box magazine. Weight is about 9.5 lbs. SIG had several thousand of these rifles left after the Mexicans were unable to take delivery. When WWI got under way the Swiss firm sold the remaining stocks to Germany. These rifles were called the Model 1915. Were all identical to the Model 1908 except for the addition of a 30-round drum magazine.

Courtesy Rock Island Auction Company

Exc.	V.G.	Good	Fair	Poor
6000	4000	2000	1000	750

FABRICA NACIONAL de ARMAS
Mexico, City

Model 1936

This bolt action rifle was chambered for the 7mm cartridge and uses a short-type Mauser action. The rifle is of Mexican design and resembles the Springfield Model 1903A1 in appearance. Barrel length is 22" with a 5-round non-detachable magazine. Tangent rear sight with "V" notch. Weight is about 8.25 lbs.

Exc.	V.G.	Good	Fair	Poor
300	270	250	160	110

Model 1954

This Mexican-produced and designed rifle also uses a Mauser action, but resembles a Springfield Model 1903A3 in appearance. The stock is laminated plywood. Barrel length is 24" and chambered for the .30-06 cartridge. Weight is approximately 9 lbs. Some of these rifles may still be in service.

Exc.	V.G.	Good	Fair	Poor
350	300	250	175	110

MACHINE GUNS

NOTE: The Mexican military has used a variety of foreign-built machine guns. The Madsen Model 1934, the Model 1896 Hotchkiss 7mm machine gun, and the Browning Model 1919, as well as the 5.56mm Ameli, the FN MAG, and the HK 21A1, and the Browning .50 M2HB. Mexico also produced its own excellent gun, the Mendoza C-1934 light machine gun and the RM2 gas operated machine gun issued in 1960.

Model 1936 • Courtesy private collection, Paul Goodwin photo

NETHERLANDS

Dutch Military Conflicts, 1870-Present

The period from 1870 to the beginning of War World I was one of economic prosperity and stablity. The Netherlands suffered economic loss during World War I because of the Allied blockade. During World War II the country suffered heavy damage and loss of life during the German occupation. After the war, the Netherlands lost many of its colonies, beginning with a war in Indonesia, which gained its independence in 1949. The independence of New Guinea followed in 1962, and Suriname in 1975. In 2001 the Dutch military had a total of 50,430 personnel. Reserves were 32,000. The army had 23,000 total personnel.

HANDGUNS

During World War II, the Dutch also used the Enfield revolver chambered for the .38 Special cartridge, as well as the Webley Model I in .38 Special, the Webley Model VI chambered for the .455 cartridge.

Since the end of World War II, the Dutch have used the Walther P5, the HK P9S, the FN High Power (both Belgian and Canadian built), the Smith & Wesson Model 19, the Colt Python (4"), the Colt Model 1911A1, the FN Model 1910, and the FN Model 1910/22.

Model 1873 (Old Model)

This solid-frame double action revolver is based on the Chamelot Delvigne design. Chambered for the 9.4mm cartridge. Fitted with a 6.3" octagonal barrel. Gate loaded non-fluted cylinder holds 6 rounds. With no ejector rod, a separate rod was required. Smooth wooden grips with lanyard ring. Was issued in 1873 and remained in service through 1945. Built by a number of different companies such as J.F.J. Bar, DeBeaumont, P. Stevens, Hembrug, etc. Military marked. Weight is about 44 oz.

Exc.	V.G.	Good	Fair	Poor
750	600	500	400	250

NOTE: An Officer's Model was also used but was not military issue and not military marked. Major differences are fluted cylinder, checkered wooden grips, and 5" barrel.

Model 1873 (New Model)

Similar to the Old Model but with 6.3" round barrel. First issued in 1909. Built by Hembrug. Military marked.

Exc.	V.G.	Good	Fair	Poor
600	500	400	300	150

Model 1873/1919

This model is based on the Model 1873 but modified to fire tear gas projectiles. Chambered for the 9.4mm cartridge but with a 12mm caliber barrel. Barrel length was only 1.9" in length with no front sight. Smooth wooden grips with lanyard ring. In service from 1919 to 1945. Built by Hembrug and military marked.

Exc.	V.G.	Good	Fair	Poor
N/A	—	—	—	—

Model 94 (Colonial Model)

This double action revolver was first issued to the Dutch Colonial Army in 1894 and remained in service until 1945. Chambered for the 9.4mm cartridge and fitted with a 4.3" barrel. Fluted cylinder holds 6 rounds. Checkered wooden grips with lanyard ring. Built by Hembrug. Military marked.

Exc.	V.G.	Good	Fair	Poor
500	400	300	200	100

SUBMACHINE GUNS

The Dutch military uses the UZI submachine gun (IMI), and several variants of the HK MP5. During World War II, the Dutch purchased a number of American made UD submachine guns in 9mm. There were no submachine guns of Dutch design issued to its military.

RIFLES

The Dutch military has used a number of different foreign-made military rifles including: FN FAL, HK PSG 1, HK 33SG1, and the U.S. M1 rifle. During WWII the Dutch used the Johnson semiautomatic rifle in its Far East colonies.

BEAUMONT/VITALI

Model 1871 Rifle

This single shot black powder rifle, chambered for the 11.3x51R cartridge, featured a heavy internally recessed two-piece bolt handle with a V-spring to activate the striker. The bolt head included the extractor. There was no ejector. Barrel length was 32.7". One-piece stock with two barrel bands. Fitted for a socket bayonet. Original rifles were issued in the white. Rear sight graduated to 1,100 meters. Weight is about 9.75 lbs.

Beaumont-Vitali Model 1871/88 • Private collection, Paul Goodwin photo

Courtesy Milwaukee Public Museum, Milwaukee, Wisconsin

Exc.	V.G.	Good	Fair	Poor
350	250	150	100	75

Model 1871 Carbine
Same as above but with 22" barrel. Also fitted for a socket bayonet.

Exc.	V.G.	Good	Fair	Poor
450	350	250	125	100

Model 1871/88
This model was a conversion to the Vitali magazine. It featured a bolt-mounted ejector and a magazine cut-off on the left side of the receiver. Magazine capacity is 4 rounds. All other specifications are the same as the Model 1871. Rear sight is graduated to 1,300 meters. Weight is approximately 10 lbs. This rifle was used by the Dutch army and remained in secondary service through World War II.

Exc.	V.G.	Good	Fair	Poor
300	200	150	100	75

Mannlicher

NOTE: Some of these rifles have a wooden block covering the left side of the magazine. These were added after 1914 to protect the magazines from damage. Rifles without this modification are refered to as the "Old Model," while rifles with the change are called "New Models." Prices listed below are for the "Old Models."

Model 1895 Rifle
This 6.5x53R rifle was produced in two versions. One for the regular army and the other for the Dutch East Indies. The colonial model has two gas escape holes in the receiver ring. The rifle is full-stocked with a half-length handguard. It is fitted with a bayonet bar. Barrel length is 31". Magazine capacity is 5 rounds and is clip loaded. After World War II, many of these rifles were rebored and converted to .303 British. Built by both Steyr and Hembrug. Weight is about 9.5 lbs.

Exc.	V.G.	Good	Fair	Poor
250	200	125	75	50

Model 1895 No. 1 Cavalry Carbine
This model featured a half stock with no handguard and sling bars on the left side. Barrel length is 17.7". Weight is about 6.75 lbs. Built by both Steyr and Hembrug.

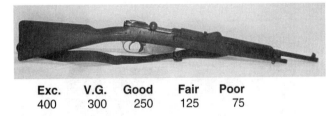

Exc.	V.G.	Good	Fair	Poor
400	300	250	125	75

Model 1985 No. 2 Gendarmerie Carbine
This model is a full-stocked version with bayonet fittings. Weight is about 7 lbs.

Exc.	V.G.	Good	Fair	Poor
400	300	250	125	75

Model 1895 No. 3 Engineer & Artillery Carbine
Similar to the No. 2 carbine but with long handguard. Weight is almost 7 lbs.

Exc.	V.G.	Good	Fair	Poor
400	300	250	125	75

Model 1895 No. 4 Bicycle Troops' Carbine
Similar to the No. 3 carbine but with handguard the same length as the stock.

Exc.	V.G.	Good	Fair	Poor
450	350	300	150	100

Model 1917
Sometimes called the "machine gunner's rifle" because ammunition was the same as the Dutch Lewis and Schwarzlose machine guns. Chambered for the 8x57 cartridge and fitted with a 31.3" barrel with quadrant sight to 2,000 meters. Similar action to the Model 1895. Weight is about 9.25 lbs. Built by Hembrug.

Exc.	V.G.	Good	Fair	Poor
300	250	200	150	100

Model 1895 No. 5 Carbine A5
This model was built by Hembrug beginning in 1930 and is a cut-down version of the Model 1895 rifle. It was issued to the Dutch Air Force. Barrel length is 17.9". Weight is about 7.75 lbs.

Exc.	V.G.	Good	Fair	Poor
550	450	300	200	100

MAUSER (FN)

M1948 Carbine
This rifle was built by FN for the Dutch police. Chambered for the 7.9x57mm cartridge and fitted with a 17.3" barrel with bayonet fittings. Full stock with pistol grip and upper handguard. Magazine capacity is 5 rounds. Marked with letter "J" or "W" with crown on receiver ring. Rear sight is V notch graduated from 200 to 1400 meters. Weight is about 7.5 lbs.

Exc.	V.G.	Good	Fair	Poor
300	240	200	125	90

MACHINE GUNS

In 1908 the Dutch adopted the Schwarzlose machine gun in 7.92Rmm, various Madsen models chambered for the 6.5mm cartridge, the Lewis gun in 6.5mm, and the Vickers Model 1918 in 7.92mm. The Dutch military has also used the FN MAG, the Bren Mark 2 in .303, and the .50 M2 HB. During World War II the Dutch also used the Johnson LMG in .30-06 as well as the Browning Model 1919 variants.

NORWAY

Norwegian Military Conflicts, 1870-Present

In 1870 Norway was ruled by Sweden. An upsurge in Norwegian nationalism forced Sweden to dissolve its ties and grant independence as a constitutional monarchy to Norway in 1905. Norway remained neutral during World War I. However, the country was occupied by Germany from 1940 to 1945 during World War II. Since the end of the war, Norway has remained independent economically and socially from the rest of Europe, having rejected membership in the European Union on two occasions.

HANDGUNS

NAGANT

Model 1883 Revolver

Adopted in 1883, this Nagant 6-round revolver has a solid frame with loading gate and mechanical rod ejection. Double action. Chambered for the 9x23R Belgian Nagant cartridge. Barrel is part round and part hexagon and is 5.5" long. Fluted cylinder and checkered wood grips with lanyard loop. Weight is about 32 oz. This model stayed in service until 1940. It was issued to both officers and NCOs.

Exc.	V.G.	Good	Fair	Poor
1250	750	400	275	150

Model 1887/93 Revolver

Similar in appearance to the Model 1883 but chambered for the 7.5x22R Norwegian Nagant cartridge. Barrel length is 4.5". Weight is about 28 oz. In service until 1940.

Exc.	V.G.	Good	Fair	Poor
1250	750	400	275	150

Model 1912/14

All of the Model 1912/14 pistols were produced by the Norwegian arsenal at Kongsberg Vapenfabrikk. The official designation of the Norwegian Colt pistol was "COLT AUTOMATISK PISTOL, MODEL 1912, CAL. 11.43 M/M." In 1917 the designation changed to "11.25 M/M AUTOMATISK PISTOL MODEL 1914." The new marking began with serial number 96 (see Table 1). For a more detailed explanation of the differences in the Norwegian pistols see Clawson's, *Colt .45 Government Models, 1912 through 1970.*

TABLE 1

DATE	SERIAL RANGE	DATE	SERIAL RANGE
1917	1-95	1929	20101-21400
1918	96-600	1932	21441-21940
1919	601-1150	1933	21941-22040
1920	1151-1650	1934	22041-22141
1921	1651-2200	1936	22142-22211
1922	2201-2950	1939	22212-22311
1923	2951-4610	1940	22312-22361
1924	4611-6700	1941	22362-26460
1925	6701-8940	1942	26461-29614
1926	8941-11820	1945	29615-30535
1927	11821-15900	1947	32336-32854
1928	15901-20100		

Kongsberg Vapenfabrikk Model M/1914 (Norwegian) copy SN 1-96

(Rarely seen) (Condition 99%-100% add 20-30%)

Exc.	V.G.	Good	Fair	Poor
3500	2200	1150	850	600

Norwegian slide legend left side • Courtesy Karl Karash

Kongsberg Vapenfabrikk Model M/1914 (Norwegian) copy SN 97-29,614, and 30,536-32,854

(Numbers must match)

Exc.	V.G.	Good	Fair	Poor
1400	900	750	600	400

Norwegian slide markings right side • Courtesy Karl Karash

Kongsberg Vapenfabrikk Model M/1914 (Norwegian) copy SN 29,615 to 30,535

Waffenamt marked on slide and barrel. Numbers must match. Waffenamt marked M/1914s outside this range are probably FAKES. Condition 99%-100% add 20-30%.

Exc.	V.G.	Good	Fair	Poor
3000	1900	1150	850	600

Kongsberg Vapenfabrikk Model M/1914 (Norwegian) copy SN 97-29614 and 30536-32854

(Numbers must match)

Notice the extended slide stop on the left side • Courtesy Karl Karash

Exc.	V.G.	Good	Fair	Poor
1400	900	750	600	400

Norwegian slide legend left side with extended slide stop • Courtesy Karl Karash

Kongsberg Vapenfabrikk Model M/1914 (Norwegian) copy SN 29615 to 30535

Waffenamt marked on slide and barrel. Numbers must match. Waffenamt marked M/1914s outside this range are probably FAKES. Condition 99%-100% add 20-30%. A little over 900 were produced.

Exc.	V.G.	Good	Fair	Poor
3000	1900	1150	850	600

SUBMACHINE GUNS

Norway used the German MP40, designated the M40, chambered for the 9x19mm Parabellum cartridge. The Norwegian military also issued the British Sten gun, as well as the HK MP5A2 and MP5A3. The Norwegian Marines use the Suomi 37/39 submachine gun.

RIFLES

The Norwegian military also uses the HK G3 rifle, the Mauser 98K converted to 7.62x51mm, as well as now-obsolete U.S. M1 Garands and U.S. M1 and M2 carbines.

REMINGTON ROLLING BLOCK

Model 1867 Rifle

Built in Norway by Christiana, Husqvarna, or Kongsberg. Fitted with a 37.3" barrel with three barrel bands and full length stock. Brass buttplate. Chambered for the 12.17x44R Norwegian Remington rimfire cartridge. Weight is about 10 lbs.

Exc.	V.G.	Good	Fair	Poor
—	650	500	300	150

Model 1888 Carbine

This model was essentially a Model 1867 fitted with a 24" barrel chambered for the 8x58R Danish Krag cartridge. Built at Kongsberg. Weight is about 8.5 lbs.

Exc.	V.G.	Good	Fair	Poor
—	800	650	425	225

JARMANN
Kongsberg

Model 1880-1882 Experimental

In 1880-1882 about 500 Jarmans were produced in Sweden for use in trials in Norway. This experimiental model used a curved 5-round box magazine mounted from the top right side of the receiver forward of the bolt handle. Chambered for the 10.15x61Rmm cartridge and fitted with a 32" barrel. Marked with Carl Gustaf markings.

Exc.	V.G.	Good	Fair	Poor

Too Rare To Price

Model 1884 Rifle

Bolt action rifle with magazine tube under barrel with 8-round capacity. Chambered for the 10.15x61R Jarmann cartridge. Full stocked with two barrel bands. Fitted with a 32.5" barrel. Weight is about 10 lbs. These rifles made at Kongsberg and marked with a "K" on the receiver ring.

Exc.	V.G.	Good	Fair	Poor

Too Rare To Price

NOTE: A carbine version was built but never adopted by Norway.

Model 1884/87

Similar to the Model 1884 but with recalibrated rear sight for smokeless powder.

Exc.	V.G.	Good	Fair	Poor

Too Rare To Price

MAUSER

K98k Reissued Short Rifle (.30-06)

The only difference between this rifle and the standard issue German model is the markings. The Norwegian word "HAER" meaning "Army" is stamped on the receiver ring. A number of other stampings that denote Norwegian military organizations may also be seen, such as: HV=Home Guard; FLY=Air Force; KNM=Navy; K.ART=Coast Artillery; NSB=Government Railway; POLITI=Police.

Exc.	V.G.	Good	Fair	Poor
300	240	190	100	70

K98k Action Military Target Rifle (Model 59)

Exc.	V.G.	Good	Fair	Poor
400	300	250	200	100

Model 84S

This rifle uses a modified Mauser 98 military action with the original markings removed. Chambered for the 7.62mm NATO cartridge and first introduced in 1984. Built by Vapensmia A/S in Norway. Fitted with a heavy barrel by the German company Heym. Has a 5-round detachable magazine. Fitted with a 6x42 Schmidt & Bender scope. Adjustable trigger. Laminated birch stock. This rifle was also sold commercially.

Exc.	V.G.	Good	Fair	Poor
1500	1150	800	500	300

KRAG JORGENSEN
See also *U.S., Rifles, Krag*

NOTE: The Norwegian Krag rifles differ from the U.S. Krags primarily in that it does not have a cartridge cutoff. The Norwegian Krags were used by the Norwegian army as its principal long arm until the Germans occupied Norway in 1940. The majority of these rifles were built at Kongsberg, although some were produced at Steyr and FN Herstal. Norwegian Krags were chambered for the 6.5x55mm Swedish Mauser cartridge.

Model 1894 Rifle

This rifle is full stocked with pistol grip and full-length handguard. Barrel length is 30". Box magazine is located in horizontal position and has a capacity of 5 rounds. Tangent rear sight. Weight is approximately 9 lbs.

Exc.	V.G.	Good	Fair	Poor
1000	750	600	400	150

Model 1923 Sniper

This model is fitted with a full stock and checkered pistol grip. Full-length handguard. Heavy barrel length is 24". Bayonet fittings on nose cap. Micrometer rear sight with aperture. Marked "M.1894" on receiver. Magazine capacity is 5 rounds. Weight is about 9 lbs. Scarce.

Exc.	V.G.	Good	Fair	Poor
3500	2250	1250	650	300

Model 1925 Sniper

Fitted with a 30" heavy barrel similar to the Model 1894 rifle but with checkered pistol grip and micrometer rear peep sight. Weight is approximately 10 lbs. Scarce.

Exc.	V.G.	Good	Fair	Poor
3500	2250	1250	650	300

Model 1930 Sniper

This model has a sporter-style half stock with checkered full pistol grip. Heavy 30" barrel. No bayonet fittings. Micrometer rear sight. Marked "M/1894/30." Weight is approximately 11.5 lbs. Scarce.

Exc.	V.G.	Good	Fair	Poor
3500	2250	1250	650	400

Model 1895 Carbine

This model is half stocked with short handguard and fitted with a 20.5" barrel. Magazine capacity is 5 rounds. Weight is about 7.5 lbs. Very similar in appearance to the U.S. Krag carbine.

Exc.	V.G.	Good	Fair	Poor
1500	850	650	400	200

Model 1897 Carbine

Similar to the Model 1895 carbine except the rear sling swivel is located near the toe of the buttstock.

Exc.	V.G.	Good	Fair	Poor
1500	850	650	400	200

Model 1904 Carbine

This model has a 20.5" barrel with full stock and upper handguard but no bayonet lug. Weight is about 8.5 lbs.

Exc.	V.G.	Good	Fair	Poor
1500	850	650	400	200

Model 1907 Carbine

Similar to the Model 1907 but with sling swivels located on rear barrel band and buttstock.

Exc.	V.G.	Good	Fair	Poor
1500	850	650	400	200

Model 1912 Carbine

Full stocked with 24" barrel and 5-round magazine. Fitted with a bayonet lug on nose cap. Weight is about 8.5 lbs.

Exc.	V.G.	Good	Fair	Poor
1200	650	450	300	150

MACHINE GUNS

Norway used the Hotchkiss machine gun, chambered for the 6.5mm cartridge, beginning in 1911, as well as the Model 1914 and Model 1918 Madsen guns. The Browning Model 1917 water-cooled gun was used by the Norwegians and designated the Model 29. After World War II the Norwegian military used the Browning Model 1919A4, as well as the MG 34 and MG 42. Currently Norway has adopted the MG 42/59 as its standard machine gun, designating it the LMG 3.

POLAND

Polish Military Conflicts, 1870 to the Postwar Period

From 1772 to 1918 Poland was part of Prussia, Austria, and Russia, and as such it did not exist as an independent state. Following World War I Poland received its independence. In 1920-21 a border dispute led to war with Russia. Poland won some of its claims in the Treaty of Riga. In 1926 Joseph Pillsudski, Chief of State since 1918, assumed dictatorial power. After his death in 1935 a military junta assumed power. In 1939 Nazi Germany invaded Poland, precipitating World War II. After the war a government was established under Soviet auspices. In 1947 government control gave the Communists full control of the country. In 1990 the first free elections were held in Poland with the election of Lech Walesa.

HANDGUNS

RADOM

Fabryka Broniw Radomu

This company was established after World War I and produced military arms for Poland. During WWII the Radom factory was operated by the Nazis. Production was not recommenced after the war.

Ng 30

A copy of the Russian Nagant revolver chambered for the 7.62mm Russian cartridge. Approximately 20,000 were manufactured during 1930 and 1936.

Courtesy Richard M. Kumor Sr.

Exc.	V.G.	Good	Fair	Poor
2000	1500	800	200	100

VIS-35

A 9mm semiautomatic pistol with a 4.5" barrel, fixed sights, and an 8-shot magazine. On this model there is no manual safety; however, a decocking lever is installed that allows the hammer to be safely lowered on a loaded chamber. Versions made prior to WWII are engraved with a Polish eagle on the slide and "FB" and "VIS" are molded into the grips. These prewar pistols are slotted for a holster stock. German production pistols were made without the decocking lever and subsequently without the stripping catch. They also eliminated the stock slot. These pistols were stamped "P35p" and bear the Waffenamt inspector's mark "WaA77." Near the end of the war, the take-down was eliminated and the grips were re-placed with crude wooden grips. The slide, barrel, and frame are all numbered to match each other.

NOTE: Prices quoted are for 1939 dated guns. Earlier years bring a significant premium.

Polish Eagle Model-1936 through 1939

Courtesy Richard M. Kumor Sr.

Exc.	V.G.	Good	Fair	Poor
1700	1400	900	350	200

Nazi Captured Polish Eagle—Waffenamt Marked

Exc.	V.G.	Good	Fair	Poor
3500	2200	1500	450	300

Nazi Polish Eagle (Navy marked)

Courtesy Richard M. Kumor Sr.

Will command a premium price.

Nazi Production Model (Model 35(p))

Exc.	V.G.	Good	Fair	Poor
500	400	250	200	175

Nazi Production Model—"bnz" code

This is a late Nazi production with no other slide markings other than "bnz." A rare variation.

Courtesy Richard M. Kumor Sr.

Exc.	V.G.	Good	Fair	Poor
1750	1400	900	650	500

POLISH TOKAREV TT-33

The TT-33 (Tula Tokarev-33) pistol was designed in Russia by Fedor Tokarev and was originally standardized by the Soviet military in 1930 as the TT-30. The pistol was modified for simplified production and redesignated TT-33. The main difference between this and the earlier pistol was that the earlier gun had Browning-type locking lugs machined into the top of the barrel, while on the later version they completely surrounded the barrel. The TT-33 is a modification of the basic Browning system, but not a copy. Tokarev made several changes to the Browning design. The TT-33 fire control mechanism is removable as a unit, simplifying maintenance. The magazine feed lips are machined into the pistol frame to improve reliability. Finally, there is no safety on Soviet-manufactured TT-33s, nor on most other versions produced in former Communist Bloc countries. When Poland undertook production of the TT-33, their manufacturers made some improvements to the original design. First, they incorporated a safety lock next to the magazine release. While the lock blocks only the trigger, it is better than nothing. The "up" position is safe, while "down" is fire. The safety is easily swept off with the shooter's thumb. The Polish TT-33 also was made with an ergonomic thumb rest on the left side grip panel that makes the pistol very comfortable and easier to shoot accurately. In addition, the Polish TT-33 is made to a much higher standard than most TT-33s. The slide is a very close fit to the frame; there is virtually no play between the two components. Trigger pull on our example is a very crisp and consistent five pounds. The finish is an even deep satin blue. There are no machine marks on the pistol's exterior and the interior is almost as well finished as the exterior. The Polish TT-33 is a significant improvement over the original and probably represents the best example of the type ever manufactured.

Charlie Cutshaw

VIS-35 Reissue

This is an exact copy of the original VIS-35 pistol. Limited to 100 pistols with less than that number imported into the U.S. The importer, "Dalvar of USA," is stamped on the barrel.

NIB	Exc.	V.G.	Good	Fair	Poor
2300	—	—	—	—	—

Model 64

A PPK size pistol chambered for the 9mm Makarov cartridge. Rare.

NIB	Exc.	V.G.	Good	Fair	Poor
900	750	600	400	300	—

Tokarev (Pistolet TT)

Polish copy with manual safety. Well made.

Exc.	V.G.	Good	Fair	Poor
350	300	250	125	100

P-83

This pistol is chambered for the 9x18 (Makarov) cartridge. It is fitted with a 3.5" barrel and has a double action trigger with decocker. Magazine capacity is 8 rounds. Weight is about 25 oz. Black oxide finish. Developed in the early 1970s, it is similar to a Makarov pistol except it is built from stampings. Used by Polish army and security forces.

NOTE: A commercial version is chambered for the 9x17 Short (.380) cartridge.

NIB	Exc.	V.G.	Good	Fair	Poor
250	200	—	—	—	—

P-93

Similar to the P-83 differing only in cosmetics but chambered for 9mm Makarov only. The decocking lever is on the frame instead of the slide. Barrel length is 3.9". Black oxide finish.

NIB	Exc.	V.G.	Good	Fair	Poor
350	275	200	150	—	—

MAG-95

This pistol is chambered for the 9mm Parabellum cartridge and fitted with a 4.5" barrel. Magazine capacity is 15 rounds. Trigger is double action with external hammer. Weight is about 38 oz. Black oxide finish. Optional 20-round magazine. In use by Polish forces on NATO duty.

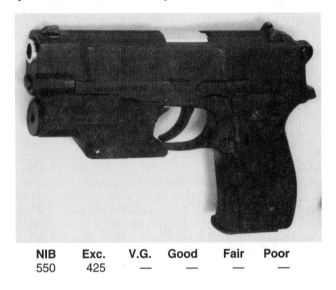

NIB	Exc.	V.G.	Good	Fair	Poor
550	425	—	—	—	—

SUBMACHINE GUNS

NOTE: Poland was supplied with Soviet made PPSh M1941 and PPS M1943 submachine guns.

M1943/52

This gun is a Polish-built modification of the Soviet PPS M1943 submachine gun in 7.63mm caliber. It is select fire and is fitted with a 9.5" barrel. Magazine capacity is a 35-round box. Rate of fire is about 600 rounds per minute. Weight is approximately 8 lbs. Wooden buttstock.

Polish Model 1943/52 • Courtesy Thomas Nelson, *World's Submachine Guns, Vol. I*

Pre-1968

Exc.	V.G.	Fair
7500	6500	6000

Pre-1986 conversions

Exc.	V.G.	Fair
N/A	N/A	N/A

Pre-1986 dealer samples

Exc.	V.G.	Fair
N/A	N/A	N/A

WZ-63

Introduced in 1964, this submachine gun is a small, almost pistol-size weapon chambered for the 9x18mm Makarov cartridge. It is fitted with a 6" barrel with folding metal butt. The folding is designed to be used as a front vertical grip, if desired.

A noticeable spoon-shaped muzzle compensator is used. Magazine is a box type with 15- or 25-round capacity. Rate of fire is about 600 rounds per minute. Weight is approximately 4 lbs.

Pre-1968

Exc.	V.G.	Fair
10000	9000	8500

Pre-1986 conversions

Exc.	V.G.	Fair
N/A	N/A	N/A

Pre-1986 dealer samples

Exc.	V.G.	Fair
N/A	N/A	N/A

RIFLES

MAUSER

NOTE: Poland began producing Mauser rifles and carbines in early 1902 at the Warsaw arsenal.

M98 Rifle

This rifle is similar to the German Gew 98 with a tangent rear sight instead of the German style. Nearly full stock with pistol grip and finger grooves on the forend. Half length upper handguard.

Exc.	V.G.	Good	Fair	Poor
325	200	125	90	60

M98AZ Rifle

This rifle is the same as the German Model 98AZ. In addition to the standard placement of sling swivels, a sling bar is fitted to the left side of the stock. Polish wood is used on the stock in place of walnut.

Polish M98AZ • Courtesy Richard M. Kumor Sr.

Exc.	V.G.	Good	Fair	Poor
400	325	250	175	100

Wz 29 Short Rifle

This rifle was built at the Radom factory. Barrel length is 23.6" and caliber is 7.92x57mm. Straight bolt handle. Almost full stock with pistol grip and grasping grooves on the fore stock. A sling bar is fitted to the left side of the stock. Tangent leaf rear sight graduated to 2000 meters. Weight is about 9 lbs.

Exc.	V.G.	Good	Fair	Poor
300	200	150	100	60

Wz 98a Rifle

Exc.	V.G.	Good	Fair	Poor
375	300	250	150	90

Wz 29 .22 Caliber Training Rifle

Exc.	V.G.	Good	Fair	Poor
2000	1500	900	—	—

Kbk 8 Wz 31 .22 Caliber Training Rifle

Exc.	V.G.	Good	Fair	Poor
2000	1500	900	—	—

Polish Wz 29 • Courtesy Richard M. Kumor Sr.

Wz 48 .22 Caliber Training Rifle
Produced after World War II as a training rifle.

Polish Wz 48 Training Rifle • Private collection, Paul Goodwin photo

Exc.	V.G.	Good	Fair	Poor
250	150	100	—	—

Model 1891 Polish Nagant
A 7.62mm caliber bolt action rifle with a 28.75" barrel, 5-shot integral magazine, ladder rear sight, and a full-length stock secured by two barrel bands. Blued with a walnut stock.

Polish Model 1891 • Courtesy Richard M. Kumor Sr.

Polish Model 1891 close-up of bayonet and fittings • Courtesy Richard M. Kumor Sr.

Exc.	V.G.	Good	Fair	Poor
150	125	100	75	50

NOTE: Add $150 to $250 for correct bayonet.

Polish Model 1891/30 Sniper Rifle
These are the Soviet rifles used by the Poles but refinished. Polish sniper rifles are identified by the serial numbered mounting rails being the same as the scope.

Exc.	V.G.	Good	Fair	Poor
1200	900	700	N/A	N/A

Model 1891/98/25 Polish Nagant
The production of these rifles started in the early 1920s at the Warsaw arsenal. Chambered for the 7.92mm cartridge but fitted with a bayonet lug and stamped with a small crowned Polish Eagle on receiver and bolt. It has a 23.5" barrel with 5-round non-detachable box magazine. Leaf rear sight. Weight is approximately 8 lbs. A very rare variation. Original, unaltered examples will command a premium price. About 77,000 of these rifles were produced.

Courtesy Richard M. Kumor Sr.

Exc.	V.G.	Good	Fair	Poor
500	450	400	—	—

Polish Model 1944 Nagant
Produced in Poland after the end of World War II until about 1962. Polish markings on the receiver, stock, and barrel. Poland's East Bloc code was "11."

Exc.	V.G.	Good	Fair	Poor
200	150	100	—	—

KbKg Model 1960 or PMK-DGN and PMKM
All of these rifles are copies of AK-47 variations. Both the PMK and PMKM are sometimes equipped with grenade launchers fitted to the muzzle.

Pre-1968

Exc.	V.G.	Fair
30000	27500	25000

Pre-1986 conversions

Exc.	V.G.	Fair
N/A	N/A	N/A

Pre-1986 dealer samples

Exc.	V.G.	Fair
N/A	N/A	N/A

MACHINE GUNS

NOTE: Poland used a variety of foreign-built machine guns prior to World War II. Some of these were the Browning Model

PMK-DGM • Courtesy West Point Museum, Paul Goodwin photo

1917s and the BAR. Both of these guns were chambered for the 7.92mm cartridge. After the war Poland used Soviet-issued weapons.

Polish BAR (Wz 28)

This Polish BAR was chambered for the 7.92x57mm cartridge with skids on its bipod instead of spikes and a bipod attached to the gas regulator instead of the muzzle. Barrel length is 24" with AA ring sight base. Approximately 12,000 Polish-built BARs were produced between 1930 and 1939. These guns are marked "R.K.M. BROWNING WZ. 28 P.W.U.F.K. (DATE) (SERIAL NUMBER)" located on the receiver. A number of these guns (est. 500) saw service in the Spanish Civil War and were used by German military forces.

Pre-1968

Exc.	V.G.	Fair
15000	13000	11000

Pre-1986 conversions

Exc.	V.G.	Fair
N/A	N/A	N/A

Pre-1986 dealer samples

Exc.	V.G.	Fair
4000	3500	3000

Polish Wz 28 • Courtesy private NFA collection • Paul Goodwin photo

ROMANIA

Romanian Military Conflicts, 1870-Present

In 1861 the principalities of Moldavia and Walachia (formerly under Russian control) were united to form Romania, which became independent in 1878. In 1881 Romania became the Kingdom of Romania. Romania was involved in the Second Balkan War in 1913 with Serbia, Greece, and Turkey against Bulgaria for a larger share of Macedonia. Romania and its allies defeated Bulgaria. This Balkan conflict helped to hasten the Balkan nationalism that precipitated World War I. In 1916 Romania joined forces with the Allies against Austria-Hungary and Germany. At the conclusion of World War I, Romania was ceded additional land, but its history was marked by increased domestic turmoil and violence. In the 1930s, the rise of the Iron Guard, a fascist organization, overthrew the Romanian king and established a dictatorship. Romania joined Germany against Russia in 1941. Soviet troops entered Romania in 1944 and shortly after the end of World War II a Communist government took power. While Romania was part of the Soviet empire it maintained a certain independence, especially in its foreign policy. In 1990 an election was held that ousted most of the Communists from the government but failed to find solutions to domestic unrest and strife.

HANDGUNS

Steyr Hahn Model 1911
Chambered for the 9mm Steyr cartridge, this pistol was made by Steyr for the Romanian military in 1913 and 1914, as well as other military forces. This particular model is marked with Romanian crest over 1912 on left of slide. Some of these pistols were used by Romanian military during World War II.

Exc.	V.G.	Good	Fair	Poor
450	375	300	250	150

Beretta Model 1934 Romanian Contract
This model is identical to the Beretta Model 1934 except the slide is marked "9mm Scurt" instead of "9mm Corto." Built for the Romanian military in 1941 with an estimate of approximately 20,000 manufactured in Italy.

Exc.	V.G.	Good	Fair	Poor
475	425	325	225	125

Model 74
A Romanian copy of the Walther PP chambered for the 7.65mm (.32 ACP) cartridge. This pistol has an aluminum frame and is similar to the FEG Hungarian R61 with the exception of a heel-type magazine release.

Exc.	V.G.	Good	Fair	Poor
175	150	125	100	80

Soviet TT33 (Copy)
This model is not fitted with a safety and has no import stamp. It is original military issue.

Exc.	V.G.	Good	Fair	Poor
800	700	600	500	300

NOTE: For pistols with safety and import stamp deduct 75%.

Soviet PM (Copy of Makarov)
Fitted with a safety but with no import stamp.

Exc.	V.G.	Good	Fair	Poor
400	350	300	200	100

SUBMACHINE GUNS

Before 1939 Romania acquired Beretta 9mm Model 1938A submachine guns. After 1939 the Romanian armed forces used the Beretta 38/42 in 9mm Parabellum. Then after the war Romania adopted the Czech VZ24 and VZ26 guns.

Orita M 1941
This gun was manufactured in Romania at Cugir Arsenal. It is similar to the MP 41 but uses magazines that are similar in appearance to the German model but are not interchangeable with it. Fitted with a one-piece wooden stock. Chambered for the 9mm Parabellum cartridge. Semiautomatic or full auto fire. The rear leaf and ramp sight is quite large and located well forward on the barrel. Barrel length is 11.25". Magazine capacity is 25 rounds. The gun has a cycle rate of about 600 rounds per minute. Weight is approximately 7.75 lbs.

RIFLES

PEABODY

Romanian Rifle (1867-1868)
Chambered for the .45 Romanian centerfire cartridge and fitted with a 32.25" barrel. Blued barrel with casehardened furniture. Full stock with two barrel bands. Oiled wooden stocks. A total of 25,000 rifles were made in serial range 21,000 to 52,000.

Exc.	V.G.	Good	Fair	Poor
—	1500	1000	500	200

PEABODY-MARTINI
Witten, Germany

Model 1879 Peabody-Martini Rifle
Made in Germany and based on the Turkish Model 1874 rifle. Chambered for the 11.43x60R Peabody-Martini cartridge. Fitted with a 33.25" barrel. Full stocked with two barrel bands. Weight is about 9.5 lbs.

Exc.	V.G.	Good	Fair	Poor
—	850	500	300	150

MANNLICHER

Model 1892
Introduced in 1892 and built by Steyr, this turn bolt rifle is chambered for the 6.5x53Rmm cartridge. This model is full stocked with straight grip and half-length handguard. Fitted with a cleaning rod and bayonet fittings. Barrel length is 28.5". Leaf rear sight. Clip loaded magazine has a 5-round capacity. Weight is about 9 lbs. Marked "OE" over "W.G." on receiver ring and "MD. 1892" on left side of receiver.

Exc.	V.G.	Good	Fair	Poor
200	150	100	75	50

Model 1893
This is an improved version of the Model 1892 with stacking hook added and bolt modifications to prevent faulty assembly. Other specifications are the same as the Model 1892.

Exc.	V.G.	Good	Fair	Poor
175	125	90	75	50

Model 1893 Carbine

This is a short version of the Model 1893 rifle with 17.7" barrel. No handguard and no bayonet fittings. Weight is approximately 7.25 lbs.

Exc.	V.G.	Good	Fair	Poor
300	200	150	100	75

MAUSER

VZ24 Short Rifle

This model is a copy of the Czech VZ24 Short Rifle. The only difference is the Romanian crest on the receiver ring.

Exc.	V.G.	Good	Fair	Poor
350	280	200	140	80

STATE FACTORIES

Romanian Mosin-Nagant M1944

These rifles are marked on the receiver with a small arrowhead in a triangle below a wreath with the letters "RPR." Romanian stocks are marked with a "C" in a diamond. These rifles were produced in the 1950s.

Exc.	V.G.	Good	Fair	Poor
200	150	100	75	50

PSL Sniper Rifle (misnamed FPK)

This model is chambered for the 7.62x54Rmm cartridge and fitted with a modified AKM-type receiver. Magazine capacity is 10 rounds. Buttstock is similar to the Soviet SVD but with a molded cheekpiece. The muzzle brake is of Romanian design. Equipped with a telescope sight. Weight is about 10.5 lbs.

Exc.	V.G.	Good	Fair	Poor
800	700	550	400	200

SKS

A Romanian-manufactured version of the Russian rifle.

Exc.	V.G.	Good	Fair	Poor
200	150	125	100	75

AK-47 (semiautomatic version)

Romanian copy of the Soviet AK-47.

Exc.	V.G.	Good	Fair	Poor
300	250	200	150	100

AKM

Copy of the Soviet AKM except for a noticeable curved-front vertical fore grip formed as part of the forend.

Courtesy West Point Museum, Paul Goodwin photo

Pre-1968

Exc.	V.G.	Fair
8500	8000	7500

Pre-1986 conversions

Exc.	V.G.	Fair
N/A	N/A	N/A

Pre-1986 dealer samples

Exc.	V.G.	Fair
N/A	N/A	N/A

AKM-R

This a compact version of the Soviet AKM with an 8" barrel and side-folding metal butt. Magazine capacity is 20 rounds. Chambered for the 7.62x39mm cartridge. Rate of fire is about 600 rounds per minute. Weight is approximately 7 lbs.

Pre-1968

Exc.	V.G.	Fair
9000	8500	8000

Pre-1986 conversions

Exc.	V.G.	Fair
N/A	N/A	N/A

Pre-1986 dealer samples

Exc.	V.G.	Fair
N/A	N/A	N/A

AK-74

Similar to the Soviet 5.45x39mm version of this model but with a full-length handguard. Forend is fitted with vertical foregrip. Produced with metal or wooden buttstock. Semiautomatic version only.

Exc.	V.G.	Good	Fair	Poor
300	250	200	150	100

MACHINE GUNS

The Romanians used Soviet-built RPDs, SGMs, PK, PKB, PKS, PHTs, and the Soviet-made DShK 38/46.

RPK (Romanian Manufacture)

Copy of Soviet RPK.

Pre-1968

Exc.	V.G.	Fair
17000	15000	12000

Pre-1986 conversions

Exc.	V.G.	Fair
8000	7500	7000

Pre-1986 dealer samples

Exc.	V.G.	Fair
4500	4000	3500

Romanian Schwarzlose converted to 7.62 caliber with larger waterjacket and metal belt • Courtesy Robert E. Naess

RUSSIA
Former USSR/Warsaw Pact

Russian/Soviet Military Conflicts, 1870 - 2000

After the Crimean War, 1854-1856, Russian expansion continued into Caucasus, Turkestan, and eastern Asia. Alexander II was assassinated in 1881. Oppressive imperial rule followed under Alexander III and Nicholas II. The Russo-Japanese War of 1905 led to the Revolution of 1905, the results of which forced Nicholas to grant a Parliament and constitution. World War I led to the collapse of imperial rule and the country was thrown into revolution in 1917. During World War I, Russia had a total of 12,000,000 military personnel with 5,300,000 killed or wounded.

Lenin took control, but civil war lasted until 1920 when the Soviet regime emerged victorious. In 1922 Russia became part of the USSR. Despite a non-aggression treaty with Hitler, Russia was invaded by Nazi Germany in 1941. Russian military forces fought several famous battles against the Germans throughout the war. In 1945 Russian forces entered Berlin and forced the Allies to partition Berlin and later Germany. A total of 30,000,000 people served in the Russian military during the war. Of that number, 11,000,000 were killed, but the number of wounded is unknown. Civilian casualties are estimated at 6,700,000.

From the end of World War II, military forces of the USSR and Warsaw Pact nations were engaged in numerous military adventures. Perhaps the best known was the ten year struggle in Afghanistan. In 1991 the USSR collapsed and Russia resumed her autonomy. Since that time Russia has been engaged in trying to control rebellious ethnic areas of the country from gaining independence, namely Chechnya and Tatarstan. As of 2001 Russia had 977,100 personnel on active duty. Active duty army was 321,000 personnel. Russia has 20,000,000 reserve forces.

HANDGUNS

NOTE: Russia contracted for a number of Smith & Wesson revolvers over a period of years. The number of these revolvers purchased by Russia was about 350,000. These revolvers were made for the Russian military and are covered under *U.S., Handguns, Smith & Wesson*.

NAGANT

Model 1895 "Gas Seal" Revolver

A 7.62mm caliber single or double action revolver with a 4.35" barrel and 7-shot cylinder. Called a Gas Seal because as the hammer is cocked, the cylinder is moved forward to engage the barrel breech forming a seal between the cylinder and the barrel. Blued with either walnut or plastic grips. Weight was approximately 28 oz. In service from 1895 to approximately 1947.

Built by Nagant Brothers in Liege, Belgium. The Russians also built the gun under license at their arsenal in Tula.

Exc.	V.G.	Good	Fair	Poor
200	150	100	75	50

Mosin-Nagant Model 1895 • Paul Goodwin photo

NOTE: Single action only versions are much less encountered and will command a 50% premium. Prices reflect revolvers that have original finish, and are not arsenal refinished.

A Model 1895 Nagant Training Revolver in .22 caliber sold at auction for $977.50. Condition is very good. Rock Island Auction Company, September 2002

THE NAGANT GAS SEAL REVOLVER

As you read this, remember the saying, "An ingenious solution to a non-existent problem." In 1891 Tsarist Russia adopted the Mosin-Nagant rifle, which combined a bolt action designed by Captain Sergei I. Mosin and a magazine developed by the Belgian firm of Leon Nagant et Freres. The Belgians took this opportunity to offer their newest revolver, which used the basic Nagant design of a DA/SA trigger mechanism and a solid frame with a pivoting ejector rod housed in a hollow cylinder pin. But the revolver offered to the Russians differed in that when the hammer was cocked, the cylinder moved forward over the end of the barrel inserting the cartridge's long neck into the forcing cone where, upon firing, it expanded to form a gas seal. The theory was that this provided extra velocity to the bullet while decreasing fouling. Being the revolver fired a 108 grain, 7.62mm projectile the whole point is sort of moot. But the Russians adopted it as the Revolver Sistemy Nagana obr. 1895 and manufacture began at the Tula arsenal where it would continue until 1945. The obr. 1895 I tested was made in 1944 and was in excellent condition. It must be understood that pulling the trigger not only cocks the hammer and rotates the cylinder, but also pushes it and the recoil plate forward and holds them in place-against the pressure of a V-shaped mainspring of truly heroic proportions. Combined with Soviet "war-time quality," the result was the DA trigger pull from hell. At seven yards, I found it almost impossible to keep my rounds on an IPSC target. Switching to SA mode, the obr. 1895 proved pleasant to shoot and quite accurate, but when all is said and done I'd rather have had an S&W Victory Model any day!

Paul Scarlata

Model 1895 Nagant .22 Caliber
As above but chambered for .22 caliber cartridges. Converted at the Tula arsenal from surplus 7.62mm revolvers. Used as a training revolver from 1925 to 1947.

Exc.	V.G.	Good	Fair	Poor
650	500	350	250	100

Model 1895 Nagant (KGB)
This is a standard Nagant with the important exception of a 3.5" barrel and shorter grip frame. Used by the Russian secret police during the Stalin years. Extremely rare. Proceed with caution.

Nagant KGB Model • Courtesy Richard M. Kumor Sr.

Exc.	V.G.	Good	Fair	Poor
2000	1500	1000	—	—

FN 1900 Russian Contract
An unknown number of these FN pistols were purchased by the Russian government. Little information is known. Proceed with caution.

FN Model 1900 Russian Contract Pistol • Courtesy Richard M. Kumor Sr.

Exc.	V.G.	Good	Fair	Poor
1000	700	500	300	200

SOVIET STATE FACTORIES

Tokarev TT-30 & TT-33
Fyedor Tokarev was a Russian weapons designer who began his career at the Sestroretsk rifle factory in 1907. He was responsible for the development of machine guns, pistols, and automatic rifles. The TT series of pistols were just some of his designs.

In 1930 the TT-30 was adopted, and in 1933 a slightly modified version, the TT-33, was introduced. A 7.62mm semiautomatic pistol with a 4.5" barrel and 8-shot magazine. This model was produced in a number of communist countries. Each country had its own model designation for the pistol. In Poland and Yugoslavia it is called the M57; in Hungary it was known as the M48; in China the M51 and M54; and in North Korea the M68. The North Korean M68 differs from the other Tokarevs in the location of the magazine release and the elimination of the barrel locking link.

NOTE: Add 50% for TT-30, for cut-aways add 200%.

TT-33 • Courtesy Richard M. Kumor Sr.

Exc.	V.G.	Good	Fair	Poor
350	300	250	125	100

NOTE: In 1941 the German army continued to manufacture Russian pistols, namely the TT-33. It was designated the Pistol 615 (r). Add 50% for these examples.

Tokarev Model R-3
A training version of the TT Tokarev pistols chambered for the .22 caliber cartridge.

Exc.	V.G.	Good	Fair	Poor
650	550	400	300	150

Tokarev Model R-4
A long barrel target version of the TT Tokarev pistol chambered for the .22 caliber cartridge.

Exc.	V.G.	Good	Fair	Poor
650	550	400	300	150

TK TOZ (Tula Korovin)
A .25 caliber pocket pistol produced by the Soviet arsenal at Tula. Fitted with a 2.7" fixed barrel. Magazine capacity is 8 rounds. Weight is approximately 14 oz. Used by military officers and police units. Produced from 1926 to about 1935.

Courtesy Orvel Reichert

Courtesy Orvel Reichert

Exc.	V.G.	Good	Fair	Poor
450	375	300	200	100

Makarov
This semiautomatic pistol is similar in appearance to the Walther PP pistol and is chambered for the 9mm Makarov (9x18mm) cartridge. It has a double action trigger and is fitted with fixed sights. Barrel length is 3.6" and overall length is 6.4". Weight is approximately 25 oz. Magazine capacity is 8 rounds.

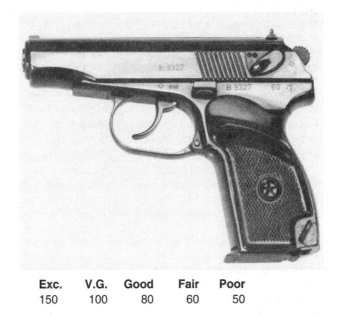

Exc.	V.G.	Good	Fair	Poor
150	100	80	60	50

Stechkin
A select fire pistol chambered for the 9x18 Makarov cartridge. Fitted with a 5.5" barrel and a 20-round magazine. Rate of fire is about 750 rounds per minute. Weight is approximately 36 oz. This was the standard service pistol of the Soviet army between 1955 and 1975. A wooden stock/holster is supplied with the pistol.

NOTE: It is not known how many, if any, of these machine pistols are in the U.S. and are transferable. Prices listed below are estimates only.

Pre-1968 (Extremely Rare)

Exc.	V.G.	Fair
30000	—	—

Pre-1986 conversions

Exc.	V.G.	Fair
N/A	N/A	N/A

Pre-1986 dealer samples

Exc.	V.G.	Fair
N/A	N/A	N/A

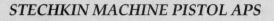

STECHKIN MACHINE PISTOL APS

There is rumored to be a fully transferable pre-1968 Stechkin Machine Pistol in private hands in the United States, but I have never run across it nor spoken to anyone else who has seen it. This would mean that all of the known Stechkins are "Post-1986 Dealer Samples," only available to active Class 3 dealers in the course of their law enforcement business. A small group of 8 or 9 was imported directly to a US Government agency in the mid 1990s, and fifty guns were brought into the US FTZ for resale in the early 1990s by Long Mountain Outfitters. Of these, 23 were brought in live to Class 3 dealers or law enforcement agencies as post-86 dealer samples; the other 27 came in as "parts sets" with torched receivers. All were East Block arsenal refinished to like-new condition. Some of the parts sets were reportedly manufactured into semi auto "Short Barreled Rifles" and registered in the NFRTR. Others were used to make display "non" guns, and some Class 2 manufacturers made and registered a few into post-1986 dealer samples. All of the imports had the reddish plastic stock, not the wooden or wire stock.

The Stechkin, in 9mm Makarov (9x18mm), is a very controllable machine pistol. When the rear slot is locked onto the buttstock, and proper hand placement (firing hand on grip, other hand on center of stock pressing it to the shoulder) is used, very accurate bursts may be fired. The recoil is less than that of a 9mm Parabellum (9x19mm) machine pistol such as the Beretta 93R, which could be a function of the mass of the Stechkin pistol and its somewhat lower rate of fire.

We took one of the Stechkins and had Jim Ryan rebarrel it to .380 ACP, with an extended and threaded barrel. A Gemtech sound suppressor was installed. The purpose of this experiment was to see if there could be a weapons platform here that was modular, small, accurate, and very quiet. The experiment worked quite well, but we took the Stechkin back to its original caliber after not finding much interest in the law enforcement community.

Dan Shea

Stechkin with stock • Courtesy Thomas Nelson, *The World's Machine Pistols, Vol. II*

SUBMACHINE GUNS

PPD-1934/38 (Pistol Pulyemet Degtyarev)

Introduced in 1938 and based on the Bergman MP28 submachine gun. Select fire. The buttstock is wooden. Barrel is 10.5" with perforated barrel jacket and tangent sight. Chambered for the 7.62 Soviet pistol cartridge. Magazine capacity is 25-round box or 71-round drum. Rate of fire is approximately 800 rounds per minute. Weight is about 8.5 lbs.

Pre-1968

Exc.	V.G.	Fair
8000	7000	6000

Pre-1986 conversions

Exc.	V.G.	Fair
N/A	N/A	N/A

Pre-1986 dealer samples

Exc.	V.G.	Fair
N/A	N/A	N/A

PPD-1940

First produced in 1940, this Russian-built submachine gun is chambered for the 7.62 Soviet pistol cartridge. The gun was fitted with a 71-round drum magazine and 10" barrel. The rate of fire was 800 rounds per minute. The serial number and factory code are located on top of the receiver. Weight is about 8 lbs. Production ceased in 1941.

Pre-1968

Exc.	V.G.	Fair
8500	8000	7500

USSR, ca. 1939. This Soviet naval infantryman is ready to deal with any close-range threat with his PPD-1940 submachine gun and an RGD-33 grenade with serrated fragmentation sleeve • Thomas B. Nelson Collection/Robert Bruce Military Photo Features

PPsh-41 (Pistol Pulyemet Shpagin)

This Russian select fire submachine was produced from 1941 until 1947. About five million were built and many were sold throughout the world. Some were converted from the 7.62 pistol cartridge to the 9mm cartridge by Germany. The gun could use a 71-round drum magazine or a 35-round box magazine.

PPD-1940 • Courtesy West Point Museum, Paul Goodwin photo

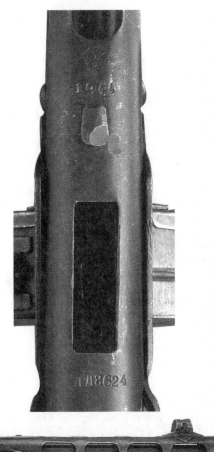

Pre-1986 conversions

Exc.	V.G.	Fair
6000	5500	5000

Pre-1986 dealer samples

Exc.	V.G.	Fair
N/A	N/A	N/A

PPsh41/Viet Cong • Paul Goodwin photo

Rate of fire was 900 rounds per minute. The barrel was 10.3" long with slotted barrel jacket and weighed almost 8 lbs. Early models had a tangent back sight while most were fitted with a two-position, flip-up rear sight. Markings are located on the receiver.

NOTE: A German conversion 9mm kit was made for this gun. The kit uses MP-40 magazines. Very rare. Too rare to price.

Courtesy Richard M. Kumor Sr.

THE PPS 1943

When it comes to the small arms produced in the Soviet Union, they all shared some common characteristics. They generally function well regardless of condition, they were simple in construction, and usually they were cheap to produce. The PPS 1943 was the odd duck of World War II Russian submachine guns because it was developed in a city under a long and brutal siege, Leningrad. Nonetheless, it was an excellent submachine gun with very few faults. The PPS 1943 fired full-auto only from an open bolt, but the cyclic rate of fire (650 rpm) was slow enough the experienced operator could easily trigger off single rounds instead of multi-shot bursts. Made totally from stamped steel construction, the PPS 1943 did not have a fixed ejector. Instead, the main operating guide rod served as the ejector when the bolt was fully rearward. Unlike the folding stock on the MP-40, the folding stock on the PPS 1943 was rigid when extended and did not flop around when folded over the receiver. The safety was very similar in operation to that found on the American Garand M-1 rifle in that it was pushed forward from inside the triggerguard. The PPS 1943 used a two position feed, dual column, stamped sheet metal curved box magazine that held 35 rounds of the 7.62x25mm Russian ammunition. A muzzle brake was incorporated in the stamped steel design of the gun, but it is questionable if it was even needed due to the low recoil of the lightweight, but high velocity, Russian ammo. The biggest negative with any PPS 1943 was the vibration felt when shooting the PPS 1943 from the shoulder and the operator's cheek is tight against the sheet metal strut. It would make the fillings hurt in your teeth. The PPS 1943 was an extremely good open bolt submachine gun in terms of its design, reliability, and operation, but while the ammo offered great penetration (it will easily shoot through mild steel 1/4th of an inch thick) it was not known for its stopping power.

Frank James

Pre-1968

Exc.	V.G.	Fair
8500	8000	7500

Pre-1986 conversions

Exc.	V.G.	Fair
7000	6500	6000

Pre-1986 dealer samples

Exc.	V.G.	Fair
N/A	N/A	N/A

PPS 1943 (Pistol Pulyemet Sudaev)

Chambered for the 7.62 pistol cartridge this full automatic only submachine gun is fitted with a 10" barrel with slotted barrel jacket and 35-round box magazine. The receiver and jacket are stamped out of one piece of sheet steel. The metal butt folds behind the ejection port. Rate of fire is about 700 rounds per minute. Weight is approximately 7.5 lbs. Introduced in 1943 as an improvement over the PPsh-41.

PPS 1943 • Courtesy Steve Hill, Spotted Dog Firearms

PPS 1943 • Paul Goodwin photo

Pre-1968

Exc.	V.G.	Fair
7500	7000	6500

Pre-1986 conversions

Exc.	V.G.	Fair
6000	5500	5000

Pre-1986 dealer samples

Exc.	V.G.	Fair
N/A	N/A	N/A

RIFLES

BERDAN

Berdan Model 1870 (Berdan II)

After Colt had built and supplied the Russians with the first Berdan rifles, BSA of Birmingham, England, produced another 30,000. BSA, in 1871 and 1872, also provided the tooling and machinery so that the Russians could build their own version of the Berdan. A total of 3,500,000 Russian Berdans were built at the arsenals in Ishevsk, Sestroryetsk, and Tula. This single-shot model had an octagon receiver with a short bolt handle. Caliber was 10.66x57Rmm with a barrel length of 32.5". Marked with the Russian arsenal on top of the receiver ring flat. These rifles saw service as late as World War I. Some captured Russian rifles were issued to German units during WWI.

Exc.	V.G.	Good	Fair	Poor
750	600	400	300	100

Berdan Model 1870 • Courtesy West Point Museum, Paul Goodwin photo

MOSIN-NAGANT

The first Mosin-Nagant rifles were developed at Tula by Sergi Mosin. The feed system was developed by Belgian designer Leon Nagant. The Russians had inadequate production facilities to build these rifles so many of them were produced by Chatelleraut, Remington, and Westinghouse. SIG made barrels for the rifles and Valmet, Tikkakoske rebuilt and modified Russian rifles. The Mosin-Nagant was also produced in Poland, Hungary, Romania, and China. For history and technical details see Terence W. Lapin's, *The Mosin-Nagant Rifle*, North Cape Publications, 1998.

NOTE: During World War II the Germans captured thousands of Russian weapons. Many of these were Russian Mosin-Nagant rifles. These rifles were reissued with German code numbers to designate them as foreign equipment (*Fremdgerat*). Part of the code included the lower case (r) denoting that the rifle was Russian.

Model 1891

A 7.62x54Rmm caliber bolt action rifle with a 31.6" barrel, 5-shot integral magazine, ladder rear sight, and a full-length stock secured by two barrel bands. Blued with a walnut stock. The Model 1891, before 1918, was fitted with an octagonal receiver ring with a heavyweight rear barrel section behind the rear sight. Pre-1908 version did not have upper handguards. Post-1908 rifles had sling swivels mounted through slots in the butt and forearm. Front sight was an unhooded blade while the rear sight was a ramp and leaf affair. Weight of these rifles was about 9.5 lbs. Used extensively in the Russo-Japanese War of 1904-1905. A total of over 9,000,000 of these rifles were built between 1892 and 1922.

German military designation 252 (r).

Exc.	V.G.	Good	Fair	Poor
150	125	100	75	60

NOTE: Some Model 1891 rifles captured by Austria were converted to take the 8x50R Austrian cartridge. These examples are extremely rare and command a $300 premium.

Model 1891 Dragoon Rifle

Same as above but for a 28.75" barrel. Fitted with a short handguard with sling slots in buttstock and forend. Weight was reduced to about 8.5 lbs. Replaced the Model 1891 rifle as standard issue after 1920.

German military designation 253 (r).

Exc.	V.G.	Good	Fair	Poor
200	150	125	75	60

Model 1891 Cossack Rifle

This variant is almost identical to the Dragoon Rifle but instead is fitted with a tangent rear sight. The rifle was not issued with a bayonet.

German military designation 254 (r).

Exc.	V.G.	Good	Fair	Poor
200	150	125	75	60

Model 1891/30 Rifle

This is an improved version of the Model 1891 Dragoon rifle. The older hexagon receiver is replaced with a cylindrical one. It has a 28.7" barrel with metric rear tangent sights. Front sight is hooded. The bayonet ring was changed to a spring loaded catch type. Five-round magazine. Weight is about 8.7 lbs. Introduced in 1930. Over 17,000,000 of these rifles were produced between 1930 and 1944.

Exc.	V.G.	Good	Fair	Poor
150	125	100	75	60

Model 1891/30 Sniper Rifle w/3.5 power P.U. scope

This is a Model 1891/30 with a scope attached to the left of the receiver, and a longer turned-down bolt handle. Fitted with iron sights.

NOTE: There are a number of Czech CZ 54 and CZ 57 sniper rifles based on the Mosin, as well as Finnish sniper rifles based on the Mosin. All examples, if extant, are worth a mini-

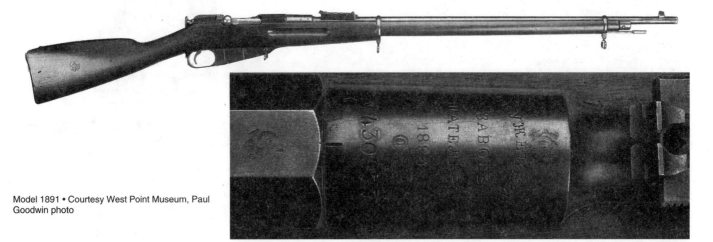

Model 1891 • Courtesy West Point Museum, Paul Goodwin photo

mum of 100% premium over the Russian Model 1891/30 PU. Deduct 50% for imported rifles.

Courtesy Richard M. Kumor Sr.

Exc.	V.G.	Good	Fair	Poor
1200	900	700	N/A	N/A

Model 1891/30 Sniper Rifle w/4 power P.T. scope (Rare)

This is a Model 1891/30 with a scope attached. This scope was used until about 1940. Most, but not all, of these scopes are dated 1921 to 1935 and made by Carl Zeiss in Jena, Germany.

Close-up of P.E. scope • Courtesy Richard M. Kumor Sr.

NOTE: Deduct 50% for imported rifles.

Exc.	V.G.	Good	Fair	Poor
2000	1700	1100	N/A	N/A

Soviet Union, WWII. A pair of Red Army sharpshooters with M1891/30 sniper rifles (note special elongated and turned-down bolt handles) equipped with telescopic sights • Thomas B. Nelson Collection/Robert Bruce Military Photo Feature

Model 1907/1910 Carbine

As above, with a 20" barrel and modified sights. No bayonet fittings. Leaf sight is graduated in Russian arshins form of measurement from 400 to 2,000. Weight is 7.5 lbs.

German military designation 453 (r).

Exc.	V.G.	Good	Fair	Poor
175	150	125	100	75

Model 1938 Carbine

This model replaced the Model 1907/1910 carbine. It is fitted with a 20" barrel. Rear tangent sight is in meters from 1 through 10. No bayonet fittings. Weight is about 7.5 lbs. Produced from 1939 to 1944. Very few were produced in 1945. About 2,000,000 were produced.

German military designation 454 (r).

Exc.	V.G.	Good	Fair	Poor
375	250	150	100	75

NOTE: Many Model 91/30 rifles were arsenal converted to M38 carbine configuration. These may be marked M91/59. Conversions done in Bulgaria, Czechoslovakia, and possibly the Soviet Union.

Model 1944 Carbine

This was the last Mosin-Nagant. It was fitted with a folding bayonet hinged at the barrel muzzle. The barrel was about 1/2" longer than the Model 1938 carbine. Rear tangent sight is in meters from 1 through 10. With the bayonet this carbine weighed about 9 lbs. This model was copied by the Chinese and designated the Type 53. This model was also made in Poland and Romania. The Russian Model 1944 Carbine was used in Afghanistan in the 1980s and by Palestinian guerrilla groups, also in the 1980s.

NOTE: Add 15% for no import markings.

Exc.	V.G.	Good	Fair	Poor
200	150	125	75	50

Model 1907/1910 carbine with receiver markings • Paul Goodwin photo

Model 1944 carbine with receiver markings • Paul Goodwin photo

Soviet Union, WWII. Soviet artillerymen in action. The soldier in the foreground carries a Model 1944 carbine slung over his back • Thomas B. Nelson Collection/Robert Bruce Military Photo Features

TOKAREV

Fyedo Vassilevich Tokarev designed not only the Tokarev rifle in 1938 and 1940, but the pistol and machine gun that bear his name as well. An experimental model, the Model 1930 was built for military trials. The Model 1935, fitted with a 17.75" barrel, was built for trials but was not successful. Only about 500 were produced.

M1938 Rifle (SVT)

A 7.62x54Rmm caliber gas-operated semiautomatic or select fire rifle with a 24" barrel with muzzle break and 10-shot magazine (15 rounds in select fire). Cleaning rod in stock. Blued with a two-piece hardwood stock extending the full-length of the rifle. Upper handguard is 3/4 length of barrel. Weight is about 8.5 lbs. Manufactured from 1938 to 1940. Approximately 150,000 of these rifles were manufactured.

NOTE: Add 300% for Sniper variation.

Courtesy Richard M. Kumor Sr.

M1938 Sniper • Courtesy Richard M. Kumor Sr.

Exc.	V.G.	Good	Fair	Poor
1000	800	600	200	1000

M1940 Rifle (SVT)

An improved semiautomatic version of the M1938 with half stock and half-length slotted handguard with a sheet metal handguard and muzzle brake. Ten-round magazine. Weight is about 8.5 lbs. Approximately 2,000,000 were produced.

NOTE: Add 50% for no importer marking. Add 300% for Sniper variation.

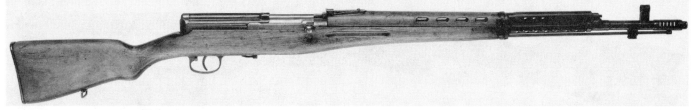

M1940 Rifle • Courtesy Rock Island Auction Company

CAUTION: All Tokarev SVT carbines (18.5" barrel) encountered with "SA" (Finnish) markings were altered to carbine configuration by their importer and have little collector value. It is believed that few, perhaps 2,000, SVT 40 carbines were ever made by the USSR.

Courtesy Richard M. Kumor Sr.

Exc.	V.G.	Good	Fair	Poor
400	350	300	200	150

Eastern Front, ca. 1944. With a 7.62mm Tokarev SVT-40 semiautomatic rifle slung on his back, a Red Army soldier cautiously moves forward under enemy artillery fire • Thomas B. Nelson Collection/Robert Bruce Military Photo Features

DRAGUNOV

Yevgeni Fyordorov Dragunov was born in 1920. He was in the Soviet army from 1939 to 1945. After the war he worked in the Izhevsk rifle factory where he designed and developed the Dragunov rifle.

SVD Sniper Rifle

This model, developed as a replacement for the Mosin-Nagant Model 1891/30 Sniper rifle, was introduced in 1963. It is chambered for the 7.62x53R cartridge. It is fitted with a 24.5" barrel with prong-style flash hider and has a skeleton stock with cheek rest and slotted forearm. Semiautomatic with an action

SHOOTING THE SOVIET SVD DRAGUNOV

It would be hard to come up with a sniper rifle more derided here in the West than the Snayperskaya Vintovka Dragunova. Yet in Russian service, among actual combat veterans, "Oar," as it's referred to, is both well respected and highly popular. Designed by the late Evgeniy Dragunov, whose biathlon rifles have taken Olympic Gold, the SVD is a lightweight self-loading sharpshooter's rifle issued at the platoon level. A simple and reliable design, it's well suited for its intended task of fire support. Chambered for the venerable 7.62x54R cartridge, over the years it's had two dedicated sniper loads developed for it: the 7N1 and the 7N14. These both drive 152 grain FMJBT's at 2723 fps and substantially increase the accuracy of this rifle. In the hands the SVD is both light and handy, compared to a conventional Western sniper rifle, and carries well. Operating it is similar to running a Kalashnikov Avtomat. Simply rock a loaded 10 round magazine into place, snap the stiff and inconveniently placed safety lever down to "Fire," then retract and release the bolt. Settling down behind the rifle one notices that the forend is comfortable and shaped to fit the hand, unlike Western designs which tend to be blocky and fit only for sandbags. The pistolgrip properly places the trigger finger, and the cheekrest provides a good cheekweld, but most will find the stock too short. The optics, while old and low powered (4x), provide a large field of view and have a user friendly reticle system. SVD's triggers are usually pretty good with a pull weight running from 2-3 pounds. Recoil is fairly light, allowing a rapid follow-up shot if required. While not as accurate as Western bolt guns, nonetheless the SVD is rugged, reliable, easy to reload, and, with its dedicated sniper loads, capable of bringing a man down at 800+ yards.

David Fortier

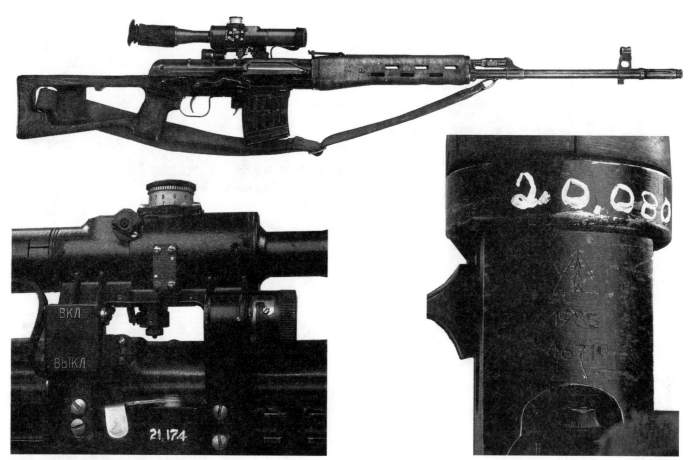

Soviet SVD Sniper • Courtesy West Point Museum, Paul Goodwin photo

closely resembling the AK series of rifles. A PSO-1 telescope sight with illuminated reticle is supplied with the rifle from the factory. This sight is fitted to each specific rifle. Magazine capacity is 10 rounds. Weight is about 9.5 lbs. This rifle is made under license in China, Iran, and Romania.

Exc.	V.G.	Good	Fair	Poor
4000	3500	3000	—	—

SIMONOV

Sergei Simonov was born in 1894 and later became a master gunsmith. He worked in a machine gun factory in the 1920s. He designed and developed several different firearm designs including the rifle that bears his name.

Simonov AVS-36

First built in Russia in 1936, this rifle is chambered for the 7.62x54R Soviet cartridge. Fitted with a 24.3" barrel with muzzle break and a 20-round magazine. This automatic rifle has a rate of fire of 600 rounds per minute. It weighs 9.7 lbs. Production ceased in 1938.

AVS-36 • Courtesy Steve Hill, Spotted Dog Firearms

Pre-1968

Exc.	V.G.	Fair
10000	9500	9000

Pre-1986 conversions

Exc.	V.G.	Fair
N/A	N/A	N/A

Pre-1986 dealer samples

Exc.	V.G.	Fair
N/A	N/A	N/A

SKS

Introduced in 1946 this 7.62x39mm semiautomatic rifle is fitted with a 20.5" barrel and 10-shot fixed magazine. Blued with oil finished stock and half-length upper handguard. It has a folding blade-type bayonet that folds under the barrel and forearm. Weight is about 8.5 lbs. This rifle was the standard service arm for most Eastern Bloc countries prior to the adoption of the AK-47. This rifle was also made in Romania, East Germany, Yugoslavia, and China.

NOTE: The importation of Chinese SKS rifles in very large quantities has resulted in an oversupply of these rifles with the result that prices are less than $150 for guns in excellent condition. However, this situation may change and, if that occurs, the price will adjust accordingly. Study local conditions before purchase or sale of this firearm.

KALASHNIKOV

Mikhail Kalashnikov was born in 1920. He was drafted into the Soviet army in 1939. He won the Order of the Red Star for bravery in combat during the German invasion of Russia in 1941. He became an amateur gun designer and after several unsuccessful attempts developed the AK series of rifles for the 7.62x39mm cartridge.

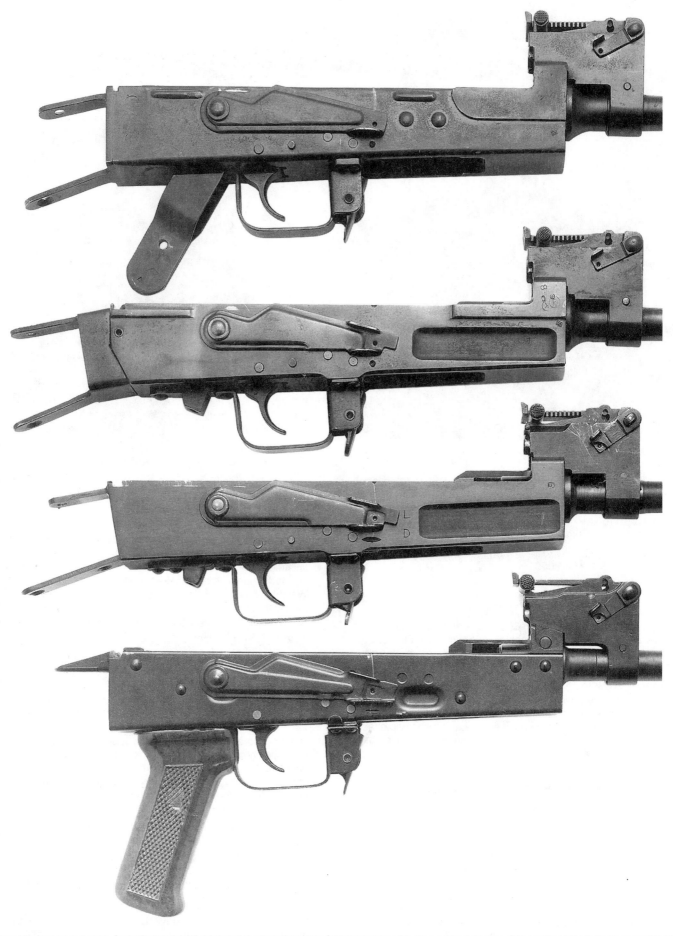

Four AKs from top to bottom: Soviet first model with fabricated sheet steel receiver; Soviet second model with machined receiver; Chinese Type 56 with 2nd type machined receiver; bottom later perfected stamped receiver • Courtesy Blake Stevens, *Kalashnikov: Arms and the Man*, Ezell

Avtomat Kalashnikov AK-47

Designed by Mikhail Kalashnikov and first produced in 1947, the Russian AK-47 is chambered for the 7.62x39mm cartridge and operates on a closed bolt principal. Select fire. The standard model is fitted with a 16" barrel and a fixed beech or birch stock. Early rifles have no bayonet fittings. Magazine capacity is 30 rounds. Rate of fire is 700 rounds per minute. Rear sight is graduated to 800 meters. The bolt and carrier are bright steel. Weight is 9.5 lbs. Markings are located on top rear of receiver. This model was the first line rifle for Warsaw Pact. The most widely used assault rifle in the world and still in extensive use throughout the world.

North Korean AK-47 • Photo courtesy private NFA collection

Pre-1968

Exc.	V.G.	Fair
21000	12000	9500

Pre-1986 conversions

Exc.	V.G.	Fair
6500	6000	5750

Pre-1986 dealer samples

Exc.	V.G.	Fair
5000	4000	3750

AK-S

A variation of the AK rifle is the AK-S. Introduced in 1950, this rifle features a folding steel buttstock which rests under the receiver.

AK-S • Courtesy West Point Museum, Paul Goodwin photo

Pre-1968

Exc.	V.G.	Fair
21000	12500	9500

Pre-1986 conversions

Exc.	V.G.	Fair
6500	6000	5500

Pre-1986 dealer samples

Exc.	V.G.	Fair
5000	4000	3750

AKM

This variation of the AK-47, introduced in 1959, can be characterized by a small indentation on the receiver above the magazine. Pressed steel receiver with a parkerized bolt and carrier. Laminated wood furniture and plastic grips. The forend on the AKM is a beavertail-style. The rear sight is graduated to 1000 meters. Barrel length and rate of fire was the same as the AK-47 rifle. Several other internal production changes were

made as well. Model number is located on the top rear of the receiver. Weight is approximately 8.5 lbs.

Photo courtesy private NFA collection

WHAT'S IT LIKE: THE AK-47

Fifty million Kalashnikovs can't be wrong and it is the world's most ubiquitous military small arm. Gas-operated and firing from the closed-bolt position, the *Automat Kalashnikov* (AK) has a much-copied rotary bolt that is piston-actuated. The pinned and riveted, sheet metal receivers of the AKM series most often are seen with a five-component mechanical device that delays hammer drop until the complete cessation of all bolt-carrier bounce.

Probably the world's most reliable infantry rifle, the Kalashnikov falls short only in the areas of ergonomics and accuracy. The selector lever, on the right side of the receiver body, clatters excessively when manipulated.

AK magazines, although rugged and more reliable than those of the M16, must be rocked forward to remove and rearward to insert. As a consequence, tactical reloads are slow and awkward for all except highly trained operators. The open U-notch rear sight is far inferior to the M16 peep aperture and can only be adjusted for elevation.

Kalashnikov triggers are notorious for horrendous and variable creep with sudden, uncontrolled let-off. Except for the Yugoslav variants, AK buttstocks are too short for most Westerners. All models of the Kalashnikov exhibit excessive flash signatures. Few AKs will shoot better than 5-6 MOA at 100 meters and Ivan apparently feels that's close enough for government work. The Yugoslav AK is an exception as its stamped, sheet metal receiver body has a thickness of 1.5mm (that of all other AKs is 1mm) and this extra rigidity substantially increases its accuracy potential. The wound ballistics potential of the boat-tail 7.62x39mm is mediocre, while that of the 5.45x39mm bullet encountered in the AK74 more or less matches the performance of the 5.56x45mm projectile (both M193 and M855 types). At about 600 rpm, the cyclic rate is on the edge of being somewhat too high for tight burst groups by all but experienced personnel.

Peter Kokalis

Pre-1968

Exc.	V.G.	Fair
15000	11500	11000

Pre-1986 conversions

Exc.	V.G.	Fair
6500	6000	5750

Pre-1986 dealer samples

Exc.	V.G.	Fair
8000	8000	7500

AKM-S

In 1960 the AKM-S was introduced which featured a steel folding buttstock as seen on the AK-S. Weight is approximately 8 lbs.

AKM-S • Courtesy West Point Museum, Paul Goodwin photo

Pre-1968

Exc.	V.G.	Fair
17000	12500	11500

Pre-1986 conversions

Exc.	V.G.	Fair
7500	7000	6500

Pre-1986 dealer samples (Rare)

Exc.	V.G.	Fair
8000	8000	7500

AK-74 Assault Rifle

Similar to the AK-47 but chambered for the 5.45x39mm cartridge. Magazine capacity is 30 rounds. Barrel length is 16.35". Select fire with semiauto, full auto, and 3-shot burst. Weight is about 8.9 lbs. Rate of fire is approximately 650 to 700 rounds per minute.

NOTE: There are no known original Soviet transferable examples in the U.S. Prices below are for pre-1986 conversions only using AKM receiver and original parts.

Courtesy Steve Hill and Doug McBeth, A.S.D. Firearms

Pre-1968

Exc.	V.G.	Fair
N/A	N/A	N/A

Pre-1986 conversions

Exc.	V.G.	Fair
9000	8500	8000

Pre-1986 dealer samples

Exc.	V.G.	Fair
N/A	N/A	N/A

AK-74 (Semiautomatic only)

Introduced in 1974, this rifle is chambered for a smaller caliber, the 5.45x39.5mm, than the original AK-47 series. It is fitted with a 16" barrel with muzzle brake and has a 30-round plastic magazine. The buttstock is wooden. Weight is approximately 8.5 lbs.

In 1974 a folding stock version was called the AKS-74, and in 1980 a reduced caliber version of the AKM-SU called the AK-74-SU was introduced. No original military AK-74s are known to exist in this country.

Exc.	V.G.	Good	Fair	Poor
N/A	—	—	—	—

Afghanistan, ca. 1982. This colorfully garbed Mujhadeen fighter of the Afghan resistance against Soviet invaders is formidably armed with a captured Russian 5.45x39mm AK-74 assault rifle with undermounted 30mm single shot grenade launcher • U.S. Army Ordnance Museum/Robert Bruce Military Photo Features

AK-47 COPIES

NOTE: These are copies of the Kalashnikov designs with only minor alterations. Because original military select fire AK assault rifles are so rare this list includes *semiautomatic rifles only* unless otherwise noted. These rifles listed below are built in their country of origin and contain no U.S.-made parts, i.e. receivers, etc. Some of these rifles may not be available to the collector and are listed for reference purposes only.

BULGARIA

AK-47

This is an exact copy of the Russian AK-47.

Exc.	V.G.	Good	Fair	Poor
650	600	500	400	300

AKN-47

This is an exact copy of the Russian AKS.

Exc.	V.G.	Good	Fair	Poor
800	700	600	500	400

AK-47-MI

This is a copy of an AK-47 fitted with a 40mm grenade launcher.

AK-47-MI • Courtesy West Point Museum, Paul Goodwin photo

Exc.	V.G.	Good	Fair	Poor
N/A	N/A	N/A	N/A	N/A

AK-74/AKS-74
These are copies of the Russian models. They were also exported in 5.56x45mm caliber.

AKN-74 • Courtesy West Point Museum, Paul Goodwin photo

Exc.	V.G.	Good	Fair	Poor
N/A	N/A	N/A	N/A	N/A

CHINA
See China, Rifles.

EGYPT
MISR (Maadi)
A copy of the AKM with insignificant dimensional differences. Sometimes seen with single brace folding metal buttstock.

Pre-Ban

Exc.	V.G.	Good	Fair	Poor
1500	1200	950	750	500

ARM
This model is a MISR modified to semiautomatic only. It is fitted with a thumbhole stock. It is usually seen with a 10-round magazine.

Exc.	V.G.	Good	Fair	Poor
300	250	200	150	100

EAST GERMANY
MPiK
A copy of the AK-47 without a cleaning rod.

Exc.	V.G.	Good	Fair	Poor
N/A	N/A	N/A	N/A	N/A

MpiKS
A copy of the AKS without cleaning rod.

Exc.	V.G.	Good	Fair	Poor
N/A	N/A	N/A	N/A	N/A

MPiKM
A copy of the AKM with a cleaning rod. Early models used wooden stocks while later ones used plastic. Not fitted with a muzzle compensator.

Exc.	V.G.	Good	Fair	Poor
N/A	N/A	N/A	N/A	N/A

MPiKMS
Copy of a AKMS without shaped muzzle.

Exc.	V.G.	Good	Fair	Poor
N/A	N/A	N/A	N/A	N/A

KKMPi69
A version of the MPiKM without the gas cylinder. Chambered for the .22 caliber Long Rifle cartridge and used as a training rifle.

Exc.	V.G.	Good	Fair	Poor
N/A	N/A	N/A	N/A	N/A

HUNGARY
See Hungary, Rifles.

IRAQ
Tabuk
This model is a copy of the Soviet AKM. An export version was built in 5.56mm.

Exc.	V.G.	Good	Fair	Poor
N/A	N/A	N/A	N/A	N/A

NORTH KOREA
Type 58
This model is a copy of the Soviet AK-47 solid receiver without the finger grooves on the forearm.

Type 58 • Courtesy West Point Museum, Paul Goodwin photo

Pre-1968

Exc.	V.G.	Fair
20000	11000	8500

Pre-1986 conversions

Exc.	V.G.	Fair
5500	5000	4500

Pre-1986 dealer samples

Exc.	V.G.	Fair
5000	4000	3750

Type 68
This is a copy of the Soviet AKM-S with lightening holes drilled into the folding butt.

Exc.	V.G.	Good	Fair	Poor
N/A	N/A	N/A	N/A	N/A

POLAND
See Poland, Rifles.

ROMANIA
See Romania, Rifles.

YUGOSLAVIA
See Yugoslavia, Rifles.

MACHINE GUNS

NOTE: Russia used early Maxim guns against the Japanese during the Russo-Japanese War of 1904-1905. The Russian military also used the Madsen Model 1902 and the Colt Model 1914 during World War I, as well as the Lewis gun.

World War I Russian machine gun crew with M1905 • Robert G. Segel collection

Soviet Union, WWII. M1910 Maxim machine gun on Sokolov mount and ski-equipped carrier • Thomas B. Nelson Collection/Robert Bruce Military Photo Features

Model 1905 Maxim

The first machine gun built in Russia at the Tula arsenal. Based on the Belgian Model 1900 Maxim with 28" barrel with smooth bronze water jacket. Fed by a 250-round belt with a 450 rounds per minute rate of fire. Gun weighs about 40 lbs.

Pre-1968

Exc.	V.G.	Fair
25000	22000	20000

Pre-1986 conversions (side-plate)

Exc.	V.G.	Fair
18000	9000	8000

Pre-1986 dealer samples (Rare)

Exc.	V.G.	Fair
N/A	N/A	N/A

NOTE: For matching numbers add a 10% premium.

Model 1910 Maxim (SPM)

This is a Russian-built water-cooled machine gun chambered for the 7.62x54R cartridge. Early guns use a smooth water jacket while later ones used corrugated type. In 1941 these guns were given a large water-filling cap so that ice and snow could be used in extreme conditions. Barrel length is 28". Fed by a 250-round cloth belt. Rate of fire is approximately 550 rounds per minute. Guns weighs about 52 lbs. and the tripod weighs about 70 lbs.

Pre-1968

Exc.	V.G.	Fair
20000	18000	17000

Pre-1986 conversions (side-plate)

Exc.	V.G.	Fair
13000	12000	11000

Pre-1986 dealer samples

Exc.	V.G.	Fair
N/A	N/A	N/A

NOTE: For matching numbers add a 10% premium.

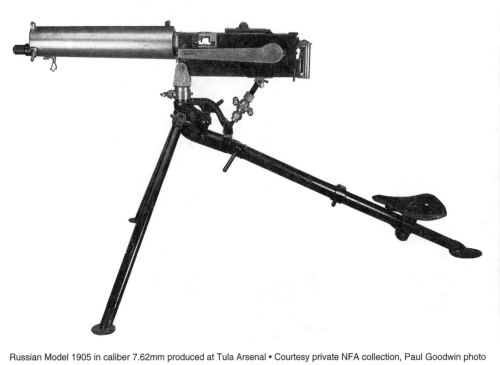

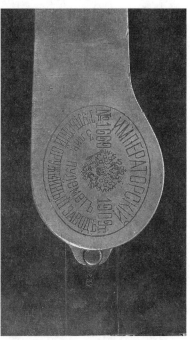

Russian Model 1905 in caliber 7.62mm produced at Tula Arsenal • Courtesy private NFA collection, Paul Goodwin photo

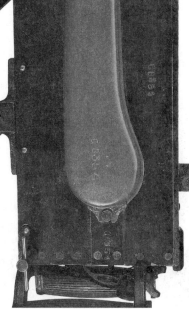

Maxim M1910 • Courtesy private NFA collection, Paul Goodwin photo

Model DP 28 (Degtyarev Pulyemet)

This was the first original Russian-designed light machine gun. Developed in 1926 by Vasily Degtyarev at the Tula Arms Factory this gun was chambered for the 7.62x54R Russian cartridge. It was an air-cooled gun with 24" finned barrel. It was fitted with a rifle-style stock and bipod. It was fed with a 47-round flat drum. Rate of fire is approximately 550 rounds per minute. Weight is about 20 lbs. Designed as a light infantry machine gun. Used by all Warsaw Pact countries.

This was the first in a series of DP variants. The DA is an aircraft mounted machine gun. The DT is a tank mounted weapon with a 60-round drum. Others are the DPM, the DTM, and the RP46.

Pre-1986 conversions (or remanufactured guns)

Exc.	V.G.	Fair
8000	7000	6500

Pre-1986 dealer samples (Rare)

Exc.	V.G.	Fair
N/A	N/A	N/A

Private NFA collection • Gary Gelson photo

Pre-1968

Exc.	V.G.	Fair
12000	10000	9000

DP • Paul Goodwin photo

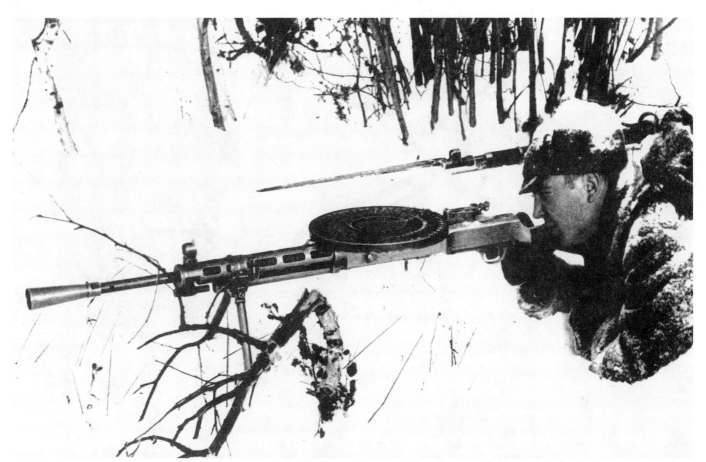

USSR, ca. 1939. Belly down in the snow, a Red Army gunner sights his DP28 light machine gun, an air-cooled weapon fed from a distinctive top-mounted pan magazine • Thomas B. Nelson Collection/Robert Bruce Military Photo Features

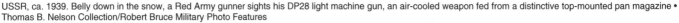

WHAT'S IT LIKE: THE SOVIET DP LMG

It was Mother Russia's Light Machine Gun during The Great Patriotic War. Vasily Alexeevich Degtyarev (1880-1949) was to be eventually responsible for the development of a wide and largely successful range of Russian small arms. Degtyarev commenced development of his LMG in 1923. The Red Army adopted it in 1927 as the DP (*Degtyareva Pekhotniy - Degtyarev Infantry*). At first the Soviet military treated the concept of the LMG with contempt, as they felt it could never replace the sustained-fire potential of the Maxim. By 1930 the DP's outstanding durability had been increased to 100,000 rounds and the parts most prone to breakage (firing pins and extractors) to 30,000 rounds.

Although clumsy by today's standards, the DP is a battle-proven design with the usual Soviet emphasis on simplicity and reliability. It has only 65 components with a design stressing manufacture by unskilled labor.

Chambered for the Russian 7.62x54R service cartridge, overall length of the DP is 50.5 inches. It features a quick-change barrel weighing 4.75 pounds. The gun weighs 26 pounds with its bipod and a magazine loaded with 47 rounds. The DP is air-cooled, gas-operated and fires from the open-bolt position. The firing pin is free to move forward and strike the primer *only* if the locking flaps on each side of the bolt body are completely engaged in their recesses, thus firing out-of-battery is not possible. There is grip safety immediately in back of the trigger guard. It can be difficult to engage. There is no provision for semiautomatic fire and the cyclic rate is about 475 rpm.

The DP's "pancake-type" drum magazine has received more than its share of criticism. It's bulky and can be easily damaged. The bipod is located just to the rear of the gas regulator. This provides adequate group dispersion with the ability to lift the weapon while in the prone position to engage targets on the flanks. Definitely ranks with the other great machine guns of World War II.

Peter Kokalis

Model 1939 DS Gun

A medium machine version of the DP 28. Two rates for fire: 550 rounds per minute and 1100 rounds per minute. Fed by a 250 round cloth belt. Weight is about 26 lbs. Limited production. No known examples in the U.S.

Pre-1968

Exc.	V.G.	Fair
N/A	N/A	N/A

Pre-1986 conversions (or remanufactured guns)

Exc.	V.G.	Fair
N/A	N/A	N/A

Pre-1986 dealer samples (Rare)

Exc.	V.G.	Fair
N/A	N/A	N/A

Model DPM

Introduced in 1944, this is a modification of the DP machine gun by placing the return spring in a tube at the rear of the receiver, sticking out over the butt. A pistol grip was added to facilitate firing. The bipod was attached to the barrel casing. No grip safety but a safety lever in its place. Barrel length is 24" and the drum capacity is 47 rounds. Rate of fire is 550 rounds per minute. Weight is approximately 27 lbs.

Pre-1968

Exc.	V.G.	Fair
15000	11000	10000

Pre-1986 conversions

Exc.	V.G.	Fair
10000	7000	6000

Pre-1986 dealer samples

Exc.	V.G.	Fair
6500	6000	5000

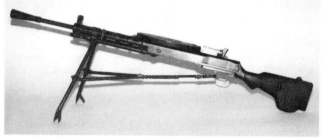

Russain DP with unusual bipod triangulation • Courtesy Robert E. Naess

Model RP-46

This gun is a version of the DP series of machine guns and is a metallic belt or magazine fed 7.62mm caliber. It was designed to be used as a company-size machine gun and is fitted with a 24" quick change heavy barrel. Introduced in 1946. Weight is about 29 lbs. Rate of fire is approximately 650 rounds per minute. The North Koreans use this same gun designated as the Type 64.

NOTE: Many RP-46s were fitted with DP or DPM components by the Soviets. These components are dated prior to 1946. The prices listed below are for RP-46 guns with RP-46 (1946) components.

Pre-1968

Exc.	V.G.	Fair
17000	16000	15000

Pre-1986 conversions (or remanufactured guns)

Exc.	V.G.	Fair
10000	9000	8000

Pre-1986 dealer samples (Rare)

Exc.	V.G.	Fair
N/A	N/A	N/A

Model RPK

Introduced around 1960 this model is the light machine gun equivalent to the AKM assault rifle. It is fitted with a 23" non-quick change barrel. It uses either a 75-round drum magazine or a 40-round box magazine. It is also capable of using the 30-round magazine of the AK and AKM rifles. This model replaced the RPD as the squad automatic weapon (SAW) of the Soviet army.

Pre-1968

Exc.	V.G.	Fair
N/A	N/A	N/A

Pre-1986 conversions

Exc.	V.G.	Fair
8000	7500	7000

Pre-1986 dealer samples (Rare)

Exc.	V.G.	Fair
4500	4000	3500

Model RPKS

This is the Model RPK with a side folding stock. All other dimensions and specifications are the same.

Pre-1968

Exc.	V.G.	Fair
N/A	N/A	N/A

Pre-1986 conversions

Exc.	V.G.	Fair
8000	5500	5000

Pre-1986 dealer samples (Rare)

Exc.	V.G.	Fair
4500	4000	3500

RP-46 • Courtesy Robert E. Naess

Model RPK • Courtesy West Point Museum, Paul Goodwin photo

Model RPK-74

Similar to the RPK but chambered for the 5.45x39mm cartridge. Select fire with 4 positions: safe, semi-auto, full auto, and 3-shot burst. Barrel length is 23.6". Magazine capacity is 45-round box magazine. Also uses a 30-round magazine. Weight is about 12 lbs. and rate of fire is approximately 650 to 700 rounds per minute.

NOTE: There are no known original Soviet transferable examples in this country. Prices below are for conversion using Russian AKM receiver and Russian parts.

Pre-1968

Exc.	V.G.	Fair
N/A	N/A	N/A

Pre-1986 conversions (A.S.D. Firearms)

Exc.	V.G.	Fair
10500	10000	9500

Pre-1986 dealer samples (Rare)

Exc.	V.G.	Fair
N/A	N/A	N/A

Courtesy Steve Hill and Doug McBeth, A.S.D. Firearms

Model PK/PKS (Pulemet Kalashnikova/Stankovy)

This is a general purpose air-cooled machine gun that is chambered for the 7.62mm Soviet cartridge. When this gun is mounted on a bipod it is designated the Model PK; when mounted on a tripod it is called a Model PKS. The operating system of this gun is the same as the AK series except turned

---

WHAT'S IT LIKE: THE SOVIET PKM GPMG

First introduced to the Soviet army in 1961, the PK GPMG (General Purpose Machine Gun) was eventually product-improved and lightened into the PKM (*Pulemet Kalashnikova Modernizirovanniy*) series. The PK was fitted with a heavy fluted barrel, feed cover fabricated from both machined and stamped components and a plain buttplate. The product-improved PKM has a lighter weight (by about a pound and a half), unfluted barrel, a feed cover constructed entirely from sheet metal components and a hinged shoulder rest fitted to the buttplate. Overall length of this machine gun is 46.2 inches. Almost four decades of fighting from arid regions to tropical jungles has demonstrated it to be flawless, with the possible exception of an overly complex feed mechanism required to accommodate the 110-year-old 7.62x54R rimmed cartridge. Weighing less than 20 pounds, the PK's most distinctive characteristic is its skeletonized buttstock, usually fabricated from wood laminate material. Bulgarian variants have reddish brown plastic buttstocks. The PK/PKM series feature chrome-plated chambers and bores, a common characteristic of

all Soviet military small arms. These guns employ the SG43 (Goryunov) non-disintegrating, metallic belts with "pull-out" links (required because of the rimmed case).

The cyclic rate is about 650 rpm and although it has no buffer system of any kind, the lack of perceived recoil when fired from the bipod is nothing short of amazing. If bursts are kept to three or fours shots, the muzzle climb is negligible. The accuracy potential when fired from its lightweight aluminum tripod, which weighs only 16.5 pounds, is more than adequate out to its effective range of approximate 800 meters. The handling characteristics are excellent, with a consequence of exceptionally high hit probability in the hands of experienced operators. This is truly an outstanding machine gun. It is gas-operated with an easily adjustable three-position regulator, has Kalashnikov-type rotary-bolt locking and fires from the open-bolt position. It will continue to serve with distinction on the battlefield well into the foreseeable future.

Peter Kokalis

upside down. It is fitted with a 26" quick change barrel and can be fed by a 100, 200, or 250 round metal belt. The rate of fire is about 700 rounds per minute. Weight is approximately 20 lbs. Introduced in 1963.

The PK, when mounted on tanks, is designated the PKT. The PKM is an improved version of the PK with lighter components. The PKMS is a PKM mounted on a tripod. The PKB is a PKM without butt, bipod, pistol grip, or trigger. Instead, a spade grip with trigger is fitted to the receiver.

Pre-1968

Exc.	V.G.	Fair
N/A	N/A	N/A

DShK 38/46

Vietnam Vets will recall the "Dishka" as a "Fifty-one", which was the way of identifying the Communist's equivalent of our venerable M2HB Browning Machine Gun, called the "Fifty". The DShK round is a bit longer and ballistically more powerful (12.7x109mm) compared to the US M2HB (12.7x99mm). The two basic ground mount configurations that are encountered are the wheeled man-towable low mount for ground contact, and when that tripod is mounted up it has an Anti-Aircraft position. There are variants that are job specific, of course. The 38 model uses different links, and a cylindrical rotating feed mechanism for the belts, while the 38/46 uses a flat shuttle style feed. Loading the "Dishka" is different from most machine guns encountered, in that it has a third "Handle" at the rear of the cradle that the operator pulls to the rear.

Placing a belt in the feed tray, grabbing the grips with one hand and pulling the charging handle to the rear where the bolt locks open doesn't really prepare the operator for what happens when he "puts the hammer down." The DShK 38/46 is one of the loudest machine guns on the battlefield or firing line, and at a civilian machine gun shoot it is a showstopper. A short burst will light up the firing line from the muzzle flash, and if APIT (Armor Piercing Incendiary Tracer) is fired then the target impact area will light up with a brilliant flash on each hit. These are not really the most noticeable characteristics of the "Dishka" however; it is the "thump" of each round firing. This massive pressure can be felt in the belly, and God help the person without hearing protection when this beast is fired.

The complex yet brilliant Anti Aircraft sight is a dual disk with tracking that is mechanically operated by an assistant gunner/spotter, who aligns the gunner's sight with the path of the targeted aircraft, while the spotter calls out distance for lead. This sight is seldom used in ground fire at targets, with the wheeled low mount being the preferred platform. These are rare, and very special machine guns, very seldom brought out to civilian shoots partially because of their high value, but also due to the scarcity of ammunition.

Dan Shea

Pre-1986 conversions (only 1 known)

Exc.	V.G.	Fair
—	43000	—

Pre-1986 dealer samples (Rare)

Exc.	V.G.	Fair
N/A	N/A	N/A

Model DShK M38-M1938/46

Introduced in 1938 this is a heavy air-cooled gas operated machine gun chambered for the 12.7x108mm cartridge. The feed system on the early guns (M1938) uses a rotary mechanism while the later versions (M1939/46) use a conventional lever system. The barrel is 42" and finned with muzzle brake. Fed by a 50-round metal belt either from the right of left side. The rate of fire is about 550 rounds per minute. Weight of the gun is approximately 75 lbs. The mount can weigh 250 lbs. This was the primary heavy machine gun in Korea in 1950-1953, and it was used both as a ground gun and as an anti-aircraft gun. The gun is mounted on a wheeled carriage or a heavy tripod.

Courtesy Steve Hill, Spotted Dog Firearms

Pre-1968 (Very Rare)

Exc.	V.G.	Fair
—	35000	30000

Pre-1986 conversions reweld

Exc.	V.G.	Fair
—	27000	—

Pre-1986 dealer samples (Rare)

Exc.	V.G.	Fair
—	20000	20000

NOTE: Many M1938/46 guns were converted from M1938 models. It is extremely difficult to determine when the conversion was done and by whom. Proceed with caution.

Degtyarev RPD

This is a belt-fed machine gun chambered for the 7.62x39mm cartridge. It has a rate of fire of 700 rounds per minute and is fitted with a 100-round disintegrating belt carried in a drum. It has a 20.5" barrel and weighs about 15.6 lbs. This weapon was at one time the standard squad automatic weapon in the Soviet bloc. It was produced in large numbers and is still in use today in Southeast Asia and Africa.

Pre-1968 (Very Rare)

Exc.	V.G.	Fair
40000	35000	35000

Pre-1986 conversions

Exc.	V.G.	Fair
30000	18000	16000

Pre-1986 dealer samples

Exc.	V.G.	Fair
20000	20000	20000

Russian RPD • Courtesy private NFA collection, Paul Goodwin photo

Goryunov SG43

This model was the standard Soviet machine gun during WWII. Chambered for the 7.62x54R Soviet cartridge, it is fitted with a 28" smooth barrel and is fed with a 250-round metal link belt. Rate of fire is 650 rounds per minute. Its weight is about 30 lbs. Marked on the top of the receiver. In production from 1943 to 1955.

Pre-1968

Exc.	V.G.	Fair
23000	13000	12000

Pre-1986 conversions (reweld)

Exc.	V.G.	Fair
15000	13000	12000

Pre-1986 dealer samples

Exc.	V.G.	Fair
N/A	N/A	N/A

Model SGM

A modified version of the SG43 with fluted barrel and cocking handle on right side of receiver. Dust covers on both feed and ejection ports. Barrel length is 28". Weight is approximately 30 lbs. Fed by 250-round metal link belt.

There are variants of the SG43 which are the SGMT, a tank mounted version with electric solenoid. The SGMB is similar to the SGM but with dust covers over feed and ejection ports.

Pre-1968 (Very Rare)

Exc.	V.G.	Fair
30000	15000	14000

Pre-1986 conversions

Exc.	V.G.	Fair
N/A	N/A	N/A

Pre-1986 dealer samples

Exc.	V.G.	Fair
N/A	N/A	N/A

SG 43 • Courtesy private NFA collection, Paul Goodwin photo

WHAT'S IT LIKE: THE RUSSIAN RPD

The U.S. Army adopted its Squad Automatic Weapon (SAW) in 1985. Ivan Ivanovich had his SAW 35 years earlier. Development of the *Ruchnoi Pulemyot Degtyarev* (Degtyarev Light Machine Gun) commenced during World War 11. Referred to as the RPD, it was fielded in the early 1950s and became the standard SAW for the Soviet army and its satellites. It was the first belt-fed machine gun chambered for the 7.62x39mm intermediate-size cartridge. By definition, an SAW's salient features should be directed to maximizing its potential for employment at the squad level. To that end, it should be capable of sustained fire, which usually mandates belt feeding and a quick-change barrel. Other desirable traits are light weight, an intermediate-size cartridge; compactness; a sturdy bipod; high hit probability; and successful human engineering.

Gas-operated and firing from the open-bolt position, the RPD is a simple, locked-breech design with a minimum number of parts. The locking system similar to that of DP LMG used by the Soviets during WWII. Locking takes place as the slide moves forward and a solid wedge at its rear end drives between the two flapper-shaped locking lugs and forces them into the receiver's locking recesses on the side walls.

There is a three-position gas regulator. In the field, when the gun is hot, adjustment of the regulator almost always requires the use of a mallet. This is not good. However, even under conditions of the most adverse fouling, if one of the higher regulator positions is used, the RPD will operate with a high degree of reliability.

Barrel length of the RPD is 20.15 inches and both chambers and bores are chrome-lined. Barrels are not of the quick-change type and this is a major and legitimate criticism of the weapon. When the recommended rate of fire is exceeded the wooden handguards will burst in flames. The bipod is sturdy, but nonadjustable. The cyclic rate at 900 rpm is too high and this compromises hit probability.

Peter Kokalis

SPAIN

Spanish Military Conflicts, 1870-Present

During the middle of the 19th century Spain was occupied with domestic power struggles. In 1868 a constitutional monarchy was established, followed by a republic from 1873 to 1874. Spain lost its last colony, Cuba, with its defeat by the United States in the Spanish-American War of 1898. In 1928 a military dictatorship was established and a second republic was created. Spanish separatists weakened the republic with the result that a Communist government came to power. This helped to create an internal struggle that led to the Spanish Civil War, 1936 to 1939. During this conflict the Germans supported Franco with men and weapons. During World War II Spain sided with the Axis powers, but did not enter the war. Franco died in 1975. Spain joined the European Union in 1986. Spain is also a member of NATO.

HANDGUNS

NOTE: Officers in the Spanish military provided their own sidearms during the later half of the 19th century and into the early 20th century. The Spanish government provided guidelines for purchase and many Spanish officers purchased Smith & Wesson and Merwin & Hulbert revolvers. In 1884 the Spanish government directed its military officers corps to purchase the Smith & Wesson .44 Double Action Top Break built by Orbea y Compania of Eibar, Spain. It was designated the Model 1884. There were a number of Spanish gun makers building revolvers during the late 19th century, and many of these handguns were used by the Spanish military but were not marked as such. During WWI Spain provided a number of handguns to Britian, France, and other countries due to the shortage of military sidearms in those countries. We only touch on the more significant models.

It is also important to note that various Spanish manufacturers sold almost one million copies of the FN/Browning Model 1903 to the French during World War I.

Bibliographical Note: For additional historical information, technical data, and photos see Leonardo Antaris, *Astra Automatic Pistols*, Colorado, 1998.

CAMPO GIRO

Model 1910
Similar to the above, in 9mm Largo. Tested, but not adopted, by the Spanish army.

Exc.	V.G.	Good	Fair	Poor
1200	800	650	500	450

Model 1913
An improved version of the above.

Model 1913 • Courtesy James Rankin

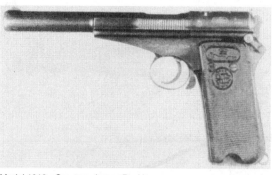

Model 1913 • Courtesy James Rankin

Exc.	V.G.	Good	Fair	Poor
950	750	650	500	450

Model 1913/16
An improved version of the above.

Courtesy James Rankin

Courtesy James Rankin

Exc.	V.G.	Good	Fair	Poor
550	450	375	300	200

ASTRA-UNCETA SA

During World War II the German army and air force purchased a number of Astra 400 and 600 pistols. They were of excellent quality.

Astra 400 or Model 1921
A 9x23 Bergman caliber semiautomatic pistol with a 6" barrel. Blued with black plastic grips. This model was adopted for use

by the Spanish army. Approximately 106,000 were made prior to 1946. Recent importation has depressed the price of these guns.

NOTE: Any with Nazi proofmarks are worth a 100 percent premium, but caution is advised because there are no known examples, even though about 6,000 pistols were delivered to the German army in 1941.

Courtesy Orvel Reichert

Exc.	V.G.	Good	Fair	Poor
350	275	150	75	40

Astra 400 Copies (Ascaso, R.E)

Top to bottom: Ascaso left side, R.E. right side, close-up of Ascaso barrel marking • Courtesy Orvel Reichert

During the Spanish Civil War, the Republican forces were unable to procure enough handguns from established weapons factories as these were in Nationalists' hands. The Republicans built their own factories to produce copies of the Spanish army's Model 1921 Astra 400. These are exact copies except for the markings.

Exc.	V.G.	Good	Fair	Poor
400	325	200	100	75

Astra 300

As above, in 7.65mm or 9mm short. A few used during World War II by German forces may bear Waffenamt marks. Between 1941 and 1944 some 63,000 were produced in 9mm Kurz, and about 22,000 were produced in 7.65mm. Approximately 171,000 were manufactured prior to 1947.

Nazi Proofed—Add 25%.

Exc.	V.G.	Good	Fair	Poor
350	300	200	150	100

Astra 600

Similar to the Model 400, but in 9mm Parabellum. In 1943 and 1944 approximately 10,500 were manufactured. Some of these World War II guns will often have Nazi proof stamp and bring a premium. An additional 49,000 were made in 1946 and commercially sold.

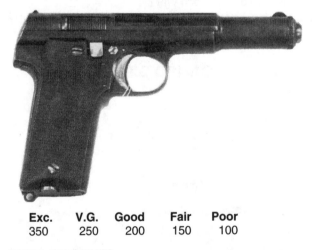

Exc.	V.G.	Good	Fair	Poor
350	250	200	150	100

ASTRA 900 SERIES

The Astra 900 series of pistols were copied from the Mauser Model 1896, but while similar in appearance to the Mauser, the Astra 900 series is mechanically quite different. Many consider the Astra 900 series as good as, or better than, its German equilvent.

NOTE: The prices listed below include original Astra matching wooden stock/holster numbered to the pistol. For pistols with detachable magazines numbered to the gun add a small premium. For non-matching stock/holster deduct $300 to $500. For Chinese stock/holsters deduct $500. Original Astra stocks are difficult to locate.

Astra Model 900

Introduced in 1928 this is similar in appearance to the Mauser C96 pistol. Fitted with a 5.5" barrel chambered for the 7.63mm cartridge and fitted with a ring hammer. Ten-round box magazine with charger loading. Weight is about 40 oz. Production discontinued in 1955. Between 1928 and 1944 almost 21,000 were manufactured. Some of these pistols (about 1,000) were purchased by the German military in France in 1943. No military acceptance marks but can be identified by serial number (see Still, *Axis Pistols*). Serial numbers 32,788 through 33,774 were used by the German army during WWII. These examples will bring a 50% premium.

NOTE: A large number of Astras exported to China are frequently found in fair to poor condition. Some of these are marked with Chinese characters. During the late 1950s a number of Chinese Astras were brought into the U.S. These pistols appear to be in much better condition.

Photo courtesy Tom Nelson, *The World's Machine Pistol and Submachine Guns, Vol. IIA*, Ironside International Publishers

Exc.	V.G.	Good	Fair	Poor
2250	1750	1000	600	300

Astra Model 901

Introduced in 1928, this is similar to the Model 900 (5.5" barrel) but with select fire capability. Fixed 10-round magazine. Many of these pistols were sold to China in the 1930s. Rate of fire is about 900 rounds per minute. Weight is about 44 oz. Only about 1,600 of these pistols were produced. Exceedingly rare. Only a tiny number of these pistols are transferable, perhaps fewer than five.

Photo courtesy Tom Nelson, *The World's Machine Pistol and Submachine Guns, Vol. IIA*, Ironside International Publishers

Pre-1968

Exc.	V.G.	Fair
7500	7000	6500

Pre-1986 conversions

Exc.	V.G.	Fair
N/A	N/A	N/A

Pre-1986 dealer samples

Exc.	V.G.	Fair
N/A	N/A	N/A

Astra Model 902

Same as above but with 7" barrel. Some went to China with various military units in the 1930s, but most remained in Spain. Weight is approximately 53 oz. About 7,000 of these pistols were built. Very rare in this country for transferable examples. Perhaps fewer than 10 known.

Photo courtesy Tom Nelson, *The World's Machine Pistol and Submachine Guns, Vol. IIA*, Ironside International Publishers

Pre-1968

Exc.	V.G.	Fair
7500	7000	6500

Pre-1986 conversions

Exc.	V.G.	Fair
N/A	N/A	N/A

Pre-1986 dealer samples

Exc.	V.G.	Fair
N/A	N/A	N/A

Astra 903/903E

This is a detachable 10- or 20-round magazine pistol developed in 1932. Fitted with a 6.25" barrel. Select fire. Some of these pistols were sold to China and others went to the German army in France in 1941 and 1942. No German acceptance proofs, but can be identified by serial number (see Still). Some 3,000 of this model were produced. It is estimated that fewer than 15 of these pistols are transferable in the U.S.

Photo courtesy Tom Nelson, *The World's Machine Pistol and Submachine Guns, Vol. IIA*, Ironside International Publishers

Pre-1968

Exc.	V.G.	Fair
8000	7500	7000

Pre-1986 conversions

Exc.	V.G.	Fair
N/A	N/A	N/A

Pre-1986 dealer samples

Exc.	V.G.	Fair
4000	3500	3000

Astra Model 904 (Model F)

Similar to the other 900 series machine pistols but chambered for the 9mm Largo cartridge and fitted with a rate reducer that reduces the rate of fire from 900 rounds per minute to approximately 350 rounds per minute. Magazine is 10- or 20-round detachable design. The Model 904 was first produced in 1933 and was the prototype of the Model F. Only 9 Model 904s were built. About 1,100 Model F pistols were issued, most of which went to the Spanish Guardia Civil. Perhaps fewer than 10 of these pistols are known to exist on a transferable basis in the U.S.

Pre-1968

Exc.	V.G.	Fair
8500	8000	7500

Astra Model F • Courtesy Chuck Karwan

Pre-1986 conversions

Exc.	V.G.	Fair
N/A	N/A	N/A

Pre-1986 dealer samples

Exc.	V.G.	Fair
4500	4000	3500

Astra A-80

A .38 Super, 9mm, or .45 caliber double action semiautomatic pistol with a 3.75" barrel and either a 9- or 15-shot magazine depending upon the caliber. Blued or chrome-plated with plastic grips. Introduced in 1982.

NIB	Exc.	V.G.	Good	Fair	Poor
450	350	300	250	200	100

Astra A-90

As above, in 9mm or .45 caliber only. Introduced in 1986.

NIB	Exc.	V.G.	Good	Fair	Poor
400	350	300	250	200	100

ROYAL

Royal machine pistols were manufactured by Beistegui Hermanos in Eibar, Spain. These were the first machine pistols made in Spain, starting in 1927. These pistols were used extensively by the Chinese during their civil wars in the 1930s and against the Japanese during World War II.

Royal MM31 (1st Model)

First produced in 1927. Chambered for the 7.63mm cartridge. The pistol was capable of selective fire and semiautomatic fire, as well as full automatic fire. Magazine capacity was 10- or 20-rounds in a fixed box magazine. Barrel lengths were 5.5" with some made in 6.3" and 7". Rear tangent sight. Rate of fire was

---

THE ASTRA MODEL F MACHINE PISTOL

The Astra Model F had a total production of only about 1100 pieces. However the Astra Model F holds a number of distinctions that make it, in my eyes, the premier machine pistol of all time. The Model F looks externally much like that most prolific of machine pistols, the Mauser Schnellfeuer "Broomhandle." Like that pistol, it has 10- or 20-round detachable magazines and a wooden holster that can serve as a detachable shoulder stock. Virtually all "Broomhandle" style machine pistols, whether made by Mauser in Germany, one of the Spanish manufacturers, or a Chinese arsenal, are chambered for the 7.63mm Mauser pistol cartridge. The sole significant exception is the Astra Model F, which is chambered for the 9mm Largo cartridge — a more versatile and generally more effective cartridge. In quality of construction the Astra Model F is second to none. It is quite literally made like a Swiss watch with jeweled internal parts of impeccable fit and finish both internally and externally. Virtually all machine pistols have one particular problem: excessively high rate of fire due to their light operating parts. Again, the sole significant exception is the Astra Model F, which has an incredibly clever rate of fire reduction mechanism under its grip. This mechanism works on a cleverly designed and beautifully made ratchet system that puts a delay in the fall of the hammer as it ticks its way through the ratchet teeth between shots. The result is a slow and controllable rate of fire that makes the Model F the easiest machine pistol to shoot well on full automatic that there is. Indeed, it is entirely possible to shoot the Astra Model F on full auto one handed with excellent control. Thus the Astra Model F garners the highest rating in quality of manufacture, usefulness of chambering, cleverness and excellence of design, and shooting performance, making it the best of the bunch in my eyes.

Chuck Karwan

about 850 rounds per minute. Production stopped on the first model in 1929 with approximately 23,000 pistols built. Extremely rare.

Pre-1968

Exc.	V.G.	Fair
20000	20000	20000

Pre-1986 conversions

Exc.	V.G.	Fair
N/A	N/A	N/A

Pre-1986 dealer samples

Exc.	V.G.	Fair
N/A	N/A	N/A

Royal MM31 (2nd Model)

This model has three variations. All were chambered for the 7.63mm cartridge and all were select fire models. All had a cycle rate of fire of about 850 rounds per minute. Early versions had either a 5.5" or 7" barrel. The last version was fitted with a 5.5" barrel only. The 1st variation had a fixed 10-round magazine while the 2nd variation had a 20-round fixed magazine. The 3rd version had a detachable 10-, 20-, or 30-round magazine. All variations were marked "MM31" or "ROYAL." Very rare.

Photo courtesy Tom Nelson, *The World's Machine Pistol and Submachine Guns, Vol. IIA*, Ironside International Publishers

Pre-1968

Exc.	V.G.	Fair
7500	6500	6000

Pre-1986 conversions

Exc.	V.G.	Fair
N/A	N/A	N/A

Pre-1986 dealer samples

Exc.	V.G.	Fair
N/A	N/A	N/A

Super Azul

This was the 4th variation of the MM31, introduced in 1931, often referred to as the Super Azul or New Model. Chambered for the 7.63mm cartridge, it was also offered in 9mm Bergmann and .38 Colt Super Automatic. Select fire. Fitted with a 5.5" barrel and a detachable magazine with a capacity of 10-, 20-, or 30-rounds. Magazine will interchange with German Mauser Schnellfeuer pistol. Rate of fire of about 850 rounds per minute. Production ceased in 1936 with the outbreak of the Spanish Civil War.

Pre-1968

Exc.	V.G.	Fair
7500	7000	6500

Pre-1986 conversions

Exc.	V.G.	Fair
N/A	N/A	N/A

Pre-1986 dealer samples

Exc.	V.G.	Fair
N/A	N/A	N/A

Royal MM34

Chambered for the 7.63mm cartridge and fitted with a 7" barrel. Fixed magazine capacity of 10 or 20 rounds. Fitted with a rate reducer in the grip. Select fire with full auto fire at various adjustable rates. Marked "MM34" on right side of frame. Extremely rare.

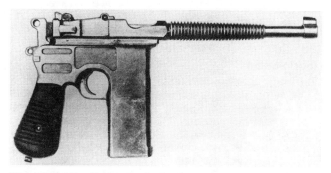

Photo courtesy Tom Nelson, *The World's Machine Pistol and Submachine Guns, Vol. IIA*, Ironside International Publishers

Pre-1968

Exc.	V.G.	Fair
7500	7000	6500

Pre-1986 conversions

Exc.	V.G.	Fair
N/A	N/A	N/A

Pre-1986 dealer samples

Exc.	V.G.	Fair
N/A	N/A	N/A

LLAMA

Model IX

Chambered for the 7.65mm Para, 9mm Largo, or .45 ACP, this model has a locked breech with no grip safety. Built from 1936 to 1954.

Exc.	V.G.	Good	Fair	Poor
325	275	200	150	100

Model IX-A

This version of the Model IX is fitted with a grip safety. Current production models are chambered for the .45 ACP only. Weighs about 30 oz. with 5" barrel.

Exc.	V.G.	Good	Fair	Poor
275	225	150	125	100

ECHEVERRIA, STAR-BONIFACIO SA

NOTE: These pistols are stamped with a letter code to denote year built: For 1938 the letter "N," up to 1945 the letter "P."

BIBLIOGRAPHICAL NOTE: For photos, production data, and in-depth history, see *Star Firearms* by Leonardo M. Antaris.

Model 1914

Similar to the Model 1908, with a 5" barrel and larger grips that have the Star name molded into them. This model was the first to have the six-pointed star surrounded by rays of light (that became the Star trademark) stamped on its slide.

The French Army purchased approximately 20,000 Model 1914s for use during World War I. These pistols had coarse checkering and no name inset into the grips. Later pistols were fitted with 5.5" barrels. Many French army magazines were stamped with "BE" in a circle. All French military pistols were finished with a highly dark blue finish. Small parts were fire blue.

Exc.	V.G.	Good	Fair	Poor
300	250	200	150	100

Model CO

First produced in 1929 and later dropped from production during the Spanish Civil War, this model was produced again in 1941. About 600 of these pistols were sold to the German military during 1941 and 1942. Chambered for the 6.35mm cartridge and fitted with a 3.3" barrel. This model stayed in production until 1956. Prices are for military examples.

Exc.	V.G.	Good	Fair	Poor
600	500	400	300	150

Modelo Militar

Represents the first pistol Star produced that was not a Mannlicher-design copy. This model was copied from the Colt 1911. It was chambered initially for the 9mm Largo in hopes of securing a military contract. When this contract was awarded to Astra, Star chambered the Model 1919 for the .38 Super and the .45 ACP, and put it on the commercial market. This model is like the Colt 1911—it has a Browning-type swinging link and the same type of lock up. However there is no grip safety, and the thumb safety functions differently. This model was produced until 1924.

Exc.	V.G.	Good	Fair	Poor
300	250	200	175	125

Star Model A

A modification of the Model 1919, chambered for the 7.63 Mauser, 9mm Largo, and 9mm Luger (scarce), as well as the rarely seen 9mm Steyr. Barrel length is 5". The slide is similar in appearance to the 1911 Colt, and the spur hammer has a small hole in it. Early models had no grip safety, but later production added this feature. Some models are slotted for addition of a shoulder stock. This model was popular with the Spanish Civil Guard as well as the Spanish air force (stamped with air force logo).

Exc.	V.G.	Good	Fair	Poor
400	300	200	150	100

Star Model A Super

An improved version of the Model A with a new takedown lever on the right side of the frame and a loaded chamber indicator.

Exc.	V.G.	Good	Fair	Poor
425	325	225	175	125

Star Model M (MD)

A select fire version of the Model A. Most were chambered for 9x23mm cartridge while some were chambered for the .45 ACP cartridge. This pistol was built during the 1930s. Some examples were sold to Nicaragua and Argentina. Rate of fire is about 800 rounds per minute. The selector switch is located on the right side of the slide. Several thousand were produced.

Star Model M • Courtesy Chuck Karwan

Pre-1968

Exc.	V.G.	Fair
7500	7000	6500

Pre-1986 conversions

Exc.	V.G.	Fair
N/A	N/A	N/A

Pre-1986 dealer samples

Exc.	V.G.	Fair
4000	3500	3000

Star Model B

Similar to the Model A. It is chambered for 9mm Parabellum and has a spur hammer with no hole. This model was introduced in 1928. Approximately 20,000 pistols were sold to the German army and about 6,000 to the German navy. These military pistols are stamped with German military acceptance stamps. About 15,000 Model Bs were sold to Bulgaria during 1943 and 1944. Also used by the German Police and the Republic of South Africa.

Courtesy Orvel Reichert

Exc.	V.G.	Good	Fair	Poor
350	250	200	175	125

Star Model B Super

Introduced in 1946, this model features a new takedown system with the lever on the right side of the frame. A loaded chamber indicator was also added. Production ended in 1983. Adopted by the Spanish army in 1946.

Exc.	V.G.	Good	Fair	Poor
400	325	250	200	100

Star Model 1941 S

This model was purchased by the Spanish air force and is stamped on the right side of the frame with the air force seal. Most of these air force pistols were produced between 1945 and 1947, with a total production of about 9,100 pistols. A large number of Model S pistols were also sold to police agencies in Spain and elsewhere. The balance of production was sold commercially. Prices listed below are for air force examples. Deduct 50% for commercial pistols.

Courtesy Richard M. Kumor Sr.

Exc.	V.G.	Good	Fair	Poor
600	400	300	200	100

Star Model SI

Chambered for the 7.65mm cartridge, this pistol was ordered by the Portuguese navy beginning in 1946. Between 1946 and 1948 a total of about 4,900 pistols were ordered for the Portuguese. Also, about 300 pistols were sold to the Chilean navy in 1964. A number of these pistols were also sold to police agencies in Spain and Europe. The balance of the Model SI production was commercial.

Exc.	V.G.	Good	Fair	Poor
500	375	300	200	100

Star Model BM

A steel-framed 9mm that is styled after the Colt 1911. It has an 8-shot magazine and a 4" barrel. It is available either blued or chrome-plated.

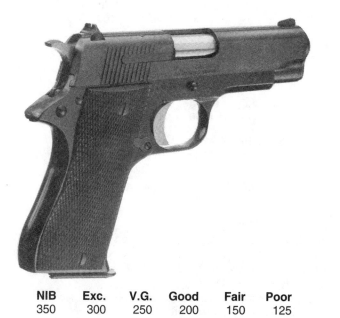

NIB	Exc.	V.G.	Good	Fair	Poor
350	300	250	200	150	125

Star Model 28

The first of Star's high-capacity 9s. It is a double action semi-automatic chambered for the 9mm Parabellum cartridge. It has a 4.25" barrel and a steel frame. The magazine holds 15 shots. The construction of this pistol was totally modular, and it has no screws at all in its design. It is blued with checkered synthetic grips and was manufactured from 1981 to 1983. Only some 16,000 pistols were built.

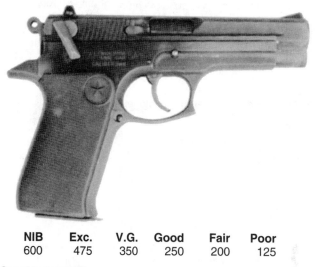

NIB	Exc.	V.G.	Good	Fair	Poor
600	475	350	250	200	125

Star Model 30M

An improved version of the Model 28 that is quite similar in appearance. It was introduced in 1982 and built until 1989. About 100,000 were manufactured.

NIB	Exc.	V.G.	Good	Fair	Poor
450	350	300	250	200	125

Star Model 30/PK

Similar to the Models 28 and 30M, with a lightweight alloy frame.

NIB	Exc.	V.G.	Good	Fair	Poor
450	350	300	250	200	125

SUBMACHINE GUNS

The Spanish made a number of submachine guns, both domestic designs and copies of foreign guns. The Spanish MP28 II was a copy of the Bergmann MP28 II in 9mm Bergmann caliber. The Model 1941/44 was a copy of the German Erma. Star made a number of submachine guns in the 1930s that were used on a limited basis in the Spanish Civil War. These were the S135, the RU35, and the TN35, all chambered for the 9x23 Largo cartridge. The first two of these models had adjustable rates of fire and the last, the TN35, had a rate of fire of about

700 rounds per minute. However, these guns were never standard issue in the Spanish army.

Star Z-45

This design is based on the German MP40 but with the cocking handle on the left side. It was fitted with an 8" barrel that was easily removable and covered by a perforated barrel jacket. The gun has a two-stage trigger: pull slightly for single shots and pull more for full automatic fire. Magazine is a 30-round box type. Gun has a rate of fire of about 450 rounds per minute. Weight is approximately 8.5 lbs. Introduced into service in 1944. This weapon is supplied with either a fixed wood stock or folding metal one. The Z-45 was the standard submachine gun of the Spanish army and was sold to Chile, Cuba, Portugal, and Saudi Arabia.

Photo courtesy Tom Nelson, *The World's Machine Pistol and Submachine Guns, Vol. IIA*, Ironside International Publishers.

Pre-1968

Exc.	V.G.	Fair
9500	8500	8000

Pre-1986 conversions

Exc.	V.G.	Fair
N/A	N/A	N/A

Pre-1986 dealer samples

Exc.	V.G.	Fair
N/A	N/A	N/A

Star Z-62

This select-fire submachine gun was introduced in 1960 and is chambered for the 9mm Largo or 9mm Parabellum cartridge. It has an 8" barrel with perforated barrel jacket. Folding metal buttstock. The box magazine has a 20-, 30-, or 40-round capacity. Rate of fire is about 550 rounds per minute. Weight is approximately 6.5 lbs. This gun was issued both to the Spanish army and the *Guardia Civil*. Marked "STAR EIBAR ESPANA MODEL Z-62" with the serial number on the left side of the magazine housing. Produced until about 1970.

Pre-1968

Exc.	V.G.	Fair
8500	7500	7000

Pre-1986 conversions

Exc.	V.G.	Fair
N/A	N/A	N/A

Pre-1986 dealer samples

Exc.	V.G.	Fair
3500	3000	2500

Star Z-70

Introduced into the Spanish army in 1971, this select-fire submachine gun is chambered for the 9x19mm cartridge, and is considered an improved version of the Z-62 with new trigger mechanism. It is fitted with an 8" barrel and has a rate of fire of 550 rounds per minute. Choice of 20-, 30-, or 40-round magazines. Folding metal stock. Weight is about 6.3 lbs. Built by Star Banifacio Echeverria in Eibar, Spain. No longer in production. Used mainly by the Spanish armed forces.

Photo courtesy private NFA collection

Pre-1968

Exc.	V.G.	Fair
N/A	N/A	N/A

Pre-1986 conversions

Exc.	V.G.	Fair
N/A	N/A	N/A

Pre-1986 dealer samples

Exc.	V.G.	Fair
3500	2500	2000

RIFLES

PEABODY

Spanish Rifle (1869)

Chambered for the .43 Spanish centerfire cartridge and fitted with a 33" barrel. Full stock with two barrel bands. Blued barrel and case hardened furniture. About 10,000 rifles were produced for the Spanish government.

Exc.	V.G.	Good	Fair	Poor
—	1750	1250	600	200

REMINGTON ROLLING BLOCK

Model 1870 Rifle

This is the standard Remington rolling block single-shot rifle with a 35" barrel. Chambered for the 11.15x57R Spanish Remington cartridge. Full stocked with three barrel bands. Weight is about 9.25 lbs. Upper tang marked Remington.

Exc.	V.G.	Good	Fair	Poor
—	—	750	400	100

Model 1870 Carbine

Same as the rifle but with 27" barrel and full stock with two barrel bands. Weight is about 8.75 lbs. Made at Oviedo Armoury from 1871 to about 1889.

Exc.	V.G.	Good	Fair	Poor
—	—	1150	600	200

Model 1870 Short Rifle

Similar to the Model 1870 pattern but with 32" barrel. Weight is about 8.75 lbs. Manufactured at Oviedo.

Exc.	V.G.	Good	Fair	Poor
—	—	900	500	150

Model 1871 Infantry Rifle

Fitted with a 37" barrel and chambered for the 11.15x57R Spanish Remington cartridge. Full stock with three barrel bands. Bayonet fittings. Weight is about 9 lbs. Built at Oviedo and Placencia armories.

Exc.	V.G.	Good	Fair	Poor
—	—	750	400	100

Model 1871 Short Rifle

As above but with 28" barrel with full stock and two barrel bands. Weight is about 8.75 lbs. Produced at Placencia Armoury.

Exc.	V.G.	Good	Fair	Poor
—	—	900	500	150

Model 1871 Cavalry Carbine

As above but with 23" barrel and half stock with sling swivels and sling bar on left side of stock. Weight is about 7.25 lbs.

Exc.	V.G.	Good	Fair	Poor
—	—	1150	600	200

Model 1871 Artillery Carbine

As above but full stocked with two barrel bands and bayonet fitting.

Exc.	V.G.	Good	Fair	Poor
—	—	1150	600	200

Model 1889 Dragoon Carbine

This model was a stort version of the Model 1871 rifle with full stock, two barrel bands, and no bayonet fittings. Barrel length is 31.5". Weight is about 8.75 lbs.

Exc.	V.G.	Good	Fair	Poor
—	—	1150	600	200

Mauser

M1891 Rifle

Based on the Turkish Model 1890 rifle with full stock and no handguard. Chambered for 7.65x53mm cartridge with barrel length of 29". Exposed 5-round box magazine. Weight is about 9 lbs.

Exc.	V.G.	Good	Fair	Poor
300	225	180	130	90

M1892 Rifle

Similar to the Model 1891 but with internal charger loaded magazine, improved extractor, and removable magazine floor plate. Chambered for 7x57mm cartridge. Half-length handguard. Barrel length is 29". Weight is about 9 lbs.

Exc.	V.G.	Good	Fair	Poor
350	260	190	130	90

M1892 Carbine

Same action as the Model 1891 rifle but full stock with nose cap, bent bolt handle, sling bar, and saddle ring. Chambered for 7x57mm cartridge. Barrel length is 17.5". Weight is about 7.5 lbs. Built by Loewe.

Exc.	V.G.	Good	Fair	Poor
300	225	180	120	80

M1893 Rifle

Built by Loewe and Oviedo this model is considered to be the "Spanish Mauser." Chambered for the 7x57mm cartridge and fitted with a 29" barrel. Buttstock has straight grip. A charger loading magazine is concealed in the buttstock. The receiver has a charger loading guide in the receiver bridge. Weight is about 8.5 lbs.

Exc.	V.G.	Good	Fair	Poor
175	140	100	80	40

M1893 Short Rifle

This is a short version of the Model 1893 rifle with a 21.5" barrel. Fitted with bent bolt and half-length handguard. Weight is about 8 lbs.

Exc.	V.G.	Good	Fair	Poor
275	210	180	110	50

M1895 Carbine

As above but with 17.5" barrel. Weight is about 7 lbs.

Exc.	V.G.	Good	Fair	Poor
300	250	185	110	80

M/G 98 Modified Rifle

Identical to the German G 98 but chambered for the 7x57mm cartridge and fitted with a tangent rear sight. Spanish markings on receiver ring.

Exc.	V.G.	Good	Fair	Poor
275	225	175	120	90

M1916 Short Rifle

This model was built by Fabrica de Armas in Oviedo, Spain, from 1916 to 1951. A shortened version of the Model 1893 rifle with 21.75" barrel and chambered for the 7x57mm cartridge. Rear sight graduated to 2000 meters. Almost full stock with upper handguard. Sight protectors on front sight. Spanish crest on receiver ring. Weight is about 8 lbs.

NOTE: Many of these rifles were converted to the 7.62mm NATO cartridge. Prices will remain about the same for these converted examples.

Exc.	V.G.	Good	Fair	Poor
200	150	100	75	40

M1916 Carbine

Produced at the Oviedo arsenal. Fitted with a 17" barrel chambered for the 7x57mm cartridge. Straight grip stock with 3/4-length stock and upper handguard. No bayonet fittings. Bent bolt handle. Weight is about 6.75 lbs.

Exc.	V.G.	Good	Fair	Poor
225	160	110	85	50

M1933 Standard Model Short Rifle

This rifle is chambered for the 7x57mm cartridge and fitted with a 22" barrel. Straight grip stock with upper handguard. Tangent leaf rear sight graduated to 2000 meters. Marked with Mauser banner over the date of manufacture on receiver. Weight is about 8.2 lbs.

Exc.	V.G.	Good	Fair	Poor
325	280	220	180	110

M1943 Short Rifle

This model replaced the Model 1916 Short Rifle. Chambered for the 7.92x57mm cartridge and fitted with a 23.6" barrel. Stock is 3/4-length with pistol grip. Straight bolt handle. Tangent leaf rear sight graduated to 2000 meters. Weight is about 8.5 lbs. Marked with Spanish crest on receiver ring.

Spanish Mauser Model 1893 • Paul Goodwin photo

Model 1943 Short Rifle • Courtesy Cherry's Fine Guns

FR 7 • Private collection, Paul Goodwin photo

Exc.	V.G.	Good	Fair	Poor
250	190	140	90	40

NOTE: This model was made for the Spanish army and air force. The army model has a bayonet lug while the air force model does not.

FR 7 Special Purpose Rifle (Training/Reserve)

An arsenal-converted (1950s) Model 1916 short rifle with 18.5" CETME barrel. Upper wooden handguard. Chambered for the .308 (7.62x51) Winchester cartridge. Weight is about 7.5 lbs.

Exc.	V.G.	Good	Fair	Poor
200	140	100	70	50

FR 8 Special Purpose Rifle (Training/Reserve)

Arsenal-converted Model 43 in the same configuration as the FR 7.

Exc.	V.G.	Good	Fair	Poor
200	140	100	70	50

CETME

CETME Autoloading Rifle (Sport)

A .308 caliber semiautomatic rifle with a fluted chamber, a 17.74" barrel, an aperture rear sight, and a 20-round detachable magazine. Black with a military-style wood stock. It is identical in appearance to the H&K 91 assault rifle.

NIB	Exc.	V.G.	Good	Fair	Poor
2500	2000	1500	900	—	—

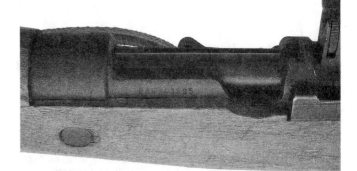

FR 8 • Private collection, Paul Goodwin photo

Model 58

Introduced in 1958 and manufactured by Centro de Estudios de Materials Especiales (CETME), this Spanish-made rifle is similar to the HK G3 rifle and is chambered for the 7.62x51mm cartridge. This is a select-fire weapon with a rate of fire of about 600 rounds per minute. The bipod, when retracted, acts as a metal forend. Barrel length is 17". Tangent rear sight. Weight is approximately 11 lbs.

CETME Model 58 • Courtesy Thomas Nelson, *The World's Assault Rifles*

Pre-1968

Exc.	V.G.	Fair
6000	5000	4500

Pre-1986 conversions

Exc.	V.G.	Fair
N/A	N/A	N/A

Pre-1986 dealer samples

Exc.	V.G.	Fair
3000	2500	2000

Santa Barbara CETME Model L

First produced in 1984, this 5.56x45mm select fire rifle was adopted by the Spanish army. It is fitted with a 15.6" barrel and 30-round magazine. It also has a fixed stock. Rate of fire is 650 rounds per minute. Weight is about 7.5 lbs. A short barrel (12.5") carbine version is known as the Model LC. Still in service.

Pre-1968

Exc.	V.G.	Fair
N/A	N/A	N/A

Pre-1986 conversions

Exc.	V.G.	Fair
N/A	N/A	N/A

Pre-1986 dealer samples

Exc.	V.G.	Fair
5000	5000	5000

MACHINE GUNS

In 1907, the Spanish used the 7mm Hotchkiss machine gun and later the Model 1914, also in 7mm. The Spanish armed forces also adopted the Madsen Model 1902 and Model 1922 guns. During the Spanish Civil War, large numbers of foreign machine guns were sent to Spain, including the Soviet Maxim Tokarev, Soviet DP guns, Czech VZ26, VZ30, and ZB53 as well as other German and Italian machine guns. At the present time the Spanish army uses the MG 42/59 machine gun.

FAO Model 59

This is a Spanish-built gun designed on the Czech ZB26. It is chambered for the 7.62mm cartridge and is belt-fed with 50-round metallic links in a drum. Full automatic fire only. Barrel length is 22" with attached bipod. Gun weighs about 20 lbs. Rate of fire is approximately 650 rounds per minute.

Pre-1968

Exc.	V.G.	Fair
16500	15500	15000

Pre-1986 conversions

Exc.	V.G.	Fair
14000	13000	11000

Pre-1986 dealer samples

Exc.	V.G.	Fair
N/A	N/A	N/A

ALFA Model 1944

This gun was designed for use as a heavy machine gun. Chambered for the 7.92x57 Mauser cartridge and fitted with a 29.5" barrel. Select fire. Fed by a 100-round metallic link belt loaded in a drum. Rate of fire is about 800 rounds per minute. Weight is approximately 28 lbs.

NOTE: The Model 44 was also supplied to Egypt with aluminum cooling fins extending the length of the barrel and large slots in the gas cylinder.

Pre-1968 (Very Rare)

Exc.	V.G.	Fair
25000	22500	20000

Pre-1986 conversions

Exc.	V.G.	Fair
15000	14000	12000

Pre-1986 dealer samples (10 known)

Exc.	V.G.	Fair
12000	11000	10000

ALFA Model 55

Introduced in 1955, this is an updated version of the Model 44 chambered for the 7.62mm cartridge and fitted with a shorter 24" ribbed barrel with a lighter tripod. Rate of fire is about 800 rounds per minute. Weight is approximately 28 lbs.

Pre-1968

Exc.	V.G.	Fair
12500	11000	9500

ALFA MODEL 1944

The far end of the Hotchkiss development includes the Spanish ALFA Oveida series of machine guns. Most are referred to as the 1944 ALFA, and there are several in the United States. I have seen two Pre-1986 Dealer Sample guns, and one Post-1986 Dealer Sample.

The ALFA uses a non disintegrating metallic link belt that sits on a spool inside of a drum mounted on the tripod. The belt is specific to the ALFA, in 8mm Mauser, and the drum will easily pass for an MG08/15 Maxim drum.

In the mid 1980s, several importers, including Sarco, brought in large quantities of ALFA tripods. These are a very compact, but heavy, tripod. They fold up into a very small package. Many have Arabic writing on them as well, from the North African contracts. These tripods were converted over to many other machine guns in the US.

ALFA machine guns are pleasant to shoot because of the tripod mount and the way that the spade grips are set in line. Recoil is dampened in the tripod, and the medium cyclic rate is smooth for the system. It is surprising that the Spanish ALFA series was not more popular.

Dan Shea

CETME Ameli • Courtesy Chuck Karwan

Pre-1986 conversions

Exc.	V.G.	Fair
8000	7000	6000

Pre-1986 dealer samples

Exc.	V.G.	Fair
N/A	N/A	N/A

Ameli

Introduced in 1980, this is a light air-cooled machine gun chambered for the 5.56x45mm cartridge. It is fitted with a 15.75" barrel with slotted jacket, carry handle, and bipod. Barrel is quick change with flash hider. Belt-fed with 100- or 200-round belts. Plastic stock with pistol grip. Rate of fire is about 900 rounds per minute. Weight is approximately 11.5 lbs. Similar in appearance to the MG42 but smaller in size.

Pre-1968

Exc.	V.G.	Fair
N/A	N/A	N/A

Pre-1986 conversions

Exc.	V.G.	Fair
N/A	N/A	N/A

Pre-1986 dealer samples

Exc.	V.G.	Fair
10500	10000	9500

SWEDEN

Swedish Military Conflicts, 1870-Present

As an outcome of the Swedish defeat against France in 1808, Sweden lost Finland to Russia but gained Norway. This union with Norway remained until 1905, when Norway was granted its independence. During the 20th century, Sweden avoided involvement in both world wars and maintained its neutrality during the Cold War. Sweden joined the European Union in 1995.

HANDGUNS

Sweden purchased a small number, about 10,000, of Walther P-38 pistols in 1939, designated the Model 39. Also, a limited number of Walther PP pistols were used by the army as well.

Model 1871

The Swedish military issued the Lefaucheux-Francotte 6-shot revolver built by Auguste Francotte in Liege, Belgium, and also by Husqvarna. The frame was solid with fixed cylinder and no mechanical ejection. Chambered for the 11mm cartridge and fitted with a 5.9" round barrel. Checkered wooden grips with lanyard loop. Six-round cylinder is non-fluted. Weight is about 41 oz. First adopted by the cavalry and then included other units as well. In use between 1871 and 1890.

Exc.	V.G.	Good	Fair	Poor
1250	750	500	350	200

Model 1863/79

This revolver is a converted pinfire to 11mm centerfire. Octagon barrel is 6.2". Smooth wooden grips with lanyard loop. Built by Lefaucheux in Paris. In use between 1879 and 1890.

Exc.	V.G.	Good	Fair	Poor
700	450	300	175	100

Model 1884

In 1884 the Swedish navy chose the French Model 1873 revolver as its issue sidearm. It was designated the Model 1884. It was chambered for the 11mm cartridge and fitted with a 4.4" half-round half-octagon barrel. Checkered wood grips with lanyard loop. It was built in St. Etienne. Used by the navy from 1884 to 1887.

Exc.	V.G.	Good	Fair	Poor
500	350	250	175	125

HUSQVARNA

Model 1887 Officer's Model

This double action revolver was chosen by the Swedish army as its official sidearm. It was a 6-shot double action Nagant design chambered for the 7.5mm cartridge with fluted cylinder. It was fitted with a 4.5" half-round half-octagon barrel. Checkered wood grips with lanyard loop. Weight is about 24 oz. The first of these revolvers were built by the Nagant brothers in Liege beginning in 1887, and starting in 1897 these guns were built at Husqvarna as well. Issued until 1947.

NOTE: Between 1897 and 1905 Husqvarna produced about 13,000 of these revolvers. They were delivered with a holster, spare cylinder, cleaning rod, and screwdriver. Many of these revolvers were also sold on the commercial market as well.

Courtesy Rock Island Auction Company

Exc.	V.G.	Good	Fair	Poor
350	200	150	100	75

Model 1907 (Browning Model 1903)

This pistol is a copy of the FN Browning Model 1903 made for the Swedish army beginning in 1907. Built by Husqvarna. It is chambered for the 9x20 Browning Long cartridge. It is identical in every way to the FN model. This pistol remained in service until 1940. Many were converted to the .380 caliber and imported into the U.S.

NOTE: If converted to .380 caliber reduce values by 50%.

Courtesy Orvel Reichert

Exc.	V.G.	Good	Fair	Poor
350	250	200	150	100

Lahti Model 40

A 9mm caliber semiautomatic pistol with a 5.5" barrel and 8-shot magazine. The grip is cut for a shoulder stock. Designed by Aimo Johannes Lahti, built with some alterations to the original design by Husqvarna and adopted as the standard Swedish sidearm in 1942. It differs from the Finnish version in that it does not have a loaded chamber indicator. The front sight is also higher. Production stopped in 1946 with some 84,000 pistols produced.

Lahti Model 40 • Private collection, Paul Goodwin photo

Exc.	V.G.	Good	Fair	Poor
450	350	275	225	150

SUBMACHINE GUNS

The Swedes used the Thompson submachine gun designated the 11mm Model 40 in limited numbers. They also used the Finnish Suomi (Model 37-39) and the Bergmann Model 34, designated the Swedish Model 39.

Carl Gustav 45

This 9mm weapon was first produced in 1945 in Sweden. This submachine gun is still in use. Models built between 1945 and 1948 are fitted with a 50-round Suomi magazine, while after 1948 guns have a 36-round two column magazine. It is used by the Swedish and Indonesian armies. Some integral silencer versions were used by Special Forces in Vietnam. Barrel is 8.25" in length. Fitted with retractable stock. Rate of fire is about 600 rounds per minute. Weight is about 8 lbs. This is the principal submachine gun in use by the Swedish army today.

Courtesy Richard M. Kumor Sr.

Carl Gustav M45/B • Photo courtesy private NFA collection

Pre-1968

Exc.	V.G.	Fair
8500	7000	6500

Pre-1986 conversions

Exc.	V.G.	Fair
5000	4500	3750

Pre-1986 dealer samples

Exc.	V.G.	Fair
3500	3000	2500

NOTE: Add 33% for M45/B model, which features a different non-removable magazine well, green finish, and improved bolt retention. There is also an M45/C that is fitted with an bayonet lug and a M45/E that is select fire.

Swedish "K" (M45/B) with integral suppressor • Courtesy West Point Museum, Paul Goodwin photo

THE SWEDISH "K"

Designed at the end of World War Two, the Swedish K — actually the Model 45/B — remained somewhat hidden from the world view until the Vietnam War because Sweden maintained a façade of neutrality. The gun, however, found favor with a number of covert operators who had to carry non-U.S.A. origin weapons. Essentially, the Swedish K was a high-class Sten gun, as it featured a tube steel receiver, a folding stock, and a very well designed dual-column, two-position feed box magazine. The Swedish K, even though it was made from stamped steel parts, had always exhibited the best in quality and manufacturing processes, a direct byproduct of being made in a country *not* at war. The Swedish K was a full-auto only weapon, but because the cyclic rate of fire was 600rpm it was not a chore to fire off single rounds versus full-auto bursts. With an empty weight of 7.62 pounds and the stock folded it was always an easy and convenient weapon to carry and store. There is a distinct similarity in appearance between the Swedish K and the Smith & Wesson Model 76, which was supposed to supplement its use in Vietnam. It seems the Swedes objected to its use in the Vietnam war so they refused to supply any more, regardless of price, to the American Special Forces. Smith & Wesson was approached and they agreed to manufacture a replacement. Unfortunately, the S&W Model 76 was never as good as the original in terms of design features, and not only that, the war ended before Smith & Wesson could deliver their ersatz Swedish K submachine guns to the American military. The Swedish K was licensed and built by Egypt and Indonesia, but none of these copies ever equaled the original in terms of quality of manufacturing or reliability and accuracy.

Frank James

RIFLES

REMINGTON

Sweden utilized the Remington rolling block rifles. Some of these were produced by Remington and others by Carl Gustav and Husqvarna.

Model 1867 Rifle

Chambered for the 12.17x42mm rimfire cartridge and fitted with a 35.5" barrel. Full stock with three barrel bands, cleaning rod, and bayonet lug on right side. Weight is about 9.25 lbs.

Exc.	V.G.	Good	Fair	Poor
—	—	600	400	100

Model 1864/68/85 Carbine

Chambered for the 12.7x42mm rimfire cartridge and fitted with a 16.5" barrel. Rear sight graduated from 250 to 800 meters. Full stock with cleaning rod and one barrel band. Built by Carl Gustav.

Exc.	V.G.	Good	Fair	Poor
—	1050	850	550	200

Model 1870

Built by Carl Gustav and Husqvarna, this model is chambered for the 12.7x42mm rimfire cartridge. Fitted with a 16.5" barrel with rear sight graduated from 250 to 900 meters. Full stock with one barrel band at the muzzle. Weight is about 6 lbs.

Exc.	V.G.	Good	Fair	Poor
—	1050	850	550	200

Model 1884 Rifle

Chambered for the 10.15x61Rmm cartridge and fitted with a 31" barrel.

Exc.	V.G.	Good	Fair	Poor
—	750	600	400	100

Model 1884 Carbine

As above but with 16.5" barrel.

Exc.	V.G.	Good	Fair	Poor
—	1050	850	550	200

Model 1889

Chambered for the 8x58Rmm Danish Krag cartridge and fitted with a 33" barrel with rear sight graduated from 300 to 2,400 meters. Full stock with two barrel bands. Sling swivel on first barrel band and in front of triggerguard. Finger grooves in stock ahead of breech and below rear sight. Bayonet lug.

Exc.	V.G.	Good	Fair	Poor
950	750	600	400	100

MAUSER

NOTE: These Mauser rifles were built either by Mauser, Carl Gustav, or Husqvarna. On the right side of the buttstock is frequently seen a tin disk with the unit number and sometimes a capital letter. The letter "I" stands for infantry "A" for artillery, "T" for reserves, and "K.FL." for marines.

M1894 Carbine

Chambered for the 6.5x55mm cartridge and fitted with a 17.5" barrel. Full stocked in European carbine-style with half-length handguard with finger grooves. Turned down bolt. Magazine capacity is 5 rounds. Leaf rear sight graduated from 300 to 1,600 meters. Weight is about 7.5 lbs. About 12,000 of these rifles were built by Mauser, the rest by the Swedish firms mentioned above.

Exc.	V.G.	Good	Fair	Poor
400	350	300	250	200

M1896 Rifle

Action similar to the Model 1894 but with a 29" barrel, full-length stock, half-length upper handguard, and bayonet lug. Rear sight graduated from 300 to 2,000 meters on Mauser and Gustav-built rifles and 100 to 800 meters on Husqvarna built rifles. Swedish crown over maker and date stamped on receiver ring. Magazine capacity is 5 rounds. Weight is about 9 lbs.

NOTE: A number of these rifles were sent to Finland during the early days of World War II to fight the Soviets. A number were also sent to Denmark as well. These Danish rifles have a Danish silver coin in the right side of the buttstock in place of the Swedish marking disk.

Courtesy Rock Island Auction Company

Exc.	V.G.	Good	Fair	Poor
200	150	100	80	60

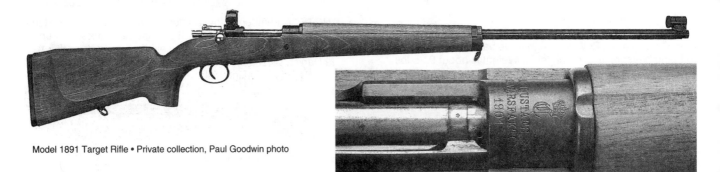

Model 1896 Sniper Rifle with M44 Scope • Courtesy Rock Island Auction Company

M1896 Sniper Rifle/M41 AGA scope
This is a Model 1896 rifle with Model 41 AGA scope mounted.

Exc.	V.G.	Good	Fair	Poor
1500	1200	850	650	500

M1896 Sniper Rifle/M42 AGA scope
This is a Model 1896 rifle with Model 42 AGA scope mounted.

Exc.	V.G.	Good	Fair	Poor
1500	1200	850	650	500

Model 1896 Target Rifle
Receiver bridge sights of different manufacturers added.

Exc.	V.G.	Good	Fair	Poor
300	250	150	100	75

Model 96-38
About 30,000 Model 1896 rifles were shortened to the same overall length as the Model 1938 Short Rifle. The straight bolt handle of the Model 1896 was retained. Weight is about 8.375 lbs.

Exc.	V.G.	Good	Fair	Poor
225	175	125	75	50

Model 38 Short Rifle
Similar to the Model 1896 but with turned-down bolt handle and barrel length of 23.5". Designed for mounted troops. There is a version of this rifle with a straight bolt handle for use by infantry troops. Magazine capacity is 5-rounds. Rear sight graduated from 100 to 600 meters. Weight is approximately 9 lbs. Built by Husqvarna.

Exc.	V.G.	Good	Fair	Poor
300	250	200	150	100

Model 38/22 Training Rifle
Similar to the Model 38 Short Rifle but chambered for the .22 caliber rimfire cartridge.

Exc.	V.G.	Good	Fair	Poor
400	325	250	200	150

M1938/40 Short Rifle (Model 40)
This model is a Swedish modified German Kar. 98k converted to the 8x63mm machine gun cartridge. The rifle was fitted with a muzzle brake to soften recoil but the cartridge was too powerful for the gun. Four-round magazine. Weight is about 9.5 lbs.

Exc.	V.G.	Good	Fair	Poor
200	150	100	80	50

M1896 Sniper Rifle/M44 AGA scope (Model 41)
A Model 1896 Rifle fitted with either a Model 44 AGA 3x65 scope, Model 42 AGA 3x65 scope, or Model 41 4x90 ZF Ajack scope.

Exc.	V.G.	Good	Fair	Poor
1500	1200	850	650	500

M1896 Military Target Rifles
A Model 1896 rifle with special micrometer target sights.

Exc.	V.G.	Good	Fair	Poor
300	250	200	150	110

Model CG-63 and CG-80 Target Rifle
Built by Carl Gustav, this rifle was chambered for the .22 rimfire, 6.5x55mm, or 7.62mm cartridge. Fitted with a medium weight 29.1" barrel. Half-length stock with half-length upper handguard. The CG-80 was not fitted with a handguard. Five round magazine. It has a turned-down bolt handle flattened on top. Generally fitted with aperture rear sight mounted on receiver bridge. Many minor variations are encountered in this rifle. Weight is approximately 9.5 lbs.

Exc.	V.G.	Good	Fair	Poor
850	700	500	300	200

Ljungman AG-42B
Designed by Eril Eklund and placed in service with the Swedish military in 1942—less than one year after it was designed. The rifle is a direct gas-operated design with no piston or rod. It is chambered for the 6.5mm cartridge and has a 24.5" barrel with a 10-round detachable magazine. This rifle has military-type sights and a full-length stock and handguard held on by barrel bands. Rear sight is graduated from 100 to 700 meters. There are provisions for a bayonet. There is also an Egyptian version of this rifle known as the "Hakim" and a Danish version that was manufactured by Madsen. The U.S. AR-15 rifles use the same type of gas system.

Model 1891 Target Rifle • Private collection, Paul Goodwin photo

AG-42B action • Courtesy Chuck Karwan

Exc.	V.G.	Good	Fair	Poor
400	325	250	150	100

MACHINE GUNS

The Swedish armed forces have utilized a wide variety of machine guns from several countries. Sweden adopted the Schwarzlose Model 14 in 6.5mm caliber, the Browning Model 1917A1 water-cooled gun (Model 36), the Browning Model 1919A6 (Model 42), the Czech VZ26 in 6.5mm caliber (Model 39), and more currently the FN MAG in 7.62mm (Model 58). These early FN MAG guns were chambered for the 6.5x55mm Mauser cartridge.

Swedish Model 36

This is the Swedish version of the Browning Model 1917 water-cooled gun. The gun shown is in a twin anti-aircraft configuration, and is too rare to price.

Pre-1968

Exc.	V.G.	Fair
15000	12500	11000

Pre-1986 conversions

Exc.	V.G.	Fair
N/A	N/A	N/A

Swedish Model 1936 Twin • Courtesy private NFA collection, Paul Goodwin photo

Pre-1986 dealer samples

Exc.	V.G.	Fair
4000	3500	3000

Swedish BAR Model 21

Designated the Swedish Kg. (*Kulsprutegevar*, light machine gun) these guns were built in Sweden under license from Colt

Model 21 Swedish BAR • Private NFA collection, Gary Gelson photo

between 1923 and 1935. Chambered for the Swedish 6.5x55mm cartridge. This model does not have a quick change barrel as originally built. A little over 8,000 of these BARs were built in Sweden during its production life.

Pre-1968

Exc.	V.G.	Fair
10000	9500	9000

Pre-1986 conversions

Exc.	V.G.	Fair
N/A	N/A	N/A

Pre-1986 dealer samples

Exc.	V.G.	Fair
4000	3500	3000

Swedish BAR Model 37

The Model 37 Swedish BAR is an improved version of the Model 21 with a screw-on receiver extension that allowed the adoption of a quick change barrel. A total of about 15,000 Model 37s were produced between 1937 and 1944.

NOTE: A number of Model 21s were refitted with quick change barrels and designated the Model 21/37.

Pre-1968 (Very Rare)

Exc.	V.G.	Fair
12000	10000	9000

Pre-1986 conversions

Exc.	V.G.	Fair
N/A	N/A	N/A

Pre-1986 dealer samples

Exc.	V.G.	Fair
3500	3250	3000

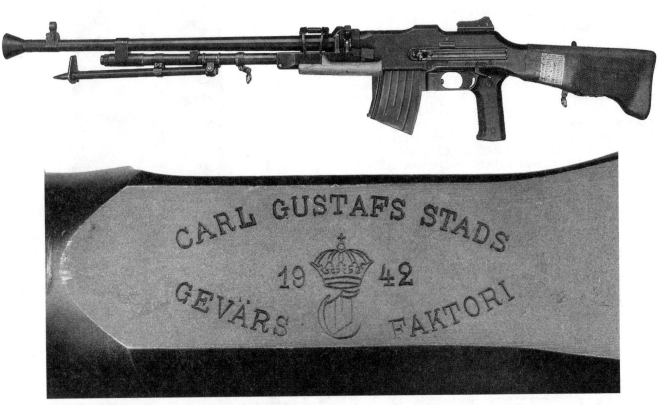

Swedish Model 1937 • Courtesy private NFA collection, Paul Goodwin photo

SWITZERLAND

Swiss Military Conflicts, 1870-Present

In 1815 Switzerland was guaranteed perpetual neutrality by the Treaty of Vienna, thus it remained neutral in both World Wars. Switzerland was not a member of the United Nations until 2002 and is not member of the EU.

National defense is based on a system of universal conscription by which every Swiss male is liable for military duty between the ages of 20 and 50. The Swiss soldier is the only soldier in the world who keeps his equipment, including arms and ammunition, at home, and who performs his obligatory duty each year in civilian clothes. Once his military rifle is issued, the Swiss soldier keeps it at home for life. In 2001, Switzerland had a total active duty military force of 3,600 personnel. Reserve forces were 351,000, of those 320,000 were in the army.

HANDGUNS

Model 1872

This Swiss Model 1872 is a 10.4mm rimfire revolver with a 6-shot fluted cylinder. It is fitted with a 5.9" octagon barrel. The frame is solid with fixed fluted cylinder and mechanical rod ejection. Checkered wood grips with lanyard loop. The revolver was built by the Belgian firm of Pirlot Freres in Liege. It was issued from 1872 until 1878. Weight is 37 oz. This was the last foreign-built handgun to be issued to the Swiss military.

NOTE: This is a very rare revolver as most were converted to centerfire with the Model 1872/78 in 1878.

Exc.	V.G.	Good	Fair	Poor
N/A	—	—	—	—

Model 1872/78

This is a centerfire converted Model 1872 in 10.4mm. This revolver was rarely used by the Swiss military.

Exc.	V.G.	Good	Fair	Poor
N/A	—	—	—	—

Model 1878

This was the first Swiss-made revolver used by the Swiss military. Made in Bern, this Schmidt-Galand-type revolver was chambered for the 10.4mm cartridge. The frame was solid with fixed cylinder and mechanical rod ejection. 4.5" octagon barrel. Checkered grips with the Swiss cross on the left side. Weight was about 35 oz. This revolver was issued to cavalry units with about 6,000 in service.

Exc.	V.G.	Good	Fair	Poor
1750	1000	600	350	250

Model 1882

This revolver was similar in appearance to the Model 1878 but was chambered for the smaller 7.5mm cartridge. It was fitted with a 4.5" octagon barrel. Early Model 1882 revolvers were fitted with hard rubber checkered grips while later guns will be seen with grooved wooden grips. This revolver was built in Switzerland at Bern or SIG. Weight is about 27 oz. This model stayed in use in the Swiss military from 1882 to as late as 1950.

Courtesy Rock Island Auction Company

Exc.	V.G.	Good	Fair	Poor
850	700	450	250	200

LUGER

WAFFENFABRIK BERN

Switzerland was the first country to adopt the Luger as a military sidearm with its contract purchase of the Model 1900 from DWM. Another contract for the Model 1906 soon followed. Because DWM could no longer supply Switzerland with Lugers during World War I, the Swiss firm of Waffenfabrik Bern (W+F Bern) produced its own version based on the Model 1906.

Bibliographical Note: For additional historical information, technical data, and photos, see Vittorio Bobba, *Parabellum; A Technical History of Swiss Lugers*, Italy, 1996.

NOTE: There are a number of sub-variations of Swiss Lugers that may affect value. It is strongly suggested that thorough research of this model be undertaken prior to a sale.

Model 1906 Bern

A Swiss-made copy of the German Model 1906 Luger. Made in caliber 7.65mm, fitted with a 4.75" barrel, and marked "WAFFENFABRIK BERN" under the Geneva cross on top of the toggle. The grips on this pistol are unique in that most are checkered walnut with a plain border on the front and rear edges. About 17,000 of these pistols were manufactured. This model was most likely produced between 1918 and 1933, and was built for the Swiss military.

Courtesy James Rankin

Exc.	V.G.	Good	Fair	Poor
4000	2750	2000	1400	1000

Model 1929

Similar to the above, with the exception that the toggle finger pieces are smooth, the grip frame is uncurved, safety lever is a flat configuration, and the grip safety is of inordinate size. Fitted with plastic grips. Chambered for caliber 7.65mm. About 30,000 of these pistols were produced. Sold both for military and commercial use.

Courtesy James Rankin

Exc.	V.G.	Good	Fair	Poor
2750	2000	1500	1200	900

SIG
Schweizerische Industrie Gesellschaft, Neuhausen am Rheinfalls, Switzerland

Biographical Note: For historical background, technical data, and photos, see Lorenz Vetter, *Das grosse Buch der SIG-Pistolen*, Verlag Stocker-Schmid AG, 1995.

NOTE: The P210 pistol was designated the SP47/8 prior to 1957, when it was renamed the P210. There are a number of production changes on this pistol that follow a chronological order.

P210

A 7.65mm or 9mm semiautomatic pistol with a 4.75" barrel and 8-shot magazine. Fixed rear sight. Blued with plastic grips. In 1996 the 9mm version was the only one imported. Weight is about 32 oz. This model was also used by the Danish army (Model 49).

NIB	Exc.	V.G.	Good	Fair	Poor
2500	1500	1300	1100	800	500

NOTE: For 1996, a .22 caliber conversion unit serialized to the gun was available. Add $600 for this option.

P 210-1

As above, with an adjustable rear sight, polished finish, and walnut grips. Imported prior to 1987. Weight is about 31 oz.

NIB	Exc.	V.G.	Good	Fair	Poor
2750	2250	1500	1150	800	—

P 210-2 (Swiss Army Model 49-SP47/8)

This model is similar to the P210-1 with the exception that it has a sandblasted matte finish and black plastic grips with fixed sights. Adopted by the Swiss army in 1947 and still in service.

NIB	Exc.	V.G.	Good	Fair	Poor
2000	1750	1350	1000	750	300

P210-3

Introduced in 1950, this model was issued to the Swiss police in Lausanne and Basel. Early examples are polished blue and later examples are sandblasted matte blue. Fixed sights. Production ceased in 1983. Very few of these pistols were sold on a commercial basis. Very scarce.

NIB	Exc.	V.G.	Good	Fair	Poor
N/A	—	—	—	—	—

P210-4

Special model produced for the West German Border Police. Fixed rear sight. Walnut grips on early models and black plastic grips on later models. Early models have blued finish while later models have sandblasted matte finish.

NIB	Exc.	V.G.	Good	Fair	Poor
2000	1750	1350	1000	750	300

P210-5

A commercial version as above, with an extended length barrel of 5.9" (150mm) or 7.1" (180mm), adjustable rear sight, target trigger, and walnut grips. Front sight is fitted to front of extended barrel, not the slide. Offered in a standard and heavy frame weight. Polished blue finish. Weight is about 35 oz. for standard weight frame.

NIB	Exc.	V.G.	Good	Fair	Poor
3500	2750	1750	1200	800	400

P210-6

A commercial version as above, with a 4.75" barrel. Front sight is fitted to slide. Adjustable rear sight on some of these variations fixed sight on others. Polished blue finish.

SIG P210-6 Commercial Version • Courtesy SIG Arms

NIB	Exc.	V.G.	Good	Fair	Poor
2750	2250	1500	1250	800	400

P210-7

This model is chambered for the .22 rimfire cartridge and fitted with a 4.75" barrel. Most of the variations of this model are built for commercial and export sales except one variation, which was built for the West German Border Guards as a practice pistol. Fixed sights. Checkered plastic grips.

NIB	Exc.	V.G.	Good	Fair	Poor
N/A	—	—	—	—	—

P220 (Swiss Army Model P-75)

Swiss army military sidearm. This is a high-quality, double action semiautomatic pistol chambered for .38 Super, .45 ACP, and 9mm Parabellum. It has a 4.41" barrel and fixed sights and features the decocking lever that was found originally on the Sauer Model 38H. There are two versions of this pistol: one with a bottom magazine release (commonly referred to as the European model) and the other with the release on the side (commonly referred to as the American model), as on the Model 1911 Colt. The frame is a lightweight alloy that is matte finished and is available in either blue, nickel, or K-Kote finish with black plastic grips. The .45 ACP magazine capacity is 7 rounds and the pistol weighs 25.7 oz.; the .38 Super magazine capacity is 9 rounds and the pistol weighs 26.5 oz.; the 9mm magazine holds 9 rounds and the overall weight is 26.5 oz. This model was manufactured from 1976 and is still in production. The 9mm version in this model is no longer in production. The prices listed below are for guns with a standard blue finish.

NOTE: For the K-Kote finish add $40, for nickel slide add $40.

MP43/44
The Swiss version of the Suomi with a bayonet lug and flip over rear sight. Built by Hispano Suiza under license from Finland. Rate of fire is about 800 rounds per minute and weight is approximately 10.5 lbs. Magazine capacity is 50-round box type.

NIB	Exc.	V.G.	Good	Fair	Poor
750	550	400	300	200	150

Swiss M43/44 • Courtesy private NFA collection, Paul Goodwin photo

SUBMACHINE GUNS

Steyr-Solothurn (Solothurn SI-100 or MP34(o))
See Austria, Submachine Guns, Steyr.

MP41/44
This model was developed by Furrer and built by W+F Bern arsenal between 1936 and 1942. Chambered for the 9mm Luger cartridge. Recoil operated with a toggle system similar to the Luger pistol but turned on its side. Slotted barrel jacket with 10" barrel with forward vertical handgrip and pistol grip wooden stock. Rate of fire is about 900 rounds per minute. Magazine capacity is 40 rounds. Very expensive to produce with the result that less than 5,000 guns were manufactured. Weight is about 11.5 lbs.

Pre-1968 (Rare)

Exc.	V.G.	Fair
9500	8500	8000

Pre-1986 conversions

Exc.	V.G.	Fair
N/A	N/A	N/A

Pre-1986 dealer samples

Exc.	V.G.	Fair
N/A	N/A	N/A

Pre-1968 (Rare)

Exc.	V.G.	Fair
9500	9000	8000

Pre-1986 conversions

Exc.	V.G.	Fair
N/A	N/A	N/A

Pre-1986 dealer samples

Exc.	V.G.	Fair
N/A	N/A	N/A

RIFLES

PEABODY

Swiss Rifle (1867)
Chambered for the .41 Swiss rimfire cartridge, this rifle was fitted with a 31.625" barrel. Full stock with two barrel bands. The barrel is blued and the furniture casehardened. On the left side of the receiver are a cross and "W" inside an oval. "Peabody" stamped on left side of receiver. About 15,000 rifles were sold to the Swiss. Serial number range: 5,500 to 21,000.

Exc.	V.G.	Good	Fair	Poor
—	1000	750	500	200

Swiss MP41 • Courtesy private NFA collection, Paul Goodwin photo

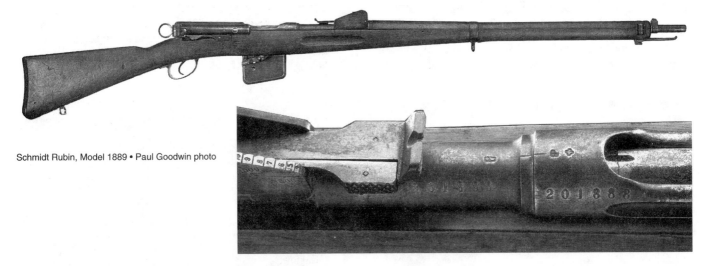

Schmidt Rubin, Model 1889 • Paul Goodwin photo

SCHMIDT RUBIN
Eidgenossische Waffenfabrik Bern
Bern, Switzerland (1875-1993)

BOLT NOTE: The bolts on this series were made stronger by shortening the overall length of the bolt and the length from the locking lug to the bolt face. These distances measure:

Model 1889: 8 3/4" overall bolt length, 7" from back of locking lug to bolt face.

Model 1889/11 and Model 1911: 8" overall bolt length, 4 1/2" from back of locking lug to bolt face.

Model 1931: 5 3/8" overall bolt length, 1/2" from back of locking lug to bolt face.

[*The above information was supplied by Simeon Stoddard.*]

Model 1889

A 7.5mm straight pull bolt action rifle with a 30.75" barrel and 12-shot magazine. Blued with a full-length walnut stock secured by two barrel bands. Approximately 212,000 were manufactured.

Exc.	V.G.	Good	Fair	Poor
300	200	175	125	90

Model 1889/96

Similar to the Model 1889 with a shortened action. The locking lug is moved forward 2 1/2" on the bolt sleeve. There were approximately 127,000 made between 1897 and 1912.

Exc.	V.G.	Good	Fair	Poor	
400	325	250	180		125

Model 1897 Cadet Rifle

A single shot Cadet Rifle with reduced overall size. These rifles were sighted for a reduced charge cartridge for target use and to reduce recoil. Approximately 7,900 were manufactured between 1898 and 1927.

Exc.	V.G.	Good	Fair	Poor
1200	1000	700	500	350

Model 1900 Short Rifle

A shortened version of the Model 1896, with a 6-shot magazine. Approximately 18,750 were manufactured between 1901 and 1911.

Exc.	V.G	Good	Fair	Poor
650	400	250	175	125

Model 1900/11 Short Rifle

Modified between 1911 and 1920 to more closely resemble the Model 1911 Carbine with new barrel and sights.

Exc.	V.G.	Good	Fair	Poor
350	250	175	125	75

Model 1905 Carbine

Adopted in 1905 as a replacement for the Mannlicher 1893. Approximately 7,900 were manufactured between 1906 and 1911.

Exc.	V.G.	Good	Fair	Poor
650	400	250	175	125

Model 1905/11 Cavalry Carbine

Modified between 1911 and 1920 to more closely resemble the Model 1911 Carbine with new barrel and sights.

Exc.	V.G.	Good	Fair	Poor
350	250	175	125	75

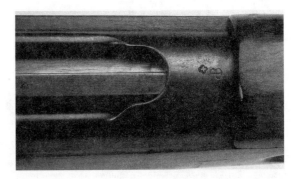

Model 1911 • Courtesy West Point Museum, Paul Goodwin photo

Model 1896/11

Updated version of the 1896 rifle to more closely resemble the Model 1911 rifle. Changes included new barrel and sight, and an inlet pistol grip into the straight 1896 stock. Modification program took place betweeen 1911 and 1920.

Exc.	V.G.	Good	Fair	Poor
250	200	150	100	75

Model 1911 Rifle

Straightened and redesigned bolt to better handle the higher performance 1911 cartridge. Magazine capacity was reduced from 12 to 6 rounds in the Model 1911. Other changes included a pistol grip and flat buttplate on the stock. Approximately 133,000 were manufactured between 1913 and 1919.

Exc.	V.G.	Good	Fair	Poor
250	175	125	75	50

Model 1911 Carbine

Same action as the Model 1911 rifle with a 23.25" barrel. Approximately 185,000 were manufactured between 1914 and 1933.

Exc.	V.G.	Good	Fair	Poor
250	150	100	80	60

NOTE: Although produced in larger numbers than the Model 1911 rifle, the carbine will command a higher price.

Model 1931 Short Rifle

Similar to the above, with a redesigned block work, 25.7" barrel, and 6-shot magazine. This was the final version of the Schmidt-Rubin design. Instead of locking lugs into the receiver, the lugs were repositioned to lock into the receiver ring thereby greatly increasing the strength of the rifle. This change also increased the length of the barrel without increasing the overall length of the rifle. Approximately 528,180 were manufactured between 1933 and 1958.

Exc.	V.G.	Good	Fair	Poor
250	175	125	75	50

Model 1931 Short Rifle with shooter added target sights

Many shooters in Switzerland have modified Model 1931s with target sights. These can range in price due to the quality of the sights added.

Prices range from $550 to $350.

Model 1931 .22 Target Rifle

This is the single-shot training version of the K31 with sights set for 50 meters.The rifle is the same overall length as the standard K31. Fitted with a highly modified bolt for the .22 caliber rimfire cartridge.

Exc.	V.G.	Good	Fair	Poor
850	750	600	350	250

Hammerili Match K31

This rifle is produced by Hammerili and is so marked on the receiver ring. These rifles have rear military sight omitted and a target sight installed at the rear of the receiver. Very limited production.

Exc.	V.G.	Good	Fair	Poor
4500	3750	3000	2000	1200

MODEL 1931 SNIPER VARIANTS

There are a number of different sniper variants to the Model 1931 rifle. The first attempt was an experimental model, the Model 1940, fitted with a Wild & Gerber scope, which was po-

---

THE SWISS SCHMIDT-RUBIN

Reportedly, the German Kaiser visited Switzerland before WWI. After reviewing an honor guard, he stopped to compliment their non-com on his men's appearance. Half-jokingly he asked the old Sergeant-Major what would their little army do if confronted by a German force twice their size. The grey-haired Sergeant thought for a moment before answering: "Then Your Highness, we would all have to fire our rifles twice!" Colonel Eduard Rubin invented the first jacketed, small caliber bullets in 1881 and in cooperation with Colonel Rudolph Schmidt, they developed Switzerland's first small caliber military rifle. The Schmidt-Rubin became the best known of the straight-pull designs developed during the 19th century. Beginning with the Infanterie Repetier Gewehr M1889 and ending with the Karabiner M.1931, they served the alpine nation's army and reserves for over a century. When I first picked up a Schmidt-Rubin Karabiner 31 and worked its bolt I said to myself, "This thing is built like a Swiss watch!" Quality of materials and workmanship were both first class. It is chambered for the 7.5mm Patrone M.11 (7.5x55 Swiss) which has a reputation as an extremely accurate cartridge. The six-round magazine is easily loaded with a unique charger made from aluminum and fiber board, while the straight-pull bolt works with an oiled smoothness that is a joy to behold. Fitted with an excellent set of sights, a very nice trigger, and above-average ergonomics, it is about as user-friendly a rifle as I've ever beheld. I fired several five-shot groups at 100 yards, the smallest of which was an impressive 1-7/8", printing directly to point of aim. You can say that Schmidt-Rubins are funny looking—but don't ever say they aren't accurate! The Swiss are proud of their ability to produce finely made military weapons and their infantrymen no doubt enjoy knowing that their weapons were not produced by the lowest bidder.

---

sitioned high above the receiver by means of an odd looking scope mount with a forehead protector attached to it. The second experimental model was the Model 1942 with a small detachable scope fitted to the left side of the receiver. All of these rifles were manfactured in small quantities.

Model 1931/42

Built by Waffenfabrik Bern on the Model 31 action and stock. Barrel length is 25.7" with 6-shot magazine. Walnut stock with handguard. This variant is fitted with a 1.8 power integral telescope attached to the left side of the receiver. It has a unique periscope type rotating objective. This rifle is also fitted with open sights to 1,500 meters.

Exc.	V.G.	Good	Fair	Poor
3500	3000	2500	1000	—

Model 1931/43

As above but with a 2.8 power telescope.

Exc.	V.G.	Good	Fair	Poor
3500	3000	2500	1000	—

Model 1931/42 Rifle • Courtesy private NFA collection, Paul Goodwin photo

Model 1955

This model, introduced in 1955, is built on a Model 1931 action. Barrel length is 25.7". A muzzle brake is fitted. This model is fitted with a 3.5 power Kern Aarau telescope mounted on the receiver bridge. Beechwood stock is 2/3 length with handguard and checkered pistol grip. Integral bipod built into midpoint of stock. Weight is about 12 lbs.

Exc.	V.G.	Good	Fair	Poor
3500	3000	2500	1000	—

MANNLICHER

Model 1893 Carbine

This is a Mannlicher straight pull design carbine with a 21.5" barrel chambered for the 7.5x53.5mm cartridge. It was the only Mannlicher adopted by Switzerland. It was fitted with a full-length stock and upper handguard. No bayonet fittings. Magazine capacity was 6 rounds and it was charger loaded. The receiver ring is marked with a small Swiss cross.

Exc.	V.G.	Good	Fair	Poor
1000	800	650	350	225

VETTERLI
Bern, SIG, Pfenninger

This rifle was invented by Friderich Vetterli at Neuhausen, Switzerland, in 1867. This was the first bolt action repeating rifle to be used as a military service weapon. It was adopted on January 8, 1869, and predated the Fruwirth by three years. It is chambered for the .41 Swiss rimfire cartridge. It has a 12-round tubular magazine that is loaded through a side gate similar to a Winchester lever action. There is a swinging cover on the loading gate. The finish is blue, with a full-length walnut stock secured by one barrel band and an endcap. There is a full-length cleaning rod located under the barrel. The receiver has a round configuration and the triggerguard has a rear spur. The rifle and its variations were built between 1869 and 1881.

Model 1869 Infantry Rifle

This model has a turn bolt action with two lugs locking into the receiver body. Full stock with no hand guard. Barrel length is 33". Cleaning rod. A swing-down loading gate is on the right

side of the receiver. Magazine capacity is 12 rounds. Weight is about 10.25 lbs.

Exc.	V.G.	Good	Fair	Poor
—	950	600	300	100

Model 1870 Cadet Rifle

Same action as the Model 1869 but single shot only. Barrel length is 26.75". Weight about 7 lbs.

Exc.	V.G.	Good	Fair	Poor

Model 1871 Rifle

Exc.	V.G.	Good	Fair	Poor
—	750	400	200	100

Model 1871 Stuzer (Short Rifle) (Sharpshooter)

This short rifle was fitted with two barrel bands on its 30" barrel. 9-round magazine. Fitted with a curved buttplate. Double set trigger. Weight is about 10 lbs.

Exc.	V.G.	Good	Fair	Poor
900	700	550	400	150

Model 1871 Carbine

The carbine has an 18.5" barrel with no bayonet fittings. Full stock with 6-round tube magazine. Rear sling swivel behind triggerguard. Weight is about 7 lbs.

Exc.	V.G.	Good	Fair	Poor
—	1500	800	400	200

Model 1878 Rifle

This model was a modified version of the Model 1878. Fitted with a full-length stock with curved buttplate and chambered for the 10.4x42R rimfire cartridge. The rear sight is graduated to 1200 meters. Barrel length is 33" with an 11-round tube magazine in the forend. Built at SIG, Neuhausen, and Bern. Weight is about 10 lbs.

Exc.	V.G.	Good	Fair	Poor
350	300	250	200	100

NOTE: There is some disagreement as to production of a Model 1878 Carbine. As a rule it is thought that some M1878 rifle barrels were cut to 18.5". These are thought to be arsenal conversions. These cut-down "carbines" are worth less than original rifles.

Model 1955 Rifle • Courtesy private NFA collection, Paul Goodwin photo

Mannlicher Model 1893 Carbine • Courtesy West Point Museum, Paul Goodwin photo

Vetterli Model 1871 Rifle • Paul Goodwin photo

Model 1878 Sharpshooter • Private collection, Paul Goodwin photo

Model 1878 Sharpshooter
Similar to the Model 1878 rifle but fitted with double set triggers and crescent butt.

Exc.	V.G.	Good	Fair	Poor
600	450	350	225	100

Model 1881 Rifle
This model is the same as the Model 1878 above with the exception of a 1600 meter graduated rear sight. Weight is about 10 lbs.

Exc.	V.G.	Good	Fair	Poor
350	300	250	200	100

Model 1881 Sharpshooter
Similar to the Model 1881 but fitted with double set triggers.

Exc.	V.G.	Good	Fair	Poor
600	450	350	225	100

SIG
Schweizerische Industrie Gesellschaft, Neuhausen am Rheinfalls, Switzerland

SSG 2000
This is a high-grade, bolt action, sniping-type rifle chambered for .223, 7.5mm Swiss, .300 Weatherby Magnum, and .308 Winchester. It has a 24" barrel and was furnished without sights. It has a 4-round box magazine. The finish is matte blued with a thumbhole-style stippled walnut stock with an adjustable cheekpiece. This model was discontinued in 1986.

NIB	Exc.	V.G.	Good	Fair	Poor
8000	6000	3500	1500	—	—

SSG 3000
Chambered for the .308 Win. cartridge, this model is fitted with a 23.4" barrel and ambidextrous McMillian Tactical stock. Magazine capacity is 5 rounds. Overall length is 46.5", and approximate weight is 12 lbs. This model comes in three different packages. They are listed below.

Level I
Base model with no bipod or scope, but with carrying case.

NIB	Exc.	V.G.	Good	Fair	Poor
2550	2000	—	—	—	—

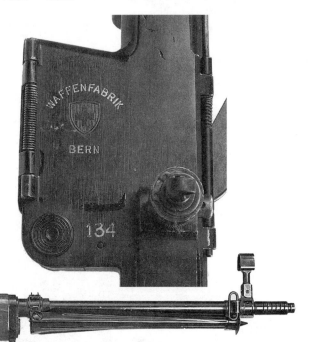

Swiss Stg Model 51 (1st Model) • Courtesy private NFA collection, Paul Goodwin photo

Level II

At this level a Leupold Vari-X III 3.5-10x40mm Duplex scope and Harris bipod with carrying case.

NIB	Exc.	V.G.	Good	Fair	Poor
3500	2750	—	—	—	—

Level III

Rifle is supplied with a Leupold Mark 4 M1-10x40mm Mil-Dot Scope with Harris bipod and carrying case.

NIB	Exc.	V.G.	Good	Fair	Poor
4500	3500	—	—	—	—

SIG AMT

This is a semiautomatic rifle chambered for the .308 cartridge. Fitted with a 19" barrel and wooden buttstock and forearm. Folding bipod standard. Box magazine capacity is 5, 10, or 20 rounds. Weight is about 10 lbs. Built from 1960 to 1974.

NIB	Exc.	V.G.	Good	Fair	Poor
4000	3700	3000	2500	1500	1000

SIG PE57

Similar to the above but chambered for the 7.5x55 Swiss cartridge.

NIB	Exc.	V.G.	Good	Fair	Poor
4500	4100	3500	2700	1700	1300

Bern Stg 51 Assault Rifle

Developed after the end of World War II; the Swiss wanted their own version of a true assault rifle. Waffenfabrik Bern was one of the companies involved in this project. The result was the Stg 51 first built in 1951. This rifle was chambered for the 7.5mm short cartridge, a special cartridge made specifically for this rifle and no longer produced. The rifle is select fire and does so in both models in closed-bolt position. A 30-round box magazine supplies the gun that has a rate of fire of about 800 rounds per minute. The barrel is 22.5" in length and is fitted with a muzzle brake/flash suppressor. A mid-barrel bipod is fitted just ahead of the forend. Weight is approximately 10.5 lbs.

A second model of this rifle was also produced with internal modifications and some small external differences. Both models were issued to the Swiss army, most likely on a trials basis. Extremely rare.

NOTE: The first model of this rifle will interchange some parts with the German FG 42. The second model will interchange all of its parts with the German FG 42.

Swiss SIG Model 51 (2nd Model) • Courtesy private NFA collection, Paul Goodwin photo

Bern Stg 51 (First Model)

Pre-1968

Exc.	V.G.	Fair
35000+	—	—

Pre-1986 conversions

Exc.	V.G.	Fair
N/A	N/A	N/A

Pre-1986 dealer samples

Exc.	V.G.	Fair
N/A	N/A	N/A

Bern Stg 51 (Second Model)

Pre-1968

Exc.	V.G.	Fair
35000+	—	—

Pre-1986 conversions

Exc.	V.G.	Fair
N/A	N/A	N/A

Pre-1986 dealer samples

Exc.	V.G.	Fair
N/A	N/A	N/A

PE57 Assault Rifle • Courtesy Chuck Karwan

Bern Stg 54 • Courtesy private NFA collection, Paul Goodwin photo

Bern Stg 54 (Sturmgewehr W+F 1954)

Introduced in 1954 and chambered for the 7.5mm cartridge, this assault rifle is fitted with a 28.4" barrel including muzzle brake. Weight is approximately 11 lbs. Rate of fire is about 800 rounds per minute. Select fire. Magazine capacity is 30 rounds. Fitted with a bipod. This was an experimental model and it was produced in a number of different variants. Extremely rare.

Pre-1968

Exc.	V.G.	Fair
Too Rare to Price		

Pre-1986 conversions

Exc.	V.G.	Fair
N/A	N/A	N/A

Pre-1986 dealer samples

Exc.	V.G.	Fair
N/A	N/A	N/A

SIG Stgw 57 Assault Rifle

This rifle is a select fire chambered for the 7.5x55mm Swiss cartridge. Barrel length is 23". Box magazine capacity is 24 rounds. Weight is about 12.25 lbs. Adopted by the Swiss army with about 600,000 of these rifles produced between 1957 and 1983. It is based on the German StG 45. The rifle has a pressed steel receiver, folding bipod, wood butt, barrel jacket, and carry handle. The muzzle is designed to act as a grenade launcher and compensator. As with all standard issue Swiss military rifles, this rifle will remain in service for the lifetime of the soldier.

Pre-1968

Exc.	V.G.	Fair
9000	8500	8000

Pre-1986 conversions

Exc.	V.G.	Fair
6000	5500	5000

Pre-1986 dealer samples

Exc.	V.G.	Fair
5000	4500	4000

SIG 550

This semiautomatic rifle is chambered for .223 cartridge and fitted with an 18" barrel.

Courtesy Rock Island Auction Company

NIB	Exc.	V.G.	Good	Fair	Poor
9000	7000	5500	3000	—	—

SIG 551

Same as above but fitted with a 16" barrel.

NIB	Exc.	V.G.	Good	Fair	Poor
9500	7500	6500	4000	—	—

SIG SG510-4

There are actually four different versions of this rifle. This version fires the 7.62x51mm cartridge and is fitted with a 19.7" barrel. A military version, adopted by the Swiss army, is called the Stgw 57(510-1). Magazine capacity is 20 rounds. Weight is 9.3 lbs. Rate of fire is 600 rounds per minute. Produced from 1957 to 1983. Markings are on left rear of receiver.

SIG SG 510-4 • Courtesy Thomas Nelson, *World's Assault Rifles*

Pre-1968 (Rare)

Exc.	V.G.	Fair
9000	8500	8000

Pre-1986 conversions

Exc.	V.G.	Fair
6000	5500	5000

Pre-1986 dealer samples

Exc.	V.G.	Fair
5000	4500	4000

SIG 530-1

This rifle is a scaled-down version of the Stgw 57 assault rifle chambered for the 5.56x45mm cartridge. Operated by a gas pistol system instead of a delayed blowback operation.

Receiver is pressed steel with synthetic butt and forend. Barrel is 18" in length with compensator and grenade launcher rings. Magazine capacity is 30 rounds. Weight is about 7.5 lbs. Rate of fire is 600 rounds per minute. There is also a folding stock version of this rifle.

SIG 530-1 • Courtesy Thomas Nelson, *World's Assault Rifles*

Pre-1968

Exc.	V.G.	Fair
N/A	N/A	N/A

Pre-1986 conversions

Exc.	V.G.	Fair
N/A	N/A	N/A

Pre-1986 dealer samples

Exc.	V.G.	Fair
N/A	N/A	N/A

SIG SG540

Designed by the Swiss (SIG) and built in Switzerland, and also built in France by Manurhin beginning in 1977. This 5.56x45mm rifle is in service by a number of African and South American countries. It is fitted with an 18" barrel, 20- or 30-round magazine and has a rate of fire of 800 rounds per minute. It is fitted with a fixed stock. Its weight is 7.8 lbs. Marked "MANURHIN FRANCE SG54X" on right side of receiver. This rifle is still in production. There are also two other variants called the SG542 and SG543.

Swiss troops with Swiss Maxim. Gun is fitted with muzzle booster or blank fire adaptor • Courtesy John M. Miller

Pre-1968

Exc.	V.G.	Fair
N/A	N/A	N/A

Pre-1986 conversions

Exc.	V.G.	Fair
N/A	N/A	N/A

Pre-1986 dealer samples (Rare)

Exc.	V.G.	Fair
7500	7500	7000

MACHINE GUNS

The Swiss adopted the Maxim machine gun in 1894. The Swiss military also used the Maxim Model 1900. More recently the Swiss have used the FN MAG in addition to its own Swiss-built guns.

Model 1911 Maxim (MG11)

Built by W+F Bern and chambered for the 7.5x55mm Swiss cartridge. Fitted with a plain steel water jacket, otherwise identical to the German MG 08. This was the standard Swiss heavy machine gun and remained in service until 1951.

Swiss Model 1911 Maxim • Courtesy private NFA collection, Paul Goodwin photo

Swiss Maxim markings • Courtesy private NFA collection, Paul Goodwin photo

Swiss Flab MG29 • Courtesy private NFA collection, Paul Goodwin photo

Pre-1968

Exc.	V.G.	Fair
10000	9000	8000

Pre-1986 conversions

Exc.	V.G.	Fair
N/A	N/A	N/A

Pre-1986 dealer samples (Rare)

Exc.	V.G.	Fair
N/A	N/A	N/A

Model Flab MG29

Developed by Adolph Furrer and built in 1929 by W+F Bern, this machine gun was chambered for the 7.5mm Swiss cartridge. Fed by metal belts. It was designed for use on armored vehicles and for anti-aircraft applications. The gun has a high rate of fire of about 1,100 rounds per minute. Weight is about 20 lbs. Rare.

Pre-1968

Exc.	V.G.	Fair
35000	32500	—

Pre-1986 conversions

Exc.	V.G.	Fair
N/A	N/A	N/A

Pre-1986 dealer samples

Exc.	V.G.	Fair
N/A	N/A	N/A

Model 25 Light

Introduced in 1926, this gun was designed as a light air-cooled gun chambered for the 7.5x55mm Swiss cartridge. The gun uses a toggle action that opens sideways. It is fitted with a 23" barrel with slotted barrel jacket, flash hider, and bipod. The buttstock is wooden. The magazine is mounted on the right side of the gun and has a capacity of 30 rounds. Rate of fire is about 450 rounds per minute. Weight is approximately 24 lbs.

Pre-1968

Exc.	V.G.	Fair
18000	15000	15000

Pre-1986 conversions

Exc.	V.G.	Fair
N/A	N/A	N/A

Pre-1986 dealer samples (Rare)

Exc.	V.G.	Fair
12500	11000	10000

Furrer M25 Light • Courtesy private NFA collection, Paul Goodwin photo

TURKEY & OTTOMAN EMPIRE

Ottoman Empire and Turkish Military Conflicts, 1870-Present

Russia and the Ottoman Empire went to war in 1877, and the Ottomans lost valuable lands and influence. These losses continued when, in 1881, Tunisia was lost to the French, and Eastern Rumelia to Bulgaria in 1885. A revolt occurred in 1909 and the Sultan was deposed, but a group of army officers known as the Young Turks were actually in control of what was left of the Empire. Pressure continued on the Ottomans with the loss of Tripoli to the Italians in 1911, and the two Balkan Wars in 1912 and 1913. With the start of World War I the Ottomans aligned with the Central Powers of Germany, Austria-Hungary, and Bulgaria. The results of World War I were a disaster for the Ottoman Empire, with the only bright spot being the Ottoman victory over Allied forces at the Battle of Gallipoli. In 1922 the Republic of Turkey was formed, ending the Ottoman Empire. Turkey remained neutral during most of World War II, until February 1945, when it declared war on Germany and Japan. After the end of the war, Turkey remained aligned with the United States and joined NATO in 1952. Beginning in 1960 and lasting almost 30 years, Turkey suffered through a number of weak governments. Turkey did not participate in the Persian Gulf War.

HANDGUNS

The Ottoman Empire purchased a number of Smith and Wesson Number 3 revolvers (*see U.S. Handguns, Smith & Wesson*). Handguns were not favored by Turkish military officers. Turkey also purchased Mauser C96 pistols (*see Germany, Handguns, Mauser*). Turkey also ordered about 70,000 Smith & Wesson Model 10 revolvers in 1980. The Turkish military also uses the Colt Model 1911A1 pistol.

Kirrikale (MKE)

Made in Ankara and Istanbul, this .380 caliber pistol is a close copy of the Walther Model PP.

Exc.	V.G.	Good	Fair	Poor
650	500	400	300	200

SUBMACHINE GUNS

Turkey uses the U.S. M3A1 submachine gun as well as the HK MP5.

RIFLES

During World War I, Turkey captured large numbers of Russian Mosin-Nagant rifles and carbines. These weapons were used by the Turks during World War I and subsequent conflicts. The Turkish crescent moon is frequently found stamped on various parts.

Over the past 40 years, Turkey has used a number of foreign-built rifles including the HK G3, the FN FAL, the M16A2, and the M1 rifle, as well as the M1 carbine.

MARTINI

Model 1874 Peabody-Martini Rifle

Chambered for the .45 Turkish centerfire cartridge and fitted with a 32.5" barrel. Blued barrel and furniture with case hardened or blued receiver. Numbered in Arabic script. About 630,000 built for Turkey for use in the Russo-Turkish wars.

Exc.	V.G.	Good	Fair	Poor
—	950	600	300	150

MAUSER

M1887 Rifle

This model is a variation of the German Model 71/84. Differences are a smaller triggerguard, a double locking bolt handle, higher comb, and 9.5x60mm Turkish blackpowder caliber. Rear sight graduated to 1,600 meters. Markings in Turkish on the receiver ring, left side rail, and rear sight. Barrel length is 30". Weight about 9.25 lbs. Tubular magazine has an 8-round capacity. About 220,000 were delivered to Turkey.

Exc.	V.G.	Good	Fair	Poor
400	350	300	200	150

M1890 Rifle

Chambered for the smokeless powder 7.65x53mm cartridge and fitted with a 29" barrel. Rear sight graduated to 2,000 meters. Weight is approximately 8.75 lbs. Markings in Turkish. Full length stock with short upper handguard. Box magazine has a 5-round capacity. About 280,000 rifles were produced for the Turkish government.

Exc.	V.G.	Good	Fair	Poor
325	280	225	180	110

M1890 Carbine

As above but with 19.5" barrel. Weight is approximately 7.75 lbs.

Exc.	V.G.	Good	Fair	Poor
400	350	300	200	150

M1893 Rifle

Similar to the Spanish Model 1893 but built with a magazine cutoff. Chambered for the 7.65x53mm cartridge and fitted with a 29" barrel. Weight is about 9 lbs. Rear sight graduated to 2,000 meters. Markings in Turkish. Full length stock with half length upper handguard. Approximately 200,000 delivered to Turkey.

Exc.	V.G.	Good	Fair	Poor
325	250	150	100	70

M1903 Rifle

Chambered for the 7.65x53mm cartridge and fitted with a 29" barrel, this model features a pistol grip full-length stock with half-length upper handguard. Magazine capacity is 5 rounds. Tangent rear sight graduated to 2,000 meters. Turkish crescent and star on the receiver. Weight is about 9 lbs. This model was the standard infantry rifle for the Turkish army from World War I to World War II.

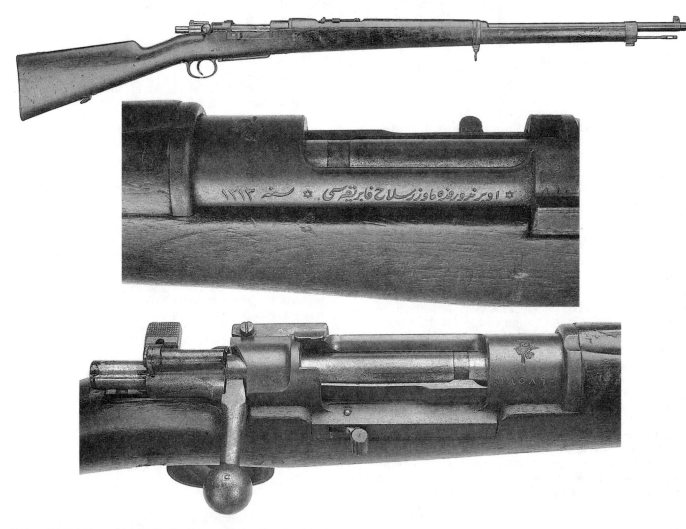

Unaltered Turkish Mauser Model 1903 rifle • Private collection, Paul Goodwin photo

Exc.	V.G.	Good	Fair	Poor
350	275	200	150	70

M1903/38 (converted to 8mm)

Exc.	V.G.	Good	Fair	Poor
250	200	140	100	40

M1905 Carbine

Fitted with a full length stock with half length upper handguard and fitted with a 21.5" barrel chambered for the 7.65x53mm cartridge. Rear sight graduated to 1,600 meters. Magazine capcity is 5 rounds. Weight is approximately 8.25 lbs. Markings in Turkish. Only about 20,000 of these carbines were produced.

Exc.	V.G.	Good	Fair	Poor
400	300	200	110	60

M98/22 Rifle

This model is a Czech Model 98/22 with Turkish or Czech markings.

Courtesy Rock Island Auction Company

Exc.	V.G.	Good	Fair	Poor
125	100	70	50	30

M38 Short Rifle

This model is an arsenal-reworked rifle with 24" barrel chambered for the 7.92x37mm cartridge. Tangent rear sight graduated to 2,000 meters. Magazine capacity is 5 rounds. Marked with the Turkish crescent and star. Weight is about 9 lbs.

Exc.	V.G.	Good	Fair	Poor
125	100	70	50	30

M38 Short Rifle with Folding Bayonet

As above but with bayonet folding under the barrel.

Exc.	V.G.	Good	Fair	Poor
150	120	80	60	30

MACHINE GUNS

During World War I Turkey acquired the German Maxim Model 08/15 in 7.92mm caliber.

The Turkish military relies on the Turkish-built, under license, German MG3, the M1918A2, the M1919 A6, and the .50 M2 HB.

UNITED STATES

U.S. Military Conflicts, 1870-Present

After the end of the American Civil War in 1865, America turned its attention back to westward expansion. The period from 1870 to 1890 was marked by a series of Indian wars that finally ended, for the most part, in 1890. The country turned its attention overseas with the annexation of Hawaii in 1898, and Puerto Rico, Guam, and the Philippines in the Spanish-American War of 1898. A brief excursion into Mexico in 1915-1916 combated the Mexican forces of Pancho Villa. In 1917 the U.S. entered World War I on the side of the Allies and withdrew from European involvement at war's end, November 11, 1918. During World War I, the U.S. had a total of 4,350,000 military personnel, and by the end of the conflict had suffered 255,896 killed and wounded. With the Japanese attack on Pearl Harbor December 7, 1941, America once again fought against foreign aggression in the Pacific and Europe. The U.S. had 16,354,000 military personnel during World War II and suffered 1,076,200 killed and wounded during that conflict. As a world power at the end of the war in August 1945, the United States found itself taking a leading role in combating the Communist invasion of Korea in 1950. A cease fire was signed July 27, 1953. After the French defeat in the Indochina War (1946-1954), the U.S. began to increase its presence in South Vietnam and with the Tonkin Gulf Resolution of 1964 the war rapidly escalated. A cease fire in 1973 ended U.S. involvement in Vietnam with the loss of over 55,000 troops. A number of military actions took place in such places as Panama (1989) and in 1991 with the Persian Gulf War, Somalia, and later in the Balkans. In 2001, total military personnel was 1,367,700. Of these, 477,800 were in the Army and 171,300 in the Marine Corp. Special Operations forces in 2001 were: Army 15,300; Navy 4,000; and Air Force 9,320.

Bibliographical Note: There a number of excellent books on general U.S. military firearms. Some of them are Bruce Canfield's *U.S. Infantry Weapons of World War I*, Mowbry, 2000, and *U.S. Infantry Weapons of World War II*, Mowbry, 1992. Norm Flayderman's *Flayderman's Guide to Antique American Firearms and Their Values*, 7th edition, Krause Publications, 1998. Thomas Batha, *U.S. Martial .22RF Rifles*, Excalibur Publications, 2000.

The famous flaming bomb ordnance mark with "U.S." stamp.

HANDGUNS

Bibliographical Note: There a number of comprehensive publications on U.S. military handguns, some of which are: *U.S. Handguns of World War II, The Secondary Pistols and Revolvers*, Charles W. Pate, Mowbray, 1999. *U.S. Military Automatic Pistols, 1894-1920*, Scott Meadows, Ellis Publications, 1993.

COLT

Bibliographical Note: There are a number of excellent books on Colt firearms, many of which cover Colt's military models. A few of these books are: John W. Brunner, *The Colt Pocket Hammerless Automatic Pistols*, Phillips Publications, 1996. Keith Cochrane, *Colt Cavalry, Artillery and Militia Revolvers*, South Dakota, 1987. Kopec, Graham, and Moore, *A Study of the Colt Single Action Army Revolver*, California, 1976. For the Colt Model 1911 references see *Colt Model 1911 section*.

NOTE: It should be pointed out that the U.S. military purchased and used a number of different Colt pistols and revolvers over the years. In some cases these handguns will be marked with military acceptance stamps or inspector's stamps. In other cases there may be no markings. The following models are some of the most often encountered military marked Colt handguns.

Early Military Model 1873-1877

The serial number range on this first run of military contract revolvers extends to #24000. The barrel address is in the early script style with the # symbol preceding and following. The frame bears the martial marking "US," and the walnut grips have the inspector's cartouche stamped on them. The front sight is steel as on all military models; the barrel length, 7.5". The caliber is.45 Colt, and the ejector rod head is the bull's-eye or donut style with a hole in the center of it. The finish

Paul Goodwin photo

features the military polish and case colored frame, with the remainder blued. Authenticate any potential purchase; many spurious examples have been noted.

Exc.	V.G.	Good	Fair	Poor
N/A	40000	25000	12000	6000

NOTE: Certain 3-digit and 4-digit serial numbers will command a substantial premium. Seek an expert appraisal prior to sale.

An Answorth inspected Colt Model 1873 sold at auction for $25,875. Fitted with 7.5" barrel and re-marked "U.S." markings. Possible connection to the Battle of Little Bighorn. Condition was good.
Rock Island Auction Company, December 1999

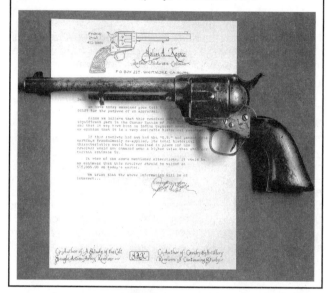

Late Military Model 1878-1891

The later Military Models are serial numbered to approximately #136000. They bear the block-style barrel address without the # prefix and suffix. The frames are marked "US," and the grips have the inspector's cartouche. The finish is the military-style polish, case colored frame, and the remainder, blued. Grips are oil-stained walnut. On the military marked Colts, it is imperative that potential purchases be authenticated, as many fakes have been noted.

Exc.	V.G.	Good	Fair	Poor
35000	20000	10000	6000	2500

NOTE: Revolvers produced from 1878 to 1885 will command a premium. Seek an expert appraisal prior to sale.

Artillery Model 1895-1903

A number of "US" marked SAAs were returned either to the Colt factory or to the Springfield Armory, where they were altered and refinished. These revolvers have 5.5" barrels and any combination of mixed serial numbers. They were re-marked by the inspectors of the era and have a case colored frame and a blued cylinder and barrel. Some have been noted all blued within this variation. This model, as with the other military marked Colts, should definitely be authenticated before purchase. Some of these revolvers fall outside the 1898 antique cutoff date that has been established by the government and, in our experience, are not quite as desirable to investors. They are generally worth approximately 20 percent less.

Courtesy Rock Island Auction Company

Exc.	V.G.	Good	Fair	Poor
—	12500	5000	2500	1500

Model 1902 (Philippine/Alaskan)

This is a U.S. Ordnance contract Model 1878. It has a 6" barrel and is chambered for .45 Colt. The finish is blued, and there is a lanyard swivel on the butt. This model bears the U.S. inspector's marks. It is sometimes referred to as the Philippine or the Alaskan model. The triggerguard is quite a bit larger than standard. About 4,600 produced in serial number range 43,401 to 48,097.

Courtesy Butterfield & Butterfield

Exc.	V.G.	Good	Fair	Poor
6000	4000	2000	1000	600

Model 1889 Navy

The 1889 Navy is an important model from a historical standpoint, as it was the first double-action revolver Colt manufactured with a swing-out cylinder. They produced 31,000 of them between 1889 and 1894. The Model 1889 is chambered for the .38 Colt and the .41 Colt cartridges. The cylinder holds 6 shots. It is offered with a 3", 4.5", or 6" barrel, and the finish was either blued or nickel-plated. The grips are checkered hard rubber with the "Rampant Colt" in an oval molded into them. The patent dates 1884 and 1888 appear in the barrel marking, and the serial numbers are stamped on the butt.

NOTE: For 3" barrel add 20%.

Exc.	V.G.	Good	Fair	Poor
—	1250	700	450	200

U.S. Navy Model

This variation has a 6" barrel, is chambered for .38 Colt, and is offered in blued finish only. "U.S.N." is stamped on the butt. Most of the Navy models were altered at the Colt factory to add the Model 1895 improvements. An original unaltered specimen would be worth as much as 50 percent premium over the altered values shown.

Courtesy Butterfield & Butterfield, San Francisco, California

Exc.	V.G.	Good	Fair	Poor
—	2500	1150	500	300

Model 1892 "New Army and Navy"

This model is similar in appearance to the 1889 Navy. The main differences are improvements to the lockwork function. It has double bolt stop notches, a double cylinder locking bolt, and shorter flutes on the cylinder. The .38 Smith & Wesson and the .32-20 were added to the .38 Colt and .41 Colt chamberings. The checkered hard rubber grips are standard, with plain walnut grips found on some contract series guns. Barrel lengths and finishes are the same as described for the Model 1889. The patent dates 1895 and 1901 appear stamped on later models. Colt manufactured 291,000 of these revolvers between 1892 and 1907. Antiques before 1898 are more desirable from an investment standpoint.

NOTE: For 3" barrel add 20%.

Exc.	V.G.	Good	Fair	Poor
1250	900	500	200	100

U.S. Navy Model

Exc.	V.G.	Good	Fair	Poor
3500	2750	1500	1000	750

Courtesy Butterfield & Butterfield, San Francisco, California

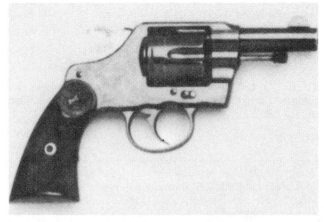

Courtesy Butterfield & Butterfield, San Francisco, California

U.S. Army Model

The initial Army purchase was for 8000 Model 1892 revolvers, almost all of which were altered to add "Model 1894" improvements. Unaltered examples will bring a premium.

Exc.	V.G.	Good	Fair	Poor
3000	2200	1250	600	300

Model 1894/96 Army Model

This model is an improved Model 1892 with a better locking mechanism for the cylinder. Many Model 1892 models were converted in this manner. By the middle of 1897, all U.S. troops were issued the Model 1894 revolver, which was the first military handgun to use smokeless powder cartridges. Marked "U.S ARMY MODEL 1894" on the bottom of the butt. The Model 1896 was identical to the Model 1894. The Model 1901 was the same as the Model 1894 with the addition of a lanyard swivel. The Model 1903 was identical to the Model 1894 with a smaller bore diameter (9.068mm) and a modified grip.

Paul Goodwin photo

Colt Model 1896 Army with cartouche • Paul Goodwin photo

Exc.	V.G.	Good	Fair	Poor
2000	1200	500	250	150

Model 1905 Marine Corps

This model is a variation of the Model 1894. It was derived from the late production with its own serial range #10001-10926. With only 926 produced between 1905 and 1909, it is quite rare on today's market and is eagerly sought after by Colt Double Action collectors. This model is chambered for the .38 Colt and the .38 Smith & Wesson Special cartridges. It holds 6 shots, has a 6" barrel, and is offered in a blued finish only. The grips are checkered walnut and are quite different than those found on previous models. "U.S.M.C." is stamped on the butt; patent dates of 1884, 1888, and 1895 are stamped on the barrel. One hundred-twenty-five of these revolvers were earmarked for civilian sales and do not have the Marine Corps markings; these will generally be found in better condition. Values are similar.

Courtesy Faintich Auction Services, Inc., Paul Goodwin photo

Exc.	V.G.	Good	Fair	Poor
4500	3500	2000	1500	750

Military Model of 1909 (New Service)

Made both in a commercial and military version, this revolver was chambered for the .45 Colt cartridge, fitted with a 5.5" barrel and walnut grips with lanyard swivel. Total military procurement was approximately 20,000 revolvers.

U.S. Army Model 1909, #30000-#50000

Marked "U.S. ARMY MODEL 1909" on butt. A total of about 18,000 were produced for the U.S. Army.

Courtesy Faintich Auction Services, Inc., Paul Goodwin photo

Exc.	V.G.	Good	Fair	Poor
3000	1500	800	300	200

U.S. Navy Model 1909, #30000-#50000

Same as above with "U.S.N." on butt. About 1,000 were produced for the U.S. Navy.

Exc.	V.G.	Good	Fair	Poor
3500	2000	1000	350	250

U.S. Marine Corps Model 1909, #30000-#50000

Checkered walnut grips. "U.S.M.C." on butt. About 1,200 were built for the Marine Corps.

Exc.	V.G.	Good	Fair	Poor
4500	2750	1350	650	450

U.S. Army Model 1917, #150000-#301000

Smooth walnut grips, 5.5" barrel, .45 ACP, model designation stamped on butt and barrel. The Model 1917 differed from the Model 1909 in that it had a shorter cylinder for half-moon clips for the .45 ACP cartridge, a wider cylinder stop lug on the sideplate, and a tapered barrel instead of a straight barrel. Blued, unpolished finish. Approximately 150,000 were purchased by the U.S. military.

Exc.	V.G.	Good	Fair	Poor
1250	850	500	300	225

A Colt U.S. Army Model 1917 sold at auction for $1,725. Condition was near mint. WWI issue with M1912 pistol belt, ammunition pouch, lanyard, and holster. Original box of ammunition.
Rock Island Auction Company, December 2001

THE COLT M1917 .45 ACP REVOLVER

The trench warfare of WWI put a huge premium on the need for effective fighting handguns for infantry troops. While the U. S. M1911 .45 ACP was unquestionably the single best of its time, they were available in insufficient supply for our needs. Fortunately, both Colt and S&W were filling large contracts with the British government for revolvers chambered for their .455 Webley cartridge. It was a relatively simple change to chamber these same revolvers for the .45 ACP cartridge once an S&W employee invented the half-moon clip to allow the revolver extractor to extract the rimless .45 ACP shell casings. The wartime production of the Colt M1917 eventually amounted to almost half of the total production of all Colt New Service revolvers. This incredibly robust and rugged revolver went on to be a standard sidearm of the U.S. Border Patrol and Post Office for many years. Many more served again as supplementary arms in WWII, particularly in military police units. Accurate, powerful, reliable, and quick to reload thanks to its half-moon clips, the M1917 was easily among the top three military revolvers of all time. While often criticized for being too large and only suitable for individuals with big hands, the simple addition of a grip adapter behind the triggerguard makes the M1917 grip comfortable for most people to handle and shoot. Famous former users of the Colt M1917 include Bill Jordan (WWII Marines), Charlie Askins (Border Patrol), and Harry Truman (WWI Army) among many others. Circa 1932 about 1000 M1917 revolvers were assembled by Colt from surplus military parts and sold commercially. In spite of their rarity, they often do not bring prices higher than nice military specimens. The Colt M1917 was easily one of the most significant revolvers in U.S. military history and arguably the best of the bunch as a combat handgun.

Chuck Karwan

Courtesy Richard M. Kumor Sr.

Exc.	V.G.	Good	Fair	Poor
550	450	275	150	100

Detective Special (Martially marked)
Chambered for the .38 Special cartridge and fitted with a 2" barrel. Blued finish with checkered cylinder latch and trigger. Checkered walnut grips. Approximately 5,000 were purchased by armed forces, mostly for military intelligence and police units.

Exc.	V.G.	Good	Fair	Poor
550	450	275	150	100

Air Crewman Special (Martially marked)
This model was especially fabricated for the Air Force to be carried by their pilots for protection. It is extremely lightweight at 11 oz. The frame and the cylinder are made of aluminum alloy. It has a 2" barrel and is chambered for a distinctive .38 Special "M41" military cartridge with a chamber pressure of 16,000 pounds per square inch. The finish was blued, with checkered walnut grips. There were approximately 1,200 manufactured in 1951 with special serial numbers A.F. 1 through A.F. 1189.

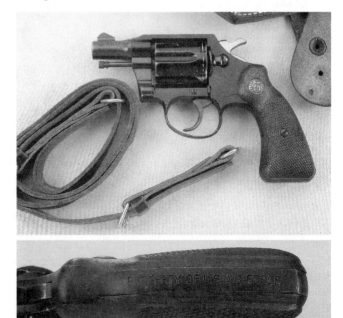

Air Crewman • Courtesy Little John's Auction Service, Paul Goodwin photo

Exc.	V.G.	Good	Fair	Poor
4500	2500	1500	800	250

Official Police (Martially marked)
This model was purchased by the military during World War II in barrel lengths of 4", 5", and 6". It has a polished blue finish. Chambered for the .38 Special cartridge. Checkered walnut grips. About 5,000 were purchased by the U.S. Army during WWII. The Defense Supply Corporation also purchased about 5,000 revolvers from Colt as well.

Exc.	V.G.	Good	Fair	Poor
750	600	400	300	150

Commando Model (Martially marked)
This model, for all intents and purposes, is an Official Police chambered for .38 Special, with 2" and 4" barrels. This model has a matte blue finish, no checkering on the cylinder latch or trigger and matte finish on top of the frame. Checkered plastic grips. Stamped "Colt Commando" on the barrel. There were approximately 50,000 manufactured from 1942 to 1945 for use in World War II.

NOTE: Add 30% for 2" barrel.

COLT SEMIAUTOMATIC PISTOLS

The Colt Firearms Co. was the first of the American gun manufacturers to take the advent of the semiautomatic pistol seriously. This pistol design was becoming popular among European gun makers in the late 1880s and early 1900s. In the United States, however, the revolver was firmly ensconced as the accepted design. Colt realized that if the semiauto could be made to function reliably, it would soon catch on. The powers that be at Colt were able to negotiate with some of the noted inventors of the day, including Browning, and to secure or lease the rights to manufacture their designs. Colt also encouraged the creativity of their employees with bonuses and incentives and, through this innovative thinking, soon became the leader in semiauto pistol sales—a position that they have never really relinquished to any other American gun maker. The Colt semiautomatic pistols represent an interesting field for the collector of Colt handguns. There were many variations with high enough production to make it worthwhile to seek them out.

Model 1900

This was the first of the Colt automatic pistols. It was actually a developmental model with only 3,500 being produced. The Model 1900 was not really a successful design. It was quite clumsy and out of balance in the hand and was not as reliable in function as it should have been. This model is chambered for the .38 Rimless smokeless cartridge. It has a detachable magazine that holds seven cartridges. The barrel is 6" in length. The finish is blued, with a case-colored hammer and safety/sight combination. The grips are either plain walnut, checkered walnut, or hard rubber. This pistol is a Browning design, and the left side of the slide is stamped "Browning's Patent" with the 1897 patent date. Colt sold 250 pistols to the Navy and 300 to the Army for field trials and evaluation. The remaining 3,300 were sold on the civilian market. This model was manufactured from 1900-1903.

NOTE: Civilian model with sight/safety combination add 40%.

Standard Civilian Production

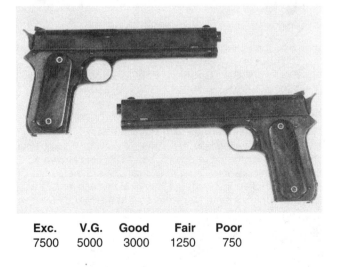

Exc.	V.G.	Good	Fair	Poor
7500	5000	3000	1250	750

U.S. Navy Military Model—250 built

Colt serial numbers 1001 to 1250 with Navy numbers, "U.S.N. 1 TO U.S.N. 250" on the left side of frame.

Model 1900 Navy model with sight safety • Paul Goodwin photo

Exc.	V.G.	Good	Fair	Poor
7500	6000	5000	2500	1000

U.S. Army Military Model—1st contract—100 built

Exc.	V.G.	Good	Fair	Poor
22000	18000	10000	4000	2000

U.S. Army Military Model—2nd contract—200 built

Exc.	V.G.	Good	Fair	Poor
20000	16000	8000	3000	1500

Model 1902 Military Pistol

This model is a somewhat larger, heavier pistol than the 1902 Sporting Pistol. It has the same .38 ACP chambering and 6" barrel, detachable magazine holding 8 rounds. The grip of this model is larger and squared off to accommodate the larger magazine, and it has a lanyard swivel on the butt. There were approximately 18,000 manufactured between 1902 and 1929. The vast majority of these pistols were commercial models.

Early Model with Front of Slide Serrated

Model 1902 U.S. military with early front slide serrations • Paul Goodwin photo

Exc.	V.G.	Good	Fair	Poor
3500	2250	1250	750	450

Standard Model with Rear of Slide Serrated

Model 1902 military with rear slide serrations • Paul Goodwin photo

Exc.	V.G.	Good	Fair	Poor
2500	1750	1000	500	400

U.S. Army Marked, #15001-#15200 with Front Serrations—200 built

Exc.	V.G.	Good	Fair	Poor
15000	12500	5000	2000	600

Model 1903 Hammerless, .32 Pocket Pistol

Courtesy Orvel Reichert

Model 1903 Hammerless with 4" barrel • Courtesy Richard M. Kumor Sr.

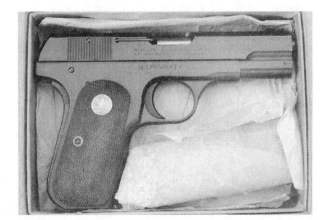

This was the second pocket automatic Colt manufactured. It was another of John Browning's designs, and it developed into one of Colt's most successful pistols. This pistol is chambered for the .32 ACP cartridge. Initially the barrel length was 4"; this was shortened to 3.75". The detachable magazine holds 8 rounds. The standard finish is blue, with quite a few nickel plated. The early model grips are checkered hard rubber with the "Rampant Colt" molded into them. Many of the nickel-plated pistols had pearl grips. In 1924 the grips were changed to checkered walnut with the Colt medallions. The name of this model can be misleading as it is not a true hammerless but a concealed hammer design. It features a slide stop and a grip safety. Colt manufactured 572,215 civilian versions of this pistol and approximately 200,000 more for military contracts. This model was manufactured between 1903 and 1945.

NOTE: A number of these pistols were shipped to the Philippine army as well as other foreign military forces, but no clear record of these shipments exist. However, about 24,000 Colt Hammerless pistols were sold to Belgium between 1915 and 1917. Serial numbers for these pistols are available (see Brunner, *The Colt Pocket Hammerless Automatic Pistols*). In addition, several thousand Colt .32 pocket pistols, as well as Colt .25 and .380 pocket models, were shipped to England during World War I. During World War II, Colt supplied about 8,000 Colt pocket pistols in various calibers to England in blued and parkerized finish marked "U.S. PROPERTY." (See Brunner.)

NOTE: Early Model 1897 patent date add 40%.
Nickel plated with pearl grips add $100.
4" barrel to #72,000 add 20%.

U.S. Military Model
Chambered for .32 caliber only and some of them marked "U.S. Property" on frame. Blue or parkerized finish.

NOTE: Pistols issued to General Officers will command a premium. Also, blued pistols will command a premium.

Model 1903, U.S. marked, issued to Gen. Ahee • Courtesy Richard M. Kumor Sr.

Exc.	V.G.	Good	Fair	Poor
1500	950	500	300	250

NOTE: *See also Belgium, Handguns, FN.*

Model 1908 Hammerless .380 Pocket Pistol

This model is essentially the same as the .32 Pocket Pistol, chambered for the more potent .380 ACP, also known as the 9mm Browning Short. Other specifications are the same. Colt manufactured approximately 138,000 in this caliber for civilian sales. An unknown number were sold to the military.

Standard Civilian Model
Nickel with pearl grips add $100.

Exc.	V.G.	Good	Fair	Poor
800	650	475	350	250

Military Model M
Some have serial prefix "M," marked "U.S. Property" on frame, blued finish.

NOTE: None of these pistols were originally parkerized.

Exc.	V.G.	Good	Fair	Poor
2500	1750	750	500	300

Model 1908 Hammerless .25 Pocket Pistol

This was the smallest automatic Colt made. It is chambered for the .25 ACP cartridge, has a 2" barrel, and is 4.5" long overall. It weighs a mere 13 oz. This is a true pocket pistol. The detachable magazine holds 6 shots. This model was offered in blue or nickel-plate, with grips of checkered hard rubber and checkered walnut on later versions. This model has a grip safety, slide lock, and a magazine disconnector safety. This was another Browning design, and Fabrique Nationale manufactured this pistol in Belgium before Colt picked up the rights to make it in the U.S. This was a commercial success by Colt's standards, with approximately 409,000 manufactured between 1908 and 1941.

NOTE: A small number of these pistols were bought by the OSS during World War II from retailers or distributors. These pistols are probably not martially marked. Beware of fakes that are marked by an engraving tool.

Courtesy Orvel Reichert

Civilian Model

Exc.	V.G.	Good	Fair	Poor
600	400	300	200	100

Military Model

"U.S. Property" stamped on right frame. Very rare.

Exc.	V.G.	Good	Fair	Poor
3750	3000	1000	450	300

Model 1905 .45 Automatic Pistol

The Spanish American War and the experiences with the Moros in the Philippine campaign taught a lesson about stopping power or the lack of it. The United States Army was convinced that they needed a more powerful handgun cartridge. This led Colt to the development of a .45-caliber cartridge suitable for the semiautomatic pistol. The Model 1905 and the .45 Rimless round were the result. In actuality, this cartridge was not nearly powerful enough to satisfy the need, but it led to the development of the .45 ACP. Colt believed that this pistol/cartridge combination would be a success and was geared up for mass production. The Army actually bought only 200 of them, and the total production was approximately 6,300 from 1905 to 1911. The pistol has a 5" barrel and detachable 7-shot magazine and is blued, with a case-colored hammer. The grips are checkered walnut. The hammer was rounded on the first 3,600 pistols and was changed to a spur hammer on the later models. The right side of the slide is stamped "Automatic Colt/Calibre 45 Rimless Smokeless." This model was not a commercial success for Colt—possibly because it has no safety whatsoever except for the floating inertia firing pin. The 200 military models have grip safeties only. A small number (believed to be less than 500) of these pistols were grooved to accept a shoulder stock. The stocks were made of leather and steel and made to double as a holster. These pistols have been classified "Curios and Relics" under the provisions of the Gun Control Act of 1968.

Civilian Model

Exc.	V.G.	Good	Fair	Poor
4000	3500	1750	950	400

Military Model, Serial #1-201

Known as the 1907 Contract Pistol, it has a lanyard loop, a loaded chamber indicator, spur hammer, and a grip safety and bears the inspector's initials "K.M."

Exc.	V.G.	Good	Fair	Poor
18000	16000	8500	2500	950

COLT 1911

Model designations and prices by Karl Karash

The popularity of the Military Colt 1911/1911A1 and its commercial Government Model sisters has recently skyrocketed to unheard of levels. The reasons for this popularity, despite general economic woes that have left the stock market in tatters, are many including the recent release of such superb movies as *Saving Private Ryan*, *We Were Soldiers*, and *The Lost Battalion*; the availability of massive amounts of WWII historical features on The History Channel; the widespread use of the Internet and Internet auctions as a tool for buying and selling collectable pistols; and probably a general realization that the heroes of WWII are dying at a geometric rate. Every 1911/1911A1 collector has his own reasons for trying to accumulate the best, the most comprehensive, and the most complete collection. Some collectors want to have one GI (Government Issue) but not necessarily original pistol that they can shoot. Others want a collection of completely original pistols in as pristine condition as is possible that they will probably never shoot, let alone touch without wearing white gloves. The vast majority of collectors want pistols in original condition and in as good of condition as they can afford. This general tendency has recently driven up the selling prices of collectible (original) Military 1911/1911A1 pistols to unheard-of levels. Prices realized on Internet auctions seem to break new records daily. These Internet auctions are especially troubling to the older collectors who are used to one-on-one buying and selling at gun shows and gun stores. Pistols sold through the Internet auctions usually have one or more pictures that can range from seemingly crystal clear (but perhaps digitally enhanced) to very fuzzy. The pictures are often of poor quality, and hide as much as they reveal. The conventional hands-on transaction, where the buyer uses his knowledge and examines the pistol live, has been replaced by an electronic process that is "Through A Glass Darkly." Nonetheless, the popularity of these auctions seems to be increasing, and the prices realized seem to be setting records. Live auctions, too, are still popular and also are realizing record prices, although probably not to the level of the Internet. The dramatic increase in collecting has been largely from new inexperienced collectors. (We were all inexperienced once.) The new (and often young) collectors usually take to the Internet as does a duck to water. Sometimes the new collector finds himself in over his head but, unlike a duck, he doesn't float. Experienced collectors know that there are a large number of refinished, restored, cold blued, altered, faked, or just plain messed-with pistols that will be represented as original. Often these undesirables can only be distinguished by a "hands on" inspection. Indeed, the army of new collectors has attracted its own group of camp followers and jackals who trail behind hoping to pick off an especially inexperienced straggler. This unsavory lot has sprung forth hoping to pass off a non-collectible, often messed-with pistol as if it was an original item. Usually the seller will attempt to take advantage of the inexperienced buyer by "spinning a yarn," as well as claiming knowledge of what an original should be. Greed has NOT gone out of fashion. The selling of collectibles is usually treated as "buyer beware," and legal redress is often impractical. In-depth knowledge and experience are the only weapons collectors have to protect themselves from the predators who are waiting to pounce. Before buying a pistol, read the books. Go to the auctions.

Attend the gun shows. Talk to and get to know other collectors. Above all, look at original pistols, as many of them as you can get to see and hold in your hands (white gloved of course) and learn what they look like. Carrying around a pair of white cotton gloves in a plastic bag is a good way to show collectors that you are serious and will not leave fingerprints on their pistols. Never pass up the opportunity to look at a collection. Never forget that an original pistol may be worth many thousands of dollars, while a similar refinished pistol would be worth only a utility shooter price. Also remember that the widespread collector interest has generated greatly inflated prices, as well as widespread counterfeiting and fakery. Only by education in depth can the collector "hold his own" with these predators and avoid costly mistakes.

There are four reference books on the Colt .45 Auto Pistol so indispensable to collecting .45s that they will be mentioned by name: *Colt .45 Service Pistols, Models of 1911 and 1911A1*, *Colt .45 Government Models (Commercial Series)*, and *Collectors Guide to Colt .45 Service Pistols, Models of 1911 and 1911A1* all by Charles Clawson. And *U.S. Military Automatic Pistols 1894-1920* by Edward S. Meadows. Currently Mr. Clawson's books are all out of print, but hopefully at least the *Collectors Guide* will be reprinted soon.

A Colt Model 1911 Winchester prototype was sold at auction for $28,600. There were also three prototype frames and slides. The frames and slides are tool room prototypes and unfinished. Acquired by Norm Flayderman from the Winchester Factory Collection. Condition of the pistol was Good wtih 80% to 85% blue.
Little John's Auction Service, Inc., November 2001

Note that since these pistols are primarily collector's items, and since originality and condition are the two factors that determine a pistol's value, the condition categories here differ from the stated categories in the front of this book. All prices are for pistols having all original parts and all finish present as factory-original finish. Broken parts, replaced parts, gun-smithing, and cold blue touch-ups will require appropriate deductions. Refinished pistols can be considered to be in or below poor condition or as non-collectible shootable pistols. Arsenal reworks are generally refinished, and while they are considered collectible pistols, they have their own categories that have values much lower than original pistols. We define the condition categories in terms of the percentage of original finish remaining: Excellent = 96% to 98% original finish, VG = 90% to 95% original finish, Good = 70% to 89% original finish, Fair = 45% to 69% original finish, and Poor condition = less than 45% original finish.

The amount of original finish can be accurately estimated by comparing the amount and thickness of the remaining finish on each part of the pistol's surface with its portion (in percent) of the total surface area. Then, add up the percents remaining. Thinning finish only counts for a portion of area covered. For example, if the finish on the front strap covers the entire surface, but the finish is only half as dense or thick as new finish, the contribution to the total is half of 7.6%, or 3.8%, and if the remainder of the pistol was as new, the pistol would have 96.2% finish.

The U.S. Military Model of 1911 was developed by a combination of the genius of John Browning plus a lot of interaction and feedback from the Ordnance Department. John T. Thompson, Lt. Colonel of the Ordnance Department, informed Colt's Patented Firearms Manufacturing Company on March 29, 1911, that the (M1911) self loading pistol had passed all prescribed tests [Editor's note: And by doing so, was adopted by The Department.] and the Department requested a quote on 30,262 pistols. The price that was finally agreed on was $14.25 per pistol and one magazine. Additional magazines were to be 50 cents each. The first 40 pistols were assembled on December 28, 1911, with an additional 11 pistols assembled the next day. The first shipment, a single wooden case of M1911 pistols serial numbered from 1 to 50, was made on January 4, 1912, from the Colt factory in Hartford, Conn., to the Commanding Officer, Springfield Armory. This single crate, marked on the outside "Serial Numbers 1 Through 50," has become "the stuff that (M1911 collectors') dreams are made of." The M1911 pistol was the most advanced self loading pistol of its time and in the eyes of many, it has remained so to this date. Yet while this is probably an exaggeration, elements of its design have become adopted in most subsequent self-loading designs. While hundreds of minor manufacturing and ergonomic changes have been made, only one functional change was made to the M1911 during its manufacture from 1911 to 1945. Removal of the original dimpled magazine catch required pushing the entire catch body into the frame far enough that the fingers could grasp and turn the protruding portion until the tooth of the catch lock left its groove in the receiver. Upon coming free, the catch lock and spring (propelled by the energy stored in the spring), often flew out of sight and landed in a mud puddle. At about serial number 3190, the design was changed and a slot was cut in the magazine catch body as well as in the head of the magazine catch lock. This greatly facilitated the disassembly of the pistol, as well as reduced the chances of losing a part. Yet Colt's manufacturing changes, Ordnance Department mandated changes (including 1911/1911A1 improvements), marking, commercial derivatives, and part variations used during manufacture by the various suppliers, amounted to over 200 variations; enough to keep even the most ardent collector in pursuit for decades.

COLT FOREIGN CONTRACT 1911 PISTOLS

NOTE: These foreign contract pistols are included as military pistols despite their commercial serial numbers. The majority of these pistols were used by foreign governments as military, police, or other government agency sidearms.

First Argentine Contract C6201-C6400

These pistols were delivered to the two Argentine battleships under construction at two U.S. shipyards. Rarely seen better than Good. Many of these pistols have been reblued and parts changed. Reblue = Fair/Poor.

Courtesy Karl Karash collection

Exc.	V.G.	Good	Fair	Poor
N/A	1200	700	500	300

Second Argentine Contract C20001-C21000

Most of these pistols have been reblued and had parts changed. Reblue = Fair/Poor.

Exc.	V.G.	Good	Fair	Poor
1800	1200	750	450	275

Subsequent Argentine 1911 Contracts after C21000

Many of these pistols have been reblued and parts changed. Reblue = Fair/Poor.

Exc.	V.G.	Good	Fair	Poor
1800	1200	750	450	275

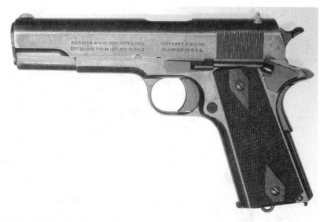

Courtesy Karl Karash collection

Courtesy Karl Karash collection

Canadian Contract (About 5000 pistols from C3000 to C14000)

Many pistols have owner's markings applied. (Condition 99%-100% add 20-30%)

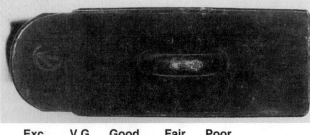

Exc.	V.G.	Good	Fair	Poor
3000	1800	950	550	300

First and Second British .455 Contract (200 pistols from W19000 to W19200) and 400 from W29001 to W29444

All "JJ" marked. Many pistols have owner's markings applied. (Condition 99%-100% add 20-30%)

Exc.	V.G.	Good	Fair	Poor
3500	2100	950	675	550

NOTE: Many of the .455 caliber pistols have been converted to .45 caliber by replacing their barrels. Converted pistols are usually considered no better than Good condition.

WWI British Contracts

This series is chambered for the British .455 cartridge and is so marked on the right side of the slide. The British "Broad Arrow" property mark will often be found. These pistols were made from 1915 to 1918. Some pistols are RAF marked on the left side of the frame. (add 30% for RAF.) RAF pistols normally have an endless welded steel ring through the lanyard loop. Many of these pistols have been reblued. Reblued=Fair/Poor. (Condition 99%-100% add 20-30%)

Left side of frame stamped "RAF" • Courtesy Karl Karash collection

Right side of slide stamped "CALIBER .455" • Courtesy Karl Karash collection

Exc.	V.G.	Good	Fair	Poor
2500	1700	750	675	500

French Contract (5000 pistols between C17800 and C28000)

Very seldom seen. (Condition 99%-100% add 20-30%)

Exc.	V.G.	Good	Fair	Poor
4500	2500	1150	750	500

1911 Russian Order

This variation is chambered for .45ACP and has the Russian version of "Anglo Zakazivat" stamped on the frame (English Order). There were about 51,100 pistols between serial C21,000 and C89,000 shipped. This variation is occasionally encountered today, and a few have been recently imported from Russia. At least one example is known that bears the Finnish arsenal mark "SA." This pistol may have been captured by the Finns as Russia invaded Finland prior to WWII. There could be thousands of these in warehouses ready to be released on the market. A precipitous drop in value might result. One should be extra cautious if contemplating a purchase, as fakes have been noted. However, original pistols in V.G. or better condition are in high demand despite the market uncertainties. (Condition 99%-100% add 20-30%)

Courtesy Karl Karash collection

Exc.	V.G.	Good	Fair	Poor
5000	3300	2250	1500	950

> A Colt Government Model Russian Order pistol, described as excellent overall with 97-98% original blue, slightly worn at the muzzle with a few scattered spots of surface rust, was sold at auction for $5,175. Rock Island Auction Company, December 2002

Kongsberg Vapenfabrik Model M/1912 (Norwegian) Contract SN 1-96

(Rarely seen) (Condition 99%-100% add 20-30%)

Exc.	V.G.	Good	Fair	Poor
3500	2200	1150	850	600

MODEL 1911 AUTOMATIC PISTOL, U.S. MILITARY SERIES

Colt Manufacture

Marked "MODEL OF 1911 U.S. ARMY" on right slide, "UNITED STATES PROPERTY" on left front frame until about Serial Number 510,000, then above trigger right. Serial number located on right front frame until Serial Number 7500, then above trigger right. Pistols have high polish and fire blue small parts until Serial Number 2400, then finish changed to non-reflective dull blue. Double diamond grips throughout. Dimpled mag catch from 1-3189, dimpled/slotted mag catch from 34190 to about 6500, and slotted thereafter. Lanyard loop magazine (3 types) until about Serial Number 129,000. Type 1 (stepped base until about Serial Number 4500, Type 2 (keyhole until about Serial Number 35000), and Type 3 (plain). Thereafter, two-tone non-looped magazine used through end of 1911 production.

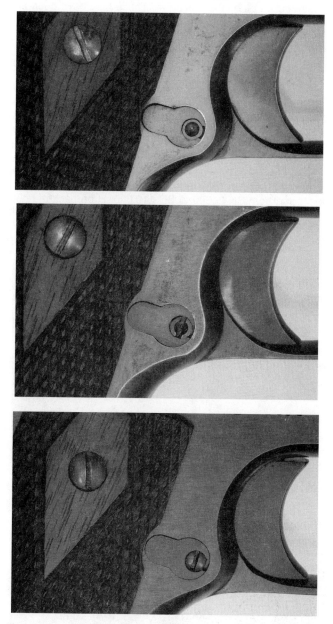

Mag catches • Courtesy Karl Karash collection

Model 1911 U.S. Army marked • Paul Goodwin photo

Serial Number 43 was shipped in first case of 50 pistols on January 4, 1912 • Courtesy Karl Karash collection

Below SN 101 "LARGE" "UNITED STATES PROPERTY" and other unique features

Unmarked fully blued barrel. (Condition 99%-100% add 20-30%)

Courtesy Karl Karash collection

Exc.	V.G.	Good	Fair	Poor
30000	12000	6000	4500	2500

Courtesy Karl Karash collection

Three Digit "MODEL OF 1911 U.S. ARMY" marked slide. SN 100 through SN 500.

Unmarked fully blued barrel until SN 400. H (with serifs) marked on rear of barrel hood until SN 500. (Condition 99%-100% add 20-30%)

Exc.	V.G.	Good	Fair	Poor
12000	6000	4000	2200	1200

Three Digit "MODEL OF 1911 U.S. NAVY" marked slide. SN 501 through SN 1000.

H (with serifs) marked on rear of barrel hood (fully blued). Some seemingly original early NAVY pistols have been observed with the later dull finish. These may have been finished, assembled, and shipped out of sequence. (Later dull finish in the range where mirror and fire blue is expected, under SN 2400, less 65%.) (Condition 99%-100% add 30-70%)

Exc.	V.G.	Good	Fair	Poor
15000	9000	6000	3200	2000

Model 1911 U.S. Navy marked • Paul Goodwin photo

Four Digit "MODEL OF 1911 U.S. ARMY" marked slide. With fire blue parts.

SN 1001 to 1500, 2001 to 2400, after SN 2,400, no fire blue and dull finish. (No fire blue after SN 2400, less 50%.) H (with serifs) marked on rear of barrel hood until SN 7500. Some seemingly original early ARMY pistols have been observed with the later dull finish. These may have been finished, assembled, and shipped out of sequence. (Later dull finish in the range where mirror and fire blue is expected, under SN 2400, less 65%.) (Condition 99%-100% add 20-30%)

Exc.	V.G.	Good	Fair	Poor
11000	6000	4000	2500	1500

1913 production USMC SN 3501 to 3800

Rarely seen and often well used. (Condition 99%-100% add 20-30%)

Exc.	V.G.	Good	Fair	Poor
9000	5000	4000	2500	1500

Courtesy Karl Karash collection

Four Digit "MODEL OF 1911 U.S. NAVY" marked slide.

SN 1501 to SN 2000, After SN 2400, no fire blue and dull finish. H (with serifs until SN 7500, no serifs after SN7500) marked on rear of barrel hood (fully blued). Five groups: (1501-2000, 2501-3500, 4501-5500, 6501-7500, and 8501-9500.) Some seemingly original early Navy pistols have been observed with the later dull finish. These may have been finished, assembled, and shipped out of sequence. (Later dull finish in the range where mirror and fire blue is expected, under SN 2400, less 65%.) (Dull finish no fire blue, less 40%, above SN 2400.) (Condition 99%-100% add 20-30%)

Exc.	V.G.	Good	Fair	Poor
17000	9500	6500	3900	2800

Five Digit Colt "MODEL OF 1911 U.S. ARMY" marked slide.

No fire blue, and dull finish. H (without serifs) marked on rear of barrel hood until about SN 19500. P (without serifs) marked on rear of barrel hood, H visible through ejection port from about SN 19500 to SN 24600. H P (horizontal) visible through eject port from SN 24600 to SN 110,000. H on back of hood add 15%. P on back of hood add 30%. (Condition 99%-100% add 20-30%)

Exc.	V.G.	Good	Fair	Poor
4000	2800	2500	1500	750

1913 production SN 36401 to 37650 USMC shipment.

Slide marked "MODEL OF 1911 U.S. ARMY" on ALL ORIGINAL USMC shipped pistols. (Any "USMC" marked 1911 pistol should be considered a FAKE. Same as five digit ARMY, but add 45%. Rarely seen and often well used.

Courtesy Karl Karash collection

Five Digit "MODEL OF 1911 U.S. NAVY" marked slide.

4 groups: SN (10,501-11,500, 12,501-13,500, 38,001-44,000, 96,001-97,537)

Exc.	V.G.	Good	Fair	Poor
5600	4200	2800	2000	1100

Six Digit "MODEL OF 1911 U.S. NAVY" marked slide.

SN (109,501-110,000). These 500 NAVY marked pistols were shipped to the Brooklyn Navy Yard for the Naval Militia and are more often found than most other batches. These are the only NAVY marked pistols to bear the JMG cartouche.

Exc.	V.G.	Good	Fair	Poor
5300	3500	2400	1800	1000

Springfield Armory "MODEL OF 1911 U.S. ARMY"

Dull finish, ALL parts MUST be Springfield marked. Made in four SN groups: 72571-83855, 102597-107596, 113497-120566. (Condition 99%-100% add 20-30%) Springfield Armory 72571 to about 75000 with short stubby hammer add 15%. (Condition 99%-100% add 20-30%)

Courtesy Karl Karash collection

Exc.	V.G.	Good	Fair	Poor
7000	5000	3300	2200	1100

Remington UMC "MODEL OF 1911 U.S. ARMY"

Dull finish, ALL parts MUST be Remington made. Most examples seem to have a deteriorated finish, probably due to poor surface preparation. EEC accepted and marked. Mainspring housing "E" marked, barrels "P" marked. Most pistols show thinning finish as well as flaking with little apparent wear. Pistols numbered in their own block of numbers from 1 to 21676 in large gothic letters. Almost never seen in better than Excellent condition. Beware of refinished pistols masquerading as original. Very late pistols show a one-line right side marking (add 15%).

Courtesy Karl Karash collection

Remington U.S. Model 1911, marked "Remington/UMC" • Paul Goodwin photo

Exc.	V.G.	Good	Fair	Poor
5000	3200	2100	1500	1000

1911 Colt "NRA" marked pistol

An unknown number of shipped Colt 1911 pistols were taken from stores and sold to NRA members. These pistols ranged from about SN 70,000 to the high 150,000 range. Pistols were marked N.R.A. under the serial or at the right front of the frame. The number is unknown, perhaps 300. Both crude and clever fakes abound. (Condition 99%-100% add 20-30%) So few of these rare pistols have been sold publicly that these prices are intended as a rough guide only.

Courtesy Karl Karash collection

Exc.	V.G.	Good	Fair	Poor
6500	4200	2700	1700	1000

1911 Springfield "NRA" marked pistol

An unknown number of shipped Colt 1911 pistols were taken from stores and sold to NRA members. These pistols ranged from about SN 70,000 to the high 129,000 range. Pistols were marked N.R.A. under the serial or at the right front of the frame. The number of N.R.A. marked Springfields is unknown, but based on observed pistols, it is perhaps 600. Both crude and clever fakes abound. (Condition 99%-100% add 20-30%)

Courtesy Karl Karash collection

Exc.	V.G.	Good	Fair	Poor
7000	5000	3300	2200	1100

North American Arms of Montreal QB "1911"
Made for U.S. but none delivered to Army. Less than 100 pistols assembled from parts. Rarely seen. Numbered on trigger under left grip and on left rear slide. Similar to five-digit Colt "ARMY" marked slide, but add 500%. (Condition 99%-100% add 20-30%) So few of these pistols have been sold publicly that these prices are intended as a rough guide only.

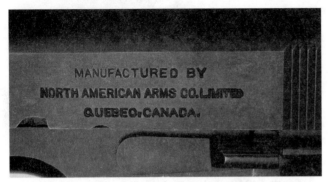

1911 North American Arms of Montreal • Courtesy Karl Karash collection

Exc.	V.G.	Good	Fair	Poor
25000	17000	11500	9000	6000

Six Digit Colt 1915 - 1918 "MODEL OF 1911 U.S. ARMY" marked slide.
Dull blue finish. Vertically oriented "P H" or "H P" marked on barrel, visible through eject port from about SN 110,000 to SN 425,000. Slides marked "MODEL OF 1911 U.S. ARMY" on ALL ORIGINAL USMC shipped pistols. Any "USMC" marked 1911 pistol should be considered a FAKE. (Condition 99%-100% add 20-30%)

Exc.	V.G.	Good	Fair	Poor
3300	2500	1800	1350	975

The following categories are listed relative to the pricing of the previous "Six Digit" SN Colt 1915-1918 "MODEL OF 1911 U.S. ARMY" marked slide:

SA suspended serial numbers assigned to Colt, shipped as replacement frames add 25%

1916 production with "S" marked frame, slide, and barrel add 60%

1916 production with partial "S" marked frame, slide, or barrel add 35%

1916 production with normally marked frame, slide, and barrel add 20%

1917 production 151187 to 151986 USMC shipment add 35% (Often well used)

1917 production 185801 to 186200 USMC shipment add 35% (Often well used)

1917 production 209587 to 210386 USMC shipment add 35% (Often well used)

1917 production 210387 to 215386 replacement frames add 35% (Rarely seen)

1917 production 215387 to 216186 USMC shipment add 35% (Rarely seen)

1917 production 216187 to 216586 ARMY transferred from USMC add 15% (Rarely seen)

1917 production 216587 to 217386 USMC shipment add 25% (Rarely seen)

1917 production 223953 to 223990 NAVY (ARMY marked) add 15%

1917 production 232001 to 233600 NAVY (ARMY marked) add 15%

1918-1919 production with eagle over number acceptance mark
Often called the Black Army because the coarse wartime finish appeared almost black. The black finish started about SN 375000. No inspector's cartouche from about serial number 302,000 to end of 1911 production (625,000). Barrel marked with overalls H P through about SN 425000. Interlaced HP (horizontal orientation) visible through ejection port from about SN 425000 to end of 1911 production. (If flaking present deduct 25%, watch out for reblue if no flaking present.) (Condition 99%-100% add 20-30%)

Courtesy Karl Karash collection

Exc.	V.G.	Good	Fair	Poor
3600	2500	1700	1250	800

4 Digit X Numbered Rework
These pistols were renumbered when their original serial numbers were either defaced, obliterated, or became too light to read during rebuilding or refinishing. The four digit X prefix serial numbers (X1000 through X4385) were assigned after WWI (1924) and were used by Springfield through 1953. All are considered "Arsenal Refinished."

Exc.	V.G.	Good	Fair	Poor
1100	850	700	575	475

"Military to Commercial Conversions"
Some 1911 military pistols that were brought home by GIs were subsequently returned to the Colt factory by their owners for repair or refinishing. If the repair included a new barrel, the pistol would have been proof fired and a normal verified proofmark affixed to the triggerguard bow in the normal commercial practice. If the pistol was refinished between 1920 and 1942, the slide would probably be numbered to the frame again in the normal commercial practice. Slides were numbered on the bottom disconnector rail during part of 1920, and after that they were numbered under the firing pin stop plate. These pistols are really a re-manufactured Colt pistol of limited production and should be valued at least that of a contemporary 1911A1 commercial pistol. (Pistols without VP or numbered slide usually cannot be authenticated, deduct 60%). Very seldom seen. (Condition 99%-100% add 30%).

Exc.	V.G.	Good	Fair	Poor
2000	1400	1100	800	575

SERIAL NUMBERS ASSIGNED TO M1911 AND 1911A1 CONTRACTORS

Year	Serial No.	Manufacturer
1912	1-500	Colt
	501-1000	Colt USN
	1001-1500	Colt
	1501-2000	Colt USN
	2001-2500	Colt
	2501-3500	Colt USN
	3501-3800	Colt USMC
	3801-4500	Colt
	4501-5500	Colt USN
	5501-6500	Colt
	6501-7500	Colt USN
	7501-8500	Colt
	8501-9500	Colt USN
	9501-10500	Colt
	10501-11500	Colt USN
	11501-12500	Colt
	12501-13500	Colt USN
	13501-17250	Colt
1913	17251-36400	Colt
	36401-37650	Colt USMC
	37651-38000	Colt
	38001-44000	Colt USN
	44001-60400	Colt
1914	60401-72570	Colt
	72571-83855	Springfield
	83856-83900	Colt
	83901-84400	Colt USMC
	84401-96000	Colt
	96001-97537	Colt
	97538-102596	Colt
	102597-107596	Springfield
1915	107597-109500	Colt
	109501-110000	Colt USN
	110001-113496	Colt
	113497-120566	Springfield
	120567-125566	Colt
	125567-133186	Springfield
1916	133187-137400	Colt
1917	137401-151186	Colt
	151187-151986	Colt USMC
	151987-185800	Colt
	185801-186200	Colt USMC
	186201-209586	Colt
	209587-210386	Colt USMC
	210387-215386	Colt Frames
	215387-216186	Colt USMC

Year	Serial No.	Manufacturer
1917	216187-216586	Colt
	216587-216986	Colt USMC
1918	216987-217386	Colt USMC
	217387-232000	Colt
	232001-233600	Colt USN
	233601-594000	Colt
	1-13152	Rem-UMC
1919	13153-21676	Rem-UMC
	594001-629500	Colt
	629501-700000	Winchester (Assigned)
1924	700001-710000	Colt
1937	710001-711605	Colt
	711606-712349	Colt USN
1938	712350-713645	Colt
1939	713646-717281	Colt USN
1940	717282-721977	Colt
1941	721978-756733	Colt
1942	756734-793657	Colt
	793658-797639	Colt USN
	797640-800000	Colt
	S800001-S800500	Singer
	H800501-H801000	H&R (Assigned, none delivered)
	801001-856100	Colt
1943	*856405-916404	Ithaca
	*916405-1041404	Remington-Rand
	*1041405-1096404	Union Switch
	1088726-1092896	Colt
	1096405-1208673	Colt
	1208674-1279673	Ithaca
	1279674-1279698	Replacement numbers
	1279699-1441430	Remington-Rand
1944	1441431-1471430	Ithaca
	1471431-1609528	Remington-Rand
	1609529-1743846	Colt
	1743847-1816641	Remington-Rand
	1816642-1890503	Ithaca
	1890504-2075103	Remington-Rand
	2075104-2134403	Ithaca
1945	2134404-2244803	Remington-Rand
	2244804-2380013	Colt
	2380014-2619013	Remington-Rand
	2619014-2693613	Ithaca

* Colt duplicated other manufacturers serial numbers

A Colt Model 1911 belonging to Major Theodore "Dutch" Van Kirk, navigator on the "Enola Gay" atomic bomb mission was sold at auction for $32,312. Condition was Fair with 20% original parkerized finish. This pistol was carried on other important combat missions as well.
Butterfield & Butterfield, June 2002

MODEL 1911A1 AUTOMATIC PISTOL MILITARY MODEL

COLT FOREIGN CONTRACT 1911A1 PISTOLS

These foreign contract pistols are included as military pistols despite their commercial serial numbers. These pistols were supplied by Colt to foreign governments as military, police, or other government agency sidearms. Many of these pistols have recently been imported into the USA, but only a few have been in "collectible, original" condition. Most have been refinished and sold at utility prices. The prices that the handful of original pistols sell for have been kept down by their poorer brothers and sisters. These original finish pistols, when found, may be some of the few bargains out there.

Argentine Army Modello 1927

Serial numbered 1 through 10000. Marked "EJERCITO ARGENTINO. Colts Cal.45 MOD.1927" on the right slide, and "Colts Pt. F.A. MFG. Co….etc." on the left slide. VP marked under left stock. Serial numbered on top of slide, under mainspring housing. Most of these pistols have been reblued and original finish pistols are very rare. Prices shown are for original pistols and the common reblued pistols would be equal to the Fair/Poor categories, depending on appearance.

Exc.	V.G.	Good	Fair	Poor
1000	700	500	400	300

Argentine Army "SIST.COLT CAL. 11.25mm MOD 1927"

Serial numbers extend over 112000. Made in Argentina under Colt license. This is a high quality 1911A1 copy with parts that generally interchange with Colt's 1911A1s. Marked "SIST.COLT CAL.11.25mm MOD 1927" on the right slide, and "D.G.F.M.-(F.M.A.P.)." on the left slide. Serial numbered on top of slide, frame, and barrel. Many of these pistols have been reblued, although original finish pistols are often seen. Prices shown are for original pistols and the more common reblued pistols would be equal to the Fair/Poor categories, depending on appearance.

Exc.	V.G.	Good	Fair	Poor
550	450	350	270	225

Argentine Navy, Coast Guard, Air Force, or Army Contract "Government Model"

Pistols serial numbered from about C130000 to about C190000. Marked "Armada Nacional," "Marina Argentina," "Aeronautica Argentina" or "Ejercito Argentina" on the right slide, and "Colts Pt. F.A. MFG. Co….etc." on the left slide. VP marked on left triggerguard bow. Serial numbered and marked as were normal commercial pistols. Most of these pistols have been reblued and original finish pistols are seldom seen. Prices shown are for original pistols and the common reblued pistols would be equal to the Fair/Poor categories, depending on appearance.

Exc.	V.G.	Good	Fair	Poor
1000	700	600	500	400

Argentine Navy, Coast Guard, Air Force, or Army Pistols

Serial numbered through about 112000. Marked "Armada Nacional," "Marina Argentina," "Aeronautica Argentina," or "Ejercito Argentina" on the right slide, and "D.G.F.M.-(F.M.A.P.)." on the left slide. Most of the recent imports of these pistols have been reblued and collectable original finish pistols are seldom seen except when from older collections. Prices shown are for original pistols, and the common reblued pistols would be equal to the Fair/Poor categories, depending on appearance.

Argentine Seal • Courtesy Karl Karash collection

Exc.	V.G.	Good	Fair	Poor
550	450	350	270	225

Argentine Navy "Government Model" With Swartz Safety

Serial numbered from about C199000 to about C2010001. Marked "Republica Argentina, Armada Nacional-1941" on the right slide, and "Colts Pt. F.A. MFG. Co….etc." on the left slide. VP marked on left triggerguard bow. Serial numbered and marked as were normal 1941 commercial pistols. Most or all of these pistols have the Swartz safeties. Most of these pistols have been reblued or parkerized when imported, and original finish collectable pistols are very rare. Prices shown are for original pistols, and the common reblued pistols would be equal to the Fair/Poor categories, depending on appearance. The very rare Swartz safeties (only a few thousand total were produced) in these pistols are under-appreciated by most collectors, and make this variation highly undervalued, especially for the few original finish pistols. The Swartz firing pin block safety can be observed by pulling the slide back all the way and looking at the top of the frame. A Swartz safety equipped 1911A1 pistol will have a second pin protruding up, next to the conventional disconnector pin. This second pin pushes a spring-loaded piston in the rear part of the slide that is visible when the slide is pulled back and the slide is viewed from underneath. This piston, in turn, blocks the firing pin when relaxed. A second Swartz safety (the Swartz Sear Safety) is usually built into pistols equipped with the Swartz firing pin block safety. The sear safety can sometimes be detected by the drag marks of the notched sear on the round portion of the hammer that the sear rides on. Pulling the hammer all the way back will expose these drag marks if they are visible. Presence of the drag marks however, does not insure that the Swartz modified sear safety parts are all present.

Exc.	V.G.	Good	Fair	Poor
1800	1300	900	700	500

Brazilian Army Contract "Government Model"

Pistols serial numbered from about C190000 to about C214000. Marked "Ejercito Brazilia" on the right slide, and "Colts Pt. F.A. MFG. Co….etc." on the left slide. VP marked on left triggerguard bow. Serial numbered and marked as were normal commercial pistols. Only a few of these complete pistols have made it to the USA, but many slides were sold as surplus parts when Brazil converted from .45 Cal to 9mm. Most or all of these slides have been reblued and original finish pistols are very rarely seen. Prices shown are for original pistols, and the common reblued pistols would be equal to the Poor category or below, depending on appearance. Separate slides would have the value of a high quality "after market" part.

Exc.	V.G.	Good	Fair	Poor
1200	900	700	500	400

North of Cam Lo, RVN, 3 Mar 67. 2LT J.E. Garney, commander of 1st Platoon, A Co., 1st Bn., 9th Marine Regt., 3rd Marine Division, encourages his men forward against NVA troops during Operation Prairie II. His .45 caliber M1911A1 auto pistol is ready to go with hammer fully cocked • USMC/National Archives/Robert Bruce Military Photo Features

COLT MANUFACTURE

Service Model Ace

In 1937 Colt introduced this improved version of the Ace pistol. It utilizes a floating chamber invented by David "Carbine" Williams, the firearms designer who invented the M1 carbine while serving time on a southern chain gang. This floating chamber gave the Service Model Ace the reliability and feel that the public wanted. The serial number is prefixed by the letters "SM." The external configuration is the same as the Ace, and the slide is marked "COLT SERVICE MODEL ACE .22 LONG RIFLE." Colt sold most to the Army and a few on a commercial basis. There were a total of 13,803 manufactured before production ceased in 1945. (99%-100% finish add 33%)

Parkerized Pistols (after about serial # SM3840)

Exc.	V.G.	Good	Fair	Poor
2600	1700	1050	600	450

Blued Pistols (before serial # SM3840)

Exc.	V.G.	Good	Fair	Poor
3500	2000	1250	800	600

Transition Model of 1924

SN 700,001 to 710,000. Some pistols below 700,100 rumored to have numbered slides (not verified). Made in 1924. All were accepted by Walter T. Gordon and marked with the "G" forms the outer circle is seen through about SN 7022000. The second type has an outer circle around the "G." Brushed blue finish, all 1911A1 features (arched mainspring housing, short checkered trigger, long tang on grip safety, trigger finger cutouts, full checkered walnut grips, etc.). However, they retained the "MODEL OF 1911 U.S. ARMY" slide marking. No verified proof or final inspector's mark on triggerguard bow, interlaced "H P" and "K" marked barrel, and serifed "H" over firing pin stop plate. (Add 30% for 99%-100% finish.)

Courtesy Karl Karash collection

First Type acceptance markings • Courtesy Karl Karash collection

Exc.	V.G.	Good	Fair	Poor
4000	2900	2050	1500	1000

First Transition Model of 1937

SN 710,001 to about 711,001. Numbered slide under firing pin stop plate. No "P" marking on frame or slide. Brushed blue finish, all 1911A1 features (arched mainspring housing, short checkered trigger, long tang on grip safety, trigger finger cutouts, full checkered walnut grips, etc.). However, they retained the "MODEL OF 1911 U.S. ARMY" slide marking. Verified proof and final inspector's mark on triggerguard bow. "COLT .45 AUTO" marked magazine floorplate with flattened letters and "COLT .45 AUTO" marked barrel. Extremely rare. (Add 40% for 99%-100% finish.) So few of these pistols have sold publicly that these prices are intended as a rough guide only.

Exc.	V.G.	Good	Fair	Poor
7000	4500	3250	2100	1475

Second Transition Model of 1937

About SN 711,001 to 712,349. Numbered slide under firing pin stop plate. "P" marking on frame and top of slide. Brushed blue finish, all 1911A1 features (arched mainspring housing, short checkered trigger, long tang on grip safety, trigger finger cutouts, full checkered walnut grips, etc.). However, they retained the "MODEL OF 1911 U.S. ARMY" slide marking. Verified proof and final inspector's mark on triggerguard bow. "COLT .45 AUTO" marked magazine floorplate with flattened letters and "COLT .45 AUTO" marked barrel. Extremely rare. (Add 40% for 99%-100% finish.) So few of these rare pistols have sold publicly that these prices are intended as a rough guide only.

Exc.	V.G.	Good	Fair	Poor
7000	4500	3250	2100	1475

Model of 1911A1, 1938 Production

SN 712,350 to 713,645. Numbered slide under firing pin stop plate. "P" marking on frame and top of slide. No markings on right side of slide. Brushed blue finish, all 1911A1 features (arched mainspring housing, short checkered trigger, long tang on grip safety, trigger finger cutouts, full checkered walnut grips, etc.). Right side of frame is marked "M1911A1 U.S. ARMY" forward of the slide stop pin, and "United States Property" behind the slide stop pin. Verified proof and final inspector's mark on triggerguard bow. Most are "H" marked on left side by magazine catch. "COLT .45 AUTO" marked magazine floorplate with flattened letters and "COLT .45 AUTO" marked barrel. Extremely rare. (Add 50% to 100% for 99%-100% finish.) So few of these rare pistols have been sold publicly that these prices are intended as a rough guide only.

Exc.	V.G.	Good	Fair	Poor
12500	8500	5500	4000	2750

NOTE: All Military .45 cal. pistols manufactured during and after 1938 are designated and marked "1911A1" and include all the 1911A1 features.

Model of 1911A1, 1939 Production (1939 NAVY)

SN 713,646 to 717,281. Numbered slide under firing pin stop plate. "P" marking on frame and top of slide. No markings on right side of slide. Brushed blue finish. Shortened hammer. Right side of frame is marked "M1911A1 U.S. ARMY" forward of the slide stop pin, and "United States Property" behind the slide stop pin. Verified proof and final inspector's mark on triggerguard bow. Full checkered walnut grips. Most are "H" marked on left side by magazine catch. "COLT .45 AUTO" marked magazine floorplate with flattened letters, and "COLT .45 AUTO" marked barrel. Rare. (Add 30% for 99%-100% finish.)

Exc.	V.G.	Good	Fair	Poor
3600	2700	1900	1050	700

Model of 1911A1, 1940 Production (CSR)

SN 717,282 to 721,977. Numbered slide under firing pin stop plate. "P" marking on frame and top of slide. No markings on right side of slide. Brushed blue finish. Shortened hammer. Right side of frame is marked "M1911A1 U.S. ARMY" forward of the slide stop pin, and "United States Property" behind the slide stop pin. Verified proof and final inspector's mark on triggerguard bow. "CSR" (Charles S. Reed) marked on left side below slide stop. "COLT .45 AUTO" marked magazine floorplate with flattened letters, and "COLT .45 AUTO" marked barrel. Full checkered walnut grips but some pistols may have early brittle plastic grips. Rare. (Add 30% for 99%-100% finish.)

Courtesy Karl Karash collection

Exc.	V.G.	Good	Fair	Poor
3300	2500	1800	1200	850

Model of 1911A1, 1941 Production (RS)

SN 721,978 to 756,733. Numbered slide under firing pin stop plate. "P" marking on frame and top of slide. No markings on right side of slide. Brushed blue finish through about SN 736,000. Parkerizing was used thereafter until the end of Colt production. Any Colt pistol after about SN 737,000 with a blued finish is likely to be a FAKE. Shortened hammer. Right side of frame is marked "M1911A1 U.S. ARMY" forward of the slide stop pin, and "United States Property" behind the slide stop pin. Verified proof and final inspector's mark on triggerguard bow. "RS" (Robert Sears) marked on left side below slide stop starting at about SN 723,000, ending about 750,500. After about SN 750,500, pistols were marked "WB" (Waldemar S. Broberg). "COLT .45 AUTO" marked magazine floorplate with flattened letters, and "COLT .45 AUTO" marked barrel. Early pistols may have wood grips, later pistols have hollow back (without ribs) plastic grips. Prices are for blued finish. (Parkerized finish less 40%.) Rare. (Subtract 5% to 10% for British proofs, most collectors prefer virgin pistols. Add 30% for 99%-100% finish.)

Exc.	V.G.	Good	Fair	Poor
3200	2550	1750	1250	875

Model of 1911A1, 1942 Production (WB)

SN 756,733 to about 856,100. Numbered slide under firing pin stop plate. All subsequent Colt made 1911A1 pistols have a "P" marking on frame and top of slide. No markings on right side of slide. Parkerized finish. Shortened hammer. Right side of frame is marked "M1911A1 U.S. ARMY" forward of the slide stop pin, and "United States Property" behind the slide stop pin. Colt plastic stocks with wide rings around screws. Verified proof and final inspector's mark on triggerguard bow, and "COLT .45 AUTO" marked barrel. "WB" (Waldemar S. Broberg) marked on left side below slide stop "COLT .45 AUTO" marked magazine floorplate with flattened letters, sand blasted bottom. (Subtract 5% to 10% for British proofs, most collectors prefer virgin pistols. Add 30% for 99%-100% finish.)

Exc.	V.G.	Good	Fair	Poor
1650	1350	1150	950	725

Model of 1911A1, 1942 NAVY

3982 pistols shipped to Naval supply depots, Oakland, Calif., and Sewalls Point, Va. Numbered SN 793658 to SN 797639. Numbered slide under firing pin stop plate. "P" marking on frame and top of slide. No markings on right side of slide. Parkerized finish. Shortened hammer. Right side of frame is marked "M1911A1 U.S. ARMY" forward of the slide stop pin, and "United States Property" behind the slide stop pin. Verified proof and final inspector's mark on triggerguard bow. "WB" (Waldemar S. Broberg) marked on left side below slide stop. "COLT .45 AUTO" marked magazine floorplate with flattened letters, sand blasted bottom, and "COLT .45 AUTO" marked barrel. (Subtract 5% to 10% for British proofs, most collectors prefer virgin pistols. Add 30% for 99%-100% finish.)

Exc.	V.G.	Good	Fair	Poor
2100	1650	1350	1100	875

Model of 1911A1, Singer Manufacturing Co., Educational Order 1942

Exactly 500 pistols accepted and shipped. "J.K.C." (John K. Clement) marked on left side below slide stop. At least two un-numbered (and not marked United States Property) pistols were made and retained by employees. Slightly dull blue finish, brown plastic hollow-back grips, unmarked blue magazine, wide spur hammer, checkered slide stop, thumb safety, trigger, and mainspring housing. About 100 of the original 500 are known. Very Rare and most highly desired. Exercise caution when contemplating a purchase as fakes, improved, and reblued models abound. Be extra cautious with an example that is 98% or better. (Add 50% for 99%-100% finish. Original pistols un-numbered or numbered with out-of-sequence numbers subtract 50% to 70%. Subtract 5% to 10% for British proofs, most collectors prefer virgin pistols. Reblued, restored subtract 90% to 95%.)

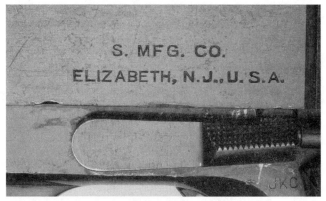

Singer Legend • Courtesy Karl Karash collection

Exc.	V.G.	Good	Fair	Poor
30000	22000	17500	13500	9000

Rock Island Arsenal Replacement numbers

SN 856,101 to 856,404. Replacement numbers issued to allow a pistol whose number had been defaced or worn away during refinishing to be numbered again. Very rare; only one known.

Exc.	V.G.	Good	Fair	Poor
1300	1000	750	650	500

Model of 1911A1, Military. 1943 Production (GHD marked)

SN 867,000 to about 1,155,000. Colt had its own serial numbers assigned within this range, but in addition, Colt duplicated Ithaca's serial numbers between 865,404, and 916,404 as well as Remington Rand's between 916,405 and 958,100, and US&S's between 1,088,726 and 1,092,896. Numbered slide under firing pin stop plate until about SN 1,140,000. "P" marking on frame and top of slide. Parkerized. Right side of frame is marked "M1911A1 U.S. ARMY" forward of the slide stop pin, and "United States Property" behind the slide stop pin. Verified proof and final inspector's mark on triggerguard bow. "GHD" (Guy H. Drewry) marked on left side below slide stop. Plain blued or contract magazine, and "COLT .45 AUTO" marked barrel. Colt plastic stocks with wide rings around screws. Add 15% for matching numbered slide. (Subtract 5% to 10% for British proofs, most collectors prefer virgin pistols. Add 30% for 99%-100% finish.) Colt in Ithaca or Remington Rand range add 10%, Colt in U.S.& S range add 20%.

Exc.	V.G.	Good	Fair	Poor
1500	1250	1000	850	700

Model of 1911A1, Commercial to Military Conversions. 1943 Production

(A few were WB marked, most were GHD marked.) SN 860,003 to about 867,000. Numbered slide under firing pin stop plate. "P" marking on frame and top of slide. Commercial markings on right side of slide. Parkerized finish over previously blued finish. Original Commercial SN peened and restamped with military numbers. Most have the Swartz grip safety cutouts in slide and frame but not the Swartz parts. None of the Commercial to military conversions have the Swartz "sear safety." No slides marked "NATIONAL MATCH" have been reported. If any exist, an NM slide pistol would command a premium. Shortened hammer. Right side of frame is marked "M1911A1 U.S. ARMY" forward of the slide stop pin, and "United States Property" behind the slide stop pin. Verified proof and final inspector's mark on triggerguard bow. "GHD" (Guy H. Drewry) marked on left side below slide stop "COLT .45 AUTO" marked magazine floorplate with flattened letters, sand blasted bottom. Colt plastic stocks with wide rings around screws. (Subtract 5% to 10% for British proofs, most collectors prefer virgin pistols. Add 30% for 99%-100% finish. Add 10%-30% for NM marked slide.)

Courtesy Karl Karash collection

Exc.	V.G.	Good	Fair	Poor
2000	1650	1375	1150	825

Model of 1911A1, Military with Commercial Slide. 1943 Production (GHD marked)

SN 867,000 to about 936,000. Perhaps a few hundred total. Numbered slide under firing pin stop plate. "P" marking on frame and top of slide. Commercial markings on right side of slide. Parkerized finish over previously blued finish (slide only). Most have the Swartz grip safety cutouts in slide but not in frame. None have the Swartz parts. Frames are generally new military manufacture. Shortened hammer. Right side of frame is marked "M1911A1 U.S. ARMY" forward of the slide stop pin, and "United States Property" behind the slide stop pin. Verified proof and final inspector's mark on triggerguard bow. "GHD" (Guy H. Drewry) marked on left side below slide stop. May have "COLT .45 AUTO" marked magazine floorplate with flattened letters with sand blasted bottom or plain blued magazine. Colt plastic stocks with wide rings around screws. Barrels marked "COLT .45 AUTO." (Add 30% for 99%-100% finish. Add 35% for Canadian Broad arrow/C.)

Exc.	V.G.	Good	Fair	Poor
1800	1450	1250	1000	775

Model of 1911A1, Canadian Broad Arrow/C marked 1943 Production

Marked on the left rear and left frame. 1515 pistols (GHD marked) SN 930,000 to about 939,000. Numbered slide under firing pin stop plate. "P" marking on frame and top of slide. Commercial markings on right side of slide on a few, otherwise blank. Parkerized finish. Right side of frame is marked "M1911A1 U.S. ARMY" forward of the slide stop pin, and "United States Property" behind the slide stop pin. Verified proof and final inspector's mark on triggerguard bow. "GHD" (Guy H. Drewry) marked on left side below slide stop. All appear to have British proofs as well. A few pistols in "Fair" condition have recently been sold at auction without British proofs. These pistols were used in Canadian prisons and recently released. Beware non-British marked Canadian pistols in better than "Good" condition, as some of these same former prison pistols have appeared in "New" condition. Barrels marked "COLT .45 AUTO." Most have plain blued magazine. Colt plastic stocks with wide rings around screws. (Add 30% for 99%-100% finish. Add 25% for numbered commercial slide.)

Courtesy Karl Karash collection

Exc.	V.G.	Good	Fair	Poor
2100	1750	1250	1000	825

Model of 1911A1, Military. 1944 Production (GHD marked)

SN 1,155,000 to about 1,208,673, and 1,609,529 to 1,720,000. Un-numbered slide. "P" marking on frame and top of slide. Parkerized. Right side of frame is marked "M1911A1 U.S. ARMY" forward of the slide stop pin, and "United States Property" behind the slide stop pin. Verified proof and final inspector's mark on triggerguard bow. "GHD" (Guy H. Drewry) marked on left side below slide stop. Barrels marked "COLT .45 AUTO." Plain blued or contract magazine. Colt plastic stocks with wide rings around screws. (Subtract 5% to 10% for British proofs, most collectors prefer virgin pistols. Add 30% for 99%-100% finish.)

Exc.	V.G.	Good	Fair	Poor
1400	1250	1050	900	725

Model of 1911A1, Military. 1945 Production

(GHD marked but a few were J.S.B. marked, see below, and a few were un-inspected.) SN 1,720,000 to 1,743,846, and 2,244,804 to 2,368,781. Un-numbered slide. "P" marking on frame and top of slide. Parkerized. Right side of frame is

marked "M1911A1 U.S. ARMY" forward of the slide stop pin, and "United States Property" behind the slide stop pin. Verified proof and final inspector's mark on triggerguard bow. "GHD" (Guy H. Drewry) marked on left side below slide stop. Plain blued or contract magazine. Early barrels marked "COLT .45 AUTO," later examples marked with a "C" in a square. Colt plastic grips with wide rings around screws. (Subtract 5% to 10% for British proofs, most collectors prefer virgin pistols. Add 30% for 99%-100% finish.)

Exc.	V.G.	Good	Fair	Poor
1400	1250	1050	900	725

Model of 1911A1, Military. 1945 Production

(A few thousand were J.S.B. marked.) Around SN 2,360,600. Un-numbered slide. "P" marking on frame and top of slide. Parkerized. Right side of frame is marked "M1911A1 U.S. ARMY" forward of the slide stop pin, and "United States Property" behind the slide stop pin. Verified proof and final inspector's mark on triggerguard bow. "JSB" (John S. Begley) marked on left side below slide stop. Plain blued or contract magazine. Barrels marked with a "C" in a square. Colt plastic grips with wide rings around screws. Extremely rare! (Add 100% for J.S.B. marking. Subtract 5% to 10% for British proofs, most collectors prefer virgin pistols. Add 30%-50% for 99%-100% finish.)

Exc.	V.G.	Good	Fair	Poor
3800	2750	2200	1700	1400

Colt, Model of 1911A1, Military. 1945 Production

(Un-inspected and usually no ordnance wheel.) Around SN 2,354,000. Un-numbered slide. "P" marking on frame and top of slide. Parkerized. Right side of frame is marked "M1911A1 U.S. ARMY" forward of the slide stop pin, and "United States Property" behind the slide stop pin. Verified proof and final inspector's mark on triggerguard bow. Plain blued or contract magazine. Barrels marked with a "C" in a square. Colt plastic grips with wide rings around screws. Very rare. (Subtract 5% to 10% for British proofs, most collectors prefer virgin pistols. Add 30% for 99%-100% finish.)

Exc.	V.G.	Good	Fair	Poor
1600	1200	800	650	400

Ithaca Gun Co. 1943-1945 Production

FJA inspected, un-numbered slide. Right side of frame is marked "M1911A1 U.S. ARMY" forward of the slide stop pin, and "United States Property" behind the slide stop pin. Plastic Keyes Fibre grips, stamped trigger, flat sided hammer, late pistols had serrated flat sided hammer, HS marked barrel, contract magazine. A few early pistols had an I prefix Serial Number. A few into the 1.28 million range had the "MODEL OF 1911 U.S. ARMY" on the right side of the slide. A few thousand early pistols were made with reclaimed WWI Colt frames ("H" marked on top of frame, and heart shaped cutouts). Add 50% for Colt frame. (Subtract 5% to 10% for British proofs, most collectors prefer virgin pistols.) (Add 40% for 99%-100% finish. Add 20% for "MODEL OF 1911A1 U.S. ARMY" marked slide. Add 15% for DU-LITE finish, below about SN 950,000. Add 150% for I prefix.)

Exc.	V.G.	Good	Fair	Poor
1050	950	850	675	600

Remington Rand Co. 1942-1943 Production

"NEW YORK" (Type I) marked slide. FJA inspected, un-numbered slide. Right side of frame is marked "M1911A1 U.S. ARMY" forward of the slide stop pin, and "United States Property" behind the slide stop pin. DU-LITE (blued over sand blasting) finish. Plastic Keyes Fibre grips with no rings around screws. Milled trigger, flat sided hammer, "COLT .45 AUTO" marked barrel, contract magazine. Fine checkered mainspring housing. (Subtract 5% to 10% for British proofs, most collectors prefer virgin pistols. Add 40% for 99%-100% finish.)

Courtesy Karl Karash collection

Exc.	V.G.	Good	Fair	Poor
2000	1100	900	825	750

Remington Rand Co. 1943 Production

Large "N.Y." (Type II) marked slide. FJA inspected, un-numbered slide. Right side of frame is marked "M1911A1 U.S. ARMY" forward of the slide stop pin, and "United States Property" behind the slide stop pin. DU-LITE (blued over sand blasting) finish. Plastic Keyes Fibre grips with small rings around screws. Stamped trigger, flat sided hammer, "HS" marked barrel, contract magazine. Fine checkered mainspring housing. (Subtract 5% to 10% for British proofs, most collectors prefer virgin pistols. Add 40% for 99%-100% finish.)

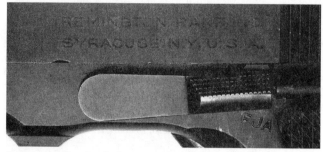

Courtesy Karl Karash collection

Exc.	V.G.	Good	Fair	Poor
1400	1100	900	825	750

Remington Rand Co. 1943-1945 Production

Small "N. Y." (Type III) marked slide. FJA inspected, un-numbered slide. Right side of frame is marked "M1911A1 U.S. ARMY" forward of the slide stop pin, and "United States Property" behind the slide stop pin. Parkerized (phosphate over sand blasting) finish. Plastic Keyes Fibre grips with small rings around screws. Stamped trigger, flat-sided hammer, "HS" marked barrel, contract magazine. Serrated mainspring housing. (Subtract 5% to 10% for British proofs, most collectors prefer virgin pistols. Add 40% for 99%-100% finish.)

Courtesy Karl Karash collection

Exc.	V.G.	Good	Fair	Poor
1050	900	820	750	675

Remington Rand Co. 1942-1945 Production

Numbered Presentation pistol (all observed are Type III) marked slide. They were usually disposed of as give-aways to contracting personnel and employees, however several remained in the company safe long after WWII until they were eventually sold. No inspector, un-numbered slide. The only frame marking is a two or three digit number above trigger right. Parkerized (phosphate over sand blasting) finish. Plastic Keyes Fibre grips with small rings around screws. Stamped trigger, flat-sided hammer, "HS" marked barrel, contract magazine. Serrated mainspring housing. (Add 30% for 99%-100% finish.)

Exc.	V.G.	Good	Fair	Poor
2400	2000	1550	1300	1100

Remington Rand Co. 1942-1945 Production

ERRS prefix Presentation pistol (all observed are Type III) marked slide. They were usually disposed of as give-aways to contracting personnel and employees, however several remained in the company safe long after WWII until they were eventually sold. No inspector, un-numbered slide. The only frame marking is a two or three digit number with the "ERRS" prefix above trigger right. Parkerized (phosphate over sand blasting) finish. Plastic Keyes Fibre grips with small rings around screws. Stamped trigger, flat-sided hammer, "HS" marked barrel, contract magazine. Serrated mainspring housing. Popular wisdom seems to be that "ERRS" meant "Experimental Remington Rand"; however, there seems to be no evidence to support that notion. The true meaning of ERRS may never be known. (Add 30% for 99%-100% finish.)

Exc.	V.G.	Good	Fair	Poor
2800	2150	1800	1300	1100

UNION SWITCH SIGNAL CO.

Swissvale, Pennsylvania. 55,000 pistols total delivered in 1943. US&S pistols have become one of the most sought after of all the 1911/1911A1 pistols.

Courtesy Karl Karash collection

Union Switch Signal Co. 1943 Production. Type I

(No "P" on frame or slide. From SN 1,041,405 to about 1,060,000 with probable overlap. RCD inspected, un-numbered slide. Right side of frame is marked "M1911A1 U.S. ARMY" forward of the slide stop pin, and "United States Property" behind the slide stop pin. DU-LITE (blued over sand blasting) finish. Plastic Keyes Fibre grips with or without rings around screws. Stamped, blued trigger, flat-sided hammer, "HS" marked barrel, contract magazine. Checkered mainspring housing. (Add 40% for 99%-100% finish.)

Courtesy Karl Karash collection

Exc.	V.G.	Good	Fair	Poor
2500	1950	1700	1300	1100

Union Switch Signal Co. 1943 Production. Type II

("P" on top edge of slide.) From about SN 1,060,000 to about 1,080,000 with probable overlap. RCD inspected, un-numbered slide. Right side of frame is marked "M1911A1 U.S. ARMY" forward of the slide stop pin, and "United States Property" behind the slide stop pin. DU-LITE (blued over sand blasting) finish. Plastic Keyes Fibre grips with or without rings around screws. Stamped, blued trigger, flat sided hammer, "HS" marked barrel, contract magazine. Checkered mainspring housing. (Add 40% for 99%-100% finish.)

Courtesy Karl Karash collection

Exc.	V.G.	Good	Fair	Poor
2500	1950	1700	1300	1100

Union Switch Signal Co. 1943 Production. Type III

"P" on frame and slide in the normal locations. From about SN 1,080,000 to 1,096,404 with probable overlap. RCD inspected, un-numbered slide. Right side of frame is marked "M1911A1 U.S. ARMY" forward of the slide stop pin, and "United States Property" behind the slide stop pin. DU-LITE (blued over sand blasting) finish. Plastic Keyes Fibre grips with or without rings around screws. Stamped, blued trigger, flat-sided hammer, "HS" marked barrel, contract magazine. Checkered mainspring housing. (Add 40% for 99%-100% finish.)

Courtesy Karl Karash collection

Exc.	V.G.	Good	Fair	Poor
2500	1950	1700	1300	1100

Union Switch Signal Co. 1943 Production. Exp.

About 100 Pistols. ("EXP" on frame partially under right grip.) These pistols generally have some defect about them which may have caused them to be rejected and written off. They were generally disposed of as give-aways to contracting personnel and employees. No inspector, un-numbered slide. Some pistols were finished with the DU-LITE process (blued over sand blasting) that closely resembled the finish of the delivered military pistols. The "EXP" and serial number marking was hand applied and is partially obscured by the right stock panel. Other EXP marked pistols were blued over such heavy buffing that the pistols have an amateur look about them. This, along with the crudeness of the markings, might lead one to question the authenticity of the blued EXPs. However, most evidence indicates that they are indeed genuine US&S made pistols. Popular wisdom seems to be that "EXP" meant "Experimental"; however, there seems to be no evidence to support that notion. Plastic Keyes Fibre grips with or without rings around screws. Stamped, blued trigger, flat-sided hammer, "HS" marked barrel, contract magazine. Checkered mainspring housing. (Add 40% for 99%-100% finish. Subtract 50% for blued or buffed.) Most have type II slides.

Courtesy Karl Karash collection

Exc.	V.G.	Good	Fair	Poor
4000	2650	2200	1800	1500

7 Digit X Numbered Rework

These pistols were renumbered when their original serial numbers were either defaced, obliterated, or became too light to read during rebuilding or refinishing. The seven digit X prefix serial numbers (X2693614 through X2695212) were assigned to various arsenals from 1949 to 1957. Some of the reworks are done in small batches and are more distinctive and collectable than the 4 digit X numbers. Each batch of pistols may have unique characteristics as they are done at different times by various arsenals. All are considered "Arsenal Refinished."

Courtesy Karl Karash collection

Exc.	V.G.	Good	Fair	Poor
1100	850	700	500	350

State of New York Government Model

Serial number 255000-C to about 258000-C with factory roll mark "PROPERTY OF THE STATE OF NEW YORK" with a verified proof and "government model" marking. A few of the parts were leftover military. This is a state militia pistol. (99% to 100% finish add 33%. For the few consecutive pairs known add 15% premium. A few match pistols were made by Al Dinan in the early 1960s; add 15%.)

Courtesy Karl Karash collection

Exc.	V.G.	Good	Fair	Poor
1100	800	600	500	350

Military National Match

These are .45 caliber pistols rebuilt from service pistols at Springfield Armory between 1955 and about 1967. These pistols were built and rebuilt each year with a portion being sold to competitors by the NRA. Each year improvements were added to the rebuild program. Four articles in the *American Rifleman* document these pistols well: August, 1959; April, 1963; June, 1966; and July, 1966. Many parts for these pistols have been available and many "look-alike" pistols have been built by basement armorers. Pistols generally came with a numbered box or papers. Less box and papers deduct 40%. When well worn these pistols offer little advantage over a standard pistol. Pistols must be in original match condition to qualify as Military National Match pistols.

Courtesy Karl Karash collection

Exc.	V.G.	Good	Fair	Poor
2000	1600	1200	1000	700

SMITH & WESSON

NOTE: For historical information, photos, and technical data, see Jim Supica and Richard Nahas, *Standard Catalog of Smith & Wesson 2nd Ed.,* Krause Publications.

.38 Safety Hammerless Army Test Revolver

There were 100 sold to the U.S. government in 1890. They have 3rd Model features but are in the 2nd Model serial number range, 41333-41470. Fitted with 6" barrels and marked "US."

CAUTION: Be very wary of fakes. Seek an expert appraisal prior to a sale.

Exc.	V.G.	Good	Fair	Poor
10000	7000	5000	3000	2000

Model 3 American 1st Model

This model represented a number of firsts for the Smith & Wesson Company. It was the first of the top break, automatic ejection revolvers. It was also the first Smith & Wesson in a large caliber (it is chambered for the .44 S&W American cartridge as well as the .44 Henry rimfire on rare occasions). It was also known as the 1st Model American. This large revolver is offered with an 8" round barrel with a raised rib as standard. Barrel lengths of 6" and 7" were also available. It has a 6-shot fluted cylinder and a square butt with walnut grips. It is blued or nickel-plated. It is interesting to note that this model appeared three years before Colt's Single Action Army and perhaps, more than any other model, was associated with the historic American West. There were only 8,000 manufactured between 1870 and 1872.

U.S. Army Order—Serial Number Range 125-2199

One thousand (1,000) produced with "U.S." stamped on top of barrel; "OWA" on left grip.

Exc.	V.G.	V.G	Good	Fair
15000	9500	7500	3250	2500

NOTE: Add 10% premium for original nickel finish.

Model 3 Russian 1st Model—Cyrillic

This model is quite similar in appearance to the American 1st and 2nd Model revolvers. S&W made several internal changes to this model to satisfy the Russian government. The markings on this revolver are distinct, and the caliber for which it is chambered, .44 S&W Russian, is different. There were approximately 20,000 Russian-contract revolvers. The serial number range is 1-20000. They are marked in Russian Cyrillic letters. The Russian double-headed eagle is stamped on the rear portion of the barrel with inspector's marks underneath it. All of the contract guns have 8" barrels and lanyard swivels on the butt. These are rarely encountered, as most were shipped to Russia. The commercial run of this model numbered approximately 4,655. The barrels are stamped in English and include the words "Russian Model." Some are found with 6" and 7" barrels, as well as the standard 8". There were also 500 revolvers that were rejected from the Russian contract series and sold on the commercial market. Some of these are marked in English, some Cyrillic. Some have the Cyrillic markings ground off and the English restamped. This model was manufactured from 1871 to 1874.

Russian Contract Model—Cyrillic Barrel Address

Exc.	V.G.	Good	Fair	Poor
—	8500	6000	2000	—

Model 3 Russian 2nd Model—Foreign Contracts

This revolver was known as the "Old Model Russian." This is a complicated model to understand as there are many variations within the model designation. The serial numbering is quite complex as well, and values vary greatly due to relatively minor model differences. Before purchasing this model, it would be advisable to secure competent appraisal as well as to read reference materials solely devoted to this firearm. This model is chambered for the .44 S&W Russian, as well as the .44 rimfire Henry cartridge. It has a 7" barrel and a round butt featuring a projection on the frame that fits into the thumb web. The grips are walnut, and the finish is blue or nickel-plated. The triggerguard has a reverse curved spur on the bottom. There were approximately 85,200 manufactured between 1873 and 1878.

Courtesy Jim Supica, Old Town Station

Russian Contract Model

70,000 made; rare, as most were shipped to Russia. Cyrillic markings; lanyard swivel on butt.

Exc.	V.G.	Good	Fair	Poor
—	5000	3750	1500	—

1st Model Turkish Contract

.44 rimfire Henry, special rimfire frames, serial-numbered in own serial number range 1-1000.

Exc.	V.G.	Good	Fair	Poor
—	6750	4750	1750	—

2nd Model Turkish Contract

Made from altered centerfire frames from the regular commercial serial number range. 1,000 made. Use caution with this model.

Exc.	V.G.	Good	Fair	Poor
—	6500	4500	1500	—

Japanese Govt. Contract

Five thousand made between the 1-9000 serial number range. The Japanese naval insignia, an anchor over two wavy lines, found on the butt. The barrel is Japanese proofed, and the words "Jan.19, 75 REISSUE July 25, 1871" are stamped on the barrel, as well.

Exc.	V.G.	Good	Fair	Poor
—	4000	3250	1200	—

Model 3 Russian 3rd Model—Foreign Contracts

This revolver is also known as the "New Model Russian." The factory referred to this model as the Model of 1874 or the Cavalry Model. It is chambered for the .44 S&W Russian and the .44 Henry rimfire cartridge. The barrel is 6.5", and the round butt is the same humped-back affair as the 2nd Model. The grips are walnut and the finish is, blue or nickel-plated. The most notable differences in appearance between this model and the 2nd Model are the shorter extractor housing under the barrel and the integral front sight blade instead of the pinned-on one found on the previous models. This is another model that bears careful research before attempting to evaluate. Minor variances can greatly affect values. Secure detailed reference materials and qualified appraisal. There were approximately 60,638 manufactured between 1874 and 1878.

Turkish Model

Five thousand made of altered centerfire frames, made to fire .44 rimfire Henry. "W" inspector's mark on butt and "CW" cartouche on grip. Fakes have been noted; be aware.

Exc.	V.G.	Good	Fair	Poor
—	4750	3000	1200	—

Japanese Contract Model

One thousand made; has the Japanese naval insignia, an anchor over two wavy lines, stamped on the bottom of the frame strap.

Exc.	V.G.	Good	Fair	Poor
—	3500	2250	1000	—

Russian Contract Model

Barrel markings are in Russian Cyrillic. Approximately 41,100 were produced.

Exc.	V.G	Good	Fair	Poor
—	4500	3750	1500	—

Model 3 Russian 3rd Model (Loewe & Tula Copies)

The German firm of Ludwig Loewe produced a copy of this model that is nearly identical to the S&W. This German revolver was made under Russian contract, as well as for commercial sales. The contract model has different Cyrillic markings than the S&W and the letters "HK" as inspector's marks. The commercial model has the markings in English. The Russian arsenal at Tula also produced a copy of this revolver with a different Cyrillic dated stamping on the barrel.

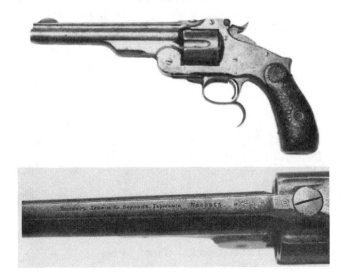

Courtesy Mike Stuckslager

Loewe

Exc.	V.G	Good	Fair	Poor
—	3750	2500	1000	—

Tula

Exc.	V.G	Good	Fair	Poor
—	4000	2750	1100	—

Model 3 Schofield

In 1870 Major George W. Schofield heard about the new S&W Model 3 revolver and wrote to the company expressing a desire to be an exclusive sales representative for them. At that time S&W was earnestly attempting to interest the government in this revolver and obviously felt that the Major could be of help in this endeavor, perhaps because his brother, General John Schofield, was president of the Small Arms Board. Major Schofield was sent one Model 3 revolver and 500 rounds of ammunition free of charge. After testing the revolver, Schofield felt that it needed a few changes to make it the ideal cavalry sidearm. With the company's approval, Schofield made these changes and secured patents. The company eventually began production of what became known as the Model 3 Schofield 1st Model. The Major was paid a 50 cent royalty per revolver. The eventual production of this model ran to a total of 8,969, with the last one sold in 1878. What was hoped to be the adopted government-issue sidearm never materialized—for a number of reasons. First, the Colt Single Action Army being used by the cavalry had a longer chamber than the S&W and could fire the Schofield ammunition. The Schofield could not fire the longer Colt .45 cartridges. This resulted in disastrous mix-ups on more than one occasion, when Colt ammunition was issued to troops armed with the Schofields. The company was not happy about paying the 50 cent royalty to Major Schofield. Sales of their other models were high and they simply did not care about this model, so they eventually ceased its production. It was a popular model on the American frontier and is quite historically significant.

Model 3 Schofield 1st Model

The modifications that made this model differ from the other Model 3 revolvers were quite extensive. The Schofield is chambered for the .45 S&W Schofield cartridge. The top break latch was moved from the barrel assembly to the frame. It was modified so that the action could be opened by simply pulling back on the latch with the thumb. This made it much easier to reload on horseback, as the reins would not have to be released. A groove was milled in the top of the raised barrel rib to improve the sighting plain. The extractor was changed to a cam-operated rather than rack-and-gear system. The removal of the cylinder was simplified. There were 3,000 contract Schofields and 35 commercial models. The contract revolvers were delivered to the Springfield Armory in July of 1875. These guns are stamped "US" on the butt and have the initials "L" and "P" marking various other parts. The grips have an inspector's cartouche with the initials "JFEC." There were 35 1st Models made for and sold to the civilian market; these revolvers do not have the "US" markings. The Schofield has a 7" barrel, 6-shot fluted cylinder, and walnut grips. The 1st Model is blued, with a nickel-plated original finish gun being extremely rare.

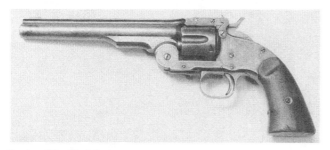

Courtesy Mike Stuckslager

"US" Contract-3,000 Issued

Exc.	V.G.	Good	Fair	Poor
—	9500	4250	1750	1000

Civilian Model, No "US" markings

35 made—very rare, use caution. **UNABLE TO PRICE**. At least double the military model values. Expert appraisal needed.

Model 3 Schofield 2nd Model

The difference between the 1st and 2nd Model Schofield revolvers is in the barrel latch system. The 2nd Model latch is rounded and knurled to afford an easier and more positive grip when opening the revolver. A group of 3,000 of these revolvers was delivered to the Springfield Armory in October of 1876, and another 2,000 were delivered in 1877. These 2nd Model contract revolvers were all blued. There were an additional 649 civilian guns sold as well. The civilian models were not "US" marked and were offered either blued or nickel-plated. A total of 8,969 Model 3 Schofield 2nd Models were manufactured. The last sale was recorded in 1878.

Courtesy Jim Supica, Old Town Station

"US" Contract—4,000 Issued

Exc.	V.G.	Good	Fair	Poor
—	8500	3750	1750	950

Civilian Model—646 Made

Exc.	V.G.	Good	Fair	Poor
—	8500	3750	1750	950

Model 3 Schofield—Surplus Models

Many Schofields were issued to various states under the Militia Act, some of which were used in the spanish American War. After the government dropped the Schofield as an issue cavalry sidearm, the remaining U.S. inventory of these revolvers was sold off as military surplus. Many were sold to dealers such as Bannerman's or Schuyler, Hartley & Graham, two large gun dealers who then resold the guns to supply the growing need for guns on the Western frontier. Schuyler, Hartley & Graham sold a number of guns to the Wells Fargo Express Co. Almost all of these weapons had the barrels shortened to 5", as were many others sold during this period. Some were nickel plated. Beware of fakes when contemplating purchase of the Wells Fargo revolvers.

Wells Fargo & Co. Model

Exc.	V.G.	Good	Fair	Poor
—	5500	2500	1500	900

Surplus Cut Barrel—Not Wells Fargo

Exc.	V.G.	Good	Fair	Poor
3000	1800	1400	1100	800

New Model No. 3 Single Action

Always interested in perfecting the Model 3 revolver, D.B. Wesson redesigned and improved the old Model 3 in the hopes of attracting more sales. The Russian contracts were almost filled so the company decided to devote the effort necessary to improve on this design. In 1877 this project was undertaken. The extractor housing was shortened, the cylinder retention system was improved, and the shape of the grip was changed to a more streamlined and attractive configuration. This New Model has a 3.5", 4", 5", 6", 6.5", 7", 7.5", or 8" barrel length with a 6-shot fluted cylinder. The 6.5" barrel and .44 S&W Russian chambering is the most often encountered variation of this model, but the factory considered the 8" barrels as standard and these were kept in stock as well. The New Model No. 3 was also chambered for .32 S&W, .32-44 S&W, .320 S&W Rev. Rifle, .38 S&W, .38-40, .38-44 S&W, .41 S&W, .44 Henry rimfire, .44 S&W American, .44-40, .45 S&W Schofield, .450 Rev., .45 Webley, .455 MkI and .455 MkII. They are either blued or nickel-plated and have checkered hard rubber grips with the S&W logo molded into them or walnut grips. There are many sub-variations within this model designation, and the potential collector should secure detailed reference material that deals with this model. There were approximately 35,796 of these revolvers manufactured between 1878 and 1912. Nearly 40 percent were exported to fill contracts with Japan, Australia, Argentina, England, Spain, and Cuba. There were some sent to Asia, as well. The proofmarks of these countries will establish their provenance but will not add appreciably to standard values.

Standard Model—6.5" barrel, .44 S&W Russian

Courtesy Mike Stuckslager

Exc.	V.G.	Good	Fair	Poor
—	3700	2000	1000	—

Japanese Naval Contract

This was the largest foreign purchaser of this model. There were over 1,500 produced with the anchor insignia stamped on the frame.

Courtesy Mike Stuckslager

Exc.	V.G.	Good	Fair	Poor
—	3700	2000	1000	—

Japanese Artillery Contract

This variation is numbered in the 25,000 serial range. They are blued, with a 7" barrel and a lanyard swivel on the butt. Japanese characters are stamped on the extractor housing.

Exc.	V.G.	Good	Fair	Poor
—	5000	2500	1250	—

Maryland Militia Model

This variation is nickel-plated, has a 6.5" barrel, and is chambered for the .44 S&W Russian cartridge. The butt is stamped "U.S.," and the inspector's marks "HN" and "DAL" under the 1878 date appear on the revolver. There were 280 manufactured between serial numbers 7126 and 7405.

Exc.	V.G.	Good	Fair	Poor
—	12500	6000	3000	—

NOTE: Rarity makes valuation speculative.

Australian Contract

This variation is nickel-plated, is chambered for the .44 S&W Russian cartridge, and is marked with the Australian Colonial Police Broad Arrow on the butt. There were 250 manufactured with 7" barrels and detachable shoulder stocks. The stock has the Broad Arrow stamped on the lower tang. There were also 30 manufactured with 6.5" barrels without the stocks. They all are numbered in the 12,000-13,000 serial number range.

NOTE: The total number of the revolvers made is greater than the number mentioned, but no exact number can be given.

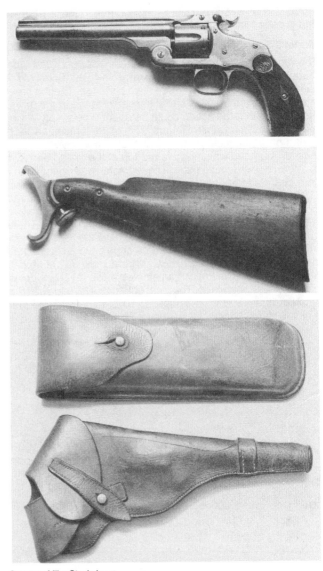

Courtesy Mike Stuckslager

Revolver with stock and holsters

Exc.	V.G.	Good	Fair	Poor
—	8000	4750	2750	—

NOTE: Deduct 40% for no stock.

A Smith & Wesson New Model No. 3 Australian with match numbered holster and shoulder stock sold at auction for $12,650. Nickel finish was good. Faintich Auction Service, October 1999

Paul Goodwin photo

Argentine Model

This was essentially not a factory contract but a sale through Schuyler, Hartley & Graham. They are stamped "Ejercito/Argentino" in front of the triggerguard. The order amounted to some 2,000 revolvers between the serial numbers 50 and 3400.

Exc.	V.G.	Good	Fair	Poor
—	7000	3500	1750	—

Turkish Model
This is essentially the New Model No. 3 chambered for the .44 rimfire Henry cartridge. It is stamped with the letters "P," "U" and "AFC" on various parts of the revolver. The barrels are all 6.5"; the finish, blued with walnut grips. Lanyard swivels are found on the butt. There were 5,461 manufactured and serial numbered in their own range, starting at 1 through 5,461 between 1879 and 1883.

Courtesy Mike Stuckslager

Exc.	V.G.	Good	Fair	Poor
—	7000	3500	1750	—

U.S. Revenue Cutter Service (U.S. Coast Guard)
This model was issued to the U.S. Revenue Cutter Service as a standard issue sidearm. Fitted with 5", 6", or 6.5" barrels. The revolver is not marked but there are known serial numbers that identify this as a military variation. Consult an expert prior to sale, or see *Standard Catalog of Smith & Wesson* for a list of known serial numbers.

Exc.	V.G.	Good	Fair	Poor
—	12500	5000	2750	—

New Model No. 3 Frontier Single Action
This is another model similar in appearance to the standard New Model No. 3. It has a 4", 5", or 6.5" barrel and is chambered for the .44-40 Winchester Centerfire cartridge. Because the original New Model No. 3 cylinder was 1-7/16" in length this would not accommodate the longer .44-40 cartridge. The cylinder on the No. 3 Frontier was changed to 1-9/16" in length. Later, the company converted 786 revolvers to .44 S&W Russian and sold them to Japan. This model is either blued or nickel-plated and has checkered grips of walnut or hard rubber. They are serial numbered in their own range from 1 through 2072 and were manufactured from 1885 until 1908. This model was designed to compete with the Colt Single Action Army but was not successful.

Courtesy Mike Stuckslager

.44-40—Commercial Model
Exc.	V.G.	Good	Fair	Poor
—	5000	2500	1250	—

Japanese Purchase Converted to .44 S&W Russian
Exc.	V.G.	Good	Fair	Poor
—	4000	2000	1000	—

.38 Hand Ejector Military & Police 1st Model or Model of 1899
This was an early swing-out cylinder revolver, and it has no front lockup for the action. The release is on the left side of the frame. This model is chambered for the .38 S&W Special cartridge and the .32 Winchester centerfire cartridge (.32-20), has a 6-shot fluted cylinder, and was offered with a 4", 5", 6", 6.5", or 8" barrel in .38 caliber, and 4", 5", and 6-1/2" in .32-20 caliber. The finish is blued or nickel-plated; the grips, checkered walnut or hard rubber. There were approximately 20,975 manufactured between 1899 and 1902 in .38 caliber; serial number range 1 to 20,975. In the .32-20 caliber, 5,311 were sold between 1899 and 1902; serial number range 1 to 5311.

Courtesy Mike Stuckslager

Commercial Model
Exc.	V.G.	Good	Fair	Poor
750	650	600	450	350

U.S. Navy Model
One thousand produced in 1900, .38 S&W, 6" barrel, blued with checkered walnut grips, "U.S.N." stamped on butt, serial number range 5000 to 6000.

Courtesy Rock Island Auction Company

Exc.	V.G.	Good	Fair	Poor
2500	1750	800	500	300

U.S. Army Model

One thousand produced in 1901, same as Navy Model except that it is marked "U.S.Army/Model 1899" on butt, "K.S.M." and "J.T.T." on grips, serial number range 13001 to 14000.

Exc.	V.G.	Good	Fair	Poor
2750	2000	950	600	300

.38 Hand Ejector Military & Police 2nd Model or Model of 1902—U.S. Navy Model

Chambered for .38 Long colt cartridge with Navy serial number range 1001 to 2000. Marked "u.s.n." with anchor stamped on butt. Smith & Wesson serial number stamped on front tang in the 25001 to 26000 serial range. Some 1025 revolvers were produced.

Courtesy Rock Island Auction Company

Exc.	V.G.	Good	Fair	Poor
2750	2000	900	500	300

.45 Hand Ejector U.S. Service Model of 1917

WWI was on the horizon, and it seemed certain that the United States would become involved. The S&W people began to work with the Springfield Armory to develop a hand-ejector model that would fire the .45-caliber Government cartridge. This was accomplished in 1916 by the use of half-moon clips. The new revolver is quite similar to the .44 Hand Ejector in appearance. It has a 5.5" barrel, blued finish with smooth

Paul Goodwin photo

walnut grips, and a lanyard ring on the butt. The designation "U.S.Army Model 1917" is stamped on the butt. After the war broke out, the government was not satisfied with S&W's production and actually took control of the company for the duration of the war. This was the first time that the company was not controlled by a Wesson. The factory records indicate that there were 163,476 Model 1917s manufactured between 1917 and 1919, the WWI years. After the war, the sale of these revolvers continued on a commercial and contract basis until 1949, when this model was finally dropped from the S&W product line.

Military Model

Exc.	V.G.	Good	Fair	Poor
750	500	300	200	150

Commercial Model

High gloss blue and checkered walnut grips.

Exc.	V.G.	Good	Fair	Poor
600	450	300	200	150

.455 Mark II Hand Ejector 1st Model

This model was designed the same as the .44 Hand Ejector 1st Model with no caliber stamping on the barrel. It has a barrel length of 6.4". Of the 5,000 revolvers produced and sold, only 100 were commercial guns, the rest were military. Produced between 1914 and 1915. The commercial model is worth a premium.

Exc.	V.G.	Good	Fair	Poor
1000	750	400	300	200

.455 Mark II Hand Ejector 2nd Model

Similar to the first model without an extractor shroud. Barrel length was also 6.5". Serial number range was 5000 to 74755. Manufactured from 1915 to 1917.

Exc.	V.G.	Good	Fair	Poor
900	650	300	200	150

Model 10 (.38 Military & Police)—Military Marked

This model has been in production in one configuration or another since 1899. It was always the mainstay of the S&W line and was originally known as the .38 Military and Police Model. The Model 10 is built on the K, or medium frame, and was always meant as a duty gun. It was offered with a 2", 3", 4", 5", or 6" barrel. Currently only the 4" and 6" are available. A round or square butt is offered. It is chambered for the .38 Special, .38 S&W, and .22 rimfire and is offered in blue or nickel-plate, with checkered walnut grips. The Model designation is stamped on the yoke on all S&W revolvers. This model, with many other modern S&W pistols, underwent several engineering changes. These changes may affect the value of the pistol and an expert should be consulted. The dates of these changes are as follows:

10-None-1957	10-3-1961	10-5-1962
10-1-1959	10-4-1962	10-6-1962
10-2-1961		

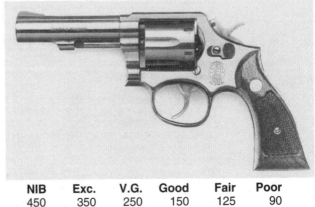

NIB	Exc.	V.G.	Good	Fair	Poor
450	350	250	150	125	90

Victory Model

Manufactured during WWII, this is a Model 10 with a sand-blasted and parkerized finish, a lanyard swivel, and smooth walnut grips. The serial number has a V prefix. This model was available in only 2" and 4" barrel lengths. The Victory Model was discontinued on April 27, 1945, with serial number VS811,119.

Victory Model marked "N.Y.M.I." • Courtesy Richard M. Kumor Sr.

Navy marked Smith & Wesson Victory model • Courtesy Amoskeag Auction, Co., Inc.

Exc.	V.G.	Good	Fair	Poor
300	200	150	100	75

NOTE: Top strap marked Navy will bring a 75% premium. Navy variation with both top strap and side plate marked will bring a 100% premium. Navy variation marked "N.Y.M.I." will bring a 125% premium. Revolvers marked "U.S.G.C." or "U.S.M.C." will bring a premium of unknown amount. Exercise caution.

Model 11 (.38/200 British Service Revolver)

First produced in 1938, S&W manufactured these revolvers for the British Commonwealth in 4", 5", or 6" barrels. Early models are bright blue, later models are parkerized. Square butt with checkered walnut grips. Lend Lease guns marked "UNITED STATES PROPERTY." Production ended in 1945 with 568,204 built. Nicknamed the .38/200 British Service Revolver. Smith & Wesson began producing this model again in 1947 and sold many of these throughout the 1950s and 1960s when production ceased again in 1965. There are several rare variations of this model that will greatly affect its value. Consult an expert if special markings and barrel lengths are encountered.

Exc.	V.G.	Good	Fair	Poor
350	250	200	100	75

USAF M-13 (Aircrewman)

From 1952 to about 1957 the Air Force purchased a large quantity of Model 12s with alloy frames and cylinders. They were intended for use by flight crews as survival weapons in emergencies. This model was not officially designated "13" by S&W, but the Air Force requested these revolvers be stamped "M13" on the top strap. This model was rejected by the Air Force in 1960 because of trouble with the alloy cylinder.

NOTE: Beware of fakes. Seek expert advice before purchase.

Exc.	V.G.	Good	Fair	Poor
900	650	500	350	200

Model 39 Steel Frame

Semiautomatic pistol chambered for the 9mm cartridge. Fitted with a 4" barrel, walnut stocks, blue finish, and adjustable rear sight. Military version of this pistol has a dull blue finish, no walnut grips, with double action trigger. Manufactured from 1954 to 1966. Some of these military models are found without serial numbers. A special variation was used with a suppressor in Vietnam, and modified with a slide lock for single shot. Named the "Hush Puppy."

NOTE: Pricing does not include the suppressor.

Exc.	V.G.	Good	Fair	Poor
1200	900	700	500	300

Model 56 (KXT-38 USAF)

Introduced in 1962, this is a 2" heavy barrel built on the K frame. It is chambered for the .38 Special. There were approximately 15,000 of these revolvers built when it was discontinued in 1964. It was marked "US" on the backstrap. A total of 15,205 were produced, but most were destroyed.

NIB	Exc.	V.G.	Good	Fair	Poor
Too Rare To Price					

HIGH STANDARD

Model B-US

A .22 Long Rifle caliber semiautomatic pistol with a 4.5" round tapered barrel and a 10-shot magazine. A version of the Model B with slight modifications to the frame. U.S. marked Model Bs will be found in both original Model B frame and Model B-US frame. An estimated 14,000 made for the U.S. government 1942-1943. Black, monogrammed hard rubber grips. Blued finish. Black checkered hard rubber grips. Type II takedown only. Most are marked "PROPERTY OF U.S." on the top of the barrel and on the right side of the frame. Crossed cannon ordnance stamp usually found on the right side of the frame. Box with papers add premium of 20%. Most guns are found in serial number range from about 92,344 to about 111,631.

Courtesy Rock Island Auction Company

Exc.	V.G.	Good	Fair	Poor
725	475	275	180	150

Model USA—Model HD

Similar to the Model HD with 4.5" barrel and fixed sights, checkered black hard rubber grips and an external safety. Early models blued; later model parkerized. Introduced 1943; approximately 44,000 produced for the U.S. government. Most are marked "PROPERTY OF U.E." on the top of the barrel and on the right side of the frame. Crossed cannon ordnance stamp usually found on the right side of the frame. Box with papers add 20% premium. Most pistols are found in serial number range from about 103,863 to about 145,700.

Exc.	V.G.	Good	Fair	Poor
750	550	400	250	175

Model USA—Model HD-MS

A silenced variation of the USA Model HD. Approximately 2500 produced for the OSS during 1944 and 1945. 6.75" shrouded barrel. Early pistols blued; later pistols parkerized. Only a few registered with BATF for civilian ownership. All NFA rules apply. Box with papers will bring a 10% premium. Most guns are found in serial number range from about 110,074 to about 130,040.

Model HD-MS • Courtesy Chuck Karwan

Exc.	V.G.	Good	Fair	Poor
6000	5000	—	—	—

Supermatic S-101

A .22 Long Rifle caliber semiautomatic pistol with 10 round magazine. Medium weight round barrel with blued finish, adjustable sights, brown plastic thumb rest grips. Grooved front and back straps on frame. The 6.75" barrel incorporates a muzzle brake with one slot on either side of the front sight. Marked "U.S." on the left side of the frame, above and in front of the triggerguard with characters approximately .150" high. Box with papers will bring a 13 percent premium. Most guns found in serial number range beginning at about 446,511.

Catalog # 9119—1954 to 1957.

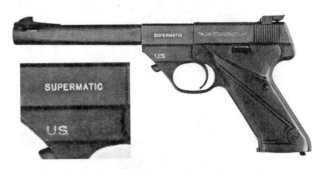

Supermatic "US" marked • Courtesy John J. Stimson Jr.

Exc.	V.G.	Good	Fair	Poor
700	400	275	195	150

Supermatic Citation Model 102 & 103

As above but with tapered barrel with an enlarged register at the muzzle end to hold a removable muzzle brake; adjustable sights; 2 and 3 oz. adjustable weights; checkered plastic grips, and blued finish. Grooved front and rear straps on frame. Marked "U.S." on left side of frame, above and in front of the triggerguard in characters approximately .150" high. Box with papers add 13 percent premium.

Catalog # 9260—1958 to 1963.

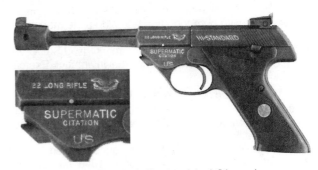

Supermatic Citation "US" marked • Courtesy John J. Stimson Jr.

Exc.	V.G.	Good	Fair	Poor
700	500	400	325	200

Supermatic Tournament 102 & 103

As above but with round tapered barrel. Blued finish, adjustable sights, checkered plastic grips. Smooth front and back straps on frame. Marked "U.S." on left side of frame, above and in front of the triggerguard in characters approximately .150" high.

Two different models catalog numbers 9271 and 9274. A contract in 1964 had mostly 9271 with some 9274. A contract in 1965 was all #9274. Catalog #9271 has a 6.75" barrel. Specifics of the #9274 are presently unknown.

Box with papers add 13 percent premium.

Catalog # 9271—1958 to 1963.

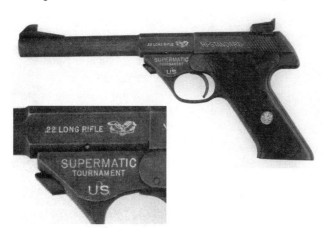

Supermatic Tournament "US" marked • Courtesy John J. Stimson Jr.

Exc.	V.G.	Good	Fair	Poor
575	400	290	200	175

T-3

A semiautomatic double action pistol made under contract to the U.S. government on a development contract. All types are blowback design. A preliminary model gun exists in the white in a private collection. No serial number and no folding triggerguard. The other pistols all have folding triggerguards for use with gloved hands. These guns are also blowback design and have barrels with angular grooves in the chamber to reduce recoil. Fitted with a 4" barrel. Made in three distinct types.

Type 1 pistols were probably made in a lot of four pistols each with a 7-round single column magazine. Serial number 1 does not include the plunge to increase the trigger pull when the trigger guard is folded. The magazine release for the Type 1 is like other High Standard pistols. Grips are checkered black plastic. Serial number 2 is in the Springfield Museum. Serial numbers 1, 3, and 4 are in private collections.

T-3 Type 1 • Courtesy John J. Stimson Jr.

Type 2 pistols were probably built in a lot of four pistols with a 7-round single column magazine. The magazine release on Type 2 pistols is located in the frame where the triggerguard meets the front grip strap. The 2nd type incorporated a thicker triggerguard and a wider frame and slide. Serial numbers 1, 2, and 3 are in the Springfield Museum, while serial number 4 is in a private collection.

T-3-Type 2 • Courtesy John J. Stimson Jr.

Type 3 pistols have a 13-round double-column magazine with a Type 2 triggerguard and magazine release. The magazine is similar to the Browning High Power. The frame and slide are wider than Type 2. One is known to exist in the Rock Island Arsenal Museum and the other is in a private collection. There are two others believed to exist.

Exc.	V.G.	Good	Fair	Poor
8500	7750	—	—	—

HECKLER & KOCH
See also-Germany

H&K Mark 23 Model O (SOCOM)

Very similar to H&K's U.S. government contract pistol developed for U.S. military special operation units. Chambered for the .45 ACP and fitted with a 5.87" barrel, this pistol has a polymer frame with steel slide. Magazine capacity is 10 rounds on civilian models and 12 rounds on military models. Barrel is threaded for noise suppressor. Weight is about 42 oz. Limited availability in fall 1996 to about 2,000 pistols.

NIB	Exc.	V.G.	Good	Fair	Poor
2250	1750	1250	—	—	—

WHAT'S IT LIKE: THE MARK 23 PISTOL & SUPPRESSOR

There is no question that the Mark 23 is a very large pistol. Some jokingly call it the only crew-served pistol in military service. It was designed for specific operational requirements that called for it to perform flawlessly in limited situations. Despite its size and weight, the pistol is extremely accurate and reliable. It should be because it's built like a truck. The companion suppressor, built by Knight Armament, is also over-built. It is also very quiet when fired wet (water). When the Mark 23 pistol and the Mark 23 suppressor are joined together, then the reason for its existence becomes quite clear. This combination makes for an incredibly accurate and quiet pistol. It is possible to make head shots at 50 yards if the shooter does his part. Recoil is almost non existent and muzzle jump is eliminated. In many cases the addition of a suppressor to a pistol is an afterthought with the result that the pistol does not function as well together as alone. That is plainly not the case with the Mark 23. Alone the pistol is big and bulky. With the suppressor attached it becomes a deadly combination of accuracy and stealth. One note of caution: With the suppressor in place the pistol becomes extremely dirty after about 20 rounds. While this does not seem to affect reliability, it is always a good idea to clean the pistol thoroughly before storage.

Ned Schwing

Mark 23 Suppressor

This is the same suppressor as sold to the U.S. military for use on the Mark 23 pistol. This unit can be fitted to the threaded barrel of the Mark 23 and be adjusted for point of aim. With water the dB sound reduction is 33-35dB. Produced by Knight Armament Corp. of Vero Beach, Fla. This suppressor, with a different piston assembly, can be fitted to the USP Tactical.

NIB	Exc.	V.G.	Good	Fair	Poor
1500	—	—	—	—	—

NOTE: Suppressors require a Class III transfer tax. All NFA rules apply to the sale or purchase of these suppressors.

BERETTA
See also-Italy

Model M9 Limited Edition

Introduced in 1995 to commemorate the 10th anniversary of the U.S. military's official sidearm, this 9mm pistol is limited to 10,000 units. Special engraving on the slide with special serial numbers. Slide stamped "U.S. 9MM M9-BERETTA U.S.A.-65490."

Saudi Arabia, 1990, Operation Desert Shield. A U.S. soldier carefully aims his M9 pistol during live fire training in preparation for the liberation of Kuwait. This 9mm semiauto pistol is commercially available as the Beretta Model 92F • U.S. Department of Defense/Robert Bruce Military Photo Features

U.S. Beretta Model M9 • Paul Goodwin photos

Standard Model

NIB	Exc.	V.G.	Good	Fair	Poor
750	600	400	300	200	100

Deluxe Model—Walnut grips with gold plated hammer and grip screws.

NIB	Exc.	V.G.	Good	Fair	Poor
850	700	450	350	200	100

SAVAGE

Model 1907/10/11

Manufactured in 1905 in .45 ACP, this pistol was tested in the U.S. Army trials. A few were sold commercially. It weighs 32 oz., and has an overall length of 9". Magazine capacity is 8-rounds. Checkered two-piece walnut grips. Blued finish. An improved version was built in 1910 and another version was built in 1911. This last version was a completely redesigned pistol: the Model 1911. Some 288 pistols were built in three different versions. Once the Army trials were over, Savage refinished the pistols with a matte blue finish and sold some of them commercially.

Courtesy James Rankin

Model 1907 Test Pistol

Manufactured in 1907 in .45 ACP, this pistol was tested in the U.S. Army trials. About 290 pistols were produced for these trials. Double stack magazine held 8 rounds.

Exc.	V.G.	Good	Fair	Poor
12500	10000	9500	6000	2000

Model 1910 Test Pistol

This was a modified Model 1907 with a heavier slide, which was not concave like the Model 1907. There were a total of nine Model 1910s built.

Exc.	V.G.	Good	Fair	Poor
		Too Rare To Price		

Model 1911 Test Pistol

This example was completely modified with a longer and thinner grip. Checkered wood grips were attached by friction instead of screws, the slide release was modified, a full grip safety was added, and a heavier serrated hammer (cocking lever) was added. Four of these pistols were built. Serial #1 has never been located.

Exc.	V.G.	Good	Fair	Poor
		Too Rare To Price		

Model 1907 Portuguese Contract

Similar to the commercial guns but with a lanyard ring like the French contract model. Original Portuguese pistols will have the Portuguese Crest on the grips. Only about 1,150 of these pistols were produced. Very rare. Proceed with caution.

Exc.	V.G.	Good	Fair	Poor
1500	1000	750	600	300

Model 1917

This semiautomatic pistol is chambered for the 7.65mm cartridge. It is fitted with an external hammer and without the grip safety. The form of the grip frame as been widened. Manufactured between 1917 and 1928. This pistol was sold to the French government during World War I and used by the French military. Approximately 27,000 of these pistols were sold to France. See also *France, Handguns, Savage.*

Exc.	V.G.	Good	Fair	Poor
275	225	175	100	75

STURM, RUGER & CO.

Mark I Target Pistol (U.S. marked)

This is a semiautomatic target pistol with 6.88" barrel and target sights. Stamped "U.S." on top of receiver. First produced in 1956. Blued finish. Rebuilt or refinished pistols may be parkerized and stamped with arsenal stamp.

Exc.	V.G.	Good	Fair	Poor
800	600	400	250	150

GUIDE LAMP
Division of General Motors

Liberator

A .45 ACP caliber single shot pistol with a 3.5" smooth bore barrel and overall length of 5.5". This pistol is made primarily of stampings and was intended to be air dropped to partisans in Europe during WWII. The hollow grip is designed to hold a packet of four extra cartridges. Originally packaged in unmarked cardboard boxes with an illustrated instruction sheet.

Courtesy Richard M. Kumor Sr.

NIB	Exc.	V.G.	Good	Fair	Poor
2500	1200	750	400	300	175

A Liberator pistol sold at auction for $1,955. Original box, instruction sheet, 10 rounds, wooden extractor, dated 1942. Condition was very good.
Amoskeag Auction Company, May 2002

SUBMACHINE GUNS

Bibliographical Note: For historical information, technical data, and photos, see Tracie Hill, *Thompson: The American Legend*, Collector Grade Publications, 1996.

Colt 9mm (Model 635)

Based on the M16, this submachine gun is chambered for the 9mm cartridge. It was first produced in 1990. It has the capability of semi-automatic or full automatic fire. The barrel length is 10.125" with a 20- or 32-round magazine. The gun is fitted with a retractable stock. As with the M16, this gun fires from a closed bolt. Weight is about 6.5 lbs. Rate of fire is about 900 rounds per minute. "SMG" and serial number are marked on left side of magazine housing. Used by the U.S. military, although not in any official capacity, and other countries military forces.

This model has several other variants:

Model 634—As above but with semi-automatic fire only.
Model 639—Same as the M635 but with 3-round burst.
Model 633HB—Fitted with 7" barrel and hydraulic buffer.
NOTE: See also *U.S., Rifles, M16.*

Photo courtesy private NFA collection

Pre-1968

Exc.	V.G.	Fair
N/A	N/A	N/A

Pre-1986 conversions, for OEM add 20%

Exc.	V.G.	Fair
6500	6000	5500

Pre-1986 dealer samples

Exc.	V.G.	Fair
N/A	N/A	N/A

Ingram Model 10

Chambered for the 9mm or .45 ACP cartridge, this submachine gun is fitted with a 5.7" barrel and a 30-round magazine. It has a rate of fire of 1,100 rounds per minute. The empty weight is approximately 6.3 lbs. This submachine gun was used by various government agencies in Vietnam. A version chambered for the .380 cartridge is known as the Model 11.

Photo courtesy private NFA collection

Pre-1968

Exc.	V.G.	Fair
1500	1200	1000

Pre-1986 conversions

Exc.	V.G.	Fair
N/A	N/A	N/A

Pre-1986 dealer samples

Exc.	V.G.	Fair
N/A	N/A	N/A

Quantico, VA, Sept. 1943. USMC Master Gunnery Sergeant Kravits demonstrates the M55 Reising submachine gun with its characteristic folding wire stock • USMC/National Archives/Robert Bruce Military Photo Features

Reising 50/55

First built in 1941, the gun was chambered for the .45 ACP cartridge. It was first used by Marines in the Pacific but failed to be combat reliable. The Model 50 was fitted with a wooden buttstock and 10.8" barrel. Magazine capacity was 12 or 20 rounds. Rate of fire was 550 rounds per minute. The gun has a select fire mechanism for single round operation. Marked "HARRINGTON & RICHARDSON WORCESTER MASS USA" on the top of the receiver. Weight was about 6.75 lbs.

The Model 55 is the same mechanism but with a wire folding stock and no muzzle compensator. The weight of the Model 55 was 6.25 lbs. About 100,000 Reising Model 50s and 55s were built between 1941 and 1945 when production ceased.

NOTE: Commercial guns will bring less than military marked guns. Add about 25% for U.S. martially marked guns.

Courtesy Richard M. Kumor Sr.

Pre-1968

Exc.	V.G.	Fair
3500	3000	2500

Pre-1986 conversions

Exc.	V.G.	Fair
N/A	N/A	N/A

Pre-1986 dealer samples

Exc.	V.G.	Fair
1750	1500	1250

THOMPSON SUBMACHINE GUNS

Text and prices by Nick Tilotta

Thompson Model 1921AC/21A, 1921/28 Navy

The first Thompsons to come to market were the Model 1921s, manufactured by Colt Patent Firearms for Auto Ordnance Corporation in New York, New York. Between March 1921 and April 1922 15,000 guns were built. Of those 15,000 manufactured, only about 2,400 weapons exist in a transferable state today. Transferable, meaning weapons that can be bought, sold, or traded legally within the U.S. Three models of the Model 1921 were produced. The Model 1921A had a fixed front sight and a rate of fire of 800 rounds per minute. The Model 1921AC has a Cutts compensator instead of a fixed front sight and an 800-rounds-per-minute rate of fire. The Mod-

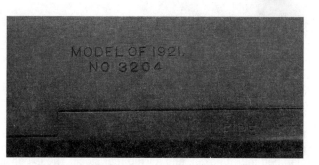

Thompson Model 1921 with close-up of receiver stamping • Paul Goodwin photo

el 1928 Navy was fitted with a Cutts compensator and a heavier actuator that reduced the rate of fire to 600 rounds per minute. All of these Navy models had the number "8" stamped crudely over the number "1" on the left side of the receiver. Of the 15,000 Colt Model 1921s produced, approximately 25% were Model 1921As, 33% were Model 1921ACs, and 41% were 1928 Navys. A handful of Model 1927s were manufactured by Colt and left the factory as semiautomatics. However, the ATF considers these guns machine guns and requires that all NFA rules apply. These Model 1927s are quite rare and represent only about 1% of total production. They do not seem to sell for the same dollar figures that the machine guns do.

All Colt-manufactured Thompsons were bright blued; none were parkerized. All had walnut stocks, grips, and forearms manufactured by Remington. With the exception of a few prototypes, all Colt Thompsons were chambered for the .45 ACP cartridge. All internal parts were solid nickel and all barrels were finned. All weapons had a Lyman rear sight assembly. A removable rear stock was standard. All weapons were marked with a "NEW YORK, USA" address on the right side of the receiver. "COLT PATENT FIREARMS" was marked on the left side of the receiver. These Colt Thompsons would accept a 20- or 30-round box magazine as well as a 50-round "L" drum or 100 round "C" drum. Weight is about 10.75 lbs. Prices below are for original Colt guns with original parts and finish.

NOTE: Model 1921As, early serial numbers, previous ownership, and documentation can dramatically add to the prices below. In addition, missing components, re-barreled weapons, etc, will see a substantial reduction in price, as these orginal components are almost extinct. Re-finishing or re-bluing will result in a substantial reduction in value by as much as 50%.

Pre-1968

Exc.	V.G.	Fair
25000	17500	12000

Pre-1986 conversions

Exc.	V.G.	Fair
N/A	N/A	N/A

Pre-1986 dealer samples

Exc.	V.G.	Fair
N/A	N/A	N/A

Thompson Model 1928 Commercial/1928A1 Military

The next limited run of Thompsons came just before and right at the beginning of WWII. This version is called the Model 1928AC or Commercial model. These weapons were assembled by Savage Arms in Utica, New York, using original Colt internal components. The receivers were still marked with the New York address but void of any "Colt" markings. Most weapons were simply marked "MODEL 1928." The first of these guns have blued receivers and blued barrels. The second run had parkerized receivers and blued barrels. These guns are quite rare and command premium prices.

At the outbreak of WWII, the demand for the Thompson gun soared. A brake lining facility in Bridgeport, Conn., was acquired to accommodate the increased demand for production. Three models of Thompsons were born in this WWII era. The first was the Model 1928A1 Thompson. This version was a copy of the Model 1928 Navy Colt Thompson. Most were parkerized with much less detail paid to fine machining. This gun was assembled in two locations: Utica, N.Y., and Bridgeport, Conn. Receivers produced in Utica were marked with an "S" prefix in front of the serial number. Receivers marked with an "AO" prefix were produced in Bridgeport. Receivers were marked on the right side "AUTO ORDNANCE CORPORATION, BRIDGEPORT, CT," no matter where the receiver was manufactured. The Utica, N.Y., plant concentrated its efforts on manufacturing components while the Bridgeport facility concentrated on assemblies. As production increased, the Model 1928A1 lost many of its "unnecessary" components such as the finned barrel, the costly Lyman sight, and finely checkered selector switches. Approximately 562,000 Thompsons were produced in the Model 1928A1 configuration. All of the weapons were parkerized, and some have finned barrels and some have smooth barrels. Some of these guns were also fitted with Lyman sights, some have a stamped "L" type sight that may or may not have protective ears. As a general rule of thumb, most Model 1928 Commercial guns were fitted with a vertical foregrip while most Model 1928A1 guns were fitted with a horizontal forearm, and all had removable butt stocks. Used by Allied forces during WWII. Used both 20- or 30-round box magazines and 50 or 100 round drum magazines.

Thompson Model 1928 Commercial

Pre-1968

Exc.	V.G.	Fair
25000	17500	12500

Pre-1986 conversions

Exc.	V.G.	Fair
N/A	N/A	N/A

Pre-1986 dealer samples

Exc.	V.G.	Fair
12000	8500	6500

Thompson Model 1928A1 Military

Pre-1968

Exc.	V.G.	Fair
15000	10000	8500

Pre-1986 conversions

Exc.	V.G.	Fair
N/A	N/A	N/A

Pre-1986 dealer samples

Exc.	V.G.	Fair
8000	6000	5000

Germany, 1945. Expended cases fly as Army PFC William F. Doty pumps .45 cal. slugs into enemy positions near the Sigfried Line. His Thompson submachine gun may be an M1 or M1A1 model • U.S. Army Signal Corps/National Archives/Robert Bruce Military Photo Features

Thompson M1/M1A1

In April 1942, the M1 Thompson was introduced. It was a simplified version of the Model 1928 with a smooth barrel, stamped rear "L" sight, and a fixed rear stock. The expensive Model 1928-type bolt assembly was modified to simplified machining procedures. The result was a repositioned cocking knob on the right side of the receiver. Some 285,000 M1s were produced before being replaced by an improved version, the "M1A1," in April 1942. This version of the Thompson has a fixed firing pin machined into the bolt face, and had protective ears added to the rear sight assembly. All M1 Thompsons were fitted with a horizontal forearm and fixed butt stock. Approximately 540,000 M1A1 Thompsons were produced before the end of WWII. All M1 and M1A1 Thompsons used stick or box magazines only.

NOTE: Many of these weapons were reworked by a military arsenal during the war and may have been refinished; however, it does not significantly reduce the value of the gun. In addition to the rework, many of the serial numbered lower assemblies were not assembled with the correct serial numbered receiver. Although this may disturb some collectors, it should not significantly devalue the weapon. A very small percentage of these weapons were marked "US PROPERTY" behind the rear sight and this increases the value by as much as $1,000.

THE THOMPSON M1A1

The 1911 pistol is "the" classic American handgun and the Thompson submachine gun is "the" classic American submachine gun. Of all the Thompson submachine guns made over the first half of the 20th Century, the military M1A1 World War II version was by far the most practical. The M1A1 was designed to be manufactured in the simplest manner possible with the fewest number of internal parts. It was the version carried by Tom Hanks in "*Saving Private Ryan*" and was carried by several characters in the HBO series "*Band of Brothers.*" In the view of many, the biggest improvement with the M1A1 Thompson over the more elegant 1928 model was the elimination of the controversial Blish lock. This created a more reliable weapon and one with fewer parts. Also not found on the M1A1 Thompson was the Cutts compensator, the ribbed barrel, the detachable stock, or the ability to accept 50-round and 100-round drum magazines. The M1A1 Thompson used only 20-round and 30-round stick magazines. The big negative with any Thompson subgun was its weight. At 10.45 pounds empty, the M1A1 Thompson was a heavy submachine gun. Add to this the weight of six or eight fully loaded 30-round magazines at 1.6 pounds each and it is easy to sympathize with all those Dogfaces who marched across France, Belgium, and Germany. The big positive with the M1A1 Thompson was its reliability. If all the parts were correct, these guns always worked. Additionally, with its .45 ACP chambering it was one of the hardest hitting submachine guns in small arms history, and in the hands of someone familiar with its heavy first shot bolt throw, it was accurate. It was not difficult to engage human targets at 100 yards with short bursts of full-auto fire. The cyclic rate of fire was 700 rpm. Over 1.5 million examples were produced by the time production ended in 1944.

Frank James

Courtesy Richard M. Kumor, Sr.

Pre-1968

Exc.	V.G.	Fair
13000	10000	8000

Pre-1986 conversions

Exc.	V.G.	Fair
N/A	N/A	N/A

Pre-1986 dealer samples

Exc.	V.G.	Fair
6500	5000	4000

Third Generation Thompsons

In 1975, the Auto Ordnance Corp., West Hurley, New York, began production of the new Model 1928 Thompson. It was an attempt to produce a version of the Thompson for the civilian collector as well as a limited number of law enforcement sales. The early weapons were manufactured from surplus WWII components and were quite acceptable in quality. As time wore on, however, many of the components were of new manufacture and lesser quality. Between 1975 and 1986, approximately 3,200 models of the 1928 were produced. Some of these guns were commemorative models. The weapons had finned barrels, flip-up rear leaf sights, removable stocks, and blued finish. In 1985 and 1986, approximately 600 versions of the M1 Thompson were built. These were actually a version of the M1A1 military Thompson with blued finish. With the exception of a short production run for export in 1992, production of these weapons was banned in May 1986 by Federal law. All receivers were marked "AUTO-ORDNANCE WEST HURLEY, NEW YORK" on the right side of the receiver and "THOMPSON SUB-MACHINE GUN, CALIBER .45 M1" on the left side. All serial numbers carried the letter "A" suffix. A very limited number of .22 caliber models were produced in the Model 1928 configuration, but had limited success in the market.

Thompson Model 1928—West Hurley

Pre-1968

Exc.	V.G.	Fair
9000	8000	6000

Pre-1986 conversions

Exc.	V.G.	Fair
N/A	N/A	N/A

Pre-1986 dealer samples

Exc.	V.G.	Fair
4500	4000	3000

Thompson Model M1—West Hurley

Pre-1968

Exc.	V.G.	Fair
8000	7000	5500

Pre-1986 conversions

Exc.	V.G.	Fair
N/A	N/A	N/A

Pre-1986 dealer samples

Exc.	V.G.	Fair
4000	3500	2750

Thompson Model 1928 .22 caliber—West Hurley

Pre-1968

Exc.	V.G.	Fair
7000	6000	4500

Pre-1986 conversions

Exc.	V.G.	Fair
N/A	N/A	N/A

Pre-1986 dealer samples

Exc.	V.G.	Fair
3500	3000	2500

UD (United Defense) M42

Built by Marlin for U.S. military forces beginning in 1942. Designed by Carl Swebilius, founder of High Standard. Well constructed of excellent materials. Chambered for the 9mm Parabellum cartridge. Select fire with rate of fire of 700 rounds per minute. Barrel length was 10.8". Weight is about 9 lbs. Markings on left side of receiver are "UNITED DEFENSE SUPPLY CORP/US MODEL 42/MARLIN FA CO NEW HAVEN." Magazine capacity is 20 rounds. Limited quantities produced with an estimate of about 15,000 produced. It seems that the majority were built to be sold to the Netherlands during WWII but, because of the war, they could not be delivered, so most were shipped to the American OSS for use in Europe and the Far East. These guns saw a lot of action during the war.

Private NFA collection, Gary Gelson photo

Pre-1968

Exc.	V.G.	Fair
8500	8000	7500

Pre-1986 conversions

Exc.	V.G.	Fair
N/A	N/A	N/A

Pre-1986 dealer samples

Exc.	V.G.	Fair
N/A	N/A	N/A

US M3

First produced in the U.S. in 1942, this submachine gun was chambered for the .45 ACP or 9mm cartridge (special conversion kit). It is similar in concept to the British Sten gun. It was fitted with an 8" barrel and folding metal stock. The box magazine capacity was 30 rounds. The rate of fire was 400 rounds per minute. Weight of the M3 was about 8 lbs. It was produced until 1944. Marked "GUIDE LAMP DIV OF GENERAL MOTORS/US MODEL M3" on top of the receiver. Approximately 600,000 M3s were produced. Built by the Guide Lamp Division of General Motors.

NOTE: A suppressed version of this gun was built for the OSS in World War II, and used for covert operations in Vietnam as well. Too rare to price.

US M3 • Courtesy Richard M. Kumor Sr.

Pre-1968

Exc.	V.G.	Fair
10000	9500	9000

Pre-1986 conversions (or current U.S. manufacture)

Exc.	V.G.	Fair
7000	6500	6000

Pre-1986 dealer samples

Exc.	V.G.	Fair
5000	4500	4000

U.S. M3 with silencer • Courtesy Chuck Karwan

Pre-1968

Exc.	V.G.	Fair
12500	10500	9500

Pre-1986 conversions (or current U.S. manufacture)

Exc.	V.G.	Fair
N/A	N/A	N/A

Pre-1986 dealer samples

Exc.	V.G.	Fair
6500	5500	5000

Ft. Benning, Ga., 1952. An Army Ranger trainee prepares to fire an M3A1 submachine gun, a simplified version of the M3 characterized by elimination of the cocking handle in favor of a finger groove on the bolt • U.S. Army Signal Corps/National Archives/Robert Bruce Military Photo Features

US M3A1

Similar to the M3 but with significant changes and improvements. This model has a larger ejection port, the retracting handle has been eliminated, a finger hole is used for cocking, disassembly grooves were added, a stronger cover spring was installed, a larger oil can is in the grip, a stock plate and magazine filler were added to the stock, and a guard was added for the magazine catch. First produced in 1944. Approximately 50,000 M3A1s were built. This version was built by Guide Lamp and Ithaca.

US M3A1 • Photo courtesy private NFA collection

THE M3A1 GREASE GUN

World War II witnessed the apogee of pistol caliber submachine guns in terms of sheer numbers and the different countries producing them. The emphasis in each combatant country was on volume and not quality per se, but the American-produced "Grease Gun" or M3 and M3A1 also exhibited some quality characteristics like accuracy and reliability for a gun produced so cheaply. The weapon itself cost the government something in the neighborhood of $12 (1944 era dollars). The M3A1 was a further refinement of the original M3. The biggest difference was the elimination of the crank handle used to cock the bolt. (It fired from an open bolt.) Instead, a larger ejection port, complete with cover, was substituted and the operator simply reached in, hooked a finger into the recess on the bolt, and pulled it backward. Construction of the M3A1 consisted of two half-shells welded together to form the round body of the receiver. The magazine was essentially a scaled-up version of the same one used for the MP-40 in that it was a dual column, single position feed magazine. A better magazine could have been chosen. The safety for the weapon was the ejector port cover because when closed a stud on the cover engaged a recess in the bolt to prevent movement. When the bolt was retracted and the cover closed, this stud prevented forward movement of the bolt. The M3A1 Grease Gun was made totally from stamped metal parts, but in the hands of a dedicated operator it could demonstrate surprising accuracy. The low cyclic rate of fire (350 to 450 rpm) allowed anyone the chance to shoot single rounds on this full-auto only weapon. The M3A1 weighed 8.15 pounds unloaded, and approximately 646,000 M3s and M3A1s were manufactured at Guide Lamp (a division of General Motors) in Anderson, Indiana, during World War II.

Frank James

RIFLES

PEABODY
Providence, Rhode Island

These rifles were made by the Providence Tool Company from 1866 to 1871. Total production for all models was approximately 112,000. These rifles were produced in a wide variety of calibers and used by military forces in Canada, Spain, Switzerland, and others. They were also issued to three state militias: Connecticut, Massachusetts, and South Carolina.

NOTE: U.S. and Canadian marked will bring a premium over foreign marked rifles of about 20%.

Rifle

This is a lever-action, top-loading rifle with side hammer. Full stocked with two barrel bands. The front sight also serves as a bayonet fitting. Weight is about 10 lbs. The .45-70 caliber is the most sought after chambering. Also chambered for the .50-60 Peabody Musket rimfire. In general, European calibers denote foreign military contracts.

Exc.	V.G.	Good	Fair	Poor
—	1750	1150	500	200

NOTE: Canada acquired 3,000 rifles in .50-60 caliber in 1865. Switzerland acquired 15,000 rifles in .41 Swiss rimfire in 1867. Romania acquired 25,000 rifles in .45 Romanian centerfire. France acquired 39,000 rifles during the Franco-Prussian War. Some rifles were chambered for the .43 Spanish centerfire cartridge and some were chambered for the .50-79 cartridge.

Carbine

This version has the same action but is half stocked with a single barrel band. Chambered for the .45 Peabody rimfire cartridge. Fitted with a 20" barrel. Weight is about 8.5 lbs.

Exc.	V.G.	Good	Fair	Poor
—	2250	1500	750	300

Model 1874 Peabody-Martini Rifle

This rifle was almost identical to the British Martini-Henry Mark I rifle (.45 Martini Henry cartridge). Built by the Providence Tool Company, it was not adopted by any U.S. military. About 600,000 were sold to the Turkish military and used in the Russo-Turkish War, 1877-1878. Marked "PEABODY-MARTINI PATENTS." Rifle chambered for the .45 Turkish caliber and fitted with a 32.5" barrel with two barrel bands. Full stock. Weight is about 8.75 lbs.

Exc.	V.G.	Good	Fair	Poor
—	950	600	300	150

NOTE: A few rifles were chambered for the .50-70 Gov't. cartridge.

Model 1874 Peabody-Martini Carbine

As above but with 21.5" barrel and one barrel band. Half stocked. Fitted with a saddle ring.

Exc.	V.G.	Good	Fair	Poor
—	1250	800	400	200

NOTE: Some of the rifles and carbines were sold to the Japanese Navy and exhibit both Turkish and Japanese markings.

Model 1879 Peabody-Martini Rifle

See Romania, Rifle, Peabody-Martini.

PEDERSEN, JOHN D.
Denver, CO & Jackson, WY

John D. Pedersen was the inventor and designer of the Pedersen device that consisted of a conversion unit to be installed in a modified Springfield .30-06 bolt action rifle. This device allowed the rifle to function as a semiautomatic. At the end of World War I the idea was discarded. During the 1920s, Pedersen and John Garand began working on a new semiautomatic military rifle for U.S. forces. Pedersen's design was chambered for the .276 caliber and his rifle eventually lost out to Garand's rifle, the M1. The Pedersen rifles and carbines appear to be part of a test group for military trials. Total number built is unknown.

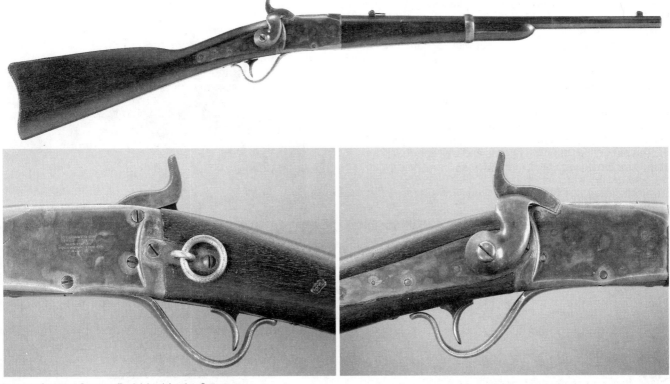

Peabody Carbine • Courtesy Rock Island Auction Company

Pedersen Carbine • Courtesy West Point Museum, Paul Goodwin photo

NOTE: Thanks to Jim Supica for his research into the Pedersen rifle and carbine that appeared for sale in his Old Town Station Dispatch.

NOTE: Most Springfield-manufactured Pedersen rifles are so rare as not to be available to the collector. Therefore, only those rifles made by Vickers are listed.

Pedersen Rifle
Chambered for .276 Pedersen cartridge. Marked "PEDERSEN SELF LOADER PA/VICKERS-ARMSTRONG LTD." on the left side of the receiver. In oval over chamber marked "C/2." Rare.

Exc.	V.G.	Good	Fair	Poor
12500	7500	—	—	—

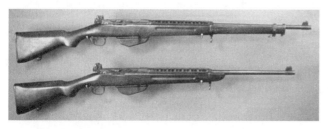

Pedersen rifle at top, carbine at bottom • Courtesy Jim Supica, Old Town Station

Pedersen Carbine
Same caliber and markings as rifle, but with 23" barrel. Rare.

Exc.	V.G.	Good	Fair	Poor
15000	8500	—	—	—

SPRINGFIELD ARMORY
This was America's first federal armory. It began producing military weapons in 1795 with the Springfield Model 1795 musket. The armory has supplied famous and well-known military weapons to the United States military forces throughout its history. The armory was phased out in 1968. The buildings and its collections are now part of the National Park Service.

BIBLIOGRAPHICAL NOTE: For further information, technical data, and photos, see the following: Robert W.D. Ball, *Springfield Armory Shoulder Weapons, 1795-1968*, Antique Trader Books, 1997. Blake Stevens, *U.S. Rifle M14 From John Garand to the M21,* Collector Grade Publications. William S. Brophy, *The Springfield 1903 Rifles*, Stackpole Books, 1985. Bruce Canfield, *A Collector's Guide to the '03 Springfield*, Andrew Mowbray Publishers, 1991.

Joslyn Breech-Loading Rifle
Until recently, this rifle was considered a post-Civil War breechloading conversion of a muzzleloading musket, but information developed since the 1970s indicates that this was the first true breechloading cartridge rifle to be made in quantity by a national armory, circa 1864. Actions were supplied to the Springfield Armory by the Joslyn Firearms Co. where they were assembled to newly made rifles designed for the action. Chambered for the 50-60-450 Joslyn rimfire cartridge, with a 35.5" barrel with three barrel bands, the uniquely shaped lock with eagle ahead of the hammer, "U.S./Springfield" on the front of the lock, with "1864" at the rear. Walnut stock specially made for the barreled action and lock. Converted to 50-70 centerfire will command approximately $100 more.

Exc.	V.G.	Good	Fair	Poor
—	2250	1000	700	400

Joslyn Breechloading Rifle • Courtesy West Point Museum, Paul Goodwin photo

Model 1866 Breechloading rifle with lock • Paul Goodwin photo

Model 1865 U.S. Breech-Loading Rifle, Allin Conversion, aka First Model Allin

Designed in .58 caliber rimfire, with a 40" barrel with three flat barrel bands. The breechlock is released by a thumb latch on the right side, pivoted upward, with the firing pin contained within the breechblock. 5,000 Model 1861 percussion muskets were altered using this method at the Springfield Armory circa 1865. The breechblock is unmarked, while the lock is marked with the eagle ahead of the hammer, as well as "U.S./Springfield," with all specimens dated 1865 at the rear.

Exc.	V.G.	Good	Fair	Poor
—	4500	3000	1500	1200

Model 1866 U.S. Breech-Loading Rifle, Allin Conversion, aka Second Model Allin

Produced in .50 caliber centerfire, with a 40" barrel with a .50 caliber liner tube inserted and brazed, walnut stock with three barrel bands with band springs. Differences between the First and Second Model Allin include a lengthened bolt, a firing pin spring, and a stronger internal extraction system. The breechblock is marked with "1866" over an eagle, while the lock bears standard Springfield markings with either an 1863 or 1864 date. A total of 25,000 Model 1863 percussion muskets were thus altered at the Springfield Armory around 1866.

Exc.	V.G.	Good	Fair	Poor
—	3500	2000	800	500

Model 1867 U.S. Breech-Loading Cadet Rifle

This model is a .50 caliber centerfire, 33" barrel, two band, scaled down version of the Model 1866 Second Model Allin "trapdoor." No sling swivels; a narrow triggerguard. The breechblock has a blackened finish, with deeply arched cut-outs on both sides of the underside, leaving a narrow flat ridge in the center. The breechblock is marked 1866/eaglehead. The lock plate was made especially for this rifle and is noticeably thinner. The plate is marked with the usual eagle and "US/Springfield," with the date "1866" behind the hammer. About 424 rifles were produced at the Springfield Armory between 1876 and 1868.

Exc.	V.G.	Good	Fair	Poor
—	10000	7500	3000	800

Model 1868 Rifle

This is a single shot Trapdoor rifle chambered for the .50 caliber centerfire cartridge. It features a breechblock that pivots forward when a thumblatch at its rear is depressed. It has a 32.5" barrel and a full-length stock held on by two barrel bands. It has iron mountings and a cleaning rod mounted under the barrel. It features an oil-finished walnut stock. The lock is marked "US Springfield." It is dated either 1863 or 1864. The

breechblock features either the date 1869 or 1870. There were approximately 51,000 manufactured between 1868 and 1872.

Courtesy Little John's Auction Service, Inc., Paul Goodwin photo

Exc.	V.G.	Good	Fair	Poor
—	2000	1250	500	350

Model 1869 Cadet Rifle

This is a single shot trapdoor rifle chambered for .50 caliber centerfire. It is similar to the Model 1868 with a 29.5" barrel. There were approximately 3,500 manufactured between 1869 and 1876.

Courtesy Little John's Auction Service, Inc., Paul Goodwin photo

Exc.	V.G.	Good	Fair	Poor
—	2500	1500	500	200

Model 1870

There are two versions of this Trapdoor breechloader—a rifle with a 32.5" barrel and a carbine that features a 22" barrel and a half-stock held on by one barrel band. They are both chambered for .50 caliber centerfire and feature the standard Springfield lock markings and a breechblock marked "1870" or "Model 1870." There were a total of 11,500 manufactured between 1870 and 1873. Only 340 are carbines; they are extremely rare.

Rifle

Courtesy Milwaukee Public Museum, Milwaukee, Wisconsin

Exc.	V.G.	Good	Fair	Poor
—	3000	1750	800	500

Carbine—Very Rare

Exc.	V.G.	Good	Fair	Poor
—	12500	9500	3500	1500

Model 1871 Rolling Block U.S. Army Rifle

This model is a .50 caliber centerfire, 36" barrel, with two barrel bands, and rolling block action. Sights, sling-swivels, and most other details as for the Model 1870 Remington U.S. Navy rifle. Case-hardened frame, bright finished iron mountings. Two piece walnut stock. Known as the "locking action" as the hammer went to half cock when the breechblock was closed. No serial numbers. Left side of frame marked "Model 1871." Right side marked with eagle over "U.S./Springfield/1872." On the tang, marked "REMINGTON'S PATENT. PAT.MAY 3D, NOV. 15TH, 1864, APRIL 17TH, 1868." About 10,000 rifles were produced between 1871 and 1872 under a royalty agreement with Remington Arms Co.

Exc.	V.G.	Good	Fair	Poor
—	4000	1750	750	500

Model 1871 Ward-Burton U.S. Rifle

A .50 caliber centerfire, 32.63" barrel secured by two barrel bands. This is an early bolt action, single shot rifle, with the cartridge loaded directly into the open action, with cocking on the closing of the bolt. Walnut stock, sling swivels on the forward barrel band and the front of the triggerguard. Not serially numbered. The top of the bolt marked, "WARD BURTON PATENT DEC. 20, 1859-FEB. 21, 1871." Left side of the action marked with American eagle motif and "US/SPRINGFIELD." 1,011 rifles (32.625" barrel) and 316 carbines (22" barrel) produced at the Springfield Armory basically as a trial weapon.

Courtesy Bob Ball

Rifle

Exc.	V.G.	Good	Fair	Poor
—	3500	2000	750	400

Carbine

Exc.	V.G.	Good	Fair	Poor
—	6500	2750	950	450

Model 1873

This is a Trapdoor breechloading rifle chambered for the .45-70 cartridge. The rifle version has a 32.5" barrel with a full-length stock held on by two barrel bands. The carbine features a 22" barrel with a half-stock held on by a single barrel band, and the cadet rifle features a 29.5" barrel with a full length stock and two barrel bands. The finish of all three variations is blued and case-colored, with a walnut stock. The lock is marked "US Springfield 1873." The breechblock is either marked "Model 1873" or "US Model 1873." There were approximately 73,000 total manufactured between 1873 and 1877.

NOTE: Prices listed below are for rifles in original configuration.

Rifle—50,000 Manufactured

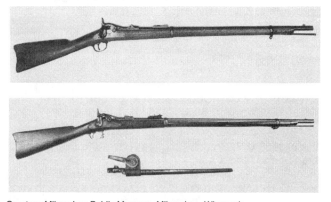

Courtesy Milwaukee Public Museum, Milwaukee, Wisconsin

Exc.	V.G.	Good	Fair	Poor
—	2500	1000	400	200

Carbine-20,000 Manufactured

Exc.	V.G.	Good	Fair	Poor
—	8500	4000	1750	700

Cadet Rifle-3,000 Manufactured

Exc.	V.G.	Good	Fair	Poor
—	1500	750	600	300

Model 1875 Officer's Rifle

This is a high-grade Trapdoor breechloader chambered for the .45-70 cartridge. It has a 26" barrel and a half-stock fastened by one barrel band. It is blued and case-colored, with a scroll engraved lock. It has a checkered walnut pistol grip stock with

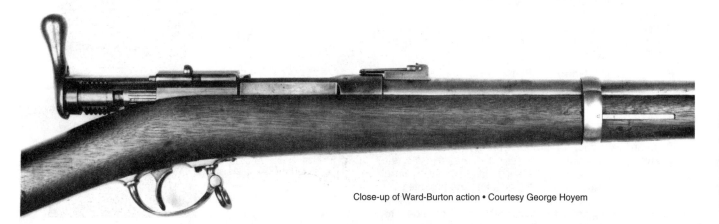

Close-up of Ward-Burton action • Courtesy George Hoyem

Springfield Model 1873 Carbine with lock • Paul Goodwin photo

a pewter forend tip. There is a cleaning rod mounting beneath the barrel. This rifle was not issued but was sold to army officers for personal sporting purposes. There were only 477 manufactured between 1875 and 1885.

Exc.	V.G.	Good	Fair	Poor
45000	35000	15000	8000	3500

Model 1875 Lee Vertical Action Rifle

A .45-70 centerfire, 32.63" barrel secured by two barrel bands. Martini-style dropping block action, with a unique, centrally mounted hammer with an exceptionally long spur. In order to open the breech, the hammer must be given a sharp blow with the heal of the hand; the insertion of a cartridge will automatically close the breech, while the hammer is cocked by hand. All blued finish. Stacking and sling swivel on upper band, with sling swivel on triggerguard. Serially numbered 1 through 143 on the internal parts only. Upper tang marked, "U.S. PAT. MAR 16, 1875," no barrel proofmarks; inspector's initials "ESA" in an oval on the stock. 143 rifles produced in 1875 at the Springfield Armory, basically as a trials weapon.

Exc.	V.G.	Good	Fair	Poor
7500	5500	2500	1500	1000

Model 1877

This is a Trapdoor breechloading rifle chambered for the .45-70 cartridge. It was issued as a rifle with a 32" barrel and a full-length stock held on by two barrel bands, a cadet rifle with a 29.5" barrel, and a carbine with a 22" barrel, half-stock, and single barrel band. This version is similar to the Model 1873. In fact, the breechblock retained the Model 1873 marking. The basic differences are that the stock is thicker at the wrist and the breechblock was thickened and lowered. This is basically a mechanically improved version. There were approximately 12,000 manufactured in 1877 and 1878.

Rifle—3,900 Manufactured

Exc.	V.G.	Good	Fair	Poor
—	3000	1750	1250	650

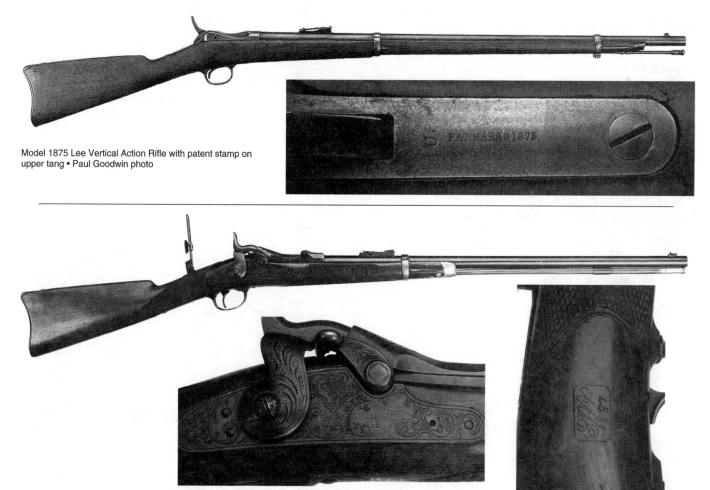

Model 1875 Lee Vertical Action Rifle with patent stamp on upper tang • Paul Goodwin photo

Model 1875 Officer's Rifle • Courtesy West Point Museum, Paul Goodwin photo

Model 1877 Cadet Rifle • Paul Goodwin photo

Cadet Rifle—1,000 Manufactured

Exc.	V.G.	Good	Fair	Poor
—	3000	1750	1250	650

Carbine—4,500 Manufactured

Courtesy Milwaukee Public Museum, Milwaukee, Wisconsin

Exc.	V.G.	Good	Fair	Poor
—	6500	3000	1250	850

Model 1879 (Model 1873/1879)

This is essentially a Model 1873 with 1879 improvements. The most noticeable improvement is that the receiver is wider and thicker so that it is no longer flush with the barrel, which results in a two-step junction between barrel and receiver. These guns are found in the 100,000 to 280,000 serial number range.

Exc.	V.G.	Good	Fair	Poor
—	2500	1000	400	200

Model 1880

This version features a sliding combination cleaning rod/bayonet that is fitted in the forearm under the barrel. It retained the 1873 breechblock markings. There were approximately 1,000 manufactured for trial purposes in 1880.

Courtesy Milwaukee Public Museum, Milwaukee, Wisconsin

Exc.	V.G.	Good	Fair	Poor
—	4750	2000	1000	500

Model 1881 Marksman Rifle

This is an extremely high-grade Trapdoor breechloading rifle chambered for the .45-70 cartridge. It has a 28" round barrel and is similar to the Model 1875 Officer's Rifle in appearance.

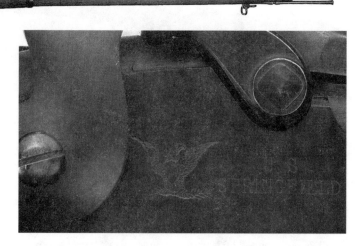

It features a full-length, high grade, checkered walnut stock held on by one barrel band. It has a horn Schnabel forend tip. The metal parts are engraved, blued, and case-colored. It has a vernier aperture sight as well as a buckhorn rear sight on the barrel and a globe front sight with a spirit level. There were only 11 manufactured to be awarded as prizes at shooting matches.

CAUTION: This is perhaps the supreme rarity among the Trapdoor Springfields, and one should be extremely cognizant of fakes.

Exc.	V.G.	Good	Fair	Poor
—	75000	60000	20000	5000

Model 1881 Long Range Rifle

This model is a Model 1879 chambered for the .45-80 cartridge. The barrel has six groove rifling. The stock has a shotgun butt with Hotchkiss buttplate. Some of these rifles had uncheckered walnut stock with detachable pistol grip and Sharps peep and globe sights. According to Flayderman, this rifle falls between serial numbers 162000 and 162500. It is estimated that less than 200 were produced between 1897 and 1880.

Exc.	V.G.	Good	Fair	Poor
—	27500	12500	5000	2000

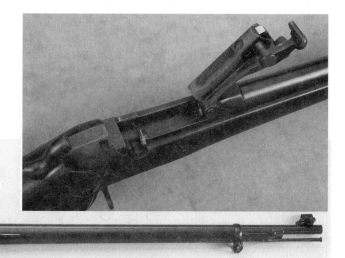

Model 1881 Long Range Rifle • Courtesy Little John's Auction Service, Inc., Paul Goodwin photo

A Long Range Trapdoor rifle based on the Model 1879 was sold at auction for $11,000. Original configuration with proper stampings. Caliber is 45-80. Condition was excellent with 98% blue.
Little John's Auction Service, Inc., April 2002

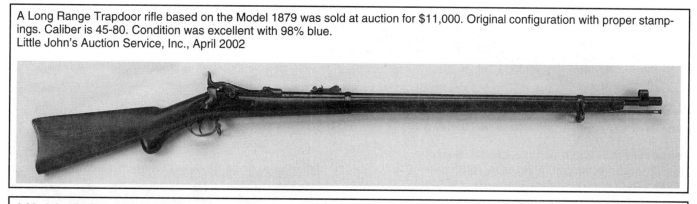

A Model 1881 Trapdoor Marksman rifle was sold at auction for $77,000. Condition was very good to excellent. This is an extremely rare Springfield.
Little John's Auction Service, Inc., April 2002

THE SPRINGFIELD TRAPDOOR

Ah the innocence, and stupidity, of youth. It is a miracle any of us survive it! The 1950s were a good news, bad news situation for those of us youngsters that were deeply involved in firearms and shooting. Great guns, single action and double action sixguns, semi-automatics, rifles of every kind imaginable were readily available. However, money was a lot harder to come by then than it is now. Springfield '03s, Enfields, 1911s, S&W 1917s, could be had for anywhere from $7.50 to $15, and if they were really in near-perfect condition, possibly $30. Old guns were also everywhere: early Colt Single Actions, cap and ball revolvers, Winchester leverguns, and of course, Springfield Trapdoors. My main interest then, as it is now, was sixguns. However, as I removed the Springfield Trapdoor from the rack and looked at it, I was intrigued by the size of the cartridge it used. This was the first time I had ever seen a .45-70, so

for $15 and another $5 for a box of 20 cartridges, I was in the big bore rifle business. That particular Springfield rifle was an 1884 Model, and when I think about it today, I realize how dumb this teenager really was. It still had most of the original bluing, the stock had a few dings and the minor wear that comes with normal use: however, the barrel was perfect. Brand-new, no pitting, sharp rifling perfect. It was obvious that this single-shot .45-70 had been well taken care of. I wish I could tell you I still had it. I don't even remember what I traded it off for. I've never ever seen another one in such shape that didn't command a very high dollar price. I still shoot a Trapdoor, an excellent shooting Trapdoor; however, it is a replica carbine that cost me thirty times what I paid for the original. We live and, hopefully, learn. My only solace is that $450 today is less than $15 was then.

John Taffin

Model 1882 U.S. Magazine rifle, Chaffee-Reese • Paul Goodwin photo

Model 1882 U.S. Magazine Rifle, Chaffee-Reese

A .45-70 caliber centerfire, 27.78" barrel secured by two barrel bands. One of the early bolt action repeaters, with the cartridges carried in a tubular feed in the butt. Iron mountings, with a blued finish, walnut stock, stacking swivel and sling swivel on the upper barrel band, and a sling swivel on the front of the triggerguard. Not serially numbered. Left side of breech marked "US SPRINGFIELD, 1884," the barrel marked "V.P." with eagle head proof. Unfortunately, most rifles found are lacking the feed mechanism in the butt, which lowers the value approximately 15%. 753 rifles were produced at the Springfield Armory in 1884.

Courtesy Rock Island Auction Company

Springfield Model 1884 • Paul Goodwin photo

Exc.	V.G.	Good	Fair	Poor
3000	2500	2000	900	750

Model 1884

This is also a breechloading Trapdoor single shot rifle chambered for the .45-70 cartridge. It was issued as a standard rifle with a 32.75" barrel, a cadet rifle with a 29.5" barrel, and a military carbine with a 22" barrel. The finish is blued and case-colored. This model features the improved Buffington rear sight. It features the socket bayonet and a walnut stock. There were approximately 232,000 manufactured between 1885 and 1890.

A Springfield Model 1884 rifle was sold at auction for $6,037.50. It was the property of Captain Leonard Wood, later General Wood, with a letter dated 1893. Stock cartouche "SWP/1887." Condition was good. Amoskeag Auction Co. Inc., March 2000

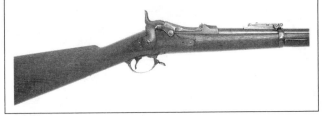

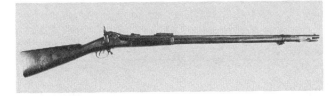

Courtesy Bob Ball

Rifle-200,000 manufactured

Exc.	V.G.	Good	Fair	Poor
—	1750	750	500	200

Cadet Rifle—12,000 manufactured

Exc.	V.G.	Good	Fair	Poor
—	1100	600	400	200

Carbine—20,000 manufactured

Exc.	V.G.	Good	Fair	Poor
—	3000	1500	700	250

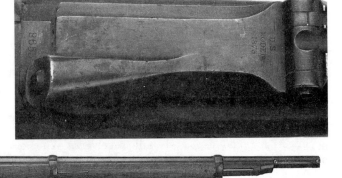

Springfield Fencing Musket, Type I • Paul Goodwin photo

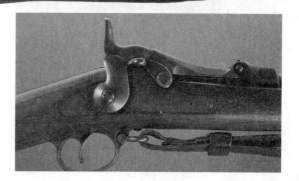

Model 1888 Rifle with ramrod bayonet • Courtesy Rock Island Auction Company

Model 1886 Experimental "Trapdoor" Carbine, aka Experimental Model 1882 third/fourth type

Apparently both of these designations are misnomers, as the weapon was officially referred to as the "24" Barrel Carbine. Collectors now call it the Model 1886 to conform to the year of manufacture. The most outstanding feature is the almost full length stock with uncapped, tapered forend. The single upper barrel band is fitted with a bent, or wraparound swivel to facilitate insertion in a saddle scabbard. Lower swivel on butt, with a sling ring and bar on the left side. Cleaning rod compartment in the butt. Buffington-type Model 1884 rear sight marked XC on leaf. About 1,000 produced during 1886.

Exc.	V.G.	Good	Fair	Poor
—	6500	3000	1100	500

Model 1888

This version is similar to its predecessors except that it features a sliding, ramrod-type bayonet that was improved so that it stays securely locked when in its extended position. The breechblock was still marked "Model 1884." This was the last Springfield Trapdoor rifle produced. There were approximately 65,000 manufactured between 1889 and 1893.

Exc.	V.G.	Good	Fair	Poor
—	1750	750	350	200

Trapdoor Fencing Musket

This is a non-gun that was used by the Army in teaching bayonet drills. They had no desire to damage serviceable rifles during practice, so they produced this version to fill the bill. There were basically four types produced.

Type I

This version is similar to the Model 1873 rifle without a breech or lock. The finish is rough, and it is unmarked. It was designed to accept a socket bayonet. One should secure a qualified appraisal if a transaction is contemplated. There were 170 manufactured in 1876 and 1877.

Exc.	V.G.	Good	Fair	Poor
—	1150	500	400	300

Type II

This version is basically a Model 1884 with the hammer removed and the front sight blade ground off. It accepted a socket bayonet that was covered with leather and had a pad on its point.

Exc.	V.G.	Good	Fair	Poor
—	750	300	250	200

Type III

This version is similar to the Type II except that it is shortened to 43.5" in length. There were approximately 1,500 manufactured between 1905 and 1906.

Exc.	V.G.	Good	Fair	Poor
—	950	450	350	300

Type IV

This version is similar to the Type III except that the barrel was filled with lead. There were approximately 11,000 manufactured between 1907 and 1916.

Exc.	V.G.	Good	Fair	Poor
—	550	300	250	200

Model 1870 Rolling Block

This is a single shot breechloading rifle with a rolling-block action. It is chambered for .50 caliber centerfire and has a 32.75" barrel. It has a full-length forend held on by two barrel bands. The finish is blued and case-colored, with a cleaning rod mounted under the barrel. The stock and forend are walnut. The frame is marked "USN Springfield 1870." There is an anchor motif marked on the top of the barrel. It also features government inspector's marks on the frame. This rifle was manufactured by Springfield Armory under license from Remington Arms Company for the United States Navy. The first 10,000 produced were rejected by our Navy and were sent to France and used in the Franco-Prussian War. For that reason, this variation is quite scarce and would bring a 20% premium. There was also a group of approximately 100 rifles that were converted to the .22 rimfire cartridge and used for target practice aboard ships. This version is extremely rare. There were approximately 22,000 manufactured in 1870 and 1871.

Courtesy Milwaukee Public Museum, Milwaukee, Wisconsin

Standard Navy Rifle

Exc.	V.G.	Good	Fair	Poor
—	2250	950	500	250

Rejected Navy Rifle

Exc.	V.G.	Good	Fair	Poor
—	1750	700	400	200

.22 Caliber

Exc.	V.G.	Good	Fair	Poor
—	6000	2500	900	600

U.S. Krag Jorgensen Rifle

NOTE: This firearm will be found listed in its own section of this text.

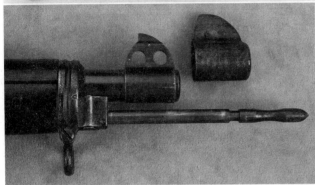

Model 1903 with rod bayonet • Courtesy Little John's Auction Service, Inc., Paul Goodwin photo

SPRINGFIELD MODEL 1903 & VARIATIONS

These rifles were built by Springfield, Remington, Rock Island Arsenal, and Smith-Carona.

Model 1903

This rifle was a successor to the Krag Jorgensen and was also produced by the Rock Island Arsenal. It was initially chambered for the .30-03 Government cartridge and very shortly changed to the .30-06 cartridge. Its original chambering consisted of a 220-grain, metal jacket soft-point bullet. The German army introduced its spitzer bullet so our government quickly followed suit with a 150-grain, pointed bullet designated the .30-06. This model has a 24" barrel and was built on what was basically a modified Mauser action. It features a 5-round integral box magazine. The finish is blued, with a full length, straight-grip walnut stock with full handguards held on by two barrel bands. The initial version was issued with a rod-type bayonet that was quickly discontinued when President Theodore Roosevelt personally disapproved it. There were approximately 74,000 produced with this rod bayonet; and if in an unaltered condition, these would be worth a great deal more than the standard variation. **It is important to note that the early models with serial numbers under 800,000 were not heat treated sufficiently to be safe to fire with modern ammunition.** There were a great many produced between 1903 and 1930. The values represented reflect original specimens; WWII alterations would be worth approximately 15% less.

Rod Bayonet Version (Original & Unaltered)

Exc.	V.G.	Good	Fair	Poor
35000	20000	15000	12500	10000

NOTE: For rifles restored to Rod Bayonet configuration but in orginal condition deduct 85%.

Rod Bayonet Model 1903 (Altered to Model 1905 in .30-03)

Exc.	V.G.	Good	Fair	Poor
25000	15000	7500	4000	1500

Rod Bayonet Model 1903 (Altered to Model 1905 in .30-06)

Exc.	V.G.	Good	Fair	Poor
4750	3000	1500	850	500

Model 1903 Rifle with 1905 Modifications

This model was built in Springfield between 1905 to 1906. Chambered for .30-03 cartridge. Overall barrel length is 24.206" (chamber & bore length is 23.949"). These rifles were newly manufactured and therefore are unaltered. No ramrod bayonet. Model 1905 front and rear sight. Front barrel band is a double strap with bayonet stud and stacking swivel. There is a Model 1905 knife bayonet designed for this model. Rear sight graduated to 2,400 yards with a silver line above and below peep sight aperture. Very Rare.

Original & Unaltered Examples

Exc.	V.G.	Good	Fair	Poor
22500	15000	8000	3000	1000

Altered to .30-06

Exc.	V.G.	Good	Fair	Poor
4000	2500	1200	800	400

Model 1903 Rifle (Altered from Model 1905 in .30-06)

This model was altered to accept a new pointed bullet that required a shortened cartridge case. This required a shorter chamber. The barrel was shortened by setting it deeper into the receiver by .200" therefore making the overall barrel length 24.006" in length (chamber & bore length is 23.749"). This new cartridge was adopted in 1906 and called the "Cartridge, Ball, Caliber 30, Model 0f 1906." or more commonly known as the .30-06. The rear sight base was also moved forward .200" of an inch and a new graduated rear sight up to 2,700 yards was installed. According to Flayderman the easiest way to determine a Model 1905 altered rifle "... is to remove the upper barrel band to see if a plugged hole appears 1/4" forward of the present upper band screw hole."

Model 1903 altered from Model 1905 • Courtesy Little John's Auction Service, Inc., Paul Goodwin photo

Exc.	V.G.	Good	Fair	Poor
3500	2750	1000	700	500

Model 1903 with Model 1905 Modifications • Courtesy Little John's Auction Service, Inc., Paul Goodwin photo

Model 1903 Rifle (1907-1910 in .30-06)

This variation was built both by Springfield and Rock Island. It features a stock with a square corner beside the receiver ring on the right side, a smooth and pointed trigger, smooth buttplate, the bolt handle is not bent back, blued metal. The receiver has a black or mottled finish. Early examples do not have a cross bolt in the stock while rifles built after 1908 have a single cross bolt. About 130,000 were produced in serial number range 269000 to 400000. Original examples are rare as most were arsenal rebuilt with parkerized finish and new features.

Model 1903 dated 1909 • Courtesy Little John's Auction Service, Paul Goodwin photo

Exc.	V.G.	Good	Fair	Poor
3500	2750	1250	750	500

Haiti, ca. 1919. U.S. Marines, armed with M1903 rifles and a Lewis machine gun, search for bandits • USMC/National Archives/Robert Bruce Military Photo Features

Model 1903 Rifle (1910-1917 in .30-06)

This variation features a stock with tapered rather than square corner on right side of receiver ring. The trigger is serrated and not pointed. Checkered buttplate, bolt handle is not bent back, and metal is blued. Stock has a single cross bolt. Most were arsenal rebuilt. About 250,000 were manufactured between serial numbers 385000 to 635000. Between 1910 and 1913, these rifles were also built by Rock Island.

NOTE: A small number of these rifles were sold to civilians through the DCM program. They are marked "NRA" on the triggerguard. These examples are worth approximately 20% more.

A Springfield Model 1903 dated 11-16 sold at auction for $3,450. Condition is 95% original blue. Stock is excellent. Crisp "J.F.C." cartouche. Correct leather sling. Amoskeag Auction Co. Inc., January 2003

Courtesy Little John's Auction Service, Inc. • Paul Goodwin photo

Exc.	V.G.	Good	Fair	Poor
3500	2750	1000	700	500

Model 1903 Rifle (1917-1921 in .30-06)

This variation features a parkerized finish with smooth buttplate, many have smooth triggers that have a thick contour. Two cross bolts in stock. This particular variation does not have the attention to detail and finish that peacetime rifles have. Many of these rifles were arsenal rebuilt. About 590,000 of this variation were manufactured between serial numbers 635,000 to 1225000.

NOTE: Rifles built between 1917 and 1918 will bring a 20% premium.

Exc.	V.G.	Good	Fair	Poor
3500	2700	1200	700	500

Model 1903 Rifle (1921-1929)

This variation features parkerized metal finish with checkered buttplate and serrated triggers. Stock have grasping grooves and straight grips. Many of these rifles were arsenal refinished and reassembled with different combinations of parts. About 80,000 were manufactured between serial numbers 1200000 and 1280000.

Exc.	V.G.	Good	Fair	Poor
3000	2250	900	700	500

France, 1918. A pair of U.S. Army soldiers maintain a watch on German lines from the protection of a deep trench. An M1903 rifle is close at hand. Note the M1903 bayonet on the sentry's cartridge belt • U.S. Army Signal Corps/National Archives/Robert Bruce Military Photo Features

Model 1903 Rifle Stripped for Air Service

Special 29" stock, 5.75 upper handguard specially made for this rifle, solid lower barrel band retained by screw underneath, rear leaf sight shortened and altered to open sight with square notch. 25-round extension magazine used. Some 910 rifles produced during the first half of 1918, with serial numbers ranging between 857000 and 863000; all barrels dated in first half of 1918. A very rare and desirable rifle, with the magazine almost impossible to find. Values shown include magazine.

Model 1903 with Air Service magazine • Courtesy Richard M. Kumor Sr.

Exc.	V.G.	Good	Fair	Poor
20000	12500	7500	3500	1000

Model 1903 Mark 1

This version is similar to the original except that it was cut to accept the Pedersen device. This device allows the use of a semiautomatic bolt insert that utilizes pistol cartridges. The rifle has a slot milled into the receiver that acts as an ejection port. The device was not successful and was scrapped. There were approximately 102,000 rifles that were produced with this millcut between 1918 and 1920.

Pedersen Device • Paul Goodwin photo

NOTE: The values given are for the rifle alone—not for the device. Rifle must contain all original Mark I parts. For rifles with the device and magazine add $35,000; for rifles with the device but no magazine add $30,000; for the metal carrying scabbard add $7,500.

Paul Goodwin photo

Exc.	V.G.	Good	Fair	Poor
2500	2000	1500	1200	600

Model 1903 Sniper Rifle

Selected Model 1903 rifles were fitted with telescopic sights from 1907 to 1919; apparently 25 rifles so equipped in 1906, but the type of scope has not been definitely identified. If proven original to the period, specimens would be worth more than shown in the values guide. 400 rifles were fitted with the Warner-Swasey Model 1906, 6-power telescope sight in 1911, with the sights marked Model 1908, as well as with the full Warner-Swasey markings. Scope numbers do not match the rifle numbers. Rifles fitted with this Model 1908 scope will bring approximately 30% more than the values shown. Approximately 5000 rifles were fitted with the Model 1913 Warner-Swasey telescopic sight up to 1919; similar to the Model 1908, they were only 5.2 power. When originally fitted, the scopes were numbered to the rifles; however, scopes were sold separately from the rifles as surplus and were never numbered. These were later fitted to other weapons and the chance of finding matching numbers greatly decreases. Values shown are for original guns with original, matching telescopes.

The U.S. Marine Corps also had its own versions of the Model 1903 Sniper. Early rifles were fitted with a Winchester A5 5X scope or a Lyman 5A 5X scope. Later examples were fitted with a Unertl 8X scope marked "USMC." All Marine Corps scopes had target bases.

Courtesy Bob Ball

Exc.	V.G.	Good	Fair	Poor
6750	5500	4250	2500	1500

NOTE: A few Model 1903 and 1903A1 rifles will have barrels marked "USMC" and the date. These barrels were installed by the Sedgley Company. Add a premium of about 15% for these barrels.

France, 1918. Private Leo Hahn, champion marksman of Intelligence Detachment, Company L, 127th Infantry, peers through the telescopic sight on an M1903 rifle. Hahn is credited with killing two German snipers in two days • U.S. Army Signal Corps/National Archives/Robert Bruce Military Photo Features

Model 1903 A1

This version is a standard Model 1903 rifle that was fitted with a Type C, semi-pistol grip stock. All other specifications were the same except for a checkered butt and serrated trigger.

Exc.	V.G.	Good	Fair	Poor
2000	1250	750	500	400

WORLD WAR II MODEL 1903s

For a complete explanation, with photos and techanical data see Bruce Canfield's, *U.S. Infantry Weapons of World War II.*

According to Canfield, the majority of World War II Model 1903 rifles were rebuilt. The extent varied from rifle to rifle. Look for the following alterations:

1. Refinished metal with greenish parkerizing.

2. Stock and handguard replaced or refinished. Replacement stock lacked finger grooves.

3. Replacement barrels were made by Springfield, Sedgley, and High Standard. Two-digit date stamped on new barrels.

4. A gas escape hole was added, but not to all WWII receivers.

5. Component parts were sometimes of a later vintage.

Model 1903 (Remington, WWII)

Remington began production of the Model 1903 in November 1941. These very early rifles are identical to the Rock Island Model 1903. About 1,273 of these early rifles were produced. The balance of Remington Model 1903 rifles were built using less expensive methods. Tolerences were eased and more stamped parts were employed. These rifles were stamped "Remington Model 1903," and small parts were stamped "R." These early Remington rifles will be found in serial number range 3,000 to about 3,050,000.

Exc.	V.G.	Good	Fair	Poor
400	350	300	200	100

NOTE: Very early Remington rifles, the first 1,273, will bring a premium over the later rifles.

Model 1903 (Remington, WWII, Modified)

This version of the Model 1903 was a further attempt to reduce cost and increase production. The right gas escape hole was eliminated, and a number of machining operations were omitted. This version is known as the Model 1903 Modified. These rifles are found in serial number range 3,050,000 to about 3,365,000.

Exc.	V.G.	Good	Fair	Poor
400	350	300	200	100

Model 1903 A3

This version was introduced in May of 1942 for use in WWII. It basically consisted of improvements to simplify mass production. It features an aperture sight and various small parts that were fabricated from stampings; this includes the triggerguard, floorplate, and barrel band. The finish is parkerized. Receiver ring is marked "03-A3." This model was manufactured by Remington and Smith Corona.

Courtesy Bob Ball

Exc.	V.G.	Good	Fair	Poor
400	350	300	200	100

Hanenburg, France, February 1945. A soldier at the 45th Infantry Division Sniper School during intensive live fire training with the M1903A4 sniper rifle and telescopic sight • U.S. Army Signal Corps/National Archives/Robert Bruce Military Photo Features

Model 1903 A4

Most of these rifles were marked "A3" and not "A4." The markings were rotated to the side in order not to be covered by the scope mount. This is a sniper-rifle version of the Model 1903. It is fitted with permanently mounted scope blocks and furnished with a telescopic sight known as the M73B1. This scope was manufactured by Weaver in El Paso, Texas, and was commercially known as the Model 330C. The rifle has no conventional iron sights mounted. This model was built by Remington.

NOTE: For those few rifles marked "A4" add a premium of 10%.

Rifle with WWII M73B1 scope • Courtesy Richard M. Kumor Sr.

Model 82 scope circa post-Korean War • Courtesy Richard M. Kumor Sr.

Model 84 scope circa Korea and Vietnam wars • Courtesy Richard M. Kumor Sr.

Exc.	V.G.	Good	Fair	Poor
2200	1800	1000	550	350

NOTE: For rifles with M84 scope deduct $250.

A Remington Model 1903 A4 Sniper Rifle sold at auction for $2,415. Condition was 95% parkerized finish. M84 scope wtih 95% finish. Includes sling and canvas scope case. Amoskeag Auction Co. Inc., May 2002

Model 1903 NRA National Match

This version was based on a standard 1903 service rifle that was selected for having excellent shooting qualities. The parts were then hand-fit, and a special rifled barrel was added that was checked for tolerance with a star gauge. The muzzle of this barrel was marked with a special star with six or eight rays radiating from it. These NRA rifles were drilled and tapped to accept a Lyman No. 48 rear sight. They are marked with the letters "NRA" and have a flaming bomb proofmark on the triggerguard. There were approximately 18,000 manufactured between 1921 and 1928.

NOTE: Prices are for verifiable samples.

Exc.	V.G.	Good	Fair	Poor
3000	2400	2000	1400	800

Model 1903 A1 National Match

Basically the same as the Model 1903 National Match rifle except for the "C" type, or pistol grip stock, without grasping grooves. Bolts and stocks numbered to the receiver. "P" in a circle proof on the underside of the pistol grip, with either a "DAL" in a rectangular cartouche, or S.A./SPG in a square cartouche. Rifles will be found with either a regular or reversed safety. Approximately 11,000 produced with a serial number range from 1285000 to 1532000.

NOTE: Prices are for verifiable samples.

Exc.	V.G.	Good	Fair	Poor
4000	3000	2000	1200	600

Model 1903 Style National Match Special Rifle

This rifle is identical to the National Match, but with a completely different buttstock configuration identical to the Model 1922 NRA. Large shotgun type steel buttplate; full pistol grip. About 150 rifles produced during 1924.

Model 1903 National Match Special Rifle • Courtesy Butterfield & Butterfield

NOTE: Prices are for verifiable samples.

Exc.	V.G.	Good	Fair	Poor
8500	6500	5500	3500	2500

Model 1903 Style "NB" National Match Rifle

This rifle produced with the "B" type stock with more drop than standard, suitable only for off-hand shooting; pistol grip configured with a noticeably squared profile. Deep checkered buttplate. Circle "P" proof in underside of pistol grip. About 195 rifles built between 1925 and 1926.

NOTE: Prices are for verifiable samples.

Exc.	V.G.	Good	Fair	Poor
8500	6500	5500	3500	2500

Model 1903 NRA Sporter

This version is similar to the National Match rifle but features a half-length, Sporter-type stock with one barrel band. It also features the Lyman No. 48 receiver sight. This version was produced for commercial sales. There were approximately 6,500 manufactured between 1924 and 1933.

NOTE: Prices are for verifiable samples.

Exc.	V.G.	Good	Fair	Poor
2600	2200	1800	1400	800

Model 1903 NBA Sporter Rifle

The barrel, action, and sights of this rifle are identical to the Model 1903 NRA Sporter rifle above. However it is fitted with a "B" type stock. Grasping grooves and squared pistol grip profile. Circle "P" proof in the underside of the pistol grip. 589 rifles produced at the Springfield Armory during 1925 and 1926.

NOTE: Prices are for verifiable samples.

Exc.	V.G.	Good	Fair	Poor
8500	6500	5500	3500	2500

Model 1903 Heavy Barreled Match Rifles

These rifles were made in a bewildering number of types and variations. Commonly encountered are the style "T" with NRA type stocks. Barrels, which came in three lengths, 26", 28", and 30", measured .860" at the muzzle and 1.250" at the breech. Lyman 48 rear sight; Winchester globe front sight on a modified B.A.R. front band, telescope blocks on the receiver and barrel. Some fitted with adjustable hook type buttplates,

Model 1903 NRA Sporter • Courtesy Little John's Auction Service, Inc., Paul Goodwin photo

Model 1903 "NB" National Match showing markings • Paul Goodwin photo

set triggers, Garand speed locks, as well as cheekpieces (all commanding premium dollars). INTERNATIONAL MATCH rifles (worth at least double the values shown) have many variant features which were changed annually at the request of the individual shooter. These features include palm rests, double set triggers, beaver-tail forends, checkered pistol grips, Swiss style buttplates, etc. Generally the Winchester 5A telescopic sight was used. These rifles are considered rare. Another variation is the 1922 MATCH SPRINGFIELD RIFLE with NRA type stock with grasping grooves, a 24" barrel with service type front sight mount and small base integral with the barrel, as well as telescopic blocks on the barrel. 566 rifles produced at the Springfield Armory between 1922 and 1930.

NOTE: Values shown here are for the standard heavy barrel match rifle without any special features.

Exc.	V.G.	Good	Fair	Poor
7000	5500	4000	2500	1500

Model 1903 .22 Caliber Gallery Practice Rifle "Hoffer-Thompson"

This practice rifle differed from the standard issue '03 as follows: the barrel bored and rifled to .22 caliber, the breech chambered for the Hoffer-Thompson cartridge holder, the rear sight graduated to 240 yards, the mainspring shortened, the stocks generally found without cross bolts or the circle "P" on the underside of the pistol grip. Receivers produced after 1901 usually are marked with ".22" on the top of the bridge. About 15,525 rifles were produced at the Springfield Armory between 1907 and 1918.

Exc.	V.G.	Good	Fair	Poor
3250	2200	1400	1000	700

A Model 1903 Gallery Practice Rifle "Hoffer-Thompson" sold at auction for $5,500. Condition was near mint. Little John's Auction Service, Inc., April 2002

Model 1917

In 1917, when the United States entered WWI, there was a distinct rifle shortage. There were production facilities set up for the British pattern 1914 rifle. This "Enfield" rifle was redesigned to accept the .30-06 cartridge and was pressed into service as the U.S. rifle Model 1917. This rifle appears similar to the British pattern 1914 rifle. In fact, they are so similar that in WWII, when over a million were sold to Britain for use by their Home Guard, it was necessary to paint a 2" stripe around the butt so that the caliber was immediately known. The barrel length is 26", and it has a 6-round integral box magazine. The finish is matte-blue, with a walnut stock. Towards the end of production parkerized parts were added. The breech is marked "U.S. Model 1917." This was a robust and heavy-duty rifle, and many are used in the manufacture of large-bore custom rifles to this day. There were approximately 2,200,000 manufactured by Remington, Winchester, and Eddystone between 1917 and 1918. The majority were produced at Eddystone, Pennsylvania.

During World War II all parts were parkerized, and barrels were supplied by the Johnson Automatics Company as a result of the rebuild.

NOTE: Add 30% for Winchester and Remington models.

Model 1917 Rifle (Winchester) • Courtesy Rock Island Auction Company

Remington Model 1917 Receiver Markings • Courtesy Karl Karash

Exc.	V.G.	Good	Fair	Poor
600	500	350	200	150

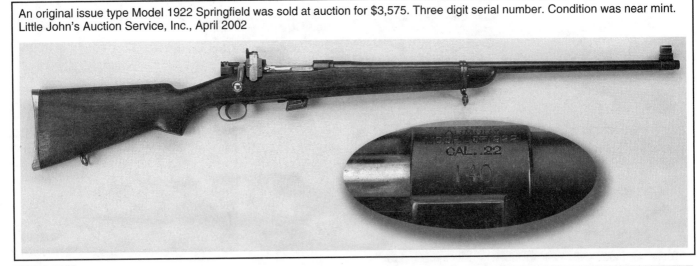

An original issue type Model 1922 Springfield was sold at auction for $3,575. Three digit serial number. Condition was near mint. Little John's Auction Service, Inc., April 2002

Model 1922

This is a bolt-action training rifle chambered for the .22 rimfire cartridge. It appears similar to the Model 1903 but has a 24.5" barrel and a half-length stock without hand guards, held on by a single barrel band. It has a 5-round detachable box magazine. The finish is blued, with a walnut stock. The receiver is marked "U.S. Springfield Armory Model of 1922 Cal. 22." It also has the flaming bomb ordnance mark. There were three basic types of the Model 1922: the standard issue type, the NRA commercial type, and the models that were altered to M1 or M2. There were a total of approximately 2,000 manufactured between 1922 and 1924. The survival rate of the original-issue types is not large as most were converted.

Issue Type

Exc.	V.G.	Good	Fair	Poor
800	650	450	250	200

Altered Type

Exc.	V.G.	Good	Fair	Poor
450	350	250	200	150

NRA Type—Drilled and Tapped for Scope

Exc.	V.G.	Good	Fair	Poor
700	550	400	200	150

Model 1922 M1

This version is quite similar to the Model 1922, with a single-point striker system and a detachable box magazine that does not protrude from the bottom of the stock. The finish is parkerized and the stock is made of walnut. There were approximately 20,000 manufactured between 1924 and 1933.

Courtesy Little John's Auction Service, Inc., Paul Goodwin photo

Unaltered Type

Exc.	V.G.	Good	Fair	Poor
750	650	550	300	200

Altered to M2

Exc.	V.G.	Good	Fair	Poor
450	350	250	200	150

Unaltered NRA Type

Exc.	V.G.	Good	Fair	Poor
650	550	450	300	250

NRA Type Altered to M2

Exc.	V.G.	Good	Fair	Poor
550	500	400	300	250

Model M2

This is an improved version of the Model 1922 M1 that features an altered firing mechanism with a faster lock time. It has a knurled cocking knob added to the bolt and a flush-fitting detachable magazine with improved feeding. There were approximately 12,000 manufactured.

Exc.	V.G.	Good	Fair	Poor
600	500	400	300	200

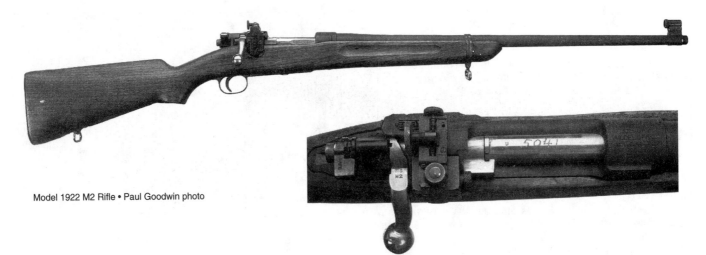

Model 1922 M2 Rifle • Paul Goodwin photo

A Springfield Model M2 was sold at auction for $2,200. Barrel dated 1937. Original sights. Condition was 95% parkerized finish. Serial number 2.
Amoskeag Auction Company, Inc., November 2001

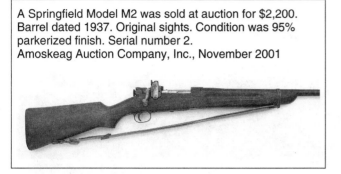

U.S. Rifle M1 (Garand)
Springfield Armory was one of the manufacturers of this WWII service rifle. It is listed in the Garand section of this text.

Springfield M21 Sniper Rifle
This is the sniper rifle version of the M14 rifle with ART II scope. Early models were fitted with an M84 scope and Griffin & Howe mounts. This scope was followed by the ART I and finally the ART II scope in the early 1970s.

M21 with ART II scope and case • Courtesy Richard M. Kumor Sr.

NOTE: Prices are for verifiable and registered samples.

Exc.	V.G.	Good	Fair	Poor
7000	5500	4000	—	—

KRAG JORGENSEN
The first smallbore, bolt action repeating rifle that used smokeless powder that was adopted by the U.S. government as a service rifle. It was adopted as the Model 1892 and was similar to the rifle being used by Denmark as a service rifle. All of the Krag-Jorgensens were manufactured at the Springfield Armory. There are 11 basic variations of Krag Rifles, and all except one are chambered for the .30-40 Govt. cartridge. They are bolt actions that hold 5 rounds in the unique side-mounted hinged magazine. All of the Krags have walnut stocks and handguards that are oil-finished. They all have dark gray case-hardened receivers and blued barrels. See also *Denmark, Rifles, Krag Jorgensen.*

Bibliographical Note: For historical information, technical data, and photos, see Lt. Col. William Brophy's, *The Krag Rifle*, Gun Room Press, 1985.

NOTE: One should be aware that there have been many alterations based on the Krag rifle by many gunsmiths through the years, and the one consistency is that all of these conversions lowered the value of the rifle and rendered it un-collectible. Proceed with caution. Prices listed are for original rifles as they left the factory.

Model 1892
Approximately 24,500 of these rifles produced, dated 1894, 1895, and 1896. They have 30" barrels and are serial numbered from 1-24562. Nearly all were converted to the latter Model 1896, and the original 1st Type is extremely scarce.

1st Type
Serial numbered from 1-1500 and is dated 1894 only. It features a wide upper barrel band and a brass tipped one-piece cleaning rod mounted under the barrel. There is no compartment in the butt, and the muzzle is not crowned and appears flat. The upper handguard does not extend over the receiver, and the buttplate is flat, without a compartment. One should be wary of fakes and secure expert appraisal if a transaction is contemplated. Unaltered specimens are extremely rare.

Exc.	V.G.	Good	Fair	Poor
—	30000	20000	6500	3000

2nd Type
Similar to the 1st Type, with a front barrel band that is cut out in the center and does not appear solid. The cleaning rod is a one piece steel type. The serial number range is 1500-24562, and the dates 1894 or 1895 are stamped on the receiver and the stock. Again be wary of fakes. This is a rare rifle.

Exc.	V.G.	Good	Fair	Poor
—	10000	7500	4000	1500

Model 1892 Altered to 1896 Model
Encompassed nearly the entire production run of the Model 1892 Krag rifle. They still bear the dates 1894, 1895, and 1896 on the receiver; but they do not have a one piece cleaning rod under the barrel, but instead a 3 piece type inserted into the buttstock, and the hole in the stock has been plugged. The front barrel band was changed. The top handguard covers the receiver, and the buttplate is curved at the bottom. The muzzle is crowned.

Exc.	V.G.	Good	Fair	Poor
—	850	400	250	150

A Model 1892 Krag, 1st Type, sold at auction for $27,500. Two digit serial number. Condition was near mint.
Little John's Auction Service, Inc., April 2002

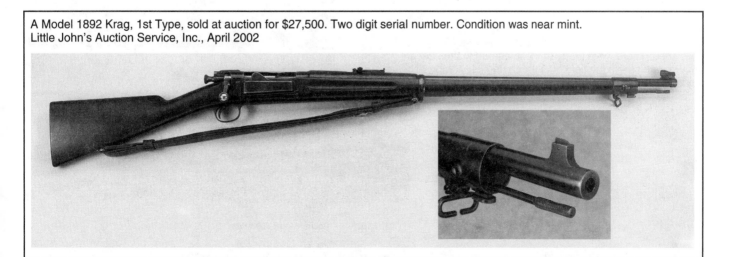

Krag Model 1892 2nd Type • Paul Goodwin photo

Model 1895 Carbine (Variation)

Marked "1895" and "1896" on the receiver—without the word "Model." They were produced before the Model 1896 was officially adopted, and they are serial numbered from 25000 to 35000. They are similar to the Model 1896 Carbine, with a smaller safety and no oiler bottle in the butt.

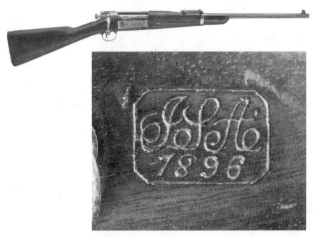

Model 1895 Carbine • Courtesy Rock Island Auction Company

Exc.	V. G.	Good	Fair	Poor
—	3000	1250	650	300

Model 1896 Rifle

Similar to the altered Model 1892 and has a 30" barrel with the cleaning kit in the butt. The rear sight was improved, and the receiver is marked "U.S. Model 1896" and "Springfield Armory." Lightning cuts were made in the barrel channel to reduce weight. A total of about 62,000 Model 96 rifles were produced in the same serial number range as the Model 1896 carbine of 37,240 to 108,471. The stock is dated 1896, 1897, and 1898. There were many of these altered to the later stock configurations—in the field or at the Springfield Armory. These changes would lower the value, and one should secure expert appraisal on this model.

Courtesy Richard M. Kumor Sr.

Exc.	V.G.	Good	Fair	Poor
—	1750	750	400	250

Model 1896 Carbine

Similar to the 1896 Rifle, with a 22" barrel and half-length stock held on by one barrel band. There were approximately less than 20,000 manufactured between 1896 and 1898, and the serial number range is 35000-90000. There were many rifles cut to carbine dimensions—be wary of these alterations!

Courtesy Jim Supica, Old Town Station

Exc.	V.G.	Good	Fair	Poor
—	3000	1250	650	300

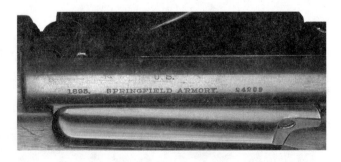

Altered Model 1896 • Paul Goodwin photo

Cuba, 1897. Frank W. Knapp of the 4th Virginia Volunteers, armed with a Krag rifle • U.S. Army Center of Military History/Robert Bruce Military Photo Features

Model 1896 Cadet Rifle

A rare variation produced for use by the Military Academy at West Point. The dimensions are the same as the 1896 Rifle with a one-piece cleaning rod under the barrel and the 1896-type front band. There were 400 manufactured, and most were altered to standard configuration when they were phased out in 1898. Extremely rare in original and unaltered condition.

Exc.	V.G.	Good	Fair	Poor
—	—	37500	15000	—

Model 1898 Rifle

This model is similar to the Model 1896 in appearance except that the receiver is marked "U.S./Model 1898." The bolt handle was modified, and the sights and handguards were improved. There were 330,000 manufactured between 1898 and 1903, and the serial number range is 110000-480000.

Exc.	V.G.	Good	Fair	Poor
—	1750	750	300	150

Model 1898 Carbine

Similar to the rifle, with a 22" barrel and a bar and ring on the left side of the receiver. There were approximately 5,000 manufactured in 1898 and 1899. The serial range is 118000-134000. Again, be aware that many of the rifles have been converted to carbine dimensions over the years. When in doubt, secure an independent appraisal.

Courtesy Little John's Auction Service, Inc., Paul Goodwin photo

Exc.	V.G.	Good	Fair	Poor
—	3000	1500	750	400

Model 1898 Carbine 26" Barrel

An attempt to satisfy both the infantry and the cavalry. There were 100 manufactured for trial, and the serial number range is between 387000-389000. Be wary of fakes.

Courtesy Little John's Auction Service, Inc., Paul Goodwin photo

Exc.	V.G.	Good	Fair	Poor
—	17500	7500	2500	900

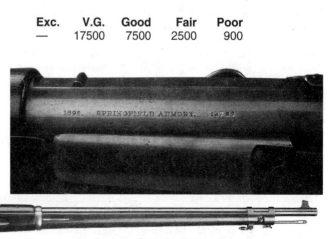

Model 1896 Cadet Rifle • Courtesy West Point Museum, Paul Goodwin photo

A Model 1898 Krag rifle was sold at auction for $5,500. Condition was near mint.
Little John's Auction Service, Inc., April 2002

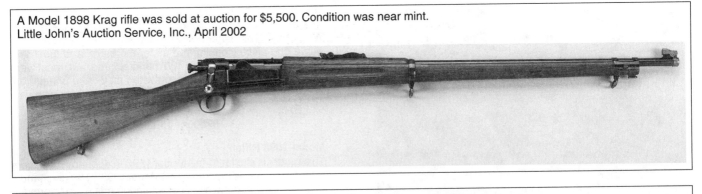

A Krag Model 1898 Practice rifle was sold at auction for $4,675. Condition was mint. Very rare.
Little John's Auction Service, Inc., April 2002

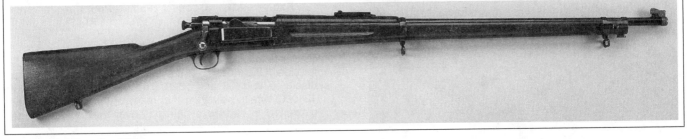

Model 1898 Practice Rifle

The only Krag not chambered for the .30-40 cartridge. It is chambered for the .22 rimfire and was designed as a target-practice rifle. It has a 30" barrel and is identical in exterior appearance to the Model 1898 Rifle. The receiver is marked the same as the standard model—with "Cal .22" added. There were approximately 840 manufactured in 1906 and 1907. Serial numbers are above 475,000.

Exc.	V.G.	Good	Fair	Poor
—	4500	2000	850	300

Model 1899 Carbine

The last of the Krags. It is similar to the 1898, with the "Model 1899" stamped on the receiver and a 2" longer stock. There were approximately 36,000 manufactured between 1900 and 1903. Serial numbers observed are between 222,609 and 362,256. These numbers are part of the Model 1898 rifle series.

Courtesy Milwaukee Public Museum, Milwaukee, Wisconsin

Exc.	V.G.	Good	Fair	Poor
—	2000	850	600	350

M1899 Krag Cavalry Carbine

Towards the end of the 19th Century, rifles firing high-velocity ammunition began replacing black powder weapons in virtually every army. The U.S. Army jumped on the smokeless powder bandwagon in 1890 and began testing repeating rifles. In 1892, Ordnance settled on the Danish Krag-Jorgensen in .30-40 caliber. There were a number of versions of the Krag, beginning with the M1892 rifle and ending with the subject of this essay, the M1899 Cavalry Carbine. About 36,000 M1899 Carbines were manufactured between 1899 and 1904. The Krag action is one of the smoothest ever designed. The Krag feeds from an unusual horizontal magazine that opens from the side. There is no provision for reloading using stripper clips, a decided disadvantage in combat. The sights consist of a blade front and small notch rear sight with a tiny pivoting aperture. The Krags all featured a magazine cutoff intended to prevent soldiers from wasting ammunition. The M1899 was very well-made. There are no machining marks whatsoever,

save for a few marks on the upper surface of the loading gate. Although well made, the Krag suffered from a cartridge that was ballistically inferior to almost every other military cartridge in the world. In addition, the action had only a single locking lug, making it incapable of firing higher pressure ammunition. This was the Krag's major downfall. A high-velocity .30-40 cartridge was developed, but it had to be withdrawn from service because the Krag action wasn't sufficiently strong to accommodate it. Because of the mild .30-40 cartridge and the carbine's light weight, shooting the M1899 is very pleasant. Recoil is mild and the little carbine handles like a modern sporting arm, which is how most Krags ended their days. Because most Krags were long ago converted to sporting rifles, original military examples are not as common as later rifles such as the M1903. Moreover, the .30-40 cartridge is ballistically inferior to both .30-06 and .308 ammunition.

Charlie Cutshaw

Model 1899 Philippine Constabulary Carbine • Courtesy Rock Island Auction Company

Model 1899 Philippine Constabulary Carbine

Approximately 8,000 modified to accept the knife bayonet at the Springfield Armory and the Rock Island Arsenal. The Springfield pieces are marked "J.F.C." on the stock. This model has a 22" barrel with the full, but shortened, stock of the rifle held on with two barrel bands. One must exercise extreme care as many rifles were altered in a similar manner at later dates.

NOTE: Prices are for verifiable samples.

Exc.	V. G.	Good	Fair	Poor
—	2500	1250	600	300

Arsenal Conversions

In the 1920s, the Department of Civilian Marksmanship had a number of Krag rifles converted for their use. These are Model 1898 rifles shortened to 24" and fitted with Model 1899 Carbine stocks. Some of these rifles were also fitted with rifle stocks shortened to carbine length. These conversions are beginning to be regarded as legitimate variations by some collectors of Krag rifles.

Exc.	V.G.	Good	Fair	Poor
—	450	250	175	100

COLT

NOTE: For historical information, technical details, and photos, see Blake Stevens' and Edward Ezell's, *The Black Rifle: M16 Retrospective*, Collector Grade Publications, 1994.

Berdan Single Shot Rifle (M.1870)

This is a scarce rifle on today's market. There were approximately 30,200 manufactured, but nearly 30,000 of them were sent to Russia. This rifle was produced from 1866-1870. It is a trapdoor-type action chambered for .42 centerfire. The standard model has a 32.5" barrel; the carbine, 18.25". The finish is blued, with a walnut stock. This rifle was designed and the patent held by Hiram Berdan, Commander of the Civil War "Sharpshooters" Regiment. This was actually Colt's first cartridge arm. The 30,000 rifles and 25 half-stocked carbines that were sent to Russia were in Russian Cyrillic letters. The few examples made for American sales have Colt's name and Hartford address on the barrel.

NOTE: For information on Russian-built Berdan rifles, see *Russia, Rifles, Berdan.*

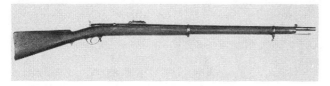

Courtesy Milwaukee Public Museum, Milwaukee, Wisconsin

Rifle Russian Order, 30,000 Manufactured

Exc.	V.G.	Good	Fair	Poor
—	2000	750	450	—

Carbine Russian Order, 25 Manufactured

Exc.	V.G.	Good	Fair	Poor
—	6000	3000	1250	—

Rifle U.S. Sales, 100 Manufactured

Exc.	V.G.	Good	Fair	Poor
—	5000	2250	1250	—

Carbine U.S. Sales, 25 Manufactured

Exc.	V.G.	Good	Fair	Poor
—	9500	4500	2000	—

Colt-Franklin Military Rifle

This is a rifle that was not a successful venture for Colt. The patents were held by William B. Franklin, a vice-president of the company. This was a bolt-action rifle with a primitive, gravity-fed box magazine. It is chambered for the .45-70 government cartridge, has a 32.5" barrel, and is blued, with a walnut stock. The rifle has the Colt Hartford barrel address and is stamped with an eagle's head and U.S. inspector's marks. There were only 50 of these rifles produced, and it is believed that they were prototypes intended for government sales. This was not to be, and production ceased after approximately 50 were manufactured in 1887 and 1888.

Exc.	V.G.	Good	Fair	Poor
—	8500	4500	2000	—

Lightning Slide Action, Medium Frame

This was the first slide action rifle Colt produced. It is chambered for .32-20, .38-40, and .44-40, and was intended to be a companion piece to the SAAs in the same calibers. The rifle has a 26" barrel with 15-shot tube magazine; the carbine, a 20" barrel with 12-shot magazine. The finish is blued, with case-colored hammer; the walnut stock is oil-finished; and the forend is usually checkered. The Colt name and Hartford address are stamped on the barrel along with the patent dates. There were approximately 89,777 manufactured between 1884 and 1902. The military variant is listed below.

Military Rifle or Carbine

Chambered for .44-40 caliber, fitted with short magazine tube, bayonet lug, and sling swivels. These guns are fitted with various barrel lengths.

Exc.	V.G.	Good	Fair	Poor
—	4500	2000	1000	600

U.S. M14/M14E2

Based on the famous M1 Garand design this select fire rifle is chambered for the 7.62x51mm cartridge. It has a 21.8" barrel and a 20-round magazine. It weighs approximately 11.2 lbs. Rate of fire is about 750 rounds per minute. Marked "US RIFLE 7.62MM M14" on the rear top of the receiver. Production began in 1957 and ceased in 1963. Produced by Harrington & Richardson (537,512 total production) stamped "HRA," Springfield (167,172 total production) stamped "SA," Winchester (356,510 total production) stamped "66118" or "OM," and TRW (319,163 total production) stamped "TRW." The M14E2 version is a light machine gun variant with bipod, folding forward hand grip, and muzzle compensator.

NOTE: A sniper version of this rifle was designated the M21 and fitted with a Leatherwood telescope sight. *See that listing.*

Courtesy Richard M. Kumor Sr.

Pre-1968

Exc.	V.G.	Fair
8500	8000	7500

Pre-1986 conversions
(or U.S. manufacture/M1A Springfield Armory)

Exc.	V.G.	Fair
4500	4250	4000

Pre-1986 dealer samples

Exc.	V.G.	Fair
N/A	N/A	N/A

Tan Dinh Island, Mekong Delta, Vietnam, 26 March 1968. Navy SEALs dodge flying debris as a demolition charge destroys an enemy bunker. The man on the left is armed with an M16 rifle with two 20-round magazines taped together for quick change in a firefight • U.S. Navy Historical Center/Robert Bruce Military Photo Features

M16 ASSAULT RIFLE

The M16 rifle has a great many variations and configurations. Some of these variations are available to the collector and others are so rare as to be, for practical purposes, unavailable to the collector. Nevertheless, we think it important to include as many variations as may be encountered by the collector. Some of the more common ones will be priced while others, because of their rarity, will not show a value. Keep in mind that the M16 series of rifles is comprised of two main parts: the upper receiver and lower receiver. The upper receiver is not considered a firearm by the ATF and is not registered. Nor is the upper receiver marked or serial numbered to the lower receiver. Conversely, the lower receiver is serial numbered and marked with its model designation. It is therefore quite possible for upper receivers to be matched to lower receivers that are not in an original factory configuration. In order to be factory original, both upper and lower receivers must be configured at the factory prior to shipment. This is sometimes impossible to determine. It is therefore highly recommended that an expert be consulted prior to a sale to help determine originality.

THE U.S. RIFLE M14

Sandwiched chronologically between the incredibly important M1 Garand of WWII and Korean War fame and the M16 from the Vietnam era to the present, the M14 is one of the most under-appreciated service rifles in U.S. history. Whereas the M1 served as our primary service rifle for over twenty years, and the M16 has held that role for over thirty, the M14 barely lasted ten years, primarily because of political considerations rather than lack of excellence. Its service was so short that many units, particularly from the reserve components, went directly from the M1 to the M16 and were never issued M14s. Though long ago ousted as a primary Army and Marine service rifle, variations of it, the M21 and M25 sniper rifles, served for more than twenty years and the M14 still serves today as the standard rifle of U.S. Navy security forces, boarding parties, EOD, and SEALs. A scoped variation is also still in service as the Marines' "Designated Marksman's Rifle." While there are several 7.62mm NATO semiautomatic military rifles that are as good as the M14, there are none that are better. It is accurate, extremely durable, and among the most reliable and effective military rifles ever fielded. I can say this with considerable authority since I carried and used the M14 extensively in combat in Vietnam as well as in other military service. Accurized variations of the M14 and its civilian equivalent, the Springfield Armory M1A, have garnered more medals and records in service rifle competition in the last three plus decades than any other rifle. Basically little more than an improved M1 Garand with a detachable magazine, the M14 deserves much more credit for its excellence and accomplishments than it has ever received.

Chuck Karwan

Early AR-15 Model 01 • Paul Goodwin photo

MODEL NOTE: On early models, the "A" suffix usually means it has a forward assist and the "B" suffix usually means it has a burst mechanism. Model numbers began with the 600 series, then the 700 series, which are based on the M16A2. The 800 series models are grenade launchers (M203). The 900 series models have flat top upper receivers and removable carry handles. The following are model designations with Colt nomenclature:

XM16 became the M16
XM16E1 became the M16A1
M16A1E1 became the M16A2
M16A2E4 became the M16A4

NOTE: As a general rule of thumb, "U.S. Property" marked guns will bring a premium, in some cases a substantial one, depending on model and configuration. These premiums will be so stated where applicable. The M16 was also produced by GM's Hydramatic division and Harrington & Richardson, Inc. Production began in late 1968. M16s from either manufacturer are rarely encountered. Rifles made by H&R will bring about 85% of a comparable Colt M16, while the Hydramatic rifles will bring almost double that of a Colt M16. This premium does not apply to rifles that have been re-welded.

M16A2 MODIFICATIONS:
1. Flash suppressor is now a muzzle brake.
2. Barrel is heavier with rifle twist changed from 1 in 12 to 1 in 7.
3. Front sight is a square post adjustable for elevation.
4. Handguards are interchangeable ribbed top and bottom halves.
5. The circumfrence of the slip ring is now canted for a better grip.
6. Upper receiver is strengthened at the front attachment point to the lower receiver, as well as a fired case deflector behind the ejection port.
7. Completely redesigned fully adjustable rear sight.
8. Forward assist is now a round button type.
9. Pistol grip has a thumb swell and is made from stronger nylon with checkering on both sides.
10. Change lever is now, SAFE, SEMI, and BURST on most but not all A2 models.
11. The stock is stronger and 5/8" longer.
12. Buttplate is squared and checkered with internal storage cavity.

M16A1 with Colt AR-15 markings with M203 grenade launcher • Paul Goodwin photo

Colt M16 NOTE: The Colt M16 comes in a variety of configurations (upper receivers), some of which are mentioned here. It is important to note that these configurations are based on the same lower receiver. In the case of civilian ownership, the lower receiver is the registered part of the firearm as far as the BATF is concerned. Therefore, it is possible, with a registered lower receiver, to interchange upper receiver components to a wide variety of different configurations from 9mm to .223 LMG uppers. Be aware that this interchangeability works best with Colt parts.

Bibliographical Note: For a full and complete description with photos, see Dan Shea's *Machine Gun Dealers Bible*, 4th edition, Moose Lake Publishing. See Blake Stevens and Edward Ezell, *The Black Rifle, M16 Retrospective*, Collector Grade Publications, for an in depth examination of the history and development of the M16.

600 Series

Colt/Armalite AR-15/M16 Model 601

This rifle was first produced in 1960 with many variants following. Chambered for the 5.56x45mm cartridge it has a 20.8" barrel with flash hider. Magazine capacity is 20 or 30 rounds. Weight is 7 lbs. Rate of fire is 800 rounds per minute. Used extensively in Vietnam and now throughout the world. Some were marked "COLT AR-15 PROPERTY OF US GOVT.M16 CAL 5.56MM" on left side of magazine housing, but early guns were not marked "US Property." There is a wide variation in prices and models. Prices listed below are for the standard rifle.

AR-15 markings • Courtesy James Alley

Pre-1968

Exc.	V.G.	Fair
8000	7500	7000

Pre-1986 conversions, for OEM A1 add 40%

Exc.	V.G.	Fair
5000	4500	4000

Pre-1986 dealer samples

Exc.	V.G.	Fair
4000	3500	3250

Colt Model 602

This U.S. ("US Property") model was fitted with a 20" barrel. It has no forward assist. Select fire in full or semiauto.

Colt Model 603 (M16A1)

This U.S. ("US Property") model has a 20" barrel with forward assist. Barrel has a 1 in 12 twist rate. Select fire in full or semiauto.

Pre-1968

Exc.	V.G.	Fair
10000	9500	9000

Pre-1986 conversions, for OEM A1 add 40%

Exc.	V.G.	Fair
5000	4500	4250

Pre-1986 dealer samples

Exc.	V.G.	Fair
5000	4500	4250

Colt Model 604 (M16)

This U.S. ("US Property") Air Force model has a 20" barrel with a 1 in 12 twist. No forward assist. Select fire in full and semiauto.

Pre-1968

Exc.	V.G.	Fair
10000	9500	9000

Pre-1986 conversions, for OEM A1 add 40%

Exc.	V.G.	Fair
5000	4500	4250

Pre-1986 dealer samples

Exc.	V.G.	Fair
5000	4500	4250

Colt Model 605A CAR-15 Carbine

This U.S. ("US Property") version is the short barrel (10") version of the rifle with a forward assist. A select fire in full and semiauto.

CAR-15 • Courtesy James Alley

Pre-1968

Exc.	V.G.	Fair
N/A	N/A	N/A

Pre-1986 OEM/Colt

Exc.	V.G.	Fair
12500	11000	9000

Pre-1986 dealer samples

Exc.	V.G.	Fair
N/A	N/A	N/A

Colt Model 605B

This U.S. ("US Property") version is the same as above but with semiauto, full auto, and burst (3 round) select fire. No forward assist.

Pre-1968

Exc.	V.G.	Fair
12500	11000	9000

Pre-1986 conversions, for OEM A1 add 40%

Exc.	V.G.	Fair
6000	5500	5000

Pre-1986 dealer samples

Exc.	V.G.	Fair
5000	4500	4250

Colt Model 606

This is the export version of the Model 616.

Pre-1968

Exc.	V.G.	Fair
10000	9500	9000

Pre-1986 conversions, for OEM A1 add 40%

Exc.	V.G.	Fair
5000	4500	4250

Pre-1986 dealer samples

Exc.	V.G.	Fair
5000	4500	4250

Colt Model 606B

As above, but with burst version.

Pre-1968

Exc.	V.G.	Fair
10000	9500	9000

Pre-1986 conversions, for OEM A1 add 40%

Exc.	V.G.	Fair
5000	4500	4250

Pre-1986 dealer samples

Exc.	V.G.	Fair
5000	4500	4250

Colt Model 607

This U.S. ("US Property") version is an SMG with sliding buttstock and 10" barrel. Designed for use by tank, helicopter, and APC crews. Length with stock closed is 26", with stock extended about 28.7". Weight is about 5.3 lbs.

Pre-1968

Exc.	V.G.	Fair
10000	9500	9000

Pre-1986 conversions, for OEM A1 add 40%

Exc.	V.G.	Fair
5000	4500	4250

Pre-1986 dealer samples

Exc.	V.G.	Fair
5000	4500	4250

Colt Model 608 Survival Rifle

This rifle was built in prototype only and its design was for use by aviation personnel. Fitted with a 10" barrel, cone shaped flash suppressor, short fixed buttstock, round handguard, no forward assist, no bayonet lug, and short pistol grip. Overall length is 29". Weight was slightly more than 4.7 lbs. Designed to be broken down to fit the standard USAF seat pack. Fewer than 10 manufactured.

Colt Survival Rifle Model 608 • Courtesy James Alley

Pre-1968

Exc.	V.G.	Fair
N/A	N/A	N/A

Pre-1986 OEM/Colt

Exc.	V.G.	Fair
15000	—	—

Pre-1986 dealer samples

Exc.	V.G.	Fair
N/A	N/A	N/A

Colt Model 609 (XM177E1)

This a U.S. Army version of the Commando with an 11.5" barrel with a 1 in 12 twist rate. This model has a forward assist. Select fire in full auto or semiauto.

Markings for U.S. property for Commando model • Courtesy James Alley

Pre-1968

Exc.	V.G.	Fair
N/A	N/A	N/A

Pre-1986 OEM/Colt

Exc.	V.G.	Fair
15000	12500	11000

Pre-1986 dealer samples

Exc.	V.G.	Fair
N/A	N/A	N/A

Colt Model 610 (GAU-5/A)

This is the U.S. Air Force version of the XM177 Commando with 10" barrel with 1 in 12 twist and no forward assist. Select fire in full auto or semiauto.

Pre-1968

Exc.	V.G.	Fair
N/A	N/A	N/A

Pre-1986 OEM/Colt

Exc.	V.G.	Fair
15000	12500	11000

Pre-1986 dealer samples

Exc.	V.G.	Fair
N/A	N/A	N/A

Colt Model 613

This is export version of the 603.

Pre-1968

Exc.	V.G.	Fair
10000	9500	9000

Pre-1986 conversions, for OEM A1 add 40%

Exc.	V.G.	Fair
5000	4500	4250

Pre-1986 dealer samples

Exc.	V.G.	Fair
5000	4500	4250

Colt Model 614

This is the export version of the Model 604.

Pre-1968

Exc.	V.G.	Fair
10000	9500	9000

Pre-1986 conversions, for OEM A1 add 40%

Exc.	V.G.	Fair
5000	4500	4250

Pre-1986 dealer samples

Exc.	V.G.	Fair
5000	4500	4250

Colt Model 616

This U.S. ("US Property") version is fitted with a 20" heavy barrel with 1 in 12 twist rate. No forward assist. Select fire in full auto or semiauto.

Pre-1968

Exc.	V.G.	Fair
10000	9500	9000

Pre-1986 conversions, for OEM A1 add 40%

Exc.	V.G.	Fair
5000	4500	4250

Pre-1986 Dealer samples

Exc.	V.G.	Fair
5000	4500	4250

Colt Model 619

This is the export version of the 609.

Pre-1968

Exc.	V.G.	Fair
10000	9500	9000

Pre-1986 conversions, for OEM A1 add 40%

Exc.	V.G.	Fair
5000	4500	4250

Pre-1986 dealer samples

Exc.	V.G.	Fair
5000	4500	4250

Colt Model 621

This U.S. ("US Property") version is fitted with a 20" heavy barrel with 1 in 12 twist. It is fitted with a forward assist. Select fire in full auto or semiauto.

Pre-1968

Exc.	V.G.	Fair
10000	9500	9000

Pre-1986 conversions, for OEM A1 add 40%

Exc.	V.G.	Fair
5000	4500	4250

Pre-1986 dealer samples

Exc.	V.G.	Fair
5000	4500	4250

Colt Model 629 (XM177E2)

This is the U.S. Army version of the Commando with 11.5" barrel with 1 in 12 twist. Sliding butt stock. Fitted with a forward assist. Select fire in full auto or semiauto. Equipped with a 4.5" flash suppressor. Weight is about 6.2 lbs without magazine.

Pre-1968

Exc.	V.G.	Fair
N/A	N/A	N/A

Pre-1986 OEM/Colt

Exc.	V.G.	Fair
15000	13000	12000

Pre-1986 dealer samples

Exc.	V.G.	Fair
N/A	N/A	N/A

Colt Model 630 (GAU-5/A/B)

This is the U.S. Air Force version of the XM177E1 with 11.5" barrel with 1 in 12 twist. No forward assist. Select fire in full auto or semiauto.

Pre-1968

Exc.	V.G.	Fair
N/A	N/A	N/A

Pre-1986 OEM/Colt

Exc.	V.G.	Fair
15000	12500	11000

Pre-1986 dealer samples

Exc.	V.G.	Fair
N/A	N/A	N/A

Colt Model 639

This is the export version of the Model 629.

Pre-1968

Exc.	V.G.	Fair
N/A	N/A	N/A

Colt Model 629 (XM177E2) • Courtesy James Alley

Pre-1986 OEM/Colt

Exc.	V.G.	Fair
15000	13000	12000

Pre-1986 Dealer samples

Exc.	V.G.	Fair
N/A	N/A	N/A

Colt Model 645 (M16A2)

This model is an improved variation of the M16A1 Standard rifle with a 1 in 7" barrel twist and a heavier 20" barrel. A case deflector is mounted on the right side. Sights are an improved version of the standard M16 type. Forward assist. Improved flash suppressor, buttstock, and pistol grip. First produced in 1982. *See list of M16A2 modifications on prior page.*

Pre-1968

Exc.	V.G.	Fair
N/A	N/A	N/A

Pre-1986 OEM/Colt

Exc.	V.G.	Fair
9000	8500	8000

Pre-1986 dealer samples

Exc.	V.G.	Fair
N/A	N/A	N/A

Colt Model 646 (M16A3)

This is the U.S. ("US Property") version of the M16A3 except that there is no 3-round burst but full auto and semiauto.

Colt Model 649 (GAU-5/A/A)

This is the U.S. Air Force version of the XM177E2 with 11.5" barrel with 1 in 12 twist rate and no forward assist. Select fire with full auto and semiauto. Equipped with a 4.5" flash suppressor.

Pre-1968

Exc.	V.G.	Fair
N/A	N/A	N/A

Pre-1986 OEM/Colt

Exc.	V.G.	Fair
15000	12500	11000

Pre-1986 dealer samples

Exc.	V.G.	Fair
N/A	N/A	N/A

Colt Model 651

This is the export version of the rifle with 14.5" barrel.

Pre-1968

Exc.	V.G.	Fair
12500	11000	9000

Pre-1986 conversions, for OEM A1 add 40%

Exc.	V.G.	Fair
6000	5500	5000

Pre-1986 dealer samples

Exc.	V.G.	Fair
5000	4500	4250

Colt Model 652

This is the export version of the rifle with 14.5" barrel and no forward assist.

Pre-1968

Exc.	V.G.	Fair
12500	11000	9000

Pre-1986 conversions, for OEM A1 add 40%

Exc.	V.G.	Fair
6000	5500	5000

Pre-1986 dealer samples

Exc.	V.G.	Fair
5000	4500	4250

Colt Model 653

This is the export version of the rifle with 14.5" barrel and sliding buttstock.

Pre-1968

Exc.	V.G.	Fair
12500	11000	9000

Pre-1986 conversions, for OEM A1 add 40%

Exc.	V.G.	Fair
6000	5500	5000

Pre-1986 dealer samples

Exc.	V.G.	Fair
5000	4500	4250

Colt Model 655 (Sniper)

This was a U.S. ("US Property") prototype version with a 20" barrel with a 1 in 9 twist rate. It has a forward assist. The upper receiver has a high profile scope mount and was to have been fitted with a Leatherwood Realist scope and Sionics suppressor. Select fire with full auto or semiauto.

Colt Model 656 (Sniper)

Same as above but with a special low profile upper receiver with no carry handle and low profile scope mount.

700 Series-Export Versions of the M16A2

Colt Model 701 Export Rifle

This is the M16A2 with 20" barrel and all the A2 features. Weight is about 7.5 lbs.

Colt Model 703 Test Model

This is a test model with a gas piston designated the M703/16A2. Test model used an AK type bolt and carrier. Test model is not priced.

Colt Model 703 Export Rifle

[There are two different types of 703s. Colt used the same model designation twice. See above.] Select fire with semi, 3-round burst, and full auto. The Export Model is an M16A2 style rifle.

Pre-1968

Exc.	V.G.	Fair
N/A	N/A	N/A

Pre-1986 OEM/Colt

Exc.	V.G.	Fair
15000	12500	11000

Pre-1986 dealer samples

Exc.	V.G.	Fair
N/A	N/A	N/A

Colt Model 707 Export rifle

This is a M16A2 with 20" A1 style barrel with 1 in 7 twist rate. Select fire with semi, 3-round burst. Weight is about 7.5 lbs.

Pre-1968

Exc.	V.G.	Fair
10000	9500	9000

Pre-1986 conversions, for OEM A1 add 40%

Exc.	V.G.	Fair
5000	4500	4250

Pre-1986 dealer samples

Exc.	V.G.	Fair
5000	4500	4250

Colt Model 711 Export Rifle

This model is the same as the M16A2 but fitted with M16A1 sights and standard weight M16A1 barrel.

Model 711 • Courtesy James Alley

Pre-1968

Exc.	V.G.	Fair
10000	9500	9000

Pre-1986 conversions, for OEM A1 add 40%

Exc.	V.G.	Fair
5000	4500	4250

Pre-1986 dealer samples

Exc.	V.G.	Fair
5000	4500	4250

Colt Model 713 Export Rifle

This model is fitted with an M16A1 upper receiver with case deflector 20" A1 barrel with 1 in 7 twist. Buttstock is A2 type. The compensator is A2 type with A2 lower receiver with select fire in semi and 3-round burst. Weight is about 7 lbs.

Pre-1968

Exc.	V.G.	Fair
10000	9500	9000

Pre-1986 conversions, for OEM A1 add 40%

Exc.	V.G.	Fair
5000	4500	4250

Pre-1986 dealer samples

Exc.	V.G.	Fair
5000	4500	4250

Colt Model 723 Export Carbine

This model is an M16A2 carbine with lightweight 14.5" barrel, M16A1 sights, and telescoping stock. Select fire in semiauto and full auto.

Pre-1968

Exc.	V.G.	Fair
12500	11000	9000

Pre-1986 conversions, for OEM A1 add 40%

Exc.	V.G.	Fair
6000	5500	5000

Pre-1986 dealer samples

Exc.	V.G.	Fair
5000	4500	4250

Colt Model 725 Export Carbine

Same as the Model 723 but with semiauto and three-round burst select fire.

Pre-1968

Exc.	V.G.	Fair
12500	11000	9000

Pre-1986 conversions, for OEM A1 add 40%

Exc.	V.G.	Fair
6000	5500	5000

Pre-1986 dealer samples

Exc.	V.G.	Fair
5000	4500	4250

Colt Model 727 Carbine

This is the M16A2 version of the M4 Carbine. Fitted with a 14.5" barrel capable of accepting the M203 grenade launcher. Rifling twist is 1 in 7". Sliding buttstock. Rate of fire is 700 to 950 rounds per minute. Select fire in semiauto and full auto. Weight is about 5.65 lbs without magazine.

Pre-1968

Exc.	V.G.	Fair
12500	11000	9000

Pre-1986 conversions, for OEM A1 add 40%

Exc.	V.G.	Fair
6000	5500	5000

Pre-1986 dealer samples

Exc.	V.G.	Fair
5000	4500	4250

M16A2 Model 727 • Courtesy James Alley

M16A2 Model 723 and Model 733 • Courtesy James Alley

Colt Model 733 Export Commando

This model is the M16A2 Commando with an 11.5" barrel, M16A1 sight, telescoping butt.

Pre-1968

Exc.	V.G.	Fair
N/A	N/A	N/A

Pre-1986 OEM/Colt

Exc.	V.G.	Fair
15000	12500	11000

Pre-1986 dealer samples

Exc.	V.G.	Fair
N/A	N/A	N/A

Colt Model 741 Export Heavy Barrel

This is an M16A2 with 20" heavy barrel that is magazine fed. Designed as a SAW (Squad Automatic Weapon). Weight is about 10 lbs.

Pre-1968

Exc.	V.G.	Fair
10000	9500	9000

Pre-1986 conversions, for OEM A1 add 40%

Exc.	V.G.	Fair
6000	5500	5000

Pre-1986 dealer samples

Exc.	V.G.	Fair
5000	4500	4250

Colt Model 750 LMG (*See U.S., Machine Guns*)

Colt Model 720 M4 (Original Version)

This is a short barrel version of the M16 with collapsible stock. Chambered for 5.56x45mm cartridge. It is fitted with a 14.5" barrel and has a magazine capacity of 20 or 30 rounds. Its rate of fire is 800 rounds per minute. Weight is about 5.6 lbs. Marked "COLT FIREARMS DIVISION COLT INDUSTRIES HARTFORD CONN USA" on the left side of the receiver, with "COLT M4 CAL 5.56MM" on the left side of the magazine housing. In use with American military forces as well as several South American countries.

Photo courtesy private NFA collection

Pre-1968

Exc.	V.G.	Fair
N/A	N/A	N/A

Pre-1986 conversions or OEM/Colt (Rare)

Exc.	V.G.	Fair
12500	11000	9000

Pre-1986 dealer samples

Exc.	V.G.	Fair
N/A	N/A	N/A

900 Series

Colt Model 920—M4

This model is the current U.S. ("US Property") version of the flat top carbine with 14.5" barrel with a 1 in 7 twist rate, forward assist, sliding buttstock, and A2 improvements. Select fire with 3-round burst and semiauto.

Model M1 Heavy Assault Rifle • Courtesy James Alley

Colt Model 921—M4A1

This U.S. ("US Property") model is the same as the Model 920, except it is full auto with no burst feature.

Colt Model 945—M16A4

This U.S. ("US Property") version is the flat top version of the M16A2.

Specialty Series

Colt CAR-15 Model M1 Heavy Assault Rifle

This was a prototype with a heavy AR-15 20" barrel. Fires from a closed bolt. Uses standard M16 magazines. Weight without magazine is about 7.6 lbs. Semi or full auto fire. Rate of fire is approximately 800 to 850 rounds per minute.

Colt CAR-15 Model M2 Beltfed Heavy Assault Rifle

Similar to the M1 version with the addition of a removable belt feeding mechanism designed by Rob Roy. Weight is about 8.3 lbs. Also feeds from standard M16 magazines. Less than 20 M2s were built.

Pre-1968

Exc.	V.G.	Fair
N/A	N/A	N/A

Pre-1986 OEM/Colt

Exc.	V.G.	Fair
30000+	—	—

Pre-1986 dealer samples

Exc.	V.G.	Fair
N/A	N/A	N/A

M2 Belt fed with close-up • Courtesy James Alley

Colt Firing Port weapon • Courtesy James Alley

Colt M231 Firing Port Weapon

This gun was never assigned a Colt model number but was fitted with a 15.6" barrel and a 1 in 12 twist rate. It fired from an open bolt in full auto only. It had no sights or buttstock. All original Colt firing port guns have an "F" prefix as part of the serial number and are marked "US PROPERTY."

Pre-1968

Exc.	V.G.	Fair
N/A	N/A	N/A

Pre-1986 OEM/Colt

Exc.	V.G.	Fair
15000	12500	11000

Pre-1986 dealer samples

Exc.	V.G.	Fair
N/A	N/A	N/A

Colt ACR Advanced Combat rifle

This model was built in prototype only and was designed to fire special duplex cartridges. It was fitted with a 20" barrel, flattop receiver with special rib designed by Abderdeen Human Engineering Labs. It has a sliding buttstock with a hydraulic buffer. Select fire in full auto or semiauto.

Pre-1968

Exc.	V.G.	Fair
N/A	N/A	N/A

Pre-1986 OEM/Colt

Exc.	V.G.	Fair
	Too Rare To Price	

Pre-1986 dealer samples

Exc.	V.G.	Fair
N/A	N/A	N/A

Colt CMG-1

One prototype was built of this model. It was a belt-fed light machine gun designed by Rob Roy and fitted with a 20" barrel with a 1-in-12 twist. Rate of fire of 650 rounds per minute. Weight is about 12.5 lbs. Fires from an open bolt. Designed to be used as a tripod mount, bipod mount, vehicle mount, or solenoid fixed machine gun.

Colt CMG1 • Courtesy James Alley

Colt CMG-2

This was an improved version of the CMG-1 designed by George Curtis and Henry Tatro. Approximately 6 were produced, 5 in 5.56 NATO and 1-in-7.62 NATO. It was fitted with a 20" quick change barrel with a 1 in 8.87" twist for the 68 grain GX-6235 bullet. Hydraulic buffer in buttstock. Bipod. Weight was about 15 lbs. Cycle rate is about 650 rounds per minute. It is fed by a 150-round belt fed drum magazine. These prototypes were built by Colt between 1967 and 1969.

Colt CMG 2 • Courtesy James Alley

Pre-1968

Exc.	V.G.	Fair
N/A	N/A	N/A

Pre-1986 OEM/Colt

Exc.	V.G.	Fair
40000+	—	—

Pre-1986 dealer samples

Exc.	V.G.	Fair
N/A	N/A	N/A

NOTE: There is little in the way of sales history, though there have been guns offered for sale in the $40,000 to $75,000 range on rare occasions.

M16 Rimfire Conversion Kits

There are several different conversion kits featuring different designs both adapted by the U.S. military. Both of these kits use a 10-round magazine but are not interchangeable with each other. The first is the Rodman design, known as the Air Force Model, built by OK Industries, New Britain, CT and the second is the M261 built by the Maremont Corp., Saco, ME. TM 9-6920-363-12 was issued with the M261 conversion kit. The Atchisson Mark I and Mark II kits and the Atchisson Mark III made by Jonathan Ciener, Inc., are also used by military forces in the U.S. and as well as by foreign governments. The Ciener kit was introduced about 1988 and is designed to be used in both the M16 and AR15 rifles, both semi-automatic fire and full auto fire. Rate of fire is between 700 and 800 rounds per minute in the M16.

NOTE: Colt built a conversion kit produced for commercial sale but this kit was not adopted by the military.

Ciener Kit Mark III

Exc.	V.G.	Good	Fair	Poor
200	150	—	—	—

Colt AR-15 and Colt Sporter Terminology

There are three different and distinct manufacturing cycles that not only affect the value of these rifles but also the legal consequences of their modifications.

Pre-Ban Colt AR-15 rifles (Pre-1989): Fitted with bayonet lug, flash hider, and stamped AR-15 on lower receiver. Rifles that are NIB have a green label. It is legal to modify this rifle with any AR-15 upper receiver. These are the most desirable models because of their pre-ban features.

Colt Sporters (Post-1989-pre-September, 1994): This transition model may or may not have a bayonet lug, but it does have a flash hider. There is no AR-15 designation stamped on the lower receiver. Rifles that are NIB have a blue label. It is legal to modify this rifle with upper receivers made after 1989, i.e., pre-ban. These rifles are less desirable than pre-ban AR-15s.

Colt Sporters (Post-September, 1994): This rifle has no bayonet lug, no flash hider, and does not have the AR-15 designation stamped on the lower receiver. Rifles that are NIB have a blue label. It is legal to modify this rifle only with upper receivers manufactured after September 1994. These rifles are the least desirable of the three manufacturing periods because of their lack of pre-ban military features and current manufacture status.

AR-15 SERIES

AR-15 Sporter (Model #6000)

A semiautomatic rifle firing from a closed bolt was introduced into the Colt product line in 1964. Similar in appearance and function to the military version, the M-16. Chambered for the .223 cartridge. It is fitted with a standard 20" barrel with no forward assist, no case deflector, but with a bayonet lug. Weighs about 7.5 lbs. Dropped from production in 1985.

NIB	Exc.	V.G.	Good	Fair	Poor
2100	1500	1100	700	600	400

AR-15 Sporter w/Collapsible Stock (Model #6001)

Same as above but fitted with a 16" barrel and sliding stock. Weighs approximately 5.8 lbs. Introduced in 1978 and discontinued in 1985.

NIB	Exc.	V.G.	Good	Fair	Poor
2150	1600	1200	800	600	400

AR-15 Carbine (Model #6420)

Introduced in 1985 this model has a 16" standard weight barrel. All other features are the same as the previous discontinued AR-15 models. This version was dropped from the Colt product line in 1987.

NIB	Exc.	V.G.	Good	Fair	Poor
1600	1350	1000	800	600	400

AR-15 9mm Carbine (Model #6450)

Same as above but chambered for 9mm cartridge. Weighs 6.3 lbs.

NIB	Exc.	V.G.	Good	Fair	Poor
2500	2000	1200	900	700	400

AR-15A2 (Model #6500)

Introduced in 1984, this was an updated version with a heavier barrel and forward assist. The AR sight was still utilized. Weighs approximately 7.8 lbs.

NIB	Exc.	V.G.	Good	Fair	Poor
1800	1500	1100	750	550	400

AR-15A2 Govt. Model Carbine (Model #6520)

Added to the Colt line in 1988, this 16" standard barrel carbine featured for the first time a case deflector, forward assist, and the improved A2 rear sight. This model is fitted with a 4-position telescoping buttstock. Weighs about 5.8 lbs.

NIB	Exc.	V.G.	Good	Fair	Poor
2500	2000	1250	950	700	500

AR-15A2 Gov't. Model (Model #6550)

This model was introduced in 1988; it is the rifle equivalent to the Carbine. It features a 20" A2 barrel, forward assist, case deflector, but still retains the bayonet lug. Weighs about 7.5 lbs. Discontinued in 1990.

NIB	Exc.	V.G.	Good	Fair	Poor
2300	2000	1250	950	700	500

AR-15A2 H-Bar (Model #6600)

Introduced in 1986, this version features a special 20" heavy barrel. All other features are the same as the A2 series of AR15s. Discontinued in 1991. Weighs about 8 lbs.

NIB	Exc.	V.G.	Good	Fair	Poor
1950	1750	1500	950	700	500

AR- 15A2 Delta H-Bar (Model #6600DH)

Same as above but fitted with a 3x9 Tasco scope and detachable cheekpiece. Dropped from the Colt line in 1990. Weighs about 10 lbs. Equipped with a metal carrying case.

NIB	Exc.	V.G.	Good	Fair	Poor
2800	2000	1500	1200	850	600

Sporter Lightweight Rifle

This lightweight model has a 16" barrel and is finished in a matte black. It is available in either a .223 Rem. caliber (Model #6530) that weighs 6.7 lbs., a Model #6430 w/A1 sights, 9mm caliber weighing 7.1 lbs., or a Model #6830 7.65x39mm that weighs 7.3 lbs. The .223 is furnished with two five-round box magazines as is the 9mm and 7.65x39mm. A cleaning kit and sling are also supplied with each new rifle. The buttstock and pistol grip are made of durable nylon and the handguard is reinforced fiberglass and aluminum lined. The rear sight is adjustable for windage and elevation. These newer models are referred to simply as Sporters and are <u>not</u> fitted with a bayonet lug and the receiver block has different size pins.

NIB	Exc.	V.G.	Good	Fair	Poor
1350	1100	900	650	400	300

NOTE: The Model 6830 will bring about $25 less than the above prices. For post-9/94 guns deduct 30%.

Sporter Target Model Rifle (Model #6551)

This 1991 model is a full size version of the Lightweight Rifle. The Target Rifle weighs 7.5 lbs. and has a 20" barrel. Offered in .223 Rem. caliber only with target sights adjustable to 800 meters. New rifles are furnished with two 5-round box magazines, sling, and cleaning kit. Same as the Model 6550 except for a rib around the magazine release.

NIB	Exc.	V.G.	Good	Fair	Poor
1350	1100	900	650	400	300

NOTE: For post-9/94 guns deduct 30%.

Sporter Match H-Bar (Model #6601)

This 1991 variation of the AR-15 is similar to the Target Model but has a 20" heavy barrel chambered for the .223 caliber. This model weighs 8 lbs. and has A2 sights adjustable out to 800 meters. Supplied with two 5-round box magazines, sling, and cleaning kit.

NIB	Exc.	V.G.	Good	Fair	Poor
1500	1200	900	650	400	300

NOTE: For post-9/94 guns deduct 35%.

Sporter Match Delta H-Bar (Model #6601 DH)

Same as above but supplied with a 3x9 Tasco scope. Has a black detachable cheekpiece and metal carrying case. Weighs about 10 lbs. Discontinued in 1992.

NIB	Exc.	V.G.	Good	Fair	Poor
1800	1500	1100	850	600	400

Match Target H-BAR Compensated (Model MT6601C)

Same as the regular Sporter H-BAR with the addition of a compensator.

NIB	Exc.	V.G.	Good	Fair	Poor
1250	900	750	—	—	—

Sporter Competition H-Bar (Model #6700)

Introduced in 1992, the Competition H-Bar is available in .223 caliber with a 20" heavy barrel counterbored for accuracy. The carry handle is detachable with A2 sights. With the carry handle removed the upper receiver is dovetailed and grooved for Weaver-style scope rings. This model weighs approximately 8.5 lbs. New rifles are furnished with two 5-round box magazines, sling, and cleaning kit.

NIB	Exc.	V.G.	Good	Fair	Poor
1800	1300	950	700	500	350

NOTE: For post-9/94 guns deduct 35%.

Sporter Competition H-Bar Select w/scope (Model #6700CH)

This variation, also new in 1992, is identical to the Sporter Competition with the addition of a factory mounted scope. The rifle has also been selected for accuracy and comes complete with a 3-9X Tasco rubber armored variable scope, scope mount, carry handle with iron sights, and nylon carrying case.

NIB	Exc.	V.G.	Good	Fair	Poor
1900	1500	1150	850	600	400

Match Target Competition H-BAR Compensated (Model MT6700C)

Same as the Match Target with a compensator.

NIB	Exc.	V.G.	Good	Fair	Poor
1250	900	—	—	—	—

AR-15 Carbine Flat-top Heavyweight/Match Target Competition (Model #6731)

This variation in the Sporter series features a heavyweight 16" barrel with flat-top receiver chambered for the .223 cartridge. It is equipped with a fixed buttstock. Weight is about 7.1 lbs.

NIB	Exc.	V.G.	Good	Fair	Poor
1250	1000	800	600	400	300

NOTE: For post-9/94 guns deduct 30%.

AR-15 Tactical Carbine (Model #6721)

This version is similar to the above model with the exception of the buttstock which is telescoping and adjusts to 4 positions. Chambered for the .223 cartridge with a weight of about 7 lbs. A majority of these guns were for law enforcement only.

NIB	Exc.	V.G.	Good	Fair	Poor
3500	3000	2500	—	—	—

Colt Accurized Rifle CAR-A3 (Model CR6724)

This variation was introduced in 1996 and features a free floating 24" stainless steel match barrel with an 11 degree target crown and special Teflon coated trigger group. The handguard is all-aluminum with twin swivel studs. Weight is approximately 9.26 lbs.

NIB	Exc.	V.G.	Good	Fair	Poor
1200	1000	800	550	—	—

U.S. CALIBER .30 CARBINE

Bibliographical Note: There are a number of variations, sights, stock configurations, etc., that are too numerous to cover in this publication. It is strongly recommended that for additional historical information, technical data, and photos see Larry L. Ruth's, *War Baby!, The U.S. Caliber .30 Carbine*, Collector Grade Publications, 1992.

This carbine was designed by William Roemer, Edwin Pugsley, and others at the Winchester Repeating Arms Company in late 1940 and early 1941. The only feature that can be credited to David Marsh "Carbine" Williams is the short stroke piston design. The U.S. M1 Carbine was produced by a number of manufacturers as listed below. The M1 A1 version was produced by Inland. The selective fire version is known as the Model M2. The exact number of carbines produced is unknown but approximately 6,000,000 carbines were built during World War II.

NOTE: Deduct 50% for imports.

U.S. M3 Carbine

This model is identical to the select fire M2 carbine with the exception of no rear sight and the scope mount to support a variety of scopes for specific uses.

U.S. M3 Carbine • Paul Goodwin photo

Pre-1986

Exc.	V.G.	Fair
4000	3500	3000

Pre-1986 conversions

Exc.	V.G.	Fair
3000	2750	2500

Pre-1986 dealer samples

Exc.	V.G.	Fair
2500	2750	2500

M3 Carbine with scope • Courtesy Richard M. Kumor Sr.

NOTE: For M3 Carbines with infra red scope add $1,000.

U.S. M2 Carbine

First produced in 1944 this select fire rifle is the automatic version of the famous M1 carbine. It has a 17.8" barrel and a 15- or 30-round magazine. It is chambered for the .30 Carbine cartridge (7.62x33mm). Its rate of fire is 750 rounds per minute. Weight is about 5.25 lbs. Marked "U.S.CARBINE CAL .30 M2" on top of chamber. Saw limited use in World War II but was widely used by American forces during Korea.

Pre-1968

Exc.	V.G.	Fair
6000	5500	5000

Pre-1986 conversions

Exc.	V.G.	Fair
3000	2750	2500

Pre-1986 dealer samples

Exc.	V.G.	Fair
2500	2750	2500

U.S. M1 Carbine

Introduced in 1941, this is a semiautomatic, gas operated carbine with a 18" barrel and a magazine capacity of 15 or 30 rounds. Half stocked with upper handguard and single barrel band. Bayonet bar located on barrel. Flip up rear sight. Chambered for the .30 U.S. Carbine cartridge. Weight is about 5.25 lbs. Widely used by U.S. military forces during World War II.

NOTE: Prices are for carbines in World War II factory configuration.

Inland

Exc.	V.G.	Good	Fair	Poor
1000	800	500	350	250

Underwood

Exc.	V.G.	Good	Fair	Poor
1100	750	550	400	275

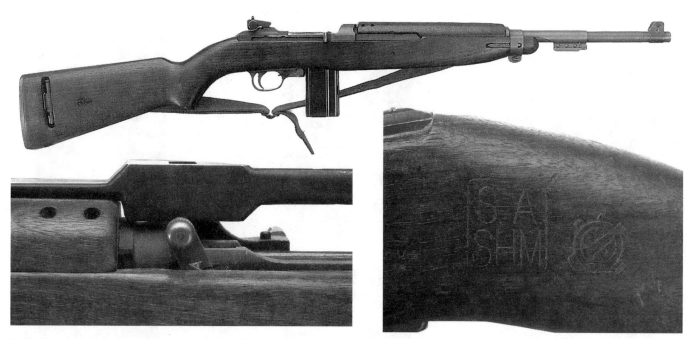

U.S. M2 Carbine, with selector switch and cartouche • Paul Goodwin photo

German infantry during Battle of the Bulge, the rear man is carrying a U.S. M1 carbine • Courtesy John M. Miller

M1 Carbine manufacturer's stampings • Courtesy Karl Karash

(Winchester) round. This was accomplished at first with a chamber insert, and later with new replacement barrels in the Nato caliber. The Navy modified rifles can be found of any manufacture, and in any serial number range. As a general rule, Navy rifles with new barrels are worth more due to their better shooting capabilities. Paper work and original boxes must accompany these rifles to obtain the values listed.

U.S.N. Crane Depot rebuild

Exc.	V.G.	Good
1250	1000	900

AMF rebuild

Exc.	V.G.	Good
1150	1000	900

H&R rebuild

Exc.	V.G.	Good
1000	900	800

Springfield Armory Production

Exc.	V.G.	Good
1250	1000	900

A Springfield M1 Garand Navy converted rifle sold at auction for $3,350. Condition is 98% arsenal refinish. Amoskeag Auction Company, January 2003

Gas trap sn: ca 81-52,000

Values shown for original rifles. Most all were updated to gas port configuration. Look out for reproductions being offered as original rifles! Get a professional appraisal before purchasing.

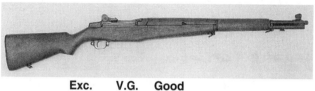

Exc.	V.G.	Good
40000	35000	25000

M1 Garand Gas Trap close-up • Courtesy Chuck Karwan

Gas tap/modified to gas port

These rifles should have many of their early parts.

Exc.	V.G.	Good
5000	3500	2500

Pre-Dec. 7, 1941 gas port production sn: ca 50,000-Appx. 410,000

Exc.	V.G.	Good	Fair	Poor
2000	1500	1000	750	650

WWII Production sn: ca 410,000-3,880,000

Exc.	V.G.	Good	Fair	Poor
1250	1000	900	750	500

POST WWII Production sn: ca 4,200,000-6,099,361

Exc.	V.G.	Good	Fair	Poor
1000	800	650	500	450

Winchester Production

Winchester produced around 513,00 M1 rifles during WWII. Their first contract was an educational order in 1939. This contract was for 500 rifles and the gauges and fixtures to produce the rifles. Winchester's second contract was awarded during 1939 for up to 65,000 rifles. Winchester M1's are typified by noticeable machine marks on their parts, and did not have the higher grade finish that is found on Springfield Armory production. Watch for fake barrels, and barrels marked "Winchester" which were produced in the 1960s as replacement barrels.

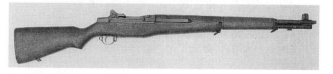

Winchester Educational Contract sn: 100,000-100,500

Exc.	V.G.	Good	Fair	Poor
10000	9000	7500	5000	4000

Winchester sn: 100,501-165,000

Rifles of this serial number range were produced from Jan. 1941 until May 1942.

Exc.	V.G.	Good	Fair	Poor
3000	2500	2000	1500	750

Winchester sn: 1,200,00-1,380,000

Rifles in this serial number range were produced from May 1942 until Aug. 1943.

Exc.	V.G.	Good	Fair	Poor
2500	2000	1800	1000	750

Winchester sn: 2,305,850-2,536,493

Rifles in this serial number range were produced from Aug. 1943 until Jan. 1945.

Exc.	V.G.	Good	Fair	Poor
2250	1850	1250	900	550

Winchester sn: 1,601,150-1,640,000

Rifles in this serial number range were produced from Jan. 1945, until June 1945. These are often referred to as Win-13's because of the revision number of the right front receiver leg.

Exc.	V.G.	Good	Fair	Poor
2800	2500	2000	1500	850

Harrington & Richardson Production

Between 1953 and 1956, Harrington & Richardson produced around 428,00 M1 rifles.

Exc.	V.G.	Good	Fair	Poor
1000	750	650	450	350

International Harvester Corp. production

Between 1953 and 1956, International Harvester produced around 337,000 M1 rifles. International at several different times during their production purchased receivers from both Harrington & Richardson and Springfield Armory. Always check for Springfield Armory heat lots on the right front receiver leg.

International Harvester Production

Exc.	V.G.	Good	Fair	Poor
1200	800	600	400	350

International Harvester/with Springfield Receiver (postage stamp)

Exc.	V.G.	Good
1800	1250	900

International Harvester/with Springfield Receiver (arrow head)

Exc.	V.G.	Good
1850	1200	1000

International Harvester/with Springfield Receiver (Gap letter)

Exc.	V.G.	Good
1250	1000	900

International Harvester/with Harrington & Richardson Receiver

Exc.	V.G.	Good
1250	1050	850

M1 Experimental with one-piece upper handguard made of fiberglass • Courtesy Richard M. Kumor Sr.

British Garands (Lend Lease)

In 1941 and 1942, the U.S. sent a total of 38,000 M1 Garands to England under the Lend Lease program. These rifles were painted with a red band around the front of the handguard the numerals :30" or "300" in black. The buttstock is stamped with a U.S. Ordnance cartouche and the initials "GHS" under "SA." Most known examples are found in the serial number range 3000000 to 600000. When these rifles were sold and imported back into the U.S., they were stamped with either London or Birmingham proof stamps.

Exc.	V.G.	Good	Fair	Poor
2250	2000	1500	1000	750

M1 Garand Cutaway

Used by factories and military armorer's to facilitate training.

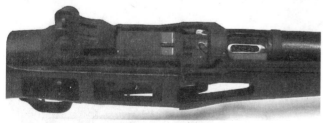

M1 Garand cutaway • Courtesy Richard M. Kumor Sr.

Exc.	V.G.	Good	Fair	Poor
3000	2500	1000	600	500

NOTE: For examples with documentation add 300%.

SCOPE VARIANTS (SNIPER RIFLES)
M1C

Springfield Armory production only. Serial number range is between ca 3,200,000 and 3,800,000. This variant is very rare with only around 7,900 produced. Should be mounted with M81, M82 or M84 scope with 7/8" scope rings. The scopes alone are worth $700 to $800 alone. Ask for government relicense paperwork, and have a serial number check run before purchase is made. If provenance can not be established, then rifles are worth the value of their individual parts, under $2000.

M1C serial number markings and cartouche • Paul Goodwin photo

Exc.	V.G.	Good
10000	8000	5000

A Springfield M1C Garand Sniper Rifle was sold at auction for $8,050. Produced in 1945 and rebuilt in 1952. New in box with paperwork, accessories, and M84 scope. All numbered to the rifle. Condition is 99%.
Rock Island Auction Company

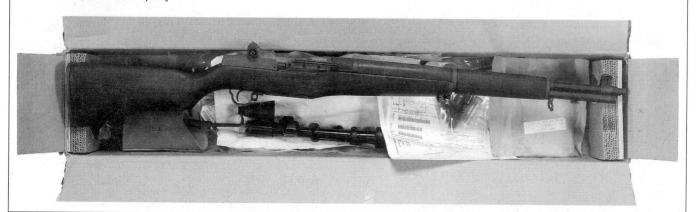

Springfield M1C rifle • Paul Goodwin photo

Garand M1 cutaway • Paul Goodwin photo

MC 1952 (USMC Issue)

Same production range as above. Should be equipped with 1" scope mount and Kollmorgen scope. These rifles will command a premium. This is the rarest of the M-1 Snipers.

Courtesy Richard M. Kumor Sr.

Close-up of MC 1952 scope and mount • Courtesy Richard M. Kumor Sr.

Korea, May 29, 1951. SFC Jack Moore, of the 187th Regimental Combat Team, draws a bead on an enemy soldier with a telescope-equipped M1 rifle. Note the cone shaped flash hider on the muzzle. His spotter, also armed with an M1, is not identified • U.S. Army Signal Corps/National Archives/Robert Bruce Military Photo Features

M1D

This model can be found by any manufacturer and in any serial number range. This mounting system was designed by John Garand, and consists of a mounting block on the rear of the barrel. The rear hand guard is shortened and the mount attaches with a large single screw system. The modification could be made on the field repair level. It is not known how many rifles were modified, but it is very likely that they numbered into the tens of thousands. If the rifle does not come with paperwork, it is only worth the value of its parts alone, under $1200. The Model 82 scope is worth between $500 and $700.

Courtesy Richard M. Kumor Sr.

Exc.	V.G.	Good
3000	2500	1500

National Match Type I
Produced on Springfield Armory receivers and in serial number ranges from ca 5,800,000 to around 6,090,000. All parts are available to reproduce both types of national match rifles. To obtain values listed these rifles must come with original paperwork.

Exc.	V.G.	Good
3000	2500	1800

National Match Type II
Produced on Springfield Armory receivers, they can be found in any serial number range. These rifles should come with papers to receive values listed.

Exc.	V.G.	Good
8500	6500	5000

KNIGHT'S MANUFACTURING CO.

SR-25 Lightweight Match (U.S. Navy, Mark 11 Model O)
This .308 rifle is fitted with a 20" free floating barrel. No sights. Weight is about 9.5 lbs. Adopted by U.S. Navy. Commercial version is the same except for the markings on the receiver.

NIB	Exc.	V.G.	Good	Fair	Poor
2995	2250	1500	900	—	—

JOHNSON AUTOMATICS MFG. CO.

Model 1941
This is a recoil-operated semiautomatic rifle chambered for the .30-06 cartridge and fitted with a rotary 10-round magazine. It has a half stock with perforated handguard. Used by the U.S. Marines, Dutch Colonial forces, and U.S. special forces during World War II. Fitted with a 22" barrel and chambered for the .30-06 cartridge. Right side of the receiver is marked

THE M1 GARAND

George S. Patton called it the greatest battle instrument ever devised. Millions of soldiers swore by it. It served as the basis for both the Italian BM-59 and the short lived American M14. The M1 Garand remains an American small arms icon that lives on in the hearts of American shooters and will do so for the foreseeable future. There is no such thing as perfection, but the Garand comes close. The only major modification needed to perfect it was the addition of a 20-round magazine, which Beretta accomplished better than Springfield Armory, at the same time converting M1s to 7.62mm NATO. The current commercial version of the short-lived M14 is called the M1A for, but, the M14 is essentially no more than a modified M1. The M1 was designed by John C. Garand, an eccentric Canadian who moved to the U.S. and went to work at Springfield Armory. His genius extended to much more than firearms. When Garand designed the rifle that bears his name, Springfield engineers told him that it couldn't be manufactured. Garand then designed the tooling to make the rifle, proving them wrong. Early Garands had a few problems, one of them critical. Early operating rods had the disconcerting habit of breaking, sending the handle back into the shooter's face. Several soldiers were actually killed before the cause was discovered and rectified. This was the only major fault in the rifle's design, although minor modifications were carried out over the entire lifespan of the M1. As WWII was drawing to a close, an M1 with a 20-round magazine was developed. 500,000 of the modified rifles were ordered, but the war's end caused the order's cancellation. Although the M1 fires the powerful .30-06 cartridge, the gas action coupled with the long operating rod and the 10-pound weight of the rifle, soften recoil. The M1 remains one of the most pleasant-shooting high-powered rifles ever manufactured.

Charlie Cutshaw

"CRANSTON ARMS CO." Parkerized finish. Checkered metal buttplate. Adjustable rear sight is graduated in meters. Bayonet fitted to barrel. Barrel is easily removed which was a plus for airborne Marine units. Weight is about 9.5 lbs.

NOTE: Rifles with a verifiable U.S. Marine Corp provenance will bring a premium.

Exc.	V.G.	Good	Fair	Poor
3750	3000	2000	1000	500

M1 Grand National Match • Paul Goodwin photo

A Johnson Model 1941 rifle was sold at auction for $3,737.50. Condition was excellent arsenal refinish. Rock Island Auction Company, December 2001

REMINGTON'S ROLLING BLOCK RIFLE

In this line of work, we pundits learn early on to avoid the use of superlatives. But I'm going to throw caution to the wind and state that the Remington Rolling Block was the MOST popular single-shot military rifle of the 19th century! I base this upon the fact that between 1865 and 1916, no fewer then fifteen countries (and probably more) used them. Remington not only produced in excess of two million units, but also licensed manufacture to a half dozen foreign countries. Designed in the early 1860s by Leonard Geiger, Remington purchased the rights to the design in 1863 and sold numbers to the U.S. Army, Navy and state militias. During the 1800s, they saw combat in Latin America, Europe, the Middle East, Africa, Asia and China and some were used by France and Russia during WWI. They were chambered for military cartridges ranging from the .56-60 Spencer up to the 7x57 Mauser. Years ago, my older brother purchased a surplus Argentinian Fusil Remington Modelo 1875 chambered for the 11x58R (11mm Spanish Remington) cartridge. Operation was simplicity personified: you cocked the hammer, rolled back the block, inserted a thumb-sized cartridge and snapped the block shut. The only safety device was the half cock notch on the hammer. After firing, you recocked the hammer and opened the block whereupon the empty case was extracted. While the trigger pull could be diplomatically described as gritty, using blackpowder handloads, we managed to fire a number of acceptable groups at 100 yards. But what was the most fun was offhand shooting at a large boulder on the range backstop. You would aim, pull the trigger and then squat down under the cloud of blackpowder smoke to watch the cast lead bullet go splat on the boulder. Scientific research? Not really. . . but it sure was a hell of a lot of fun!

Paul Scarlata

REMINGTON ARMS COMPANY, INC.

U.S. Navy Rolling Block Carbine

A .50-70 caliber single shot rolling block carbine with a 23.25" round barrel. A sling ring is normally fitted to the left side of the frame and sling swivels are mounted on the barrel band and the bottom of the butt. Inspector's markings are to be found on the right side of the frame as well as the stock. Blued, case hardened with a walnut stock. The barrel is marked "Remington's Ilion, N.Y. U.S.A." along with the patent dates. Approximately 5,000 were manufactured in 1868 and 1869.

Exc.	V.G.	Good	Fair	Poor
—	—	3500	1250	350

Model 1867 Navy Cadet Rifle

A .50-45 caliber single shot rolling block rifle with a 32.5" barrel and full length forend secured by two barrel bands. Markings identical to the above with the exception that "U.S." is stamped on the buttplate tang. Blued, case hardened with a walnut stock. Approximately 500 were made in 1868.

Exc.	V.G.	Good	Fair	Poor
—	—	2750	1200	400

Rolling Block Military Rifles

Between 1867 and 1902 over 1,000,000 rolling block military rifles and carbines were manufactured by the Remington Company. Offered in a variety of calibers and barrel lengths, the values listed below are for full length rifles. Foreign contract models are listed under country.

NOTE: Carbines are worth approximately 40% more.

Courtesy Milwaukee Public Museum, Milwaukee, Wisconsin

Exc.	V.G.	Good	Fair	Poor
—	—	750	400	100

Remington-Keene Magazine Rifle

A bolt-action rifle chambered for the .40, .43, and .45-70 centerfire cartridges with 22", 24.5", 29.25", or 32.5" barrels. It is readily identifiable by the exposed hammer at the end of the bolt. Blued, case hardened hammer and furniture, with a walnut stock. The receiver marked "E. Remington & Sons, Ilion, N.Y." together with the patent dates 1874, 1876, and 1877. The magazine on this rifle was located beneath the barrel and the receiver is fitted with a cut-off so that the rifle could be used as a single shot. Approximately 5,000 rifles were made between 1880 and 1888 in the following variations:

Sporting Rifle-24.5" Barrel

Exc.	V.G.	Good	Fair	Poor
—	1750	1200	500	200

Army Rifle

Barrel length 32.5" with a full-length stock secured by two barrel bands. Prices are for martially marked examples.

Courtesy Milwaukee Public Museum, Milwaukee, Wisconsin

Exc.	V.G.	Good	Fair	Poor
—	3500	2000	850	300

Navy Rifle
As above, with a 29.25" barrel. Prices are for martially marked examples.

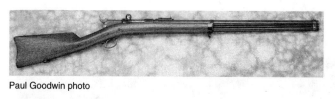

Paul Goodwin photo

Exc.	V.G.	Good	Fair	Poor
—	4750	3000	1500	750

Carbine
As above, with a 22" barrel and a half-length forend secured by one barrel band.

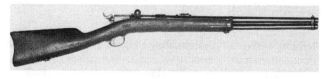

Courtesy Milwaukee Public Museum, Milwaukee, Wisconsin

Exc.	V.G.	Good	Fair	Poor
—	3250	1500	750	350

Frontier Model
As above, with a 24" barrel and half-length forend secured by one barrel band. Those purchased by the United States Department of the Interior for arming the Indian Police are marked "U.S.I.D." on the receiver.

Exc.	V.G.	Good	Fair	Poor
—	—	5500	3000	850

Remington-Lee Magazine Rifle
Designed by James Paris Lee, rifles of this type were originally manufactured by the Sharps Rifle Company in 1880. The Remington Company began production of this model in 1881 after the Sharps Company ceased operations. Approximately 100,000 Lee magazine rifles were made between 1880 and 1907. Their variations are as follows:

Model 1879 U.S. Navy Model
Barrel length 28", .45-70 caliber with a full-length stock secured by two barrel bands. The barrel is marked with the U.S. Navy Inspector's Marks and an anchor at the breech. The receiver is marked "Lee Arms Co. Bridgeport, Conn. U.S.A." and "Patented Nov. 4, 1879." Approximately 1300 were made.

Paul Goodwin photo

Exc.	V.G.	Good	Fair	Poor
—	3500	1750	750	250

Model 1882 Army Contract
This model is identifiable by the two grooves pressed into the side of the magazine. The receiver is marked "Lee Arms Co. Bridgeport Conn., U.S.A." and on some examples it is also marked "E. Remington & Sons, Ilion, N.Y. U.S.A. Sole Manufactured & Agents." Barrel length 32", caliber .45-70, full-length stock secured by two barrel bands. U.S. Inspector's marks are stamped on the barrel breech and the stock. Approximately 750 were made

Paul Goodwin photo

Exc.	V.G.	Good	Fair	Poor
—	3500	1750	750	300

Model 1885 Navy Contract
As above, with the inspection markings (including an anchor) on the receiver ring and the left side of the stock. Approximately 1,500 were made.

Exc.	V.G.	Good	Fair	Poor
—	3500	1750	750	300

Model 1882 & 1885 Military Rifles
Barrel length 32", full-length stock secured by two barrel bands, chambered for .42 Russian, .43 Spanish, .45 Gardner or .45-70 cartridges. The values for those rifles not in .45-70 caliber would be approximately 25% less than those shown below. Approximately 10,000 Model 1882 rifles were made and 60,000 Model 1885 rifles. The two models can be differentiated by the fact that the cocking piece on the bolt of the Model 1885 is larger. The majority of these rifles were made for foreign contracts and commercial sales.

Exc.	V.G.	Good	Fair	Poor
—	—	950	400	150

Model 1899
Designed for use with smokeless and rimless cartridges, this model is marked on the receiver "Remington Arms Co. Ilion, N.Y. Patented Aug. 26th 1884 Sept. 9th 1884 March 17th 1885 Jan 18th 1887." Produced from 1889 to 1907 in the following variations:

Model 1885 Navy Contract • Courtesy Rock Island Auction Company

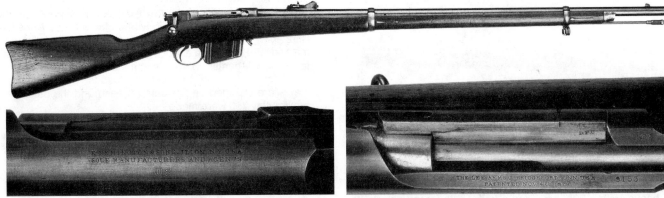

Model 1882 Military Rifle • Courtesy West Point Museum, Paul Goodwin photo

Military Rifle

Barrel length 29", 6mm USN, .30-40, .303, 7x57mm or 7.65mm caliber with a full-length stock secured by two barrel bands.

Paul Goodwin photo

Exc.	V.G.	Good	Fair	Poor
—	1000	450	200	100

NOTE: Add $250 if U.S. marked.

Military Carbine

As above, with a 20" barrel and a 3/4 length carbine stock secured by one barrel band.

Exc.	V.G.	Good	Fair	Poor
—	1500	800	300	100

Remington-Mannlicher Berthier Bolt-Action Rifle (Model 1907/1915)

Produced for the French government, this rifle has a 31.5" barrel of 8mm Lebel caliber and a full-length stock secured by two barrel bands. The barrel marked "RAC 1907-15" and the left side of the receiver marked "Remington M'LE 1907-15." Several thousand were manufactured between 1907 and 1915.

Paul Goodwin photo

Exc.	V.G.	Good	Fair	Poor
—	700	350	150	100

Remington-Mannlicher Berthier Bolt-Action Carbine (Model 1907/1915)

As above but 24.5" barrel. Half stock with one barrel band.

Exc.	V.G.	Good	Fair	Poor
—	800	450	200	125

Remington/Westinghouse Mosin-Nagant Bolt-Action Rifle

Produced for the Imperial Russian government, this rifle has a 32" barrel of 7.62x54mm R caliber with a full-length stock secured by two barrel bands. The barrel is marked "Remington Armory" with the date of manufacture and the receiver ring is stamped with the Russian coat-of-arms. Approximately 3,000,000 were made between 1916 and 1918.

Paul Goodwin photo

Exc.	V.G.	Good	Fair	Poor
500	400	300	100	75

A Remington Mosin-Nagant rifle was sold at auction for $1,725. Two digit serial. Condition is 95% blue and wood. Rock Island Auction Company, September 2002

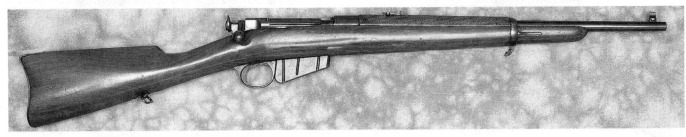

Remington Model 1899 Military Carbine • Paul Goodwin photo

U.S. Model 1917 Magazine Rifle

Produced for the United States government by Eddystone as the principal manufacturer and also by Remington and Winchester. This rifle has a 26" barrel of .30-06 caliber and a full length stock secured by two barrel bands. Those sold to the British government during WWII are often found with a 2" wide red and white painted stripe around their magazine, which was intended to show that they were chambered for the .30-06 cartridge instead of the .303 British cartridge. Total production was 2,200,000.

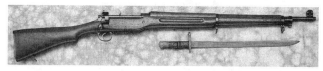

Paul Goodwin photo

Exc.	V.G.	Good	Fair	Poor
550	450	375	150	100

MODEL 1917 ENFIELD

Let's get right to the point. The M1917 is actually a better combat rifle than the venerable M1903 Springfield. This isn't heresay—it is a fact. Some 2 million M1917s were manufactured by Eddystone, Remington and Winchester during World War I as compared to only 800,000 M1903 rifles. The vast majority of American Doughboys went to war with the M1917, including Medal of Honor winner Sergeant Alvin York. General of the Armies "Blackjack" Pershing ordered that M1903s be relegated to rear area troops while M1917s be conserved for front line units. In the early 1920s, there were so many M1917s and the rifle was so respected that the Army seriously considered replacing the M1903 with it. Only internal Army politics saved the M1903. Now for some details as to why the M1917 is superior as a combat rifle. First is magazine capacity. The M1917 holds six cartridges rather than the M1903's five, although when loading with stripper clips this is academic. The M1917's action is stronger and more reliable than the M1903's. The M1917 cocks on closing, eliminating the resistance needed to cock the action as the bolt handle is raised. The cock on the closing action was deliberately chosen to enhance extraction and the primary extraction force of the M1917 is much stronger than the M1903, increasing reliability. The M1917's sights are far better than the M1903 sights. The M1917 has a large aperture rear sight that speeds target acquisition. For enhanced accuracy, the rear sight is simply flipped up to employ a sliding aperture sight that is just the right diameter for long range combat shooting. The M1917's front sight is protected by heavy "ears" that positively prevent damage, unlike the M1903, whose front sight is exposed. We could go on, but space limits us to cover only the high points of the M1917's superiority. The M1903 went on to become a military small arms icon while the M1917 was essentially forgotten.

Charlie Cutshaw

France, 1918. An American soldier in full marching order with U.S. Model 1917 "Enfield" rifle at right shoulder arms. This excellent bolt action rifle, based on the British Pattern 14, was issued in much greater numbers to Doughboys in WWI than the more famous Springfield M1903 • U.S. Army Signal Corps/National Archives/Robert Bruce Military Photo Features

Model 513-T

This is a bolt action .22 caliber training rifle with oil finished walnut stock and checkered steel butt. Barrel length is 26.75" and detachable magazine capacity is 6 rounds. Rear sight is an adjustable Redfield Model 75 RT. Most, but not all, of these rifles are drilled and tapped for telescope mounting blocks. Receiver is stamped "us property". Some of these rifles will have the arsenal rebuilder stamped on the barrel. About 70,000 of these rifles were produced under government contract from 1942 to 1944.

Exc.	V.G.	Good	Fair	Poor
800	600	500	300	200

Model 700 (M40)

This is a military version of the commercial Remington bolt action rifle. It was issued without sights and a 10x scope, chambered for the .308 (7.62x51 Nato) cartridge. Barrel length is 24". Magazine capacity is 5 rounds. Walnut stock with oil finish. Scope is a Redfield 3-9X Accu-Range. Buttplate, triggerguard and floorplate are aluminum. Weight is about 14 lbs with scope. Marked, "US RIFLE M40" with the serial number over the chamber. First issued in 1966. Weight is about 9.25 lbs. Primarily used the U.S. Marine Corp.

Model 513-T • Paul Goodwin photo

In 1977, an improved version of this rifle was issued known as the M40A1. Same barrel length and scope butt-fitted with a synthetic McMillan camouflage stock, Pachmayr brown recoil pad and steel triggerguard and floorplate. In 1980, the Marine Corp began using Unertl 10X scope with mil-dot reticle with Unertl base and rings.

NOTE: Prices listed below are for verifiable samples.

Exc.	V.G.	Good	Fair	Poor
5000	3500	2500	1500	1000

Remington Model 700P Rifles
Remington's line of law enforcement rifles are also used by a variety of military forces. Rifles purchased under contract will be marked for the country and service of origin. Models purchased by commercial means will not be marked.

Model 700 Police LTR (Lightweight Tactical Rifle)
Fitted with a fluted 20" barrel and chambered for the .308 or .223 cartridge this rifle weighs about 7.5 lbs. Synthetic stock.

NIB	Exc.	V.G.	Good	Fair	Poor
700	550	—			

Model 700 Police
This model is fitted with a 26" barrel and chambered for the .308 and .223 cartridges in a short action or 7mm Rem. Mag., .300 Win. Mag., or .300 Rem. Ultra Mag. in a long action. Weight is about 9 lbs. Synthetic stock.

NIB	Exc.	V.G.	Good	Fair	Poor
630	500	—	—	—	—

Model 700 TWS (Tactical Weapons System)
Chambered for the .308 cartridge and fitted with a 26" barrel this model also features a Leupold Vari-X II 3.5x10 scope, a Harris bipod, quick adjustable sling. and a Pelican hard case. Weight of rifle is about 10.5 lbs.

Courtesy Remington Arms

NIB	Exc.	V.G.	Good	Fair	Poor
N/A	—	—	—	—	—

Model 700 VS LH
This model is a left hand version of the Model 700m Police.

NIB	Exc.	V.G.	Good	Fair	Poor
630	500	—	—	—	—

Model 40-XB KS
Two versions of this rifle are offered. In the single shot version it is chambered for the .223, .308, and .300 Win. Mag. calibers. In the repeating version it is chambered in the .223 or .308 calibers. All versions are fitted with a 27.25" barrel. Weight is about 10.25 lbs. Martially marked rifles will command a premium over retail prices.

NOTE: Retail prices range from $1,200 to $1,500 depending on configuration and finish.

PARKER HALE

Model 85 Sniper
Built by the Gibbs Rifle Co. in Martinsburg, West Virginia, this Parker-Hale designed bolt action rifle is chambered for the .308 cartridge and fitted with a 27.5" barrel with a telescope and bipod. Box magazine capacity is 10 rounds. Weight is about 12.5 lbs. First produced in 1986.

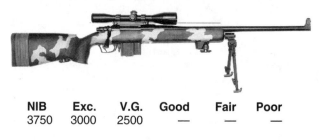

NIB	Exc.	V.G.	Good	Fair	Poor
3750	3000	2500	—	—	—

SAVAGE

Model 1899-D Military Musket
Chambered for .303 Savage only with 28" barrel. Fitted with full military stocks. Produced from 1899 to 1915. Several hundred produced for Canadian Home Guard during WWI. These will have rack numbers on the buttplate.

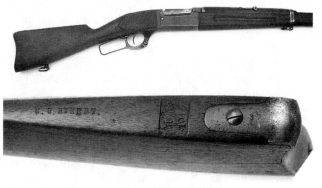

Photo courtesy Amoskeag Auction Company

Exc.	V.G.	Good	Fair	Poor
3000	2000	1500	700	300

A Savage Model 1899 Military Musket was sold at auction for $3,737.50. Condition was very good. Rock Island Auction Company, December 2001

WINCHESTER REPEATING ARMS COMPANY

NOTE: The U.S. government purchased many different Winchester rifles over the years for a wide variety of purposes. During World War I, the Model 1894 carbine was purchased by the government as well as small numbers of the Model 1907 and the Model 1910 self loading rifles. There is evidence that the U.S. Coast Guard purchased several thousand of Model 1906 .22 caliber rifles for use during World War I. The Model 52 bolt action rifle was first designed by Winchester in hopes of a government contract as a military training rifle, but the end of World War I precluded that goal. During World War II, the U.S. government purchased the Winchester Model 74 .22 caliber rifles from 1941 to 1943. It is possible that many Winchester rifles were purchased by the U.S. military for assorted purposes from guard duty to pest control. Many of these rifles will be martially marked and their value has increased over the standard civilian rifle.

Bibliographical Note: For more historical information, technical data, and photos see Bruce Canfield's, *A Collector's Guide to Winchester's in the Service.* Also Thomas Henshaw, *The History of Winchester Firearms,* 1866-1992, Winchester Press, 1995. George Madis, *The Winchester Book,* 1985.

Model 1873 Musket

This rifle was fitted with a 30" round barrel and chambered for a variety of calibers at the customer's request. Nominal calibers are: .44-40, .38-40, and .32-20. Magazine capacity was 17 rounds. Muskets were fitted with almost full length wooden stocks with cleaning rod and bayonet fittings. Many of these muskets were sold under contract to foreign governments. Survival rate is very low.

1st Model

Exc.	V.G.	Good	Fair	Poor
—	—	8500	4000	1000

2nd Model

The dust cover on the Second Model operates on one central guide secured to the receiver with two screws. The checkered oval finger grip is still used, but on later Second Models this is changed to a serrated finger grip on the rear of the dust cover. Second Models are found in the 31000 to 90000 serial number range.

Courtesy Rock Island Auction Company

Exc.	V.G.	Good	Fair	Poor
—	—	5000	2000	1000

3rd Model

The central guide rail is still present on the Third Model, but it is now integrally machined as part of the receiver. The serrated rear edges of the dust cover are still present on the Third Model.

Exc.	V.G.	Good	Fair	Poor
—	—	4000	1500	700

Model 1876

Musket, 32" round barrel with full-length forearm secured by one barrel band and straight grip stock. Stamped on the barrel is the Winchester address with King's patent date. The caliber marking is stamped on the bottom of the receiver near the magazine tube and the breech end of the barrel.

First Model

As with the Model 1873, the primary difference in model types lies in the dust cover. The First Model has no dust cover and is seen between serial number 1 and 3000.

Musket

Exc.	V.G.	Good	Fair	Poor
—	—	9500	4000	1500

Second Model

The Second Model has a dust cover with guide rail attached to the receiver with two screws. On the early Second Model an oval finger guide is stamped on top of the dust cover while later models have a serrated finger guide along the rear edge of the dust cover. Second Models range from serial numbers 3000 to 30000.

Musket

Exc.	V.G.	Good	Fair	Poor
—	—	9500	4000	1500

Third Model

The dust cover guide rail on Third Model 76s is integrally machined as part of the receiver with a serrated rear edge on the dust cover. Third Model will be seen from serial numbers 30000 to 64000.

Musket

Exc.	V.G.	Good	Fair	Poor
—	—	9500	4000	1500

Model 1886

Based on a John Browning patent, the Model 1886 was one of the finest and strongest lever actions ever utilized in a Winchester rifle. Winchester introduced the Model 1886 in order to take advantage of the more powerful centerfire cartridges of the time.

Musket, 30" round barrel, musket style forearm with one barrel band. Military style sights. About 350 Model 1886 Muskets were produced. This is the most rare variation of all Winchester lever action rifles.

Musket

Exc.	V.G.	Good	Fair	Poor
—	—	15000	7000	2500

Model 1895 U.S. Army Musket

U.S. Army Musket, 28" round barrel chambered for the .30-40 Krag. Came equipped with or without knife bayonet. These muskets were furnished to the U.S. Army for use during the Spanish-American War and are "US" marked on the receiver.

Exc.	V.G.	Good	Fair	Poor
—	4250	2000	1000	500

Model 1895 Russian Musket

Russian Musket, similar to standard musket but fitted with clip guides in the top of the receiver and with bayonet. Chambered for the 7.62x54mm R cartridge. Approximately 294,000 Model 1895 Muskets were sold to the Imperial Russian Government between 1915 and 1916. The first 15,000 Russian Muskets had 8" knife bayonets, and the rest were fitted with 16" bayonets. Some of these rifles went to Spain in its Civil War in 1936-1939.

Exc.	V.G.	Good	Fair	Poor
—	3500	1500	650	300

Model 1885 (Single Shot)

The High Wall musket most often had a 26" round barrel chambered for the .22 caliber cartridge. Larger calibers were available as were different barrel lengths. The High Wall Musket featured an almost full length forearm fastened to the barrel with a single barrel band and rounded buttplate.

The Low Wall musket is most often referred to as the Winder Musket named after the distinguished marksman, Colonel C.B. Winder. This model features a Lyman receiver sight and was made in .22 caliber.

Close-up of Hotchkiss 1st Model action • Courtesy George Hoyem

Close-up of Hotchkiss 2nd Model action • Courtesy George Hoyem

Close-up of Hotchkiss 3rd Model action • Courtesy George Hoyem

U.S. and Ordnance markings will appear on rifles purchased by the government.

High Wall Musket

Exc.	V.G.	Good	Fair	Poor
—	2500	1200	900	700

Low Wall Musket (WinderMusket)

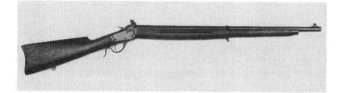

Courtesy Buffalo Bill Historical Center, Cody, Wyoming

Exc.	V.G.	Good	Fair	Poor
—	2000	800	400	250

Winchester Hotchkiss Bolt Action Rifle

This model is also known as the Hotchkiss Magazine Gun or the Model 1883. This rifle was designed by Benjamin Hotchkiss in 1876, and Winchester acquired the manufacturing rights to the rifle in 1877. In 1879, the first guns were delivered for sale. The Hotchkiss rifle was a bolt-action firearm designed for military and sporting use. It was the first bolt-action rifle made by Winchester. The rifle was furnished in .45-70 Government, and although the 1884 Winchester catalog lists a .40-65 Hotchkiss as being available, no evidence exists that such a chamber was ever actually furnished. Two different types of military configurations will be seen:

1. Carbine, 24" round or 22-1/2" round barrel with military style straight grip stock. Chambered for the 45-55 cartridge.
2. Musket, 32" or 28" round barrel with almost full length military-style straight grip stock. Winchester produced the Model 1883 until 1899, having built about 85,000 guns. Chambered for the 45-70 cartridge.

First Model

This model has the safety and a turn button magazine cut-off located above the triggerguard on the right side. The carbine has a 24" round barrel with a saddle ring on the left side of the stock. The musket has a 32" round barrel with two barrel bands, a steel forearm tip, and bayonet attachment under the barrel. The serial number range for the First Model is between 1 and about 6419.

Army Rifle

These Army models are marked with the inspector stamping of "ESA/1878" on the left side of the stock. Production total of 513 rifles.

Courtesy Butterfield & Butterfield, San Francisco, California

Exc.	V.G.	Good	Fair	Poor
—	5500	3500	900	500

Carbine-501 Carbines produced.

Exc.	V.G.	Good	Fair	Poor
—	4500	2750	900	500

Navy Rifle-1,474 produced

Exc.	V.G.	Good	Fair	Poor
—	4250	2250	900	500

Musket

Exc.	V.G.	Good	Fair	Poor
—	2500	1500	700	300

Second Model

On this model the safety is located on the top left side of the receiver, and the magazine cutoff is located on the top right side of the receiver to the rear of the bolt handle. The carbine has a 22-1/2" round barrel with a nickeled forearm cap. The musket now has a 28" barrel. Serial number range for the Second Model runs from 6420 to 22521.

Carbine-400 produced

Exc.	V.G.	Good	Fair	Poor
—	5000	3000	900	500

Musket

Exc.	V.G.	Good	Fair	Poor
—	3000	1750	750	350

Third Model

The Third Model is easily identified by the two-piece stock separated by the receiver. The carbine is now fitted with a 20" barrel with saddle ring and bar on the left side of the frame. The musket remains unchanged from the Second Model with the exception of the two-piece stock. Serial numbers of the Third Model range from 22552 to 84555.

Army Rifle

Exc.	V.G.	Good	Fair	Poor
—	3000	1750	750	350

Courtesy Butterfield & Butterfield, San Francisco, California

Musket

Exc.	V.G.	Good	Fair	Poor
—	3000	1750	750	350

Winchester-Lee Straight Pull Rifle

This rifle was a military firearm that Winchester built for the U.S. Navy in 1895. The Navy version was a musket type with a 28" round barrel and musket style forearm and plain walnut pistol grip stock. In 1897, Winchester offered a commercial musket version for public sale as well as a Sporting Rifle. All of these guns were chambered for the 6mm Lee (.236 Caliber) cartridge. The Sporting Rifle featured a 24" round barrel with plain walnut pistol grip stock and finger grooves in the forearm. Built from 1895 to 1905, Winchester sold about 20,000 Lee rifles; 15,000 were sold to the U.S. Navy, 3,000 were sold in the commercial version, and 1,700 were Sporting Rifles.

NOTE: Commercial and Sporting rifles will not have martial markings, inspector markings, or bayonet fittings.

U.S. Navy Musket

Exc.	V.G.	Good	Fair	Poor
—	2750	1500	700	500

NOTE: Some of these muskets were stored on the U.S. battleship Maine. Records of serial numbers exist to authenicate these muskets. Add a premium of 50% for these examples.

Model 65 with USMC markings • Courtesy private collection, Paul Goodwin photo

HARRINGTON & RICHARDSON, INC.

Reising Model 60

A .45 ACP caliber semiautomatic rifle with an 18.25" barrel and a 12- or 20-round detachable magazine. Blued, with a walnut stock. It operates on a retarded blowback system and was developed to be used as a police weapon. Manufactured between 1944 and 1946.

Courtesy Richard M. Kumor Sr.

Exc.	V.G.	Good	Fair	Poor
1500	1200	500	250	100

Model 65 Military

A .22 l.r. caliber semiautomatic rifle with a 23" barrel and Redfield peep sights. Blued, with a walnut stock. Manufactured between 1944 and 1956.

NOTE: Add 100% if USMC marked.

Exc.	V.G.	Good	Fair	Poor
500	300	200	125	90

BARRETT F.A. MFG. CO.

Model 95 (M 107 Sniper Weapon System)

Introduced in 1995, this .50 caliber BMG bolt action model features a 29" barrel and a 5-round magazine. Scope optional. Weight is 22 lbs. Adopted by the U.S. Army in 2000 as an anti-

material weapon out to 1,500 plus meters. This model differs from the commercial version in that it breaks down into two smaller sections; it is fitted with an 11.5" optical rail, has one takedown pin, detachable bipod with spiked feet, is fitted with front and rear iron sights, and has adjustable scope rings.

NIB	Exc.	V.G.	Good	Fair	Poor
4500	4000	3000	2000	—	—

SHOTGUNS

For a more detailed historical and technical account of U.S. military shotguns see Bruce Canfield's, *A Collectors Guide to United States Combat Shotguns*, Andrew Mobray, 1999. Also Thomas F. Swearengen, *The World's Fighting Shotguns*, Vol. IV, Ironside International Publishers, 1978.

WINCHESTER

Model 1897 Trench Gun (Model 1917)

Slide action hammer gun 12 gauge, 20" barrel bored to shoot buckshot, plain walnut modified pistol grip stock with grooved slide handle. Solid frame (WWI) or takedown (WWII). Fitted with barrel hand guard and bayonet. This model was furnished to the U.S. Army for trench work in World War I. It was not listed in Winchester catalogs until 1920. This model was also used in large numbers in WWII, Korea, and Vietnam. Prices below are for U.S. marked guns.

Model 97 Solid Frame-World War I

Exc.	V.G.	Good	Fair	Poor
5000	3500	2000	1000	700

Model 97 Take Down-World War II

Exc.	V.G.	Good	Fair	Poor
4500	3000	1800	800	650

NOTE: Add about $200 for Winchester marked bayonet.

Model 12 Trench Gun

Slide action hammerless gun 12 gauge, 20" barrel bored to shoot buckshot, plain walnut modified pistol grip stock with grooved slide handle. Solid frame or takedown. Fitted with barrel hand guard and bayonet. Finish is blued. This model was furnished to the U.S. Army for trench work in World War I and World War II. Prices below are for U.S. marked guns.

Exc.	V.G.	Good	Fair	Poor
4500	3000	1800	800	650

NOTE: Add about $200 for Winchester marked bayonet.

Winchester Model 1897 Trench Gun • Courtesy Rock Island Auction Company

A Winchester Model 97 Trench Gun was sold at auction for $6,900. Martial markings. Built around 1944. Bayonet and scabbard. Condition is 98%.
Rock Island Auction Company, May 2002

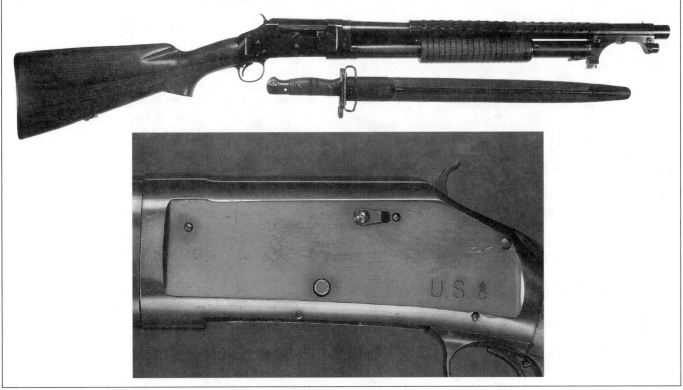

A Winchester Model 12 Trench Gun was sold at auction for $4,600. Condition was excellent. Late World War II production with correct martial markings. Includes sling and Winchester M1917 bayonet.
Rock Island Auction Company, December 2001

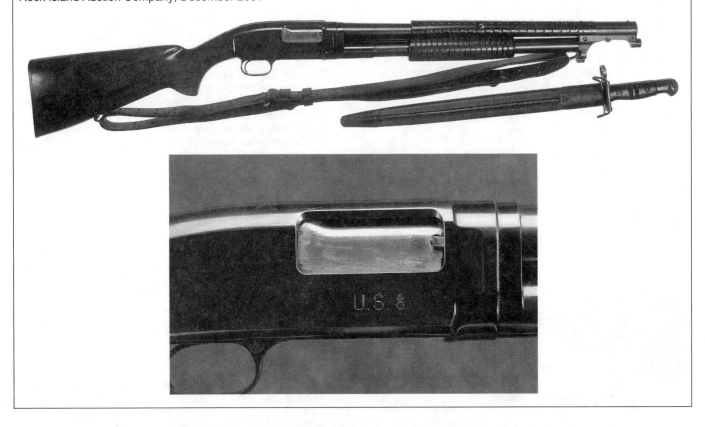

Remington Model 10 Trench Gun • Paul Goodwin photo

REMINGTON

Model 10 Trench Gun

Slide action 12 gauge shotgun with 23" round barrel. No checkering on buttstock. Wooden handguard and bayonet lug. Prices below for shotgun only with military markings.

Exc.	V.G.	Good	Fair	Poor
15000	12500	10000	7500	5000

Model 11 Military Riot Gun

This is a 12 gauge 20" barrel shotgun used during WWI. Most were blued, some were Parkerized when rebuilt. Military markings with stock cartouche. Many thousands were sold to the military and are often encountered.

Exc.	V.G.	Good	Fair	Poor
750	550	400	300	150

NOTE: A long barrel version of the Model 11 was used by the military for aeriel gunnery practice. these examples will bring less.

Model 31 Military Riot Gun

This model was to replace the Model 10. Built in a short barrel (20") riot configuration, there were about 15,000 of these shotguns bought by the military but most were in the longer barrel lengths used for training. Stocks were not checkered. Martially marked.

Exc.	V.G.	Good	Fair	Poor
1500	1000	750	500	350

Model 870 Mark I

This is a slide action 12 gauge shotgun with Parkerized finish. Fitted with an 18" round barrel. Prices are for military marked guns.

Exc.	V.G.	Good	Fair	Poor
5000	3500	2000	1250	850

NOTE: The Model 870 is still purchased by the U.S. military in a number of different configurations. The key to the correct designation of these more current shotguns lies with the military markings.

Model 11-87P

This is a semi-automatic 12 gauge shotgun with an 18" barrel and 7-round magazine extension. Fitted with synthetic stock. Purchased by various branches of the U.S. military, this shotgun may be found in a number of different configurations. All will be military marked.

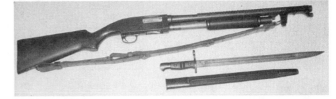

Exc.	V.G.	Good	Fair	Poor
750	600	400	300	150

SAVAGE

Model 720 Military Riot Gun

A semiautomatic 12 gauge shotgun similar in design to the Remington 11 and the Browning A-5. Some 15,000 of these shotguns were sold to the military during WWII. Martially marked. One of the more rare WWII shotguns.

Exc.	V.G.	Good	Fair	Poor
2500	1850	1500	850	500

STEVENS

Model 520 U.S. Marked Trench Gun

A slide action shotgun manufactured from 1930 to 1949. Chambered for the 12 gauge shell and fitted with a 20" barrel with cylinder choke. Fitted with a metal handguard and Stevens designed bayonet adapter. Used extensively in WWII. About 35,000 of these guns were purchased by the government during the war. Blued finish. Trench guns were fitted with metal handguards and bayonet adapters. There is also a military version without handguard called a Riot Gun. These models will also have military markings. Riot guns will bring less than Trench Guns.

Exc.	V.G.	Good	Fair	Poor
1750	1350	850	500	350

Model 620 U.S. Marked Trench Gun

Courtesy Richard M. Kumor Sr.

Exc.	V.G.	Good	Fair	Poor
2000	1600	1100	600	300

NOTE: Add $150 for bayonet.

Stevens .22/.410 Shotgun-Rifle combination

This was the precursor to the Model 24. First made in 1940 with a Tenite stock, this combination gun was used by some bomber crews during WWII. According to Savage records the U.S. government purchased about 10,000 of these guns during the war as well as some years after as some of these guns were marked "USAF."

Exc.	V.G.	Good	Fair	Poor
N/A	—	—	—	—

MOSSBERG

Model 590 Special Purpose (ATP8)

Fitted with a 20" shrouded barrel, bayonet lug, parkerized or blued finish. Speed feed stock and ghost ring sights. Introduced in 1987. Weight is about 7.25 lbs. Military marked. This gun is also offered in a commercial version.

NIB	Exc.	V.G.	Good	Fair	Poor
350	275	200	175	125	100

Model 11 Military Riot Gun • Courtesy West Point Museum, Paul Goodwin photo

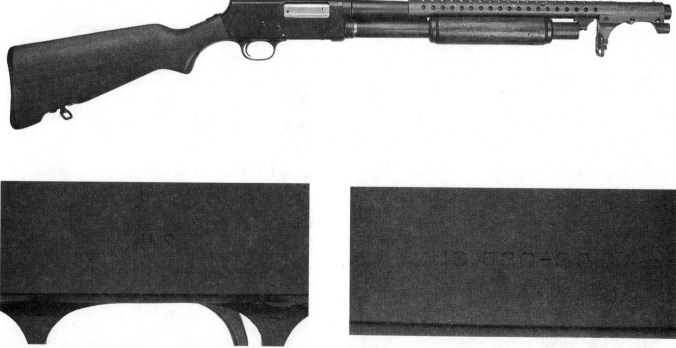

Model 520 Trench Gun • Courtesy West Point Museum, Paul Goodwin photo

Model 590A1

A 12 gauge slide action shotgun fitted with an 18" barrel. This model differs from the commercial one by having an aluminum trigger housing instead of plastic, an aluminum safety instead of plastic, and a heavy walled barrel. The finish is Parkerized and military marked.

Exc.	V.G.	Good	Fair	Poor
350	300	250	200	100

Model RI 96

Essentially a modified Mossberg Model 9200 semiauto gas operated 12 gauge shotgun with 3" chamber fitted with an 18" barrel thicker than standard. Five round magazine. Military contract number on barrel and receiver with "US" suffix to serial number. Black phosphate finish. Issued to army special operations units in South America.

Exc.	V.G.	Good	Fair	Poor
N/A	—	—	—	—

MOSSBERG RI 96 "JUNGLE GUN"

Mossberg's short-lived Model 9200A1 "Jungle Gun" tactical shotgun was based on a military model that was produced in small numbers in 1996 for counter-narcotics operations in Central America, hence the name "Jungle Gun" for commercial variants. Unfortunately, the civilian versions were not exact replicas of the military guns and the "Jungle Gun" wasn't commercially successful. On the other hand, the military version, designated Model RI 96, passed the same 3,000 round reliability test as the earlier M590 pump action gun. The actual military RI 96 differs from the commercial 9200A1 in several ways, however. The RI 96 has a heavier barrel than the civilian version. The RI 96 safety selector and triggerguard are steel instead of plastic. The RI 96 shell elevator is thicker and heavier. Most important, though, is the gas system, which on the RI 96 ensures near 100 percent reliability with just about any type of shotgun shell imaginable, regardless of the gun's position. The RI 96 can be fired with one hand or from the hip with complete reliability. The author tested an RI 96 military contract gun and found it to be 100 percent reliable with shotgun shells ranging from Number 9 shot light target loads to three inch magnum 000 buckshot. The gas operation also substantially reduced felt recoil, making the RI 96 more easily controllable and pleasant to shoot than traditional pump-action guns. Since only about 400 RI 96s were manufactured for the military and most went to South America where they saw hard use, the chances of encountering an actual RI 96 in good condition are slim. Given the low production numbers and the fact that only a few authentic RI 96s exist in private hands, the RI 96 should be of great interest to Mossberg collectors. Besides the differences mentioned above, each authentic RI 96 is marked as such on both barrel and receiver and also with the military contract number, DAAE20-96-P-0363.

Charlie Cutshaw

ITHACA

For a more detailed description of Ithaca military shotguns see Walter Snyder's book, *Ithaca Featherlight Repeaters...the Best Gun Going: A Complete History of the Ithaca Model 37 and the Model 87*, Cook and Uline Publishing, 1998.

Model 37 Military Marked Trench Gun (WWII)

This is one of the scarcest military shotguns. It was built in three different configurations; 30" barrel, 20" barrel, and 20" barrel with handguard and bayonet lug (Trench Gun). A scarce shotgun, proceed with caution.

Model 37 with 20" barrel and release papers • Courtesy Richard M. Kumor Sr.

Exc.	V.G.	Good	Fair	Poor
10000	7500	5000	2500	1500

NOTE: Add $200 for government release papers and 150% for Trench Gun configuration.

Model 37 Military Marked Trench Gun (Vietnam)

Same as above but built from 1962 to 1963. Fitted with 20" barrel. Stock was not checkered and had oil finish. Receiver had "US" stamped. Highest serial number reported is S23710.

Exc.	V.G.	Good	Fair	Poor
3500	2500	1800	900	750

Model 37 Military Marked Trench Gun (Navy Contract)

Similar to the Model 37 Trench gun but built in 1966-1967 for the U.S. Navy Ammunition Depot. About 3,000 were built. Based on the Model 37 M&P model.

Exc.	V.G.	Good	Fair	Poor
5000	3500	2500	1250	900

BENELLI

M4 Super 90 (M1014)

Adopted by the U.S. Marine Corps this 12-gauge shotgun features a choice of three modular buttstock and two barrel configurations. Action is semi-auto or slide action. Top mounted Picatinny rail. Barrel length is 18.5". Magazine capacity is 6 rounds. Ghost-ring sights. Black MILSPEC finish. Weight is about 8.4 lbs. Matte black finish. Deliveries in 2000. This model will be available in a modified form for commercial sale after military and law enforcement contracts are filled.

NIB	Exc.	V.G.	Good	Fair	Poor
N/A	—	—	—	—	—

MACHINE GUNS

Bibliographical Note: For historical information, technical data, and photos see James Ballou, *Rock in a Hard Place; The Browning Automatic Rifle*, Collector Grade Publications, 2000. Wahl and Toppel, *The Gatling Gun*, New York, 1965.

Colt Gatling Gun

First invented by American Dr. Richard J. Gatling in 1861, this is a multi-barrel (6 to 10 barrels) hand-cranked machine gun. Several different models were developed and built in the 1860s with some used in the American Civil War. Some of these early guns were chambered for the .58 caliber, while a few others were chambered for the 1" shell. The classic Gatling gun is the Model 1874 chambered for the .45-70 cartridge. There are several other models such as the Model 1879, Model 1881, the Model 1892, Model 1895, and the Model 1903. Some of these guns were tripod-mounted while others were mounted on gun carriages, and still others were deck-mounted for ship-board use. Some of the Gatling guns have exposed barrels while others are enclosed in a brass jacket. The Model 1877 bulldog is fitted with five 18" barrels enclosed in a brass jacket. The Model 1893 Police has six 12" barrels in .45-70 and weighs about 75 lbs. These guns are marked with a brass plate on top of the receiver, "GATLING'S/BATTERY/GUN 9 (PATENT DATES) MADE BY COLT'S/PT. FIRE ARMS MFG. CO./HARTFORD, CONN.U.S.A."

NOTE: As an interesting aside, Gatling guns are still in use by military forces but are now electrically powered (GEC M134/GAU-2B Minigun) and capable of a rate of fire of 6,000 rounds per minute using the 7.62x51 cartridge.

Values for these guns are difficult to establish. Gatling guns in excellent condition in .45-70 caliber can bring between $75,000 to $200,000 and even more.

Colt Gatling Model 1883 • Photo courtesy Butterfield & Butterfield

Colt Model 1895

Designed by John Browning and built by Colt, this is a gas operated air-cooled belt-fed gun chambered for the .30-03, 6mm U.S.N., and .30-40 cartridges as well as the .30-06 (called the Model 1906 cartridge) in later applications. Rate of fire is about 450 rounds per minute. Called the "potato digger" because of its back and forth motion and proximity to the ground. This was the first non-mechanical firing machine issued to the U.S. military. It saw limited use during the Spanish-American War, the Boxer Rebellion, and as a training gun during World War I.

NOTE: See also *Colt/Marlin Model 1914/1915*

Pre-1968 (rare)

Exc.	V.G.	Fair
15000	13000	12000

Pre-1986 conversions

Exc.	V.G.	Fair
N/A	N/A	N/A

Pre-1986 dealer samples

Exc.	V.G.	Fair
N/A	N/A	N/A

Colt Model 1895 • Courtesy Butterfield & Butterfield

NOTE: The .30-03 cartridge was the original and earlier version of the .30-06 cartridge. Guns chambered for the older .30-03 cartridge will function and fire the .30-06 cartridge (accuracy suffers) *but the reverse is not true*. Sometimes the .30-03 cartridge is referred to as the .30-45. Both of these cartridges replaced the older .30-40 Krag as the official military round.

Colt Maxim 1904

This belt-fed machine gun was originally chambered for the .30-03 cartridge and then altered to the .30-06. Built on the standard Maxim M1900 pattern. Barrel length is 28.5". Rate of fire is about 500 rounds per minute. Fed by a 250 round cloth belt. Primarily used as a training gun during World War I. A total of 287 of these guns were produced. Weight is approximately 75 lbs.

Pre-1968 (very rare)

Exc.	V.G.	Fair
40000	35000	30000

Pre-1986 conversions

Exc.	V.G.	Fair
N/A	N/A	N/A

Pre-1986 dealer samples

Exc.	V.G.	Fair
N/A	N/A	N/A

Maxim Model 1904 • Robert G. Segel collection

Model 1909 Benet-Mercie Machine Rifle

Developed by the French firm Hotchkiss and built in the U.S. by Colt's and Springfield Armory, this air cooled gas operated automatic rifle is fed by a 30-round metal strip. Chambered for the .30-06 cartridge. Rate of fire was about 400 rounds per minute. Weight of gun was approximately 27 lbs. This gun was equipped with a Model 1908 Warner & Swasey telescope. This model was used against Mexican bandits in 1915 and 1916 by the U.S. Army and in France during the early stages of World War I. However, it did not prove to be reliable and was soon replaced by the Hotchkiss and Vickers guns. About 670 were produced by both Colt and Springfield.

Model 1909 Benet-Mercie • Robert G. Segel collection

Model 1909 Benet-Mercie Warner & Swasey telescope sight • Robert G. Segel collection

A U.S. Army cavalry officer tries his hand at firing the Benet-Mercie Model 1909 Machine Rifle, a .30-06 caliber version of the French Light Hotchkiss. This serviceable weapon got an undeservedly bad reputation in the Mexican Punitive Expedition of 1916 due primarily to poor training and maintenance • U.S. Army Signal Corps/National Archives/Robert Bruce Military Photo Features

Pre-1968 (Rare)

Exc.	V.G.	Fair
9000	8000	7000

Pre-1986 conversions

Exc.	V.G.	Fair
N/A	N/A	N/A

Pre-1986 dealer samples

Exc.	V.G.	Fair
N/A	N/A	N/A

Browning M1917 & M1917A1

Based on John M. Browning's original automatic weapon design it was chambered for the .30-06 cartridge. This water-cooled gun is fitted with a 23.8" barrel and has a rate of fire of 500 rounds per minute using a cloth belt. Its empty weight for the gun only is 33 lbs. The M1917A1 tripod weighs about 53 lbs. Marked "US INSP BROWNING MACHINE GUN US CAL 30 MODEL OF 1917." This gun was produced by various manufacturers from 1917 to 1945.

About 56,000 were built prior to the end of WWI although a few saw actual combat service. In the mid 1930s, a few minor modifications were made to the gun and it became known as the Model 1917A1. These modifications are as following:

The most important legacy of the Model 1917 Browning is that it led to the use of this gun as the air-cooled Model 1919. During its production life the gun was built by Colt, Remington, and Westinghouse.

Browning Model 1917 (Westinghouse) (The ID number on the side plate is a Numrich Arms registered serial number, not an original factory Model 1917 number) • Courtesy private NFA collection, Paul Goodwin photo

A gunner's view of the Browning Model 1917 during World War II in Germany • Courtesy John M. Miller

Pre-1968

Exc.	V.G.	Fair
20000	18000	16000

Pre-1986 conversions
(Non-martial current U.S. manufacture)

Exc.	V.G.	Fair
13000	12000	11000

Pre-1986 dealer samples

Exc.	V.G.	Fair
N/A	N/A	N/A

Browning Model 1917A1 • Robert G. Segel collection

Browning .30 Aircraft M1918

This was a modified M1917 water-cooled gun to air-cooled for aircraft use. The water jacket was removed and replaced with a slotted barrel jacket and spade grips. This model is referred to as the M1918M1.

Browning .30 Aircraft M1918 Fixed

As above but made as new in the same configuration with spade grips.

Browning .30 Aircraft M1919 Flexible

Same as M1918 but newly made with spade grips.

Browning M1919 A1

First utilized in 1931, this gun was a M1919 tank gun modified for ground use. It was fitted with a removable butt with a hand grip under the receiver. The barrel jacket was slotted. The front sight was mounted on the front of the receiver. Chambered for the .30-06 cartridge. Barrel length is 18". Fed with a 250-round cloth belt. Cycle rate of about 600 rounds per minute. Weight is about 40 lbs with tripod.

Browning M1919 A2

Introduced in 1931, this gun was intended for cavalry use. The front sight was mounted on the barrel jacket. There was no butt stock. The gun was issued with the M2 tripod. Otherwise, this model is an improved M1919A1.

Browning M1919 A3

There were 72 trials samples built. This gun was essentially a M1919A2 with the front sight moved back to the receiver.

Browning M1919 A4

This air-cooled gun is chambered for the .30-06 cartridge and fitted with a 23.8" barrel. It has a rate of fire of 500 rounds per minute and is fed with a cloth belt. Weight is about 31 lbs.

Marked "BROWNING M1919A4 US CAL .30" on the left side of the receiver. First produced in 1934, it is still in use today. There were a number of earlier variations of this model beginning with the M1919 aircraft gun and several improvements leading to the A4 version.

The Model 1919 was used in WWII as an infantry weapon, tank gun, and even in aircraft (M2). It has seen service all over the world in untold conflicts. Many arms experts think of the A4 version as the definitive .30 caliber machine gun.

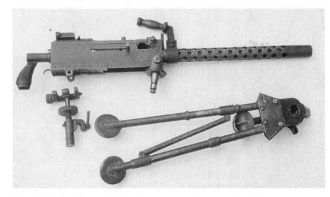

Courtesy Richard M. Kumor, Sr.

Pre-1968

Exc.	V.G.	Fair
10000	9000	9000

Pre-1986 conversions
(Non-martial current U.S. manufacture)

Exc.	V.G.	Fair
8000	7500	7000

Pre-1986 dealer samples

Exc.	V.G.	Fair
5000	4500	4500

Browning M1919 A5

This gun is an modified version of the M1919A4 for use with the M3 light tank. It was fitted with a special bolt retracting slide. Weight is about 30 lbs.

Browning M1919 A6

This model is a M1919 A4 fitted with a shoulder stock, flash hider, and bipod. Its weight is 32 lbs. Produced from 1943 to 1954. Marked "US INSP BROWNING MACHINE GUN US CAL 30" on the left side of the receiver.

Browning Model 1919A6 • Robert G. Segel collection

Pre-1968

Exc.	V.G.	Fair
10000	9000	9000

Pre-1986 conversions
(Non-martial current U.S. manufacture)

Exc.	V.G.	Fair
7000	6800	6500

Pre-1986 dealer samples

Exc.	V.G.	Fair
5000	4500	4500

Okinawa, May 1945. A U.S. Army soldier poses with the tough and reliable Browning .30 caliber M1919 machine gun, newly modified to A6 configuration with addition of a bipod and buttstock to assist portability in the assault • U.S. Army Signal Corps/National Archives/Robert Bruce Military Photo Features

Browning .30 Aircraft M2

This gun was designed for airplane use in 1931. It rate of fire is higher than the ground gun version; 1,000 to 1,200 rounds per minute. Chambered primarily for the .30-06 cartridge but some were chambered for the .303 British round for that country's use. The gun is fed from either the left or right side as determined by the situation. It was originally designed in two configurations; as a flexible gun (for an observer) with hand grips and hand trigger or as a fixed or wing type with a back plate without hand grips. The recoil buffer in the flexible type is horizontal while the fixed gun has a vertical type buffer. Weight is about 21 lbs. Barrel length is 23.9".

Browning M2 machine gun (tripod used for photo purposes) • Courtesy Robert G. Segel

Pre-1968

Exc.	V.G.	Fair
10000	9000	8500

Pre-1986 conversions
(Non-martial current U.S. manufacture)

Exc.	V.G.	Fair
8000	7000	6000

Pre-1986 dealer samples

Exc.	V.G.	Fair
5000	4500	4000

Browning Tank M37

This gun is a version of the M1919A4 adopted for tank use. Feed mechanism was designed to be used from either side.

Pre-1968

Exc.	V.G.	Fair
10000	9000	8500

Pre-1986 conversions
(Non-martial current U.S. manufacture)

Exc.	V.G.	Fair
8000	7000	6000

Pre-1986 dealer samples

Exc.	V.G.	Fair
7500	7000	7000

MG 38

Similar in appearance to the Model 1917 (water cooled) but with several modifications such as an improved bolt handle. The MG 38 is fitted with a pistol grip back plate while the MG 38B has a double grip (spade type) black plate. Fed from a 250-round belt. Weight of MG 38 is about 35 lbs, while the MG 38B weighs about 36.5 lbs. Barrel length is 24". This gun was utilized for several different purposes and therefore has different tripods depending on the application. Rate of fire is between 400 and 650 rounds per minute.

Courtesy Robert E. Naess

Model 1924

A commercial version of the Model 1917. Some interior modifications.

Model 1928

A commercial version of the Model 1917 with interior modifications.

Pre-1968

Exc.	V.G.	Fair
10000	9000	8500

Pre-1986 conversions
(Non-martial current U.S. manufacture)

Exc.	V.G.	Fair
8000	7000	6000

Pre-1986 dealer samples

Exc.	V.G.	Fair
5000	4500	4000

MG 40

This is the commercial version of the M2 .30 caliber aircraft gun.

Pre-1968

Exc.	V.G.	Fair
10000	9000	8500

Pre-1986 conversions
(Non-martial current U.S. manufacture)

Exc.	V.G.	Fair
8000	7000	6000

Pre-1986 Dealer samples

Exc.	V.G.	Fair
5000	4500	4000

Browning .50 M1921

Introduced in 1925, this heavy machine gun is water cooled and recoil operated. Chambered for the .50 Browning cartridge. Rate of fire is about 450 rounds per minute. Barrel length is 36". Fed by a cloth belt. Weight of gun is 66 lbs.

Browning .50 M1921 A1

An improved version of the M1921 with a compound leverage cocking handle.

Alaska, 1942. A water-cooled .50 cal. Browning M2 machine gun on M2 antiaircraft tripod protecting resupply operations against the threat of possible attack by Japanese fighter planes. This heavy hitter is fed from 200 rounds of belted ammunition on a reel in the M2 chest on the left, and steel links are collected in the canvas bag on the right for reloading. Two rubber hoses attached to the water jacket provide a circulating flow of cooling water for sustained fire • U.S. Army Signal Corps/National Archives/Robert Bruce Military Photo Features

Browning .50 M2

Introduced in 1933, this gun is an improved version of the M1921 with a water jacket that extends past the muzzle. Fitted with spade grips and fed from either side. Early guns had a 36" barrel later guns were fitted with a 45" barrel. Intended for antiaircraft use with a special mount for that purpose. Weight of gun was 100 lbs while the tripod weighed about 375 lbs. Cycle rate is about 650 rounds per minute. Fed by a 110-round metal link belt.

Browning M2/M2HB .50

This is an air-cooled .50 caliber machine first produced in 1933. It has a 44.5" barrel and weigh about 84 lbs. Its rate of fire is 500 rounds per minute. It is belt-fed. Marked "BROWNING MACHINE GUN CAL 50 M2 "on the left side of the receiver. Approximately three million were produced. The gun was produced by Colt, FN, Ramo, Saco, and Winchester.

It is one of the most widely used and successful heavy machines ever produced. Besides being utilized as an aircraft, ground and vehicle weapon, the M2 is also used as an antiaircraft gun in single, twin, and four-barrel configurations. The M2 was additionally configured as a water-cooled gun for sustained fire. The commercial designation for this model was the MG 52A. Widely used throughout the world and is still in use today and still in production in the UK, USA, and Belgium.

The .50 caliber cartridge was first adopted in 1923 after extensive research by John M. Browning, Winchester, and Colt. The cartridge, like many with military applications, has a wide variety of variations.

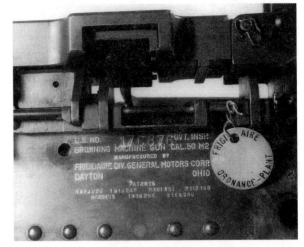

Browning M2 water-cooled anti-aircraft gun • Robert G. Segel collection

Pre-1968

Exc.	V.G.	Fair
15000	14000	13000

Pre-1986 conversions
(Non-martial current U.S. manufacture)

Exc.	V.G.	Fair
12000	11000	10000

Pre-1986 dealer samples

Exc.	V.G.	Fair
N/A	N/A	N/A

NOTE: For original M2 water-cooled guns add $10,000 to pre-1968 prices.

MG52-2A TORA TORA GUN

"Fat Alice" was our gun. We didn't like the name, really, we hesitated to say it in public, I considered not saying it here. However, that was her name. Crew served weapons are usually nicknamed by the crew that operates them-it is an old and venerable tradition. And, much like a tough Indian Brave might get stuck with "Waddling Duck" or "Runs Naked Through The Flowers" due to a mistimed naming dream, once a name is on a weapon, it usually sticks. The late David "Caveman" Wilson, a USMC veteran of Chu Lai and Indian Country, former president of the North Country Machine Gun Shoots, latched on to my old "Tora Tora" mounted MG52-2A as crew chief, and immediately christened her "Fat Alice." The name stuck, just like the "Tora Tora" moniker to the US M3 AA mount, from the movie of that same name.

Weighing in at 800 or so pounds, "Fat Alice" was a piece of work to set up. On a Saturday when we all were lacking in sensible things to do, Dave might call and see if "Fat Alice" could come out to play. If so, we would gather some friends and break down the tripod setup, load up some linked fifty caliber ammo, and head out to a sandpit. Setup took about twenty minutes, filling the water jacket and pump, then preparing to shoot. Normally, we would go out and blast with American 180s, M16s, and whatever else came to mind before we gave "Alice" a run. At a buck a round or so, it was an expensive hobby.

We almost always started the early North Country Shoots in New Hampshire by letting a youngster open with a volley from "Alice." This was because it was a most impressive weapon, and easily controlled. The multiple firing control positions allow for the system to be fired from almost any angle, and the excellent locking traverse and elevation system keep it under control. You can literally lock the gun down, stand behind it, and fire bursts one handed. It was also a gun you could "ride," you could get on the controls with your central body, both hands on the grips, and fire intuitively at the targets, your body being hammered with the recoil and explosions you could feel in your belly. Many people likened it to riding an old Harley.

When ammunition was available inexpensively, we would fire long bursts at old cars in the sandpits, or at mile away quarry walls. With APIT ammunition, the red tracer and large white burst on the targets was awe inspiring.

Shooting the Water Cooled fifty caliber Browning was a labor intensive task, but we all have fond memories of our afternoons in the mountains of New Hampshire with "Fat Alice," good friends, and piles of brass on the ground.

Dan Shea

Korea, December 1951. A .50 caliber M2HB machine gun has been equipped for long range sniping by addition of a telescopic sight. The heavy, tripod-mounted Browning with its precise traversing and elevating mechanism and powerful cartridge is a good choice for such duties • U.S. Army Signal Corps/National Archives/Robert Bruce Military Photo Features

Browning Automatic Rifle (BAR)

This is gas-operated machine gun chambered for the .30-06 cartridge. Fitted with a 23.8" barrel and a 20-round magazine, it weighs about 16 lbs. Its rate of fire is 500 rounds per minute. Marked "BROWNING BAR M1918 CAL 30" on receiver it was produced from 1917 until 1945, but saw service in the Korean War.

This Browning-designed rifle was built by Colt, Marlin, and Winchester. It has several variations from the original M1918 design. About 50,000 Model 1918 BARs saw service in Europe during World War I. The M1918A1 was first built in 1927 and has the buttplate hinged shoulder support. The bipod has spiked feet and is attached to the gas cylinder. It too is select fire. Weight for the M1918A1 is 18.5 lbs. The M1918 A2 was first built in 1932 and is fitted with a bipod with skid feet attached to the flash hider. There is a monopod beneath the buttstock. The rear sight is from a Browning M1919A4 machine gun and is adjustable for windage. This version has a rate of fire regulator that sets the rate between 450 and 650 rounds per minute. Weight for this variation is 19.5 lbs. During World War II approximately 188,000 Model 1918A2 BARs were produced. The last version is called the M1922 and was built in limited numbers. It is similar to the M1918 but with a heavy finned barrel. The bipod is attached to the barrel. Barrel length is 18" with rate of fire of 550 rounds per minute.

Photo courtesy Jim Thompson

Pre-1968

Exc.	V.G.	Fair
20000	17500	16000

Pre-1986 conversions

Exc.	V.G.	Fair
10000	9000	8000

Pre-1986 Dealer samples

Exc.	V.G.	Fair
10000	9000	8500

Johnson M1941 & 1944

Chambered for the .30-06 cartridge, the Model 1941 was fitted with a wooden buttstock while the Model 1944 had a metal stock. Barrel length was 21.8". The M1941 had a rate of fire of 600 rounds while the M1944 had an adjustable rate of fire between 200 and 900 rounds per minute. Fed by a side

Browning BAR in action, January 30, 1951, Korean front • U.S. Army photograph

Browning Automatic Rifle cutaway with markings • Paul Goodwin photo

mounted 20-box magazine. Weight is about 14 lbs. Produced for the Marine Corps until 1945. Marked "LIGHT MACHINE GUN JOHNSON AUTOMATICS MODEL OF 1941" above the magazine housing. About 10,000 Model 1941 guns were built.

This is an interesting model because it fires from an open bolt for full auto fire and a closed bolt for single shots. The M1941 was built by Cranston & Johnson and the M1944 was built by Johnson.

Johnson Model 1941

Pre-1968

Exc.	V.G.	Fair
10000	9000	9000

Pre-1986 conversions

Exc.	V.G.	Fair
N/A	N/A	N/A

Pre-1986 dealer samples

Exc.	V.G.	Fair
N/A	N/A	N/A

Stoner Model 63/63A

Developed in 1963 as a further evolution to the Model 63 with an improved stainless steel gas system and different style safety per U.S. Marine Corp specifications. This machine gun is chambered for the 5.56x45mm cartridge. It has an overall length of 40.24", a barrel length of 21", and a weight of approximately 11 lbs. Its rate of fire is 700 rounds per minute. It can function as a belt feed gun or can be fed by a top mounted magazine. It was used by both the U.S. Navy and Marine Corps during the Vietnam conflict. Production stopped in the early 1970s. The gun was produced by Cadillac Gage Co.

NOTE: This model is really a weapons system that is capable of a number of different configurations from carbine to machine gun. Also note that Model 63 components will not always interchange with Model 63A guns.

Johnson Model 1944 • Courtesy private NFA collection, Paul Goodwin photo

Stoner Model 63 Carbine • Courtesy West Point Museum, Paul Goodwin photo

Stoner Model 63A • Photo courtesy private NFA collection

Pre-1968 (Very rare, less than 6 known)

Exc.	V.G.	Fair
45000	40000	35000

Pre-1986 conversions (Non-martial current U.S. manufacture)

Exc.	V.G.	Fair
35000	30000	25000

Pre-1986 dealer samples

Exc.	V.G.	Fair
27500	25000	20000

NOTE: Deduct 33% for Stoner Model 63. There are more Model 63s availabe (transferable) than Model 63As.

Mekong Delta, Vietnam, May 1970. This Navy SEAL is waist deep in mud after jumping from an insertion craft at the start of another patrol. His Mark 23 Stoner light machine gun with bottom-mounted belt box is held high to avoid contamination • U.S. Navy Historical Center/Robert Bruce Military Photo Features

THE M60 MACHINE GUN

The M60 machine gun served as the primary general purpose machine gun for the U. S. Army and Marines for nearly forty years. It has also been used extensively by Australia, South Korea, and a number of our other allies. It was our primary machine gun throughout Vietnam and Desert Storm. It was used as a light machine gun, a medium machine gun, a helicopter door gun, and in several vehicular and aircraft mounts. While well trained and dedicated operators could keep the M60 working reasonably reliably, it is amazing that this decidedly mediocre machine gun could last so long in service. Indeed many are still in service today. The M60 suffered from a wide variety of poor features. These included: a quick detachable barrel with its bipod attached to the barrel so that if you carried a spare barrel you also had to carry the extra weight of a spare bipod, sights on the barrel that were not adjustable so that if you changed the barrel you lost the weapon's zero, a feed tray cover that if it was closed with the bolt forward would damage the feed mechanism, a trigger group and gas system that had to be held together with twisted wires to keep from accidentally disassembling itself, and other idiotic peculiarities. If that were not enough, the gun was overly sensitive to dirty ammunition and dirty or corroded belt links. After decades of putting up with its problems, eventually an improved M60E3 was developed that corrected most, but not all, of these problems but created one or two new ones. Currently, the M60 is being replaced in the U. S. service by the much better M240 machine gun which is nothing more than a variation of the FN MAG 58 machine gun which was rejected in favor of the M60 back in the 1950s. Historically significant, but mediocre in performance, the M60's long service is quite unexplainable.

Chuck Karwan

Armalite AR-10 • Courtesy West Point Museum, Paul Goodwin photo

U.S. M60

Chambered for the 7.62x51mm cartridge, this machine gun entered U.S. service in the late 1950s. It was fitted with a 22" barrel and a rate of fire of 550 rounds per minute using a disintegrating link belt system. The weight of the gun is 24.4 lbs. Used extensively by U.S. forces in Vietnam. Still in production and still in service with U.S. forces (Marine Corp) and many others around the world. The early M60 guns were built by Bridge & Inland.

Pre-1986 OEM/Maremont manufacture

Exc.	V.G.	Fair
22500	20000	17500

Pre-1986 conversions

Exc.	V.G.	Fair
15000	13000	12000

Pre-1986 Dealer samples

Exc.	V.G.	Fair
N/A	N/A	N/A

U.S. M60E3

This is an improved version of the M60 with a lightweight shorter 17" barrel. The forearm is replaced with a forward pistol grip with heat shield. The feed system has been modified to allow the cover to be closed when the bolt is forward. The gas system has been modified as well. Weight has been reduced to about 18 lbs. This model was in service with the U.S. Marine Corp, Navy, and Air Force. Built by both Maremont and Saco.

M60-E3 • Photo courtesy private NFA collection

Pre-1986 OEM/Maremont manufacture

Exc.	V.G.	Fair
30000	27500	25000

Armalite AR-10

Chambered for the 7.62x51mm cartridge, this select fire machine gun was fitted with a 19.8" barrel and had a 20-round magazine. Rate of fire is 700 rounds per minute. Weight is 9 lbs. Marked "ARMALITE AR10 MANUFACTURED BY AL NEDERLAND" on left side of magazine housing. Produced from 1958 to 1961. This gun was adopted by Burma, Portugal, Nicaragua, and Sudan. It was produced in limited numbers.

Pre-1968 (Very rare)

Exc.	V.G.	Fair
15000	15000	14000

Pre-1986 conversions

Exc.	V.G.	Fair
7500	6500	5000

Pre-1986 Dealer samples

Exc.	V.G.	Fair
2500	2500	2000

Armalite AR-15

Introduced in 1957, this select fire rifle was fitted with a plastic butt and handguard. The rear sight also acted as a carry handle. The cocking handle was located at the rear of the receiver. The 20" barrel was fitted with a flash hider. It was a gas operated mechanism with rotating bolt. This design eventually became the U.S. military M16 rifle. Weight is about 6.25 lbs. Rate of fire was about 800 rounds per minute.

Pre-1968

Exc.	V.G.	Fair
12000	11000	10000

Pre-1986 conversions

Exc.	V.G.	Fair
N/A	N/A	N/A

Pre-1986 dealer samples

Exc.	V.G.	Fair
N/A	N/A	N/A

Armalite AR-18

First produced in 1964 and chambered for the 5.56x45mm cartridge. Side-hinged plastic butt stock. Gas operated and select fire. Rate of fire is about 800 rounds per minute. Barrel length is 18.25". Weight is about 7 lbs. Magazine capacity is 20, 30, or 40 round detachable magazines. Designed to be a less expensive alternative to the AR-15. Built by ArmaLite. Rare

Pre-1968 (Very rare)

Exc.	V.G.	Fair
15000	15000	14000

Pre-1986 conversions

Exc.	V.G.	Fair
7500	6500	5000

Pre-1986 dealer samples

Exc.	V.G.	Fair
7500	7500	7000

ARMALITE AR-18/AR-180

The select fire AR-18 and semiautomatic AR-180 were developed by Armalite in the late 1960s as an alternative to the AR-15/M16. The concept was a rifle made of sheet metal stampings that could be manufactured virtually anywhere without the need for forgings and expensive tooling as required for the earlier AR-15. Even the fire control components of the AR-18/180 were made of sheet metal, including the hammer and sear. The magazine release was also made of sheet metal, necessitating a different magazine retention method. This consisting of a small slot in the right side of the magazine which was never fully satisfactory because it rubbed against the magazine surface, binding and making insertion and withdrawal difficult. Otherwise, the AR-15 and AR-18 magazines are identical. AR-15 magazines can occasionally be encountered with this small slot on the right side. These are magazines intended to be used in either the AR-15 or AR-18. The AR-18's basic design is actually superior to the earlier AR-15, which is flawed by its Ljungmann-type gas operating system that dumps fouling back into the receiver, causing carbon buildup and requiring intensive maintenance. The AR-18 uses a piston and operating rod gas system that eliminates the AR-15's problems. AR-18s were initially produced in Costa Mesa, California, and then under contract by Howa of Japan and later by Sterling of Britain. Although it was a basically superior design as compared to the AR-15, the AR-18 was overshadowed by the earlier rifle and was never fully developed. The AR-18 did, however, achieve the dubious honor of being a favorite of Irish Republican Army terrorists. Armalite has recently reintroduced the semiautomatic AR-180 with a polymer lower receiver that uses standard AR-15 magazines and fire control components. This new version of rifle retains the best features of the original, while curing its few problems, although it lacks the original's bayonet lug and folding stock.

Charlie Cutshaw

Colt/Marlin Model 1914/1915

This was a Browning design that was first produced in 1895. Nicknamed the "Potato Digger" because of its swinging arm bolt driver. It was air cooled and fired a variety of calibers both for the military and commercial sales. The Model 1914 was converted to fire the .30-06 cartridge. Rate of fire was about 450 rounds per minute. Barrel length was 28". Belt-fed by 250 round cloth belt. The Model 1915 had cooling fins added to the barrel. The gun was built from 1916 to 1919.

Pre-1968

Exc.	V.G.	Fair
10000	9000	8000

Pre-1986 conversions

Exc.	V.G.	Fair
N/A	N/A	N/A

Pre-1986 dealer samples

Exc.	V.G.	Fair
N/A	N/A	N/A

Robert G. Segel collection

Marlin Model 1914 • Paul Goodwin photo

Canadian soldiers on the firing line with the "Potato Digger" • Robert G. Segel collection

Marlin Model 1917

This model is an improved Potato Digger with a gas pistol and cylinder fitted underneath the barrel. Chambered for the .30-06 cartridge. Designed for use in aircraft with long finned aluminum radiator around the barrel, and in tanks with a heavy armored barrel jacket. Barrel length is 28". Fed by a 250-round cloth belt with a rate of fire of approximately 600-rounds per minute. Weight is about 22 lbs.

Pre-1968

Exc.	V.G.	Fair
9000	8000	7000

Pre-1986 conversions

Exc.	V.G.	Fair
N/A	N/A	N/A

Pre-1986 dealer samples

Exc.	V.G.	Fair
N/A	N/A	N/A

Savage-Lewis Model 1917

This a .30-06 caliber Lewis gun made by Savage during World War I. About 6,000 of these guns were chambered for the .30-06 caliber cartridge and used by the U.S. Marines and Navy until World War II. The U.S. Army purchased 2,500 of the guns but most of these Army guns were used for training purposes. See *Great Britain, Machine Guns, Lewis 0.303in., Mark I.*

Marlin Model 1917 Tank Gun • Courtesy private NFA collection, Paul Goodwin photo

Pre-1968

Exc.	V.G.	Fair
17500	15000	13000

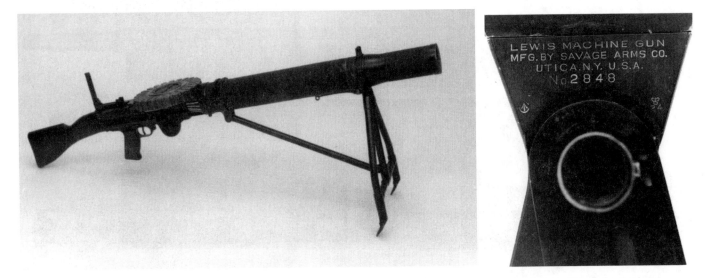

Savage-Lewis Gun • Robert G. Segel collection

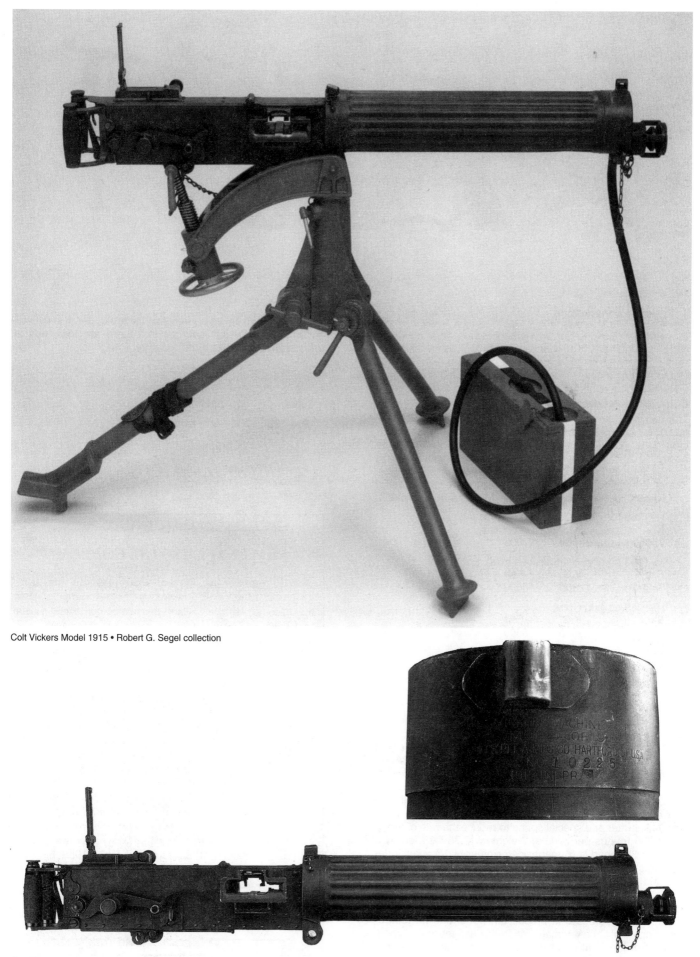

Colt Vickers Model 1915 • Robert G. Segel collection

Colt Vickers Model 1915 with markings • Paul Goodwin photo

Colt LMG (RO-750)

Pre-1986 conversions

Exc.	V.G.	Fair
12000	11000	10000

Pre-1986 dealer samples

Exc.	V.G.	Fair
N/A	N/A	N/A

Colt-Vickers Model 1915

This gun is similar to the British Vickers but built by Colt in Hartford, CT. Many of these Colt Model 1915 guns were rebuilt aircraft guns. About 12,000 were produced by Colt during the period 1915 to 1918 but few of these were original Colt-built ground guns and many of those were destroyed after the war. Therefore, original Colt-Vickers ground guns are very rare and quite desirable. See also Great Britain, Machine Guns, Vickers.

Pre-1968 (original Colt ground gun)

Exc.	V.G.	Fair
22500	20000	17000

Pre-1968 (Colt rebuilt aircraft gun)

Exc.	V.G.	Fair
14000	12000	10000

Pre-1986 conversions

Exc.	V.G.	Fair
10000	9500	8500

Pre-1986 dealer samples

Exc.	V.G.	Fair
N/A	N/A	N/A

Colt LMG (RO-750)

First introduced in early 1986, this M16A2 light machine gun was designed as a squad automatic weapon (SAW). SAWs are designed to provide a more sustained fire capability than the standard M16 rifle. Similar in appearance to the M16A2 rifle, this model features a 20" heavy hammer forged barrel upper made by Diemaco with square handguard and vertical handgrip. The lower receiver fires from an open bolt full auto only and is marked, "SAFE AND FIRE." The fixed stock houses a hydraulic buffer and special spring to reduce the rate of fire to about 650 rounds per minute. Weight is 12.75 lbs. Fed by a standard 30-round M16 magazine or other high capacity devices such as the 100 round Beta C magazine. In use by the U.S. Mar*ine Corp. and other military forces in Central and South America and the Middle East. The Colt LMG was also utilized by the Canadian forces supplied by Colt licensee Diemaco of Canada. Still in production, but under the reintroduced name of Colt Automatic Rifle with changes to the bipod, removal of the front carry handle, and improvements in the handguard heat shield as well as a flat top upper. It is estimated by knowledgeable sources that there are less than 20 transferable examples in this country.

Pre-1968

Exc.	V.G.	Fair
N/A	N/A	N/A

Pre-1986 OEM (Very rare)

NIB	Exc.	V.G./Fair
15000	12500	N/A

Pre-1986 dealer samples

Exc.	V.G.	Fair
N/A	N/A	N/A

WHAT'S IT LIKE: THE COLT LMG

With a rate of fire of about 650 rounds per minute, a weight of 13 lbs, and a very large barrel diameter, this machine gun this extremely accurate out to 400 yards and beyond. Equipped with a mini A.C.O.G. scope in 3 power by Trijicon, this gun was able to consistently score hits with 10 and 15 rounds burst on target from 400 yards with ease. This gun needs a quality scope like the Trijicon to bring out its full capabilities. This kind of accuracy with a light machine gun is nothing short of amazing. Recoil is very light with the result that aim is not disturbed during fire. All of this in full automatic fire. Even with sustained burst from a 100-round Beta C magazine heat dissipation was excellent as was accuracy. The open bolt system and the heavy 20" barrel makes this gun a very effective SAW. Many who have fired both the FN Minimi and the FN Mag prefer the Colt LMG for its accuracy and ease of operation. Only a handful of transferable examples exist in this country due to the small window between introduction of this gun in very early 1986 and the May, 1986 ban on additional transferable machine guns to the civilian market. Some operators refer to the gun as the "full auto target rifle."

Ned Schwing

YUGOSLAVIA-SERBIA

Yugoslavian-Serbian Military Conflicts, 1870-Present

Once part of Turkey, then an autonomous state, Serbia became a kingdom in 1882. After the Balkan Wars of 1912 and 1913, Serbia emerged as a Balkan power. The Assassination of Austrian Archduke Francis Ferdinand by a Serbian nationalist precipitated World War I when Austria declared war on Serbia. After the war, Serbia became part of what is now Yugoslavia. During World War II, Serbia allied itself with the Germans. After the war, Serbia became a republic of Yugoslavia in 1946. In the early 1990s Serbia wanted greater independence from Yugoslavia with the result of war in that region between Bosnia, Croatia, and Yugoslavia. The area is still unsettled.

Yugoslavia's existence began after World War I when it officially became identified as Yugoslavia in 1929. This period was marked by regional tensions and border disputes. In 1939, Yugoslavia aligned itself with the axis powers. The country was invaded by Germany in 1941 and partisan forces led by Marshal Tito battled the Germans and then each other in a civil war to determine control of the country after the Germans were driven out in 1944. In 1945, Tito came to power and ruled until his death in 1980. In 1990, the communist party ceded control with Serbian president Milosevic eventually coming to power. In 1995, Serbia, Croatia, and Bosnia signed a treaty ending its conflict.

NOTE: In the 1870s, military arms were produced at Kragushevat, the national arsenal in Serbia. In the 1920s, it was often referred to as Voini Techiki Zavod. This factory was destroyed during World War II. Production of weapons since World War II is at the state arms factory of Zavodi Crena Zastava, Kragujevac, often shortened to "ZCZ." After 1990, the name was changed to Zastava Arms.

HANDGUNS

At the end of World War I Yugoslavia acquired a large number of Austrian Model 12 Steyr pistols in 9mm. The Yugoslavians have also used the FN-built M1935 pistol in 9x19 caliber.

Model 1875

This is a double action solid frame with fixed cylinder and mechanical rod ejection. Cylinder holds 6 rounds and is chambered for the 11mm cartridge. Checkered wood grips with lanyard loop. Octagon barrel is 6.2" long. Built by Auguste Francotte in Liege, Belgium. In use from 1875 to 1919.

Exc.	V.G.	Good	Fair	Poor
900	700	450	250	125

Model 1876

This model is built on a modified Lefaucheux-Chaineux solid frame with swing-out cylinder. The non-fluted cylinder is chambered for the 11mm cartridge. The half-round half-octagon barrel is 4.4". Checkered wood grips with lanyard loop. Built by Manufacture d'Ares, St. Etienne, France. In service with the Serbian army from 1876 to 1919.

Exc.	V.G.	Good	Fair	Poor
850	600	425	250	125

Model 1891

Built on the Nagant-Model 1887 frame, this double action model is chambered for the 7.5mm cartridge. Fluted cylinder. The 4.5" barrel is 3/4 octagon and 1/4 round. Checkered grips with lanyard loop. Built by the Nagant brothers in Liege, Belgium. The Serbian army used this revolver from 1891 to 1945. Revolver has cyrillic markings on the frame.

Exc.	V.G.	Good	Fair	Poor
2000	1000	500	350	225

Model 1898

This revolver is the same as the Austrian Model 1898, built by Rast & Gasser in Wien (Vienna), Austria. This model was built on the Schmidt-Galand double action solid frame with swing-out 8-round cylinder with multiple ejection. Chambered for the 8mm cartridge and fitted with a 4.5" round barrel. Checkered wooden grips with lanyard loop. Weight is about 33 oz.

Exc.	V.G.	Good	Fair	Poor
450	300	200	150	100

Model 1910 FN Browning

Adopted by Serbia and used in World War I. Chambered for 7.65mm cartridge and fitted with a 3.5" barrel. Magazine capacity is 7 rounds. Weight about 21 oz. The principal difference between this model and its predecessors is that the recoil spring on the Model 1910 is wrapped around the barrel. This gives the slide a more graceful tubular appearance instead of the old slab-sided look. This model has the triple safety features of the 1906 Model 2nd variation and is blued with molded plastic grips. The pistol has the Yugoslavian crest on the slide and cyrillic lettering on the slide. This model was adopted by police forces and some military units around the world. It was manufactured between 1912 and 1954.

Courtesy Orvel Reichert

Exc.	V.G.	Good	Fair	Poor
450	300	200	150	125

Model 1922 FN Browning

Adopted by Yugoslavia in the 1930s in 9mm short (.380). Fitted with a 4.5" barrel and a magazine capacity of 9 rounds. Fitted with a grip safety. Yugoslavian crest on top of slide. Weight is about 25 oz. Approximately 60,000 of these pistols were produced for the Yugoslavian military between 1922 and 1925. These pistols were also used by the German occupation forces, but are not marked with German acceptance or proof stamps.

Exc.	V.G.	Good	Fair	Poor
650	500	400	300	150

Tokarev copy (Model 70)

This is a Yugoslavian copy of the Soviet TT33 in 9x19mm.

Exc.	V.G.	Good	Fair	Poor
500	400	300	200	100

Tokarev copy (Model 57)

This is a Yugoslavian copy of the Soviet Tokarev, but with a 9-round magazine in 7.62x25mm.

Exc.	V.G.	Good	Fair	Poor
1200	850	700	500	200

Tokarev copy (Model 65 for export)

This is a copy of the Tokarev in 9mm Parabellum.

Exc.	V.G.	Good	Fair	Poor
500	400	300	200	100

SUBMACHINE GUNS

Prior to World War II, Yugoslavia adopted the Erma submachine gun. After the war, Yugoslavia used the German Mp38 and Mp40. The Yugoslavian army also used British Sten guns and Beretta submachine guns as well. As a communist state, the Yugoslavians were supplied with Soviet PPDs and PPSh41 guns.

Yugoslav Model 49

Similar in appearance to the Soviet PPSh41 this gun is chambered for the 7.62 Soviet cartridge. Barrel is 10.5" and the rate of fire is 700 rounds per minute. It is fitted with a wooden stock. Weight is approximately 9.4 lbs.

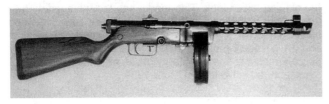

Photo courtesy private NFA collection

Pre-1968

Exc.	V.G.	Fair
7500	7000	6500

Pre-1986 conversions

Exc.	V.G.	Fair
5500	4500	4000

Pre-1986 dealer samples

Exc.	V.G.	Fair
5500	4500	4000

Yugoslav Model 56

The Model 56 is chambered for the 7.62 cartridge, and is fitted with a metal folding stock and 9.8" barrel. Magazine capacity is 35 rounds. Weight is about 6.6 lbs. Rate of fire is 600 rounds per minute.

Photo courtesy private NFA collection

Pre-1968

Exc.	V.G.	Fair
8500	7500	6000

Pre-1986 conversions

Exc.	V.G.	Fair
6500	5500	5000

Pre-1986 dealer samples

Exc.	V.G.	Fair
3500	3200	3000

RIFLES

MAUSER

NOTE: Most of these early Mauser rifles were used by the Serbian armed forces through World War I. The Model 24 was adopted by Yugoslavia.

M78/80 Rifle

A modified G 71 rifle with 30.7" barrel with two barrel bands. Turn bolt action. Single shot in 10.15x62.8mm caliber. Weight is about 10 lbs. Fitted with a long receiver tang to support rearward bolt travel. Marked in cyrillic or German on left side rail.

Exc.	V.G.	Good	Fair	Poor
450	350	300	200	—

M1884 Koka Carbine

Chambered for 10.15mm black powder cartridge and fitted with an 18.375" barrel with turn bolt action. Tubular magazine holds 5 rounds. Full-length stock with front sling swivel on left side of barrel band and real swivel on bottom on buttstock near wrist. Weight is about 8 lbs. Marked "MODEL 1884" on right side of butt. About 4,000 were built by Mauser at its Oberndorf factory.

Exc.	V.G.	Good	Fair	Poor
400	350	300	250	200

M1899 Rifle

Produced by DWM with a full-length stock with straight grip. Barrel length is 29". Chambered for 7x57mm cartridge. Adjustable rear sight graduated to 2000 meters. Serbian crest marked on receiver ring. Magazine capacity is 5 rounds. Weight is about 9 lbs.

Exc.	V.G.	Good	Fair	Poor
350	300	250	200	100

M1899c Rifle

Chambered for either the 7.92x57mm cartridge or the 7.65x53mm cartridge and fitted with a 23.25" barrel with full-length stock with pistol grip with finger grooves. Magazine capacity is 5 rounds. Weight is about 8.5 lbs. Straight bolt handle. Marked with Serbian crest on receiver ring.

Exc.	V.G.	Good	Fair	Poor
350	275	225	150	90

Model 24 Short Rifle • Courtesy Rock Island Auction Company

M1908 Carbine

This 7x57mm caliber model is fitted with a full-length pistol grip with finger grooves. Barrel length is 17". Upper handguard extends to the lower barrel band. Bolt handle is bent. No bayonet fittings. Weight is about 6.8 lbs.

Exc.	V.G.	Good	Fair	Poor
400	325	280	210	90

M1910 Rifle

This is the standard export German Model 1910 rifle. Fitted with a 29.13" barrel and full-length stock with pistol grip. The nose cap has a bayonet lug on its bottom. Chambered for the 7x57mm cartridge. Weight is about 9 lbs. Marked with Serbian crest on receiver ring.

Exc.	V.G.	Good	Fair	Poor
350	280	200	130	80

M90 (t) Short Rifle

A Yugoslavian model that was received from the Turks following WWI. Rebarreled for 7.92x57mm and cut to 23.25".

Magazine capacity is 5 rounds. Tangent rear sight graduated to 2000 meters. Weight is about 8.5 lbs.

Exc.	V.G.	Good	Fair	Poor
325	250	200	130	80

M03 (t) Short Rifle

Turkish Model 1903 converted to 7.92x57 caliber.

Exc.	V.G.	Good	Fair	Poor
325	250	200	110	70

M24 Short Rifle

This model has a full-length stock with pistol grip. Upper handguard goes from the receiver to upper barrel band. Fitted with 23.25" barrel and chambered for the 7.92x57mm cartridge. Tangent rear sight graduated to 2,000 meters. Weight is about 8.5 lbs. Yugoslavian crest over model designation on left side of receiver.

Exc.	V.G.	Good	Fair	Poor
350	275	225	100	60

M24 Carbine

Similar to the above model but with 16.75" barrel. Bayonet fittings are on nose cap. Weight is about 7.25 lbs.

Exc.	V.G.	Good	Fair	Poor
375	300	250	150	100

FN M30 Short Rifle

This model has a full-length stock with pistol grip. Straight bolt handle. This model is the standard FN Model 1930 configuration.

Exc.	V.G.	Good	Fair	Poor
275	200	125	70	40

FN M24 Carbine

Full stock with pistol grip and 17.5" barrel. Caliber is 7.92x57mm. Turn bolt action. Tangent leaf sight graduated to 1,400 meters. Yugoslavian crest of top of receiver ring. Weight is about 8 lbs.

Exc.	V.G.	Good	Fair	Poor
300	200	150	100	75

M1948 98k Short Rifle

This model is similar to the German 98k carbine. Almost full-length stock with pistol grip and short upper handguard. Hooded front sight with tangent leaf sight to 2000 meters.

Model 1948 Short Rifle • Courtesy Rock Island Auction Company

YUGOSLAV M48

The Yugoslavian M48 represents the last production version of the Mauser M98, and while it is similar to the German original, it is not the same. The major difference between the M48 and the K98 is the receiver, which is slightly shorter in the Yugoslavian version. Otherwise, there are only detail differences between the two rifles. The M48 was produced at Kragujevac Arsenal and is designated the M48 Short Rifle. A simplified version designated the M48A was also produced. The M48 is marked with the Yugoslavian Communist crest on the receiver ring and "Preduzece 44" in cyrillic on the left side of the receiver. The M48 that we evaluated for this article was one of the "new" rifles that have recently been imported. It is soundly made with matching serial numbers on the receiver, bolt, floorplate and buttstock. The rifle came with a bayonet that did not match the rifle's serial number, although some are available with matching bayonets. Our M48 had obviously been placed in storage shortly after manufacture. There were no signs of use anywhere on the rifle and the action had the typical stiffness characteristic of new military bolt action rifles. Instead of the characteristic German cut in the stock to clear the turned down bolt handle, the M48 bolt handle has the bottom half of the knob machined flat to accomplish the same purpose. Trigger pull is heavy, but crisp. The M48 we received required thorough cleaning prior to shooting. The stock was also new and was unfinished. The stock was so rough that there were splinters protruding in some areas. It was necessary to carefully sand the stock to preserve markings and then give it a linseed oil finish. Once the rifle was serviced and broken in, shooting was typical K98 and was as good as any military variant.

Charlie Cutshaw

Chambered for 7.92x57mm with 5-round magazine. Weight is about 10 lbs. Communist Yugoslavian crest on receiver ring.

Exc.	V.G.	Good	Fair	Poor
250	175	100	80	50

M24/52C Short Rifle
This is an arsenal reconditioned Model 24 short rifle with communist Yugoslavian crest on the receiver ring.

Exc.	V.G.	Good	Fair	Poor
200	150	100	70	40

Model 59/66
This is a Yugoslavian copy of the Soviet SKS rifle. The major difference between the two is a gas shut-off valve on the gas cylinder and an integral grenade launcher fitted to the barrel.

Exc.	V.G.	Good	Fair	Poor
1500	1200	850	500	250

Model 64
This is a Yugoslavian copy of the Soviet AK-47, but with a 19.7" barrel with built-in grenade launcher sights that pivots on the barrel.

Pre-1968

Exc.	V.G.	Fair
16000	14000	12000

Pre-1986 conversions

Exc.	V.G.	Fair
N/A	N/A	N/A

Pre-1986 dealer samples

Exc.	V.G.	Fair
N/A	N/A	N/A

NOTE: Add 20% for folding stock.

Zastava M70B1
This Yugoslavian copy of the AK-47 rifle was first produced in 1974. It is chambered for the 7.62x39mm cartridge and is fitted with a 16.2" barrel. Its rate of fire is 650 rounds per minute. Weight is about 8 lbs. This model features a folding grenade sight behind the front sight. When raised, it cuts off the gas supply to the cylinder redirecting it to the launcher. This is the standard Yugoslav service rifle. Still in production.

Pre-1968

Exc.	V.G.	Fair
N/A	N/A	N/A

Pre-1986 conversions

Exc.	V.G.	Fair
N/A	N/A	N/A

Pre-1986 dealer samples

Exc.	V.G.	Fair
7500	6500	5500

M70B1 (Semiautomatic version)

Exc.	V.G.	Good	Fair	Poor
2350	2150	1850	900	500

M70AB2
Copy of the Soviet AKM-S. *See Russia, Rifles.*

M76 Sniping Rifle
This is a copy of a Soviet AKM with a 21.5" barrel and wooden butt. The rifle is fitted with iron sights and a telescope mount. Semiautomatic operation. Chambered for the 8x57mm cartridge. Weight is about 9.5 lbs. Prices listed below are for rifles with correct matching military scope.

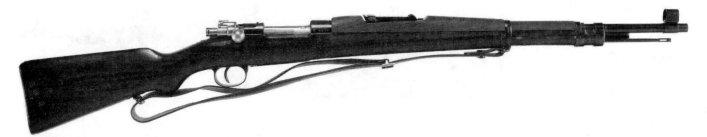

Mauser Model 24/52C • Courtesy Rock Island Auction Company

M76 with correct military scope • Courtesy Steve Hill

Exc.	V.G.	Good	Fair	Poor
2500	2000	1500	—	—

NOTE: For rifles without scope deduct $1,500. For rifles with commercial scopes but marked M76B deduct $1,000. For rifles in .308 caliber without scope deduct 70%.

M77B1 (Semiautomatic)

Copy of the Soviet AKM with a fixed wooden butt, straight 20-round magazine, and 16.4" barrel. Weight is about 8.5 lbs. Prices listed are for semiautomatic version.

Exc.	V.G.	Good	Fair	Poor
2250	1650	1100	800	300

M77 B1 Assault Rifle

Copy of the Soviet AKM with a fixed wooden butt, straight 20-round magazine, and 16.4" barrel. Rate of fire is about 700 rounds per minute. There are examples in this country chambered for .308 and .223. Weight is about 8.5 lbs.

NOTE: For rifles chambered for .223 add 75% premium.

Pre-1968

Exc.	V.G.	Fair
N/A	N/A	N/A

Pre-1986 conversions

Exc.	V.G.	Fair
N/A	N/A	N/A

Pre-1986 dealer samples

Exc.	V.G.	Fair
4500	4000	3500

MACHINE GUNS

Between the two world wars, Yugoslavia used the Schwarzlose M07/12, the Maxim 08, and the Madsen. After World War II, Yugoslavia used the MG34 and MG42 as well as some Soviet machine guns. The principal Yugoslavian machine is its own produced MG 42 designated the Model 53.

Yugoslavia also acquired several thousand U.S.-made Browning Model 1919 machine guns prior to 1964 as well as the .50 M2HB Browning heavy machine gun.

ZB30J

This was the primary light machine gun used by Yugoslavian forces prior to World War II. It is a modified copy of the Czech ZB30 gun chambered for the 7.92mm cartridge. The primary difference between the ZB30 and ZB30J is the knurled barrel ring in front of the receiver on the ZB30J.

Pre-1968

Exc.	V.G.	Fair
20000	18500	17000

Pre-1986 conversions

Exc.	V.G.	Fair
16500	15500	14000

Pre-1986 dealer samples

Exc.	V.G.	Fair
N/A	N/A	N/A

INDEX